LAW'S FUTURE(S)

Law's Future(s)

British Legal Developments in the 21st Century

EDITED BY

David Hayton

Professor of Law
King's College London

• HART •
PUBLISHING
OXFORD – PORTLAND OREGON
2000

Hart Publishing
Oxford and Portland, Oregon

Published in North America (US and Canada) by
Hart Publishing c/o
International Specialized Book Services
5804 NE Hassalo Street
Portland, Oregon
97213-3644
USA

Distributed in the Netherlands, Belgium and Luxembourg by
Intersentia, Churchillaan 108
B2900 Schoten
Antwerpen
Belgium

Hart Publishing Ltd is a specialist legal publisher based in Oxford, England.
To order further copies of this book or to request a list of other
publications please write to:

Hart Publishing Ltd, Salter's Boatyard, Oxford OX1 4LB
Telephone: +44 (0)1865 245533 or Fax: +44 (0)1865 794882
e-mail: mail@hartpub.co.uk
WEBSITE: http//:www.hartpub.co.uk

British Library Cataloguing in Publication Data
Data Available
ISBN 1 84113–100–8 (cloth)

Typeset in Minion
by Hope Services (Abingdon) Ltd.
Printed and bound in Great Britain on acid-free paper by
Biddles Ltd, Guildford and King's Lynn
www.biddles.co.uk

FOREWORD

The Society of Public Teachers of Law consider that, as we commence the 21st Century, there should be a review of the prospect ahead. In the light of past experience how will or should the law develop to cope with the ever-increasing pace of change as society changes and human expectations become greater?

Some improvements—or changes to use a more neutral term—in the law can, perhaps, be seen as almost bound to come, but others require informed speculation by knowledgeable experts, some of whom may even set an agenda for what needs to be considered and what goals should be set.

Teachers of Law, in particular, are in a position to view where the law is too constrained and where there are inconsistencies in what the law is seeking to achieve. However, it is not just substantive law topics that need to be addressed, but also the legal system and procedure and the role of the legal profession. With that in mind Sir Richard Scott joined the team of contributors to consider what needs to be tackled in fundamental reforms of our litigation procedures.

No doubt lawyers will read chapters on their own specialist areas with particular interest; they should not, however, restrict their reading to those. Hardly any chapter is an island unaffected by developments canvassed in other chapters. A few intended chapters have not materialised in the time constraints required to have the book launched to mark the Society's first Annual Conference in the new Millennium; illness and pressures of other commitments inevitably have some effect.

Nonetheless, the editor has brought together a distinguished team who have reflected on and written about contemporary ideas and possible future developments in so many areas—from the conflict of laws and European law to environmental labour and public law, to the criminal law and character evidence and criminal procedure. There is something for everyone.

The book provides many insights and challenges; it will provoke much reflection and discussion. Perhaps it will make even more interesting reading in twenty years' time.

Slynn of Hadley
August 2000

CONTENTS

LIST OF CONTRIBUTORS

Andrew Ashworth
Vinerian Professor of English Law, All Souls College, Oxford

Stephen Bailey
Professor of Public Law, University of Nottingham

Rebecca Bailey-Harris
Professor of Law, University of Bristol

Nicholas Bamforth
Fellow in Law, The Queen's College, Oxford

Kit Barker
Lecturer in Law, University of Southampton

John Birds
Professor of Commercial Law, University of Sheffield

Anthony Bradney
Professor of Law, University of Leicester

Margaret Brazier
Professor of Law, University of Manchester

Richard Card
Professor of Law, De Montfort University

Elizabeth Cooke
Lecturer in Law, University of Reading

Fiona Cownie
Senior Lecturer in Law, University of Leicester

Keith Ewing
Professor of Public Law, King's College London

Conor Gearty
Professor of Human Rights Law, King's College London

Nicola Glover
Lecturer in Law, University of Liverpool

Desmond Greer
Professor of Common Law, The Queen's University of Belfast

Brigid Hadfield
Professor of Law, University of Essex

Jonathan Harris
Reader in Law, University of Nottingham

David Hayton
Professor of Law, King's College London

Dr Jo Hunt
Lecturer in Law, University of Leeds

John Jackson
Professor of Public Law, The Queen's University of Belfast

Tim Jewell
Lecturer in Law, University of Southampton

John Lowry
Reader, University of Warwick

Laura Macgregor
Dundas & Wilson Lecturer in Commercial Law, University of Glasgow

Judith Masson
Professor of Law, University of Warwick

David McClean
Professor of Law, University of Sheffield

Gillian Morris
Professor of Law, Brunel University

David Oughton
Professor of Commercial Law, De Montfort University

John Parkinson
Professor of Law, University of Bristol

Alan Paterson
Professor of Law, University of Strathclyde

Colin Reid
Professor of Environmental Law, University of Dundee

Sir Richard Scott
Vice Chancellor, Chancery Division of the High Court

Jo Shaw
Professor of European Law, University of Leeds

Lionel Smith
Fellow, St Hugh's College, Oxford

Brenda Sufrin
Reader in Law, University of Bristol

Phil Thomas
Professor of Law, Cardiff Law School

Joseph Thomson
Regius Professor of Law, University of Glasgow

Adam Tomkins
Fellow, St Catharine's College, Oxford

Martin Wasik
Professor of Law, Keele University

Sally Wheeler
Professor of Law, Business and Society, University of Leeds

Richard Whish
Professor of Law, King's College London

Sarah Worthington
Senior Lecturer, London School of Economics

1

British University Law Schools in the Twenty-First Century

ANTHONY BRADNEY AND FIONA COWNIE

The Way We Were

British university law schools now are very different places from that which they were twenty or thirty years ago. Changes have been quantative and, more importantly, qualitative. Even those academics who have lived through the changes that the past twenty to thirty years have brought to universities may underestimate and misunderstand the precise scale and nature of those changes.[1] This is unfortunate because an understanding of these changes is vital if we are to predict the future course of law schools; the past points to the future.[2]

The Growth of Law Schools

In 1975, the date of the Wilson and Marsh survey of university and polytechnic law schools, there were 31 British university law schools.[3] There were also 17 polytechnic law schools.[4] Now, in the year 2000, there are 85 university law

[1] Trow, in his discussion of the changing nature of higher education, observes "[m]any academics . . . do not draw the full implications of growth nor see its logical consequences" (M Trow, *Problems in the Transition from Elite to Mass Higher Education* (Carnegie Commission on Higher Education, 1973), p. 27).

[2] "Time present and time past/Are both perhaps present in time future/And time future contained in time past" (T S Eliot, "Burnt Norton" in "Four Quartets") or, more succinctly, "No story begins nowhere" (S Rushdie *Haroun and the Sea of Stories* (London, Granta Books, 1990), p. 86.

[3] Wilson and S Marsh, "A Second Survey of Legal Education in the United Kingdom" (1975) 15 *JSPTL* 239 at 250 and 314. Wilson and Marsh looked at the position of law schools in England, Scotland and Wales. To their figures we have added the law school at Queens University Belfast.

[4] Wilson and Marsh, *supra* n. 3, at 255. We have excluded Ealing and Mid-Essex because, although Wilson and Marsh note that law degrees were being awarded at these places, the institutions were colleges rather than polytechnics.

schools, the binary divide between polytechnics and universities having been formally abolished by the Further and Higher Education Act 1992 and the Further and Higher Education (Scotland) Act 1992.[5] In 1975 there were 692 full-time academics working in British university law schools.[6] In 1996 the Harris and Jones survey concluded that there were 2,440 full-time academics in British university law schools.[7] Increases in the number of legal academics have been more than matched by increases in the number of full-time students. In 1975 the number of full-time law students stood at 8,660.[8] In 1996 the number had grown to 34,466, with a 50 per cent increase in the numbers between 1993 and 1996.[9] This 300 per cent growth in the number of students in university law schools is not just the result of the abolition of the binary divide and the creation of new law schools. Individual law schools have themselves grown greatly in size. In Wilson and Marsh's 1975 survey only two law schools, Oxford and Cambridge, had over 600 students, whilst the median group was those law schools having between 250 and 300 students.[10] By 1996 the average size of student body for a law school was 382; a figure which is larger than that for all but three university law schools in 1975.[11] This growth shows no clear signs of abating. Even the few years since the Harris and Jones survey have seen the creation of new undergraduate law courses in institutions which hitherto had not offered law degrees.[12]

Just as the size and number of university law schools has grown in the last two decades so the range of their activities has increased. In 1975 the principal activities of university law schools were research and teaching undergraduate law courses. Indeed even the idea that the university law school's remit

[5] Harris and Jones in 1996 noted that there were 83 British university law schools in 1996 (P Harris and M Jones, "A Survey of Law Schools in the United Kingdom, 1996" (1997) 31 *The Law Teacher* 38 at 44 and 67). To this we have added Birkbeck College, which has a law department although it offers only part-time degrees and was thus excluded from the Harris and Jones survey, and the University of Sunderland which opened its law department after the Harris and Jones survey. We have not included the Open University because, although it now offers an LLB it does not, in any usual sense of the phrase, have a law school.

[6] Wilson and Marsh, *supra* n. 3, at 268 and 317. (There are no figures available for the number of full-time staff at Queens University at this date.) There were also 411 full-time staff in polytechnic law schools (Wilson and Marsh, *ibid.*, at 271).

[7] Harris and Jones, *supra* n. 5, at 82. This figure excludes the staff at Birkbeck College.

[8] Wilson and Marsh, *supra* n. 3, at 249. (Once again there are no figures for students at Queens University at this date.) There were also 2,779 students in polytechnic law schools at this time (Wilson and Marsh, *ibid.*, at 255).

[9] Harris and Jones, *supra* n. 5, at 67.

[10] Wilson and Marsh, *supra* n. 3, at 250.

[11] Harris and Jones, *supra* n. 5, at 66. (Only 58 institutions responded to this part of the Harris and Jones survey.) Wilson and Marsh, *supra* n. 3, at 250.

[12] At, for example, the Open University and the University of Sunderland. In addition to this, as the "Constituency News" section of almost any issue of the *SPTL Reporter* will testify, institutions which have already offered law degrees are constantly in the business of expanding either the number of students on the their extant degree programmes or adding new programmes, combining the study of law with some other subject, or both.

extended beyond undergraduate teaching into research was, at that time, not uncontroversial. Whilst Wilson and Marsh's survey observed that "[a]ll university law teachers are expected to undertake research" Bridge, writing at the same time, said that "[i]f academic lawyers are honest they will admit that there is still too little legal research being done".[13] Arguably, at this time, research had a formal but not a substantive place on the agendas of many university law schools and many academics. Comparatively few law schools in 1975 attempted postgraduate teaching on any scale. In total there were only 924 students registered for postgraduate work with 75 per cent of those being registered in Cambridge, Oxford or the University of London and 45 per cent of that total being registered at London.[14] Vocational law teaching in university law schools was limited to a relatively small-scale involvement in continuing professional development. Polytechnic law schools, in some instances, taught students on the Law Society's Part II Course but polytechnic law departments were not university law departments, the binary divide pointing to real differences in the self-perceived missions of the two types of institutions, and not even polytechnic law schools taught students on the Bar's Part II Course.[15] Now very few university law schools do not have a postgraduate programme.[16] Harris and Jones reported a total of 3,749 full-time postgraduate students with 67 per cent being taught outside Cambridge, Oxford and the University of London.[17] Teaching on vocational courses now includes the Bar Vocational Course as well as the Law Society Legal Practice Course and goes on in some of the old university law schools as well as in a larger number of new university law schools.[18] Research has increased in quantity with more

[13] Wilson and Marsh, *supra* n. 3, at 272; J Bridge "The Academic Lawyer: Mere Working Mason or Architect?" (1975) 91 *LQR* 488 at 494.

[14] Wilson and Marsh, *supra* n. 3, at 263–4.

[15] In 1975, seven polytechnic law schools provided Law Society Part I and Part II courses (Wilson and Marsh, *ibid.*, at 302–3). The divide in mission between the polytechnic and university law school at this time is illustrated by Boucher's statement that "[a] polytechnic library aims at a full-exploited working collection rather than the vast research-oriented collection of a university library" (H Boucher, "Law Collections in Polytechnic Libraries" (1979) 13 *The Law Teacher* 174). See also, P Leighton, "New Wine in Old Bottles or New Wine in New Bottles?" (1998) 25 *Journal of Law and Society* 85.

[16] Even comparatively new law schools such as, for example, the University of Luton now offer a variety of postgraduate programmes. In the Harris and Jones survey only six new universities reported that they did not have postgraduate provision (Harris and Jones, *supra* n. 5, at 68 and 70).

[17] Harris and Jones, *ibid.*, at 77, 78 and 79.

[18] In 1996, 17 new and two old universities taught the Common Professional Examination course whilst 12 new and five old universities taught the Legal Practice Course (Harris and Jones, *ibid.*, at 68 and 71). The vast majority of student provision was found in new universities in both instances with 87.7 per cent of CPE students being taught in new universities and 74 per cent of LPC students being taught in new universities (Harris and Jones, *ibid.*, at 77 and 80). Four new universities and one old university now offer the Bar Vocational Course (http://www.barcouncil.org.uk/).

academics bringing an ever more diverse range of techniques to an ever increasing range of topics.[19]

Elite and Mass Education

That law schools have grown is not a new phenomenon nor is it necessarily of great significance. Wilson and Marsh, in their 1975 survey, note that their results show an in increase in size in almost all areas when their figures were compared with Wilson's 1966 survey.[20] However, the recent growth in the size of university law schools, which mirrors a similar or even greater growth in the size of their parent institutions, signals for many people a change in the nature of university education. Because of the level of participation in higher education that has been achieved in the United Kingdom, an elite system of higher education, it is argued, has become a mass system.[21]

It is clear that university law schools have experienced more than an increase in size during the last few decades. The institutional and cultural context in which they operate has also greatly changed. Law schools of the 1970s had neither Teaching Quality Assessment nor the Research Assessment Exercise. Their parent universities were not subject to the host of external audits that have now become common. Within law schools academic staff, at least once they had passed probation, were not subject to regular appraisal exercises. League tables barely existed and comparatively few students paid fees. Once law schools operated within a system where "development [was] initiated from below"; now some would argue that they, like other parts of the university, "make choices within boundaries [set by those outside universities] that discriminate against some decisions while encouraging others".[22]

Many of the contextual changes which law schools have experienced seem to add weight to the argument that there has been a change in the nature of university legal education from an elite system to a mass system. Trow, writing in 1973 and basing his observations largely on the experience of the USA, argued that increasing the percentage of the population attending courses in institutions of higher education to above 15 per cent of an age grade produced a

[19] 1,295 academics were registered for the 1996 Research Assessment Exercise in law (P Birks, "The Academic and the Practitioner" (1998) 18 *Legal Studies* 397 at 406). On the diversification of legal scholarship see further below.

[20] Wilson and Marsh, *supra* n. 3, *passim*; J Wilson, "A First Survey of Legal Education in the United Kingdom" (1966) *JSPTL* 1.

[21] See, for example, L Wagner, "A Thirty-Year Perspective: From the Sixties to the Nineties" in T Schulter (ed.), *The Changing University?* (Buckingham, The Society for Research into Higher Education/Open University Press, 1995) and J Daniel, "The Challenge of Mass Higher Education" (1993) 18 *Studies in Higher Education* 197.

[22] E Tapper and B Salter, "The Changing Idea of University Autonomy" (1995) 20 *Studies in Higher Education* 59 at 70.

number of changes in the qualitative character of higher education. Courses, he argued, become modular, there is a greater emphasis on learning skills rather than knowledge, a growing number of students work whilst pursuing their academic studies, student backgrounds (both academically and socially) become less homogeneous, less and less teaching takes the form of small-group instruction, institutions become more diverse in their missions and academic administration becomes more bureaucratised and less collegial.[23] Higher education in Great Britain has long since passed the 15 per cent participation point. Trow's observations about the resultant change in the nature of higher education will chime with the experience of many academics working in university law schools.

The recent history of British university law schools has set a trajectory for their path in the future. Upon their face the combination of growth in size, increase and diversification of function and changes in the bureaucracy to which the law school is subject seem indicative of a move in university law schools away from an elite system towards a mass system. If this is so this chapter should be a discussion of the ways in which British university law schools will have to change over the next two decades in order to accommodate themselves to the demands of a mass system together with some remarks on what will happen when there is a move from a mass to a universal system.[24] In this chapter, however, we will argue that whilst such an analysis captures some elements which are significant for the future of British university law schools it also over-simplifies both how law schools have been affected by change and what they will become in the future, neglecting in particular the strength of the internal culture of law schools which has preserved many aspects of elite education.

Scholarship and Teaching

The Challenge to Doctrinalism

In terms of the approach taken to legal education, the major change in the last twenty years has been the replacement of a dominant doctrinal paradigm with a multiplicity of approaches to teaching and studying law. While there is much evidence to suggest that doctrinalism is still perceived as the dominant mode of delivery of legal education by some, there is also considerable evidence

[23] M Trow, *Problems in the Transition from Elite to Mass Higher Education* (Carnegie Commission on Higher Education, 1973), pp 7–20.

[24] Trow argues that this transition takes place when 50 per cent of an age grade attend courses in an institution of higher education (Trow, *supra* n. 23, at 7).

which suggests that other approaches are gaining ground and that "black letter law" in fact no longer holds unquestioned sway in the way it used to do.[25] Socio-legal studies, in particular, has developed rapidly, especially since the establishment of the Socio-Legal Studies Association (SLSA) in 1990.[26] In 1994, when the Economic and Social Research Council published its review of socio-legal studies, it noted that socio-legal studies had achieved "a very wide dispersal among UK higher education institutions", with at least 65 universities and five independent research institutes conducting socio-legal research.[27] Interest in socio-legal studies has been characterised as "the emergence of a new legal paradigm" and socio-legal scholarship has been described as "the most important scholarship currently being undertaken in the legal world".[28] While the precise extent of the influence of socio-legal studies remains a matter of debate, it is clear that with, for example, an association whose membership which has grown from zero to 500 in ten years, and an annual conference attended by as many academics as attend the annual conference of the much longer-established Society of Public Teachers of Law, socio-legal studies has come of age, and represents a major challenge to doctrinalism at the very heart of the law school, both in terms of research and in teaching.[29]

Socio-legal studies is not the only source for change in patterns of scholarship and teaching within the law school. Feminism too has had considerable impact on the law school. While no-one could argue that it is fully part of the mainstream, McGlynn's empirical data reveals its growing influence in British law schools.[30] She notes that while the Harris and Jones survey, carried out in 1996, found 15 law schools offering courses which could be clearly identified as feminist in nature, her own data, collected in 1997, revealed that 24 law schools offer courses which adopt a gender/feminist perspective.[31] Since both sets of data appear to concentrate on whole courses which explore feminism,

[25] See for example, G Jones, "'Traditional' Legal Scholarship" in P Birks (ed.), *Pressing Problems in the Law Volume Two: What Are Law Schools For?* (Oxford, OUP, 1996); P Birks, "The Academic and the Practitioner" (1998) 18 *Legal Studies* 397; W Twining, *Blackstone's Tower: The English Law School* (London, Sweet and Maxwell, 1994), p. 130. For a more detailed development of this argument see A Bradney "Law as a Parasitic Discipline" (1998) 25 *Journal of Law and Society* 71.

[26] P Thomas, "Socio-Legal Studies: The Case of Disappearing Fleas and Bustards" in P Thomas (ed.), *Socio-Legal Studies* (Aldershot, Dartmouth, 1997), p. 10; this chapter contains a brief discussion of the recent development of socio-legal studies.

[27] ESRC, *Review of Socio-Legal Studies: Final Report* (Swindon, ESRC, 1994), p. 24 and Appendix 1.

[28] Thomas, *supra* n. 26, at 19; R Cotterell, *Law's Community: Legal Theory in Sociological Perspective* (Oxford, Clarendon Press, 1995), p. 314.

[29] Information provided by Ann Mumford, the Membership Secretary of the SLSA; we would like to express our gratitude for her assistance. For further discussion of the impact of socio-legal studies on the law school see P Thomas and S Wheeler ch 14.

[30] C McGlynn, *The Woman Lawyer: Making the Difference* (London, Butterworths, 1998).

[31] McGlynn, *ibid.*, at 14.

they necessarily ignore the extent to which it may be used as a significant part of other courses, suggesting that the impact of feminism on the law school is likely to be more widespread than revealed by these surveys. The increasing influence of feminism on legal education is also reflected in the establishment of a journal, *Feminist Legal Studies*, and in the fact that publications which adopt a feminist perspective can now be found on the lists of all the major publishers and in a wide range of law journals. Critical Legal Studies (CLS) has also emerged during the last twenty years as a challenge to the monopoly of doctrinalism. While CLS in Britain has had considerably less influence than it has in the USA, it has nevertheless developed into a distinctive part of the law school scene.[32] CLS in Britain has spawned an annual conference, a new journal (*Law and Critique*), as well as monographs, such as those published by Pluto Press, which cover the "core" subjects or other subjects which are taught in most law schools.[33] Like feminism, the influence of CLS over the last twenty years has spread far beyond those law schools with which it is primarily associated. In scholarship the trajectory set by the last twenty for the next twenty years is one of increasing pluralism.

The Changing Nature of Law Teaching

The last decades of the twentieth century have seen traditional teaching practices within the law school being challenged by the emergence of the legal skills movement. The concept of "legal skills" includes both clinical legal education and a skills-based approach to teaching law.[34] In clinical legal education students are involved in running a law clinic, either with "live" clients or by means of simulations and role plays; the intent being, proponents argue, to develop both academic and vocational skills.[35] A skills-based approach to the teaching of academic law, on the other hand, involves fusing "legal" skills such as legal reasoning and legal research, with general transferable "academic" skills, such

[32] For a discussion of the recent history of CLS in the USA, see A Austin, *The Empire Fights Back: Outsiders and the Struggle Over Legal Education* (New York, New York University Press, 1998).

[33] See, for example, J Conaghan and W Mansell, *The Wrongs of Tort* (2nd edn., London, Pluto Press, 1999) and K O'Donovan, *Family Law Matters* (London, Pluto Press, 1993). (Harris and Jones found that family law was taught in 83.1 per cent of all law schools (Harris and Jones, *supra* n. 5, at 51)).

[34] "Legal skills" is also the term used to refer to courses which teach "lawyering" skills, often referred to as the DRAIN skills (drafting, research, advocacy, interviewing and negotiation); the classic example of this approach in English legal education can be found in N Gold, K Mackie and W Twining. *Learning Lawyers' Skills* (London, Butterworths, 1989).

[35] See for example H Brayne, N Duncan and R Grimes, *Clinical Legal Education: Active Learning in Your Law School* (London, Blackstone Press, 1998) ch. 2, and J MacFarlane "The Clinical Legal Education Evaluation Project" (1990) *The Law Teacher* 65.

as critical analysis or writing skills.[36] The continuing interest in clinical legal education has resulted in the establishment of the Clinical Legal Education Organisation (CLEO) in 1994.[37] However, full-blown clinical legal education continues to be pursued only in a small minority of law schools. In 1994 only about 10 per cent of law schools ran live clinics.[38] However, the Harris and Jones survey found that the penetration of legal skills teaching was much greater than this, with 56.6 per cent of law schools teaching drafting, interviewing, advocacy and negotiation as part of their undergraduate law degrees.[39] The incorporation of skills teaching in the wider sense of a skills-based approach to teaching was much more widespread, with Grimes and others finding that nearly all law schools incorporate some skills teaching into their degree programmes.[40]

The apparent growth in enthusiasm for the inclusion of skills in the curriculum appears to be related to a number of influences external to law schools. Skills are clearly valued in teaching quality assessment processes, as reflected, for example, in the current draft of the law benchmark, which refers both to "general transferable intellectual skills" and to "key skills", such as communication and literacy.[41] Commentators have also noted the influence of other external pressures, such as employer-led demands for "practical relevance" and various government initiatives, such as Enterprise in Higher Education and the PICKUP (Professional, Industrial and Commercial Updating) scheme.[42]

At the same time as law schools appear to have been embracing skills-based teaching, some commentators have been engaged in an extensive examination of the law degree as a form of liberal education. A central recommendation of the Lord Chancellor's Advisory Committee on Legal Education and Conduct, *First Report on Legal Education and Training*, was that "the degree course should stand as an independent liberal education in the discipline of law, not tied to any specific vocation".[43] Hepple, in his examination of the Report, has argued for the development of a broad, liberal legal education which teaches students to engage in rigorous legal argument, but which also teaches them to

[36] See J Webb and C Maugham, *Teaching Lawyers' Skills* (London, Butterworths, 1996).

[37] See Webb and Maugham, *supra* n. 36, at xx.

[38] R Grimes *et al*, "Legal Skills and Clinical Legal Education: A Survey of Undergraduate Law School Practice" (1996) 30 *The Law Teacher* 447.

[39] Harris and Jones, *supra* n. 5, at 49–50. Vocational skills teaching was not evenly distributed; 79 per cent of new university law schools, but only 34 per cent of those in old universities, incorporated these skills into the curriculum (Harris and Jones *ibid.*).

[40] See Grimes *et al*, *supra* n. 38, at 48.

[41] The draft benchmark can be found on the QAA website at http://www.qaa.ac.uk

[42] See Webb and Maugham, *supra* n. 36, at xxi and A Boon, "History is Past Politics: A Critique of the Legal Skills Movement in England and Wales" (1998) 25 *Journal of Law and Society* 151 at 158.

[43] ACLEC, *First Report on Legal Education and Training* (London, ACLEC, 1996), p. 57.

view legal problems from the appropriate social, political or economic perspective, which develops their awareness of the value of comparative law, as well as providing them with sufficient knowledge of theory to make connections between the particular and the general and which also addresses ethical problems, so that students have an awareness of the obligations lawyers owe not just to their clients but to society as a whole.[44] Developing the idea of what a liberal education in law means, Brownsword has argued that the aim of law schools should be not merely to produce really good lawyers, but to produce really good citizens.[45]

Scholarship and Teaching: the Future for the Law School

For some the changes heralded by the development of serious alternatives to traditional doctrinal research and teaching are worrying and threatening. Sherr explores, among a number of other possibilities, the idea that, now that law schools are far less constrained by the requirements of the legal profession, law teachers are worried that the law degree will melt into some sort of general social science degree. "Many are saying if we do not have some guidance, some standards, some 'core', how will we know what is a law degree and what is not?".[46] Equally, Hepple notes that practitioners fear that they:

> "will have trainees who know nothing of breach of contract or tort, let alone estates in land or constructive trusts. Instead they will be expected to employ or give pupillages to a cynical bunch of post-modern theorists, who know little law".[47]

Brownsword's concern, on the other hand, is that

> "in teaching-led law schools, academics will not be resourced in a way that enables them to respond to the liberal mission, while, in research-led law schools, research-active academics who could respond to this mission will have other priorities".[48]

In looking at scholarship and teaching the past tells us that there will be a diverse future for university law schools but gives little clue as to whether the

[44] B Hepple, "The Liberal Law Degree" (1996) 55 *CLJ* 470 at 480–5.

[45] R Brownsword "Teaching Contract: A Liberal Agenda" in P Birks (ed.), *Examining the Law Syllabus: The Core* (Oxford, Oxford University Press, 1992), p. 42. See also R Brownsword, "Law Schools for Lawyers, Citizens and People" in F Cownie (ed.), *The Law School: Global Issues, Local Problems* (Aldershot, Ashgate, 1999), pp. 26, 29; A Bradney, "The Quality of Teaching Assessment in English Law Schools" (1996) 30 *The Law Teacher* 150 and H Collins, "Aims of Teaching the Law of Contract" in P Birks (ed.), *supra* n. 45, at 14.

[46] A Sherr, "Legal Education, Legal Competence and Little Bo-Peep" (1998) 32 *The Law Teacher* 37 at 53.

[47] Hepple, *supra* n. 44, at 480.

[48] R Brownsword, "Law Schools for Lawyers, Citizens and People" in F Cownie (ed.), *The Law School: Global Issues, Local Problems* (Aldershot, Ashgate, 1999), at 27.

system will survive that diversity as a system or whether it will become a set of contending divided institutions.

Audit and Academic Culture

A Culture of Audit?

A superficial analysis would suggest that the trajectory set by the past appears to indicate ever-increasing external control of the life of the university law school during the next two decades. Benchmark standards are due to be implemented in the immediate future. The next Research Assessment Exercise is in 2001. Law schools will be the subject to Quality Assurance Agency review between 2002 and 2003. The noose of external audit is, it seems, being tied ever tighter. On this analysis, by 2020 legal academics can expect to be little more than labourers on a knowledge and teaching production line. "I'm just an employee, like your father at the steel plant" says Roger Lambert, a Professor of Divinity, in John Updike's 1986 New England novel *Roger's Version*.[49] Mass education in university law schools it seems heralds a sea-change in the university's culture and will mean, in future, that we will all be workers in higher education's equivalent of a steel plant. Closer examination of the implementation of audit processes in university law schools, however, suggests a rather different picture for the future.

In 1989, writing after a number of attacks on the autonomy of universities and university law schools, McAuslan argued that:

> "there is a crisis looming in legal education. . .unless those who are professional legal educators adopt a proactive approach to the crisis, we will inevitably be driven to adopting a reactive approach which will do irremediable harm to legal education and scholarship".[50]

McAuslan identified the failings of university law schools as lying in two directions; first, that they and their professional associations failed to respond to official and unofficial reports on matters that affected legal education and secondly, that legal academics failed to think about legal education "on any kind of coherent collective basis and I would venture to suggest on an individ-

[49] J Updike, *Roger's Version* (London, Andre Deutsch, 1999), p. 62. In fact the novel shows that Lambert misunderstands his own position in the University and that his role as an academic is in fact very different from that of an employee in a steel plant. See further A Bradney and F Cownie, "Working on the Chain Gang?" (1996) II(2) *Contemporary Issues in Law* 15 at 30.

[50] P McAuslan, "The Coming Crisis in Legal Education" (1989) 16 *Journal of Law and Society* 310.

ual basis".[51] McAuslan's propositions were plausible, although perhaps overstated, at his date of writing. Law schools at this date did comparatively little to defend their tribal culture from external attack.[52] The reaction of the community of academic legal scholars to external interventions over the decade following his article have meant that a very different picture is to be found in the present day.

In 1988 only eight law schools or professional associations representing legal academics made representations to the Marre Committee when it considered university legal education.[53] The Committee's subsequent report was critical of university law schools. The Committee concluded that, amongst other things, university law schools "should be made aware of the inadequacies of students entering the vocational stage and should make concerted efforts to meet these deficiencies" and sought to retain constraints on the independence of law schools recommending that "the concept of the core subjects should be retained".[54] In 1996 35 law schools or professional associations representing legal academics made representations to ACLEC when it was preparing its report on legal education.[55] ACLEC took a much more positive attitude towards university law schools than Marre had done. It concluded that:

> "the strait-jacket of subject prescription must be lifted. We recommend that law schools should be left to decide for themselves, in the light of their own objectives, which areas of law will be studied in depth".[56]

Comparison of the legal academic community's reaction to Marre and ACLEC is illustrative of a general change in legal academic politics during the 1990s. Whereas once the community largely ignored external bodies, perhaps correctly judging that they would have little effect on the university (the Marre Report's recommendations resulted in no changes to university legal education), the community now seeks to manage change by making early interventions. These interventions have not affected the fact of increasing amounts of external audit of university law schools but they have altered the impact of that audit.

An illustration of the change in way in which the academic community of legal scholars now manages its affairs can be seen in the way in which the Research Assessment Exercise has been implemented. The Research

[51] McAulsan, *ibid.*, at 311 and 312.

[52] On the idea of the division of the university into different academic tribes see T Becher, *Academic Tribes and Territories* (Buckingham, SRHE/Open University Press, 1989).

[53] *A Time for Change: Report of the Committee on the Future of the Legal Profession* (The Marre Report) (London, The General Council of the Bar and The Law Society, 1988) Appendix B.

[54] The Marre Report, *supra* n. 53, at 121.

[55] *First Report on Legal Education and Training* (The ACLEC Report) (London, The Lord Chancellor's Advisory Committee on Legal Education and Conduct, 1996), Appendix B.

[56] The ACLEC Report, *ibid.*, at 64.

Assessment Exercise was originally introduced in response to a government perception that new mechanisms were needed to ensure that funds set aside for research were "effectively deployed" in universities.[57] For the then Government, "effective deployment" meant that "higher education [had] to contribute more effectively to the improvement of the performance of the economy".[58] In the context of legal scholarship such a demand could be interpreted as a call for more writing which would directly assist the legal professions. Thus, from the Government's point of view, the Research Assessment Exercise should have increased the amount of research that was of direct utility for the professions. In practice most legal academics have "felt that the RAE discouraged the writing of professional practice books".[59] Not all legal academics have welcomed this, arguing that the RAE has resulted in what they would call "applied research" being devalued.[60] Nonetheless the important point for analysis here is that the RAE's judgements have been made by a panel comprised of academics, who in turn were nominated by academics, and their audit judgement was made using criteria which were probably antithetical to those intended by the external body (in this case the Government) whose pressure led to the introduction of the audit.[61] Audit has not changed the fundamental nature of academic culture; rather, arguably, it has enhanced it.

One resource for resistance to external pressure in the present day is that fact that, contrary to McAuslan's analysis of the situation in the late 1980s, the RAE panel's work is not now done in the context of a community which, collectively and individually, fails to analyse the nature of legal education. On the contrary, legal education now forms a discrete area of research and scholarship with its own journals, monographs, subject groupings and conferences.[62] Like most areas of scholarship or research, issues relating to university legal education are highly contested topics but that contest serves to delimit the parameters of academic thinking about university legal education and, through the contest, clarify and deepen that thinking. This thinking in turn contributes to debates within professional associations. In one sense this rising field of research into legal education brings nothing new to the law school. There has always been thinking and writing about legal education in universities and this writing and

[57] *The Development of Higher Education into the 1990s* (Cmnd 9524, 1985), para 9.11.

[58] *The Development of Higher Education into the 1990s, ibid.*, at para 1.2.

[59] K Campbell, D Vick, A Murray and G Little, "Journal Publishing, Journal Reputation and the United Kingdom's Research Assessment Exercise" (1999) 29 *Journal of Law and Society* 470 at 475.

[60] See, for example, A Hicks "Legal Practice is an Academic Matter" *SPTL Reporter* (Spring 1995) 6.

[61] A similar argument could be made with respect to the application of the Teaching Quality Assessment exercise to university law schools. See further A Bradney "The Quality of Teaching Quality Assessment in English Law Schools" (1996) *The Law Teacher* 150.

[62] On the growth of legal education as a sub-discipline within law see further A Bradney "The Rise and Rise of Legal Education" (1997) 4 *Web Journal of Current Legal Issues*.

thinking has been an important part of the culture of those engaged in university legal education.[63] However, the greater quantity and higher general quality of work in this area now helps law schools to acquire a clearer sense of their own identity and a surer sense of their own purpose.

The lesson for the future to be derived from this example of the implementation of the RAE is not that over the next two decades law schools will increasingly be driven to do things that they do not want to in response to outside pressures but that they can retain a substantial degree of control over their own destinies if they are willing to invest the time and effort that is necessary in managing the process of audit.[64]

The above is not to argue that audit, and probably increasing degrees of audit, will not be a feature of the next two decades. Moreover it is clear that the various forms of audit imposed on university law schools have worsened the quality of academic's lives and will probably continue to do so. The RAE itself is commonly seen as being a largely deleterious exercise by both the academic legal community and the wider academic community.[65] Academics in law schools as much as academics elsewhere are subject to increasing degrees of stress. Rose reports university teachers as being the fifth most stressed occupational group out of a total number of 143 occupational groups surveyed.[66] However, the stress occasioned by audit should not be taken as being indicative of a successful attempt to control the direction or focus of academic lives.

The Occupational Culture of the Law School

Research into the work of universities has been consistent in showing that the occupational culture of academics is far more important in determining behaviour than any hierarchical or managerial controls, whether these come from inside or outside the universities.[67] Thus, for example, even in the new

[63] Blackstone's lecture on the nature of university legal education, "On the Study of Law", was given and published in 1752 (W Blackstone, *Commentaries on the Laws of England* (16th edn, T Cadell and J Butterworth, London, 1825), p. 3).

[64] In this instance the specific time and effort being that expended by professional associations who ensured that those nominated to serve on the RAE panel were acceptable to the academic community at large.

[65] See, for example, D Wick, A Murray, G Little and K Campbell, "The Perceptions of Academic Lawyers Concerning the Effects of the United Kingdom's Research Assessment Exercise" (1998) 25 *Journal of Law and Society* 536 and T Smith, "The UGC's Research Rankings Exercise" (1987) 41 *Higher Education Quarterly* 303.

[66] M Rose "Future Tense . . . Are Growing Occupations More Stressed-out and Depressive?" (2000) (www.bath.ac.uk/~hmjr).

[67] This point is not unique to the universities. Holdaway has shown that the occupational culture of junior police officers is more important in determining their behaviour than is either statute or the instructions of their senior officers (S Holdaway, *Inside the British Police* (Oxford, Basil Blackwell, 1983).

university sector, where both the culture and form of university governance is more managerial and more bureaucratic than that within the old university sector, Trowler has shown that the internal cultural imperatives of the academic body subvert management or audit controls.[68] It is his perception of the strength of this culture which led Trow to argue that many of the Dearing Committee recommendations were doomed to failure because they rested on the premise that change could be imposed on the academic community.[69] Trow argued that, on the contrary, change which was change in substance, rather than change in form, either came from within the academic community or not at all. Similarly, Becher has argued that audit only becomes acceptable when it is managed in a collegial way.[70]

What will be important for the direction of university law schools over the next two decades is not the process of audit but the internal culture of university law schools. Historically, other academics have been critical of university law schools, seeing them as alien intruders within the academy. Veblen, writing in 1918, argued that because of its concern with vocational training, the law school had as little a place within the university as did a fencing school.[71] In Becher's description of the university some eleven years ago he quotes one academic as describing academic lawyers as "an appendage to the academic world".[72] Historically, such hostile comment has not been limited to those outside the law school. Bridges' comments, twenty-five years ago, on the limited research aspirations of academic lawyers have already been noted and the anti-intellectual tendencies of academic lawyers in the recent past have also been the subject of comment.[73] However, the present culture of university law schools and the likely culture two decades from now is, in general, very different from that to be found in the past.

Twining, using unpublished data provided by Halsey from work done for his survey published as "Decline of Donnish Dominion", notes that:

> "in almost all key respects his [Halsey's] profile of academic lawyers in 1989 very closely resembled the profile of the academic profession as a whole, especially colleagues in the Humanities and Social Sciences".[74]

[68] P Trowler, *Academics Responding to Change* (Buckingham, SRHE/Open University Press, 1998).

[69] M Trow, "The Dearing Report: A Transatlantic View" (1998) 52 *Higher Education Quarterly* 93.

[70] T Becher, "Making Audit Acceptable: A Collegial Approach to Quality Assurance" (1992) 46 *Higher Education Quarterly* 47

[71] T Veblen, *The Higher Learning in America* (New York, Augustus M Kelly, Bookseller, 1919), p. 211.

[72] T Becher, *Academic Tribes and Territories* (Buckingham, SRHE/Open University Press, 1989), p. 30.

[73] A Bradney, "Legal Education in the 21st Century" in J Grant *et al* (eds), *Legal Education 2000* (Aldershot, Gower, 1988).

[74] W Twining, *Blackstone's Tower* (London, Stevens and Sons/Sweet and Maxwell, 1994), p. 202.

Perhaps the most important findings, in the light of the critical comments noted above, were the fact that academic lawyers devoted the same amount of time to research as their colleagues and, if anything, produced slightly more publications.[75] Academic lawyers, in other words, valued the academic side of their job as highly as anyone else within the university. Leighton, Mortimer and Whatley's 1995 survey similarly provides evidence to illustrate a change in the culture of law schools. Only 10 per cent of their respondents thought membership of the academic community to be unimportant or irrelevant to their work whilst 88 per cent of respondents thought that the opportunity of doing research was either essential or important in their jobs.[76] Similarly, there is some evidence to indicate a general improvement of the standard of academic qualifications held by those working in university law schools. Twining's 1989 data suggested that those in law schools had far fewer doctorates than those outside but the 1995 Leighton, Mortimer and Whatley study showed a considerable increase in numbers with research qualifications.[77] The law school is becoming ever more centrally part of the university.

In important respects the changing nature of academic culture in university law schools represents a distancing of the law school from the legal professions. In 1989 the Committee of Heads of University Law Schools issued a policy statement, saying that full-time academic work was not compatible with "significant" employment elsewhere, thus making combining academic life and practice more difficult.[78] More respondents rated the opportunity to do consultantcy as being irrelevant than virtually any other aspect of academic life in the Leighton, Mortimer and Whatley survey.[79] Writing and scholarship is ever less concerned with practitioners and academics are increasingly less likely to have had experience of legal practice.[80] Yet there is a need for caution when describing this aspect of the change in academic culture. Work done for the

[75] Twining, *ibid.*, at 203.

[76] P Leighton, T Mortimer and N Whatley, *Law Teachers: Lawyers or Academics?* (London, Cavendish, 1995), pp. 53–4. 28 per cent of respondents said that they were presently engaged in consultancy whilst 75 per cent said that they were engaged in research (Leighton, Mortimer and Whatley, *ibid.*, at 41).

[77] Twining's figures showed that 11.8 per cent of those in law schools had doctorates compared with 58.4 per cent in the rest of the university (Twining, *supra*, n. 74, at 203). Leighton, Mortimer and Whatley found that 22 per cent of their respondents had Masters of Philosophy or doctorates in law and 4 per cent had the same qualifications in other disciplines (Leighton, Mortimer and Whatley, *supra* n. 76, at 18).

[78] Committee of Heads of University Law Schools, *Academic Staff Recruitment and Retention* (1989), p. 8.

[79] Leighton, Mortimer and Whatley, *supra* n. 76, at 55.

[80] K Campbell, D Vick, A Murray and G Little, "Journal Publishing, Journal Reputation and the United Kingdom's Research Assessment Exercise" (1999) 29 *Journal of Law and Society* 470 at 475; according to Leighton, Mortimer and Whatley, 40 per cent of their respondents did not have professional legal qualifications and less than half of those who did have such qualifications had practised for any significant time (Leighton, Mortimer and Whatley, *supra* n. 76, at ix).

professions now includes not just writing but also studies of the nature of professional activity.[81] Work by academics in the professions includes not only those academics who are still active practitioners but also those who are trainers and significant numbers who hold judicial office.[82] The change in academic culture has seen less engagement with the professions but, at the same time, a broadening of that engagement. The law school of 2020, if this trend continues, will still devote some of its time to the professions, but what it does with the professions will be very different from the old diet of writing, practice and continuing professional development, and what it does with the professions will be done, at least largely, because of the contribution it can make to academic scholarship.[83]

Diversity and Discord

Treating legal academics as a members of a single community with a single culture is, in some ways, problematic. We have already noted continuing divisions in the nature of legal scholarship and changes in the balance of power between those different forms of scholarship. There are long-established institutional differences between law schools in Scotland and those in England and Wales. The university law schools of Northern Ireland have a rather different role in their community to those elsewhere in the United Kingdom. The formal abolition of the binary divide has not been translated into a substantive abolition of this divide.[84] Equally there are continuing gender differences between the experience of male and female academics.[85] A short chapter of this kind can do little to acknowledge the diversity that is now to be found in the various missions of university law schools, the individual background and aspirations of

[81] For example, V Johnston and J Shapland, *Developing Vocational Training for the Bar* (Sheffield, Faculty of Law University of Sheffield, 1990).

[82] See, for example, M Partington, "Academic Lawyers and Legal Practice in Britain: A Preliminary Analysis" (1988) 15 *Journal of Law and Society* 374.

[83] Thus, for example, Johnston and Shapland's survey of the nature of barrister's work, *supra* n. 81, undoubtedly had pragmatic significance for the Bar when they addressed the question of course content for the Bar Vocational Course. More important for the academic community was the insight that the survey gave us into the question of what it meant to be a lawyer within the modern legal system.

[84] Harris and Jones found it necessary to report the new university and old university results for many aspects of their survey of university law schools because of the differences between the two sectors (P Harris and M Jones, "A Survey of Law Schools in the United Kingdom, 1996" (1997) 31 *The Law Teacher* 38).

[85] See, for example, F Cownie, "Women Legal Academics—A New Research Agenda?" (1998) 25 *Journal of Law and Society* 102; Leighton, Mortimer and Whatley, *supra* n. 76, and C McGlynn, *The Woman Lawyer* (London, Butterworths, 1998), ch. 2.

academic staff and the range of students in all kinds of courses. Yet that diversity is both an important new feature of university law schools and one that is likely to continue over the next two decades. Most university law schools entered the RAE in 1996 but not all did so. Academic research is now an ever more dominant part of the culture of law schools. It does not follow, however, that all law schools or all academics will follow this route. A dominant culture is not the only culture. Some law schools have already identified teaching goals that are, because of their large-scale resource implications, probably incompatible with the pursuit of a significant quantity of research. The Open University is an institution which now offers undergraduate law without employing a single full-time legal academic and with a course which is restricted to the "core" subjects for the purposes of professional practice.[86] For each example of what law schools are like now, and what they are likely to become, it is possible to find counter-examples. Nor are any of the present divides immutable. What divides us in 2000 is different from that which will divide us in 2020. Once, for example, research was mainly a feature of old university law schools; now, increasing numbers of new university law schools are entering significant numbers of staff in the RAE and some are creating specific research units within their law school. Law schools which have a research mission will be a feature of 2020 and will dominate academic legal culture but they are unlikely to be the only kind of law school and, if present trends are maintained, not all old university law schools will have a research mission and some, perhaps many, new university law schools will have such a mission.[87] What is at issue is whether, in that divergence in mission, university law schools will continue to have sufficient unity to oppose external interference whilst, at the same time, pursuing different and sometimes antithetical, or even hostile, intellectual agendas.

[86] http://pcbs042.open.ac.uk/law/

[87] Evidence for this is to be found in changes in RAE ratings for various law schools over the last two exercises.

2

Legal System and Procedure

SIR RICHARD SCOTT

Every civilised country needs a civil justice system. Its function is to provide a means whereby citizens can have their disputes resolved without having to resort to self-help. Everyone who has been to a school or grown up in a large family will have understood from an early age that recourse to a superior authority to settle disputes is to be avoided if possible. It is a recourse of last resort. But the need to place limitations on self-help is also something that is, or should be, learned very early in life. The interests of every society, whether school or country, demand that, if a reasonable and acceptable compromise cannot be reached between disputing parties, a means of dispute resolution other than use of the strong-arm must be available to them.

A state of affairs under which self-help in the resolution of civil disputes were the order of the day would be chaotic. A trader with an unpaid debt will probably start by writing to his debtor asking for payment. If payment is not forthcoming the demands are likely to become increasingly peremptory. Eventually the trader may need, if he is to obtain payment, to do something more. What he must do is to have recourse to the civil justice system, obtain an order against the debtor for payment of the debt and then execute the judgment in one or other of the ways the law permits. What he must not do is employ strong-arm men to visit the debtor and to extract payment by force or by threats of force. If he does so he, and his strong-arm men, may find themselves in the criminal courts. It is reasonable to regard the provision of an accessible and fair civil justice system as an obligation imposed on the State as a *quid pro quo* for the ban which the State imposes on the use by its citizens of forcible self-help. It follows that if a civil justice system is to discharge its essential function it must use procedures which are, and are perceived to be, fair to the disputants and efficient in resolving disputes. In addition, and just as important, the system must be reasonably accessible to all citizens who need to use it. These three features, fairness, efficiency and accessibility are, I suggest, the touchstones by which to measure the adequacy of a civil justice system.

As is well known, the first stage of Lord Woolf,s *Access to Justice* reforms was introduced on 26 April 1999 and, at the time of writing, we have had some ten months' experience of the new system. It is still too early to be sure to what extent the new system is achieving the improvements intended; it can at least be said, however, that the forecasters of gloom and doom have not yet been able to claim any tributes to their prescience and wisdom. In the meantime it is possible, and, perhaps, instructive, to measure up the reformed system against the three attributes that I have mentioned, fairness, efficiency and accessibility.

The first two of these, fairness and efficiency, go hand in hand. Both procedural efficiency and procedural fairness may be obtained at too high a cost to the other. The trick is to strike the right balance. I think this is probably so in every justice system in every country. In this country our civil justice system is, basically, adversarial in character. The essence of an adversarial system is that each side prepares its case which is presented to an impartial court whose task is to choose which of the two cases, on the facts and in law, is to be preferred. The function of the court in a true adversarial system is not to seek the truth in any absolute sense but simply to judge between the two sides. In such a system the court does not take the initiative in preparing the case for trial, does not interfere with the parties, choices of witnesses, cannot decline to hear admissible evidence, does not inform itself in advance about the facts of the case or issue which is to be heard or about the relevant law and certainly does not carry out any independent research into the legal principles applicable to the case. The court simply judges which of the rival cases presented by the litigants is to be preferred.

Provided that each side has sufficient notice of the factual case the opposing side is to present in order to be able properly to deal with it, an adversarial system as I have described it may be thought to be fair. But it is fair only if each of the disputing parties has the same knowledge of the relevant facts, the same ability to look at the relevant documents and the same access to the witnesses of fact as the other. For the system to operate fairly, the litigation must take place, as it is sometimes put, on a level playing field. A level playing field can be provided for by procedural rules for disclosure of documents, rules for the names and statements of witnesses to be exchanged in advance of the hearing, rules enabling information about the facts known to one side but not to be other to be disclosed. Procedural rules imposed on one party in order to assist the other in order to make the litigation fair, in order to provide the level playing field, is bound to make some inroads into the strict concept of adversarial litigation under which a previously uninformed court simply chooses between the rival cases that the parties choose to present. The multitude of procedural powers, starting with powers to order discovery, that were conferred on the civil courts over the period between the Common Law Procedure Act 1854 and the introduction of the Civil Procedure Rules (SI 1998/3132) on 26 April 1999, were for the most part, conferred on a basis consistent with the adversarial system, namely, that the powers would not be exercisable otherwise than on the application of a litigant. The notion of the court exercising its procedural powers of its own initiative would have been heresy under the old Supreme Court or County Court Rules.

Nonetheless, the procedural powers bestowed on the court, the exercise of which was discretionary not obligatory, from time to time placed the court in the position of making procedural decisions that neither litigant had sought. If one party applied for discovery, or for further and better particulars of a pleading, or for the adjournment of the trial, or for anything else, the application would be dealt with on an adversarial basis. Each side would present its case on the issue in question. But the court would not be obliged to confine itself to choosing which of the cases it preferred. It could produce a compromise between the rival contentions, order some of the discovery sought but not all, agree to an adjournment on conditions, make an "unless" order, and so on. The concept of case management by the court did not begin on 26 April 1999. It was, I think, a concept born when discretionary procedural powers first began to be available to the courts.

Over the period between the time when I began practice at the Bar, 1960, and, say, 1999, there was a steady increase in the degree of control exercised, or available to be exercised, by the courts over the progress of cases from their inception to trial. There were, no doubt, many reasons for this increase, but among them, in my view, were the increasing factual complexity of cases, the growing proliferation of documents, the curse of the photocopier, increasing pressure on judicial resources and on courts, and ever increasing litigation costs. A response to these pressures became necessary. Some procedural steps in the litigation were made automatic, rather than being left to the parties to apply for if they wished. Automatic discovery after close of pleadings was introduced, a summons for directions within a set period of close of pleadings had to be issued, together with potentially severe sanctions if the required steps were not taken. In the county courts the automatic strike-out of proceedings was prescribed if a strict timetable of steps to be taken was not complied with (see Order 17, rule 11 of the County Court Rules 1981 (SI 1981/1687)). These rules, in attempting to dictate to the parties how they should conduct the litigation, were inconsistent with an adversarial system. Nor did they succeed in preventing many cases being left inactive, gathering dust, for far too long. In the case of the County Court automatic strike-outs, the rules led to an intolerable burden on the courts which had to deal with re-instatement applications from litigants whose only error was in the choice of their legal adviser. The procedural rules would, if they had been properly complied with, have led to efficient litigation conducted fairly on a level playing field. In the event, however, they failed to ensure fairness, for justice delayed is justice denied, and certainly did not ensure efficiency. The problem was not any deficiency in the substance of the procedural powers of the court, but was that the court had not been given power to use its procedural powers on its own initiative. The adversarial system under which the parties were able to decide for themselves on the steps they would take and on what applications to make and when to make them failed to ensure a consistently efficient preparation of cases for trial. The discretionary powers of the court could only be exercised on an application from one of the parties. The adversarial system remained intact.

One of the most radical changes introduced by the Civil Procedure Rules, a change which has had much less publicity than it deserves, is that, for the first time, all the procedural powers available to the court can be exercised on the court,s own initiative (see CPR 3.3). The implications of this change are far-reaching. Consider, for example, some of the powers that procedural judges can now exercise without any prior application from any of the parties.

The court can strike out a claim as being vexatious or bound to fail (CPR 3.4). The court can give summary judgment against the claimant or against the defendant (CPR 24). The court can direct a preliminary issue to be tried (CPR 3.1(l)). The court can order an additional party or parties to be joined (CPR 19.1). The court can order a party to provide to the other side an estimate of his costs already incurred and likely to be incurred in the future (section 4 of the Practice Direction to CPR 43). The court can consolidate claims and separate out particular issues to be tried separately (CPR 3.1(g) and (i)). The court can exclude admissible evidence (CPR 32.1), control expert evidence, or direct that only a single joint expert may give evidence (CPR 35.4 and 35.7). The court can stay the proceedings for up to a month in order to encourage the parties to try mediation (CPR 26.4). The court may do all or any of these things of its own initiative and even in the face of opposition from the parties. We no longer have, in the strict sense, an adversarial system. We do not have an inquisitorial system either. The court has no power itself to investigate the facts of the case. The court,s role, being neither inquisitorial nor confined to its adversarial role of referee, has become managerial.

It is not only in the procedural stages leading up to the trial that the court,s role has ceased to be strictly adversarial. The days of a trial taking place before an uninformed judge who has no prior knowledge of the case have gone forever. This departure from adversarial principle predated the Civil Procedure Rules but has been underlined and confirmed by them. In 1983, when I was appointed a judge in the Chancery Division, there was a highly respected and experienced Chancery judge still on the Bench who not only did not pre-read before the commencement of a hearing but expressed the view that it was positively wrong to do so. The plaintiff or applicant was entitled, he thought, to come into court and present his case to a judge with no pre-conceived view about the issues and whose mind, apart from being full of legal learning, was as a blank sheet of paper. This is the purist's view of the adversarial system. But it is a view that was fatally undermined by the advent of skeleton arguments. Skeleton arguments are pointless without some reference to the facts. They will refer also to the leading cases on which the author will rely or which he will seek to distinguish. They are an invitation to the judge to read into the case before the hearing commences. Every judge is now expected to accept this invitation. Skeleton arguments are expected to include a reading list for the judge, identifying the documents that the judge should read in advance in order to understand the issues and the arguments. The skeletons are now required to include an estimate of the time the judge will need in order to read the material set out in the reading list. This estimate is necessary so that the Clerk of the Lists will know when to place the case papers before the judge. The judge must be given time to read the material before the hearing begins.

An obvious, and intended, consequence of this pre-reading is that the judge will have formed a view about the case before the hearing begins. His view will not be a concluded view; his mind must be kept open until he has heard the evidence and the parties' arguments. But his mind will certainly not be a blank sheet of paper.

Another consequence of the pre-reading is that the judge, if he has time, is quite likely to have done some research on his own into the legal issues. Judges are all ex-litigators of experience. That that is so is, I believe, one of the strengths of our system. It is not in the least uncommon for a judge to recall authority bearing upon the case but which has not been referred to in the skeletons. The judge is likely to refresh his memory about such an authority or to pursue a particular line of legal inquiry which is prompted by the facts of the case but not dealt with in the skeletons. So, by the time the hearing commences, the judge may not only have a preliminary view but a view based on a line of authority not dealt with in the skeletons. This state of affairs is plainly inconsistent with an adversarial system under which the judge simply reacts to the cases presented by the parties.

The changes to which I have referred, the departures from a strict adversarial system are intended to, and I do not doubt will, improve the efficiency of the litigation process. But it is important that they should not lead to unfairness. And because the procedures built into our system in order to ensure fairness are, for the most part, designed to achieve fairness in an adversarial system, it is I think, very important that special attention should be paid to the need for fairness in connection with those rules and procedures that represent a departure from the adversarial system.

So far as the exercise by the court of powers on its own initiative is concerned, CPR 3.3 contains rules designed to achieve fairness. Either the parties must be given a suitable opportunity to make representations before the order is made or, alternatively, a party affected by the order must be given an opportunity to apply to have the order set aside or varied (see CPR 3.3(3) and (5)). These rules provide a framework which ought to prevent court intervention from becoming unfair.

As to the exercise of particular powers, the rules are less explicit as to what should be done to ensure fairness. The overriding objective, set out in CPR 1, must be the guide. And it must be borne in mind that the object of the Civil Procedure Rules is not absolute justice but justice proportionate to what is at stake in the litigation. In litigation where many millions of pounds are at stake it might well be unjust to deny the parties the right to rely on the evidence of expert witnesses of their choice. But in a case where the amount at stake is not more than £15,000, and where the use of separate experts, one for each side, would be likely to cause the hearing to last longer than a day and disqualify it from the fast track, it might be positively unjust to allow multiple experts.

If the court is responding to an application made by a party, it may be that fairness requires no more than that proper notice of the application be given to the other side and that a proper opportunity to make representations in opposition to the application be provided. The application notice will have set out the remedy the applicant is seeking and the applicant's written evidence will have disclosed the material being relied on in support. But where the court is proposing to exercise a power on its own initiative, it will be necessary, in my opinion, for a full statement of the court's reasons for so proposing to be supplied to the parties. It is as necessary for a party to know the case he is to meet where the proposal to make the order comes from the court as it is where the proposal comes from a litigant. There is nothing inherently unfair in the interventionist powers given to the court by the CPR, but great care must, in my view, be taken to ensure that the court does not act on its own initiative in a manner that is unfair. As Bridge LJ (as he then was) observed in *Goldsmith* v. *Sperrings* [1977] 1 WLR 508, the rule, *audi alterem partem*, applies to points taken by the court as well as to points taken by opposing litigants. Judges should bear this in mind when proposing to exercise powers on their own initiative. Apart from anything else, Article 6 of the European Convention on Human Rights 1950 will, as from 2 October 2000, require them to do so.

In my opinion, not in the least a disinterested one, the Civl Procedure Rules, the new civil justice system, measures up, on paper at least, to the criteria of fairness and efficiency. Whether the new rules will do so in practice will depend upon the manner of their implementation. There is no reason why they should not do so.

Some of the implications of the departure from an adversarial system that the new rules represent have not yet been fully realised. I will give two examples.

It is often desirable in the interests of efficient case management in a complex case to assign at an early stage a particular judge to deal with, or to supervise, its case management and to deal with any applications for interim remedies, such as injunctions, security for costs or the like. Where that has been done, representations are not infrequently made by parties asking for the trial judge to be someone other than the assigned judge. The reason usually given is that the assigned judge will have learnt too much about the case. He may have made rulings against one or other, or all, of the parties. He may have expressed some view about the case adverse to one of the parties. By the time the trial comes to be heard, the impartiality of the assigned judge may, so it is argued, have become suspect. Similar representations are sometimes made after a hotly contested and highly contentious interlocutory application has been heard. A direction is sought for some other judge to be the trial judge. These are representations which hark back to the days when the trial judge's mind was supposed to be like a blank sheet of paper. They reflect a mind-set consistent with an adversarial system of litigation which we no longer have. Unless there is reason to doubt the ability of the assigned judge to maintain an open mind about the issues still to be decided—in which case he should be relieved of his position as the assigned judge—he is, for the very reason that he knows more about the case than anyone else, ideally placed to conduct the trial. The parties are not entitled to expect to open their cases before an uninformed judge.

The other example relates to what is sometimes called "litigation privilege". Litigation privilege has grown out of legal professional privilege and is, I believe, a product of the adversarial system. The importance in the public interest of lawyer/client privilege is undoubted and I need not take time to defend it. Lawyer/client privilege gives the client the right to withhold from disclosure his instructions to his lawyers and his lawyers' advice to him, whether given in documentary or oral form. Litigation privilege would extend that right to all documents brought into existence for the purposes of the litigation. But this makes sense only in the context of a strict adversarial system. Under such a system, each side prepares its case, the identity of witnesses need not be disclosed, the evidence the witnesses can give can be kept under wraps until they appear in the witness box. Litigation privilege is consistent with such a system. But that system, as I have already remarked, has gone forever. Compulsory exchange of witness statements pre-dated the Civil Procedure Rules. Exchange of experts, reports has been required for some considerable time, but exchange of other witnesses, statements only relatively recently. These rules had, well before 26 April 1999, become commonplace. They are plainly not consistent with litigation privilege. Nonetheless, if a party requests disclosure of earlier drafts of a disclosed witness statement, the request is likely still to be met by a plea of litigation privilege. And the plea is likely to succeed. Litigation privilege has been raised as an objection to the rule regarding an expert witness to state the substance of the instructions pursuant to which he wrote his report (CPR 35.10). An authoritative ruling on this point is still awaited but, in my opinion, the objection should be rejected. The justification of litigation privilege in the context of the civil justice system now in place needs, I believe, to be re-thought. I do not believe there is any longer any public interest justification for it. The public interest reasons supporting lawyer/client privilege are as powerful as ever. But the changes in the rules for the conduct of civil litigation have removed, in my opinion, whatever justification for litigation privilege there may previously have been. If the implications of our departure from an adversarial system are not thought through, there is a danger that the fairness and efficiency of the new system may in some respects be undermined.

The third criterion by which the new system must be measured is accessibility. As to this, the new system stands, in my view, in some danger of failing satisfactorily to meet the criterion. The cost of litigation is continuing to constitute an obstacle to the ability of most citizens of this country to have access to justice.

Lord Woolf, in formulating his proposed reforms, had the cost of litigation very much in mind. He recommended the introduction of the „fast track‰ for litigating cases of a modest amount at a fixed cost. The Civil Procedure Rules incorporate a fast track system. The fast track is available for cases where not more than £15,000 is at stake and which are estimated to last no longer than one day. But the fixed cost recommendation has not yet been implemented. There is a fixed fee for advocates at the fast track hearing but all the other costs of the litigation are at large. Moreover, the costs of all litigation, including fast track litigation, are likely to be increased as from 2 April 2000. Two changes come into effect on that date. First there will be widescale withdrawal of legal aid as a means whereby those of slender means can fund civil litigation. Legal aid will not disappear entirely, but it will be withdrawn from the vast majority of cases where previously it was available. The substitute means of funding civil litigation, intended to take the place of legal aid, will be conditional fee agreements and after-the-event insurance. Conditional fee agreements, under which the lawyers will recover nothing if their client fails but up to double the rate of normal fees if their client succeeds, are now authorised for practically all types of litigation. And, as from 2 April 2000, the amount of the uplift (subject to the powers of costs judges to cut down percentage uplifts fixed at an unreasonably high levels) will be recoverable under a costs order made against the losing party. So, too, will the insurance premium, paid to effect an after-the-event insurance policy to protect the insured against his costs liability if he should fail in the action, be recoverable.

These changes may make it impossible for an ordinary person of modest means to contest an action against an opponent funded under a conditional fee agreement. Such a person can, in theory, protect his position by effecting insurance to cover his costs liability in the event he loses the litigation. But for many people the premiums payable may be too high. And a person funded by a conditional fee agreement, usually a claimant, may be unable to pay the premium for a policy to protect himself against the liability to pay the costs of the other side that he will incur if his action should fail.

These are very real problems. How they will appear after 2 April 2000 is to some extent a matter of speculation, but that they will render the courts inaccessible to many people is a very real fear.

Then there is the issue of court fees. These are about to be substantially increased. In the totality of litigation costs, court fees are likely to represent only a small proportion. But an increase in fees may drive from the courts those whose ability or willingness to pay for litigation had already become marginal. The "straw that breaks the camel's back" will be only a trivial proportion of the total load. So, too, with court fees.

While, therefore, the civil justice system and procedures that are now in place comply with the criteria of fairness and efficiency and go some way towards controlling the costs of litigation, the accessibility of the system to ordinary people seems to me to be in some danger. This is no time for complacency.

3

Self-regulation and the Future of the Profession

ALAN PATERSON

An invitation to consider the future of the legal profession and its regulation even for as short a period as the next twenty years is one to be regarded with the circumspection of one of Princess Liu's suitors in "Turandot". At best it is an opportunity to look foolish and at worst to jeopardise one's intellectual credibility. As Mark Twain is reputed to have observed, "it is dangerous to prophesy, particularly about the future". Certainly the speed of change in the last twenty years offers little by way of comfort. Back then complacency and anti-competitive practices were the order of the day. Scale fees, unchallenged monopolies and a ban on advertising ruled the roost. Self-regulation was simply unquestioned. Had it been so, the puzzled respondent would have replied that the profession's right to regulate itself was a vital part of being a profession, and was clearly in the public interest since (1) only peers were in a position to judge their fellows, (2) peers were more likely to be tough on errant lawyers than outsiders and thus standards in the profession would be higher, (3) it was cheaper than the alternatives, and (4) it was quicker and more effective than the alternatives.[1]

How different appears the scene today. The criticisms of self-regulation are much more to the fore: that it can be a cloak for rent-seeking if not profiteering, for regulatory capture, ineffective disciplinary procedures and anti-competitive practices.[2] More active consumer movements and a global

[1] The arguments in favour of self-regulation in the case of professions can be found in P Slayton and M J Trebilcock (eds), *The Professions and Public Policy* (Toronto, University of Toronto Press, 1976); A Ogus, *Regulation: Legal Form and Economic Theory* (Oxford, Clarendon Press, 1994), p. 107 and M Seneviratne, *The Legal Profession: Regulation and the Consumer* (London, Sweet and Maxwell, 1999), pp. 26–28.

[2] Such arguments can be found in a range of modern writings including Ogus, *supra* n. 1, at 108, Seneviratne, *supra* n. 1, at 28–9 and D Rhode, "Policing the Professional Monopoly" (1981) 34 *Stanford Law Review* 1.

movement in favour of freer trade have led governments of all political hues to embrace deregulation to a greater or lesser degree with respect to the profession worldwide. In the United Kingdom the process has been particularly striking, with scale fees going, advertising coming and monopolies being removed or eroded. However, the problems of information asymmetry between lawyers and clients which justified regulation in the first place have led to re-regulation in the shape of public protection measures—ethical codes, legal services ombudsmen, penalties for "shoddy work" and financial services regulation. Despite this, or perhaps because of this, in a number of Commonwealth jurisdictions we have seen active debates within the profession as to the merits of retaining self-regulation.[3] In England and Wales the debate has perhaps been fiercest as first, the National Consumer Council and then, successive Legal Services Ombudsmen have pointed to the continuing failures of the Solicitors' Complaints Bureaux and its successor, the Office for the Supervision of Solicitors,[4] to cope with the level of complaints against the profession. At the same time the Solicitors Indemnity Fund has been given its marching orders and the Lord Chancellor has taken powers in the Access to Justice Act 1999[5] to appoint a Legal Services Complaints Commissioner with the power to step in when a professional body is not handling complaints' effectively and efficiently, and to curb the Society's use of members' subscriptions to fund publicity campaigns against government policy (for example, cutbacks in civil legal aid).

Regulation, Self-regulation and changes thereto

The foregoing suggests that over time intervention ebbs and flows in relation to the market for the services of legal professionals as it does in other service

[3] For Australia, see C Parker, "Competing Images of the Legal Profession: Competing Regulatory Strategies" (1997) 25 *International Journal of the Sociology of Law* 385 and C Parker, "Law Deregulation Via Business Deregulation" (1999) 6 *International Journal of the Legal Profession* 175. For Canada, see H W Arthurs, "The Dead Parrot: Does Professional Self-Regulation Exhibit Vital Signs?" (1995) 33 *Alberta Law Review* 800 and W H Hurlburt, *The Self-Regulation of the Legal Profession in Canada and in England and Wales* (Alberta, Law Society of Alberta and Alberta Law Reform Institute, 2000). In England and Wales there has been a Law Society Discussion Paper, *Regulation of Solicitors* (London, Law Society, 1999) as well as many short pieces in the *Law Society's Gazette*, *The Lawyer* and the *New Law Journal*. In Scotland , an article by Ewan Kennedy, "A Time for Change" (1998) 43 *Journal of the Law Society of Scotland* 20 (November) sparked a series of articles and letters in the succeeding six months. The Scottish Consumer Council at the same time published a highly critical report on complaint handling by the Law Society of Scotland and called for the establishment of an independent complaints handling body.

[4] See R Moorhead, S Rogers and A Sherr, *Willing Blindness: OSS Complaints Handling Procedures*, RRPU Research Study No. 37 (London, The Law Society, 2000).

[5] See ss. 51–52 and 47.

markets. Whether we see our era as one of regulatory flux with regulatory, deregulatory and re-regulatory shifts occurring in close proximity,[6] or as a circle or spiral from self-regulation to regulation to de-regulation,[7] the essential questions being debated are the same. Which regulatory strategies are the most effective and in what circumstances? Applied to the world of the lawyer, we wish to know where we should be going in regulatory terms and where we probably are going.

The normative issue cannot be settled by fiat. In part it turns on which model of professionalism one espouses, since regulation lies at the heart of the principal theories of the profession and professionalism in the ideological marketplace of today, touching as it does on autonomy, public protection and competition. In terms of the dominant orthodoxy of the 1980s and early 1990s, the Abel/Larson market control thesis is that[8] "the power to engage in self-regulation is one of the goals that motivates an occupation to seek professional status. The efficacy of self-regulation is one of the measures by which outsiders judge whether a profession deserves that status".[9] However, Abel believes that professionalism as a method of organising the profession is dying[10]—as de-regulation and external forces have stripped the profession of much of its ability to control the market. Abel does not regret this—since in his opinion self-regulation by the profession, including its ethical codes and rules[11]—has been a thin disguise for self interest. Abel's allegation that the profession's commitment to ethics dwindles with the loss of market control is more a cynical observation than a condemnation, for in his view the route forward is less regulation, including self-regulation.[12]

Terence Johnson[13] too gives regulation pride of place in his arguments on occupational control. For him, the information asymmetry between the specialist and the client has to be resolved in one of three ways: first, by the body of specialists acting collegiately to define the legal needs of the public and how they will be met—these Johnson deems to be the true professionals. Secondly, the client can control the interface through patronage as corporate clients frequently do. Finally, the relationship can be regulated by a third party mediating control over both the professional and the client e.g. the Legal Services Commission in legal aid cases. For Johnson only collegiate control is truly

6 See, e.g. I Ayres and J Braithwaite, *Responsive Regulation* (New York, Oxford University Press, 1992), p. 7.

7 See, e.g. National Consumer Council, *Models of Self Regulation* (London, NCC, 1999), p. 4.

8 R L Abel, *The Legal Profession in England and Wales* (Oxford, Blackwell, 1988).

9 *Ibid.*, at 248.

10 R L Abel, "The Decline of Professionalism?" (1986) 49 *Modern Law Review* 1.

11 R L Abel, "Why Does the ABA Promulgate Ethical Rules?" (1981) 59 *Texas Law Review* 639.

12 R L Abel, "Transnational Law Practice" (1994) 44 *Case Western Reserve Law Review* 737.

13 T Johnson, *Professions and Power* (London, Macmillan, 1972).

professional and thus he, like Abel and Kritzer[14] sees us as entering an era of post-professionalism as the profession loses its market control, and as the Internet provides a boost to de-professionalisation by reducing the knowledge gap between the professional and the client. The cultural theorists,[15] however, share a relativist notion of professionalism with regulation in the guise of competing perceptions of professional responsibility being their central thrust.[16] Aspects of regulation are even more central to the neo-contractualist model of professionalism which pits the expectations of the State, society and clients of competence, a service ethic and public protection (e.g. professional responsibility, mandatory insurance, compensation funds and ombudsmen) against the profession's desire for high status, reasonable rewards, limited competition and autonomy/self regulation.[17] Unlike the earlier "social contract" version of functionalist thinkers, the neo-contractualist concept of professionalism is a dynamic one which is re-negotiated over time. In their view this has been happening, particularly in the past fifteen years, when consumers and the State have pushed for a redressing of a perceived imbalance in self-regulation in favour of the profession.[18]

Even to hazard a guess as to the form of regulation which is most appropriate for the legal profession of the future, requires one first to decide the directions in which the profession is going.

Changes in the Profession

Intra-Profession Competition

De-regulation of many of the anti-competitive practices within the legal professions around the world over the past twenty-five years has led to a level of competition within these professions that is unlikely to be quickly reversed.[19]

[14] H M Kritzer, "The Future of Legal Practice: Surviving in the Post-Professional World" (1999) 33 *Law and Society Review* 000.

[15] The most prominent thinkers in this camp are R Nelson, D Trubek and R Solomon, *Lawyers' Ideals and Lawyers Practice* (Ithaca, Cornell University Press, 1992).

[16] T Schneyer, "Professionalism as Politics" in Nelson, Trubek and Solomon (eds) *supra* n. 15.

[17] A A Paterson, "Professionalism and the Legal Services Market" (1996) 3 *International Journal of the Legal Profession* 137.

[18] Neo-contractualist thinking also appears in the writings of T Halliday, *Beyond Monopoly* (Chicago, University of Chicago Press, 1987); R Dingwall and P Fenn, "A Respectable Profession?" (1987) 7 *International Review of Law and Economics* 51; M Seneviratne, *supra* n. 1, and A Boon and J Levin, *The Ethics and Conduct of Lawyers* (Oxford, Hart Publishing, 1999), p. 48.

[19] The Irish Government is in the process of passing legislation to make advertising by Irish lawyers illegal. This move, which swims against the general trend with respect to lawyer advertising in the Anglo-American world, has been prompted by the Irish Government's perception that too much litigation against them has been inspired by entrepreneurial lawyers.

The consequent increase in business pressures has undoubtedly reduced the comfort zone in smaller provincial and high street firms, even before the impact of the legal aid reforms had been fully felt.[20] For corporate and large city firms, declining client loyalty, beauty parades, tendering, mergers, lateral hires, attenuated promotion structures and partnership rewards related to individual performance,[21] have become the order of the day. The era of wide-spread unsung *pro bono* work across the profession has long since succumbed to the more commercially-minded climate that now prevails. *Pro bono* is indeed still to be found amongst the larger city firms in North America and London, though public relations as much as altruism lies at its roots. Hanlon[22] describes these developments as the gradual replacement of the "traditional" professionalism of service, based on the perceived needs of the citizen, by a new commercialised professionalism where services are tailored to the client's ability to pay. Whether or not these two forms of professionalism are as starkly differentiated as Hanlon portrays, it is probably the case, as he asserts, that the corporate firms have welcomed the commercial ethos of the "new" professionalism more than the high street firms.[23] Certainly the whole profession has had to learn to live with the ongoing tension between business priorities and professional priorities—a tension which regulation in the shape of professional ethics strives to hold in balance.[24] There is nothing to suggest that this tension, and with it the significance of professional ethics, will diminish in the next decade.

Heterogeneity of the Profession

The growth of the legal professions around the world following the post-War "baby-boom" has brought with it an increasing heterogeneity. Not only has the gender balance in the profession dramatically changed in the past quarter-century, so too has the ethnic balance and, most striking of all, the size

[20] H Sommerlad, "Managerialism and the Legal Profession" (1995) 2 *International Journal of the Legal Profession* 159.

[21] While the "eat what you kill" philosophy of partnership remuneration is gaining ground in the largest UK law firms, it is far from the dominant reward mechanism in the Anglo-American legal world, although it prevails amongst the largest accounting firms: G Hanlon, *Lawyers, the State and the Market* (London, Macmillan, 1999), pp. 140–1.

[22] Hanlon, *ibid.*, at 140–2.

[23] See Hilary Sommerlad, "Managerialism and the Legal Profession: A New Professional Paradigm", (1995) 2 *International Journal of the Legal Profession* 159.

[24] Suggestions that competition is leading to reduced standards have not been borne out . Thus interviews conducted by the author for an ESRC study of competition amongst conveyancers revealed that more short cuts had been taken a few years earlier at the height of the property boom than in the more competitive recession era that followed: F Stephen, J Love and A Paterson, *The Regulation and Deregulation of Markets for Legal Services in the United Kingdom* (ESRC Research Report, 1994).

differential between firms.[25] Heinz and Laumann[26] have described this latter phenomenon in terms of the two hemispheres—personal service versus the corporate sector. Certainly, as Nelson[27] and Hanlon[28] have shown, the largest corporate firms in North America and England and Wales have moved to abandon or downgrade personal service work. However, not all large firms have given up private client work. Equally some large firms are provincial generalists rather than corporate specialists, or regional firms rather than national ones. Thus in Leeds, the largest legal market outside London, of the big six law firms, two are probably genuinely national firms, one is staunchly regional and the other three are somewhere in between.[29] Even legal aid firms are no longer a homogeneous grouping. Franchising and now contracting is encouraging the development of legal aid megaliths covering large regions as well the niche practitioner in mental health. Not even the small or solo firms are homogeneous. Some are generalist "Jacks and Jills of all trades" whilst others are niche firms specialising in criminal legal aid, mental health, licensing, employment, patents and intellectual property, immigration etc. Indeed, the diversity of firm specialisms, structures, profitability, governance and missions strongly suggest that the bi-polar model of Heinz and Laumann is too simplistic.

This is not to deny that the corporate law firm is a highly distinctive specialism. Increasingly, corporate clients are demanding more commercially-led legal advice, causing the firms symbiotically to re-structure themselves along market or sectoral lines.[30] Moreover, with the emergence of the mega-law firms[31] has come the dramatic increase in the proportion of employed lawyers to principals. Abel[32] and Kritzer[33] see the fact that lawyers are increasingly employees of bureaucratically organised law firms and institutions as a threat to professionalism. However, the same phenomenon holds true for large

[25] In 1971, no UK law firm had more than 30 partners, and fewer than 100 firms in the USA were larger than this. By 1999, 100 firms in the United Kingdom had 30 partners and 17 had over 100 partners, the largest having over 2,000 fee earners . At the same time the proportion of sole practice law firms rose to over 40 per cent in the United Kingdom as did the proportion of 2–4 partner firms. With 5–9 partner firms running at 11 per cent of all UK firms, the 10 or more partner firms represented only 6 per cent of UK law firms, although containing 38 per cent of all private practitioners. See (1999) *The Lawyer* 100 and A A Paterson, T St JN Bates, and M R Poustie, *The Legal System of Scotland* (4th edn, Edinburgh, W.Green, 1999), p. 266.

[26] J P Heinz & E O Laumann, *Chicago Lawyers* (New York, Russell Sage Foundation, 1982).

[27] R L Nelson, *Partners with Power* (Berkeley, University of California Press, 1988).

[28] See *supra* n. 21, at 124.

[29] A Townsend, "Leeds United against City Rivals" (2000) 14 *The Lawyer* 26.

[30] Hanlon, *supra* n. 21, at 135. Even the English Bar is not immune from such pressures. In 1999 a merger mania seemed to infect a number of Chambers gearing up to meet the specialist needs of corporate clients and lawyers.

[31] See M Galanter and T Palay, *Tournaments of Lawyers* (Chicago, University of Chicago Press, 1991).

[32] R Abel, "The Decline of Professionalism" (1986) 49 *Modern Law Review* 1.

[33] H Kritzer, *supra* n. 14.

accounting firms, not to mention all the doctors and nurses who work in hospitals.

The increasing heterogeneity of the profession poses particular regulatory problems. Is the level of diversity and pluralism such that the profession can no longer reasonably be described as one profession? [34] As the different sectors of the profession evolve in divergent directions so too will their views on professional ethics.[35] Indeed, to the cultural theorists as we have seen, professionalism is now only a meaningful concept at the level of different professional sectors. Will this then mean that regulation at least in terms of professional ethics can no longer hope to cover the whole profession? On the one hand we have commentators who argue that corporate lawyers now have more in common with accountants than with their smaller counterparts.[36] Yet differences on ethical issues between the self-styled elite members of the profession and those who do the "dirty work" of the profession,[37] or between corporate lawyers and trial lawyers,[38] have an ancient pedigree. Moreover, it can also be argued that the core values of the legal profession—commitment to the rule of law; fiduciary duties such as confidentiality; independence from clients and from the State—remain for the whole profession and differentiate them from other professions such as accountancy.

Inter-Profession Competition

If competition within the profession has increased in the past quarter-century, so too has competition between the legal profession and other professional and occupational groupings operating in the legal services market. In one sense this is not new—Scottish solicitors having spawned the first accountants many years ago, have a long track record of losing markets to other providers in the fields of banking, insurance, insolvency, tax advice, estate agency and financial services. However, it was the advent of deregulation that served as a clarion call to the legal profession to resist further predatory attacks. The price competition which followed the announcement that the conveyancing monopoly would go in England and Wales reduced conveyancing fees by

[34] See C Glasser, "The Legal Profession in the 1990s" (1990) 10 *Legal Studies* 1; Hanlon, *supra* n. 21, at 161 "It seems that the legal profession is slowly fragmenting".

[35] See T Schneyer, *supra* n. 16.

[36] e.g. R Lee, "From Profession to Business" (1992) 19 *Journal of Law and Society* 31 and G Hanlon, "A Fragmenting Profession—Lawyers, The Market and Significant Others" (1997) 60 *Modern Law Review* 798.

[37] See A A Paterson, *supra* n. 17; J Carlin, *Lawyers on their Own* (Rutgers, Rutgers University Press, 1962).

[38] See J Carlin, *Lawyers' Ethics* (New York, Russell Sage Foundation, 1966) and Schneyer, *surpa* n. 16.

30 per cent[39] before the first licensed conveyancer had begun to practice. The parallel campaign by solicitors to obtain rights of audience in the higher courts was but a new phase in a long running war with the Bar. Their victory was more apparent than real—the economics of the respective overheads of solicitors and barristers has entailed that in neither England nor Scotland have the solicitors made significant inroads into the Bar's territory. Nevertheless, what little ground had been gained on the Bar has to be set against the ground that has been lost on a number of other fronts—a trend that is likely to continue in the next decade.

Kritzer argues that post-professionalisation entails that as in medicine, specialist para-professionals or non-professionals will begin to supplant qualified lawyers.[40] Claims agents and mediators are providing competition for litigators and contracts for the not-for-profit sector are a key plank of the Community Legal Services programme in England and Wales. In the corporate sector, accountants are no longer satisfied with tax advice, management consultancy, insolvency and litigation support. Arthur Anderson's intent to create and own the largest global firm of lawyers is setting the benchmark for the remainder of the "big five" to follow suit.[41] We will return to these developments when we consider corporate governance and multi-disciplinary partnerships (MDPs), however the diversification in bodies seeking to operate in the legal services market brings with it regulatory challenges. Sooner or later the pressure to create a single regulator for all providers of legal services will tell on the State.[42] Indeed the President of the English Law Society in 1999 used just this argument to propose that the Law Society should be that single regulator, much to the irritation of the Bar.[43]

Changing Forms of Governance

High on the agenda of the "big five" accounting firms and the largest English corporate law firms in the past decade has been the desire to change the forms of corporate governance of UK partnerships. In some respects the accounting firms are already ahead of their legal rivals because they have been operating modern management structures for longer. However innovative corporate lawyers have been in the services they have provided since "Big Bang", their

[39] See S Domberger and A Sherr, "Competition in Conveyancing" (1987) 8:3 *Fiscal Studies* 17.

[40] Kritzer, *supra* n. 14, argues that the delegation of routine tasks to para-legals opens the door to clients wanting direct access to para-professionals on cost grounds.

[41] Klegal, the UK law firm established by KPMG, moved in August 1999 to link up with a "top 25" American international law firm: (1999) *The Lawyer* (9 August).

[42] In the United Kingdom the Legal Services Ombudsman has already been given a residuary jurisdiction over solicitors, barristers/advocates and licensed/qualified conveyancers.

[43] See C Smith, "Papering Over the Cracks" (1999) *The Lawyer* (8 November), 12.

approach to corporate governance has been relatively conservative.[44] Larger law firms have long had a departmental structure, but it is only in the last few years that we have seen firms restructuring from departments or groupings based on legal specialisms to groups based on client market sector.[45] Here the lawyers are belatedly following the accountants' lead in organising to suit the client market. Yet they continue to lag behind in adopting the proactive, prophylactic legal risk assessment strategies which corporate clients are seeking rather than the reactive firefighting which is still all too prevalent.

Even at the executive level there is much for the law firms to learn. Only now is Clifford Chance adopting a UK corporate-style structure by electing a governing board from the international partnership with scope for non-executive "directors" from outwith the firm.[46] Of course it is already open to law firms in the United Kingdom to operate as limited liability companies but the disclosure requirements and tax disadvantages that this would entail have dissuaded them from going down this route. A new form of limited liability partnership[47] has been the object of desire for the large accounting and law firms. Available in most of the USA, this form of business organisation preserves the personal assets of partners (as opposed to those of the firm) from seizure in the event of a catastrophic negligence claim against the partnership. With the UK Government Bill on this issue currently making slow progress, the corporate giants in accounting and law have been threatening to re-register with a domicile in Jersey[48] or in one of the states of the USA.[49] However, the Inland Revenue already treats American Limited Liability Partnerships (LLPs) as companies for taxation purposes and has indicated that it would treat UK partnerships which re-register in Jersey or the USA to acquire LLP status, in the same way. There is also scepticism that the English courts will permit corporate firms to hide behind a foreign "flag of convenience".[50] Nevertheless, the UK Government is under pressure to move on this

[44] Typically, even the largest law firms have a considerably flatter management structure than their more hierarchical accounting rivals, where equity partners constitute less than 5 per cent of the professional staff.

[45] See Hanlon, *supra* n. 21, at 132–6.

[46] (1999) *The Lawyer* (2 August), 1.

[47] Existing limited liability partnerships under the Limited Partnerships Act 1907 are of little use for professional partnerships, as limited liability applies only to partners who do not engage in management.

[48] See P Morris and J Stevenson, "The Jersey Limited Liability Partnership" (1997) 60 *Modern Law Review* 538 and C Waelde and J Birrell, "New Era in Partnership Law" (1999) 44 *Journal of the Law Society of Scotland* 27.

[49] One of the byproducts of the Clifford Chance merger with Rogers and Wells in the USA is that the joint firm will be domiciled in New York and thus qualify as a New York LLP. Commentators are divided as to the efficacy of this change in limiting the partners' liability in the eyes of an English court.

[50] See J Payne, "Limited Liability, Within the Grasp of Professional Partnerships?" (1996) 17 *The Company Lawyer* 278.

issue and to ensure that the resulting legislation does not disadvantage UK-based firms as compared with their American counterparts. The regulatory challenge, of course, is to avoid advantaging the corporate partnerships over the wider public and consumer interest.[51]

Ultimately the question for the lawyers of the future will be, what is the most advantageous method of organising one's form of practice?

Multi-Disciplinary Partnerships

If the accounting firms have been pressing the Government for limited liability partnership, they have been equally vociferous in their pursuit of multi-disciplinary partnerships. The logic is stark. If corporate deals require a team of specialists from a range of professions, why not bring the team together on an ongoing basis rather than on the current *ad hoc* basis. At best this would enhance the quality and experience of the team, at worst it would force clients to accept less than the strongest available team. Depending on one's standpoint it is either a case of providing a better service to corporate clients by casting aside outmoded disciplinary boundaries or an example of greed masquerading as the pursuit of the public interest. And that is surely the key point. Is it the suppliers who are crying out for MDPs or the clients?[52]

While it may be clear where the interests of the accountants—the profession best able to exploit MDPs and to control the largest ones—lie, it is far harder to gauge where the interests of clients or the wider public truly lie.[53] After twenty years of debate[54] we seem no nearer to establishing the answer to either of these questions. Amongst lawyers there are many shades of grey with respect to MDPs. But whether one is an enthusiast or an opponent, there is unanimity as to the need to guard against the potential dangers associated with them: the threat to independence and integrity; conflicts of interest; issues of legal professional privilege and confidentiality; reduction in choice and tying-in;

[51] Suggestions for enhancing client protection include disclosure, a £5 million bond, two-year clawbacks of partners' drawings and the retention of personal liability for a partner's own defaults and negligence: Waelde and Birrell, *supra* n. 48.

[52] A number of surveys of clients have been conducted in a variety of jurisdictions, including the United Kingdom, Ontario and New South Wales. All have proved inconclusive. While medium-sized businesses are said to see the advantages of a "one-stop-shop", the large conglomerates are thought to value the cross-checking and rivalry that exists between differing professional groupings in an *ad hoc* multi-disciplinary team created for a particular transaction. It was partly the lack of hard evidence of client demand which persuaded the Scots Law Society working party on MDPs to reject their introduction in March 2000.

[53] In fairness to accountants it should be said that the World Trade Organisation, the OECD, the Office of Fair Trading and several governments have also been pressing for the introduction of MDPs.

[54] MDPs were considered by both the Royal Commission on Legal Services in England and in Scotland in 1979 and 1980 respectively.

threats to professional standards and even to the identity of the profession. Equally, there is a widespread suspicion that the spirit, if not the letter, of the existing regulatory prohibitions against MDPs that exist around the world is increasingly being circumvented. Certainly the "big five" accounting firms have been pursuing a twin-track strategy of pushing governments and legal professions around the world to accept "the inevitable" by removing the anti-competitive restrictions against MDPs, whilst at the same time they have been establishing or "buying over" their own law firms with whom they have a close relationship.[55] Faced with such incrementalist tactics and a slow but perceptible global movement in favour of relaxing the restraints against MDPs[56] the pragmatists in the legal profession[57] have begun to argue that the public interest would best be served by accepting the inevitable and trying to get the regulatory framework sorted out while the legal profession has some power to influence the situation.[58] This is reinforced by the fact that in most jurisdictions the relative smallness of the largest law firms will entail that they are vulnerable to the economic blandishments that the large accounting firms have to offer. Only in the USA and England are the biggest law firms sufficiently large enough and profitable enough to resist the economic muscle of the "big five". Even here the lawyers would be well advised against complacency.[59]

The arrival on the global legal scene of MDPs as significant players *de facto*, if not *de jure*, will pose major regulatory challenges for the legal profession and society at large. Who should regulate them and by what ethical standards, are but two of the more obvious ones. Frequently the solution proffered is that each profession in an MDP should regulate its own members. However, as

[55] The "big five" experimented with such associated law firms in Paris and then expanded into the rest of Europe. Already the largest law firms in France, Spain and Scotland are associated with large accounting firms.

[56] MDPs in some form or other are now permitted in Germany, the Netherlands, Upper Canada, New South Wales, Victoria, New Zealand, Washington DC and are under active consideration in North America, the United Kingdom and most of Europe.

[57] See ACLEC, *Report on Multi-Disciplinary Practice* (London, ACLEC, 1999); J Eliott, "MDPs—Threat or Opportunity ?" (1999) 44 *Journal of the Law Society of Scotland* 16.

[58] Thus in Washington DC MDPs have been allowed but only to provide legal services, in New South Wales MDPs are only allowed if they are controlled by lawyers, and in Upper Canada the MDPs must only offer legal services *and* be controlled by lawyers. In moving the acceptance by the American Bar Association of the report of its Commission on MDPs which would have allowed MDPs, the President of the ABA Philip Anderson observed, "The response of 'I don't like it' won't make it go away. I don't like it either, but its here, and its here to stay . . . Someone will write the rules . . . the Lawyers should write the rules" (1999) 85 *American Bar Association Journal* 23 (September). A somewhat similar philosophy of fatalistic pragmatism was probably what lay behind the decision of the Law Society of England and Wales to accept MDPs in principle in October 1999. However, against the global tide, the Scots Law Society's Working Party on MDPs rejected them in March 2000 as not being in the public interest.

[59] The defection of the former managing partner of Clifford Chance, Tony Williamson, to Anderson Legal in November 1999 is likely to have sent shock waves through the top ten law firms in London.

Boon and Levin have argued,[60] it is difficult to see how multi-disciplinary partnerships could function with different professional staff being subject to different regulatory regimes and ethical standards. What if some of the professionals are largely unregulated? Transparency—telling the clients the different standards to which each member of staff dealing with their business will be held—is impractical. This would be a recipe for confusion amongst clients and "buck-passing" by staff and their professional bodies or insurers whenever a complaint arose. The public interest seems to require a single set of standards for all professional staff in an MDP. The easiest way to achieve this is to adopt the ethical precepts of one profession. But which one? Given that lawyers offer a greater degree of client confidentiality because of a stricter regime over conflicts of interest and the operation of lawyer/client privilege, they would argue that their code should prevail in any MDP where there are lawyers.[61] This is hardly likely to appeal to the self-confident, aggressively entrepreneurial "big five" accounting firms. A more logical route would be to develop a composite code for professionals in an MDP, but the danger here would be "Esperanto ethics"—a solution which fails because staff perceive themselves as lawyers, accountants, surveyors etc rather than members of a new profession, the MDP worker. Indeed, if the professionals did not react in this way, MDPs would threaten the autonomy and corporate identity of the existing professions. Moreover, who would draft such a code? A collaboration between the leading professions? A new regulatory agency representing each profession? Would that body also police MDPs? Perhaps it is not surprising that reform in this area is proving so problematic.

If MDPs are problematic in regulatory terms they are equally so for notions of professionalism. In Johnson's terms a new super-regulator for MDPs would be a further incursion of mediative control and further erosion of the collegiate forms of professionalism. Abel, as we have seen,[62] would see the reduction of most lawyers in MDPs to employee status as a development that diminishes professionalism.[63] Neo-contractualists on the other hand would point to an erosion of key elements on both "sides" of the tacit understanding between the State, the public and the legal profession,[64] such as status, autonomy and public protection. Left unchecked, the commercial pressures at the heart of the drive for MDPs could, in neo-contractualist eyes, threaten such core values of

[60] A Boon and J Levin, *The Ethics and Conduct of Lawyers* (Oxford, Hart Publishing, 1999), p. 85.

[61] This was the route that appealed to ABA Commission on MDPs who wished all professionals in an MDP to be governed by the lawyers' ethical rules. Certainly the auditor's duty to disclose seems sufficiently at odds with the lawyer's duty of confidentiality to suggest that auditing and advocacy are incompatible functions for an MDP.

[62] See *supra* n. 32.

[63] R Abel, *The Legal Profession in England and Wales* (Oxford, Basil Blackwell, 1988), p. 306.

[64] See A A Paterson, *supra* n. 17.

the legal profession as independence, professional integrity, and commitment to the rule of law. Cultural theorists, however, would focus on the competing concepts of appropriate professional behaviour when an MDP encounters ethical difficulties such as confidentiality or conflict of interest. Abbott, conversely would regard the emergence of a new breed of provider in the legal services market as a vindication of his thesis that professions are defined by the territorial battles which they fight.[65]

Globalisation

If European law firms are concerned as to the predatory muscle of the large accounting firms in the guise of MDPs, they are equally concerned by the move of the top ranked American and UK legal firms into global markets. Once again the blandishment to clients is the "one-stop-shop", only this time it is the law firms that are making the offer. Strictly speaking globalisation is the creation of a global commercial and financial market. Like e-commerce, globalisation owes much to the telecommunications and information technology breakthroughs of recent years which have transcended the world's time zones. Large accounting and law firms are attracted by the globalisation of financial markets for several reasons. They want first, to have a presence in the major capital markets (e.g. New York, London and Tokyo) to gain or maintain a share of the international legal business; secondly, to provide an international standard of service in countries where the local Bar lack the necessary expertise e.g. Eastern Europe or Latin America; thirdly, to follow large clients into foreign markets for fear of losing their custom to other international competitors and to provide them with a one-stop-shop of legal services—the comfort factor of a familiar culture and a consistency of quality.[66] Strictly speaking only a relatively few really large law firms and accounting firms in England and the USA are likely to aspire to become truly global players in the international legal services market.[67] However, considerably more have been pursuing internationalisation or transnational practice with a presence in several countries. Indeed

[65] A Abbott, *The System of Professions* (London, University of Chicago Press, 1988).

[66] R Vineburg, "Globalisation of the Legal Profession" (1995) 23 *International Business Lawyer* 514.

[67] Clifford Chance's merger with Rogers and Wells is likely to be the first of a steady trickle of transatlantic mergers designed to create an Anglo-American axis as the fulcrum from which to launch more global initiatives. The trend may even accelerate if more multi-national conglomerates follow the example of BP and Proctor and Gamble in transferring their in-house legal function from a regional to a global structure with a major reduction in the size of their out—house legal panel. On the other hand there are notable sceptics as to the likely success of global law firms including Professor John Kay, head of the Oxford Business School, see (1998) *The Lawyer* (10 November). Moreover some multi-national corporations have reinforced Professor Kay's thesis by preferring to instruct local niche firms rather than more expensive global law firms: (2000) *The Lawyer*, (17 January), 16.

there is a bewildering array of vehicles to achieve this: [68] strategic alliances, clubs, networks; "best friends"; exclusive referral arrangements; affiliation; joint ventures; branch offices; or a full blown multi-national partnership.[69]

Globalisation and internationalisation of legal practice[70] inevitably bring with them regulatory headaches. In the early days they involved little more than practising domestic law in another jurisdiction. In such a scenario regulation was originally a matter for the home jurisdiction, including its standards of professional responsibility. However, concerns amongst local lawyers about competition in key areas e.g. unauthorised practice of law, litigation, transfer of real property, and advice on local law, led to the now established double deontology rule. This requires lawyers in international firms operating in other jurisdictions, whether as foreign legal consultants or through locally qualified lawyers, to comply with both the local ethical code of whatever jurisdiction the firm is in as well as that of its home jurisdiction.[71] This somewhat cumbersome arrangement stems from the requirements of the International Bar Association's International Code of Ethics, and in Europe from the CCBE Code of Conduct and EU law.[72]

The position is further complicated by the fact that transnational law firms have increasingly been practising international law, whether like EU law it is a supranational law or focused on the conflicts between the laws of different jurisdictions. Today the list of international specialisms is wide-ranging: e.g. international arbitration, telecommunications, global tax, mergers and acquisitions, privatisations, derivatives, intellectual property, trade and investment,

[68] Whether by relocation of lawyers from home, or acquisition of a local firm. See Ward Bower, "International Expansion of Law Firms" (1992) *International Legal Practitioner* 42.

[69] See R G Lee, "From Profession to Business" (1992) 19 *Journal of Law and Society* 31 and J Flood, "Megalawyering in the Global Order" (1996) 3 *International Journal of the Legal Profession* 169.

[70] For detailed discussions of the internationalisation of legal practice, see D Trubek, Y Dezalay, R Buchanan and J Davis, "Global Restructuring and the Law" (1994) 44 *Case Western Reserve Law Review* 407; R L Abel, "Transnational Law Practice" (1994) 44 *Case Western Reserve Law Review* 737; Special Issue on "The Globalisation of the Legal Profession" (1995) 23 *International Business Lawyer* 501–48; J Flood, "Megalawyering in the Global Order" (1996) 3 *International Journal of the Legal Profession* 169 and T Halliday and L Karpik, "Postscript: Lawyers, Political Liberalism and Globalisation" in Halliday and Karpik (eds), *Lawyers and the Rise of Western Political Liberalism* (Oxford, Clarendon Press, 1977).

[71] As Clifford Chance has recently found to its cost when it announced its merger with Rogers and Wells and Punder Volhard Weber Axster in the world's press. The same advert in the same format was unproblematic in New York, Washington and England but was challenged under the stricter rules on self-promotion by law firms in Germany.

[72] Comite Consultatif des Barreaux Europeens, *Code of Conduct for Lawyers in the European Community* and Art. 4 of the Lawyers' Services Directive 77/249/EEC. The CCBE Code, rule 3.8.3, allows a transnational lawyer who is practising in a host country to reach agreement with his/her home jurisdiction and the host jurisdiction that he/she will be governed solely by the ethical provisions of the host country.

global finance, global project financing and international banking.[73] To the extent that such activities are supranational they are currently little regulated except by the home jurisdiction of the transnational firm, while for other transactions problems of multiple deontology may exist.[74]

Small wonder that the some have been calling for greater harmonisation of national conduct standards or even a Global Code of Legal Ethics.[75] However, academic commentary on this proposal has been sceptical. Economides and Webb consider the proposal to beg the question as to whether there are universal values on which to base a common professional order.[76] Arthurs[77] is more cynical. For him the drive for a international code is a sop in place of more effective collective action. It would, he believes, send reassuring messages to transnational corporations and covertly advance the interests of the transnational firms. For such a code to be effective it would have to constrain the activities of the transnational firms, yet in Arthurs' eyes these are the very firms which have influence with the IBA and the CCBE. It would be more effective, he asserts, if the firms were to encourage provisions in their own domestic Codes to deal with transnational legal practice. Boon and Flood share the scepticism as to the achieveability of "universal ethics".[78] Having discussed the structure and content of the CCBE and IBA Codes, they note that neither code has a serious regulatory function since there are no provisions for enforcement except to the extent that either has been incorporated into the ethical rules of the domestic jurisdiction.[79] Moreover, they note that ethical codes reflect the professional legal cultures which prevail in particular jurisdictions, pointing to incompatibilities in practice which will inhibit any prospect of a "universal ethic". And yet, and yet, the authors also point to the movement towards a universal global culture which may eventually lead to a globalised professional ethics.

How, then, should the transnational activities of lawyers be regulated in future? The "market control" view is that since transnational clients are primarily multinational corporations with in-house counsel there are few asymmetries of information or inequalities of bargaining power. Accordingly, Abel favours deregulation, with host jurisdictions leaving the practice of foreign law

[73] See W Matteson, "Building an International Practice" (1995) 23 *International Business Lawyer* 516.

[74] Here global ethics becomes akin to the conflict of laws.

[75] See e.g. J Toulmin, "A Worldwide Common Code of Professional Ethics?" (1991–92) 15 *Fordham International Law Journal* 673. The harmonisation principle is enshrined in the CCBE Code.

[76] K Economides and J Webb, "Codification of Professional Duties" (1999) 2 *Legal Ethics* 1.

[77] H Arthurs, "A Global Code of Legal Ethics for the Transnational Legal Field" (1999) 2 *Legal Ethics* 59.

[78] A Boon and J Flood, "Globalisation of Professional Ethics?" (1999) 2 *Legal Ethics* 29.

[79] Here the CCBE Code has had a bigger impact, having been incorporated into a number of domestic jurisdictions.

unregulated and foreign and transnational lawyers being disciplined in their home jurisdiction.[80] Johnson for similar reasons would favour deregulation, despite the vacuum that would leave for patronage control of the global lawyers. The cultural theorists[81] would claim that professionalism for transnational lawyers derives from transnational practice and should be regulated by a transnational body. Thus if, as some have argued,[82] the affinities between the cultures and working practices of the Anglo-American corporate law firms and accounting law firms continue to grow, a transnational consensus on ethical regulation will emerge.[83] What is not clear is what the mechanism for enacting or policing such a "globalised ethic" might be. Similarly, neo-contractualists, whilst able to identify the transnational lawyers and clients in their tacit "understanding", would point to a lack of an equivalent to the State or the public to be parties to the ongoing negotiation as to the parameters of transnational professionalism. The problem is akin to regulating and policing the Internet.[84] There is no world government, no global professional body with the legislative competence or the political and economic muscle to enact and enforce a globalised legal ethic. Until such body emerges, progress will depend on the fate of the World Trade Organisation, treaties such as GATT and the willingness of nation states to cover transnational legal practice in their domestic ethical codes; the irony being that professional elites seeking a global order may struggle to carry their professions with them,[85] whilst any jurisdiction which becomes too proactive in seeking to regulate transnational practice in ways that the megalaw firms dislike will provoke a flight of its domestically registered transnational firms to the flags of convenience of less intrusive jurisdictions.[86]

The Impact of Technology

Whilst most of the changes in the profession set out above are so well established as to brook no debate, there remains a vibrant and healthy debate as to

[80] Abel, *supra* n. 73, at 763.

[81] R Nelson and D Trubek, "Arenas of Professionalism" in Nelson, Trubek and Solomon, *supra* n. 15.

[82] e.g. Toulmin, *supra* n. 75.

[83] This tendency can be exaggerated. The ease with which Lord Millett in the *Bolkiah* case dismissed decades of North American jurisprudence on conflict of interest in a single line of his judgment suggests that even in the Anglo-American world of transnational legal practice there is much room for convergence: [1999] 1 All ER 517 at 527b.

[84] See A Murray, D Vick and S Wortley, "Regulating E-commerce" (1999) 13 *International Review of Law Computers & Technology* 127. "The supranational nature of the Internet yields a strange dichotomy of a medium , which is at the same time highly regulated yet subject to minimal policing".

[85] A Boon and Jennifer Levin, *The Ethics and Conduct of Lawyers in England and Wales* (Oxford, Hart Publishing, 1999), p. 412.

[86] The ability of transnational law firms to adopt flags of convenience undermines the credibility of Abel's minimalist deregulation proposals.

the likely impact of the final change—the effect of advances in technology on the legal profession of the future. Richard Susskind threw down the gauntlet with his seminal work, *The Future of Law*.[87] In it he argues that in future there will be three kinds of legal service:[88]

(1) Traditional high value, personalised service from skilled practitioners. IT will speed up the delivery of this "high-end work", providing it at lower cost with greater consistency and to a higher quality. The role of IT, however, will be to automate existing methods of legal service delivery rather than to innovate through the development of new forms of delivery.
(2) Commoditised legal service. Much of the standard, repetitive work of today's lawyers will be commoditised as debt collection already is, with para-legal staff handling large caseloads with the aid of IT to provide pre-packaged productised services. Susskind's view is that this disintermediation of legal advisors will reduce the need for legally qualified staff in firms and that generalist practitioners will be hit hardest by this development.
(3) The latent legal service. If lawyers are concerned by Susskind's first two predictions, they should be cheered by his last. His view is that technology and the Internet in particular will open up the myriad of situations which currently exist for legal advice which go by default because seeking legal advice is too costly, time-consuming or inconvenient. Although such automation of the advice-giving function will undoubtedly operate in areas typically covered by legal aid,[89] Susskind reports that his views on the latent legal market have had the greatest resonance with the in-house counsel of large corporate conglomorates.[90] For Susskind the latent legal market, closely connected as it is to unmet legal need, represents a major opportunity for the profession of key significance to itself and to society. He suspects that it will be the entrepreneurs who will seek to exploit the latent legal market, by providing affordable, easy access to legal services using the Internet's strengths as a marketing tool. It will be a proactive legal service—a legal guidance system. Lawyers tapping into this market by harnessing technology will become legal information engineers[91] who will interpret and repackage statutes and case law into a format suitable for a legal information service which will be provided not on a one on one basis as at present, but on-line. As Susskind notes,

[87] Oxford, Clarendon Press, 1996.
[88] *Ibid.*
[89] Or at least the areas that used to be covered by civil legal aid prior to the implementation of the Access to Justice Act 1999.
[90] See Susskind, "The Future of Law Revisited" extended preface to the paperback edition of *The Future of Law* (Oxford, Clarendon Press, 1998), p. l.
[91] See *supra*, n. 87, 270.

> operating at the level of generalisations rather than specific cases is alien to practising lawyers, though not to academics. The greatest challenge for the profession posed by the latent legal market is that the disappearance of the middle men—disintermediation—will open the door to new providers of legal services, such as publishers, or the not-for-profit sector. It may well be that the large accounting and consulting firms will come to dominate the latent legal market, relegating lawyers to the role of technicians or salaried partners in MDPs dominated by accountants.[92]

Susskind's work has provoked considerable debate amongst both the profession and academia. Practitioners in a wide variety of legal fields acknowledge the general soundness of his thesis but point to reasons why their particular specialism alone will remain untouched by the tide of technological change sweeping over the rest of the profession. Susskind notes the irony but is unpersuaded. Another group of critics claim that he is exaggerating the speed of change, but Susskind is careful not to put precise dates as to when his anticipated paradigm shift in the provision of legal services will take place. Others, still, point to the added value which lawyers provide including: sorting the relevant from the irrelevant, using their "knowhow" to enhance efficiency and to increase client benefits and reduce client costs, and drawing on their experience, insight and judgement.[93] Susskind does not deny the added value that lawyers can bring over the "punchy, practical and jargon-free" guidance which will be provided on the information highway. He asserts, however, that either the pervasive effect of technologically driven information systems will sweep lawyers from centre stage in dispensing legal assistance[94] whatever the added value of the traditional mode of providing legal assistance, or that legal advice on the Internet will not be a competitor to conventional service but an additional resource for clients who cannot afford to pay for the traditional lawyer's services. For Susskind is in no doubt, the Internet lawyer "may deliver a rougher and readier legal service but . . . that should be far better than no access to justice at all".[95]

Susskind's conclusion here accords well with the community legal services proposals contained the White Paper on legal aid in 1998[96] and the Access to Justice Act 1999. However, for our purposes the key aspect of his thesis is the extent to which technology will transform or replace traditional aspects of legal practice. Certainly, we can already see the large city firms using technological advances to enhance legal services provision through data transfer to

[92] *Ibid.*, at 273.

[93] See E Greenebaum, "Is the Medium the Message?" (1999) 6 *International Journal of the Legal Profession* 197.

[94] See R Susskind, "Reply" (1999) 6 *International Journal of the Legal Profession* 208.

[95] See *supra* n. 87, at 214.

[96] *Modernising Justice* (London, Lord Chancellor's Department, 1998).

clients, litigation support, document assembly, interactive on-line services and even e-mail. Equally he is right to expect some commodification of more routine legal tasks. Susskind and Kritzer[97] may even be right to predict that technology will help new suppliers (not necessarily law firms) to enter specialised legal markets using para-legals and technology to threaten the legal professionals currently colonising that field just as guilds were replaced by the industrial revolution. However, the limited achievements of artificial intelligence in the legal sphere in the last twenty years do not suggest that we are likely to witness the wholesale demise of legal advice-giving by lawyers in favour of a computer in the foreseeable future. It is unclear, therefore, that generalised legal advice on the Internet will really drive out traditional legal services to a significant degree in the next ten to fifteen years although it may well make inroads into the latent legal market. There remains the delivery of traditional legal services on the Internet. This has hardly begun in the United Kingdom[98] but there is a growing band of lawyers in the USA who are now exploring this mode of delivering legal services. It is likely that this trend will continue but again its impact may be greater in the latent legal market. Finally, we should not overlook the fact that research has confirmed that the bulk of the work of solicitors is not legal research and advice-giving but routine administration, negotiation and client-handling, areas where technology's contribution in the short to medium term may be automation rather than innovation.

The implications of technological change for regulatory reform are unclear. Internet provision of legal services may involve crossing numerous state boundaries by providers who are not legally qualified in these states. Already in the USA such cases have begun to raise questions of unauthorised practice of law. This problem may be easier to overcome in the European Union because of the mutual recognition and freedom of establishment Directives. For traditional services its impact may only relate to issues such as value rather than hourly billing, and confidentiality of electronic communications. Commoditised legal services and the latent legal market may also raise issues of unauthorised practice and the scope of the monopolies.

Regulatory Options

In the light of the foregoing excursus on the future of the profession in the coming decade, what can we tell about the changes in the regulation of the

[97] H Kritzer, *supra* n. 14.
[98] Although it is a long-term goal for Community Legal Services.

profession which are likely to occur during this period? Inevitably it is easier to identify the options rather than the actual outcome that history will record ten to twenty years hence. In terms of the regulatory cycle, as the Thatcherite era demonstrated, substantial deregulation of the profession is not a long term option[99] since information asymmetry entails that the market is unable to control for quality. Full-scale State regulation has little more support. Leaving aside the threat that this might pose to an independent profession, the risks of regulatory "capture", the lack of internalisation and the cost of State regulation, are thought to reduce its attractions as a way of regulating the profession. This leaves independent regulation and self-regulation. The former has support from a number of quarters[100] but there is less consensus as to the appropriate form. Locating day-to-day regulation, supervision and discipline with the courts has a long historical tradition around the world. Equally it has as often been abandoned, since it is best suited for the regulation of court lawyers (although it undermines their independence), and is an impractical option for the regulation of today's large and specialist profession, unless the court delegates the task to a separate agency. Conferring full-scale investigation and discipline powers on a Legal Services Ombudsman has its attractions but would involve an exponential increase in resources—extracted with reluctance from the profession, and a significant change of function. A similar model would be to create an equivalent to the General Medical Council to handle discipline and regulation, with the professional body playing a purely trade union function,[101] though this is sometimes classified as a variant on self-regulation, depending on the membership of the Council and how it is selected. As with the GMC, however, increasingly regulators are being expected to tackle information asymmetry by moving into the field of quality audit as well as discipline. The merits of an "Ofsted" for lawyers as a method of ensuring quality and compliance are unclear, and in any case, as with all independent regulators, it would leave the *quis custodiet* question—who regulates the regulators—unanswered.[102]

Ironically, therefore, despite all the criticism that it has attracted, self-regulation is probably still the favoured option by most of the profession and its critics. Not, however, in the "traditional" version which prevailed from the 1930s to the 1980s with its associated restrictive practices. The neo-contractualist[103]argument for a re-negotiation of the "regulatory bargain" implicit in professionalism to achieve an improved balance between deregulation, self-regulation and independent regulation in the public interest seems to

[99] For a more sophisticated account of the drawbacks of deregulation, see Nicolson and Webb, *op.cit.* p.114.

[100] See Arthurs, *supra* n. 3; Kennedy, *supra* n. 3, and A Arora and A Francis, *The Rule of Lawyers* (London, the Fabian Society, 1998).

[101] Arora and Francis, *supra* n. 100.

[102] See Nicolson and Webb, *supra* n. 99, at 92.

[103] See Paterson, *supra* n. 17.

resonate on a wide front.[104] Most commentators[105] are agreed that professional self-regulation should operate within a broader, multi-layered[106] regulatory framework involving e.g. courts, competition authorities, legal services ombudsmen, legal services commissions, and financial services regulators.[107] Whether this form of self-regulation is best described as "coerced",[108] "mandated",[109] "modulated", "regulated",[110] or "sanctioned",[111] turns on points of emphasis, but cannot hide the degree of parallel thinking that exists in this area. Each is endorsing the view that a broad, multi-layered, statutory regulatory framework can overcome the drawbacks associated with voluntary self-regulation. Inevitably the commentators do have points of difference. Shapland[112] sees the professional bodies as acting as "intermediate regulators" under coercion from the ultimate regulators, rather than in partnership or conjunction with them—a stance that Hanlon[113] likens to Johnson's "mediative" control of the professional grouping. Seneviratne[114] and Nicolson and Webb[115] argue for self-regulation to be transparent and open to public scrutiny, while the latter also argue for accountability and reflexivity. It is their pursuit of reflexivity, even more than transparency and accountability, which places Nicholson and Webb firmly in the camp of responsive regulation.[116]

[104] Similarly, in 1997 the President of the GMC called for a new regulatory agreement between his profession, the State and society, to make self-regulation effective: D Irvine, "The Performance of Doctors" (1997) 314 *BMJ* 1540.

[105] e.g. Boon and Levin, *supra* n. 85, at 66, Dingwall and Fenn, *supra* n. 18, Hurlburt, *supra* n. 3, Nicolson and Webb, *supra* n. 99, at 219, A Ogus, *Regulation*, *supra* n. 1, Paterson, *supra* n. 17, J Shapland, "Self-Regulation of the Professions", unpublished paper at ESRC Regulatory Policy Seminar Group conference, Strathclyde University 20–21 April 1995, and Seneviratne, *supra* n. 1, at 219.

[106] The bewildering array of existing regulators of the legal profession are set out in R Baldwin, *Regulating Legal Services* (London, Lord Chancellor's Department, 1997).

[107] At the transnational level also the norm is multiple deontology and competing national and international regulators. However, there are centripetal forces which push towards fewer or even a single regulator for the legal services market e.g. the regulatory challenges posed by MDPs or by new players in the legal services market attracted by the growth in conditional fees. In 1999 the President of the English Law Society made a pitch for the Society to be the single regulator for all legal services providers, one year after the President of the English Institute of Chartered Accountants had called for the establishment of a super watchdog to police the regulation of all the professions (*Lawtel*, News Page, June 1998). At the transnational level, as we have seen, the search is on for a uniform code to govern transnational legal practice akin to a new *lex mercatoria* (see Arthurs, 1999, *supra* n. 77).

[108] Ayres and Braithwaite, *supra* n. 6, Nicolson and Webb, *op.cit.*, Shapland, *supra* n. 105.

[109] Nicolson and Webb, *supra* n. 99.

[110] P Dry, "Independence is Essential" (1999) 44 *Journal of the Law Society of Scotland* 12.

[111] Nicholson and Webb, *supra* n. 99.

[112] See *supra* n. 105.

[113] See *supra* n. 21, at 95.

[114] See *supra* n. 1, at 219.

[115] See *supra* n. 99, at 94.

[116] See e.g. Ayres and Braithwaite, *supra* n. 6, Parker, *supra* n. 3, and Nicholson and Webb, "Institutionalising trust: Ethics and the Responsive Regulation of the Legal Profession" (1999) 2 *Legal Ethics* 148.

This school of thought argues that regulators should use a pyramid of strategies in a dialogue with the regulated, keeping the strongest sanctions in reserve, to encourage the profession to accept voluntary reform in the public interest. Parker advocates this approach to professional regulation in preference to neo-contractualism which she brands as "far too static and statist" and too trusting in the effectiveness of the "social bargain".[117] This is an unfair reading of Paterson, at least, who specifically denies that neo-contractualists need to believe in the actual fairness of the social or regulatory bargain,[118] and who stresses both that the "bargain" involves society, the State and clients as well as the profession, and the dynamic nature of the "bargain" which is subject to ongoing re-negotiation. Indeed, the latter process may involve exactly the sorts of dialogue that Parker[119] and Nicolson and Webb[120] are seeking. Thus the neo-contractualists argue the public interest case for lay participation in the drafting as well as the enforcement of regulatory standards, precisely because the regulatory bargain concerns the interests of the public in relation to the profession—the very thesis of the responsive regulation school. True, the neo-contractualist engages in the dialogue, not to make regulation more effective, but to encourage the profession to offer more competence, more access and better public protection to society, i.e. a better bargain; however, there is a much greater degree of overlap and compatibility between the schools than Parker allows for. Certainly in terms of the future, both hold in reserve the option of independent or State regulation, should a profession's efforts to reform its disciplinary processes prove ultimately elusive.[121]

Conclusion

It is clear then, that the future of the profession and its regulation may take a variety of forms. At one extreme (a somewhat pessimistic one from the profession's perspective, at least) the profession in its current guise would disappear or suffer a gradual demise, with:

- conveyancing and other routinisable legal services being appropriated by the financial institutions and non-lawyers harnessing technology allied to para-legals to develop a commoditised legal service;

[117] *Ibid.*, at 399.

[118] See *supra* n. 17, at 140.

[119] See *supra* n. 3, at 403.

[120] See *supra* n. 99, at 93–4, and *supra* n. 116, at 162–66.

[121] A viewpoint shared by the LSO and the Lord Chancellor, as successive Annual Reports of the English Legal Services Ombudsman and ss. 51 and 52 of the Access to Justice Act 1999 have made clear.

- transnational and large-scale corporate work becoming the purview of MDPs controlled by accountants;
- latent legal services being provided by publishers, and
- dispute resolution being squeezed by ADR, diversion and the disappearance of civil legal aid.

The rump of the profession would handle litigation in the higher courts with the remainder scattered as employees throughout the legal services sector. Regulation of such a scaled down and demoralised profession would occur within the context of developing a coherent regulatory framework for a diverse range of providers of legal services with less in common with each other than today's legal profession. Competing self-regulatory agencies would be the order of the day.[122]

Less apocalyptic, but perhaps as damaging in the long run, would be the triumph of the centrifugal over the centripetal forces, leading the profession to fragment into a range of sub-specialisms with overlapping values but no shared conception of professionalism.[123] Robbed of its cohesion and core values, the authority of a once—proud calling would diminish, hastened by its members' relegation to the status of technicians in corporate work or MDPs , or the willingness of its corporate elite to re-register abroad under a flag of convenience to evade domestic regulation. In such a scenario the triumph of ethical relativism might tilt the tenuous balance between commercial pressures and professional values in the direction of the former. Regulation would either be sucked into the minutiae of competing professional factions or take the form of the appointment of single (independent) regulator to paper over the cracks.

Fortunately, there are more optimistic scenarios (from the profession's perspective). Self-regulation may yet survive as the profession responds to the pressure for responsive regulation. The neo-contractualists' re-negotiated regulatory bargain may convince the State, society and the profession that its core values of independence, integrity, public service and a commitment to the rule of law mark it out as a profession that deserves to survive. Equally vital to the future success of the profession is the need to convince the many sub-specialisms within the profession that such core values provide a unifying cement that surpasses their desire to be free from the rule of the Law Society or wedded to other providers who have moved into the legal services market in recent times.

[122] Ironically for the profession, Dingwall and Fenn, *supra* n. 18 and Ogus, *supra* n. 1, would argue that such competition works against restrictive practices and is therefore in the public interest.

[123] A scenario foreshadowed by Glasser, 1990, *supra* n. 34, and S Mayson, "The Future of the Legal Profession" (1992) 1 *Nottingham Law Journal* 1.

Finally, at the other (most optimistic) extreme for the profession we might see:

- markets regained for the profession from other providers as a result of entrepreneurial initiatives;
- new markets colonised by the profession e.g. the latent legal market, by harnessing the new technologies;
- transnational and large-scale corporate work predominantly in the hands of the megalaw firms and MDPs controlled by lawyers;
- dispute resolution and ADR remaining under the control of the profession;
- self-regulation within a broader regulatory framework being preferred to more independent and more intrusive forms of regulation

More realistically, the eventual scenario in ten or twenty years time will turn out not to resemble any of these. Whether the scenario which finally emerges will be in the public interest must remain a moot point.

4

Constitutional and Human Rights Law

CONOR GEARTY AND ADAM TOMKINS

Introduction

There is a sense in which every chapter in this book could be about human rights law. If we had to make one prediction about the future of UK law over the coming two decades or so it would be that rights-talk (and, increasingly, rights law) will figure ever more intrusively. Human rights might not come to dominate UK law, but they are set to become a domineering presence over it.

We write here under the heading: "Constitutional and Human Rights Law". The noun "law" reflects our belief that human rights law (as opposed to human rights) is a deeply technical subject, often quite distant from the noble political ideas of radical eighteenth century philosophy which fathered it. The "constitutional" dimension reflects our belief that a collection such as this should include at least some passing reference to the constitution, but more broadly we felt that, as public lawyers, one of the more arresting lessons of the Human Rights Act 1998 has already been how much the Act speaks to certain other areas of law more fundamentally than it appears to relate to constitutional law. While it might initially have been assumed that it would be constitutional lawyers who would embrace the Human Rights Act as a new aspect of their discipline, on further analysis it turns out that family lawyers, criminal procedure lawyers, and specialists in the law of evidence will all have to confront the Human Rights Act more immediately and more urgently than will constitutional lawyers. But one critical task which the Human Rights Act will perhaps set constitutional lawyers, more pressingly than they are used to, is to crystallise the scope of their subject. In a sense, therefore, there is a critical tension in our title, which raises the two questions on which we focus in this chapter. First, what is it to be a constitutional lawyer in the opening decades of the new century? And secondly, where in the legal system will the Human Rights

Act bite hardest, if it is not to be in the arena of constitutional law? It is to the first of these questions that we now turn.

The Future of Constitutional Law

Surveying the most recent catalogues of the United Kingdom's major publishers of law books, one would have thought that constitutional law somehow no longer existed as a field of academic research, but had been replaced by a subject called constitutional reform.[1] No-one would deny that the Labour Government elected in 1997 has indeed embarked on an ambitious programme of legislative reforms, some of which will have a profound impact on the future of constitutional governance in the United Kingdom. The combined effect of devolution, reform of the House of Lords, freedom of information, and incorporation of (most of) the European Convention on Human Rights 1950 will be significant and long term.

A State of Constant Flux

However, while all this is true, a sense of perspective is called for. The constitution is not being re-written. It is not even being written. It will remain uncodified and customary. Power will continue to flow down from the Crown, as neither the personal powers of the monarch, nor the executive prerogative powers of her ministers feature as items for "modernization" on the Government's constitutional reform agenda (subject, of course to any possible intrusion of the Human Rights Act in this area). Constitutional conventions (the non-legal rules of constitutional behaviour) will continue to serve as a fundamental source of the United Kingdom's constitutional authority, with ministerial responsibility continuing to hold pole position in the list of merely conventional, yet nonetheless essential, principles of the constitution.[2] Similarly, each of the three broad institutions of the State—the legislature, the

[1] See, for example, R Blackburn and R Plant (eds), *Constitutional Reform: The Labour Government's Constitutional Reform Agenda* (London, Longman, 1999); The University of Cambridge Centre for Public Law, *Constitutional Reform in the United Kingdom: Practice and Principles* (Oxford, Hart Publishing, 1998); and R Hazell (ed.), *Constitutional Futures: A History of the Next Ten Years* (Oxford, Oxford University Press, 1999).

[2] See Sixth Report of the Committee on Standards in Public Life (Chairman, Lord Neill), *Reinforcing Standards* (Cm 4557, January 2000). See also D Oliver, "Ministerial Accountability: What and Where are the Parameters?" and D Woodhouse, "Individual Ministerial Responsibility and a 'Dash of Principle'", both in D Butler, V Bogdanor, and R Summers (eds), *The Law, Politics, and the Constitution: Essays in Honour of Geoffrey Marshall* (Oxford, Oxford University Press, 1999).

executive and the judiciary—will continue to play the same essential role as before. Parliament remains sovereign (even after the Human Rights Act).[3] The executive remains dominated by party (even after devolution).[4] And the judiciary remains limited in the ways in which it can review acts of the legislature or of the executive, although it is in this aspect of constitutional governance that things have changed most, as we shall see.

Vast swathes of the constitution will carry on much as before. From time to time small, pragmatic changes may be made (as before), but by and large, the civil service, political parties, the institutions and agencies of national security, the process of making delegated legislation, the role of the European Union in UK constitutional law, the law of local government, and the prevalence of audit as a technique of administrative regulation will continue as before: all of these and more will look in the opening years of the twenty-first century much as they did in the closing years of the twentieth. But constitutional continuity will be a theme to be found not only of the United Kingdom's institutions of government, but also in its doctrines. Constitutional law teachers will continue to be able to structure their subject around the same broad themes with which we have grown familiar since the time of Dicey: the sovereignty of parliament, the rule of law, the separation of powers, ministerial responsibility, constitutional monarchy, and limited democracy. Such a list would make as coherent a series of chapters in a textbook on constitutional law now as it would have done half a century ago.

This is not to say, of course, that nothing has changed or will change. Viewed historically this is not at all surprising. In the last three decades of the twentieth century, significant changes were made to the constitution by all the leading players on the constitutional stage. As far as Parliament is concerned, legislation such as the European Communities Act 1972 and the Police and Criminal Evidence Act 1984 has had a profound effect on aspects of constitutional law. Parliament also passed legislation privatising much of what the State formerly owned industrially, and in doing so has created a new species of administrative regulator in the form of Oftel, Ofgas, and their various cousins in electricity, water, and rail, spawning a vast amount of academic research—in law schools and elsewhere—in the rejuvenated field of regulation. Such regulation-related activity and scholarship has made a significant contribution to the further development of our understanding of such matters as rule-making, enforcement, participation and control of power, themes which are of central concern to constitutional law.[5]

[3] See K Ewing, "The Human Rights Act and Parliamentary Democracy" (1999) 62 *MLR* 79.

[4] As witness, for example, the disagreement within the Labour Party over who should be the First Minister of Wales (first Ron Davies, then Alun Michael, and finally the popular choice, Rhodri Morgan), and over who should be the Labour candidate for Mayor of London.

[5] See R Baldwin and C McCrudden (eds), *Regulation and Public Law* (London, Weidenfeld and Nicolson, 1987); A Ogus, *Regulation: Legal Form and Economic Theory* (Oxford, Oxford University Press, 1994); and J Black, *Rules and Regulators* (Oxford, Oxford University Press, 1997).

In terms of changes made by successive governments, in the 1970s the Labour administrations in power during that decade radically extended the role of trade unions in government decision-making and policy development.[6] In the 1980s, during the Thatcher period, considerable reforms to the structure and indeed to the ethos of the civil service were introduced, with the creation of the so-called Next Steps agencies and the growth in the use of short-term contracts and performance-related pay.[7] And in the 1990s John Major's ministers repeatedly attempted to redraw the boundaries of their constitutional responsibilities to Parliament by seeking to make a variety of amendments to the convention of individual ministerial responsibility.[8]

Finally, the judges, too, have over the years seen important changes made to the role that they play within the constitution. Judicial review of the exercise of prerogative powers was extended by the House of Lords in the GCHQ case in 1984;[9] ministers were tied more tightly to the rule of law by the extension in 1993 of the courts' ultimate coercive jurisdiction (contempt of court) to cover the wrongdoings of officers of the Crown;[10] and around this time significant moves were also made to enhance the ability of the courts to hold high-handed ministers to constitutional account when Parliament fails to do so—most notoriously in the narrowly won *Fire Brigades Union* case.[11]

The Blair Reforms

How, then, are we to read the various constitutional reforms which have been introduced under the Labour Government headed by Tony Blair? The Labour administration's package of constitutional reforms can be viewed in two ways. The first of these involves not seeing it as a package at all, but rather viewing each of the various reforms as a discrete and separate entity in itself. On this view, while the various measures of constitutional reform do to some extent relate to one another, this is more by accident than by design. Thus, each of the main reforms was arrived at via quite disparate routes. Those who led the fight for Scottish devolution, for example, were substantially different both in terms of personnel and as regards political purpose from those who campaigned so vigorously for the incorporation of the European Convention on Human

[6] See K Ewing, "The Politics of the British Constitution" [2000] PL (forthcoming). See also P Birkinshaw, I Harden and N Lewis, *Government by Moonlight: The Hybrid Parts of the State* (London, Unwin Hyman, 1990).

[7] For a survey of the constitutional implications of the changes to the civil service made by the Thatcher and Major Governments, see A Tomkins, *The Constitution after Scott: Government Unwrapped* (Oxford, Oxford University Press, 1998), ch. 2.

[8] For a full account, see Tomkins, *ibid.*, ch. 1.

[9] *Council of Civil Service Unions* v. *Minister for the Civil Service* [1985] AC 374.

[10] *M* v. *Home Office* [1994] 1 AC 377.

[11] *R* v. *Secretary of State for Home Affairs, ex parte Fire Brigades Union* [1995] 2 AC 513.

Rights.[12] It is also clearly the case that some of the Blair Government's reforms are closer to Blair's own political heart than are others. Devolution was largely inherited from the John Smith era, and reform of the House of Lords was an even more long-standing Labour commitment. Enacting a bill of rights based on the ECHR may have been a cause to which Blair more clearly allied himself, although here again he was building on an earlier commitment made by John Smith. From this perspective, therefore, it would be a mistake to imagine that the various constitutional reforms introduced by the Blair Government were designed to fit together to form one perfectly coherent, single whole.

However, it is also the case that, despite their differing origins, there is nonetheless a sense in which taken together the bundle of reforms can indeed sensibly be viewed as possessing a degree of cohesion. The multiple components of reform can be seen as constituting a package of more or less integrated modernisation, informed throughout by a common set of constitutional and political values. Institutionally this appearance manifests itself in the form of the Cabinet Committee on the constitution, presided over by the Lord Chancellor, Lord Irvine of Lairg. But more significantly, it could be argued that conceptually the various items on the Blair Government's agenda of constitutional change are, despite their disparate origins, tied together by a number of common threads.

Four such common threads can be identified: first, a theme of decentralisation (which applies to Scottish, Northern Irish and Welsh devolution, to the establishment of the Greater London Authority and its mayor, and to the reorganisation and rejuvenation of regional development agencies in England); secondly, a theme of the radical enhancement of the constitutional role of the judiciary (which can be seen from granting to the judges such matters as the enforcement of the Human Rights Act, discussed below, and the policing of boundary disputes between Westminster and the devolved institutions under the Scotland Act 1998 and the Government of Wales Act 1998); the third theme is that of according new rights to the people (under both the Human Rights Act and the freedom of information legislation); finally, there is the theme of streamlining Parliament, in the combined senses of modernising the procedures of the House of Commons, tinkering with composition and membership of the House of Lords, and continuing to think about whether to invite the electorate to make changes to the electoral system for the House of Commons.

[12] See M Foley, *The Politics of the British Constitution* (Manchester, Manchester University Press, 1999), esp ch. 4. See also N Walker, "Constitutional Reform in a Cold Climate: Reflections on the White Paper and Referendum on Scotland's Parliament", in A Tomkins (ed.), *Devolution and the British Constitution* (London, Key Haven, 1998).

From Constitutional Pragmatism to Liberal Constitutionalism?

Each of these four themes is a key component of liberal constitutionalism, and it is this fact which might well turn out to have the most telling impact on the future of UK constitutional law. The reason for this is that the values of liberal constitutionalism are different from the values traditionally associated with constitutionalism in the United Kingdom. Liberal constitutionalism is a complex set of ideas, on which there is a significant and growing literature,[13] but for our purposes its three most salient characteristics are: first, the belief in the supremacy of a written (that is to say, codified) constitutional text; secondly, the notion that government should be a task for three separate but equal bodies: a legislature, an executive, and a judiciary; and thirdly, the idea that the relationship between the individual and the State is best expressed in terms of a series of fundamental or constitutionally entrenched civil or human rights, and that these rights should be enforceable by the judiciary. It follows that, if our analysis of the Blair Government's constitutional reform programme is correct, the lasting impact of that programme might well be to alter the values on which the United Kingdom's constitution has traditionally been based. For all the ebbing and flowing of the constitutional tides over the course of the decades preceding 1997, this would be an achievement which could not be claimed by any other government since the emergence of democracy in the early twentieth century.

What were the values of UK constitutionalism in the twentieth century, from which it may be that a new constitutional order is at least partly resiling? Four can be readily identified. First there was the central importance attached to the sovereignty of the one Parliament over the entire union: England, Wales, and Scotland (and, during times of direct rule, also Northern Ireland).[14] Secondly there was the authority of the Crown: the United Kingdom as constitutional monarchy; ministers being ministers of the Crown (and obtaining significant powers through the prerogative); civil servants being servants of the Crown rather than regular employees; and even judges, let us not forget, adjudicating upon legal disputes in the *Royal* Courts of Justice. Thirdly there was the idea that such royal power, especially where exercised on the monarch's behalf by his or her ministers, should be subject to the principle of responsible

[13] See for example the extensive bibliography in M J C Vile, *Constitutionalism and the Separation of Powers* (2nd edn., Indianapolis, Liberty Fund, 1998).

[14] In the closing years of the century, the sovereignty of parliament became subject to the growing influence of the European Union on UK public law. This started, ironically enough, with an Act of Parliament (the European Communities Act 1972), but for a famous illustration of how painfully UK lawyers adjusted to the new regime, see the long and drawn-out *Factortame* saga: especially *R* v. *Secretary of State for Transport, ex parte Factortame (No. 1)* [1990] 2 AC 85 and *(No. 2)* [1991] 1 AC 603.

government. This was a notion of responsibility which was owed by ministers *to Parliament.* Just as the succession to the throne itself has since 1701 been a matter upon which Parliament may legislate,[15] so too is it now the case that the exercise by the Crown's ministers of their powers is something which it is for Parliament to monitor. Whereas twentieth century UK constitutionalism privileged the idea of government accountability to Parliament, conversely it never developed any sophisticated notion of government responsibility to law.[16] Indeed, it has been a striking feature of twentieth century UK constitutionalism that there has been only a relatively weak principle of legality[17]—hence the idea, as John Griffith so famously described it, of the "political constitution".[18] The final value of UK constitutionalism in the twentieth century was, as suggested above, a commitment to democracy. But this was only a limited democracy. Democracy in twentieth century UK law did not extend far—either in terms of representation or as regards participation. Certainly, democracy was not the only source of constitutional legitimacy or authority. Tradition, convention, the heredity principle, and patronage were also significant players.

Will these values survive the revisionist agenda of the Blair Government? It is already clear that at least three of them will not, or at least not in the form we knew them before 1997. Of the four key values of the twentieth century constitution identified here, only the second (the authority of the crown) remains untouched by the hand of modernisation.[19] The sovereignty of

[15] See the Act of Settlement 1701. See also the Bill of Rights 1689.

[16] Even supposed breakthroughs were vastly more limited than they first appeared to the headline writers. In *M* v. *Home Office, supra* n. 10, the House of Lords unanimously proclaimed that the courts could find a minister of the Crown in contempt of court. But it should not be forgotten that in the same case the Lords also declared (1) that even if a minister were found in contempt of court he or she could not be judicially punished for it; (2) that even though ministers of the Crown could be found in contempt of court the Crown itself could not be; and (3) that even in the late twentieth century it was still the law that "the Crown may do no wrong". For a fuller analysis, see A Tomkins, "Crown Privileges", in M Sunkin and S Payne (eds), *The Nature of the Crown* (Oxford, Oxford University Press, 1999), ch. 7.

[17] The essence of the rule of law is that government may do nothing without specific, direct legal authority: *Entick* v. *Carrington* (1765) 19 St Tr 1030. This is an easy enough rule for any government with a majority in the House of Commons to negotiate: see, among many examples, Home Secretary Michael Howard's reaction to losing the *Fire Brigades Union* case (*supra* n. 11). He simply introduced legislation in Parliament, which Parliament passed, to achieve the same result as he had previously (and unlawfully) attempted to achieve through other means: see Criminal Injuries Compensation Act 1995 (see C Harlow and R Rawlings, *Law and Administration* (2nd edn., London, Butterworths, 1997), p. 617). Several cases in the late twentieth century indicated that even though the rule of law was already weak, the courts would readily dilute it further: see, for example, *Malone* v. *Metropolitan Police Commissioner* [1979] Ch 344, and *R* v. *Secretary of State for the Home Department, ex parte Northumbria Police Authority* [1989] 1 QB 26.

[18] J A G Griffith, "The Political Constitution" (1979) 42 *MLR* 1.

[19] Though it is interesting to note that the Crown is subject to the Human Rights Act: see s. 22(5).

parliament must now face the combined challenges not only of the European Union, but also of having newly established legislatures elsewhere within the kingdom and, perhaps even more significantly, of having the further pressure of the judiciary breathing down its neck, ready to step in with its declarations of incompatibility whenever Parliament is judged to have overstepped the human rights mark.[20] As for responsible government, ministers will remain collectively and individually responsible to Parliament, but at the same time their constitutional responsibilities to the courts will be augmented as the rule of law is strengthened, section 6 of the Human Rights Act 1998, for example, providing that "it is unlawful for a public authority to act in a way which is incompatible with a Convention right". This is a provision which will be policed not by Parliament, but by the courts.

The relationship between democracy and the constitution has also been reworked through the changes which the Blair Government has introduced. The freedom of information legislation, while significantly less far-reaching than were the Government's initial proposals,[21] nonetheless crystallises the people's right to accurate information about what their government has done in their name, at least in certain circumstances. Further, the devolution and regional government packages (all of which were introduced with the express consent of the people in a series of referendums in Scotland, Wales, Northern Ireland and London) bring government closer to the people that elect it. At the same time, the authority previously attained from heredity is being diluted—albeit rather more gradually than some would have liked. The monarchy remains unaffected, but at least in the House of Lords there have since 1999 been only ninety-two hereditary peers, as opposed to the 647 who had enjoyed voting rights in the national legislature before the House of Lords Act 1999. It is but a small step, and there is at the time of writing no firm indication as to when (if ever, under the present Government) a second step might be attempted, but it is at least an indication that as we enter the twenty-first century, the House of Lords is preparing itself, at last, to leave the nineteenth.

To clarify, we are not arguing that through the Blair Government's reforms, the United Kingdom has finally reached the holy grail of liberal constitutionalism. The United Kingdom remains some distance from that outcome. Of the three cardinal principles of liberal constitutionalism only one has been legally recognised, and even that only in a partial manner. There remains no sign at all of a written constitution. The separation of powers (in the Madisonian sense of there being three powers, kept separate from one another in terms

[20] Human Rights Act, s. 4.

[21] The Government introduced its Freedom of Information Bill into the House of Commons on 18 November 1999. Its earlier proposals were set out in the White Paper, *Your Right to Know* (Cm 3818, December 1997).

both of function and personnel, with each having the constitutional responsibility of checking and balancing the other two) remains as far away from UK constitutionalism as ever. Only the protection of civil rights—the third and final element of liberal constitutionalism—is with us, and even that only in a limited way. It is to this, the most dramatic of the Blair Government's reforms from the legal perspective, that we now turn.

The Human Rights Act 1998

Two assumptions underpinned the push for incorporation of the European Convention on Human Rights into UK domestic law. These were, firstly that civil liberties and human rights protection had been seriously eroded in the United Kingdom during the 1980s and 1990s and secondly, that the European Convention on Human Rights and in particular the case law of the European Court of Human Rights offered a better guarantor of basic freedoms in the United Kingdom than the then prevailing *status quo*. We shall briefly consider the validity of these two assumptions before analysing the construction of the Human Rights Act 1998 and what its enactment suggests for the future.

The Supposed Erosion of Civil Liberties

It is a commonly held view that the 1980s was a time when unparalleled damage was done to civil liberties protection in UK law. This may be true, but the question is begged as to when exactly was the high point with which the substantive consequences of this decline can be compared. The freedom enjoyed by the few in the pre-democratic era can hardly count, since the liberties of the many were then arbitrarily restricted by the authority of the military, backed up by explicitly coercive laws. The right to vote was not available on a universal basis until well into the twentieth century, after which civil liberties were regularly sharply controlled by emergency regulation. Such regulations were promulgated during the First World War,[22] during the 1920s[23] and once again during the Second World War.[24] In the inter-War period, the common law was used in a draconian way to destroy political dissent in the 1930s[25] and legislation was also frequently enacted which was subversive of civil liberties during

[22] Under the Defence of the Realm legislation regularly passed by Parliament during the war.
[23] Emergency Powers Act 1920.
[24] Defence Regulations Act 1939.
[25] *Duncan* v. *Jones* [1936] 1 KB 218; *Elias* v. *Pasmore* [1934] 2 KB 164; *Thomas* v. *Sawkins* [1935] 2 KB 249.

the same period.[26] Even in the period between the end of the Second World War and the beginning of Mrs Thatcher's time in office (in other words, for much of the Cold War period), control on industrial espionage and (from the late 1960s) the fear of terrorism meant that civil liberties were regularly under attack from many sources of authority and in many different ways.[27]

The second assumption referred to above may be easier to sustain. Certainly it was a widely held view in the 1980s and 1990s. During this period, many in the Liberal and Labour Parties, and whole sections of the legal establishment (including many senior members of the judiciary) came to believe that the European Convention on Human Rights provided a better source of protection for freedom than British domestic law. While there are valid grounds for such an argument, this view reveals only half the picture. The reality is that there is both a positive and a negative side to the ECHR's contribution to the protection of freedom. As to the former, it is clear that the European Court of Human Rights has secured significant procedural safeguards for a number of minority groups. This has been particularly so in the case of prisoners, and in the mental health and criminal justice fields.[28] Similarly, other minority groups have also been able to use such principles of Convention jurisprudence as the right to respect for privacy in Article 8 to establish some degree of personal dignity in their public lives as well as their private lives, on issues related to sexual identity for example.[29] The press has also rightly regarded the European Convention and the European Court of Human Rights as important sources of *dicta* protective of press freedom.[30]

More negatively, however, and less widely understood, perhaps, there have also been many unattractive features to the Strasbourg jurisprudence when viewed from a civil liberties perspective. In the Strasbourg version of *Brind*[31] a challenge to the media ban under Article 10 was unsuccessful with the result that not only Sinn Féin was restricted in its access to the airwaves but so also were persons holding views similar to those of Sinn Féin. The GCHQ case, in which the banning of trade unions at GCHQ was effected by ministerial diktat, survived scrutiny at the Commission stage in Strasbourg without ever reaching the Court.[32] After *Brannigan and McBride* v. *United Kingdom*,[33] the

[26] See for example the Incitement to Disaffection Act 1934; Public Order Act 1936, s. 3. See generally K D Ewing and C A Gearty, *The Struggle for Civil Liberties: Political Freedom and the Rule of Law in Britain, 1914–45* (Oxford, Oxford University Press, 2000).

[27] See generally D G T Williams, *Not in the Public Interest* (London, Hutchinson, 1967). On terrorism, see the Prevention of Terrorism (Temporary Provisions) Act 1974.

[28] See C A Gearty, "The United Kingdom" in C A Gearty (ed.), *European Civil Liberties and the European Convention on Human Rights: A Comparative Survey* (The Hague, Martinus Nijhoff, 1997).

[29] See *Norris* v. *Ireland* (1988) 13 EHRR 186.

[30] See *Sunday Times* v. *UK* (1979) 2 EHRR 245.

[31] *Brind* v. *UK* (1994) 18 EHRR CD 76.

[32] *Council of Civil Service Unions* v. *UK* (1988) 10 EHRR 269.

UK authorities were able to present seven-day detention without charge under the Prevention of Terrorism legislation as justified under Article 15(3) of the European Convention. So it has always been dangerous to expect too much from the European Convention on Human Rights, a point worth remembering when the potential of the Human Rights Act 1998 is considered, a topic to which we now turn.

Enacting the Human Rights Act 1998

The Human Rights Act went through parliament in a fairly brisk manner early on in the Government's term of office, after a somewhat cursory public debate and a White Paper published at the same time as the bill.[34] In considering the measure we need to be aware of the issues of the day that drove its content and what its political rationale was, but in doing this we also need to be mindful of the future impact of the Act, five or ten years from now. Two particular issues were of central importance when the precise content of the measure was being considered, relating to the perceived need to preserve parliamentary sovereignty and to deal with what was then believed to be a central issue, the problem of the lack of privacy rights in UK law. We shall look at each of these concerns in turn and show how the content of the Human Rights Act has been moulded by the Government's reaction to them.

Turning first to parliamentary sovereignty, in opposition, Labour had reworked clause 4 of its constitution but in doing so had there retained the idea that the party was a democratic socialist party. The Human Rights Act could only attack parliamentary sovereignty if Labour were prepared to sacrifice democratic socialism, because parliamentary sovereignty is the only probable means through which the radical changes in society that are required by democratic socialism can be advanced. In particular, the liberal constitutionalism discussed above, of which rights-talk is an exemplification, would make such a transformation of society impossible. However a "human rights" document which took a distant second place to the will of Parliament would have been attacked by many as not worthy of enactment. During the summer of 1997, the drafters of the human rights bill confronted these contradictory impulses, the liberal and the democratic socialist elements in Labour, and resolved them unambiguously at the level of theory in favour of parliamentary sovereignty, but almost equally unambiguously at the level of practice in favour of liberal constitutionalism.

[33] *Brannigan and McBride* v. *UK* (1994) 17 EHRR 539.

[34] *Rights Brought Home: The Human Rights Bill* (Cm 3782, October 1997). See for an analysis of the measure C A Gearty, "Incorporation of the European Convention on Human Rights. Some guesses about the future" in F Butler (ed.), *Human Rights For the New Millenium* (The Hague, Kluwer, 2000).

Under the Act no court will be able to strike down any provision of any Act of Parliament for having infringed a Convention right. In particular, and unusually, no court is empowered to strike down any part of even a pre-existing Act. Thus, the doctrine of implied repeal, a routine feature of English constitutional law, does not appear to apply to the Human Rights Act. All that can happen is that there can be a declaration of incompatibility, declaring that in the judge's opinion, or the judges' opinions, a piece of primary legislation infringes the Human Rights Act.[35] Such declarations will "not affect the validity, continuing operation or enforcement"[36] of the provision(s) in respect of which they are made. Moreover, the Human Rights Act can itself be repealed. After implementation it will still be possible for a political party to campaign on a series of promises which would be inconsistent with the Human Rights Act, and which would involve either the wholesale rejection of the human rights language in the courts or the repeal of the Human Rights Act itself.

New Labour has therefore preserved the key democratic principle that underpins its fundamental ideology. To this extent it is perfectly true to say that even in the field of human rights law, liberal constitutionalism does not hold full sway. But the principle of parliamentary sovereignty is now very isolated, in four ways. First, it does not apply to Scotland, Wales or Northern Ireland. All the assemblies that have been put in place under the Government's devolution plans, will be required, and all the executives, if there are any executives that service them, will be required, to act in a way which is compatible with the Convention. Secondly, there is in the Human Rights Act no suggestion that the right of the victim who has exhausted all local remedies should be disabled from taking his or her case to Strasbourg. To the extent that it involves the infringement of Convention rights, therefore, democratic socialism would have either to reject international law or at the very least it would need to deprive persons from taking cases to Strasbourg. This is unlikely.

Thirdly, this theoretical commitment to parliamentary sovereignty is further diluted by international reality, in particular in the form of an EU increasingly committed not only to market and commercial unity but also to supremacy in the field of human rights.[37] A fourth restraint on Parliament is to be found in various forms in the Human Rights Act itself. As noted above, section 3 states that all legislation, past and present, must be construed so far as is possible to be compatible with Convention rights. This is a very strong principle of statutory interpretation, far stronger than is normally found in traditional English law. Furthermore all public authorities are going to be required to act compatibly with Convention rights, under section 6(1) of the

[35] See s. 4 of the 1998 Act.

[36] See s. 4(6).

[37] Note that a Convention has been mandated by the European Council to report by the end of 2000 on the creation of a Charter of Fundamental Rights for the EU.

Act. Delegated legislation will also have to be Convention compliant. The Crown is expressly bound.[38] In practice, therefore, the effect of the Human Rights Act on executive action is likely to be profound, not least because of the breadth of the incorporated rights[39] and the requirement to have regard where relevant to the case law of the European organs that have been responsible for policing its meaning during the past four decades.[40]

We turn now to the second of the issues referred to above (i.e. privacy) and to the potentially long-term effects of the way in which this issue has been resolved in the Act. When the human rights bill was first mooted, it was clear that from the Government's perspective any proposal of this nature should have the potential to allow the creation of a new law on privacy. Such an effect would mean that the Government would not have to introduce such a measure itself, thereby avoiding a battle with a very powerful interest group that could no doubt present itself as a constitutional watchdog. The measure was in this respect an intelligent piece of political management. The route to achieving the goal of making possible the development of a covert privacy law was to write into the Act the provision that the definition of "public authority" under section 6 would include the courts.[41] The implications of this are certain to be extraordinarily interesting. Clearly this provision must mean that the courts must manage their own affairs compatibly with the Convention. Thus, for example, in the running of the court and in the administration of the court's rules, they must comply *inter alia* with Article 6(1) of the Convention. It will be interesting to see the extent to which the Woolf reforms on civil procedure can be rendered Convention-compatible. Already there is a reported case on the point.[42]

Even more interesting is the extent to which the Human Rights Act will mould the common law. Though the point is controversial,[43] it would seem that the traditional forms of that law—nuisance, trespass and so on—may well be required in future to evolve in a Convention-compatible way, with this "evolution" being assisted by the principles to be found in the European Convention. It was on this basis that Lord Irvine, in the House of Lords' debates, was able to anticipate the evolution of a privacy law through the old forms of action in nuisance being expanded to include the requirement for compliance with Article 8.[44] In the post-enactment decision of *DPP* v. *Jones*,[45] the Lord Chancellor, giving the leading speech for the majority, identified a

38 See s. 22(5) of the 1998 Act.
39 See s. 1 and Schedule 1.
40 See s. 2.
41 See s. 6(3)(a).
42 *General Mediterranean Holdings* v. *Patel* [1999] 3 All ER 673.
43 See Sir Richard Buxton, "The Human Rights Act and Private Law" (2000) 116 *LQR* 48.
44 HL Deb, vol 583, col 783 (24 November 1997).
45 [1999] 2 All ER 257.

development within the law of trespass which was independent of the Convention but which drew a kind of strength from the core values related to freedom of assembly that are to be found in Article 11. The case may turn out to be an early example of the way in which the law will develop in the future, though there are a couple of interesting dissents from judges more unfamiliar, perhaps, with the idea that public protest can in certain circumstances trump private property.

The large question begged by this discussion is whether there will develop out of the Human Rights Act a cause of action for breach of human rights. Individual victims[46] will be able to take cases against public authorities on the basis of an alleged breach under section 6 of the Human Rights Act, but the case of a private *inter partes* action would not be easy to characterise in these terms, especially if the defendant was not a "public authority" within the meaning of section 6. It would appear that there is in this sense no "pure horizontality" in the Act. It is improbable therefore that, at least in the short to medium term, the judges will read the Human Rights Act as permitting actions against private parties for breach of the Human Rights Act, or actions which require courts to provide remedies for such breaches, which would in effect amount to the same thing.[47]

The Future of Human Rights Litigation

Clearly the Human Rights Act provides opportunities for the improvement of the lot of ordinary persons, for their protection from state power, and for the improvement of their personal circumstances. If the idea of human rights is seen as being mainly concerned with the dignity of the individual, then clearly there are going to be unprecedented opportunities for advancement. The courts increasingly will be an important part of these movements. Take for example the whole question of the alleged racism of the police. That is likely to be repackaged and re-litigated as a liberty and discrimination issue under Articles 5 and 14 (with there being no guarantee as to the outcome, it should be stressed).

Operational incompetence by the police is another area where there are likely to be interesting developments. Sooner or later the question will arise as to whether the *McCann*[48] judgment's interpretation of Article 2 of the European Convention (on the right to life) is to be applied in domestic law. *McCann* was the extremely controversial Gibraltar case, in which the European Court of Human Rights held by the narrowest of margins that the British

[46] See s. 7(1) of the 1998 Act.

[47] Whether, if the courts do develop the law in this way, such a route would in turn prove to be a violation of the courts' new-found duty under s. 6 not to act in a way which is incompatible with Convention rights, remains of course to be seen.

[48] *McCann* v. *UK* (1995) 21 EHRR 97.

authorities had been culpable in having failed to organise an anti-terrorist operation properly with the consequence that people had died. An outstanding further case in the same general area is *Osman*.[49] This was an extraordinary Strasbourg decision in 1998, in which it was held that a general rule which protects a public authority, in this case the police, from an action in negligence, infringe the Article 6(1) "right of access to court", itself nowhere in the article but extrapolated from a series of cases, with the result that the inability of the applicant to sue the police for negligence in this case amounts to a breach of their rights. The case has been criticised by some within this jurisdiction but equally hailed by others as representing a human rights breakthrough in its insistence that each case of alleged negligence be properly considered on its facts.[50]

Other constitutional areas also suggest themselves as ripe for litigation under the new Act. In *Ribitsch* v. *Austria*[51] the European Court of Human Rights suggested that the onus should be on the police to explain how injuries happen in detention. Another topical example is immigration and asylum. The right to bail for immigration detainees can be repackaged as a right to liberty point under Article 5. Furthermore, how can it be argued after the Human Rights Act that a person facing expulsion to another country, where it is possible he or she will be tortured, cannot have legal aid to argue a case which might save his or her life? Other examples include workers' rights under Article 4 and the implied environment rights in Article 8.[52]

What needs to be recognised is that litigation will be part of politics in this new, partly liberal constitutional world which the Blair Government has ushered in. This requires a completely new approach to litigation in the United Kingdom and it will only be worked through over a long period of time. It is likely that academic scholarship will come more to the fore in litigation than hitherto, not least because there is likely to be a strong emphasis on comparative and European research, at least in large-scale cases. It is also clear that the Act will be used, and used successfully, by the powerful in society. Relevant rights in this context include the right to property, in Article 1 of the First Protocol; the commercial expression guarantee in Article 10; and the very strong controls on State regulation of serious crime, fraud and racketeering that are to be found in Article 6 and Article 8.[53] These are going to be much bigger inhibitions on State action than the Government has perhaps anticipated.

[49] *Osman* v. *United Kingdom* (1998) 29 EHRR 245.

[50] See T Weir, "Down Hill—All the Way?" (1999) 58 *CLJ* 4; Lord Hoffmann, "Human Rights and the House of Lords" (1999) 62 *MLR* 159; M Lunney, "A Tort Lawyer's View of *Osman* v. *UK*" (1999) 10 *KCLJ* 238.

[51] *Ribitsch* v. *Austria* (1995) 21 EHRR 573.

[52] *Lopez Ostra* v. *Spain* (1994) 20 EHRR 277.

[53] *Saunders* v. *UK* (1996) 23 EHRR 313; *Funke* v. *France* (1993) 16 EHRR 297; *Niemietz* v. *Germany* (1992) 16 EHRR 97; *Chappell* v. *UK* (1989) 12 EHRR 1; *Gasus Dosier—und Fördetechnik* v. *Netherlands* (1995) 20 EHRR 403.

We started this chapter by referring to the pervasiveness of the Human Rights Act and its great importance outside the realm of public law. An overriding impression of the Act is of its potential for complication. Will the civil law be reworked to comply with the case law of Article 6?[54] Will the whole set of criteria to determine what is and what is not a charity, be redefined to make them Article 9 compatible? Will all financial regulation have to be resynthesised to make it Convention-compatible? We are also entering a world of potentially distracting new technicalities. What is a public authority as opposed to a private body for the purposes of section 6? What kind of horizontality will there be as opposed to what kind of verticality? Will a public interest group that gets standing on the broad criteria for judicial review be able to argue a human rights point in the case, when it comes to court? Or will the standing restriction poison the argument in court, depriving the applicant of arguments that might have been available to a victim but are not available to it? What will be the relationship between judicial review and Article 6 of the European Convention on Human Rights? Almost inevitably *Wednesbury*[55] will need to be reworked so as to provide some oversight for factual error but only in cases raising a human rights-related point. So will there be different criteria for judicial review depending on the kind of issue that is raised under the case? We will return, if we are not careful, to the stymied procedural world of the first half of the twentieth century and to the tortured wrangles which ensued the introduction of the revamped Order 53 into judicial review, wrangles which the courts found themselves unable to escape for more than a decade, it should not be forgotten.[56]

Conclusion

We end with some further general points. Firstly, government will clearly want its legislation to comply with the Human Rights Act. Section 19, requiring that statements of compatibility accompany all proposed governmental legislation, is already in force and is being used. The correctness of government claims that all its proposals are compatible with the Convention remains to be tested in the courts. Given that few Acts directly mandate action, such assertions of compatibility are not surprising. The true question will be as to whether a statutory

[54] *Blackstone's Civil Practice 2000* (London, Blackstone Press, 2000) has a whole chapter devoted to "Human Rights and Civil Procedure".

[55] *Associated Provincial Picture Houses Ltd* v. *Wednesbury Corporation* [1948] 1 KB 223.

[56] See *O'Reilly* v. *Mackman* [1983] 2 AC 237; *Roy* v. *Kensington and Chelsea Family Practitioner Committee* [1992] 2 WLR 239; and *Mercury* v. *Director-General of Telecommunications* [1996] 1 All ER 575.

discretion which on its face is compatible with the Convention has on the facts before a court been exercised in a Convention-compatible way. Much will depend on the breadth accorded by the courts to section 6(2) of the Act which exempts public authorities from the requirements of section 6(1) where their action has been specifically mandated by statute: it will be on the interpretation of this sub-section that the fate of parliamentary sovereignty will depend.

Secondly, it is not improbable that there will be a renewed and growing interest in the personality and temperament of our leading judges and further pressure to infuse a higher level of accountability and representativeness into this branch of the State. The Hoffmann affair was a taster for an inevitable future;[57] if political power is relocated as between the executive and the judicial branches, it must not then be surprising that the character and ideological predispositions of those exercising this power becomes of interest to the lay citizen. Take as an example a recent report that the Charities Commission might want to reorganise its criteria on charities so as to make it more difficult for private schools to secure charitable status. That would unquestionably, sooner or later, be challenged under the Human Rights Act. Does it matter if the judge has children in private school? Or does it matter if the judge has children in a State school? The Hoffmann/Pinochet point will be everywhere.[58]

In terms of constitutional reform, the issue will not be just how the judges are selected, but also how they are made more accountable. Will there be a select committee on the judiciary? Will we quite soon have Lord Woolf or Lord Bingham or whoever it is, being required to appear before Parliament like the Cabinet Secretary, Sir Richard Wilson, defending this and that colleague's interpretation of this or that provision of the Human Rights Act? How can this be avoided? Why should it not happen? And should the law lords stay in a reformed upper house of Parliament? No doubt these are matters upon which the new joint select committee on human rights will in due course be expressing a series of views.

For now, what is clear at the turn of the millennium is that whatever its defects, the Human Rights Act 1998 is set to have a profound effect on the United Kingdom's legal system. That effect will not start from the over-arching meta-principles of the constitution and work gradually down to ground level, however. On the contrary, as we have sought to demonstrate in this chapter, the constitution might escape relatively unscathed. It is elsewhere in the legal system that the Human Rights Act will have the most pronounced effect—in family law, and in criminal and civil procedure especially. Human rights might be a principal concern of constitutionalists, but human rights law as it is set to develop under the Human Rights Act is likely to focus its energies well away from the constitution itself.

[57] See *In Re Pinochet* [1999] 2 WLR 272.

[58] See *Locabail* v. *Bayfield Properties* [2000] 1 All ER 65.

5

Legislative devolution and legal diversity: the Northern Ireland dimensions

DESMOND GREER AND BRIGID HADFIELD

Since almost anything written about Northern Ireland law in the past thirty years has begun with the *caveat* that it is "subject to the outcome of the present crisis", we feel obliged at the outset to state our basic assumption that Northern Ireland will, for the foreseeable future, remain part of the United Kingdom. We also assume, as we are bound to do, that, even in the context of the United Kingdom, there is—and will continue to be—something distinctive about Northern Ireland law. This assumption, implicit in the scheme of devolution adopted in 1920, has now been given added force by recent developments in Scotland and Wales. Political realities—and, more formally, the recent creation of a North-South Ministerial Council—also mean that regard must also be had to the future relationship between the laws of the two Irish jurisdictions. We assume finally that *all* these legal systems will for the period under consideration remain part of the European legal orders.

It is likely that the political problems of Northern Ireland will, for the foreseeable future, continue to require distinctive legal arrangements, particularly in the field of public law. But there is more to law, even in Northern Ireland, than public law, and the more general issue posed by the three dimensions in which that law will develop must be the extent to which distinctive solutions may or should be adopted across the spectrum of the wider legal system. In this sense, the future of Northern Ireland law is *not* merely a matter of local concern, but raises more fundamental questions, equally applicable throughout the United Kingdom and the Republic of Ireland, concerning the scope for legal diversity within the Europe of the twenty-first century.

Our thesis, in brief, is that the main question for consideration is not *whether* the future law of Northern Ireland will or should be distinctive from English (and Scots and Welsh) law in some respects, but rather *when* and *why*

Northern Ireland will, or at least should, go its own way. An attempt to answer these questions can only be made after a brief consideration of some general characteristics of the existing law and legal system of Northern Ireland.

The story so far

In 1920 the two new Irish jurisdictions inherited a common law tradition which, with some notable exceptions, had for many centuries been characterised by the principle of *una et eadem lex*—the *lex* in question being English law.[1] This principle was promoted prior to the Acts of Union in 1800 by formal and informal restrictions on the Irish Parliament, and by the assertion by the (English) House of Lords of the right to be the "supreme judicature" for Ireland. This is not to suggest that Irish law did not develop some distinctive features, both before and after 1800;[2] what it does signify, however, is that Ireland (unlike Scotland) did not retain a broad legal culture distinctive from that in England and Wales.

The strength of the "common law" tradition readily defeated a suggestion made in the first flush of independence that, pending the enactment of a new code of Irish law, the Free State should adopt native Irish (Brehon) law and civil law principles,[3] and led the framers of the 1922 Constitution to declare instead that "the laws [now] in force . . . shall continue to be of full force and effect until . . . repealed or amended"[4] by an Irish Parliament answerable only to the requirements of the Constitution. A similar, but more limited, principle obtained in Northern Ireland; crucially it was to operate within the United Kingdom under the system of devolution enshrined in the Government of Ireland Act 1920, but otherwise without the benefit of a written constitution.

[1] A phrase first used in 1285, when the English Council condemned the Irish custom of wardship: G Hand, *English Law in Ireland 1290–1324* (Cambridge, CUP, 1967), p. 214, who also points out (at 218) that "The Bar of the Republic of Ireland is still educated at an Inn which owns the motto, derived from the declaration of the barons at Merton in 1236, *nolumus (leges Angliae) mutari*".

[2] In particular, with reference to criminal justice, land law, family law and civil procedure. Distinctive legislation designed to resolve particular Irish problems prior to 1920 were primarily made by the United Kingdom Parliament after 1800.

[3] *The Judiciary Rules and Forms of Parish and District Courts* (1920), cited by K Boyle and D Greer, *The Legal Systems North and South* (Dublin, Stationery Office, 1983), p. 14. Any possibility of incorporating Brehon law into the common law as a form of local custom (as had been done in Wales with "the particular custom of Denbigh") was rejected by the (common law) judges in *The Case of Tanistry* (1607) Davies Rep 28.

[4] Constitution of Saorstát Éireann 1922, Art. 73, replicated in the Constitution of Ireland 1937, Art. 50.1.

The Government of Ireland Act gave the new Parliament of Northern Ireland a general power to make laws for "peace, order and good government" in respect of unenumerated transferred matters.[5] This scheme of legislative devolution was supplemented by a "hands-off" policy which successive British Governments adopted for the next forty years or more. But in practice the Unionist governments which dominated the Parliament of Northern Ireland generally followed the Westminster line, not least because of their insistence that the financial relationship between Northern Ireland and Great Britain should be governed by the principle of "parity" in taxation and social services. In many other matters, particularly those which concerned the regulation of trade and industry, there were practical advantages to be gained from uniformity of law and procedure throughout the United Kingdom.[6]

Nevertheless, there was a certain degree of local initiative, particularly in the 1960s. A survey for the Royal Commission on the Constitution characterised only one-fifth of the Acts passed by Stormont during the years 1965–1969 as "parity" legislation; two-fifths were "peculiar" to Northern Ireland and the remainder represented legislation which fell somewhere between those two categories.[7] The Commission's verdict was that "Home rule" had worked to the advantage of Northern Ireland:

> "Particularly in the large areas of government which were unaffected, or at least were not dominated, by the community problem, conspicuous progress was made . . . It must be questioned whether so much would have been accomplished . . . without a separate administration".[8]

The Commission declared in favour of continued legislative devolution; although all Northern Ireland legislation could in theory be enacted by the United Kingdom Parliament, the volume of such legislation would be such

[5] Excepted and reserved matters were enumerated, and some restrictions were also placed on the exercise of the transferred powers. The Act also assumed that the partition of Ireland was temporary and made provision for certain institutions (including a High Court of Appeal for Ireland under the House of Lords) to be developed on an all-Ireland basis, albeit *within* the United Kingdom; these latter provisions ceased to have effect on the establishment of the Irish Free State. See further B Hadfield, *The Constitution of Northern Ireland* (Belfast, SLS Publications, 1989), ch. 2.

[6] See e.g. F H Newark, "The Constitution of Northern Ireland: The First Twenty-Five Years" (1948) 8 NILQ 52 at 60: "'Step by step' is more often than not a virtue born of necessity".

[7] *Royal Commission on the Constitution: Minutes of Evidence III—Northern Ireland* (London, HMSO, 1971), Appendix II. This survey was merely quantitative; it made no attempt to assess the qualititative significance of the legislation in question. Most of the "peculiar" statutes dealt with agricultural, commercial or educational policy. But there were some notable legal "peculiarities" relating for example to the presumption of intention for murder, criminal injuries compensation, committal proceedings, the creation of a local government ombudsman and the establishment of a unified State office for the enforcement of judgments. The survey did not include those matters, particularly abortion and homosexuality, in relation to which the *absence* of equivalent Northern Ireland legislation also brought about a lack of parity.

[8] *Report of the Royal Commission on the Constitution* (Cmnd 5460, 1973), para. 1264.

that, even if variations of policy were kept to a minimum, Northern Ireland affairs would be bound to receive considerably less attention at Westminster than they had—and would—in a separate devolved legislature.

That, of course, is precisely what happened after "direct rule" was introduced in the early 1970s. Since 1972 all significant legal developments in Northern Ireland have come from London, not Belfast. Political necessity dictated that policy-making was determined primarily by successive British Governments, aided and abetted by a "democratic deficit" arising from a refusal to integrate Northern Ireland into Westminster's legislative procedures on "constitutional", political and pragmatic grounds.[9] However, the *administrative* structures of devolution (a separate Northern Ireland civil service and distinctive Northern Ireland departments) remained in place. The key consequences of "direct rule" in the present context were the lack of accountability to the Northern Ireland electorate of the ministers responsible for Northern Ireland affairs, and the bureaucratic-driven agenda for much of the other law reform *not* directly inspired by government policy. By degrees, too, the Irish Government came to be involved, at first informally and then formally, in the making of decisions which led to changes in the law of Northern Ireland. The United Kingdom's accession to the European Economic Community as from 1 January 1973[10] and the impact (or at least potential impact) of the European Convention on Human Rights 1950[11] also meant that other aspects of law-making began to pass out of local control.

We do not wish to overstate the case; many lawyers and others in Northern Ireland continued to play a significant part in law-making even under direct rule. In particular, the Order in Council procedure often allowed for widespread consultation on the proposal prior to the introduction into Parliament of a draft Order. But the effect of much of this consultation was resolved in private,[12] and it is difficult to assess its impact on the final version of legislation. Nor can we know what would have happened to Northern Ireland law if direct rule had not continued for more than twenty-five years. We cannot therefore

[9] Integration "would represent a complete reversal of the traditions of half a century [and] would impose a substantial new legislative burden on the Westminster Parliament": *The Future of Northern Ireland: A Paper for Discussion* (Belfast, HMSO, 1972), p. 21, para. 44(a).

[10] The same date as the Republic of Ireland.

[11] With particular reference to "moral" issues such as homosexuality in respect of which Northern Ireland had *not* followed developments in England and Wales, see especially *Dudgeon* v. *United Kingdom* (1981) 4 EHRR 149. This "unifying" impact of the Convention was also felt in the Republic—see especially *Norris* v. *Ireland* (1988) 13 EHRR 186.

[12] Cf. under the Northern Ireland Act 1982, the Northern Ireland Assembly until 1986 had a pre-parliamentary scrutiny role with regard to proposed Orders in Council. For an evaluation, see Hadfield, *supra* n. 5, at ch. VI. For the very limited role of the Northern Ireland Standing (and now Grand) Committee, see *ibid.*, Appendix D and HC Research Paper 94/39, Appendix 1; the Committee's new power, under HC Standing Orders 109 *et seq* have had at best a very minimal impact. Since 1994, there has also been a Select Committee for Northern Ireland Affairs.

say definitively to what extent, if at all, direct rule has reduced the extent of distinctive Northern Ireland legislation.

A broad and tentative conclusion is, however, suggested by a consideration of the mechanics of direct rule.[13] During both its phases, legislation for Northern Ireland which fell outside the (previously) devolved legislative competence had to take the form of an Act; but legislation in respect of those areas which were, actually or potentially, within the (previously) devolved legislative competence *could* (the provision was facilitative, not mandatory) be made by Order in Council. Under the Northern Ireland Act 1974, such Orders were made subject to the affirmative resolution procedure. But, for a number of years, where the Government intended to introduce a "parity" Order in Council for Northern Ireland (that is, legislation identical to the provisions of all or part of a bill applicable to England and Wales, or Great Britain), they tended in practice to include in the relevant bill a clause overriding the 1974 Act procedure by providing that the "parity" Order was to be subject only to the negative resolution procedure.

Between March 1972 and June 1998, thirty-five UK Acts applied wholly or mainly to Northern Ireland. A number of these Acts contained "parity" provisions, as, of course, did many of the other Acts (particularly in the 1990s) which applied more widely. During the same period, 568 Orders in Council were made for Northern Ireland. Unfortunately, authoritative information even as to the number of "negative resolution" Orders is not available; but it would appear that, on average, no more than four or five of the twenty-two or so Northern Ireland Orders in Council made each year between 1974 and 1998 were "parity" Orders.[14] Some affirmative resolution Orders were also parity Orders, even though not laid in accordance with the parity practice. Taking into account that many of these Orders (such as Consolidation and Appropriation Orders) were of a formal nature, it may be that another four or five Orders per year were also parity Orders. These estimates tentatively suggest that, when compared with home rule in the late 1960s, direct rule did *not* lead to a significant reduction in the amount of legislation "peculiar" to Northern Ireland. But a systematic *qualitative* analysis, heavily dependent upon the co-operation of those public bodies with the requisite information, remains to be done.

It is in any event arguable that, insofar as the distinctiveness of *any* legal system is (or should be) the product of particular problems and conditions, the

[13] For 1972–73, see Northern Ireland (Temporary Provisions) Act 1972; for 1974–98, see Northern Ireland Act 1974. The position at the time of writing is governed by the Northern Ireland Act 2000.

[14] Based on the estimate that there were 112 "negative resolution" Orders between 1974 and 1998. The only occasions on which the annual tally exceeded single figures were 1988 (13) and 1991 (10).

identity of the legislator is in theory largely irrelevant. We cannot, however, subscribe to such a pure theory of law which, in any event, is repugnant to the current belief in devolved government. Be that as it may, the most significant consequence of "the Troubles" and of direct rule in our view was the development of a broad dichotomy between high profile "public" law reform designed to address peculiar Northern Ireland constitutional and civil liberties issues and low profile "general" law reform designed to deal with matters in respect of which Northern Ireland had—or may have had—more in common with other parts of the United Kingdom. With regard to the former, the British Government was both required and prepared to devote considerable time, resources and skills to "solving" Northern Ireland's problems, in some cases by enacting legislation (for example, with reference to criminal justice or fair employment) which had no counterpart elsewhere in the United Kingdom. But other law reform for Northern Ireland was less pressing and its lower priority was often reflected in the fact that government, when it did act (for example in relation to family law and labour law), in general took the preferred road of following English precedent. Notwithstanding our tentative analysis of the *quantitative* impact of direct rule on Northern Ireland legislation, it is our contention that, with the exception of those aspects of "public" law identified earlier, the *qualitative* effect of direct rule has been to reinvigorate the policy of *una et eadem lex*.

The Government of Ireland Act 1920 also created a separate court system for Northern Ireland, but one in which virtually all decisions of the highest local court, the Court of Appeal, might be appealed to the House of Lords. Although it has been usual in recent years for one of the Lords of Appeal in Ordinary to come from Northern Ireland, the convention (in contrast to that applicable to Scottish appeals) was—and remains—that he should not sit in an appeal from Northern Ireland. In strict precedent theory, Northern Ireland courts are bound only by decisions of the House of Lords in Northern Ireland cases; but they have on occasions preferred decisions of the House in English appeals to conflicting decisions of the Northern Ireland Court of Appeal. When not constrained by the House of Lords, the Northern Ireland courts have also tended to rely on English rather than Irish decisions.[15] In any event, there have been few cases which called for judicial "activism"; appellate litigation in Northern Ireland has been generally confined to fairly routine matters argued by non-

[15] Out of almost 300 cases referred to in the headnotes of Northern Ireland cases reported during the period 1921–75, only nine were post-1920 Irish cases, and five of these were "disapproved", "doubted" or "not followed"; 180 English or Scottish cases were cited: Boyle and Greer, *supra* n. 3, at 46. The position in the South is much the same—only two of some 500 cases cited in cases reported in the Republic in 1995 came from Northern Ireland: R Byrne and J P McCutcheon, *The Irish Legal System* (3rd edn., Dublin, Butterworth, 1996), pp. 351–2. For a more detailed comparative study, see K Goodall, *Judicial Justification in the two Irish Legal Systems* (Ph.D. thesis, Queen's University Belfast, 1999).

specialist barristers and determined by judges who are required to decide cases covering a wide spectrum of the law.[16] With some notable exceptions, there has also been a certain lack of judicial self-confidence—or rather we should say a noticeable degree of judicial caution; in a divided society, it is perhaps wiser for judges to seek to maintain a studied neutrality than to be seen to be actively engaged in making new law.[17] Another result of the Troubles, which have resulted in the murder of a number of judges, is that the relaxation of the Kilmuir Rules has not led to any of the Northern Ireland judges developing the kind of high public profile associated with some leading members of the English Bench in recent years. This view of the judicial role may be contrasted with that of the Irish judges in the years after 1965, when an activist Supreme Court, often in the absence of legislative action, breathed new life into the "personal rights" provisions of the Irish Constitution.[18]

Formal and informal restraints on law-making in Northern Ireland

The brief historical sketch which we have given provides a number of pointers for the future of Northern Ireland law:

(1) For a variety of reasons which are likely to continue to have force for the foreseeable future, parity between Northern Ireland and English law will continue to account for a significant amount of "Northern Ireland" law.

(2) The areas of Northern Ireland law likely to be most distinctive from English law will continue to be those areas of law dominated by constitutional or public law considerations.

[16] Certain types of work, such as divorce cases and judicial review applications, do tend to be mainly dealt with by one particular judge. Even in such cases, however, the much larger volume of litigation in England means that cases of first impression rarely arise in Northern Ireland; but this does not necessarily mean that the principles are always applied identically in the two jurisdictions. And in a few cases, such as judicial review of the disciplinary decisions of prison governors and the drawing of inferences from the silence of a person accused of crime, the Northern Ireland judges for a time led the way.

[17] Thus, Lord Lowry is said to have displayed a "discreet talent for judicial ingenuity": Goodall, *supra* n. 15, p. 56. Cf. his Lordship's five guidelines for judicial development of the law set out in *C (A Minor)* v. *DPP* [1996] 1 AC 1 at 39.

[18] For a general survey of these cases, see e.g. J P Casey, *Constitutional Law in Ireland* (2nd edn., London, Sweet & Maxwell, 1992), chs 12–19. Cf. Osborough, "Constitutional Law—a Waning of Judicial Activism?" (1979–80) 2 *Dublin Univ Law J* 101. It has also been suggested that such "activism" is much less evident outside the constitutional sphere, and indeed Irish judges have been accused of "forensic forelock touching" in their treatment of English case law: see McCarthy J's introduction to Byrne and McCutcheon, *supra* n. 15, at i.

(3) The broader legal climate favours the continued development of a distinctive Northern Ireland law in certain "non-constitutional" areas.
(4) The extent to which such latter developments will take place is dependent upon the operation of certain formal and informal constraints on the making of law for Northern Ireland.

Formal Constraints

The dimensions of European law

To what extent is there scope for "EU" law in Northern Ireland to differ from English "EU" law? Presumably at least as far as Directives are concerned, a Northern Ireland legislative assembly (or even Westminster) might take some initiatives either of its own making or to fall into line with Irish policies (whether or not involving cross-border activities). This possibility may be assisted by the developing trend at EU level to move away from insistence on rigid uniformity and towards greater subsidiarity or at least "best-level" decision-making within (more) broadly defined parameters.

That devolution enhances the potential for divergence is perhaps best illustrated by the Concordat on the Co-ordination of European Union Policy Issues[19] and the procedures and principles there provided for the resolution of internal differences, ministerial involvement in EU decision-making and the implementation of European Union obligations. Northern Ireland was not covered by this Concordat, since devolved government was not in place when it was agreed upon. If and when there is a resumption of devolution, a similar Concordat will have to be agreed and issued; presumably, it will then also have to address the cross-border dimensions of Northern Ireland within the EU, given the continuing involvement with Northern Ireland in matters of EU concern of another sovereign State, namely Ireland, at ministerial, official and cross-border implementation body level.

Northern Ireland is also part of another European legal order through the European Convention on Human Rights and Fundamental Freedoms 1950, as implemented in Northern Ireland (as in the rest of the United Kingdom) by the Human Rights Act 1998. Judges throughout the United Kingdom (and the Republic) will be required to take the Convention jurisprudence into account in their application of the Convention; but since they will not be formally bound by such decisions, there will be some room for separate development in Northern Ireland. In addition, Northern Ireland may be expected to throw up some problems which have not been the subject of decision by the European Court of Human Rights. To what extent, then, can we expect the judges to

[19] Cm 4444 (October 1999).

develop in Northern Ireland human rights standards which differ from those in England? Four factors may be relevant here:

(1) There is to be an additional Bill of Rights for Northern Ireland supported by a Human Rights Commission (established in 1999, and with no exact parallel in England) with the powers conferred upon it by the Northern Ireland Act 1998—and in large measure operative whether or not there is devolution.
(2) The Belfast Agreement and the 1998 Act also envisage the establishment of a Joint (all-Ireland) Committee on Human Rights (once an Irish Human Rights Commission has been established).
(3) "Legimated" by the Human Rights Act, the Northern Ireland judges may be influenced by "activist" decisions of, for example, the Irish Supreme Court applying the "human rights" provisions of the Irish Constitution, not infrequently by reference to decisions of the United States Supreme Court.[20] Such decisions may encourage an approach which differs from that adopted by English judges,[21] although it is also likely that a comparative human rights jurisprudence, already evident in "common law" developments, will be given a more secure footing throughout the United Kingdom once the Human Rights Act becomes fully operative.
(4) Northern Ireland judges may consider that the European Court sets a particular standard or standards at too low a level.[22]

One thing at least is clear; the shock to the judicial system provided by the Human Rights Act will be felt as much in Northern Ireland as elsewhere in the Untied Kingdom, and the more "active" role to be played by the judges under that Act in a divided society, and in the only part of the United Kingdom (as yet) to have a Human Rights Commission, may well produce "unique" results, particularly if it transpires that there is not to be a regular and continuing devolved legislative authority.

[20] Cf. Goodall, *supra* n. 15, at 49: "Cultural and legal links with Europe and the United States have promoted social diversity and presented alternative sources of legitimacy to lend support to legal change".

[21] See e.g. *People (Att Gen)* v. *O'Brien* [1965] IR 142 (evidence obtained in breach of constitutional rights excluded unless "extraordinary excusing circumstances"); *Blake and others* v. *Attorney General* [1982] IR 117 (rent restriction legislation unconstitutional) and *In re Article 26 of the Constitution and the Matrimonial Home Bill 1993* [1994] 1 IR 305 (bill introducing automatic joint ownership of matrimonial home unconstitutional).

[22] See e.g. *R* v. *O'Halloran* [1979] NI 45 at 47, where Lowry LCJ in effect rejected the view expressed by the European Court that a distinction may be drawn between acts prohibited by Art. 3 of the European Convention and "a certain roughness of treatment".

United Kingdom law

Under the Northern Ireland Act 1998, Northern Ireland law remains divided into three categories—excepted, reserved and transferred. "Excepted" matters, which remain the sole responsibility of the United Kingdom Parliament, pertain to such "national" concerns as defence and national security, international relations and general taxation, and in these regards are much the same as Scottish "reserved" matters. But the inclusion of certain other matters, such as the appointment of judges, means that the "excepted" category (like the Scottish "reserved" list) also has some distinctive "peculiarities".

Many aspects of law (particularly the organisation of the police, police powers, the criminal law and the administration of criminal justice generally) are "reserved" to Westminster, but may be "transferred" to the Northern Ireland Assembly if (i) the Assembly has so resolved with cross-community support, and (ii) Parliament on the recommendation of the Secretary of State for Northern Ireland agrees. Pending such a transfer, legislation in respect of a reserved matter may be (i) by Act of Parliament, (ii) by Order in Council (subject to a consultation procedure), or (iii) by the Northern Ireland Assembly—but only with the consent of the Secretary of State for Northern Ireland and subject to scrutiny by Parliament. "Reserved" matters under the Northern Ireland Act 1998 are, therefore, very different in rationale from the matters which are "reserved" under the Scotland Act 1998; the latter are rather the equivalent, in principle though not in detail, of Northern Ireland "excepted" matters.

Everything which is not specified as "excepted" or "reserved" is "transferred" to the Northern Ireland Assembly; there is no explicit enumeration of transferred matters. In relation to any matter falling substantially within transferred powers, the Assembly may pass "Acts" which may modify any Act of the United Kingdom Parliament insofar as it is part of Northern Ireland law. But the Northern Ireland Act 1998 imposes some restraints on this transferred legislative competence; the Assembly may not lawfully legislate, for example, in a way which is incompatible with EU law or the European Convention on Human Rights or which discriminates on the ground of religious belief or political opinion.

The 1998 Act also envisages a strong cross-border dimension in the future development of Northern Ireland, by providing for "consultation, co-operation and action" on matters of mutual interest within the competence of the Administrations, north and south. All-Ireland cross-border implementation bodies will be set up in relation to such matters as inland waterways, food safety, trade and business development, language and some special EU programmes. Particular areas already identified for co-operation between the two jurisdictions include aspects of transport, agriculture, education, health, the environment and tourism. Although these areas may not have a strong legislative component, they do at least indicate the particular matters in which a clear, and possibly distinctive, all-Ireland dimension may be expected to develop in the near future.

Informal Constraints

Law-making in Northern Ireland is also subject to a number of informal constraints, most of which tend to lead in practice to conformity with England—or, where there is a cross-border legislative dimension, to development in an all-Ireland way.[23]

Practical politics

Legislation by its very nature is subject, in greater or lesser degree, to political constraints of one kind or another, and in general Northern Ireland legislation, whether enacted in Belfast or London, does not differ in this respect. It is clearly inappropriate in the present context to attempt to explore such matters in any detail. But the experience of the past twenty-five years, and the possibility of continued direct rule, prompt us to make two observations. Part (albeit, perhaps, a small part) of the case for legislative devolution in the United Kingdom is the overall pressure on parliamentary time at Westminster and the consequential lack of adequate time to devote to particular Northern Ireland (or Scottish or Welsh) affairs. In general, proposed legislation in respect of Northern Ireland was obviously less likely to give rise to controversy, in and out of Parliament, if it replicated, or was generally on the same lines as, legislation which had already received parliamentary assent. There must therefore have been some temptation, to put it at its lowest, to follow precedent in order to find a more "amenable" parliamentary reaction to proposed Northern Ireland legislation. The fact that such legislation assimilated Northern Irish and English law also provided a ready shield—and in some cases even a trusty sword—against opposition from particular interest groups within Northern Ireland. It is obvious that such pragmatic considerations have limited significance in respect of much legislation, and we have no means of evaluating their overall importance. But it seems reasonable to suggest that, in some cases at least, they may have some influence on legislative developments.

[23] Under the Belfast Agreement and legislation in both jurisdictions establishing the implementation bodies, this cross-border dimension is mutual and may require changes in the law of the Republic to bring about, or maintain, an all-Ireland dimension.

Financial considerations

Under the 1998 Act, the Northern Ireland Assembly, when operative, has no tax-raising powers, but it does have power to appropriate money from the Northern Ireland share of the Consolidated Fund to the public service of Northern Ireland. Law reform in Northern Ireland is, therefore, subject to the budget provided by the United Kingdom Parliament. If that budget is not increased to allow for the cost of any particular reform, the money therefor will have to be found from the existing budget, to the detriment of some existing public service or function. Current pressures to reduce the level of public spending in Northern Ireland, as in the remainder of the United Kingdom, may already be making their impact in this respect.[24] It seems likely that these considerations will continue to have some effect on the implementation or otherwise of any major legal reform likely to have significant public expenditure implications.

Commercial pressures

In commercial terms, Northern Ireland is less a separate jurisdiction than an integral part of a wider market increasingly governed by EU law. Since business and commerce are, or may be, hampered by "peculiar" laws, there is normally considerable local pressure from such quarters against any change (within EU constraints) which would put Northern Ireland significantly out of line with England or the Republic, at least if such divergence would or might increase manufacturing or service costs or otherwise complicate the conduct of business. But as we have already seen, it was precisely the economic and other factors which inhibited commercial development in Northern Ireland which in the past led to separate legislation, and calls for "special treatment" to offset disadvantageous business conditions continue to be made at regular intervals.

Professional practices

Much has been written about the "professional" weakness of a small jurisdiction such as Northern Ireland which adjoins a larger and more complex legal system with much more highly developed legal resources.[25] In this context, for example, it has often been pointed out that there are in the largest City firms

[24] For example, the future of the "common law" scheme of compensation for criminal injuries in Northern Ireland is under close government scrutiny; for the background see *Report of the Review of Criminal Injuries Compensation in Northern Ireland* (Belfast, Northern Ireland Office, 1999).

[25] See especially W L Twining and J Uglow (eds), *Law Publishing and Legal Information* (London, Sweet & Maxwell, 1981).

more solicitors—and more specialised legal expertise—than in the whole of Northern Ireland. Likewise the Northern Ireland Bar tends to be generalist, a feature encouraged by a shortage of specialised litigation and a Bar Library system which prevents the formation of specialist Chambers.

Northern Ireland does have a Law Reform Advisory Committee, charged with keeping the *civil* law of Northern Ireland under review and with making recommendations for its reform; it is an independent part-time body which has no research assistants (although it may and does appoint research consultants). Not surprisingly, the Committee has restricted itself to proposals for reform of some particular, and mainly technical, aspects of "lawyer's law".[26] The Committee functions in co-operation with a small Office of Law Reform, which also has responsibility for keeping the civil law under review "so as to ensure its systematic development and reform".[27] This Office has been active in the reform of family and property law; but it, too, has limited research resources. *Ad hoc* reform groups are also set up from time to time.

Some policy-oriented legal research is undertaken by the Northern Ireland Office and by other government departments. But, at least outside the arena of "constitutional" law reform, much of this is *ad hoc*, piece-meal or "in-house", aimed at improving the day-to-day efficiency of the legal system rather than more fundamental reform. The Belfast Agreement has meant that a number of radical proposals have been made by specially appointed committees, for example in respect of police organisation and the criminal justice system. But in areas which fall outside the Agreement, the general opinion would appear to be "our law and legal system on the whole works pretty well, and is not in need of any major changes". There is indeed some evidence which tends to support this view; but our contention is that that evidence is not sufficiently cogent to inspire confidence in such a verdict. Quite simply, there is a noticeable lack of reliable empirical evidence as to the actual working of many important aspects of the law of Northern Ireland, and the whole approach to general law reform is lacking in co-ordination and leadership.

The Foreseeable Future

Within the constraints summarised above, we may now speculate on what may happen in the foreseeable future. We can do so only in the most general of terms, given that ours is a territorial, rather than a subject-specific, contribution to this survey.

[26] See LRAC, *Ninth Annual Report 1997–1998* (HMSO, 1999). The Committee's legislative achievements to date are limited to the Business Tenancies (NI) Order 1996 and the Civil Evidence (NI) Order 1997.

[27] *The Office of Law Reform 1965–1995* (Belfast, 1995), p. 2.

There is already in existence (or in an advanced state of gestation) an extensive legislative programme for Northern Ireland which includes (*inter alia*) major reforms relating to criminal justice, the police, land law, legal services and the civil justice system, family law and environmental law. We propose to make only one comment on the proposed reforms of the police and the criminal justice system. There is the danger that this will be law reform at its most "public"; indeed, present trends portend a worrying possibility for law's future—that law reform will become a more direct instrument of "politics", rather than the embodiment of some more objective (or at least less transitory) justice. Professor A. W. B. Simpson made a similar point, albeit in a different context, as long ago as 1988:

> "What is . . . possible is that government through law will come to be more acutely in opposition to the ideal of the rule of law than is the case at present, and if this happens law, in the sense required by the ideal of the rule of law, will die".[28]

Be that as it may, reforms of the police and of the criminal justice system involve issues too complex for consideration here, and will in any case—and rightly—generate considerable attention. It is for these reasons that we prefer to concentrate on three less visible areas of law reform in Northern Ireland, representing respectively a devolved, a non-devolved and an EU matter, which in our view raise more general issues as to *when* and *why* there is a case for legal divergence.[29]

Land Law

One part of law's future in Northern Ireland has been mapped out by the Land Law Survey of 1971 and the Land Law Working Group report of 1990.[30] These Reports envisage a "root and branch" reform of the land law, consistently treated as a devolved matter and often thought to represent Northern Ireland law at its most distinctive.[31] The ultimate objective is to simplify a law largely

[28] *Invitation to Law* (Oxford, Basil Blackwell, 1988), p. 210.

[29] For a study of another devolved matter, see L Lundy, "Education and devolution: Northern Ireland" (2000) 1/2 *Education Law J* 81.

[30] Land Law Working Party, *Survey of the Land Law of Northern Ireland* (Belfast, HMSO, 1971); Office of Law Reform, *The Final Report of the Land Law Working Group* (Belfast, HMSO, 1990).

[31] See especially Wylie, "The Irishness of Irish Land Law" (1995) 46 *NILQ* 332 at 336: "Over the centuries a number of concepts emerged which, if not unique, have a particularly Irish distinctiveness. Most of these were devised by landowners and their legal advisers and given recognition by the courts. In some cases, legislators made a contribution. There were also a few instances when the Irish courts on particular points of law took a different view of the principles to be applied".

exempt from the "Birkenhead" reforms,[32] and thereby to facilitate the compulsory registration of urban land (most agricultural land having already been registered under an Act of 1891). Effective registration requires the prior removal, so far as possible, of complexities like the pyramid titles associated with such Irish peculiarities as fee farm grants and ground rents. The reformers saw their proposals as an integrated package to be enacted *en bloc*. That, however, has not occurred; instead, piecemeal legislation such as the Property (NI) Order 1997 has merely prepared the ground for the more comprehensive reforms which, presumably, will soon follow.

The proposed reforms suggest some general observations. First, they are not founded on any particular philosophy of land law either in general or for Northern Ireland in particular; the implicit assumption appears to be simply that they will clarify and simplify the law. There is no overt acknowledgement of the need to assimilate Northern Ireland law with that in England or, indeed, in the Republic. A broad assessment of the proposals is that, while they will bring Northern Ireland into line with England in some respects (and with the Republic in other respects), they will *not* do so in either case to a considerable extent. Presumably this is the result of a conscious decision to adopt what is best for the particular conditions in Northern Ireland, whatever they may be. This pragmatic approach may reflect the fact that the proposals are those of an *ad hoc* working party which was neither required to articulate, nor asked to proceed in accordance with, some more general theory of law reform.

Civil Justice

A rare statutory declaration of the principle of *una et eadem lex* appeared in the Irish Judicature Act 1877, which provided that "In making . . . Rules of Court . . . regard shall be had to the Rules of Court for the time being in force [in England] . . . so as that the pleading, practice and procedure [in Ireland] shall, so far as may be practicable and convenient, having regard to the difference of the laws and circumstances of the two countries, be the same".[33] In spite of this declaration, the Irish civil justice system developed some distinctive characteristics which were retained after 1920 in Northern Ireland. In particular, the County Courts in Northern Ireland continued a civil bill tradition dating back

[32] Professor Wylie has, however, explained that the impact of the failure to follow the English lead in 1925 should not be exaggerated, since (i) much of the Birkenhead legislation merely consolidated earlier reforms which *were* followed in Ireland, and (ii) legislation similar to or the equivalent of some of the other 1925 legislation has since been enacted in both Irish jurisdictions: see *supra* n. 31, at 333–4.

[33] Supreme Court of Judicature (Ir) Act 1877, s. 61. This provision was repealed by the Northern Ireland Act 1962 and has not been re-enacted.

to the seventeenth century (at least),[34] and when small claims courts were set up at the end of the 1970s, these too exemplified a much simpler process than their English counterparts. Civil trial by jury of personal injury actions also survived in Northern Ireland (and in the Republic) long after it had been abolished in England.[35] It was in this context that a Civil Justice Reform Group was appointed by the Lord Chancellor in 1998 "to review procedures in Northern Ireland for the administration of civil justice" with particular reference to Lord Woolf's reforms as implemented in England and Wales.

The Reform Group's final report had not been published at the time of writing; but it may reasonably be assumed that its interim report provides a guide to the final recommendations which is sufficient for our purposes. In broad terms, the Group adopted much of the Woolf "philosophy", but considered that it would not be "practicable and convenient" to follow his reforms in every respect, given the different style and pattern of civil litigation in Northern Ireland, and the fact that "innovations" such as a "fast-track" procedure were already operative.[36]

In the present context, two more general facets of the Reform Group's work attract comment. First, their analysis of the actual working of the County Court and High Court is not supported to any significant extent by independent empirical research.[37] To this extent, the case for a distinctive approach is strictly unproven—though that is not to say that it is not justified. But the point to us seems to be a general one; without adequate "proof" derived from appropriate research, who is to say whether Northern Ireland should—or should not—follow English precedent?[38]

[34] See Greer, "The Development of Civil Bill Procedure in Ireland" in J F McEldowney and P O'Higgins (eds), *The Common Law Tradition: Essays in Irish Legal History* (Dublin, Irish Academic Press, 1990), p. 27.

[35] As a result, the level of damages for pain and suffering and loss of amenities was much higher in Northern Ireland than in England, a fact recently acknowledged by the Law Commission (*Damages for Personal Injury: Non-Pecuniary Loss* (Law Com No. 257, 1999), paras 3.99–3.105). Soon after trial by judge alone was substituted in 1987, it was contended that the level of damages should be brought more into line with those in England; but Lord Lowry, the Lord Chief Justice, disagreed: "I would reject the suggestion that our calculations of general damages are 'wrong' if they do not conform to standards observed in other jurisdictions since Northern Ireland, like Scotland and the Republic of Ireland, constitutes a separate legal jurisdiction with its own judicial and social outlook": *Simpson* v. *Harland & Wolff plc* [1988] NI 432 at 440–1. The decision of the Court of Appeal in *Heil* v. *Rankin* [2000] 2 WLR 1173 *not* to implement the recommendations of the Law Commission in full has prevented a rare example of England following Northern Ireland's lead.

[36] See *Review of the Civil Justice System in Northern Ireland: Interim Report* (Belfast, NI Court Service, 1999). For a commentary, see Capper, "Keeping Woolf from the Door: The Reform of Civil Procedure in Northern Ireland" (1999) 50 *NILQ* 434. The Reform Group's *Final Report* was published in June 2000: nothing in the report affects our general analysis.

[37] The Irish Law Reform Commission have frequently made much the same point about the Republic, see e.g. *Report on Family Courts* (Dublin, LRC 52–1996), p. 122: "The lack of any independent Irish empirical research on most aspects of the operation of our legal system is a serious flaw in the policy-making process".

[38] Cf. recent proposals to amend the law of divorce in Northern Ireland follow a major multi-disciplinary research report which (*inter alia*) challenges the widely-accepted belief that

A second observation relates to the nature of law reform. It seems clear that the Woolf reforms in England were led "from the top" by a strong-minded judge who diagnosed the illness and recommended the cure. If implemented in Northern Ireland, the diluted version of these reforms will represent more of an evolutionary approach largely devised by a group drawn from the local legal profession and the judiciary. This would involve something of an anomaly, given that the civil justice system is a "reserved" matter under the Northern Ireland Act 1998. But the origin of the recommended reforms may be expected to lead them to be more readily absorbed into professional and judicial practice. But will they really work? Should the Lord Chancellor accept what he may consider to be limited recommendations which, without essential elements of the Woolf reforms, may be more susceptible to being subverted—like so many earlier proposals in England—by a profession uninhibited by strong judicial leadership? This scenario raises the possibility that local diversity may in some circumstances operate not for the benefit of society at large, but for the convenience of interested parties. On the other hand, and even if it is a matter reserved for Westminster, on what basis can the Lord Chancellor justifiably reject informed local opinion as to the best way forward?

A better theoretical model for local law reform may be provided by the treatment of the government proposal to reform legal aid in Northern Ireland by bringing it into line with recent developments in England.[39] Once again we have a radical English precedent which, in the absence of research, may be unsuitable for Northern Ireland. The Lord Chancellor has acknowledged that appropriate research must be undertaken "into how the longer term suggestions for reform . . . can be brought forward to the advantage of the public in Northern Ireland",[40] and the need for prior research has been strongly emphasised by the Legal Aid Advisory Committee.[41]

Environmental Law

Our third example of law reform in the pipeline is designed to provide an example of the legal deficit attributable in part at least to the preoccupation

Northern Ireland is extremely conservative with deep-rooted family structures bound together by strong religious beliefs: see *Divorce in Northern Ireland: Unravelling the System* (Belfast, Stationery Office, 1999) and Office of Law Reform, *Divorce in Northern Ireland: A Better Way Forward* (Belfast, Stationery Office, 1999).

[39] *Public Benefit and the Public Purse: Legal Aid Reform in Northern Ireland* (Belfast, NI Court Service, 1999).

[40] *Ibid.*, para. 15.6.

[41] See the Committee's *Response to the Government's Consultation Paper* (Belfast, 1999). A similar function could be performed *post facto* in relation to the civil justice system if the Civil Justice Council proposed by the Civil Justice Reform Group is given adequate powers and funding.

with Northern Ireland's constitutional and political problems. The verdict of the leading authorities on this area of our law is stark:

> "Despite the tidal wave of environmental law and policy which has swept across the European Community during [the past thirty years], Northern Ireland represents a pocket of inertia, stolidly resisting action based on a contemporary understanding of the environment . . . Since direct rule was reintroduced, every area of substantive environmental regulation in Northern Ireland has fallen significantly behind the standards applying in the rest of the United Kingdom, Europe and the international community. In the context of nationally generated regulatory approaches, the most prominent example of this problem is found in respect of Integrated Pollution Control, introduced in Great Britain in 1990, but still awaiting extension to Northern Ireland. Even more acute delays arise in relation to the implementation of EC environmental Directives".[42]

The reasons suggested for these delays are the impact of direct rule,[43] a shortage of "professional" resources and the fact that Northern Ireland does not have an independent environmental protection agency. The overall position has improved in recent years;[44] but there is some evidence that, in the haste to clear the backlog of unimplemented environmental Directives, serious errors are being made in transposing the substance of the law.[45] What is more:

> "Given the difficulties encountered in embracing the first stage of Community environmental law, it is highly unlikely that the Province is prepared for the rigours of the new proactive EC environmental strategy. The Commission's declared intention to focus its monitoring activities on ensuring effective implementation can only throw the profound inadequacy of the regulatory chain in Northern Ireland into even more sharp relief".[46]

Environmental law also brings us back to the Irish dimension of law reform in Northern Ireland. Cross-border co-operation has, since 1990, been facili-

[42] K Morrow and S Turner, "The More Things Change, the More They Stay the Same? Environmental Law, Policy and Funding in Northern Ireland" (1998) 10 *J Environmental Law* 41. See also "The Impact of EC Law on the Environmental Law of Northern Ireland" in J Holder (ed.), *The Impact of EC Environmental Law in the United Kingdom* (Chichester, Wiley, 1997) and more generally, *Northern Ireland Environmental Law* (Dublin, Gill and Macmillan, 1997) by the same authors.

[43] The authors note that it is settled EU law that late implementation of Directives cannot be excused simply because it is the outcome of national constitutional arrangements: see e.g. Case 283/86 *Commission* v. *Belgium* [1988] ECR 3271 and Case C-337/89 *Commission* v. *UK* [1992] 1 ECR 257.

[44] Integrated pollution control has now been introduced in Northern Ireland, but is being implemented slowly and is likely to be overtaken by a further EU Directive. See also Water (NI) Order 1999, discussed by S Turner, "Modernising the Regulation of Water Pollution in Northern Ireland" (2000) 51 *NILQ* 65 and 230.

[45] For example, in its implementation of the Groundwater Directive of 1980, the NI Department of Environment ignored a vital European Court of Justice ruling made three years earlier: Morrow and Turner, "The more things change. . . .", *supra* n. 42, at 52.

[46] *Ibid.*

tated by the European Union through the INTERREG programme. This programme coincided with the growing climate of north-south co-operation initiated by the Anglo-Irish Agreement in 1985 and consolidated by the Framework Document in 1995 and the Belfast Agreement in 1998. It is now common policy throughout the island to exploit the shared opportunities presented by mutual membership of the EU. Despite its imperfections as a tool for cross-border co-operation,[47] the first INTERREG Programme appears to have had some beneficial effect on the Irish environment; it remains to be seen how far INTERREG II will expand upon those positive results.

Securing legal diversity

In the 1830s a Royal Commission appointed by the United Kingdom Government devised a poor law scheme designed to meet the particular problems of the poor in Ireland.[48] The ambitious nature of the scheme, and its likely cost, went far beyond anything which the Government had in mind, and they procured a second report which duly "established" that what was really required in Ireland was a poor law scheme on much the same lines as that which had recently been adopted for England and Wales. Such a scheme was duly implemented in 1838. Although the Republic went its own way after 1920, the Northern Ireland Parliament did not, preferring instead to adopt a deliberate policy of following social security developments in Great Britain on a "step-by-step" basis—an application of the "parity" principle now expressly enshrined in the Northern Ireland Act 1998.

It is not immediately obvious why this should continue to be so.[49] We have sought to show that, notwithstanding various formal and informal pressures to conform to the principle of *una et eadem lex*, there remains a fair amount of legal "room" for distinctive Northern Ireland law. The most obvious areas are

[47] See e.g. D Corrigan, "Cross-Border Programmes" in K Browne and J Kennedy (eds), *Northern Ireland and the European Union: Discussion Papers on the Intergovernmental Conference and other European Issues* (Belfast, QUB Institute of European Studies, 1996).

[48] See further L Lundy, "Parity, Parrotry or Plagiarism? Legislating for the Unemployed Poor in Northern Ireland 1838–1995" in N Dawson, D Greer and P Ingram (eds.), *One Hundred and Fifty Years of Irish Law* (Belfast, SLS Publications, 1996), p. 1.

[49] Cf. the weighty arguments for retaining the parity principle, which are summarised by Lundy, who nonetheless concludes: "[W]hile endorsing the arguments for maintaining parity, it is still open to question whether social security entitlement in Northern Ireland really amounts to parity. This depends ultimately on how parity is defined and in particular, whether parity means equivalent legislation or an equivalent level of provision. It is submitted that Northern Ireland currently has parity on paper but not parity in practice . . . What is required is a recognition that the attainment of a national standard may necessitate regional variation": see *supra* n. 48, at 17–18.

those most closely connected with attempts to resolve the constitutional and political problems engendered by a divided community. We do not seek to underestimate the fundamental importance of such attempts; but we have preferred to focus on what may be regarded as more "bread-and-butter" issues which seem to us likely also to arise in other small jurisdictions, whether or not they form part of a wider system of asymmetrical legislative devolution—and particularly if, like Northern Ireland, they do not have a distinctive legal tradition. If we may be permitted to leave to one side some admittedly fundamental "constitutional" niceties, it is suggested that the example of welfare law may be used to illustrate five "conclusions" about legal diversity which appear likely to shape the future development of the law in Northern Ireland.

1. Legislative devolution does not of itself determine those areas of "local" law which are or should be distinctive. In some cases (such as the law of contract and most aspects of commercial law) the devolved legislature is likely to operate a "parity" principle. On the other hand, it may be appropriate for some "excepted" or "reserved" matters (such as the civil justice system) to be treated distinctively. The relaxation of the strict uniformity principle in EU law also suggests that the formal allocation of legislative authority is not coterminous with the need for legal diversity. Notwithstanding the progress within EU law towards a "best-level" principle of law-making or "controlled diversity", there does not yet appear to be any *a priori* principle on which to found distinctive legal provisions.[50] The problem in Northern Ireland is exacerbated by the fact that its law now has *four* dimensions—Europe, United Kingdom, Ireland and Northern Ireland—and no overarching process or mechanism for law reform. It is not suggested that some kind of blueprint should be attempted; but it should be possible to devise a framework within which future developments may take place more systematically and effectively.

2. There is an obvious need for appropriate policy-oriented research of an interdisciplinary nature to determine the extent to which Northern Ireland differs from other relevant jurisdictions, so that an informed decision may be made as to whether, and if so what, "peculiar" laws are necessary or desirable. The absence of such research not only impedes proper decision-making, but also renders law reform vulnerable to interest groups of various kinds which claim exclusive or superior knowledge as to what is or is not required or desirable.

3. Appropriate legal expertise and resources need to be made more available in order to "drive" law reform and to enable more radical solutions to be properly devised and considered and, if approved, implemented effectively.

4. There should be more open and effective consultation procedures for dis-

[50] It also appears still to be the case, as the Royal Commission on the Constitution pointed out in 1973 (*Report, supra* n. 8, at para. 1097), that "whether people [in different regions of the United Kingdom] in fact want varying standards or uniform standards is by no means clear".

cussing law reform proposals. In the recent words of the Law Reform Advisory Committee:

> "If the work of law reform is to be of value to society, recommendations for reform must be well thought out and properly researched and there must be proper consultation with interested persons and bodies to ensure workable and beneficial reforms".[51]

5. Appropriate arrangements need to be in place so that reform proposals with significant cost implications are not subject to *unnecessary* financial restrictions.

It is our contention that unless these matters are adequately addressed, the future of Northern Ireland law as a distinctive legal system will be unduly constrained.

[51] *Ninth Annual Report 1997–1998* (Belfast, Stationery Office, 1999), p. 4.

6

2001—A Scots Lawyer's Odyssey

LAURA MACGREGOR AND JOE THOMSON

Introduction

The purpose of this chapter is to take an exploratory voyage around some of the major issues which Scots lawyers face in the new millennium. The emphasis is on private law and, in particular, those areas which have not been reserved to the United Kingdom Parliament. With the advent of a Scottish Parliament, there is an exciting opportunity to reform Scots private law. But caution is also necessary. Because the Scottish Executive and Parliament are closer to the Scottish electorate and media, there is a danger of knee-jerk responses to what are perceived to be injustices inherent in the law. Hard cases, as we know, make bad common law but they can also result in bad "reforming" legislation. Indeed, the first enactment of the Scottish Parliament was a bill, which received all party support, to close a "loophole" in the Mental Health (Scotland) Act 1984, under which dangerous patients detained in the State mental hospital at Carstairs were entitled to be discharged if they could no longer benefit from treatment.[1]

However, the Scottish Parliament was not born unfettered. Both the Scottish Parliament and the Executive cannot act in a way which is inconsistent with the European Convention on Human Rights 1950.[2] There is therefore an important check on the Parliament's legislative capacity which, in this respect, is subject to judicial review. The difficulty is that the European Convention protects human rights at a minimalist standard. In some areas, Scots domestic law currently gives Scottish men and women far greater rights than those guaranteed by the Convention. For example, it is a fundamental principle of Scots criminal law that an accused cannot be convicted unless the Crown's evidence

[1] Mental Health (Public Safety and Appeals) (Scotland) Act 1999.

[2] Scotland Act 1998, s. 29(2)(d). It has been held by the Inner House of the Court of Session (Scotland) Act 1999 is not inconsistent with the European Convention: *Anderson and Reid* v. *Scottish Ministers* (16 June, 2000).

has been corroborated by at least two independent sources. The need for corroborated evidence goes beyond the minimal requirements of the right to a fair trial under Article 6 of the Convention. It is not difficult to envisage pressure for legislation to abolish the need for corroboration if, for example, the Crown fails to secure a conviction in a particularly gruesome case owing to the lack of corroborative evidence.

There is another important point. There are areas of Scots private law which have traditionally been the reserve of common law, i.e. judge-made law. The law of obligations—contract, delict and unjustified enrichment—is an example. Indeed, unlike the position in England, vast tracts of Scots criminal law, including murder, culpable homicide, rape, assault, theft and breach of the peace, are the province of the common law. While this law changes incrementally as a consequence of judicial decision, if greater—or quicker—changes are thought necessary, these will almost inevitably be achieved through legislation. The judicial function will then alter from common law inductive reasoning to statutory interpretation. There are, of course, law reform techniques which can be used to minimise this result. For example, because of the rule in *Manners* v. *Whitehead*,[3] when A had entered into a contract with B as a result of B's misrepresentation, A could not sue B for damages unless A could prove that B had acted fraudulently. With the development of liability for negligent misrepresentation, the rule in *Manners* v. *Whitehead* became increasingly anomalous. It was abolished by section 10(1) of the Law Reform (Miscellaneous Provisions) (Scotland) Act 1985, leaving the courts free to develop the law on negligent misrepresentation between parties to a contract on common law delictual principles. Nevertheless, great care should be taken before embarking on legislative reform of the common law. Judicial development has many virtues as well as disadvantages: the creative judge can use principle and precedent to mould the law to modern conditions. The resurgence of the law of unjustified enrichment in Scotland as well as England is evidence of the vitality of the common law. But, as we shall see, there are important areas where judicial developments have been unfortunate and where, in spite of genuine fears, reforming angels may have to tread.

On the other hand, where the law has a statutory basis, there is far greater scope for legislative change. There are statutory regimes of private law in Scotland where it is arguable that the rules no longer reflect the expectations of ordinary Scots. These can be overhauled without too great an intrusion into the judicial function. Here, it is thought, the Scottish Parliament will have an important role in the development of Scots private law in the twenty-first century.

[3] (1898) 1 F 171.

Some Statutory Regimes in need of Reform?

Succession

In spite—or because—of their Calvinistic and Roman Catholic heritage, Scots do not like to contemplate death. Rather than make a will, approximately 75 per cent of Scots women and men prefer to die intestate. Most of them die without knowing who will inherit their estates. The law is to be found in the Succession (Scotland) Act 1964. Under that Act, a surviving spouse appears well protected. She is entitled to the matrimonial home provided its value is less than £130,000; to furniture up to the value of £22,000, and a capital sum of £58,000 (no issue) and £34,000 (survived by issue). In addition, she is entitled to half the deceased's moveable estate (no issue) or one-third (survived by issue). After her rights have been satisfied, the estate will fall to the deceased's children. If there are no children (or grandchildren), the estate will be divided equally between the deceased's parent(s) and brothers and sisters. If the deceased was wealthy, the widow might therefore find herself driven from the former matrimonial home by her mother-in-law or sister-in-law who is the heir on intestacy. If the couple had cohabited rather than married, the surviving cohabitant is entitled to nothing, however long the period of cohabitation. Where the deceased was unmarried, and has no children, the current rules can lead to bizarre results. Consider the following case:

H and W1 had a child, S1. H left W1. H and W2 had child, S2. S1 lent W1 the deposit to purchase her council house. S1 was killed in a car crash. On intestacy, half of S1's estate goes to S2 i.e. his half-brother whom he has never known; one-quarter to H, who had left S1 and his mother, W1; one-quarter goes to W1, who will have to account to S1's estate for the loan she had received from S.

We find this result absurd as well as unjust to W1. If only S1 had made a will.

Yet Scots law hardly encourages wills. A surviving spouse and children enjoy legal rights in respect of the deceased's moveable estate: one-third or one-half (if no issue); one-third or one-half (if no surviving spouse). These rights cannot be defeated. But they are only exigible on moveable property. A testator is free to test on heritage (land/houses etc.) and could therefore defeat his family's claims by investing in land. Moreover, since legal rights only attach to moveable property owned by the testator at the time of his death, the testator could defeat them by transferring the property outright to a third party *before* he dies. Unlike the Family Law (Scotland) Act 1985 (financial provision on divorce) there is no claw-back procedure in respect of succession. Consider the following case:

H is diagnosed of terminal cancer. H transfers £250,000 of shares to M, his mistress. The share certificates are changed in favour of M. H dies. H has no further moveable property. The legal rights of his wife and children are of no value as H has no moveable estate at the time of his death.

Most persons do not go to such extremes to avoid their family's legal rights. But surely the Scots family is over-protected. Perhaps a surviving spouse's fixed share of the deceased's estate can be justified but, then, why not a fixed share for the deceased's long term cohabitee? Why should adult children enjoy a fixed share of a parent's estate, particularly when the testator wishes to benefit friends who have been helpers and companions in her old age? There is much to be said for restricting legal rights to children who were entitled to aliment from the deceased at the date of death: the obligation to aliment a child ends when the child is eighteen, but can continue to the age of twenty-five if the child is engaged in higher education or professional training.

We do not propose to suggest solutions to these problems. Our point is that much of the Scots law of succession is out of step with the lifestyle of modern Scottish families. Worse, the rules are over-complex. Worst of all, they bear little relationship to what ordinary Scots think the law is. There is clearly a case for reform.

Damages for Death

When a person dies as a consequence of personal injuries sustained through the fault of the defender, there are two possible causes of action. First, if the deceased has survived his injuries for a period before he died, his executor can sue for *solatium* (damages for pain and suffering) and loss of earnings etc. up to the date of death. If the deceased was killed outright, the executor has no title to sue. Secondly, where the deceased dies as a consequence of personal injuries his relatives have title to sue under the Damages (Scotland) Act 1976. Their claims are dependent in the sense that any defences (for example, *volenti non fit injuria* and contributory negligence) which the defender would have against an action by the deceased, are good against the relative's claim.

The 1976 Act lists the deceased's relatives. In so doing, any relationship by affinity is treated as a relationship by consanguinity, half-blood as whole blood etc. While the relatives can claim for *patrimonial* loss, i.e. when they have been financially supported by the deceased, a subgroup of relatives, the deceased's immediate family, can *in addition* sue for *non-patrimonial* loss, viz. loss of the deceased's society. The immediate family include the deceased's spouse, heterosexual cohabitant, parents and children, and children accepted by the deceased as a child of the family. But because the deceased's immediate family must be relatives within the meaning of the 1976 Act, it follows, for example, that the deceased's mother-in-law or daughter-in-law fall within that class because affinity is treated in the same way as consanguinity.[4] Conversely, the deceased's brothers and sisters are not part of the deceased's immediate family and can therefore only sue for patrimonial loss. While this result might appear bizarre, it is the inevitable consequence of a literal construction of the statutory language.

Additionally, the list of relatives is beginning to show its age. A divorced spouse of the deceased is treated as a relative but not a member of the deceased's immediate family: she can therefore sue for patrimonial loss. But given the Family Law (Scotland) Act 1985, with its emphasis on economic clean breaks on divorce, few ex-wives should be financially dependent on their ex-husbands. While the 1976 Act recognises the interests of the heterosexual cohabitant of the deceased, it does not allow the deceased's homosexual partner to sue, even when she has been financially dependent on the deceased. Yet a homosexual partner has been recognised as a member of the deceased's family for the purpose of the Rent Acts.[5]

More importantly, perhaps, how can we *compensate* for the grief and pain caused by the death of a loved one? There is something distasteful in quantifying such non-patrimonial loss.[6] The sums involved are small: £15–20,000 for a spouse, £5–20,000 for a child.[7] If such claims were abolished, we could abandon the need for a person to be a relative before there is title to sue. Instead, anyone who was financially dependent on the deceased could sue for patrimonial loss. This would not open the floodgates. Even today a relative's claim for patrimonial loss will fail, if financial dependency cannot be established.

Family Law

Over the last twenty-five years or so, family law in Scotland has been transformed. No small part of that transformation is that Scottish family law is now almost entirely based on statute. It has been argued that, unlike other areas of private law, family law is so closely interrelated with the mores and cultural values of a particular society that it cannot be changed radically. This is certainly not true of Scotland. Nor, we would suggest, is it true of England or the other European countries which have seen a remarkable degree of reform in this area in the last couple of decades. Indeed, it would appear that family law lends itself to reform, reflecting the profound changes Western societies have seen in the economic and social position of women and the move to a child-centred family culture.

[4] *Montieth* v. *Cape Insulation* 1998 SC 903; 1999 SLT 116.

[5] *Fitzpatrick* v. *Sterling Housing Association* [1998] Ch 304; [1999] 3 WLR 1113.

[6] *Beggs* v. *Motherwell Bridge Fabrications Ltd* 1998 SLT 1215.

[7] *McManus' Executrix* v. *Babcock Energy Ltd* 1999 SC 569.

While difficulties can be anticipated in respect of procedural issues, for example, at children's hearings, it is thought that most of Scots substantive family law is "Convention proof". This is because the European Convention provides a minimum platform of human rights rather than the inherently liberal nature of Scots family law. There are, of course, some areas where reform is necessary. For example, the five-year separation ground of divorce may be a breach of Article 6. The refusal to give step-parents automatic parental responsibilities and rights in respect of children who have been accepted as children of the family could be a breach of Article 8. Again, the position of the unmarried father remains difficult to justify and may fall foul of Article 8. Surely where an unmarried man is presumed to be the father of a child, he should automatically have parental responsibilities and rights. In Scots law, the presumption of paternity arises when the mother agrees that a man should be registered as the father of her child.[8] If the presumption applies, parental responsibilities and rights should follow.

As the law now stands, a father has parental responsibilities and rights if he was married to the mother at the date of conception of the child or at any time thereafter.[9] An unmarried father can obtain parental responsibilities and rights if the mother agrees or he obtains a court order giving them to him.[10] The court cannot award him parental responsibilities and rights unless he can establish that it is in the child's best interests to do so and that it is better for the child that the order be made than no order be made at all.[11] But is the unmarried father in such a different position from the married father who has automatic parental responsibilities and rights? This issue was explored in *White* v. *White.*[12]

Before discussing the case, it should be noted that under section 1(1)(c) of the Children (Scotland) Act 1995, parental responsibilities include the responsibility, "if the child is not living with the parent, to maintain personal relations and direct contact with the child on a regular basis . . . but only in so far as compliance with this section is practicable and in the interests of the child". Section 2(1)(c) of the 1995 Act gives a parent the corresponding right to maintain personal relations and direct contact with the child on a regular basis, if the child is not living with him. By section 11 of the Act, the court can make an order depriving a person of parental responsibilities and rights (section 11(2)(a)), giving a person parental responsibilities and rights (section 11(2)(b)) and regulating the *arrangements* for the child's residence and contact with the child (section 11(2)(c) and (d)).

8 Law Reform (Parent and Child)(Scotland) Act 1986, s. 5(1)(b).

9 Children (Scotland) Act 1995, s. 3(1)(b).

10 *Ibid.*, s. 11(2)(b).

11 *Ibid.*, s. 11(7).

12 1999 Fam LR 28. But cf. *H* v. *M* 2000 Fam LR 70 where the Sheriff Principle (Bowen) held that an unmarried father could apply for an order regulating contact without first obtaining the parental responsibility and the right of contact with his child.

The facts of *White* were simple. H and W were married. H had therefore the full complement of parental responsibilities and rights in respect of the children of the marriage. On divorce, a residence order was made in favour of W. The effect of the order was *not* to deprive H of his parental responsibilities and rights, although he could not *exercise* his responsibilities and rights in a way which was incompatible with the residence order made in favour of W.[13] H had difficulty seeing his children. He brought proceedings for contact in the sheriff court. There the sheriff held that since H had parental responsibilities and rights, he should be presumed to be entitled to contact with his child unless the mother could show that contact would be against the child's interests when H could be deprived of the responsibility/right to contact under section 11(2)(a). On appeal to the Sheriff Principal (Nicholson), the sheriff's decision was reversed.

Sheriff Nicholson explained that the statutory responsibilities merely articulated those which had always existed at common law. Section 1 expressly states that parental responsibilities exist "only in so far as compliance with this section is practicable and in the interests of the child". The section 2 rights only exist to implement the parental responsibilities and accordingly must be exercised in the child's interests. Although H had *prima facie* the responsibility of, and right to, contact, these were dependent on being in the interests of the child. Therefore the onus lay on H to show that contact was in the child's interests. The Sheriff Principal found support for this interpretation from the language of subsections 11(3) and (4) which provide for orders *regulating* residence and contact, as opposed to giving a right to residence or contact. In making section 11 orders, the welfare of the child is the paramount consideration and the court cannot make an order unless satisfied that it is better for the child that an order should be made than that none should be made at all.[14] Where the father is unmarried, he has to apply for parental responsibilities and rights under section 11(2)(b), when, of course, the welfare principle applies: if successful, he can then apply under section 11(2)(d) for an order regulating contact. Because of the view he had taken of sections 1 and 2, at the stage of seeking an order regulating contact, the positions of the married and unmarried father are the same. In both cases, the father would have to show that contact was in the best interests of the child: a child's future would therefore not depend on the father's status.

As a matter of statutory construction, the Sheriff Principal's reasoning is compelling. As a consequence, however, the fact that a married father has automatic parental responsibilities and rights gives him little, if any, advantage over an unmarried father. While the unmarried father must first be granted parental responsibilities and rights, both cannot have an order *regulating* the

[13] Children (Scotland) Act 1995, s. 11(11).

[14] *Ibid.*, s. 11(7)(a).

right of contact unless they can demonstrate that contact is positively in their child's interests.

In these circumstances, why give a married father automatic parental responsibilities and rights if they have no substance unless he can show that their exercise is positively in his child's interests? The sheriff's judgment recognises that *prima facie* children benefit from contact with *both* parents and that this would be reinforced by presuming that a married father, at least, should have contact unless it is *against* the child's interests. This gives his parental responsibility and right to maintain and foster his relationship with his child some substantive constant. It is consistent with the rights discourse of Article 8, unlike the appellate court's welfare-orientated approach.

It remains to be seen whether Sheriff Principal Nicholson's decision will be appealed to the Inner House. Until then, there is surely cause for concern. Would, for example, the same result have been reached if the sexes were reversed and the mother had been seeking contact with the child? Where a father pursuer has parental responsibilities and rights, why, if he must establish that their exercise is in his child's interests, does a mother defender not have to demonstrate the same? (Ironically, this was probably the case in *White,* as the mother had obtained a residence order in the earlier divorce proceedings.) What is good for the goose, should surely be good for the gander. At present, possession of the child appears to be nine-tenths of the law since the onus of satisfying the welfare principle in section 11(7) rests on the pursuer. It could be argued—though this would be contrary to Article 8—that Scots law after *White* has *in praxis* adopted the view that mothers can be trusted to exercise parental responsibilities and rights while fathers cannot, unless they can prove that it is in their children's interests to do so.

However, as in English law, the major issue, of which *White* is an illustration, is, of course, whether the welfare principle itself is inconsistent with Article 8. In our view the language of our discourse will require to be changed to ensure that it is "rights-orientated" so that parental rights cannot be "trumped" unless their exercise would be *against* the child's interests as opposed to positively in the child's interests.

Reform of the Common Law

Delict

Wrongful conception

There is one area of English law where Scots law has played a significant role in the twentieth century, viz. the development of the law of negligence. *Donoghue* v. *Stevenson*,[15] perhaps the most important decision emanating from Scotland in the last century, brought coherence and principled reasoning to the English tort of negligence as well as the Scots law of reparation. (It is often forgotten that Mrs Donoghue *lost* in the Scottish courts.) However, in Scotland *Donoghue* is now seen as a milestone which has been passed *en route* to the current chaos that passes for the "law" of negligence. Scots private lawyers are proud of *Donoghue*: we would suggest that the last contribution in the old millennium from Scotland to the law of negligence, *Macfarlane* v. *Tayside Health Board*,[16] provides less cause for celebration.

What is the extent of a doctor's liability when a sterilisation fails as a consequence of her negligence and a woman conceives an unplanned child? This was the question raised in *Macfarlane*. The pursuer had a vasectomy which failed, even although he was assured by the defender that it was safe to have intercourse with his wife without contraception. His wife conceived and gave birth to a healthy child. Both the father and the mother sued the Health Board. At first instance,[17] the Lord Ordinary (Gill) accepted that the defenders owed the couple a duty of care. However, Lord Gill denied them damages on the ground that they had not sustained any reparable loss. He refused to classify pregnancy and labour as physical injury to the mother, and he did not regard the cost of rearing the child as economic loss, since such costs were outweighed by the inestimable benefits of being the parents of a healthy child.

In the Inner House,[18] Lord Gill's decision was reversed. There it was held that the parents' rights not to have a child had been infringed, i.e. that the unplanned conception constituted *damnum* (harm) for the purpose of the law of negligence. This was a reparable interest in modern Scots law. In other words, the defenders were in breach of their duty of care to prevent the couple having a child. They were therefore liable for the foreseeable heads of loss which arose from the unwanted conception. These included the mother's pain and suffering caused by the pregnancy and birth (*solatium*) *and* the costs to the

[15] 1932 SC (HL) 31.
[16] 2000 SLT 154.
[17] 1992 SLT 211, OH.
[18] 1998 SLT 307.

parents of bringing up an unplanned child. The latter would be substantial since, as stated above, in Scots law parents are obliged to aliment their child until the age of eighteen, or twenty-five if the child is engaged in higher education or training.

The Health Board appealed to the House of Lords. There their Lordships (Lords Slynn, Steyn, Hope, Clyde, and Lord Millett dissenting) awarded the mother damages for *solatium* but unanimously refused compensation for the cost of rearing a healthy, but unplanned, child.

The House agreed that the defender owed the pursuers a duty of care. This duty was to prevent the couple conceiving a child. The issue before the court was "the extent of the losses which may properly be claimed in the circumstances of the case, rather than with the existence or non-existence of a liability to make reparation":[19] per Lord Clyde. It is important to stress that all the judges accepted that the wrong suffered by the pursuers was the unwanted conception, not the unplanned birth of the child: the unwanted conception constituted the *damnum* for which the couple could seek reparation. *Prima facie*, the pursuers were entitled to compensation for the losses which were the reasonably foreseeable and direct consequences of the unplanned pregnancy: these included *solatium* for the mother in respect of the pregnancy and birth of the child and the economic costs of the child's upbringing.

The majority of their Lordships had no difficulty in awarding *solatium* to the mother. As Lord Clyde observed, "It seems to me to be a clear example of pain and suffering such as could qualify as a potential head of damages".[20] Only Lord Millett thought that a normal pregnancy and ordinary birth were simply the price of parenthood and, as such, non-reparable. It is thought that few, if any, would disagree with the majority that a mother should obtain compensation in these circumstances. It remains to be seen what figure the court will consider to be an appropriate amount of damages.

The controversial issue before the House of Lords was whether the father and mother should recover compensation for the cost of rearing the child. The difficulty facing their Lordships was that the traditional devices for limiting damages were not applicable in this case. First, the scope of the duty of care was to prevent Mrs McFarlane from becoming pregnant: the unwanted conception was precisely what her doctors ought to have avoided. Put another way, since an unwanted conception was reasonably foreseeable as a probable consequence of the defender's carelessness, there was clearly a *breach* of the duty of care: cf. *Muir* v. *Glasgow Corpn.*[21] Secondly, as the unwanted conception was regarded as the *damnum* suffered by the pursuers, the cost of bringing up an unplanned child was both direct and reasonably foreseeable. The damages

[19] 2000 SLT 154 at 176.
[20] *Ibid.* at 176.
[21] 1943 SC (HL) 3.

were therefore not too remote: *Allan* v. *Barclay*.[22] Thirdly, the House of Lords rejected the contention that the chain of causation was broken when the couple refused to terminate the pregnancy or have the child adopted. Fourthly, the House maintained that the economic costs of the child could *not* be set off against the joy she gave to her parents (this had been the approach favoured by Lord Gill). As Lord Steyn recognised, from the perspective of corrective justice, "It requires somebody who has harmed another without justification to indemnify the other. On this approach the parents' claim for the cost of bringing up Catherine [the child] must succeed".[23]

Yet the House of Lords refused to allow the claim for the cost of alimenting the child. How was this achieved? The parents' loss was economic. Lords Slynn and Hope took the view that before economic loss should be recognised as a head of damage in a delictual claim, the *Caparo* criteria had to be satisfied, viz. that the loss was not only foreseeable and proximate but that it was fair, just and reasonable that it should be recoverable.[24] The *Caparo* criteria have hitherto been used to determine the existence of a duty of care, particularly in relation to cases of "pure" economic loss. Now it appears that it is also to be used to determine the *scope* of the duty so that a judge can exclude a head of loss which cannot be regarded as too remote under the traditional limitation devices discussed earlier.

Lords Hope and Slynn considered that it would not be fair, just and reasonable to impose upon the Health Board the costs of maintaining an unplanned, healthy child which the parents had accepted into their family. The doctors, it was contended, had not assumed responsibility for such costs. However, in our view the doctors *had* assumed responsibility for Mr and Mrs Macfarlane to the extent that they were obliged to take reasonable care to prevent her having an unwanted conception. The conception infringed their rights not to have further children. The cost of maintaining the child was not *pure* economic loss but was derivative economic loss, i.e. it *derived* from or was parasitic upon the *damnum* suffered by the pursuer. Often the *damnum* will be physical injury, but the House of Lords accepted that the unwanted pregnancy amounted to *damnum* in this case. As derivative economic loss, the extent of the defender's liability is determined by the remoteness rules, not the *Caparo* criteria. Moreover, it is ironic that the House of Lords stresses (wrongly) that the loss is purely economic when over the last few years, the House has taken pains to argue that in novel situations the criteria for the existence of a duty of care are the same regardless of the nature of the damage suffered by the pursuer: see, for example, *The Nicholas H*.[25]

[22] (1864) 2 M 873.
[23] 2000 SLT 154 at 165.
[24] *Caparo Industries plc* v. *Dickman* [1990] 2 AC 226.
[25] [1996] AC 211 per Lord Steyn at 235.

Lord Clyde's speech gives an eloquent account of why the traditional devices were inappropriate to limit the pursuer's claim for the cost of rearing the child. Instead, he refuses the claim on the ground that to allow it would not "accord with the idea of restitution or with an award of damages which does justice between both parties".[26] For Lord Clyde there must be an element of proportionality between the damages awarded and the culpability of the defender. This is the language of the law of unjustified enrichment, not delict. Delict provides reparation for damage wrongfully caused. If the defender's fault is trivial, there will usually be no breach of duty and therefore no liability. But once the defender has been negligent then she must compensate the pursuer for the foreseeable losses.

Lord Millett embraced the concept of subjective devaluation. Put simply, an individual cannot "devalue" an object which is valued by society in general. Because the birth of a healthy child is considered by society to be, on balance, beneficial, the Macfarlanes cannot devalue their daughter in order to claim compensation for her upkeep. They cannot transfer the responsibilities for alimenting their daughter to others, while having her at home.

Lord Steyn, dismissing legal rules and principles as "unrealistic and formalistic propositions", found a solution in distributive justice. Rather than a discourse on Aristotle, Lord Steyn's discussion of that concept is the view of the commuter on the Underground on whether or not the parents should succeed. Without a shred of empirical evidence, he is "firmly of the view that an overwhelming number of ordinary men and women would answer the question with an emphatic 'No' ".[27] Surely that might depend on whether the commuter has been the victim of a botched sterilisation and has an unplanned child to bring up? Nevertheless, the Macfarlanes' claim for economic loss was rejected on this ground.

In the writers' view, once it was accepted that a wrongful conception constituted an interest which was reparable in Scots law, the pursuers' should have been able to recover the cost of rearing their daughter. As explained above, the traditional tests for limiting damages were of no assistance in this case. The reasoning of the House of Lords for rejecting the claim is difficult to defend. Nevertheless, as a matter of *policy* we would suggest that the decision of the House of Lords is correct. Why should the tax-payer via the Health Board's limited resources take on the economic cost of alimenting an unplanned, but not unwanted, healthy child? What the House of Lords should have done was to reverse the Scottish courts and hold that an unwanted conception was not a reparable interest in Scots law. In other words, the infringement of the "right" to enjoy sexual intercourse without contraception was not delictual even if

[26] 2000 SLT 154 at 177. It is interesting to note that at no stage in the argument in the House of Lords: did counsel refer to the doctrine of proportionality or subjective devaluation!

[27] *Ibid.* at 165.

caused by a doctor's negligence. If so, of course, the mother's claim for *solatium* as well as the claim for economic loss would fail.

At present the law adopts a half-way house, a typical compromise. It is inelegant and illogical. Throughout their speeches, their Lordships emphasise that they are not considering the situation where the child is born handicapped. It is not clear, however, why a handicapped child is to be treated as less of a blessing than a "normal, healthy" baby; nor are we concerned with the case where a woman has conceived but is not given the opportunity to terminate her pregnancy owing to medical negligence. It will not be long before these issues will be litigated in the higher courts.

Nervous shock

In common with English law, Scots law has recently wrestled with the difficulties of liability for nervous shock. The case of *Page* v. *Smith*,[28] however, raises particular problems for Scots lawyers. The facts of the case are well known: the plaintiff was involved in a road accident caused by the defendant's negligent driving. The plaintiff did not suffer physical injury as a result of the accident, but rather a recurrence of ME which had, prior to the accident, been in remission. The House of Lords held that because the plaintiff was within the area of potential physical harm, he was to be regarded as a primary victim of the accident. Thus it was irrelevant that psychiatric injury was not reasonably foreseeable because a person of ordinary fortitude would not have suffered nervous shock in the circumstances. The foreseeability of physical injury was sufficient to permit recovery of damages.

Although this case has been discussed in recent Scottish cases,[29] in our opinion it should not be followed given that it is contrary to established principles. The difficulties are illustrated by two cases which have been important for the development of negligence or *culpa* in Scotland: *Muir* v. *Glasgow Corporation*[30] and *Hughes* v. *Lord Advocate*.[31] The former case established that a defender is only in breach of a duty of care if the harm sustained by the pursuer would have been foreseen by a reasonable person in the defender's position as a probable consequence of her conduct. The latter case added the important qualification that provided the pursuer suffers the same type of harm which was foreseeable as a probable consequence of the defender's conduct, it does not matter that the extent of the pursuer's injuries was greater than could have been anticipated or that the accident had occurred in an unforeseeable way.

[28] [1996] AC 155, [1995] 2 All ER 736.

[29] See, for example, the opinion of Lord Reed in the Outer House in *Campbell* v. *North Lanarkshire Council and others*, 30 June 1999, available at www.scotcourts.gov.uk

[30] 1943 SC (HL) 3.

[31] 1963 SC (HL) 31.

If these principles are applied to the facts in *Page* it is necessary to ask whether the recurrence of ME was foreseeable as a reasonable and probable consequence of the defender's conduct. Only personal injury was reasonably foreseeable as a reasonable and probable consequence. Therefore, either psychiatric injury must be included within the ambit of what constitutes "personal injury" or, using the *Hughes* case, psychiatric injury is to be regarded as the same type of injury as personal injury and differs only in extent. Neither of these two possibilities appears to us to be sound.

It could be argued that the case can be understood using the "thin skull rule." This rule provides that if the pursuer suffers physical injury then the defender may be liable for unforeseeable consequences due to the distinct characteristics or weaknesses of the pursuer. However, this can apply only *after* a breach of duty has been established. It provides no assistance in assimilating the *Page* case into the Scottish principles given that Mr Page suffered no physical injury.

As a decision of the House of Lords, *Page* is likely to be followed in future Scottish cases. This would be unfortunate for the reasons explored above. The possibility of *Page* becoming part of Scots law is even more real given that a future case may ultimately be heard by the House of Lords. It is notable that both of the Scottish Lords of Appeal dissented in *Page.*

Mention should also be made of the most recent analysis of nervous shock. Whilst *Page* developed the rules for primary victims, the case of *White* v. *Chief Constable of South Yorkshire Police*[32] provided an opportunity to re-examine the rules governing secondary victims most famously analysed in *Alcock* v. *Chief Constable of South Yorkshire Police.*[33] *White* has not resolved all of the problems affecting the rules on secondary victims. Consider the facts of *Vernon* v. *Bosley (No. 1).*[34] In this case, two children were drowned when the car driven by their nanny crashed into a river. Their father was called to the scene and witnessed the unsuccessful attempts to rescue his children who were trapped inside the car. The father was successful in his claim for damages given the close tie of love and affection which existed and his presence at the aftermath of the accident. However, clearly he would not have succeeded had he been informed of the accident by telephone or had he been unable to witness the scene due, for example, to being out of the country. The requirement of presence at the aftermath will undoubtedly lead to more hard cases.

Another avenue for recovery which had previously existed now seems closed, in Scotland at least. Following *Alcock*, it appeared to be possible that an onlooker witnessing an exceptionally horrific accident but who did not possess the necessary close tie of love and affection with the primary victim might still

[32] [1999] 2 All ER 1.
[33] [1992] 1 AC 310, [1991] 4 All ER 907, HL.
[34] [1997] 1 All ER 577.

recover damages for psychiatric illness caused by witnessing the accident. However, subsequent courts have held that employees who were present at particularly horrific accidents were nevertheless unable to recover any damages. In *Robertson* v. *Forth Road Bridge Joint Board*[35] an employee witnessed the death of a fellow employee who was killed when he was blown off on the Forth Road Bridge. The pursuer had socialised with the deceased with whom he had been friends for several years. The Inner House held that this was not sufficient to constitute the necessary "close tie of love and affection" and thus the pursuer was unsuccessful. Similar reasoning was applied by the Court of Appeal in the case of *McFarlane* v. *EE Caledonia Ltd*[36] where the pursuer had witnessed the Piper Alpha disaster. It is difficult to imagine a more horrific accident than those which occurred in these cases. Thus it appears that the *dicta* in *Alcock* have not created an exception in favour of the pursuer in cases where he or she witnesses a particularly horrific accident. It is unfortunate that this should be so. The factual circumstances of these two cases were, we would suggest, particularly distressing.

Unjustified Enrichment

The last twenty years have seen a resurgence of interest in the Scots law of unjustified enrichment. The most notable development is the work which has been carried out by many academics in an attempt to create a suitable taxonomy for the area. It is almost universally agreed that the existing taxonomy fails to provide a logical framework within which to analyse the principles. Although the suggested taxonomies differ widely, most begin with an analysis of the work of the Institutional writers. English lawyers had to wait until the case of *Woolwich Equitable Building Society* v. *Inland Revenue Commission*[37] for judicial recognition of the difficult process of classification and analysis which has been undertaken by writers such as Goff and Jones, Birks and Burrows. Scots lawyers, in contrast, are proud to point to the work of Institutional writers such as Stair, Erskine, and Bankton in the seventeenth and eighteenth centuries, each of whom tried not only to analyse the detail of the principles, but also to classify them. However, in this as in other areas, Scots lawyers might be accused of resting on the laurels won by the Institutional writers. It is undoubtedly the case that the field of unjustified enrichment requires a great deal of further research and analysis before it can be described as practical and rational.

[35] 1995 SC 364, 1996 SLT 263.

[36] [1994] 2 All ER 1.

[37] [1991] 4 All ER 577, [1992] 3 All ER 737, [1993] AC 70.

Many academic lawyers see the beginning of the recent interest to be two seminal articles on Scots law written by Peter Birks and published in 1985.[38] Since the publication of these articles, several commentators have analysed existing and potential taxonomies. One possibility is the enactment of a code. This possibility is a real one, given the existence of a code written by Dr Eric Clive.[39] Others have favoured a taxonomy which takes much from the current English approach.[40] However, the use of an English taxonomy has inevitable difficulties. As Niall Whitty has commented:

> "Having regard to the major differences between the Scots and English laws on enrichment and related areas of obligations and property law, it is scarcely surprising that Scots enrichment law cannot be spatchcocked into Professor Birks' taxonomy without undue and unnecessary distortion".[41]

Whitty favours the adoption of a taxonomy based on that of a civil law country, Germany: "[R]esemblances between Scots and German law are such that the Wilburg-von Caemmerer taxonomy may form a suitable model for Scots law".[42]

It would, however, be wrong to suggest that academics have achieved the only advances in enrichment law in Scotland in recent years. The judiciary have shown an increasing interest in this area and an increased willingness to develop the law in what must be described as a creative manner. The most famous example is the resolution of the question of whether an action for the return of a payment which was not due was available in cases of error of law as well as error of fact. The Scottish Law Commission had produced a detailed analysis of this issue.[43] Enactment of statutory reform was rendered unnecessary following the case of *Morgan Guaranty Trust Company of New York* v. *Lothian Regional Council.*[44] The method of achieving this result was unusual. A case from 1733 was used to redirect the course of the law. Although the case report of *Stirling of Northwoodside* v. *Earl of Lauderdale,*[45] like many reports from that era, extended to only ten words confirming "*Condictio indebiti* sus-

[38] "Restitution: a View of the Scots Law" 38 CLP 57 and "Six Questions In Search of a Subject—Unjust Enrichment in a Crisis of Identity" 30 *Juridical Review* 227.

[39] Eric Clive, "Draft Rules on Unjustified Enrichment and Commentary" (Scot Law Com DP 99, Appendix, 1994).

[40] See W J Stewart, *The Law of Restitution in Scotland* (Edinburgh, Greens, 1992, with Supplement, 1995).

[41] N R Whitty, "Issues in Scots Enrichment Law", 39 *Juridical Review* 126 at 134.

[42] *Ibid.* at 134.

[43] *Recovery of Benefits Conferred Under Error of Law* (Scot Law Com DP No. 95, 1993); *Judicial Abolition of the Error of Law Rule and its Aftermath* (Scot Law Com DP No. 99, 1996); *Recovery of Ultra Vires Public Authority Receipts and Disbursements* (Scot Law Com DP No. 100, 1996); *Report on Unjustified Enrichment, Error of Law and Public Authority Receipts and Disbursements* (Scot Law Com No. 169, 1999).

[44] 1995 SC 151, 1995 SLT 299.

[45] 1733 (Mor) 2930.

tained to one who had paid *errore juris*",[46] the Court of Session identified this case as correctly representing the principles of Scots law. The wrong-turning which the law had taken was seen to have occurred due to the influence of English law.[47] The law represented by *Stirling* was reinstated notwithstanding the more recent contrary authority. Although we might argue with the method which was used in this case, the result was welcome.

Other examples of judicial creativity can be seen in *dicta* which could be interpreted as suggesting the existence of a general enrichment action in Scots law. The existing tripartite classification of Scots enrichment law is one of its most criticised aspects. Actions must be brought within one of the "three Rs": restitution, repetition and recompense. The ambit of each action is far from clear despite the attempts of many academics to produce definitions. However, at the risk of over-simplification, restitution is the relevant action for the return of a specific thing and repetition for the return of money. Recompense is notoriously difficult to define, although Lord Hope has described it as a remedy which arises:

> "where the defender has been enriched at the pursuer's expense in implement of a supposed obligation under a contract other than by the delivery of property or the payment of money".[48]

Accordingly, the actions differ depending upon the type of benefit which must be returned. In two high-profile cases, the judges have emphasised not the tripartite division, but rather the fact that each is an expression of the general underlying principle of unjustified enrichment.[49] The Lord President (Rodger) summarised the position as follows in *Shilliday* v. *Smith*:

> "So repetition, restitution and recompense are simply examples of remedies which the courts grant to reverse an unjust enrichment, depending on the way in which the particular enrichment has arisen".[50]

Although such pronouncements undoubtedly assist in shaping the law, their utility must be limited in a practical context. The form of pleadings used in a particular case is unlikely to change without actual law reform. Solicitors will continue to consider themselves bound by the individual forms restitution, repetition and recompense. This tripartite classification which Birks originally

[46] *Ibid.*

[47] See *Glasgow Corporation* v. *Lord Advocate* 1959 SC 203 where the Inner House adopted *obiter dicta of* Lord Brougham in *Wilson & McLelland* v. *Sinclair* (1830) 4 W & S 398 and *Dixon* v. *Monkland Canal Company* (1831) 5 W & S 445.

[48] *Morgan Guaranty Trust Company of New York* v. *Lothian Regional Council* 1995 SLT 299 at 309.

[49] See Lord Rodger in *Shilliday* v. *Smith* 1998 SC 725; and Lord Hope's approval of this passage in *Dollar Land (Cumbernauld) Ltd* v. *C I N Properties Ltd* 1997 SLT 260, 1998 SC (HL) 90 at 98.

[50] 1998 SC 725 at 728.

criticised[51] is obviously in need of reform. This reform would, however, require to encompass the entire framework and not just seek to eradicate that part which dictates the type of action depending upon the form in which the benefit is received.

The judiciary is not alone in the discussion of a general enrichment action. Similar moves are afoot in academic circles, most notably in an article by MacQueen and Sellar. They suggest that recompense was, in fact, a general enrichment action.[52] Notwithstanding the identification of the historical roots of recompense, it appears unlikely that the judiciary could make the necessary leap to develop recompense in this manner. We would suggest that legislative change is required.

To summarise, the last twenty years have seen great developments, achieved by both academics and the judiciary. However, the Scots lawyer must concede that, in spite of the recent resurgence of interest, in comparison with the English principles of restitution, much work remains to be done. Scots law does not as yet have a textbook of the status of Birks' *Introduction to the Law of Restitution* or Goff and Jones' *The Law of Restitution.* Undoubtedly, many problems are caused by the small size of the Scottish jurisdiction. Fewer academics are writing about enrichment law and fewer cases exist to develop that law.

The most important question which must be asked at the beginning of the new millenium is what form should reform take? Most lawyers would agree that the distinctive nature of Scots enrichment law—established so clearly in the works of the Institutional writers—ought to be retained. In the writers' opinion, reform cannot and need not proceed by adopting an English taxonomy. This would be to reject the existing benefits and impose a taxonomy which would fit uneasily into the overall framework of Scots private law. The dangers of taking such a course of action can be seen from the furore which ensued following the case of *Sharp* v. *Thomson.*[53] Some have argued that this case illustrates the tensions caused by the presence of an English concept, the floating charge, in the Scots system of real and personal property rights.

Proceeding by way of a code is a possibility, particularly given that Dr Clive's code already exists. This code appears to have received very little consideration in published research.[54] The possibility of development in this manner could arise given Clive's current work on a Scottish Civil Code project. Whether or

[51] For example in "Six Questions" *supra* n. 38, at 237–8.

[52] H L MacQueen and W D H Sellar, "Unjust Enrichment in Scots Law" in E J H Schrage (ed.), *Unjust Enrichment: The Comparative Legal History of the Law of Restitution* (Berlin, Dunkler & Humblot, 1995).

[53] 1997 SC (HL) 66.

[54] At a seminar on 22nd October 1994, Dr Clive's code was discussed in depth: it was not well received by members of the Scottish judiciary!

not it receives the backing of the Scottish Parliament is obviously of key importance. What seems to be clear is that we cannot expect reform to be achieved by the judiciary alone. Despite the recent judicial contributions, what is required is wholesale reconsideration of the taxonomy of enrichment law.

The question of taxonomy is, in a sense, only the first step. Although it is obviously of key importance, once it is established attention must turn to the substantive principles. The majority of recent academic work, perhaps not surprisingly, has considered taxonomy alone. This has left the substantive law under-researched. As an example, although the location of recompense in the taxonomy has been considered, less attention has been given to the actual prerequisites of a recompense case. Several "marks" or "notes" of recompense have been judicially identified, but these remain controversial.[55] The importance of mistake in the application of recompense is not clear, nor is the meaning of the requirement that the actings must not be *in suo*. Indeed, little consideration has been given to the meaning of numerous judicial pronouncements suggesting that recompense is a "subsidiary" remedy. Lawyers in the new millenium must look beyond taxonomy and seek to refine the substantive principles.

Contract

Scots lawyers have been fond of pointing to the advantages of Scots contract law in comparison with English contract law notwithstanding the fact that much of the law in the two countries is similar. As an example, Scots law has never been dogged by the difficulties of consideration. Scots law contains an enforceable unilateral promise or *pollicitatio* clearly analysed by Viscount Stair.[56] A related concept, which is usually held up for general admiration, is the Scottish version of a third party right, *jus quaesitum tertio*. In contrast, the rigidity of the English privity rule led to the creation of many exceptions. These Lord Steyn has referred to (quoting Lord Diplock) as: "juristic subterfuges . . . to mitigate the effect of the lacuna resulting from the non-recognition of a *jus quaesitum tertio*".[57]

Nevertheless, Scots contract lawyers often find themselves looking enviously over the border. The lacuna recognised by Lord Steyn has now been filled by

[55] See the Lord President (Dunedin) in *Edinburgh and District Tramways Co Ltd* v. *Courtney* 1909 SC 99; the Lord Justice-Clerk (Wheatley) in *Varney (Scotland) Ltd* v. *Burgh of Lanark* 1976 SLT 46, 1974 SC 245; the Lord President (Emslie) in *Lawrence Building Co Limited* v. *Lanark CC* 1977 SLT 110, 1978 SC 30, 1979 SLT 2.

[56] *Institutions* I x 5.

[57] *Darlington Borough Council* v. *Wiltshier Northern Limited (Lowes and other third parties)* [1995] 3 All ER 895 at 905, quoting Lord Diplock in *Swain* v. *Law Society* [1982] 2 All ER 827 at 832, [1983] 1 AC 598 at 611.

the Contracts (Rights of Third Parties) Act 1999.[58] Scots lawyers are left to struggle with the under-developed common law concept of *jus quaesitum tertio.*

The difficulties surrounding the Scottish concept are the result of a historical accident. Lord Dunedin famously misinterpreted Stair's explanation of *jus quaesitum tertio.*[59] The misinterpretation surrounded the issue of irrevocability of the right. Stair's original exposition suggested that the right, once created, was irrevocable.[60] However, after commenting, "I do not think that Lord Stair meant to lay down such a proposition",[61] Lord Dunedin proceeded to hold that irrevocability is a *prerequisite* rather than a *consequence* of creation. This has led to much uncertainty, and may be one reason why there is so little evidence of the use of the right in recent cases.[62]

The solutions adopted by the English 1999 Act have much to commend them. In relation to the "crystallisation" of the third party's right, the Act provides that the right may not be rescinded without the consent of the third party if the third party communicates his assent,[63] if the promisor is aware of reliance by the third party,[64] or if the promisor can "reasonably be expected to have foreseen that the third party would rely on the term and the third party has in fact relied on it".[65] There are exceptions to these provisions, the most notable of which is that they can be overridden by a term in the contract.[66] Any Scottish reform project would do well at least to consider these possibilities.

The potential benefits of a reformed concept of *jus quaesitum tertio* are illustrated by considering the decision of the House of Lords in *BT* v. *James Thomson.*[67] This case is an example of the classic problems caused by contractual chains in a construction context and the extent to which contractual terms can affect parties who are not immediate contracting parties but are located elsewhere in the contractual chain. The possibility of a contractual rather than a delictual approach to this problem was referred to, only in passing. The House of Lords adopted a delictual solution.

[58] 1999, c. 31.

[59] See *Carmichael* v. *Carmichael's Executrix* 1920 SC (HL) 195, and comment by J T Cameron, "Jus Quaesitum Tertio: The True Meaning of Stair I,X,5", 6 *Juridical Review* 103; A Rodger, "Molina, Stair and the Jus Quaesitum Tertio", 14 *Juridical Review* 34 and 128; D N MacCormick, Jus Quaesitum Tertio: Stair v Dunedin", 15 *Juridical Review* 228.

[60] *Institutions* I x 5.

[61] *Carmichael* v. *Carmichael's Executrix* 1920 SC (HL) 195 at 199.

[62] Although see Lord Clyde in *Scott Lithgow Ltd* v. *GEC Electrical Products Limited* 1992 SLT 244 at 259 *et seq*; *Mercedes-Benz Finance Ltd* v. *Clydesdale Bank plc* 1997 SLT 905 per Lord Penrose at 912 *et seq.*

[63] Contracts (Rights of Third Parties) Act 1999, s. 2(1)(a).

[64] *Ibid.*, s. 2(1)(b).

[65] *Ibid.*, s. 2(1)(c).

[66] *Ibid.*, s. 2(3).

[67] 1999 SC (HL) 9.

Constraints of space prevent a full analysis of the issues raised by this decision. What can be said is that it represents one of the most notable lost opportunities for the judicial development of Scots law. The case was disposed of by one speech given by Lord Mackay, extending to little more than five pages, with which the four other judges (Lords Lloyd, Mustill, Cooke and Hutton) concurred. This is in stark contrast to the painstaking analysis both at first instance by Lord Rodger and on appeal by the Lord Justice-Clerk (Ross), Lord Morison and Lord Cowie. The possibility of a contractual solution had also been fully explored in an excellent article.[68]

It is also interesting to note that the delictual solution used is an example of the tendency already adverted to in this chapter, namely the application of the *Caparo* tripartite test in a situation of damage to property which one would hitherto have expected to be analysed using the *Donoghue* neighbourhood principle.

Ironically, the English Law Commission paper which preceded the 1999 Act envisaged the use of the new statutory third party right in a situation similar to that which existed in the *BT* case.[69] If we continue to solve "contractual chain" problems by expanding the law of delict, the principles of the law of negligence will, it is suggested, become even more uncertain if that is possible. The strain on the principles of the English law of tort will be less severe, simply because of the new third party right.

However, we would not wish to give the impression that much of the Scots law of contract is in need of reform. The Scottish Law Commission has been active in this area. The Contract (Scotland) Act 1997 repealed three anachronistic and impractical rules of the law of contract.[70] Scottish Law Commission Reports have been published in the areas of interpretation in private law, penalty clauses and remedies for breach of contract.[71] With the advent of the Scottish Parliament, legislation in these areas is a more realistic possibility.

The *Report on Remedies for Breach of Contract* must be singled out for praise. It analyses a very difficult area. As an example, a great deal of doubt surrounded the interplay between contractual and restitutionary remedies which may be available on breach of contract. This issue has undoubted practical relevance, particularly in a construction context. Historically, it has been difficult to identify the remedies open to a builder who was in breach of contract but

[68] J Convery, "Contractual Structures and the Duty of Care", 1997 SLT (News) 113.

[69] *Privity of Contract: Contracts for the Benefit of Third Parties* (Law Com No. 242) at para. 3.10 *et seq.*

[70] The parole evidence rule, the rule in *Winston* v. *Patrick*, and the rule against the *actio quanti minoris.* For analysis, see L Macgregor, "The Contract (Scotland) Act 1997", 42 *Journal of the Law Society of Scotland* 271–3.

[71] *Report on Interpretation in Private Law* (Scot Law Com No. 160, 1997); *Report on Penalty Clauses* (Scot Law Com No. 171, 1999); *Remedies for Breach of Contract* (Scot Law Com No. 174, 1999).

had conferred a benefit on the other contracting party.[72] Whether the builder in breach was barred from contractual remedies as a result of the principle of mutuality of contract and how any benefit to the innocent party was to be valued were issues requiring clarification. Although the Report does not recommend reform of this particular area, the thorough analysis which is provided clarifies the existing law. This is of undoubted practical use.

It is perhaps surprising that the Scottish Law Commission did not give more consideration to the possibility of restitutionary damages in contract. The reason given by the Commission for retaining a compensatory function only was that other areas of the law could carry out a function similar to restitutionary damages, "for example, the law on unjustified enrichment, the law on fiduciary duties, the criminal law or the law on declarators".[73] The Commission also indicated that the current Scottish rule was in line with that applying in most countries of the European Union and the European "Principles".[74] However, the question of restitutionary damages has been a current issue in England[75] and in the USA, and it is suggested that the Law Commission missed an opportunity to take a deeper look into whether the Scots system would benefit from reform.

Particular initiatives of the English Law Commission have also been followed closely from this side of the border. The uncertainty surrounding the enforceability of illegal contracts and extent to which parties to such a contract can avail themselves of restitutionary remedies is a problem in both the Scottish and English jurisdictions. The English Law Consultative Paper provided some very welcome suggestions for reform, particularly the enactment of a statutory discretion to govern the availability of restitutionary remedies.[76] There have been few recent Scottish cases on contractual illegality, and so the uncertainty surrounding the existing principles has gone almost unnoticed. It is hoped that the area of illegal contracts is one which will be considered by the Scottish Law Commission.

Conclusion

In this chapter, we have discussed some areas of Scots law where we anticipate change in the new millennium. The choice has not been entirely arbitrary,

[72] *Ramsay* v. *Brand* (1898) 25R 1212, 6 SLT 114; *Steel* v. *Young* 1907 SC 360, 14 SLT 660.

[73] *Discussion Paper on Remedies for Breach of Contract* (Scot Law Com No. 109, 1999), para. 8.3.

[74] O Lando and H Beale (eds), *Principles of European Contract Law Part I: Performance, Non-Performance and Remedies* (Dordrecht, 1995).

[75] See *Attorney General* v. *Blake (Jonathan Cape Ltd, third party)* [1998] 1 All ER 833.

[76] *Illegal Transactions: the Effect of Illegality on Contracts and Trusts* (Law Com Cons Paper No. 154, 1999).

reflecting the interests—as well as the expertise—of the authors. Important subjects have been omitted, in particular Scottish land law where fundamental reform is already under way.[77] The point is that interest in Scots private law is flourishing. There has been a renaissance in the literature on the subject. Led by the Lord President, Lord Rodger of Earlsferry, the Court of Session is making an immense contribution to the development of the law. The work of the Scottish Law Commission has also been extremely important. With the revival of interest in the *ius commune* in Europe, Scots lawyers have participated in many projects which have emphasised the distinctive nature of Scottish private law. We are no longer considered and, perhaps more importantly, no longer consider ourselves to be, purveyors of quaint, but anachronistic, legal rules which will, almost inevitably, be overtaken by the Anglo-American common law. To that extent, at least, Scots law can look forward to the new century with confidence.[78]

[77] Abolition of Feudal Tenure etc. (Scotland) Act 2000. The Scottish Law Commission anticipate submitting the final report and draft bill, Title Conditions etc. (Scotland) Bill, to the Scottish ministers by the end of 2000.

[78] It should be noted, however, that the learned editors of this volume still consider that the whole of Scots law can be accommodated in a single chapter of this book!

7

European Legal Studies: Then and Now

JO HUNT AND JO SHAW

"The construction of a genuine legal order is, naturally, also the construction of a genuine academic discipline".[1]

Introduction

The use of the word "genuine" in the quotation which heads up this chapter is, of course, a deliberate provocation. The study of "European law", "EC law", "Community law", "EU law" or whatever it might be termed, has been dogged, in many ways, by the grand ideas of the European Court of Justice with its well publicised rhetoric of building a "new legal order".[2] The image of the constitutionalised EC Treaty as the basis of the legal order, and the agency of the Court of Justice in constructing that image on the basis of the relatively unpromising material contained in the Treaty texts themselves, were probably amongst the most powerful factors shaping the first thirty years or so of the existence of the EU legal order.

At least, such would certainly be the orthodox view, an orthodoxy which might even go so far as to attribute a strong causality to "law" overall as a shaping factor in the development of European economic and political integration more generally. Turning the lens of that same orthodoxy to the contemporary world, it would now probably point to a range of factors which suggest some changes in the role of law: challenges to the legitimacy of the Court of Justice in tandem with wider challenges to the legitimacy of the EU as a whole after

[1] H Schepel and R Wesseling, "The Legal Community: Judges, Lawyers, Officials and Clerks in the Writing of Europe" (1997) 3 *European Law Journal* 165 at 183.
[2] Case 26/62 *Van Gend en Loos* v. *Nederlandse Administratie der Belastingen* [1963] ECR 1.

the Treaty of Maastricht ratification debacle is one good example. Another would be the endemic "flexibility" of the system, under which the legal and administrative frameworks of "Schengenland" and "Euroland" currently do not include the United Kingdom, even though it remains, of course, a full member of the EU. Equally, a survey of the discipline through the medium of a review of the available scholarly literature reveals very quickly that there appear to have been considerable changes here as well. In particular, there is now a richly varied scholarship on EU law, making use of a wide range of different research methodologies.

The hypothesis on which this chapter is based is that all of these "orthodoxies" are deserving of much closer examination before any of them can be credited with true explanatory force in the construction of the discipline. In particular, the historical elements of the emergence of the EU legal order and the academic discipline parasitic upon that order need to be disaggregated. The concept of the "early years" of what were then the European Communities and their legal order needs to be reconsidered. For example, Community law existed in some form or other from 1952[3] to 1963;[4] that is, it existed for more than ten years *before* the Court of Justice's groundbreaking approach to the interpretation of the effects of Community law in national courts began to suggest a more "federal" future for the Community legal order rather than a limited future as a "mere" international legal order. To assist the process of disaggregation, we deploy a division between the disciplinary framework and its context. Context includes not only the wider arena of European integration processes and events, but also the immediate structural context in which a discipline flourishes (or sometimes withers), namely the University system. For these purposes, we limit our discussion to the United Kingdom, its University system, and the academic discipline as rooted in that system. However, to the extent that there exists a genuinely cross-national disciplinary debate within the academic field which we inhabit, this is a rather artificial division, so far as it wrongly suggests a hermetic separation of the United Kingdom and UK-based studies of the EU. Thus in our discussion of context we highlight some of the most important cross-national influences such as personal mobility in the context of studies and work. We also indicate areas where the disciplinary framework is dependent upon a wider context of scholarship provided by interactions with legal practice, judicial practice and administrative or bureaucratic practice.

The core of the chapter is a detailed examination of the interaction between disciplinary framework and context. Through this interaction emerge the intellectual movements which characterise "the discipline" as it has developed.

[3] The date of inception of the ECSC Treaty.

[4] The date of the first "constitutionalising" decisions of the Court of Justice.

This allows us to draw some (necessarily synoptic) conclusions about whether or not there now indeed exists the famed "genuine academic discipline" and the extent to which disciplinary development is causally linked to changes in the legal and political environment as well as in the "study environment" in which the legal materials are studied. For part of the provocation intended by the use of the word "genuine" undoubtedly stems from a perception in some parts that the study of the legal part of the European integration process has undergone a somewhat stunted growth; there have been suggestions that this discipline has been slow to draw upon wider changes in the academic environment of legal studies, such as the development of theoretical or interdisciplinary perspectives, as well as to grasp fully the challenge of interrelating the law, the politics and the economics of European integration.[5] And yet, as Snyder commented some time ago, it is a field ripe for contextual and interdisciplinary study.[6]

As any such reconsideration of a discipline, its framework and its context will inevitably involve some personal position-taking, we have taken active steps to build the personal element into the structure of the chapter, rather than dissembling on this question. Thus we have based our historical "stocktaking" upon the years 1984 and 1999—the years when the two of us first took up lecturing positions in UK Universities. We are ourselves typical products of the changes in the wider system. The older one entered a lecturing post with a minimum of experience and training in research or teaching, and a minimal postgraduate education; the younger one secured a lectureship on the back of completing two postgraduate courses—a masters course and a PhD programme—and with considerable experience already of teaching and the prospects of undergoing further training through a teaching and learning certificate. These differences significantly affect our view of the world. In the first two sections of the chapter we systematically examine the context and the disciplinary framework "then and now", trying to blend the differing visions of the authors. In section 3 we bring the context and the disciplinary framework together to examine what interactions they produce in terms of understanding the emergence of the discipline itself, and its associated intellectual movements.

[5] Schepel and Wesseling, *supra* n. 1; H Schepel, "The Mobilisation of European Community Law" in J Brand and D Strempel (eds), *Soziologie des Rechts—Festschrift fur Erhard Blankenburg*, (Baden-Baden, Nomos, 1998); F Snyder, *New Directions in European Community Law* (London, Weidenfeld and Nicolson, 1990); J Shaw, "Introduction" in J Shaw and G More (eds), *New Legal Dynamics of European Union* (Oxford, Clarendon Press, 1995); J Shaw, "European Union Legal Studies in Crisis? Towards A New Dynamic" (1996) 16 *OJLS* 231; J Shaw, "Social-Legal Studies and the European Union" in P Thomas (ed.), *Socio-Legal Studies* (Aldershot, Dartmouth, 1997).

[6] Snyder, *supra* n. 5, at 9.

The Context Then and Now

Then

In 1984, claims that a "genuine legal order" had been established were already a common refrain. The fundamental building blocks of this legal order had been put in place over the previous two decades, through the familiar canon of the "constitutionalising" decisions of the Court of Justice, decisions which reveal the federalising ambitions of that institution.[7] The orthodox account of the process of European integration up until this point (and beyond) conceived of integration as a "legal process driven by legal interpretation rather than political decision".[8] Indeed, whilst the legal dimension of this process appeared in robust health, the political and economic context had been in a state of relative stagnation and inertia. The era of "eurosclerosis", of the continued dominance of the Luxembourg Accords was not yet past. In fact, contemporary assessments painted a far bleaker picture than of simply a "stagnated" EEC. The European Council meeting of December 1983, with its failure to provide solutions to the Community's budget shortfall, had been described as bringing the EEC "to the brink of the worst crisis in its short but crisis-ridden history".[9]

That said, prospects were not bleak enough to deter the accession of further Member States. The Community of the ten of 1984 would soon become that of the twelve, with the Act of Accession with Spain and Portugal being signed in 1985. 1984 could indeed be seen as something of a turning point in the economic and political fortunes of the Community. Initiatives were beginning to emerge which would result in the *relance* of the political and economic dimension. The Fontainebleu Summit of 1984 not only marked a positive step forward on the issue of the EEC's budgetary crises, but it also gave rise to the establishment of two committees, the Dooge Committee on institutional reform and the Addonio Committee on a People's Europe. 1984 was the year the European Parliament produced its draft Treaty on European Union,[10] and not least, this was also the year in which Delors was installed as President of the European Commission. Despite the stagnation of the previous years, it was at this time rare to find evidence of any real challenge being made to the legitimacy of the EEC, with the governing ideas upon which the Community was established—those of peace, prosperity, and supranationalism—still sustaining support.

[7] *Van Gend en Loos, supra* n. 1; Case 6/64 *Costa* v. *ENEL* [1964] ECR 585.
[8] *Supra* n. 1, at 166.
[9] "Editorial Comments" (1984) 21 *Common Market Law Review* 5.
[10] OJ 1984 C 77/83.

This period also bears witness to the expansion in the influence of the ever increasing number of Community level interest groups, with the industrialists' associations in particular, such as UNICE[11] and ERT,[12] set to play a crucial role in the Community's relaunch.[13] The European Court of Justice, meanwhile, was involved in a lobbying exercise of its own—the target being national judiciaries, the objective being to actively enlist their support in its endeavours. As Maher reports, the organisation of visits to the Court of Justice contributed to the emergence of a collaborative spirit between the national and Community level judiciaries. Personal contacts were formed, the Community law process demystified, and opportunities were created for the Court of Justice to bring "informal pressure to bear in order to encourage compliance with Community law".[14]

The Court's message was also taken to the law schools of Europe (and beyond), with short and long-term career moves between practice and academia a common feature of the working lives of some Court of Justice personnel. Such linkages were also seen between the academy and the Commission,[15] as well as with those in private practice.

What of the UK law school at this time? Placing it within the broader University context, the elitism in higher education of the Robbins' era continued to result in a relatively small number of Universities with relatively small law schools. Within these law schools, legal studies remained primarily doctrine-led, with a dominance of positivist theories, although critical legal studies was arriving from the USA and the sociology of law was a present, if marginal discipline. In the pre-RAE era, the entrenchment of a research culture emphasising productivity and quality was yet to take place. The methods of teaching of law remained, by and large, traditional, and it would be a decade before EC law was demanded as a foundational subject for a qualifying law degree. The Law Society's ambivalence to EEC law at this time well reflected the limited practice of EEC law within the United Kingdom.

Now

Fifteen years on, and the EEC has become, formally, a somewhat more ambitious project. During the intervening period, four major Intergovernmental Conferences have taken place,[16] with a fifth just commencing as this chapter

[11] The Union of Industrial and Employers' Confederations of Europe.

[12] The European Round Table of Industrialists.

[13] See, on the role of business organisations in the framing of the single market project, W Sandholtz and J Zysman, "1922: Recasting the European Bargain" (1989) 42 *World Politics* 95.

[14] I Maher, "National Courts as Community Courts" (1994) 14 *Legal Studies* 226 at 234.

[15] Examples of these linkages are well catalogued in Schepel and Wesseling, *supra* n. 1.

[16] Resulting in the Single European Act (1986), the Treaty on European Union (Treaty of Maastricht) (1993) and Treaty of Amsterdam (1999).

was completed in early 2000, and a new legal entity supplementing the existing supranational forms has been created. The establishment of the European Union, and the expansion of its competence into policy areas most closely associated with traditional concepts of statehood such as justice and home affairs, as well as the relatively well established area of foreign policy, have rendered legitimacy a crucial subject for debate. The easy answers of 1984 have been replaced with an ever more critical approach to the EU.[17] Increasingly, the EU's political process is called into question, the founding ideals of the enterprise are no longer seen as relevant, and law no longer provides a bedrock for integration.

In 1999, the Union of 15 is on the verge of expanding yet again to take in the first wave of applicants from the countries of Central and Eastern Europe. Its reach is expanding southwards, through the customs union with Turkey as well as accession negotiations with Cyprus and Malta, an increasingly elaborate policy on South Eastern Europe through a "stability pact" to promote reconstruction and liberal democracy, and an increased emphasis on policy towards the Mediterranean. The single market is all but realised, and EMU has become a reality, though perhaps not—yet—a success. The EU has acquired legal competence in "low politics" areas such as education policy, social policy, environmental policy and cultural policy, and the realm of "high politics" is being inhabited too—through the EU's common foreign and security policy, through the communitarisation of the Schengen process, through the formal creation of citizenship of the European Union. In all of this, however, law no longer has an assumed role of engendering "integration" if that term is understood as bringing about an ever closer convergence, of unity and uniformity. 1999 is the age of subsidiarity and of flexibility, of a Europe of "bits and pieces".[18] The variations existing between different policy domains in terms of the locus of policy responsibility contributes to a widespread confusion and disenchantment amongst the public about the role, purpose and capabilities of the EU. For "insiders", too, there is much about the present system which is likely to confound—not least the renumbering of the provisions of the Treaties accomplished by the Treaty of Amsterdam.

The EU is now widely regarded as a polity, and a sign of the maturity of this polity will be its ability to withstand the increasing criticism being levelled against it. At an institutional level, the Commission is attempting to rebuild its image following the resignations of May 1999. The European Parliament has also received its share of negative publicity, and the June 1999 elections saw low turnouts for the European parliamentary elections in many Member States.

[17] J H H Weiler, "Bread and Circus: the State of European Union", (1998) 4 *Columbia Journal of European Law* 223.

[18] D Curtin, "The Constitutional Structure of the Union: A Europe of Bits and Pieces" (1993) 30 *Common Market Law Review* 17.

The Court of Justice meanwhile is, according to some,[19] responding to increased scrutiny by retreating from its traditional activism. Yet it is still, formally, the same Court, composed of the same pattern of judges and Advocates General, assisted now by a Court of First Instance, and with a similar framework for jurisdiction, if a much higher workload.[20] The Union, however, continues to function, imperfectly perhaps, but a governance system has been created, and continues to be developed beyond the nation state.[21] Participation in this system of governance, through the medium of intensive lobbying of all EU institutions, is now the norm, involving national and supranational actors alike. This strategic use of political channels is accompanied by strategic litigation in a number of areas, such as sex equality,[22] environmental policy and consumer protection.

The radical changes taking place between 1984 and 1999 in relation to the process of European integration are matched by the developments in the University context. Law schools, and Universities as a whole are of course now more numerous, and much larger, though this expansion has been accompanied by swingeing cuts in the unit of resource. The RAE and QAA are familiar to us all, as will be benchmarking. The culture of audit and of accountability has become embedded in the University system, with significant implications for research and for teaching and learning. Reflecting the ever expanding influence of EC law onto domestic law, EC law has, since 1995, been one of the seven foundations of legal knowledge for the qualifying law degree in England and Wales (having achieved that status rather earlier in Scotland), and typically it is also a compulsory module for all law students on law degrees or mixed degrees. That practice-oriented development within the academy is matched by the emergence in recent years of a powerful European legal profession, in which a key role has been played by UK firms.

In comparison with the situation in 1984, legal studies in general are now much more pluralistic. Critical legal studies and post-modernism are credited as important approaches to the study of law, and the law-and-society, socio-legal and law-in-context movements are firmly established. Legal studies make use of, or interact positively with, many other social science or humanities discipline, and the question of "what is interdisciplinarity" is a challenging one for legal scholars. Meanwhile doctrinal studies continue to play an important

[19] R Dehousse, *The European Court of Justice: The Politics of Judicial Integration* (Basingstoke, Macmillan, 1998).

[20] See generally on the Union's judiciary: S Kenney, "The Judges of the Court of Justice of the European Communities", in S Kenney, W Reisinger and J Reitz (eds), *Constitutional Dialogues in Comparative Perspective* (London, Macmillan, 1999).

[21] M Jachtenfuchs, "Theoretical Perspectives on European Governance" (1995) 1 *European Law Journal* 115.

[22] C Barnard, "A European Litigation Strategy: the Case of the Equal Opportunities Commission" in Shaw and More, *supra* n. 5.

role, but there is now a sharper distinction between "academic" and "practice-oriented" literatures.

The Disciplinary Framework Then and Now

Then

In 1984, it would be rare to find many UK Universities offering very much more than one basic course in the law of the EEC, a course which typically could cover substantially all the basic institutional and substantive elements of the "new legal order". The titles of such courses moreover, such as "European Law" and "Common Market Law", reveal both an inexact, as well as an unduly narrow conceptualisation of the EEC legal order. Opportunities did exist in some institutions for a more advanced study of the economic law of the EEC, typically through competition law options. The demand for EEC law courses at undergraduate level was, however, low. Few institutions had made EEC law a compulsory part of the legal curriculum. Nor was there any significant integration of EEC law into other English law courses, with the exception perhaps of constitutional law.

This limited development of undergraduate study of EEC law was, unsurprisingly, matched at postgraduate level, though specialised LLMs in EEC law had been established remarkably early in the history of the discipline, notably where there were important pockets of expertise, such as at the Universities of Exeter and Edinburgh. Postgraduate study was, however, more firmly established in some other Member States, and certain institutions—most obviously the College of Europe in Brussels, and the European University Institute in Florence—were administering genuinely cross-national postgraduate courses, and, in the latter case, awarding PhDs in EEC Law.

Within the United Kingdom, the research discipline was also nascent, and the bulk of research being conducted was of a principally orthodox, doctrinal nature. The dominance of this approach to the subject matter was a response to a number of factors, not least, perhaps, the fact that many of the new teachers of EEC law were coming from a practice background. Scholarship was "close to the Court", in that EEC law was conceived of primarily as the study of the Court as judicial institution, with a primary focus being placed on the outputs of the Court. Little cross-national research was being conducted, and very little, if any, cross- and inter-disciplinary work was emerging. FIDE,[23] a federation intended to draw together national European law societies in the various

[23] *Fédération Internationale de Droit Européen.*

Member States and other countries, was holding conferences on a biennial basis (as it continues to do), but these have always been rather expensive and inaccessible to most academic lawyers. Thus the role of FIDE has disappointed as the basis for potential cross-national networking. Rather than being actively engaged in any meaningful cross-disciplinary discourse over the integration process, lawyers were perceived by non-lawyers as first and foremost providers of technical knowledge. Beyond the UK-based EEC legal scholar's natural (specialised and isolated) home of the *European Law Review* and the Netherlands-based *Common Market Law Review*, there existed limited opportunities for the broader dissemination of EEC legal writing. A review of the standard English law journals from 1984[24] reveals that only one full article directly related to EEC law was published in that year. That article, L N Brown's "Air Hostesses and Discriminating Employers" appeared in the *Modern Law Review*,[25] a journal which would continue to index articles on the EEC system under the heading "Common Market Law" until 1987. Thus, it could hardly be said that EEC law was fully integrated into the discipline of "law" as it then existed.

Now

Since 1995, competence in EC law has been a prerequisite for undergraduates seeking to graduate with a qualifying law degree in England and Wales. At undergraduate level, then, most if not all law students will follow at least a basic course introducing them to the institutions of the Community, and to fundamental issues in the substantive law of the internal market. Such courses may set their sights more broadly, if the titles which some of these courses go by indeed reflect their content, for example, the Law of the European Union, and EU Law. Occasionally, law schools choose to integrate the acquisition of this basic competence into studies of "legal system" and/or "public law". Beyond this basic competence, undergraduates, and particularly postgraduates are increasingly presented with opportunities to acquire competence in a range of advanced specialisms, such as social and employment law, competition law, the law of money, of agriculture, of the EU's external relations and trade relationships, of the environment, of Union citizenship. This broader focus has been reflected in the publication of a range of less black-letter, doctrine-led student texts, such as Shaw's *Law of the European Union*,[26] and Chalmers and Szyszczak's *EU Law*, which is self-described as being "designed for the newer types of European law courses which trace the development of

[24] *Cambridge Law Journal, Law Quarterly Review* and *Modern Law Review.*

[25] (1984) 47 *MLR* 692.

[26] (London, Macmillan, 1996).

the EU from economic to political community, as well as the more traditional courses which focus predominantly upon the law of the institutions and of the internal market".[27] In terms of the supply of courses and the expertise to teach upon, EC law in the United Kingdom has been a particular beneficiary of the symbolic support and small, but nonetheless significant, amounts of funding coming from the European Commission's "Jean Monnet Project", which has run throughout the 1990s to encourage teaching in European Union studies disciplines. A high proportion of law schools have a "Jean Monnet Chair".

The study of the influence and impact of EC law is, of course, no longer limited to courses expressly devoted to that issue. Given the reach of EC law it is, in 1999, impossible to study many fields of English law without considering the "European dimension". This has been recognised through the widespread integration of EC law into other courses, and a non-exhaustive list of these would comprise constitutional law, English legal system, contract and tort law, labour law, and company law.

The increase in provision and take up of EC law courses extends to include students from outside the law department. Increasingly, other faculties and departments are recommending a course of EC law study to their students, as can be seen particularly in the case of politics, of international relations, of business and environmental management. This exposure to EC law at undergraduate level may lead those without a first degree in law to consider postgraduate study in EC law, resulting in an increasingly diverse postgraduate student body, and facilitating inter-disciplinarity. Many UK law schools now offer a taught masters course in EC law, and most offer PhD supervision. The diversity in disciplinary backgrounds of postgraduate students is also matched by a diversity in students' nationalities, with students from other Member States as well as many third countries enrolling on UK postgraduate law degrees. This cross-national movement of students is not only one way, with UK students taking advantage of the developing postgraduate market in Germany, Scandinavia, Belgium and Netherlands. Such movement may be facilitated, for example, through students' prior involvement in an ERASMUS/SOCRATES exchange programme (and the language skills developed thereby) as well as through Universities in these countries offering tuition in English.

The profile of the EC law University lecturer is also changing. Increasingly, as in all other areas of law, new appointees are required to have a postgraduate research degree. A significant number of teaching and research staff working on EC law are not UK nationals, and a even larger number have received at least part of their legal education in another Member State. The research culture is firmly embedded within the context of both the law school and of EC/EU studies more generally, with a far broader range of substantive areas

[27] (Aldershot, Ashgate/Dartmouth, 1998).

being subject to enquiry, and a more diverse range of approaches being taken to them. The 1990s has seen the emergence of a tradition of socio-legal, theoretical and critical, law in context, and inter-disciplinary work on the EU by UK-based legal scholars.[28] Work which focuses on the workings of the Court of Justice has been joined by studies which are less "close to the Court", studies which bring in non-judicial institutions, and which explore the role of law in the wider process of EU governance.

The opportunity structures for more cross-national work have increased, for example through research-funding initiatives such as the Commission-funded Framework Four and Framework Five Programmes. In addition, legal academics are joining the ranks of political scientists, economists, international relations, sociology and regional studies scholars in umbrella associations such as UACES (the University Association for Contemporary European Studies). UACES itself is the UK wing of a wider organisation, the European Community Studies Association, and the conferences and symposia organised under their auspices have facilitated the emergence of a genuine cross-national, pluri-disciplinary debate in European Studies. This debate is also taking place in the pages of multi-disciplinary journals such as the *Journal of Common Market Studies*[29] and the *Journal of European Public Policy*. Publishing opportunities for EU legal scholars in general have expanded significantly; in addition to these multi-disciplinary outlets, new EU law journals have emerged, such as the EUI-edited *European Law Journal*,[30] and the *Yearbook of European Law*. EU law-related publications are also increasingly found in the standard UK law journals, although this assertion is not borne out by the figures for 1999, during which only one full article relating to EU law appeared in the *Modern Law Review*, the *Cambridge Law Journal*, or the *Law Quarterly Review*.[31] This anomaly is perhaps explicable by the high number of articles appearing in 1999 concerning the transposition by the United

[28] A necessarily selective set of examples of such work would include K Armstrong, "New Institutionalism and EU Legal Studies" in P Craig and C Harlow (eds), *Law Making in the European Union* (The Hague, Kluwer Law International, 1998) and "Legal Integration: Theorizing the Legal Dimension of European Integration" (1998) 36 *JCMS* 155; D Chalmers, "Accounting for 'Europe'" (1999) 19 *OJLS* 517; J Hunt, "Interdisciplinary Approaches to EU Decision Making: Law, Politics and the Multi-level 'Governance Regimes'" (2000) 9 *Current Politics and Economics in Europe* 165; N MacCormick, "Beyond the Sovereign State" (1993) 56 *MLR* 1, "The Maastricht-Urteil: Sovereignty Now" (1995) 3 *ELJ* 255; I Maher, "Community Law in the National Legal Order; A Systems Analysis", (1998) 36 *JCMS* 237; J Scott, "Law, Legitimacy and EC Governance: Prospects for 'Partnership'" (1998) 36 *JCMS* 175; J Shaw, *supra* n. 5.

[29] A special edition on "Integrating Law", edited by J Shaw and K Armstrong appeared in the (1998) 36 (2) *JCMS* 147.

[30] Devoted to the study of "law in context".

[31] C Barnard and B Hepple, "Indirect Discrimination: Interpreting *Seymour Smith*", (1999) 58 *Cambridge Law Journal* 399.

Kingdom of the European Convention of Human Rights 1950, and a possible assumption by editors that some sort of "Europe" quota was thereby fulfilled!

The Interaction of Disciplinary Framework and Context

Then

Despite the knocks received by the European integration process during the 1970s and 1980s, still dominant in 1984 at least in legal circles was the received wisdom of a "simple" teleology of integration, according to which the integration project was understood as the progressive centralisation of governmental processes and associated political and economic elements. "Integration"—understood as a unilinear process towards ever closer convergence—was still regarded as the means towards the realisation of the ends of the EEC, and this convergence was first and foremost to be realised through the vehicle of the law. Law and integration were immutably linked. As Dagtoglou declared: "the European Community's legal order simultaneously presupposes and creates unity—and vice versa".[32] In the "writing of Europe",[33] lawyers presented an image of the EU legal order as predicated on consensus, on unity and cohesion, on the centrality of law, and as bestowed with an unassailable legitimacy and authority.

The dominance of these images derived great strength from a reading of the case law of the Court of Justice as constitutionalising the EC Treaty. Constitutionalisation in this (limited) sense had everything to do with a form of "federalisation" of the treaties by the Court of Justice through the principles of direct effect and supremacy of EC law in relation to national law, and the establishment of the duties of national courts as "Community courts". It had little, if anything, to do with the classic vision of constitutionalism as limited government under the rule of law. For while the Court of Justice has long recognised a doctrine of fundamental rights as general principles of EC law (Article 164 EC, now Article 220 EC), and much was made of this doctrine in the literature, it was effectively a limited doctrine oriented towards a goal of economic integration and the limitation of the sovereignty of the Member States. Likewise, a critical debate about the scope of competence was slow to emerge, since it was not necessarily at that time assumed (prior to the first formal expansion of competence in the form of the Single European Act 1986 and

[32] P Dagtoglou, "The Legal Nature of the European Community" in Commission of the European Communities (ed.), *Thirty Years of Community Law* (Luxembourg, OOPEC, 1981), p. 40.

[33] Schepel and Wesseling, *supra* n. 1.

at a time of "Eurosclerosis") that issues of excessive competence expansion might be raised.

On the other hand, it is of interest to note that in the context of the development of internal market law, the margins of provisions such as Article 30 guaranteeing the free movement of goods (now Article 28 EC) were just beginning to be explored in the mid-1980s, after the seminal *Cassis de Dijon* case[34] opened the floodgates for economic actors to attack all manner of seemingly non-discriminatory national measures restrictive of trade. In turn, of course, the mutual recognition doctrine enunciated in *Cassis* lays one of the foundation stones of the legal and legislative techniques of the single market programme and the Commission's White Paper, due out in 1985, on *Completing the Internal Market.*[35] The success of this regulatory programme, combined with the expansions of competence which occurred in the Single European Act (e.g. the environment) and the spread of qualified majority voting foreshadowed the perceived *need* for a competence-limiting principle such as subsidiarity within the legal order. In 1984, such reasons why the fear of expansive competence might arise could only be dreamed of. On the other hand, in an example of extraordinarily prescient scholarship, 1984 was the year of the publication of the first work on "flexibility" by Ehlermann,[36] a work accompanying the first round of debate on the possibility of "two speed Europe".

These readings seem to suggest a widespread, if implicit, acceptance of one of "grand" theories of integration, namely neofunctionalism, explaining the development of integration as an immutable process of "spillover" between domains and policy areas.[37] Such an interpretation also seems mandated by a one-dimensional view of the autonomy of the Court as an institution, insulated—for the most part—from political pressures exerted by the Member States. Yet by 1984 neofunctionalism was largely discredited, or in abeyance, as an accepted explanation of the integration process amongst political science and international relations scholars. The visible dominance of Member State preferences over institutional (quasi)autonomy seemed undeniable, and some form of inter-governmental explanation of the Communities as an international organisation seemed to be demanded. Indeed, the 1980s was the era of "interdependence" theory when integration and the Communities appeared less to be subjects of study in their own right, but aspects of a wider study of

[34] Case 120/78 *Rewe-Zentrale AG* v. *Bundesmonopolverwaltung für Branntwein* [1979] ECR 649.

[35] COM(85) 310.

[36] C D Ehlermann, "How Flexible is Community Law? An Unusual Approach to the Concept of 'Two Speeds'", (1984) 82 *Michigan Law Review* 1274.

[37] B Rosamund, *Theories of European Integration* (Basingstoke, Macmillan, 2000), ch. 3.

international relations.[38] This broader intellectual environment was little reflected in studies of the law.

In terms of scholarship and the style of scholarship, it was interesting in the 1980s to witness the dominance of the English textbook tradition[39] and orthodox legal scholarship. This is neatly described as work:

> "patterned on the work of the common law judges. Such work took it for granted that in the common law—the distilled wisdom of generations of lawyers—answers were to be found for all legal problems. One started, naturally, from the cases and either developed existing doctrine in slightly different ways or tidied up the work of the less gifted of the judges".[40]

This distillation process, however, reinforced the closure of the research discipline, making it seem above all the province of specialists who have charge of a holy grail. Yet all the while, there remained subcurrents of questioning of the perceived wisdom of the scholarly approach. American legal scholarship has been an important influence, and already in 1980 Martin Shapiro had launched his celebrated attack upon the interpretation of the "constitutional" jurisprudence of the Court of Justice. He argued that:

> "[such work] is a careful and systematic exposition of the judicial provisions of the 'constitution' of the [EEC]. . . But it represents a stage of constitutional scholarship out of which American constitutional law must have passed about seventy years ago. . . It is constitutional law without politics. [The work] presents the Community as a juristic idea; the written constitution as a sacred text; the professional commentary as a legal truth; the case law as the inevitable working out of the correct implications of the constitutional text; and the constitutional court as the disembodied voice of right reason and constitutional teleology. . . [S]uch an approach has proved fundamentally arid in the study of individual constitutions."[41]

Again, this is an opening of critique which significantly foreshadows the richness of the research discipline of fifteen or twenty years later.

Now

With the constitutionalisation of the principles of subsidiarity and flexibility through the Treaties of Maastricht and Amsterdam respectively, the simple teleology of integration as a unilinear process has been all but rejected. Indeed,

[38] For an overview, see C Webb, "Theoretical Prospects and Problems", in H Wallace, W Wallace and C Webb (eds), *Policy-Making in the European Community* (2nd edn., Chichester, John Wiley, 1983).

[39] D Sugarmann, "Legal Theory, the Common Law Mind and the Making of the Textbook Tradition", in W Twining (ed.), *Common Law and Legal Theory*, (Oxford, Blackwells, 1986).

[40] J Gava, "Scholarship and Community", (1994) 16 *Sydney Law Review* 442 at 444.

[41] M Shapiro, "Comparative Law and Comparative Politics", (1980) 53 *Southern California Law Review* 537 at 538.

the very notion of "integration" itself is problematised. Concomitant with this turn has been decline in the previously paradigmatic "grand theories" of integration. Within the disciplines of political science and international relations the debate has shifted from seeking to explain the processes of integration to exploring the functioning of the EU system of governance.[42] Increasing use is made of the tools of comparative politics so as to enable the EU to be studied as a polity.[43] A similar strand of enquiry is discernible within EU legal studies, whereby instead of searching for ways to explain, and indeed to celebrate the role of law in the process of integration, attention is turning to an exploration of the ways in which the law is implicated in the processes of governance.

There is thus emerging a body of work linked by a common perspective of the EU as a complex, multi-levelled governance structure. Lawyers are contributing to the attempts which are being made to conceptualise this entity—to answer, or at least to explore, the "paradox of the European Polity" (the paradox being that the EU is at once "near-state and antithetical to stateness").[44] The study of constitutionalism now draws on wider experiences and a wider range of levels of normative understanding of polity formation, and, in institutional terms, it goes beyond a preoccupation with the Court. A first step has been to reassess the claims of the Court of Justice to have constitutionalised and federalised the European (Community) legal order. Space has been created for a more pluralistic view than that developed by the Court, one which regards the Community and national legal orders as "interacting, not hierarchical, distinct but partially independent and partially overlapping because of the incomplete but sometimes exclusive competence of the Community".[45] Moving away still further from the Court of Justice's orthodoxy are works which attempt to conceptualise the legal order(s) in ways which begin at least to overcome the dominance of the statist paradigm; with approaches being developed from, for example, systems theory,[46] social constructivism,[47] and postmodernism.[48] New constitutional principles have been conceptualised and have entered the lexicon of EU law. These include subsidiarity, flexibility, the *acquis communautaire* and "pillarisation".

[42] An accessible overview of the field of European integration theory is provided in Rosamond, *supra* n. 37.

[43] The leading proponent of this view is perhaps S Hix, *The Political System of the European Union* (Basingstoke, Macmillan, 1999).

[44] J Shaw and A Wiener, "The Paradox of 'the European Polity'" Harvard Jean Monnet Working Papers, 10/99 (www.law.harvard.edu/).

[45] I Maher, "Community Law in the National Legal Order: A Systems Analysis" (1998) 36 *JCMS* 237 at 239.

[46] Maher, *ibid.*

[47] See *supra* n. 44.

[48] I Ward, "Identity and Difference: The European Union and Postmodernism" in Shaw and More, *supra* n. 5 and the papers in P Fitzpatrick and J H Bergeron (eds), *Europe's Other: European Law Between Modernity and PostModernity* (Aldershot, Dartmouth, 1998).

Other strands of EU legal studies focus in on the operation of the polity, and once liberated from the teleology and touchstone of integration, space emerges for more critical approaches to be taken. Thus diversity and difference within the EU can be explored, as can the internal fragmentation of the EU's political and legal order. The body of work which began emerge in the late 1980s and which challenges the legitimacy and authority of the Court of Justice[49] has been joined by works which extend a more critical approach to the EU as a whole.[50]

Within EU legal studies, there is an ever broader view of what may be considered a legitimate focus for study. The previous dominance of accounts of the Court of Justice and its "history-making" jurisprudence is being challenged by work which focuses less on the Court, less on the "constitutional moments", and more on the day-to-day operation of the EU. Lawyers are turning their focus beyond the outputs of the policy process and revealing the role of the law in areas often left unexplored through traditional doctrinal legal analysis. Greater attention is being paid to the structuring role that law plays in the processes of governance, with law presented as an institution, the legal order imposing a particular organisational structure, and carrying certain normative understandings which offer both constraints and opportunities to actors involved in the policy process. This attention is coming from those both inside and outside the legal discipline, as this image of the law and its institutional significance (understood in normative, organisational and procedural terms) feeds into developments in the disciplines of political science, sociology and economics, wherein the "new institutionalist" turn posits that a greater explanatory force should be afforded to the institutional dimensions of policy arenas.[51]

Such new institutionalist perspectives on EU governance should not be equated with a necessarily formalist, legalist view of the capacity of law and legal rules for the conditioning of behaviour. Instead of a ready acceptance of the regulative effects of formal rules and laws, such perspectives seek to locate and identify those institutionalised norms which *in fact* regulate behaviour. This line of enquiry additionally opens up a vista on the increasing use of non-traditional means of regulation, particularly within the internal market context—such as through contractual methods, the concept of partnership, and soft law.

Today, the field of EU legal studies as practised by UK-based scholars embraces an astonishingly varied and diverse range of work. Doctrinal, criti-

[49] Led by H Rasmussen's *On Law and Policy in the European Court of Justice* (Dordrecht, Martijnus Nijhoff, 1986).

[50] Weiler, *supra* n. 17; see I Ward, *The Margins of European Law* (London, Macmillan, 1996) who talks of finding the "sceptic".

[51] See on the "new institutionalism", Armstrong, *supra* n. 28.

cal, positivist, sociological, feminist, postmodernist, and inter-disciplinary approaches are all represented. The nature of the EU means that it presents a very obvious meeting place for scholars from diverse disciplines to come together to address key questions—questions of power, of legitimacy, of the relationships between the Member States and the Union, and those involved in EU legal studies are increasingly participating in these pluri-disciplinary debates.

Conclusion

Are we now, therefore, in the presence of a genuine academic discipline? If we are, then the irony is that the discipline has emerged as the legal order has become increasingly problematised. That is not to suggest that EC law has become practically less important. Clearly, this is not true, as the changed world of many legal practitioners or bureaucrats can testify. However, some of the orthodoxies about its singular and consistent nature as an order, as well as about the nature of its supremacy over national law, have been challenged. Perhaps, in turn, this makes it a more "genuine" legal order: that is, a legal order better fitted to a world of complex heterarchies and inter-dependencies. A world which is beyond the binary divide of international law and national law, and where—simultaneously—the nation state can remain a powerful force or figure and yet sovereignty can be intensely challenged. To the recognition of these complexities, and their incorporation in scholarship in the EU generally and its legal order specifically, can—in our view—be ascribed a powerful causal force in the transformation of the discipline.

8

Community Competition Law: Notification and Individual Exemption—Goodbye To All That

RICHARD WHISH, BRENDA SUFRIN

Introduction

On 28 April 1999, the Commission adopted a White Paper on modernisation of the rules implementing Articles 81 and 82 of the EC Treaty.[1] The proposals, if adopted, will revolutionise the way in which EC competition law is enforced. National competition authorities and national courts will have a far more prominent rôle; they will be able to rule on the applicability to agreements of Article 81(3) as well as Article 81(1); and the existing notification system will be eliminated. The proposals are radical, imaginative and controversial.

Article 81(1) prohibits agreements, decisions by associations of undertakings and concerted practices that have as their object or effect the restriction, prevention or distortion of competition and which have an effect on trade between Member States. Agreements that infringe Article 81(1) are void and unenforceable under Article 81(2). However, Article 81(1) "may be declared inapplicable" to agreements which satisfy the criteria of Article 81(3): that they will contribute to an improvement in the production or distribution of goods or of technical or economic progress, that consumers will get a fair share of the resulting benefit, that they do not contain restrictions that are dispensable, and that they do not substantially eliminate competition in the common market. Article 82 prohibits the abuse of a dominant position. Council Regulation 17/62[2] conferred powers on the Commission to enforce the competition rules. Article 9(1) of Regulation 17/62 provides that:

[1] OJ 1999 C 132/1, [1999] 5 CMLR 208.
[2] OJ Sp.Ed. 1959–62, 87.

"Subject to review of its decision by the Court of Justice, the Commission shall have sole power to declare Article 81(1) inapplicable pursuant to Article 81(3) of the Treaty".

This monopoly over the grant of exemptions has caused substantial problems in the enforcement of the competition rules. The White Paper offers a solution which is both breathtakingly simple and yet complex in its implications: the abandonment of the Commission's monopoly and the abolition of individual exemptions altogether. The authors of this chapter strongly support the Commission's proposal, while acknowledging that numerous measures will have to be taken to ensure that the new system works efficiently and that the competition rules are applied in a consistent manner across the Community.

Summary of the Proposals

The White Paper begins by explaining that when Regulation 17/62 was adopted, it was decided that there should be a centralised authorisation system for exemption under Article 81(3) so that the Commission could create a "culture of competition" in Europe and ensure the integration of national markets. However, the centralised system devised in 1962 when there were six Member States "is no longer appropriate for the Community of today with 15 Member States, 11 languages and over 350 million inhabitants".[3] The system of exclusive notification to the Commission of agreements requiring exemption has thwarted its attempts to achieve decentralisation of the enforcement of the competition rules. Notices in 1993 and 1997 which were intended to give impetus to increased enforcement of the rules by national courts and national competition authorities (NCAs) respectively[4] "have now reached their limits within the existing legal framework".[5]

The need for the Commission to devote resources to dealing with notifications hinders it in the performance of tasks that it considers more important: dealing with cross-border cartels, maintaining competitive market structures, merger control, the liberalisation of hitherto monopolised markets and international co-operation.[6] The Commission notes the numerous steps that have

[3] White Paper, "Executive Summary", para. 5.

[4] Commission Notice on cooperation between national courts and the Commission applying Articles 81 and 82 of the EEC Treaty, OJ 1993 C 39/6; Commission Notice on cooperation between the national competition authorities and the Commission in handling cases falling within the scope of Articles 81 and 82, OJ 1997 C 313/3.

[5] White Paper, para. 39.

[6] *Ibid.*, "Executive Summary", para. 8.

been taken to alleviate the burden of notification: for example, the provision of guidance as to those agreements that fall outside Article 81(1) in a series of Notices; the adoption of block exemptions; and speedier settlement of cases, in particular by so-called "comfort letters". However, further accessions to the Community in the near future will lead to more notifications, exacerbating the Commission's problems.

In the Commission's view, the time has come for "radical reforms" to be considered; it is no longer possible to retain a centralised prior authorisation system in Brussels.[7] The notification system tends to force the Commission to adopt an essentially reactive stance, dealing with the agreements notified to it.[8] Instead, the burden of enforcement, *including a determination of whether the criteria of Article 81(3) are satisfied*, should be the prime responsibility of national courts and NCAs. The Commission therefore proposes that the notification and exemption system in Regulation 17/62 should be abolished and replaced by a Council Regulation which would render the criteria in Article 81(3) directly applicable without prior decision of the Commission. Prior authorisation would be replaced by directly applicable exceptions:[9] "Article 81 would then become *a unitary norm comprising a rule establishing the principle of prohibition unless certain conditions are met*" (Commission's own emphasis).[10] However, one particular category of agreement, partial-function joint ventures, should continue to be subject to an authorisation system.[11]

Crucially, there are two strands to this proposal: first, that the system of notification should be abandoned and secondly, that the Commission should abandon its monopoly of decision-making under Article 81(3). Early reaction to the White Paper resulted in greater concern about the former than the latter.

The Ending of the Notification and Authorisation System

The Commission notes[12] the workload and expense involved in having to notify under the existing system, but says that notification proved useful "as long as the interpretation of Article 81 and in particular of paragraph 3 was

[7] *Ibid.*, para. 40.

[8] *Ibid.*, paras 44–5, where the Commission points out that of new cases commenced between 1988 and 1998, only 13 per cent were commenced as a result of its own initiatives, whereas 58 per cent arose from notifications and 29 per cent from complaints.

[9] The White Paper considers the respective merits of the authorisation system and a directly applicable exception system at paras 55–73.

[10] White Paper, para. 69.

[11] *Ibid.*, paras 79–81 and see *infra*.

[12] *Ibid.*, para. 76.

uncertain".[13] In a system of *ex post* control, undertakings would have to make their own assessment of the compatibility of their restrictive practices with Community law, which would lighten their administrative burden, but would require them to take on added responsibility.[14]

The Commission avers that in the new system "undertakings' legal certainty will remain at a globally satisfactory level, and will in some respects even be strengthened".[15] Among the reasons given for this somewhat insouciant statement are that, after forty years of the competition rules, the conditions for the application of Article 81(3) have been largely clarified; that a new generation of block exemptions with a wider scope of application is about to come into being; that the Commission will adopt a more economic approach to Article 81(1) when dealing with individual cases (so that Article 81(3) would not be relevant to the analysis of many cases where there is no market power); and that there will be "preventive and corrective mechanisms" to ensure consistent and uniform application of Community law by national authorities and courts.

Decentralised Application of the Competition Rules

There will be a new division of responsibilities. The Commission will continue to determine competition policy in various ways.[16] It will retain the sole right to propose legislative texts, regulations (including block exemptions[17]), notices and guidelines; and will continue to adopt prohibition decisions, which will be of great importance as precedents. As it would be concentrating on the most serious restrictions of competition rather than scrutinising notified agreements which tend to be innocuous, the number of individual prohibition decisions can be expected to increase substantially.[18] However, the Commission will no longer grant individual exemptions: the whole point is that the new system will not require a constitutive act by the Commission in order to declare the prohibition of Article 81(1) inapplicable. Nevertheless the Commission says that it will sometimes adopt decisions that are not prohibition decisions, for example where new questions arise and a declaration of the Commission's position in relation to them is needed.[19]

[13] *Ibid.*, para. 77

[14] *Ibid.*

[15] *Ibid.*, para. 78.

[16] *Ibid.*, paras 83–90.

[17] However, since a constitutive act will no longer be necessary under Article 81(3), they will be block "clearances" rather than block exemptions.

[18] White Paper, para. 87.

[19] *Ibid.*, paras 88 and 89.

The Commission proposes[20] a new kind of decision, terminating proceedings that would otherwise have led to a prohibition, where suitable commitments have been offered by the parties. The possibility of fines and periodic penalty payments would have to be introduced in order to ensure that such commitments are complied with. The Commission does not say so specifically, but there is an obvious precedent for such decisions in Article 8(2) of the European Community Merger Regulation 4064/89 (the ECMR).[21]

The Commission wishes to see national competition authorities play an enhanced rôle in the application of the competition rules.[22] It notes that, although there has been pragmatic co-operation between itself and the national competition authorities (NCAs) to date, this has been limited as a result of its exclusive right to grant exemptions. For the new system to work, each NCA will have to be given the power, as a matter of domestic law, to apply Community law. At the moment, there are seven Member States (including the United Kingdom) that have not empowered their NCAs to do this, although it is arguable that Article 10 of the EC Treaty, which imposes on Member States the duty to fulfil their Community obligations and to facilitate the achievement of the Community's tasks, requires that such powers should be made available. The Commission has subsequently stated its intention that the new procedural regulation will state expressly that Member States must provide for this.

The national courts are also to play an enhanced rôle in the application of the competition rules. The Commission has for a long time been keen to see more enforcement of Articles 81 and 82 in national courts and this is seen in the 1993 Notice on Cooperation.[23] The inability of national courts to exempt agreements under Article 81(3) has been a major obstacle and there has been relatively little recourse to national courts, as discussed below. With a directly applicable exception the Commission says that parties to agreements will be able to obtain a judgment from national courts both on Article 81(1) and Article 81(3), and this will provide them with greater legal certainty; furthermore third parties will be able to obtain damages more quickly, without the national action being stayed pending a decision of the Commission on the application of Article 81(3). The judgments of national courts would be *res judicata* (subject to any appeal), and would be entitled to recognition in all other Member States of the EU and Contracting States of the EEA under the Brussels and Lugano Conventions respectively.[24]

20 *Ibid.*, para. 90.

21 Council Regulation 4064/89, OJ 1989 L 395/1, corrected version OJ 1990 L 257/13, as amended by Council Regulation 1310/97, OJ 1997 L 180/1.

22 White Paper, paras 91–8.

23 See *supra* n. 4.

24 Brussels Convention on Jurisdiction and the Enforcement of Judgments in Civil and Commercial Matters 1968; Lugano Convention 1988, OJ 1988 L 391/1.

Paragraphs 101 to 107 of the White Paper address the need to maintain consistency and uniform application of the competition rules. In one of the less convincing passages of the document, the Commission sets out various principles for the resolution of conflicts which, it claims, should allow any problems that may arise to be resolved. The Commission suggests that mechanisms should be set up to buttress the need for consistency. NCAs would have to inform the Commission of the initiation of proceedings or of the withdrawal of the benefit of block exemption.[25] The Commission would be able to take a case out of the jurisdiction of an NCA where appropriate. NCAs would also be obliged to inform the Commission of any proceedings under national law that might have implications for Community proceedings. The Advisory Committee on Restrictive Practices and Dominant Positions would have a reinforced rôle and become a full-scale forum in which important cases would be discussed irrespective of the competition authority dealing with them.[26] The Commission proposes that national courts would be obliged by regulation to make the Commission aware of any proceedings involving the Community competition rules, a precedent for which exists in paragraph 96 of the German Act against Restrictions of Competition, which obliges the German court to inform the Bundeskartellamt of any proceedings.[27] The Commission would be given the right to intervene as *amicus curiae* in domestic proceedings, and the rules in the 1993 Notice on Cooperation would also be incorporated in the regulation amending Regulation 17/62.

Implications of the Proposals

The Commission never specifically acknowledges one central problem: it does not have, and will not be given, adequate resources by the Member States to act as a pan-European competition authority. Its staffing is meagre, and its range of responsibilities vast. Without considerable new resources, the system is on the verge of collapse, in particular as ten or more further accessions to the Community are anticipated over the next decade. There is a heavy dose of pragmatism about the proposal for abandonment of notification and the pursuance of decentralisation: if Member States will not give the resources to the

[25] Provision has been made for withdrawal of block exemption by NCAs by Article 1(4) of Regulation 1215/1999, OJ 1999 L 148/1, amending Article 7 of Regulation 19/65 OJ 1965 L66/35, where an agreement has a detrimental effect on competition in a "distinct market" in that Member State; Article 6 of the new block exemption on vertical agreements, Regulation 2790/1999, OJ 1999 L 336/21, expressly provides for this.

[26] White Paper, para. 106.

[27] *Ibid.*, para. 107.

Commission, then the Commission will hand the responsibility back to the Member States.

The White Paper triggered a wide-ranging debate. Responses were submitted to the Commission by individuals, companies, trade associations, Community and national institutions and by the Member States themselves. The German Government issued a statement[28] setting out its doubts about the proposals, questioning the very legality of the suggestion that Article 81(3) could be directly applicable and that notification should be eliminated. The European Parliament investigated and presented a report on 30 November 1999 which was broadly supportive of the proposals.[29] In the United Kingdom the CBI's Position Paper of 29 September 1999 was critical of many features of the proposals, in particular on decentralisation and the abolition of notification. The House of Lords Select Committee on the European Communities published a wide-ranging Report and accompanying evidence on 29 February 2000;[30] this Report acknowledged the "bold and imaginative initiative" of the Commission,[31] but concluded that much more work needs to be done before the proposals could be implemented: otherwise, adoption of the White Paper would "involve a great step into the unknown".[32] The Report also raised the question of whether the time might not be approaching when Article 81 itself might be reformulated, so as to make it more amenable to national judges.[33]

A number of issues arise from the White Paper and the responses to it.

Is the Proposal to Make Article 81(3) Directly Applicable Lawful under the Treaty?

The initial problem to consider is whether the proposal to make Article 81(3) directly applicable is compatible with the Treaty. The first issue is textual: does the language of Article 81(3) itself lend itself to direct applicability? In paragraphs 11 and 12 of the White Paper the Commission states that, although the national delegations who met in Messina to draft the EC Treaty were agreed on the necessity of a system of competition law based on the prohibition principle, they disagreed on the method whereby the Article 81(1) prohibition could be lifted from an agreement because it satisfied the criteria set out in Article 81(3). Two choices were available. One, that an agreement that infringed Article 81(1) could escape the prohibition of that Article (and the

[28] Statement by the Government of the Federal Republic of Germany, November 1999.

[29] *Report on the Commission White Paper on Modernisation of the Rules Implementing Articles 85 and 86 of the EC Treaty* (Final A5–0069/1999).

[30] HL 33 (2000).

[31] *Ibid*, para. 145.

[32] *Ibid*, para. 147.

[33] *Ibid.*, para. 149.

voidness provided for by Article 81(2)) only where a prior authorisation was given to it by a public agency such as the Commission: a "constitutive" act was needed in order to invest the agreement with a validity that it would otherwise lack. The alternative choice was the idea of a directly applicable exception ("*de l'exception légale*"), according to which all the provisions of Article 81—both Article 81(1) and Article 81(3)—should be applied to an agreement to determine whether or not it was lawful, without the need for a positive, constitutive act. The inability to agree which of these two approaches was appropriate led to a compromise:[34] by phrasing Article 81(3) in a negative manner (Article 81(1) "may be declared inapplicable"), rather than a positive one (agreements "may be declared valid"), the choice between an authorisation system on the one hand and a directly applicable exception system on the other was left to the Community legislator, for this purpose the Council of Ministers: that choice was subsequently made in Article 9(1) of Council Regulation 17/62, which adopted a system of prior authorisation. According to this view, it remains possible to scrap prior authorisation, which was introduced only by secondary legislation, and to introduce a directly applicable exception system, which was an option provided for in the Treaty itself.

It can be argued that the text of Article 81 does not support this construction: for example Article 81(2) provides that agreements *that infringe Article 81(1)* shall be automatically void, whereas Article 81(3) provides that Article 81(1) *may be declared inapplicable*: the temporal language here suggests that a constitutive act by a public authority is needed to lift the inherent voidness of agreements that infringe Article 81(1). The point was considered by Advocate General Lagrange in *De Geus* v. *Bosch*[35] in 1962. He recognised the two possible theories, of the requirement of a constitutive effect on the one hand and of legal exception on the other. He personally thought that the legal exception approach was particularly suited to the application of the EC Treaty, since it would ensure that the questions posed by Article 81(1) and 81(3) would be examined at the same time, by the same authority or court, and that there would be no difficulty over the effects of the automatic nullity.[36] However, he accepted that the constitutive decision theory had been given the force of law by Regulation 17/62 and admitted that "it must be recognized that this accords best with the text of Article 85(3) [now Article 81(3)]". He said that:

> "The theory depending on *l'exception légale* would have required a different text, for example: 'The provisions of paragraph (1) shall be deemed not to apply . . .' or simply 'shall not apply'."[37]

[34] The disagreement was fundamentally one between Germany and France.
[35] Case 13/61 [1962] ECR 45, [1962] CMLR 1.
[36] Exactly the attractions now espoused by the Commission.
[37] [1962] ECR 45 at 67.

Professor Arved Deringer, the head of the committee which drafted Regulation 17/62, writing in 1963, thought that Article 81(3) was not susceptible to a legal exception system. He considered that removing the prohibition was a normative activity belonging to the realm of the administration and not that of the courts and that "[e]ven if the Commission had not been given exclusive jurisdiction, the national courts could only apply Article 85(3) [now Article 81(3)] if this power had been specifically conferred upon them".[38]

Since those heady days in the early 1960s when implementing powers were first made available to the Commission to enforce Articles 81 and 82, there has been little discussion of the wording of Article 81(3). Attention since then has been focused on whether the Commission would be prepared to advocate that the Council should amend Article 9(1) of Regulation 17/62 to decentralise the granting of exemption decisions to NCAs: an extension of the authorisation procedure, not a revocation of it. The Commission's proposal to render Article 81(3) directly applicable is radically different, and necessitates a careful examination of the phraseology of Article 81(3) for the first time for forty years. The issue of what exactly Article 81(3) means has awoken from a long sleep, and requires us now to put ourselves in the position of policy-makers in the late 1950s and early 1960s: the accretion of nearly 40 years of administrative experience of notification and individual exemption under Regulation 17/62 must not blind us to the possibilities that existed prior to its adoption. The authors of this chapter acknowledge the arguments on both sides, but take the view that the Treaty did indeed envisage a choice between the authorisation system and direct applicability; and predict that the Court of Justice would be likely to uphold a Council regulation that revoked Regulation 17/62 and replaced it with the system proposed in the White Paper.

The second issue in relation to the direct applicability of Article 81(3) concerns the way in which the Community legal order determines whether a Treaty provision is directly applicable in the first place. The White Paper states that:

> "the switch to such a [directly applicable exception] system can be achieved by a Council Regulation, based on Article 87 [now Article 83] of the Treaty, which would stipulate that all national authorities or courts before which the applicability of Article 85(1) of the Treaty was invoked would also consider the applicability of Article 85(3)".

Articles of the Treaty, however, have hitherto been held to be directly applicable only by a ruling of the Court of Justice, not by a decision of the Council of

[38] A Deringer, "*The Distribution of Powers in the Enforcement of the Rules of Competition under the Rome Treaty*" [1963] 1 *CMLRev* 30 at 34. Professor Deringer remains of this view: see his evidence to the House of Lords Select Committee on the European Union, 4th Report, 1999–2000, para. 31.

Ministers. Treaty Articles are silent as to their direct applicability[39] and Hartley maintains that it is probable that the authors of the original Treaties assumed that the question would be decided by national courts according to the criteria of national law.[40] The assumption of jurisdiction over this issue by the Court in *Van Gend en Loos*[41] changed the face of the Community legal order for ever. The Court's view is that, when it rules on the interpretation of a Community law provision, it is applicable even to legal relationships arising and established before the judgment, because it "clarifies and defines where necessary the meaning and scope of that rule as it must be or ought to have been understood and applied from the time of its coming into force",[42] although it can restrict the retroactivity of its judgments.[43]

The foregoing argument would suggest that the reason that Article 81(3) is not directly applicable is *not* because Article 9(1) of Regulation 17/62 gives the Commission a monopoly in deciding on its application, but because Article 81(3) has never been held to be directly applicable by the Court of Justice. The revocation of Article 9(1) of Regulation 17/62, and a stipulation in a Council Regulation that Article 81(3) was directly applicable, would and could not suffice to make it so. Of course, in the first case to come before the Court in which the issue was raised, it could determine that Article 81(3) was directly applicable, but this would only go to demonstrate that it is the Court and not the Council which decides the issue. The acquiescence of the Court should not, in the meantime, be taken for granted. It is true that in *Bosch*[44] Advocate General Lagrange was reluctant to advise the Court to find Regulation 17/62 itself to be illegal:

> "It cannot be contended that the Regulation is illegal as being contrary to the Treaty . . .; to declare such a Regulation illegal would be a step of such gravity that this Court, in my view, ought not to contemplate it except when the illegality is quite plain".

However, since those early days the Court has shown that it is not timorous of striking down Council Regulations, which it has done on several occasions.[45]

[39] The expression "direct applicability" is used here to encompass both direct applicability and direct effect: even if there is a distinction between these concepts, it is not one which is relevant in the present context . In contrast, Article 34 of the Maastricht Treaty on European Union specifically provides that decisions taken by the Member States under that Article shall not entail direct effect.

[40] T Hartley, *The Foundations of European Community Law* (4th edn., Oxford, 1998), p. 196.

[41] Case C-26/62 [1963] ECR 1, [1963] CMLR 105.

[42] Case 61/79 *Amministrazione delle Finanze dello Stato* v. *Denkavit Italiana* [1980] ECR 1205 at para. 16.

[43] See Case 43/75 *Defrenne* v. *SABENA (No. 2)* [1976] ECR 455, [1976] 2 CMLR 98 and Case C-262/88 *Barber* v. *GRE* [1990] ECR I-1889, [1990] 2 CMLR 513; W Alexander, "*The Temporal Effects of Preliminary Rulings*" [1988] *YEL* 11.

[44] Case 13/61 [1962] ECR 45 at 67.

[45] See for example Case 138/79 *Roquette Frères SA* v. Council [1980] ECR 3333; Case C-309/89 *Codorniu* v. *Council* [1994] ECR I-1853, [1995] 2 CMLR 561.

Another issue is whether the criteria for direct applicability laid down by the Court of Justice are satisfied in the case of Article 81(3). Originally, in *Van Gend en Loos*,[46] these were strict: the provision had to be clear, negative, unconditional, containing no reservation on the part of the Member State and not dependent on national implementing measures. These conditions have gradually been loosened. The watershed was *Defrenne* v. *SABENA*,[47] where the provision under scrutiny for direct applicability was expressed as a "principle", was not couched as a negative obligation and contained imprecise and undefined expressions. Since then many Treaty Articles have been held to be directly applicable. Pescatore has argued that direct effect is the normal characteristic of Community law, and that it simply comes down to a question of justiciability.[48]

The Court will deny direct applicability to provisions which require the discretionary intervention of a Member State[49] or which are aspirational in character, containing "expressions of intent, purpose and motive, rather than rules that are of direct operative effect".[50] Article 81(3) is not aspirational in this sense. It does entail the exercise of discretion: consumers must derive a "fair share" of any benefit; restrictions must not be "indispensable" and competition must not be "substantially" eliminated. However, judgments of this nature have to be made under Article 81(1), Article 82 and, indeed, under other provisions in the Treaty: Article 28, for example, requires judges to decide whether a measure has equivalent effect to a quantitative restriction, whether it comes within the so-called "mandatory requirements" or is covered by the derogation in Article 30. If Article 81(3) is not justiciable, it is not because it is aspirational, or because judges are left to make difficult decisions within a broad discretion, but because in making those decisions they may be required to balance public and private interests, and this is something which a court is inherently inappropriate to do. This brings us to a further question, which is at heart of the matter: what is Article 81(3) really about?

[46] Case C-26/62 [1963] ECR 1, [1963] CMLR 105.

[47] See *supra* n. 43.

[48] P Pescatore, "*The Doctrine of "Direct Effect": An Infant Disease of Community Law*" (1983) 8 *ELRev* 155.

[49] See for example Article 31(1) (ex Article 37(1)) imposing on Member States the obligation to "progressively adjust any State monopolies of a commercial character".

[50] Per Advocate General Mancini in Case 126/86 *Zaera* v. *Institutio Nacionale de la Seguridad Social* [1987] ECR 3697, [1989] 1 CMLR 827, in relation to Article 2, which the Court of Justice confirmed could not impose legal obligations on Member States or confer rights on individuals (para. 11).

Are National Courts Appropriate Fora for Determinations on (a) the Competition Rules Generally and (b) More Specifically on the Criteria in Article 81(3)?

The suitability of Article 81(3) for direct applicability cannot be answered without addressing the question of what, exactly, Article 81(3) is intended to achieve. This is not a new puzzle. The bifurcation of analysis between Article 81(1) and Article 81(3) has had a profound effect on the way in which competition law and practice has developed; the authorisation procedure in Regulation 17/62 has contributed to this. The possibility of exemption led to the adoption by the Commission, in particular in the early years, of a wide interpretation of the term "restriction of competition" under Article 81(1); agreements "caught in the net" of Article 81(1) could nevertheless be "rescued" by exemption under Article 81(3). This however resulted in intellectual confusion and practical problems. The intellectual confusion has been twofold: first, the failure to develop a coherent body of law on the meaning of a restriction of competition under Article 81(1); the second confusion has been in determining how the questions posed by Article 81(3) relate to the analysis of agreements under Article 81(1). It is noticeable that, nearly forty years after the competition rules were brought into force by Regulation 17/62, this confusion remains. The practical problems are the very ones that caused the Commission to adopt the White Paper and which have been rehearsed above, such as the burden of notification and the diversion of the Commission's scarce resources away from more important tasks.

As to the meaning of a restriction of competition under Article 81(1), the Community Courts have, in a number of judgments, demonstrated that not every contractual restriction is necessarily restrictive of competition and that, apart from those agreements that entail "obvious" or "hard-core" restrictions of competition such as price-fixing or market-sharing, full analysis is needed of an agreement in its factual, legal and economic context before it can be condemned under Article 81(1).[51] The Commission, also, can more easily be persuaded now than was formerly the case that an agreement is not restrictive of competition.[52] However, Article 81(1) still does not incorporate an American style "rule of reason", and undoubtedly can capture agreements that would not infringe section 1 of the Sherman Act 1890 in that jurisdiction. One cause of this is the single market imperative, which continues to have a profound influ-

[51] Case C-234/89 *Stergios Delimitis* v. *Henniger Bräu* [1991] ECR I-935, [1992] 5 CMLR 210; Case C-250/92 *Gøttrup Klim* v. *KLG* [1994] ECR I- 5641, [1996] 4 CMLR 191; Cases T-374/91 etc. *European Night Services* v. *Commission* [1998] ECR II-3141, [1998] 5 CMLR 718.

[52] See for example the joint venture decision *Re Cégétel: Vivendi/BT/Mannesmann/SBC International* OJ 1999 L 218/14, [2000] 4 CMLR 106.

ence in the EC context and which leads, for example, to the condemnation of export bans in distribution agreements that would not concern other competition authorities.[53] However, quite apart from single market considerations, the very structure of Article 81 suggests a different approach to the analysis of agreements than in the USA: there, the pro- and anti-competitive effects of an agreement must be balanced against one another in determining whether section 1 of the Sherman Act has been infringed. The bifurcation in Article 81 suggests a different approach: clearly it was envisaged that some questions would be divorced from Article 81(1) and answered by reference to the criteria in Article 81(3), but what, precisely, are those questions?

The White Paper recognises the conundrum, and concludes that if a more systematic use were made of a "rule of reason" approach under Article 81(1), analysing the pro- and anti-competitive aspects of an agreement at that stage, "Article [81](3) would be cast aside". It says that this could not happen without a revision of the EC Treaty, and that it would anyway be paradoxical since Article 81(3) contains "all the elements of a 'rule of reason'".[54] The White Paper appears to answer the "what is Article 81(3) about" question by suggesting that it provides something like the rule of reason in American law; it expressly says that Article 81(3) is "to provide a legal framework for the economic assessment of restrictive practices and not to allow the application of the competition rules to be set aside because of political considerations".[55] It is not clear to the authors of this chapter that Article 81(3) is as simple as this: as already noted, confusion surrounds this issue.

The idea that Article 81(3) brings into the equation matters other than purely competition considerations evokes horror in some quarters;[56] it runs counter to theories of competition policy which have economic efficiency as the sole goal of antitrust. However, Community competition policy does not exist in splendid isolation but in the context of the whole European adventure. It is one means by which the objectives in Article 2 of the EC Treaty can be advanced, and it co-exists, for example, with the regional, social, cultural, environmental and industrial policies of the Community. Competition policy cannot be divorced from these other policies. For example, in the early days competition policy was influenced by industrial policy, and this can still be

[53] In the United Kingdom, section 50 of the Competition Act 1998 provides that the Secretary of State may by order exclude vertical agreements from the Act: this was done in relation to the Chapter I prohibition (the domestic analogue of Article 81) for all vertical agreements other than those imposing minimum or fixed resale prices by the Competition Act 1998 (Land and Vertical Agreements) Exclusion Order 2000, SI 2000/310.

[54] White Paper, para. 57.

[55] *Ibid.*

[56] See for example E Fox in *European Competition Law Annual 1997* (Ehlermann and Laudati (eds), Hart Publishing, 1998) at 478–80.

detected in matters presented in the guise of antitrust:[57] for example Amato points to the block exemption for specialisation agreements, with its acceptance that rationalisation in production fulfils the Article 81(3) criteria, as reflecting industrial policy rather than competition thinking.[58] This has not changed: the recitals in the draft of the new block exemption for such agreements sent out for consultation on 20 January 2000 express the same policy.[59] Another example is cultural policy: in the case of the Commission's action on fixed prices for the retailing of German-language books, Commissioner Monti announced that the solution reached was fully supported by the Commissioner for Culture and Education "with whom I have maintained regular contacts on this matter".[60]

There are many instances where non-competition matters have intruded into Article 81(3). In *Metro* v. *Commission*[61] the Court of Justice considered that employment was a relevant factor under the first condition in Article 81(3), saying the agreement was "a stabilizing factor with regard to the provision of employment which, since it improves the general conditions of production, especially when market conditions are unfavourable, comes within the framework of the objectives to which reference may be had pursuant to Article 85(3) [now Article 81(3)]". When considering whether an exemption might be given to a joint venture to produce a "multi-purpose vehicle" in Portugal in *Ford/Volkswagen,* the Commission "took note" of "exceptional circumstances" in that it would bring a large number of jobs and substantial foreign investment to one of the poorest regions of the Community, promoting harmonious development, reducing regional disparities and furthering European market integration.[62] It emphasised, however, that it would not be enough to make an exemption possible unless the other conditions of Article 81(3) were fulfilled.[63] In its submissions to the CFI when the decision was challenged, the Commission argued that it was possible to take into account factors other than those expressly mentioned in Article 81(3), including, for example, the maintenance of employment.[64] The Commission has been con-

[57] Note that by Article 157 (formerly Article 130, introduced by the Maastricht Treaty) the Community's industrial policy is to be conducted "in accordance with a system of open and competitive markets".

[58] G Amato, *Antitrust and the Bounds of Power* (Hart Publishing, 1997), pp. 63–4.

[59] Recitals 8 and 3 respectively.

[60] IP/00/183 of 23 February 2000. The German Government had called upon the Commission to remember cultural policy when deciding whether to unpick the resale price maintenance scheme for German language books and the Council of Ministers has made the same point: see the Council Resolution on fixed book prices in homogeneous cross-border linguistic areas, OJ 1999 C 42/3.

[61] Case 26/76 *Metro* v. *Commission (No. 1)* [1977] ECR 1875, [1978] 2 CMLR 1 at para. 43.

[62] OJ 1993 L 20/14, [1993] 5 CMLR 617 at paras 23, 28 and 36; see also the Commission Press Release, IP/92/1083 of 23 December 1992.

[63] *Ibid.*, para. 36.

[64] Case T-17/93 *Matra Hachette* v. *Commission* [1994] ECR II-595 at para. 96.

sidering the question of exempting the collective selling of broadcasting rights for football[65] and appears unwilling to limit the analysis to "simple economic considerations", but to recognise the need to redistribute revenue in order "to promote sporting activities within the population, as well as providing for interesting sporting competitions".[66] In *Stichting Baksteen*[67] the restructuring of the Dutch brick industry involving co-ordinated closures ensuring that the restructuring "could be carried out in acceptable social conditions, including the redeployment of employees" and the agreement in question was held to promote technical and economic progress.[68] Benefits to the environment led to an exemption for an agreement between members of the European Council of Manufacturers of Domestic Appliances, announced on 11 February 2000.[69]

It is clear, therefore, that the intrusion of "non-competition factors" into decisions under Article 81(3) was not confined to the early days of EC antitrust, and the majority view seems to be that on balance Article 81(3) does admit of non-competition considerations.[70] It is interesting to note in passing that the ECMR also refers to "technical and economic progress",[71] but only as one of the "appraisal criteria" to be taken into account by the Commission when making a decision on the compatibility of a concentration with the common market, and only provided that it is to the consumers' advantage and is not an obstacle to competition; it appears from this formulation that technical and economic progress cannot trump the anti-competitive effect of the creation or strengthening of a dominant position, in the way that Article 81(3) can trump the restriction of competition under Article 81(1).[72] There is an asymmetry between Article 81(3) and the treatment of technical and economic progress in the ECMR, and Ehlermann has remarked that it may not be sustainable in the long run to have a strictly economic competition goal in the ECMR but non-economic considerations included in Article 81(3).[73]

[65] In the wake of the RPC case in the United Kingdom on the selling of broadcasting rights by the Premier League, *Re the Football Association Premier League Ltd* (28 July 1999), the Commission asked the parties to notify the relevant agreements.

[66] See Jean-François Pons, "Sport and European Competition Policy", 26th Fordham Corporate Law Institute, 14–15 October 1999.

[67] OJ 1994 L 131/15, [1995] 4 CMLR 646.

[68] *Ibid.*, paras 27–28.

[69] Commission Press Release IP/00/148.

[70] See the comments by Mario Siragusa in Ehlermann and Laudati (eds), *supra* n. 56, at 39. Jonathan Faull, giving the Burrell lecture in London, 21 February 2000, said that social policy can "reasonably credibly" be brought within Article 81(3).

[71] Council Regulation 4064/89, Article 2(1)(b).

[72] See *MSG/Media Service* OJ 1994 L 364/1, para. 100; *Nordic Satellite Distribution* OJ 1996 L 53/20; technical or economic progress under Article 81(3) may, however, have to be considered when the test in Article 2(4) of the ECMR is applied to the co-ordination aspects of a joint venture.

[73] See C-D Ehlermann in Ehlermann and Laudati (eds), *supra* n. 56, at 480.

In considering whether national courts are appropriate fora for making determinations under Article 81(3), the authors of this chapter stress that in their view the problem is emphatically *not* that economics is too difficult for judges. The issue of whether there is a restriction of competition, which is already within the ambit of national judges given that Article 81(1) is directly applicable, in itself demands economic analysis, which may be more complex than the application of Article 81(3) in its narrow "competition" sense.[74] The point is rather that, if the question asked by Article 81(3) does require the consideration of *non-competition matters*, it is arguable that this needs a public body to do it because the nature of the decision, which involves a balancing of public and private interests and of the requirements of different Community policies, is unsuited to judicial determination. Other Member States, in adopting Community style competition provisions in their domestic laws, have not taken on board the broad sweep of Article 81(3),[75] and exemptions under the Competition Act 1998 in the United Kingdom will be given by the Director General of Fair Trading, not the courts.[76] There seems little judicial enthusiasm in the United Kingdom for applying Article 81(3).[77]

To sum up: whether or not non-competition policies *should* be taken into account under Article 81(3), the conclusion must be that it is inconvenient in terms of the White Paper if they *are*, because interpreted broadly the Article 81(3) criteria are inimical to direct applicability. If the Commission says long and hard enough in the lead up to any implementation of the White Paper that the purpose of Article 81(3) is only to provide for additional economic analysis, and follows a self-denying ordinance in any exemptions it issues, that interpretation may for practical purposes become the orthodoxy. The difficulty, of course, would be if the Court were to continue to interpret Article 81(3) to admit other policies, as it has been prepared to do in the past. It is, in any event, impossible to disguise the fact that the White Paper proposals do not merely concern matters of procedure, but go to the meaning of Article 81(3) itself. It may be that the Commission should go further than the White Paper proposal and advocate the abolition of Article 81(3) altogether, leaving the entire analysis of agreement to the test set out in Article 81(1): that, however, would require a Treaty amendment.[78]

[74] For cases in the English courts where judges have shown considerable sophistication of these matters see for example *Society of Lloyds* v. *Clementson* [1995] 1 CMLR 693, [1995] CLC 117; *Higgins* v. *Marchant & Eliot Underwriting Ltd* [1996] 3 CMLR 313 QB, [1996] 3 CMLR 349, CA; *Oakdale (Richmond) Ltd* v. *National Westminster Bank plc Oakdale (Richmond) Ltd* v. *National Westminster Bank plc* [1997] EuLR 7, 40; affirmed [1997] 3 CMLR 815.

[75] This is true, for example, of the law in Germany.

[76] Competition Act 1998, s. 4.

[77] See for example Eady J in *Williams* v. *Welsh Rugby Union* [1999] EuLR 195; and the evidence of Ferris J and Laddie J to the House of Lords Select Committee, HL 33 (2000), para. 59.

[78] Note that the House of Lords Select Committee itself raised this suggestion: HL 33 (2000) at para. 149.

The Rôle of the National Courts in the Proposed New System

If one makes the assumption that Article 81(3) is capable of direct applicability, notwithstanding the foregoing arguments, it is necessary to consider how a national court would actually proceed under the new system. Under English law a court can give a ruling only where there is a genuine *lis inter partes*: it would not be able to grant a declaration to the parties to the agreement who, deprived of the possibility of notifying their agreement to the Commission for an exemption, seek a declaratory judgment instead. Furthermore, a court could pronounce on the lawfulness of an agreement only at the time of its judgment or at the time relevant to the dispute: it would not be able to rule upon the future legality of the agreement. This is very different from the content of an Article 81(3) exemption, which is stated to last for a set period of time in the future, may come with conditions and obligations attached, and can be pursuant to modifications by the parties of their agreement following negotiations with the Commission. The application of a directly applicable exception by a court is a quite different creature. It is difficult, for example, to see how a court could achieve the outcome engineered by the Commission in *British Interactive Broadcasting*,[79] where highly detailed conditions and obligations were attached to an individual exemption; of course, those who see decisions such as this as an undesirable piece of micro-regulation by the Commission rather than as a pragmatic solution to a real competition problem, might consider it to be an advantage that a national court could not achieve the same kind of outcome.

A problem with the system of notification to the Commission for exemption is that it is not conducive to the application of the competition rules in national courts. Many would-be litigants prefer to complain to the Commission. A specific problem is that if a defendant responds to a plaintiff's action[80] by lodging a notification with the Commission, the national court will normally adjourn the proceedings. As the Commission says in paragraph 100 of the White Paper, this means in practice that undertakings can bring proceedings to a halt through notification. The abolition of the notification system, and the conferment on national courts of the right to grant exemptions, would reduce the number of occasions on which this would happen: a national court could decide to proceed with a case, although if one of the parties had complained to the Commission, the national court might still prefer to await the Commission's diagnosis.

Giving the national courts the power to apply Article 81(3) will undoubtedly alter the legal culture of competition law, by making the courts full (or at

[79] *British Interactive Broadcasting/Open* OJ 1999 L 312/1 [2000] 4 CMLR 901.

[80] The pre-Woolf terminology is used as the point is Community-wide.

any rate fuller) players in the enforcement of the competition rules. The proposals in the White Paper should increase the volume of litigation involving Article 81, because the validity of agreements not falling within a block exemption will not have to be tested before the Commission and because the national court will have full jurisdiction over the disputed agreement. The more central rôle of national courts raises many issues beyond direct applicability and the nature of Article 81(3): how divergent decisions between Member States are to be avoided; whether the courts of the new Member States will be equal to the task; whether specialised courts, or at least specialist judges, should be established to deal with competition cases; and so on. Commission officials have suggested that economists might be appointed as advisers to national courts, or that there might be a standing national *amicus curiae* on issues of EC law or on economic matters.

The increased use of national courts also raises the principle of national procedural autonomy,[81] whereby it is for the national legal systems to determine how Community rights are protected, subject to the conditions that the procedures must be no less favourable than those governing similar domestic claims and that they must not render Community rights virtually impossible or excessively difficult to enforce. The principle of autonomy has already been the subject of considerable inroads,[82] and is likely to come under increasing strain, particularly with the further development of the *Francovich* case law.[83] The effect of the Commission's proposals in the White Paper would be to erode the principle further by harmonising some aspects of civil procedure. Commission officials have suggested[84] that it will be essential for all national courts to be in a position to protect rights given by Community competition law, which means being able to hear declaratory[85] and class actions, to give interlocutory relief, to give remedies against unlawfully obtained advantages and to proceed without delay. It has also been suggested that the Commission could be given the right of appeal to higher national courts against the decisions of lower courts and NCAs: a radical proposal indeed.[86] This would mean that the White Paper's move towards decentralisation of the enforcement of competition law would, ironically, provide a rôle for the Commission in national proceedings and lead to a harmonisation of procedures in an area

[81] See Case 33/76 *Rewe-Zentralfinanz eG and Rewe-Zentral AG* v. *Landwirtschaftskammer für das Saarland* [1976] ECR 1989, [1977] 1 CMLR 533 and the subsequent case law.

[82] See for example Case C-213/89 *R* v. *Secretary of State for Transport, ex parte Factortame Ltd and others* [1990] ECR I-2433, [1990] 3 CMLR 1.

[83] Cases 6 and 9/90 *Francovich and Bonifaci* v. *Italy* [1991] ECR I-5357, [1993] 2 CMLR 66.

[84] See for example J Temple Lang, paper given at the Hammond Suddards/UCL conference, London, 17 September 1999.

[85] As noted above, declaratory relief would not normally be available in the courts of England and Wales: see *supra*.

[86] See *supra*.

where hitherto the Community institutions have proceeded warily because of the principle of procedural autonomy. Similar effects would result from the proposals for NCAs, discussed below.

There is, of course, already a mechanism in place for maintaining the consistency of the interpretation of Community competition law: Article 234 EC (ex Article 177). Many of the leading competition cases were Article 234 rulings, such as *Télémarketing*,[87] *Volvo*,[88] *Delimitis*[89] and *Corbeau*.[90] The Commission clearly does not consider that Article 234 would be adequate to deal with the new dispensation. This is understandable. First, unless the point of Community law is raised before a final court there is no obligation on the national court to refer.[91] Secondly, the delays involved in obtaining a ruling from the Court of Justice are notorious, so that a national judge may prefer not to make a reference. These delays stem from the overloading of the Court of Justice, which will be exacerbated when further states accede to the EU unless radical changes are made to the "judicial architecture" of Europe. Thirdly, under an Article 234 reference the Court of Justice's rôle is to rule on the interpretation of the law, while leaving its application to the facts to the national court.[92]

Given that the CFI has developed considerable expertise in competition matters and has taken a rigorous approach to review of Commission competition decisions,[93] it might be preferable for Article 234 references to go there rather than to the Court of Justice. It is also arguable that the very nature of Article 234 references should be reconsidered, as the split between the Court of Justice's interpretation of the law and the national court's application of it is not only artificial but also adds to the expense and delay of litigation: replacement of a system in which an opinion goes back to the national court with one which actually disposes of the case would be more efficient. It cannot be expected that the Member States would agree to such a change where matters of constitutional principle were concerned, but it might be feasible in competition cases. A more radical possibility would be the establishment of a

[87] Case 311/84 *Centre Belge d'Etudes de Marché-Télémarketing* v. *Compagnie Luxembourgeoise de Télédiffusion SA and Information Publicité Benelux SA* [1985] ECR 3261, [1986] 2 CMLR 558.

[88] Case 238/87 *A B Volvo* v. *Erik Veng* [1988] ECR 6211, [1989] 4 CMLR 122.

[89] Case C-234/89 *Stergios Delimitis* v. *Henninger Bräu* [1991] ECR I–935, [1992] 5 CMLR 210.

[90] Case C-320/91 *Corbeau* [1993] ECR I-1477, [1995] 4 CMLR 621.

[91] Even in the final court there is the so-called "acte claire" doctrine pronounced in Case 283/81 *CILFIT* v. *Italian Ministry of Health* [1982] ECR 3415, although this is hedged around with conditions.

[92] Although the line between interpretation and application is famously difficult to draw: for a recent example in the competition field see Case C-266/94 *Corsica Ferries France SA* [1998] ECR I-3949, [1998] 5 CMLR 402.

[93] As in, for example, Cases T-79/89 etc. *BASF and others* v. *Commission* [1992] ECR II-315, [1992] 4 CMLR 357; Case T-68/89 *Società Italiano Vetro* v. *Commission* [1992] ECR II-1403, [1992] 5 CMLR 302; Case T-374/94 *European Night Services* v. *Commission* [1998] ECR II-1341, [1998] 5 CMLR 718.

Community competition court where national rulings could be challenged. Such an innovation would subordinate national courts to a Community court and would entail a fundamental change in the relationship between Community and national courts. However, in the context of modernisation proposals which appear inevitably to affect the relationship between Community and national institutions, nothing is so sacred that it cannot be considered.

The Position of the NCAs

It is a central plank of the White Paper that NCAs will play an enhanced rôle in the application of the Community competition rules. Although there has previously been cooperation between NCAs and the Commission, it has been limited by the Commission's monopoly on exemptions. For a long time it was suggested that NCAs should have power to grant exemptions: indeed this was what "decentralisation" meant. Under the White Paper, there will be decentralisation—but not to grant exemptions, because they will no longer be given.

The Commission is concerned, as in the case of national courts, that decentralisation should not lead to inconsistency in the application of the rules: NCAs should not take a line which does not accord with the Commission's thinking. The Commission's proposals for ensuring that this does not occur include heightened co-operation and the passing of information between the NCAs and the Commission; and the new dispensation would also involve greater cooperation between NCAs *inter se*. The objective of the Commission is to ensure that the NCAs come to the same decision as it would have done if it was handling the case. Policy will still be laid down in Brussels, only the application of that policy will be transferred to the NCAs and national courts. The inevitable result of this will be a hierarchical relationship between the Commission and the NCAs, even if the White Paper describes this hierarchy as "co-operation". In some cases there may also be the possibility of Article 234 references from NCAs to the Court of Justice. Whether or not the NCA qualifies as a "court or tribunal" depends on whether it meets the criteria in the Court of Justice's case law.[94] In the United Kingdom, it is thought that the Director General of Fair Trading (DGFT) does not, but that the Competition Commission Appeal Tribunal does.[95] The White Paper proposes that the Commission should handle some cases and the NCAs others. This would necessitate some mechanism for allocating cases, both as between the

[94] See Case 246/80 *Broekmeulen* v. *Huisarts Registratie Commissie* [1981] ECR 2311, [1982] 1 CMLR 91.

[95] In Case C-7/97 *Oscar Bronner GmbH & Co.KG* v. *Mediaprint* [1999] 4 CMLR 112 the Austrian Kartellgericht referred a question to the Court of Justice.

Commission and the NCAs and between NCAs themselves. The principles for deciding on the jurisdiction of courts over disputes laid down in the Brussels and Lugano Conventions[96] do not apply to bodies such as NCAs. The ECMR[97] lays down jurisdictional rules based on the turnover for allocating jurisdiction between the Commission and the Member States,[98] but there is no method of allocating mergers between Member States when they are below the Community dimension threshold. The new Regulation could provide for NCAs to act jointly, and such a possibility would have the beneficial effect of increasing co-operation and consistency between NCAs. It would also be possible to allocate jurisdiction on the basis of the centre of gravity of the agreement, *Schwerpunkttheorie*. Some rules for the allocation of jurisdiction *must* be laid down, however, to ensure that the "one-stop-shop" principle in regard to Article 81 is not lost.

Can the Proposal that the System of Notification Should be Scrapped Entirely be Justified?

The elimination of *mandatory* notification if exemption is to be granted has generally been welcomed;[99] however, the removal of the right to notify at all is another matter. This is more than a procedural alteration, it is a fundamental change in the way that undertakings operate in relation to the competition rules. Hitherto the problem has been that, for most agreements, an individual exemption required pre-notification to the Commission, and yet the Commission does not have the resources to deal with the volume of notifications it receives. The majority of agreements receive nothing more than a comfort letter. The system is flawed, but at least it offers a relatively safe haven. Under the proposals in the White Paper, notification will be abolished altogether: sending in a Form A/B to the Commission and relying on immunity from being fined[100] will no longer be available. In the words of the Commission at paragraph 77 of the White Paper:

[96] See *supra*, n. 24.

[97] See *supra*, n. 21.

[98] Even then there are some exceptions: Articles 9, Article 21(3) and Article 22(3) of the ECMR.

[99] Note that it is not mandatory to notify agreements that infringe Article 81, in the way that Article 4 of the ECMR makes the notification of mergers mandatory; however, for most agreements it has been mandatory to notify if exemption is sought; a major change was effected in 1999, with the adoption of Regulation 1216/99, OJ 1999 L 148/5, which enabled exemption to be sought for vertical agreements even where there has been no notification.

[100] This immunity is provided by Article 15(5) of Regulation 17/62; it can be removed by decision under Article 15(6).

"undertakings would have to make their own assessment of the compatibility of their restrictive practices with Community law, in the light of the legislation in force and the case-law".

The abolition of notification will present significant challenges to companies and their advisers. The position will be closer to that in the USA, where companies have to be more self-reliant, or else reliant on being able to sue their lawyers who may have reached a wrong judgement on the compliance of an agreement with the Sherman Act or other relevant statute.

It is reasonable to ask whether matters are quite as bad as both sides of this debate suggest. The number of notifications is not as great as a reading of the White Paper would at first suggest, although it is large enough to distract the Commission from what it considers the more important tasks of cartel-busting and investigating abuses of dominant positions. Undertakings are actually quite sensible about notifying. For a variety of reasons, the decision is frequently taken that an agreement need not be notified. Firms notify when the risk being assumed is very great, where the agreement raises genuinely new points of law and, possibly, where the advice they are receiving is poor. As a result of actions deliberately taken by the Commission, there are many situations where notification is not necessary. The latest Notice on agreements of minor importance[101] removed the turnover thresholds making it applicable to more agreements; the new block exemption on vertical agreements covers many more transactions than before;[102] the proposed new block exemptions on horizontal agreements are designed to encompass more agreements than before; and the modifications made to the "non-notifiable agreements" provision in Article 4(2) of Regulation 17[103] bring within its scope all vertical agreements not covered by the block exemption. Also 3 decades of Community case law, decisions of the Commission, other Notices, and other block exemptions, guide undertakings and their advisers as to the way in which Article 81 is to be interpreted and applied. It must be remembered that other sophisticated competition law systems, such as those of the USA, Australia and France, operate without notification. Germany, on the other hand, does have notification and so the same division between France and Germany which existed when the competition rules were being drafted in the 1950s and 1960s is still there today and reflected in the current debate.

The degree to which the directly applicable exception will create a diminution of legal certainty for undertakings should not be entirely dismissed. The Commission itself recognises that, in some cases, a decision *ex ante* may be required, for example where substantial investment is to be made in a particu-

[101] OJ 1997 C 372/13.
[102] Regulation 2790/1999, OJ 1999 L 336/21.
[103] Regulation 1216/1999, OJ 1999 L 148/5.

lar case and legal certainty on the compliance of the agreement is needed: for this reason it proposes that partial-function joint ventures would be dealt with in accordance with the procedures of the ECMR, where the system is one of prior notification followed by a binding decision. The attractions of having a joint venture classed as "concentrative" and subject to the ECMR rather than as "co-operative" and subject only to Article 81 were so great that transactions were sometimes structured to fall within the former category. Refinements to the dividing line between the categories were made in 1994[104] and the legal position substantially altered in 1997, so that all full-function joint ventures are now dealt with under the ECMR.[105] In paragraph 79 of the White Paper the Commission proposes maintaining a prior authorisation system for partial-function production joint ventures by bringing them, too, within the scope of the ECMR. The Commission suggests this because "operations of this kind generally require substantial investment and far-reaching integration of operations which makes it difficult for them to unravel afterwards at the behest of a competition authority". This is an admission that legal certainty is reduced without a prior authorisation system. Given this favoured treatment of partial-function joint ventures it can be predicted that a new tactic will emerge—the structuring of horizontal transactions not covered by block exemptions so that they can be notified under the ECMR, which can not only deliver clearance to the transaction, but clearance, in most cases, within four weeks. An irony will be that partial-function joint ventures having a Community dimension will therefore become subject to *mandatory* notification, by virtue of Article 4(1) of the ECMR, whereas under the current law notification is an option for the parties. Once joint ventures have been taken out of the picture, as well as agreements which fall within the terms of one of the block exemptions or the Commission's Notices, the types of agreement which will be subject to the system of directly applicable exception rather than authorisation will be comparatively limited; but in some cases they may possess particular features which give rise to real doubt. An alternative to scrapping the notification system would be to retain it, but to charge the notifying parties substantial fees.[106]

The Commission says at paragraph 88 of the White Paper that it *would* still take positive decisions "in the general interest" in certain cases, where a

[104] See the Commission's Notice on the interface between concentrative and cooperative joint ventures, OJ 1994 C 385/1.

[105] See Article 3(2) of Regulation 4064/89 as amended by Regulation 1310/97 and the Notice on the concept of a full-function joint venture, OJ 1998 C 66/1. By Article 2(4) of the ECMR the co-ordination aspects of such joint ventures are dealt with by applying the standards of Article 81(1) and Article 81(3), but under the procedures of the ECMR rather than those of Regulation 17/62.

[106] Precedent exists for this in the United Kingdom, both for mergers (Mergers (Fees) Regulations 1990, SI 1990/501) and under the Competition Act 1998 (Competition Act 1998 (Director's Rules) Order 2000, SI 2000/293).

transaction raises a "new" question and where "it may be necessary to provide the market with guidance". This recognises the important function which individual exemptions have played in the past in developing competition policy. "Positive decisions" of this kind would be able to contain commitments entered into by the parties in the same way that commitments can be attached to decisions under Article 6(1)(b) of the ECMR. These decisions would be of a declaratory nature, and would have the same legal effect as a negative clearance at present.

How Do the Proposals Impact upon the UK Competition Act 1998?

In the United Kingdom, the new Competition Act 1998 is designed around the idea of notification. The Act provides for notification for guidance and for notification for a decision that the Chapter I and/or Chapter II prohibitions do not apply; the consequences of each type of notification are spelt out with great particularity. The White Paper came out six months after the Royal Assent on 9 November 1998 and less than a year before it entered into force on 1 March 2000. The irony is that, having adopted a system to mimic the Community one, the United Kingdom now discovers that a mature system of competition law apparently does not need such procedures.

The procedure for notification under the Competition Act is not identical to that in Regulation 17/62: for example the latter does not provide for "notification for guidance".[107] Nevertheless the two systems have much in common, both setting up systems of prior authorisation; in each case there is the possibility of both block and individual exemptions. Section 10(1) of the Competition Act 1998 provides "parallel" exemption from the Chapter I prohibition if it is covered either by a Community block or individual exemption or has been cleared under an "opposition procedure" in a block exemption; section 10(2) provides that parallel exemption will also be available for an agreement that is not subject to EC law because it does not have an effect on inter-Member State trade, but would fall within a block exemption if it did. These "parallel exemptions" mean that a great many agreements would not have to be notified to the DGFT under the Competition Act, and obviate much of the need for the DGFT to issue block exemptions under the Act. If the Commission's proposals are implemented, there will no longer be the possibility of parallel exemption pursuant to an individual exemption, since such a creature will not exist; there will however still be block exemptions, so that parallel exemption will still have utility in those cases.

[107] See Competition Act 1998, s. 13 in relation to the Chapter I prohibition (the Article 81 equivalent) and s. 21 in relation to Chapter II (the Article 82 equivalent).

Under the White Paper proposals the DGFT would assume an enhanced rôle, since the Commission will in effect be delegating responsibility to the Member States to enforce the competition rules. At the same time, the DGFT will want to exercise the powers he now has to pursue cartels and abusive behaviour that infringe the Competition Act.

Conclusion

There are many arguments of principle in the White Paper; they are well-rehearsed, and the Commission succeeds in making a powerful argument for change. The proposals for decentralisation accord with subsidiarity, they integrate competition law more completely into the mainstream civil legal system by enabling agreements to be fully dealt with by national courts, they hand back to undertakings more responsibility for their own conduct and they bring the Commission and the NCAs together in a new way in a common enterprise.

The pragmatic arguments for ceasing notification to the Commission are overwhelming. The system does not operate at the moment as it was designed to do, and the individual exemption process embodied in Regulation 17/62 was replaced long ago by comfort letters. Matters are deteriorating, not improving, and with the new accessions to the Community looming it is clear that something fundamental has to give. Being pragmatic, the only possibility, short of a massive addition of resources for the Commission, is decentralisation. The main shock in the White Paper is not the idea of decentralisation itself, but the abolition of notification in its entirety and, with it, the system of individual exemption by an authorisation procedure; the added rôle that this gives to national *courts* is also a major change.

There is much to welcome in the proposals, but welcoming them is not to say that there are not some quite serious problems. One is the uncertainty that surrounds the rôle of Article 81(3): the case for allowing NCAs and national courts to give rulings on the criteria in that provision is more convincing if it is given a narrow, economic function rather than a broad, policy-based one. It is the view of the authors of this chapter that the one absolute essential in reforming the procedural regime for Articles 81 and 82 is to maintain the coherence and consistency in the application of competition law throughout the Community. Whether that can be done without upsetting the delicate balance between Community and Member States institutions is a challenge, but a considerable amount of work requires to be done before the new system can be introduced.

9

The Conflict of Laws

JONATHAN HARRIS AND DAVID McCLEAN

Introduction: Ever More Harmonisation?

These are heady days indeed for conflicts lawyers. Those who have recovered from the seismic shift of the core of the subject in the last fifteen years from the intricacies of the choice of law process to the jurisdictional revolution, now find themselves deluged by an avalanche of further initiatives, principally at a European level, aimed at the "harmonisation" of the subject. Before our eyes, the common law is becoming an endangered species, at least in the British Isles. We have also seen the use of the conflict of laws to promote particular commercial policies or ideologies.

If we look ahead, there will undoubtedly be more of the same for some years to come. The English courts may lose even more of their power to regulate forum choice, and a possible result would be a revived interest in choice of law techniques, especially those derived from the civil law tradition. The relentless march of harmonisation may well continue unchecked and undiluted; but it is possible that there will be a reaction. So, we may hear much more of *ordre public* in its various forms, and of mandatory rules (even those of third states). The continued capacity of the courts for creativity in the conflict of laws may depend upon their learning to exploit the potential of such concepts.

Very significant harmonisation measures have already been achieved at a European level in the past twenty years.[1] Private international law is seen as a vital tool in completing the internal market, allowing judgments to be enforced freely across Europe and enabling exporters to have their rights determined by a single legal system. At the time of writing, the Community institu-

[1] Most notably, the Brussels Convention 1968 and Lugano Convention 1988 on Jurisdiction and Enforcement of Judgments in Civil and Commercial Matters, given effect in English law by the Civil Jurisdiction and Judgments Act 1982, as amended, and the Rome Convention 1980 on the Law Applicable to Contractual Obligations, given effect by the Contracts (Applicable Law) Act 1990.

tions are taking prompt advantage of the added powers they enjoy under the Treaty of Amsterdam and show a clear intention to extend harmonisation into hitherto untouched areas.

The Treaty of Amsterdam, which entered into force on 1 May 1999, has brought judicial co-operation in civil matters having cross-border implications within the sphere of the EC Treaty, insofar as necessary for the proper functioning of the internal market.[2] The conflict of laws is expressly mentioned as an aspect of such co-operation. An Action Plan of the Council and Commission indicates that within two years of entry into force of the Treaty of Amsterdam, work on revision of the Brussels Convention 1968 and the Lugano Convention 1988 should have been completed, a legal instrument on the law applicable to non-contractual obligations drawn up ("Rome II") and necessary revisions of the Rome Convention 1980 made. Within five years, the possibility of drawing up an instrument harmonising the law applicable to divorce and another harmonising all private international law aspects of matrimonial property regimes and succession should have been evaluated. Consideration should also be given within that latter time scale to the approximation of choice of law rules concerning acquisition in good faith of tangible movable property and to improving the compatibility of civil procedures and co-operation in taking of evidence.[3]

The United Kingdom has an opt-out from Article 65 EC,[4] subject to the discretion to opt back in to individual initiatives.[5] Much will depend on how this discretion is exercised, and it is important that the matter is the subject of informed consultation and debate.

Those familiar with the work of the Hague Conference on Private International Law will find in the Action Plan much that is familiar. It has done very successful work in the areas of civil procedure and the taking of evidence abroad, of divorce, succession and matrimonial property. There would seem to be a determination on the part of the Community to replace the Hague Conventions as soon and as far as possible, and that bodes ill for the future of the Hague Conference and so for co-operation on the global level.[6]

Much of the Community programme has been taken forward already. The Commission issued a draft Regulation to replace the current Brussels

[2] Article 65 EC.

[3] Action Plan of the Council and Commission on how best to implement the provisions of the Treaty of Amsterdam establishing an area of freedom, security and justice, adopted on 7 December 1998: OJ 1999 C 19/1.

[4] Article 69 EC preserves the Protocol on the position of the United Kingdom and Ireland (for the text of which, see OJ 1997 C 340/99).

[5] It must do so within three months of the initiative being presented to the Council.

[6] Compare the apparent determination to "trump" the European Convention on Human Rights 1950, a product of the Council of Europe, by the proclamation in the year 2000 of a European Union Charter of Fundamental Freedoms.

Convention.[7] The Council has adopted a sister Regulation on jurisdiction and judgments in matters of divorce and parental responsibility for joint children ("Brussels II")[8] and a Regulation on insolvency proceedings[9] and on the service of judicial and extra-judicial documents.[10] Work on the "Rome II" Convention continues. Moreover, having already issued a Proposal for a Directive on aspects of electronic commerce,[11] the Commission is considering the extent to which current private international law rules adequately address the transnational implications of the Internet.[12]

Article 65 EC presents a real challenge to forum control. In matters falling within its scope, it appears to grant the European institutions an exclusive competence to act on behalf of their Member States in negotiation of international treaties and to represent those States at the Hague.[13] The Hague Conference would quite probably collapse were the delegations of the Member States to be replaced by a single Community team. Although the United Kingdom is unshackled by this general provision, opting in to any specific Community instrument will cede exclusive competence in that area to the European institutions. An opt-in to the Commission's proposed Regulation to replace the existing Brussels Convention and to the parallel Regulations concerning insolvency and certain matrimonial causes would drive a coach and horses through the United Kingdom's competence in the law of jurisdiction and foreign judgments.

This creates something of a dilemma.[14] To be left behind in the harmonisation stakes might be thought to reduce the attractiveness of the English courts as a centre of litigation, compared to the "advanced" jurisdictional schemes of the Regulations. To accept them takes the United Kingdom further along the

[7] For those Member States which are bound by Article 65 EC or who opt into the Regulation. See 1999 COM 348 Final, OJ 1999 C376E/1 and see the opinion of the Economic and Social Committee OJ 2000 C117/6.

[8] See Regulation 1347/2000, 2266th meeting, 29 May 2000, OJ 2000 C160/19. A revised version of the Brussels Convention was proposed by the Commission (see 1997 COM 609 Final; OJ 1998 C33/20), and the new "Brussels II" Convention (OJ 1998 C 221/1) had been adopted by the Council. Both were overtaken by the entry into force of the Treaty of Amsterdam before they could be brought into force.

[9] See Regulation 1346/2000, OJ 2000 C160/1.

[10] See Regulation 1348/2000, OJ 2000 C160/37. It appears that the United Kingdom intends to opt in to each of these initiatives: see 2229th Council Meeting of 2 December 1999 on Justice and Home Affairs (doc ref: 13461/99).

[11] 1998 COM 586 Final, OJ 1999 C 30/4; common position of Council OJ 2000 C128/32.

[12] A public hearing on jurisdiction and applicable law in electronic commerce was held by the Commission in November 1999. Its capacity to cause instantaneous harm on a global scale and the difficulties of attributing a place to contract formation, breach and to the place of a tort all need consideration.

[13] See P Beaumont, "Current Developments in EC Law: European Court of Justice and Jurisdiction and Enforcement of Judgments in Civil and Commercial Matters", (1999) 48 *ICLQ* 225, at 228–9.

[14] See the 31st Report of the House of Commons Select Committee on European Scrutiny (1998–99 Session), considering the Revision of the Brussels and Lugano Conventions.

road towards Community goals and represents a potentially fatal blow to the common law and the objectives that it pursues. The question is not whether the United Kingdom wishes to maintain a substantial degree of forum control, but whether it can afford to do so.

Harmonisation has hitherto been accommodated in English law, even if this sometimes leads to the introduction of concepts which are unfamiliar to, and sit unhappily with, the common law. But there must be limits to such changes. The present Brussels Convention, for example, contains certain key compromises. It permits derogation from the Convention by international treaty,[15] preserves a residual role for the traditional common law jurisdictional rules[16] and maintains a public policy defence to recognition of foreign judgments.[17] Reducing those forum powers still further, or removing them altogether, might be a step too far.

It is not that European initiatives lack principle; indeed they have been instrumental in introducing new values into the English conflict of laws. For example, the English conflict of laws now performs a role which it hitherto did not play, in protecting the interests of parties supposedly in need of special protection.[18] But principle is increasingly operating an international level.

Global initiatives to harmonise may offer even greater commercial rewards, but the same challenges to the autonomy of the English conflict of laws. A proposed Hague Convention on jurisdiction and judgments in civil and commercial matters[19] would partially harmonise jurisdiction rules, reduce instances of *lis alibi pendens* and facilitate recognition of foreign judgments on a scale much wider than the English common law permits. The advantages of participation are too great to ignore; but so too is the danger of loss of adequate forum autonomy, especially since future global initiatives may henceforth be negotiated collectively by the European Community on behalf of its Member States in areas within its exclusive competence. [20]

Against this backdrop, one might wonder whether the common law has any future and whether the English will in future in any sense be masters of their own proceedings. These questions will be considered in this chapter.

[15] Brussels Convention, Articles 57 and 59.

[16] *Ibid.*, Article 4.

[17] *Ibid.*, Article 27(1).

[18] Consumers and insured parties are the subject of special jurisdictional rules under the Brussels Convention, by virtue of Articles 13–15 and 7–12 respectively. Consumers and employees are the subject of special choice of law rules in the Rome Convention, by virtue of Articles 5 and 6 respectively. Protection for employees is a matter of especial controversy as some employees are both very wealthy and in a very strong bargaining position; examples range from football stars to software millionaires.

[19] Hereafter "the draft Hague Judgments Convention". It is hoped to reach agreement on the Convention at the 19th Session of the Conference in October 2000.

[20] Tactically, the United Kingdom might be better placed to opt in to the proposed Brussels Regulation on jurisdiction and enforcement of judgments in civil and commercial matters *after* it has concluded negotiations on the Hague Judgments Convention.

Jurisdiction

Even some ten or more years ago, it was evident that not everyone was convinced that the jurisdictional revolution was desirable.[21] "It can be argued that litigants want resolution of their disputes [whereas] . . . instead . . . time and money is spent on litigating about where to litigate".[22] In many ways, the current law is neither one thing nor the other, since the nature of the common law and Brussels Convention rules are so very different. The pivotal role of discretion in the *forum non conveniens*[23] doctrine allows an almost limitless number of factors to be considered, so as to exclude cases from the English courts where the natural forum clearly lies elsewhere. Not the least merit of this is that many cases where the English court would be minded to apply a foreign law on the merits can be sent to that country, so that it can apply its own law. In contrast, the rule-based approach of the Brussels Convention rules ought in theory to induce rather less litigation about whether the court should invoke its jurisdiction.[24] The defendant domicile rule,[25] which should be a strong antidote to forum shopping, receives no common law counterpart. Particular Brussels policies, such as the provisions for consumers and insured parties, which permit them to bring proceedings in their own courts in certain circumstances,[26] are not pursued at national level, so that this form of consumer protection is largely unavailable as against defendants domiciled outside Europe. In short, there is almost no cohesive jurisdictional strategy between the English common law and the Brussels Convention. Yet both systems produce, in civil or commercial matters, judgments which are freely enforceable throughout Europe.[27]

Forum Non Conveniens: A Bleak Future?

A world motivated by harmonisation, expediency and foreseeability necessarily puts the traditional common law jurisdictional rules under ever-increasing

[21] See, e.g. P Carter, "Rejection of Foreign Law: Some Private International Law Inhibitions", (1984) 55 *BYIL* 111.

[22] A Briggs, "Conflict of Laws: Postponing the Future", (1989) 9 *OJLS* 251.

[23] As expounded in *Spiliada Maritime Corp* v. *Cansulex* [1987] AC 460.

[24] Unfortunately, it has led to a vast number of cases on interpretation of the words of the Convention itself.

[25] Contained in Article 2 of the Brussels Convention.

[26] See *infra*.

[27] In matters falling within the Convention, Article 4 derogates to the common law in certain situations where the defendant is not domiciled in a Contracting State. But because the matter is *ex hypothesi* within the Convention, the judgment is still subject to the Convention enforcement regime.

strain. What price the survival of the *forum non conveniens* doctrine? Today, trends are somewhat contradictory. There has been some evidence of a desire to reduce the role of discretion, even in the English common law. The Lord Chancellor's Department contemplated the replacement of RSC Order 11, rule 1,[28] which provided for service out of the jurisdiction,[29] with new provisions which would eliminate the requirement for the claimant to obtain the court's permission to do so.[30] Any claim falling under such a head would qualify for service out, even if the claimant had not shown England to be the natural forum; it would then be incumbent on the defendant to seek a stay. There was a clear dilemma: applications for permission take time and money and are apparently rarely refused;[31] yet the more "exorbitant" the jurisdiction looks, the less likely the judgment is to be enforced in a non-Contracting State to the Brussels Convention.[32] In the event the replacement provisions added to Part 6 of the Civil Procedure Rules[33] retain the familiar requirement that permission be obtained by the claimant.

Elsewhere, however, discretion is alive, well and even over-exuberant. Recent trends in the application of the Brussels Convention show this. For example, Article 22 of the Brussels Convention, which allows a court second seised to stay its proceedings in the face of a related action abroad, has been applied in England so broadly that the temptation to reproduce the *forum non conveniens* doctrine in the guise of seeking to avoid fragmentation of related actions in different courts is significant.[34] A residual discretion to stay proceedings in favour of non-Contracting States has been read into the Convention.[35] Moreover, the inclination to restrain foreign proceedings by anti-suit injunction, even where the Convention applies, so as to prevent vexatious or oppressive conduct, has proved irresistible.[36] Even now, it is obvious that discretionary means of reasserting forum control are being sought. Further harmonisation initiatives mean that the common law is imperilled;

[28] Set out in Schedule 1 to the Civil Procedure Rules 1998, SI 1998/3132, as originally made.

[29] The manner in which the court will exercise its discretion to serve out of the jurisdiction will be determined in accordance with the principles laid down in *Spiliada Maritime Corp* v. *Cansulex* [1987] AC 460 and *Seaconsar Far East Ltd* v. *Bank Markazi Jomhouri Islami Iran* [1994] 1 AC 438.

[30] Lord Chancellor's Department Consultation Paper, *Service of Court Process Abroad* (1997).

[31] The Consultation Paper, *supra* n. 30, indicated that less than 5 per cent of *ex parte* applications in the Commercial Court for service out were refused.

[32] There is little cause for complaint, given that an English court would be equally unwilling at common law to enforce a judgment where the foreign court has taken "exorbitant" jurisdiction: *Schibsby* v. *Westenholz* (1870) LR 6 QB 155.

[33] By the Civil Procedure (Amendment) Rules 2000, SI 2000 221, effective from 2 May 2000.

[34] *Sarrio SA* v. *Kuwait Investment Authority* [1999] 1 AC 32.

[35] *Re Harrods (Buenos Aires) Ltd* [1992] Ch 72.

[36] *Continental Bank NA* v. *Aeakos Compania Naviera SA* [1994] 1 WLR 588; *Turner* v. *Grovit* [1999] 3 WLR 794; see further *infra.*

but the Brussels Convention experience suggests that the more it is pushed, the harder it will fight back.

Therein lies much of the problem of advancing the harmonisation cause. The desire to preserve a forum's interests will not lightly be quenched. This is demonstrated by the proposed Hague Judgments Convention.[37] The context in which that convention is being negotiated is very different from that of the European Community. The common law tradition is more powerfully represented, with Australia, Canada and New Zealand playing an active part in the work of the preparatory Special Commission. Even more significant is the very prominent part played by the large American delegation, which in some respects joins with other common law countries (as in the debates about *forum non conveniens*) but also has to defend its own special concerns, mainly those derived from the "due process" clause of the United States Constitution.

On first inspection, there are many parallels in the provisions of the draft Hague Judgments Convention to the Brussels Convention. The scope of the two Conventions is very similar[38] and there is every reason to suppose that the Hague Judgments Convention would be uniformly interpreted in all signatory states.[39] The defendant would ordinarily be sued in the courts of his habitual residence.[40] Familiar exceptions to that rule would be introduced.[41] There would then follow rules allocating jurisdiction in e.g. matters relating to contract and tort. But, unlike in the Brussels Convention, those rules would contain protection against a jurisdictionally competent forum arising which could not reasonably have been foreseen. For example, the torts provision[42] allows the claimant to sue where the act causing the injury occurred, or where the injury arose, but in the latter case goes on to say "unless the defendant establishes that the person claimed to be responsible could not reasonably have foreseen that the act or omission could result in injury in that State". The influence of the American doctrine of due process is evident; but the result may be to promote litigation about where litigation should occur.

Elsewhere, common law desire for discretionary control asserts itself very directly. Draft Article 22 provides that "in exceptional circumstances, the court

[37] Discussion in this chapter is based on the text of the Preliminary Draft Hague Judgments Convention adopted by the preparatory Special Commission on 30 October 1999.

[38] Although the draft Hague Judgments Convention would exclude maintenance obligations, which are within the Brussels Convention.

[39] Article 38(1) of the draft Hague Judgments Convention states that "in the interpretation of the Convention, regard is to be had to the international character and to the need to promote uniformity in its application". Article 38(2) requires that the case law of other Contracting States be taken "due account of" in the state addressed.

[40] *Ibid.*, Article 3(1).

[41] *Ibid.* These concern: exclusive jurisdiction (Article 12); submission by the defendant (Article 5); exclusive choice of court clauses for Contracting States (Article 4); consumer contracts (Article 7); and individual contracts of employment (Article 8).

[42] *Ibid.*, Article 10.

may, on application by a party, suspend its proceedings if in that case it is clearly inappropriate for the court to exercise jurisdiction and if a court of another State is clearly more appropriate to resolve the dispute".[43] This Article was the end-result (pending the final Diplomatic Conference) of intense debate, which revealed the very sharp contrast between the civil law preference for strict *lis alibi* rules, crudely summarised as "first come first served", and the common lawyers' trust in judicial discretion, which some civil law delegations feared might be held contrary to the separation of powers principle in their constitutional documents. The Article contains a severely limited version of *forum non conveniens*, specifying the factors to which the court may have regard.[44] It may be wondered whether this emasculated version of *forum non conveniens* will prove acceptable. But another view is that once the door to *forum non conveniens* is opened, however narrowly, the reality of uniform application of the Convention in Contracting States would be severely undermined with common law courts finding ways of operating their accustomed practice in *forum non conveniens* cases.[45]

The proposed Hague Judgments Convention is both more and less interventionist in the common law bases of jurisdiction than the Brussels Convention. On the one hand, it permits use of the common law bases in certain circumstances, even though the defendant is habitually resident in a Contracting State, but without guaranteeing the recognition and enforcement of the resulting judgment. On the other hand, it would take it upon itself to interfere directly in the contents and application of those bases, prohibiting use of such common law rules against defendants habitually resident in a Contracting State "if there is no substantial connection between that State and the dispute".[46] A number of "exorbitant" factors are expressly forbidden as sole bases for jurisdiction, including "the service of a writ upon the defendant in that State".[47] Yet this would greatly *increase* the role for the *forum non conveniens* doctrine in England. A claimant serving the defendant within the jurisdiction would presumably also have the burden of proof of discharging the first limb of *Spiliada* and demonstrating that England was the natural forum. Where the defendant is not habitually resident in a Contracting State, the common law is untouched. But is the English court likely to be ready to apply the

[43] Save where jurisdiction is founded on the exclusive jurisdiction provisions, choice of court clause or the consumer or employee provisions.

[44] Draft Hague Judgments Convention, Article 22(2). The factors mentioned are: inconvenience to the parties, in view of their habitual residence; location and nature of the evidence; limitation periods; and the possibility of obtaining recognition and enforcement of any decision on the merits.

[45] Certain factors are not mentioned as relevant to the decision to stay which would clearly be relevant under the traditional English common law rules. For example, the applicable law is not mentioned, nor are subjective factors which form the basis of the second limb of *Spiliada*.

[46] Draft Hague Judgments Convention, Article 18.

[47] *Ibid.*, Article 18(2)(f).

forum non conveniens doctrine differently, depending on whether it has "main" Convention jurisdiction, takes common law jurisdiction over a defendant domiciled in a Contracting State, or common law jurisdiction over a defendant not domiciled in such a State?[48]

Although harmonisation is likely to reduce the areas where the common law jurisdictional rules apply unfettered, it seems that *forum non conveniens* is far from being faced with extinction. Internationally, it may be controlled, but then allowed to extend into new areas, ensuring that an English court does not take jurisdiction over cases without a substantial connection to the dispute. If that is so, there may be further benefits. An English court might be slower to interfere in foreign proceedings[49] and more willing to recognise its judgments,[50] when it is at least satisfied that the foreign court has applied something close to its own *forum non conveniens* doctrine in deciding whether to take "exorbitant" jurisdiction.

Reverse Forum-Shopping

Anti-suit injunctions

Any system of harmonisation requires mutual confidence in the application of the jurisdictional rules in different Contracting States. As yet, the English courts have appeared unwilling to demonstrate the faith shown by the legislature. A very discernible trend in recent years has been the tendency to reassert jurisdictional control through the use of the anti-suit injunction to restrain the overseas claimant from suing in a foreign court.

A device almost calculated to cause offence in a foreign court, even if not directly addressed to it, the injunction's functions were nonetheless clear at common law. Any foreign court had, for recognition purposes, to be jurisdictionally competent in the eyes of English law. If England was the natural forum, the injunction might save the applicant the inconvenience and expense of defending the action abroad,[51] help prevent duplicated litigation and give him a means of knowing, at an earlier stage, whether the judgment would be enforced in England. But one might expect matters to be different where the Brussels Convention applies. Where the foreign court has jurisdiction under a

[48] And to whom Article 18 of the draft Hague Judgments Convention is inapplicable.

[49] The (then) absence of a *forum non conveniens* doctrine in Texas was clearly a significant factor for the Court of Appeal and the House of Lords to consider when deciding whether to restrain the Texan proceedings in *Airbus Industrie GIE* v. *Patel* [1997] 2 Lloyd's Rep 8; [1999] 1 AC 119.

[50] Taking inspiration, perhaps, from the Supreme Court of Canada's decision in *Morguard Investments Ltd* v. *De Savoye* (1991) 76 DLR (4th) 256; and see A Briggs, "Which Foreign Judgments Should We Recognise Today?", (1987) 36 *ICLQ* 240.

[51] Although not if the foreign judgment would remain enforceable in other states in which the injunction applicant held assets.

Convention to which the United Kingdom is party, second-guessing whether the foreign court has misapplied the Convention,[52] or regarding it as an abuse of process to invoke courts which clearly have jurisdiction thereunder,[53] is wholly inconsistent with the Convention's ideologies.

Yet, as the forum retains less and less direct control over its own jurisdiction, the tendency to reassert it indirectly through the injunction is obvious, and capable of operating as a loose cannon. And there lies the perennial problem. Harmonisation leads to an instinctive need for negative control. At the recognition and choice of law stage, it may take the form of a public policy defence; jurisdictionally, the anti-suit injunction is capable of performing a similar role. Moreover, the potential inclination of an English court to intervene in Hague Judgments Convention proceedings, on the basis that the foreign court should have stayed proceedings on the basis of Article 22, already casts an ominous shadow. Short of express prohibition in the legislation itself,[54] the spectre of the anti-suit injunction endangering the harmonisation process is real.

Negative declaratory relief

For many, one refreshing aspect of the Brussels Convention has been its embracing of the declaration of non-liability sought by the "natural" defendant.[55] It redresses the balance of international litigation, because it does not force the "natural" defendant to wait around to be sued in the courts of the claimant's choice. The "court first seised" rule[56] makes it especially important to get in first and there is no obvious reason why that advantage should rest with the claimant. "It is not commonly objected that a plaintiff obtains an improper advantage when he chooses a forum in which the available procedure suits him nicely".[57] The declaration is also important for the defendant in assessing his liability at an earlier stage, for the purpose e.g. of passing on liability to insurers. And, in the absence of a declaration of non-recognition of a foreign judgment being available in the English courts, it is a way for the "natural" defendant to know whether a foreign judgment would be recognised in England.

Yet, the proposed Hague Judgments Convention reasserts the view that there is something improper about the declaration. Article 21 lays down a

52 *Continental Bank NA* v. *Aeakos Compania Naviera SA* [1994] 1 WLR 588; *Turner* v. *Grovit* [1999] 3 WLR 794.

53 *Turner* v. *Grovit* [1999] 3 WLR 794.

54 Or from the European Court of Justice, in the case of the Brussels Convention.

55 A Bell, "The Negative Declaration in Transnational Litigation", (1995) 111 *LQR* 674; A Briggs and P Rees, *Civil Jurisdiction and Judgments* (2nd edn., London, LLP, 1997), pp. 281–7.

56 i.e. that where a number of Contracting States' courts are jurisdictionally competent under the Convention, only those first seised of the cause of action between the parties may actually hear the case.

57 A Briggs, "Conflict of Laws: Postponing the Future", (1989) 9 *OJLS* 251, at 254.

"court first seised" rule, adapted from the Brussels Convention, but then states[58] that this shall not apply where the action in the court first seised is for negative declaratory relief (whilst, in the court second seised, it is for substantive relief). In that case, the court *first* seised should suspend its proceedings, if the court second seised is expected to render a decision capable of being recognised under the Convention. This is likely to produce wasteful litigation. The negative declaration applicant cannot know that he has managed conclusively to invoke the English courts until the action is concluded. If the negative declaration falls back into decline, mastery of the proceedings will truly reside in the claimant. That only makes the case for an ample *forum non conveniens* doctrine and for the anti-suit injunction stronger.

Interim Relief

Whilst the future of the anti-suit injunction remains uncertain, the use of the worldwide *Mareva* injunction (or "asset-freezing order"),[59] and the English court's jurisdiction to grant interim relief in support of foreign proceedings, may now have reached its high-water mark. There is a thin line between support of and undermining foreign proceedings. Properly handled, the worldwide asset freezing order in support of English substantive proceedings can greatly assist the enforcement of an English judgment abroad. An injunction over English assets in support of foreign substantive proceedings can likewise facilitate the foreign judgment's effectiveness. But there must be limits, lest the substantive rules of jurisdiction are bypassed altogether. The European Court of Justice has recently stressed that the granting of a provisional measure pursuant to Article 24 of the Brussels Convention:

> "is conditional, *inter alia*, on the existence of a real connecting link between the subject-matter of the measures sought and the territorial jurisdiction of the Contracting State of the court before which those measures are sought".[60]

This connection would most readily be shown where the defendant's assets were within the jurisdiction.[61]

The draft Hague Convention is more radical. A court with Convention jurisdiction on the merits may grant any interim measures (presumably, even

[58] Draft Hague Judgments Convention, Article 21(6).

[59] The term now used to replace "*Mareva* injunction" in the Civil Procedure Rules 1998.

[60] *Van Uden Maritime BV* v. *Kommanditgesellschaft in Firma Deco-Lini* [1998] ECR I–7091, para. 40. Curiously, the European Court of Justice also held that Article 24 of the Brussels Convention could be used to grant such relief in support of substantive arbitration proceedings, even though arbitration falls outside the scope of the Convention by Article 1.

[61] The draft Brussels Regulation proposes no changes to the interim relief provisions: see Article 31.

if extra-territorial).[62] Courts of a state in which property is located have jurisdiction to order any provisional or protective measures in respect of that property, even where the substantive litigation is taking place abroad,[63] since this would be an aid to enforcement. In all other cases, however, such orders cannot be granted unless their enforcement is limited to the territory of that state.[64] To a considerable extent *The Siskina*[65] will rise again, in that extra-territorial relief in support of foreign proceedings may not be granted, or at least should not be enforced overseas, no matter that the defendant's connection with England might render it an appropriate forum to grant such an order. The worldwide asset freezing order in support of foreign proceedings, whose legitimacy was only fully recognised in 1997,[66] may soon be a thing of the past.

Matrimonial Status

It is not immediately obvious how family law instruments fit within Article 65 EC. In the context of the Regulation on divorce and parental responsibility, the assertion is made that "differences between certain national rules governing jurisdiction and enforcement hamper the free movement of persons and the sound operation of the internal market".[67] This link is not further explained and appears indirect only, in that one's "limping" matrimonial status around Europe may act as a disincentive to establish oneself in another country. That might appear to make the need for harmonisation of choice of law rules almost more pressing than jurisdictional rules. It also leads one to wonder where Article 65 EC will stop, if any question relating to a person's status can fall within the internal market provisions. And yet, when the original Brussels Convention was concluded, family law was excluded, because the disparity which exists between rules on status was such as to raise the spectre of wholesale refusal to recognise foreign judgments;[68] difficulties which are increased with the expansion in the number of Member States. It has been acknowledged that even today "These are not minor differences; some of them even have constitutional implications".[69] Article 27(4) of the Brussels Convention, which

[62] Draft Hague Judgments Convention, Article 13(1).

[63] *Ibid.*, Article 13(2).

[64] *Ibid.*, Article 13(3).

[65] [1979] AC 210.

[66] Civil Jurisdiction and Judgments Act 1982 (Interim Relief) Order 1997, SI 1997/302; RSC Ord. 11, r. 8A (inserted by SI 1997/415).

[67] OJ 2000 C160/19, preamble.

[68] Jenard, OJ 1979 C 59/1, at 10–11.

[69] Borras Report on the Convention on Jurisdiction and the Recognition and Enforcement of Judgments in Matrimonial Matters, OJ 1998 C 221/27, at 29, para. 4 (now superseded by the draft Brussels II Regulation: OJ 2000 C160/19).

allows a court to refuse to recognise a judgment on the basis that the court of origin determined a preliminary question of status in a sense contrary to that which would have been adopted by the court addressed, is being dropped in the draft Brussels Regulation, allegedly because "these rules are gradually being approximated in the Member States".[70] But in truth there is a long way to go. A court which loses control over the status of persons within its jurisdiction might well wonder whether too much forum autonomy has been given away.

Consumer Protection

Another issue which is currently presenting difficulties is that of the protection of weaker parties. This was not one of the specific concerns of the English jurisdictional rules, other than in the general sense of being relevant to the subjective interests of the parties under the second limb of the *Spiliada* test. Perhaps precisely because the Brussels Convention approach (and that of the proposed Hague Convention) is to reduce the discretionary element, consideration of factors relating to the parties needs to be rule-based. The consumer, for example, may sue either where the defendant is domiciled or where he himself is domiciled.[71] A jurisdiction clause agreed at the time of contracting will normally not be given effect to where a consumer is concerned,[72] even if shown to have been freely agreed upon.

However, there are problems with such rule-based approaches. They risk inflexibility and may undermine genuinely agreed bargains. There is as yet a lack of precision in international understandings of the scope of the protection that is needed. So whilst the draft Brussels Regulation proposes expansion to include all consumer contracts and abolishes the requirement that the consumer should have taken all necessary steps to conclude the contract in his home state (so as to protect consumers who are lured overseas),[73] such a provision is retained in the proposed Hague Judgments Convention.[74] Both introduce the concept of the trader's activities being "directed" at the consumer's home state, in the case of the Hague text as a conscious reflection of American notions of "doing business".[75] The problems of such a concept are manifest for transactions made via an interactive website. Potentially, the trader will find himself open to litigation in any State in which a consumer is induced to enter

[70] 1999 COM 348 Final, OJ 1999, C376E/1 commentary to Article 41 of the draft Brussels Regulation.

[71] Brussels Convention, Article 14.

[72] Subject to *ibid.*, Articles 15(1) to (3).

[73] Draft Brussels Regulation, Article 15(3).

[74] Draft Hague Judgments Convention, Article 7(1)(b).

[75] Draft Brussels Regulation, Article 15(3); draft Hague Judgments Convention, Article 7(1)(a).

into a transaction by what he finds on the website. It may tilt the balance too far, since a trader "would have to be aware of 15 different concurrent regimes in order to trade across borders".[76] Fears were raised at The Hague that some geographically remote countries, such as New Zealand, might find that companies would attempt to deny access to consumers giving an address in their territory. In the uncertainty that surrounds these issues (and given that technological change may well outstrip the capacity of international and regional organisations to revise treaties and legislative texts) the flexibility of the common law may prove a virtue.

Foreign judgments

Ever More Recognition?

If there is one goal uniting the harmonisation cause, it is a drive towards more widespread recognition of foreign judgments. The drive to negotiate a Hague Judgments Convention and to a reduction in the permissible derogations from the Brussels scheme, will almost inevitably lead to a reduced role for the common law and for the other statutory foreign judgments provisions.[77]

Developments of the Brussels scheme suggest a trend to yet further liberalisation of recognition rules and procedures. In the proposed Regulation, the already limited defences to recognition have been further restricted and procedural mechanisms further simplified. Under its provisions, a judgment must be declared enforceable immediately on completion of the necessary formalities without review of the grounds of non-enforcement, and the judgment debtor may not make any submissions on the matter. Only after registration may he appeal against enforcement.[78] Commercial pressures for trouble-free enforcement have been placed ahead of defendant protection—and matters are set to go further still. The draft Regulation contains no provision allowing a state to enter into new treaties exempting non-Member State domiciliaries from the free recognition scheme when jurisdiction is taken pursuant to Article 4 on the basis of national jurisdictional rules. Such a provision exists under Article 59 of the present Brussels Convention and has been utilised by the United Kingdom.[79]

[76] Select Committee on European Scrutiny's 31st Report (1999), considering the revision of the Brussels and Lugano Conventions.

[77] i.e. the Administration of Justice Act 1920 and the Foreign Judgments (Reciprocal Enforcement) Act 1933.

[78] Draft Brussels Regulation, Article 37.

[79] In respect of defendants based in Canada and Australia: see respectively SI 1987/468 and SI 1994/1901.

It may be found necessary to balance these changes by extending the use of other devices. Significantly, the public policy defence, omitted from an earlier proposed revised version of the Brussels Convention,[80] has resurfaced in the draft Regulation.[81] And it may in part be precisely because jurisdictional objections ordinarily have to be made prior to judgment that the anti-suit injunction has gained momentum in restraining Brussels Convention proceedings.

On the world stage, there is still a great deal to be achieved. The draft Hague Judgments Convention adopts a complex scheme under which judgments obtained on certain bases of jurisdiction are entitled to ready recognition, but this does not apply when the court of origin has exercised the right, conceded by the Convention in certain circumstances,[82] to assume jurisdiction on grounds known only to national law. In such cases, the court addressed will apply its own national law as to the recognition of foreign judgments, in England the common law rules or those under the applicable statutory scheme. Theoretically, an English court would be free to ignore a judgment given in another Contracting State on the basis of its national law, notwithstanding that it was satisfied that the latter state was the *forum conveniens*.

In the medium term, even supposing the Hague negotiations prove successful, there will be much scope for the traditional English recognition rules. However, few will doubt that there is room for revision and improvement of those rules. Given the application of the Brussels Convention recognition scheme to judgments based on national jurisdiction rules, it has not been possible to maintain the stance that uniform jurisdictional rules are a prerequisite to liberal recognition. Canada has shown that a common law country can move decisively towards more liberal recognition, extending recognition to judgments from a forum of substantial connection, even from states with quite different jurisdictional rules.[83] The centrality of *forum non conveniens* to common law jurisdiction rules has made its total absence from the recognition rules a ready source of criticism.[84] Moreover, to continue to recognise foreign judgments on the basis of the defendant's presence in the state of origin,[85]

[80] Article 37a (see 1997 COM 609 Final, OJ 1998 C33/20). This version was overtaken by the entry into force of the Treaty of Amsterdam before it itself could come into force.

[81] Although recognition would now need to be *manifestly* contrary to public policy to be refused: draft Brussels Regulation, Article 41(1).

[82] Draft Hague Judgments Convention, Article 17.

[83] See *Morguard Investments Ltd* v. *De Savoye* (1991) 76 DLR (4th) 256; *Clarke* v. *Lo Bianco* (1991) 84 DLR (4th) 244; *Moses* v. *Shore Boat Builders Ltd* (1993) 106 DLR (4th) 654; *Hunt* v. *T & N PLC* (1993) 4 SCR 289; *United States of America* v. *Ivey* (1995) 130 DLR (4th) 674.

[84] See A Briggs, "Which Foreign Judgments Should We Recognise Today?", (1987) 36 *ICLQ* 240; A Briggs, "Foreign Judgments: More Surprises", (1992) 108 *LQR* 549; J Harris, "Recognition of Foreign Judgments at Common Law—the Anti-Suit Injunction Link", (1997) 17 *OJLS* 477.

[85] Which it appears that the common law is willing to do: see *Adams* v. *Cape Industries* [1990] Ch 433.

when reliance on this as the sole basis of national jurisdiction against defendants domiciled in Contracting States is expressly forbidden in the draft Hague Judgments Convention, would be curious to say the least. There appears to be no interest in the Lord Chancellor's Department in the revision of the 1920 and 1933 schemes, but international developments may point up the eccentricity of those schemes and force the pace of reform. From the present vantage point, however, the prospect of England as a land of free-flowing (non-European) foreign judgments, devoid of any significant forum intervention, is a distant one.

Irreconcilable Judgments

Whist forum control has a tendency to reassert itself, there is undoubtedly a shared international resolve to prevent *lis alibi pendens* and to avoid irreconcilable judgments. However, the solution adopted in both the Brussels Convention and the proposed Hague Judgments Convention does cause problems. A "court first seised" rule has the unfortunate effect of creating an incentive for both parties to commence proceedings in their preferred forum, rather than to negotiate a settlement. To tackle that problem by discriminating against negative declarations is not obviously an ideal means of addressing the problem.[86] A discretion to stay proceedings is the only other obvious way to prevent the worst excesses of forum-shopping. The draft Hague Judgments Convention proposes that the court first seised rule should not apply if that court "determines that the court second seised is clearly more appropriate to resolve the dispute".[87] Once again, something close to *forum conveniens* has resurfaced.

Moreover, the Conventions are limited to *lis alibi pendens* between Contracting States, or between Brussels and Hague States.[88] There is no express general right to stay proceedings in favour of a non-Contracting State.[89] That remains the case, even if the action concerns, for example, title to land in the foreign state or a choice of court clause in favour of its courts. The risk of irreconcilable judgments between Contracting and non-Contracting States is apparent. Once again, it might take a general *forum non conveniens*

[86] See *supra*.

[87] Draft Hague Judgments Convention, Article 21(7). See also Article 22. This discretion would not apply to judgments delivered on the basis of the exclusive jurisdiction provisions, choice of court clauses, or the consumer or employee provisions.

[88] Although the details of the inter-relationship of the two Conventions are still to be ironed out: see the proposals for Article 37 in the draft Hague Judgments Convention.

[89] Although the Court of Appeal was minded to read such a right into the Brussels Convention in *Re Harrods (Buenos Aires) Ltd* [1992] Ch 72. Article 22 of the draft Hague Judgments Convention is somewhat ambiguous, in that it allows a court to suspend its proceedings "if another State has jurisdiction and is clearly more appropriate to resolve the dispute". It is not apparent whether that other state would need to be a Contracting one.

discretion, which has regard, in particular, to the enforceability of the non-Contracting State's judgment, adequately to confront the issues of *lis alibi pendens* and irreconcilable judgments.

Foreign Judgments and Choice of Law

A less apparent facilitator of free recognition in future years might emerge from harmonisation of the choice of law process. This might seem curious, given that no scheme of recognition applicable in England permits consideration of the merits of the foreign judgment. But the reality might be rather different. The applicable law exerts an influence on the decision whether to stay proceedings.[90] Furthermore, a decision that judgment of a foreign court is contrary to English public policy is likely to be made as a result of the law applied in that court. As harmonisation of choice of law develops, so the need to investigate the substantive rules applied, or to be applied, in a foreign court diminishes. Whatever its jurisdictional basis, a judgment delivered on the basis of the same law as would have been applied in the natural forum has a certain case for recognition. It might well unlock the door to even further recognition.

Choice of law

Choice of law has spent an extended period in the shadows of the law of jurisdiction and foreign judgments. But its importance to the conflicts agenda cannot be overstated, not least because the link between harmonisation and the objectives of the European movement is manifest. A trader exporting goods throughout Europe, who knows that he will be subject to the same law in whichever State he might face litigation, might trade with rather more confidence.

Forum-Shopping and the Role of the *Lex Fori*

The choice of law process can play a strong anti-forum-shopping role. Choosing one's forum can be significantly less important when the same law will resolve the dispute in all available fora. One consequence of the decline in the use of *forum non conveniens* in recent times has been that English courts are compelled to hear a broader range of cases where foreign law might be applied.

[90] See A Briggs and P Rees, *Civil Jurisdiction and Judgments* (2nd edn., London, LLP, 1997), pp. 197–8.

This is especially so, given the dominance of the domicile rule in the Brussels Convention, compared to its almost total absence as a connecting factor in commercial areas of the conflict of laws.

In the past, however, the importance attached to the *lex fori* meant that reproducing the substantive conditions applicable in the natural forum was not a primary concern. In the field of tort liability, the common law rule of double actionability, which required the defendant's conduct to constitute a tort in English law as well as giving rise to civil action in the *locus delicti*,[91] demonstrated little concern for party expectation. It was rather a blanket means of preventing a claimant from recovering in England for conduct which he would have given rise to no liability in English law.[92] Whilst the rule would hardly encourage a claimant to forum shop here, it gave every incentive to the "natural" defendant to reverse forum-shop, by seeking a declaration of non-liability.

It appears that the *lex fori* is now playing a reduced role in the modern conflict of laws. The much criticised Private International Law (Miscellaneous) Provisions Act 1995, Part III,[93] has, save in the case of defamation,[94] swept aside the common law in favour of a straight *lex loci delicti* approach. This might be the law which parties would normally expect to apply to the case; it is the law which might be regarded as having the greatest "interest" in the case; and it is the law which helps counter the worst excesses of reverse forum-shopping.[95] Harmonisation by Regulation in this area is firmly on the agenda and is most unlikely to accord a dominant role to the *lex fori*.

Protecting Party Expectations

There is little doubt that harmonisation, expediency and protecting party expectations are the order of the day, and there is little reason to suppose that this will not continue. These factors have exerted their influence most clearly in contract law. The use of the objectively applicable law as a primary choice of

[91] *Phillips* v. *Eyre* (1870) LR 6 QB 1; *Boys* v. *Chaplin* [1971] AC 356.

[92] Although its effect had been reduced by the Privy Council's decision in *Red Sea Insurance Co Ltd* v. *Bouygues SA* [1995] 1 AC 190, where it was held that, exceptionally, the first limb could be disapplied, so that appropriate cases could be governed solely by the *lex loci delicti*.

[93] See A Briggs, "Choice of Law in Tort and Delict", [1995] *LMCLQ* 519; P Carter, "The Private International Law (Miscellaneous Provisions) Act 1995", (1996) 112 *LQR* 190; J Harris "Choice of Law in Tort—Blending in with the Landscape of the Conflict of Laws?" (1998) 61 *MLR* 33; R Morse, "Torts in Private International Law: A New Statutory Framework", (1996) 45 *ICLQ* 888; A Reed, "The Private International Law (Miscellaneous Provisions) Act 1995 and the Need for Escape Devices", (1996) 15 *CJQ* 305.

[94] Which, along with certain related claims, is excluded from the 1995 Act by s. 13.

[95] Given its popularity on the world stage as a choice of law rule: see P North and J Fawcett (eds), *Cheshire and North's Private International Law* (13th edn., London, Butterworths, 1999), pp. 605–9.

law rule is extremely limited. Not only is it almost universally accepted that parties should be free to choose the law applicable to the contract, but there are also few areas to which that law will not extend.[96] Gone are the arguments about which law determines whether an international contract has been formed.[97] The "bootstraps" objection of using the law putatively applicable to a contract to determine its validity is no longer a live issue. For better or for worse, the putative applicable law is used for this question,[98] and to decide if the parties have agreed on a choice of law clause.[99] Gone too are debates abut the permissibility of changing the law,[100] or picking and choosing different parts of different legal systems to apply to the contract.[101] And gone is even the suggestion that a theoretical doctrine such as *renvoi* might have a role in the law of obligations.[102] Parties apparently expect to be subject to the domestic law of a country, and that is what they will get, even if it means applying a country's law in circumstances where it would not itself apply it. The fact that the parties may have formed no intention at all as to the applicable law is of no relevance. Nor is the fact that exclusion of *renvoi* can undermine much of the good work of harmonisation of jurisdiction and choice of law rules. It reopens the door to forum-shopping, because the law that the English court will apply will not necessarily be the same as the courts of the applicable law would apply.

In other areas, party expectation has not yet conquered all. The law of unjust enrichment is one area where considerable caution has been shown in simply applying the law of the actual or putative contract, or, in the case of restitution for wrongdoing, the *lex loci delicti.*[103] True, restitutionary obligations are not imposed consensually upon the parties; but the expectation argument might ultimately hold sway here too.[104] If the putative law of an allegedly void contract can be used to determine the validity of "contractual" obligations because the parties would so expect, its extension to other areas is not implausible. Nor, in cases of overlap between contractual and tortious claims, or where

[96] See P Nygh, *Autonomy in International Contracts* (Oxford, Clarendon Press, 1999), ch. 1.

[97] See e.g. A Jaffey, "Essential Validity of Contracts in the English Conflict of Laws", (1974) 23 *ICLQ* 1; A Jaffey, "Offer and Acceptance and Related Questions in the English Conflict of Laws", (1975) 24 *ICLQ* 603; D Libling, "Formation of International Contracts", (1979) 42 *MLR* 169; A Thomson, "A Different Approach to Choice of Law in Contract", (1980) 43 *MLR* 650; A Briggs, "The Formation of International Contracts", [1990] *LMCLQ* 192.

[98] Rome Convention, Article 8(1).

[99] Permitted by *ibid.*, Article 3(4).

[100] Permitted by *ibid.*, Article 3(2).

[101] Permitted by *ibid.*, Article 3(1).

[102] Excluded by *ibid.*, Article 15.

[103] See F Rose (ed.), *Restitution and the Conflict of Laws* (Oxford, Mansfield Press, 1995); P North and J Fawcett (eds), *Cheshire and North's Private International Law* (13th edn, London, Butterworths, 1999), ch. 20; L Collins (ed.), *Dicey and Morris, The Conflict of Laws* (13th edn., London, Sweet and Maxwell, 2000), ch. 34.

[104] See P Nygh, *Autonomy in International Contracts* (Oxford, Clarendon Press, 1999), pp. 253–7.

contractual defences are pleaded to tortious actions, can the triumph of the applicable law of the contract be ruled out.[105] It is not that principle does not compel the use of both contractual and tortious rules; it is that the parties compel the use of the expected law.

Restricting Party Autonomy

Nevertheless, it is suggested that some limits to party autonomy will continue to exist, for a number of reasons. Removal of forum control is considered desirable, until it leads to an English court having directly to apply a foreign law that is quite unsuited to its tastes. In tort, the first limb of the common law rule of double actionability stepped in to prevent this. Now, the only means of escape is to superimpose a mandatory rule on to the *lex loci delicti*, or to refuse to apply it as contrary to English public policy. Both are significant possibilities in tort, precisely for the reason that double actionability was preserved for so long: civil liberties can be compromised by a foreign law beyond the realms of acceptability to an English court. Comity is arguably more affronted by refusal to apply foreign law than by its application in a case where the claimant nonetheless fails to recover because he cannot satisfy the first limb of double actionability.

A second justifiable restriction on autonomy is the importance of theoretical doctrine. The argument that *renvoi* has no role to play in the law of obligations has not convinced everyone: "But if today we are much more concerned with getting the venue right, then it ought to follow that we are much more generally concerned with how a foreign court would itself decide a case".[106] To treat the doctrine as a quaint survivor in areas of property, succession and family law is to abandon the anti-forum-shopping cause at the last. One problem confronting the conflict of laws in tort is the unpredictability of foreseeing where the *locus delicti* might be where instantaneous means of communication are used. It should also follow that, where the use of the foreign law is justified by reasons other than party expectation and expediency, *renvoi* can be the final piece in the uniformity jigsaw.

So too with characterisation. To characterise in a manner which ignores the approach of a putatively applicable legal system is to risk applying a law where it was not intended to apply, or *vice versa*. Both *renvoi* and characterisation can serve the current aims of the conflict of laws, not undermine them. Indifference to the conditions prevailing in a foreign court suggests, far from a *laissez-faire* expectation protecting approach, overly-extensive forum control over which parts of the foreign law will be applied in England.

[105] *Ibid.*, at 234–49.

[106] A Briggs, "Conflict of Laws: Postponing the Future", (1989) 9 *OJLS* 251, at 255.

Stagnant Waters

The pace of change in so many areas should not hide the fact that there are others where very little development has occurred in recent years. Much of the law of property and succession would head such a list. Doubtless, the idiosyncrasies of property laws around the world impede progress, but the European institutions are now ready to try to harmonise.[107] It scarcely seems appropriate to an internal market that, when goods are purchased, title to them might depend not just on the place of the transaction, but also on the place of litigation. And if questions of status can be confronted by the Commission, it ought surely also to be possible to make progress on matters of succession. The possible disincentive to settle in a state in which one is not free to dispose of one's assets as one would wish is apparent.[108]

Personal Connecting Factors

Family law and succession are two of the very few areas where "personal" connecting factors still hold sway.[109] One might predict their almost total disappearance from the commercial stage. They are often difficult to determine, create problems where the parties are domiciled or habitually resident in different states and cannot readily be changed. But once again, bidding "*adieu*" to them may be too hasty. At Brussels and Hague levels, the private international law demands of electronic commerce are being investigated. A recent Hague gathering[110] concluded that in tort "it is difficult to depart from one of the two connecting factors: defendant's or victim's habitual residence".[111] This is largely because, in such instantaneous communication, the place of the tort can be almost wholly fortuitous, and because a single action has the potential to cause harm worldwide. Subjecting the defendant to a bewildering number of potentially applicable laws would be unacceptable. In the absence of other suitable candidates, it may be that electronic commerce will actually force a return to personal connecting factors to resolve the dispute.

[107] See *supra*.

[108] Even though one might wonder if it is so significant as to need addressing for the proper functioning of the internal market.

[109] See L Collins (ed.), *Dicey and Morris, The Conflict of Laws* (13th edn, London, Sweet and Maxwell, 2000), chs 17, 18 and 27.

[110] The Geneva Round Table on Electronic Commerce and Private International Law, held jointly between the Hague Conference and the University of Geneva on 2–4 September 1999.

[111] Press Release on the Geneva Round Table on Electronic Commerce and Private International Law, para. 8.

Consumer Protection

Another obvious limit to party autonomy has emerged from the Rome Convention: weaker party protection. For example, the consumer will always be accorded the protection of the mandatory rules of his habitual residence, even in the face of a choice of law clause.[112] In the absence of such a clause, the contract will be governed by the law of his habitual residence.[113] Once again, personal connecting factors have come to the fore in an area where they would previously have had no place.

More than this, however, one sees a fundamentally different role being assumed by the choice of law process. English law classically adopts a neutral approach to choice of law. Having selected a choice of law rule which, it is hoped, will lead to the application of the law most appropriate to the type of action in question, there is no further investigation of the law to which that choice of law rule leads or to the contents thereof, save in the very limited case of infringement of public policy. To restrict the application of the connecting factor of the law chosen by the parties is to make a protectionist, value judgment on the function of the choice of law process. Provided that the law is genuinely freely chosen by the parties, one might question whether such intervention is appropriate.

The response may be that the alleged neutrality of the English choice of law process has never been wholly convincing. The selection of a connecting factor is a value judgment as to the law which has the greatest claim to be applied on the facts. To determine the applicable law separately for consumer contracts is to adopt a more specific connecting factor for certain types of contract. Now that "protectionism" is an accepted aspect of both Brussels and Rome Conventions, and of the draft Hague Judgments Convention, one can expect to see more and more of it.[114] In the meantime, a dichotomy exists between harmonised rules of protection and the common law. Common law protection takes the form only of mandatory rules and public policy provisions of general application to all contracts. Though mandatory rules may concern consumer protection,[115] the English common law continues to show no sign of developing a private international law of protectionism.

[112] Rome Convention, Article 5(2). He must, of course, satisfy the pre-conditions for the application of the consumer contract provisions contained in the same subsection.

[113] *Ibid.*, Article 5(3).

[114] Its importance was stressed at the Geneva Round Table on Electronic Commerce and Private International Law on 2–4 September 1999.

[115] e.g. that contained in the Unfair Contract Terms Act 1977, s. 27(2).

Looking Forward

What then might become of choice of law? One might look forward to a choice of law process which recognises more expressly the link between jurisdictional rules and the applicable law. One might expect rules that give ever greater prominence to the parties' expectations. The drive to harmonise choice of law rules is very likely to gather pace. However, one might also anticipate that this will necessitate significant forum intervention, in order to ensure that its public policy is not infringed. It might also necessitate greater protectionism, which in turn might call for the resurgence of personal connecting factors; factors which might already have been revived by the unsuitability of attributing location to modern means of concluding international transactions. Regard to the conditions which would prevail in the courts of the applicable law may also yet give the theoretical doctrines a new lease of life.

Conclusion

The coming years seem sure to bring further harmonisation and a considerable tightening of the control of the European institutions over private international law. Rules, not discretion, are certainly the Union's order of the day. Forum control is challenged and, if the United Kingdom wishes to remain at the core of European initiatives, there may be little that can be done about it. The proposed Hague Judgments Convention further threatens some traditional bases of common law jurisdiction.

Jurisdictional reforms are driven by protecting party expectation and autonomy, whilst at the same time offering protection for weaker parties. They are driven by the desire to avoid *lis alibi pendens* and to restrict forum-shopping opportunities. They are driven by the fundamental objectives of the European institutions and the need to ensure free movement of judgments. But, at least on the global stage, they are equally driven by a desire to ensure that cases may only be heard in a forum of substantial connection; and that may be where the common law will not just survive (albeit in an adapted form), but may flourish.

Increased recognition of foreign judgments is undoubtedly a common goal. Whilst the Brussels Convention and Commonwealth developments have shown that progress can be achieved without harmonisation of national jurisdictional rules, the full fruits are unlikely to be realised without this.[116]

[116] The draft Hague Judgments Convention would appear to confirm this, insofar as judgments granted on the basis of national law jurisdictional bases are excluded from the free recognition regime by Article 24.

Nonetheless, there are dangers. The adoption of overly-extensive recognition provisions before all states are truly ready for them in likely to result in a re-emergence of public policy.

The choice of law process is no longer the core of the conflict of laws, but, if anything, harmonised, non-discretionary jurisdictional rules ought to lead the English courts to take jurisdiction in more cases where English law is not applicable. Harmonisation in this area is not just an essential aspect of the internal market; it is a complement to jurisdictional reform, in that it significantly reduces the incentives to forum shop.

To describe developments in the conflict of laws in recent years as a triumph of pragmatism over principle would be unfair. It is undoubtedly true, however, that the concerns of party expectation have pushed many theoretical and logical arguments into the background. To extend party autonomy to its limits is not, and should not be treated as, a reason to ignore theoretical underpinnings. Increasingly, private international law is being used as a tool to implement other objectives of the law. In recent years, comity has clearly exerted an increasing influence over the rules of private international law. But it is not so much harmonious relations *per se*, as the potential free trade benefits which flow from harmonious relations, which appear to drive the subject forward. In doing so, there is a tendency to overlook the traditional concerns of the *lex fori*. Yet as one looks back on, and forwards to, the evolution of the subject, one suspects that forum control will always reassert itself. It may do so through public policy, through mandatory rules, through the anti-suit injunction, through use of the *forum non conveniens* doctrine in dubious circumstances or through refusal to enforce foreign penal, revenue or public laws. The brave new world of harmonised conflict of laws might trim and refine the common law principles that have emerged in this country, but it is unlikely to oust them entirely. Complete harmonisation of the subject, with minimal derogations and limitations, is not yet in sight. Expectations and party autonomy may come to dominate the conflict of laws; but even in the face of an avalanche of European and international initiatives, mastery of one's own proceedings is not something which any state will lightly cede.

10

Public Law

STEPHEN BAILEY AND NICHOLAS BAMFORTH

Introduction

Lawyers of the future might well come to see the emergence of a distinctive system of public law as one of the more significant developments in English law in the second half of the twentieth century. The term "public law" can be used in both broad and narrow ways. Speaking broadly, the term refers to the general body of rules relating to the allocation and regulation of state power. More narrowly, it refers specifically to the determinations which courts make on an application for judicial review, and the types of interest which applicants are entitled to vindicate via judicial review.[1] It is clear that public law, understood in either sense, has developed dramatically in the twentieth century—a development which shows no signs of abating in the twenty-first. This chapter will argue that the causes of the development lie in a combination of factors: the growing power of the state; a perceived decline in the power of Parliament as a mechanism for policing the exercise of state power; and the internal dynamic of judicial review itself. The development has also continued despite the existence of a variety of judicial opinions about whether courts should be interventionist or deferential in public law cases, and about the appropriate relationship between judicial review and the political process. Although attempts have been made since 1979 to reduce the functions of the state, the growth of public law seems set to continue in the twenty-first century, not least because of the quasi-constitutional rôle allotted to the courts by the various constitutional changes which have occurred since 1997. The reasons for the growth of public law will be examined in the next two sections of the chapter, after which we will assess the variety of judicial attitudes to the permissible development of public law, the current position and prospects for the future.

[1] We use the term "public law" given the overlap between constitutional and administrative law: see Paul Craig, *Public Law and Democracy in the United Kingdom and the United States of America* (Oxford, Clarendon Press, 1990), pp.1–3.

Public law and the rôle of the state

There has been some debate about whether the massive growth in state functions in the United Kingdom up until 1979—to encompass, for example, the provision of education and health care, together with the regulation of working conditions, planning and (to a certain extent) trade—should more accurately be seen as a product of the twentieth century, or as originating rather earlier in the nineteenth.[2] Whichever answer is correct, it should be clear that the state is nowadays responsible for significant areas of life for which it would not have assumed responsibility at the start of the nineteenth century.[3] This growth in the state's rôle and responsibilities has been of profound importance in relation to the development of public law. Carol Harlow and Richard Rawlings have suggested that "[b]ehind every theory of administrative law there lies a theory of the state".[4] We might also say, more broadly, that the precise *contours* of any given system of public law are likely to develop and to alter according to prevailing perceptions—among the judiciary, legislators and sometimes commentators—about the appropriate rôle and powers of the state vis-à-vis its citizens and about the need either to control or to empower the state (or specific parts of it) to act.[5] There may sometimes be time lags between changes in the basic rôle and powers of the state, changes in perceptions of that rôle and consequent changes in the rules of public law. There will also be divergences of opinion about whether the preferable means of control are of a political character and exercised via the political process (for example, by enhancing the rôle of Parliamentary scrutiny of government), or whether they should be of a legal character and exercised by the courts, or whether there should be some combination of controls.[6] Nonetheless, given public law's

[2] Compare, for example, Oliver MacDonagh, "The Nineteenth-Century Revolution in Government: A Reappraisal" (1958) 1 *Historical Journal* 52; Henry Parris, "The Nineteenth-Century Revolution in Government: A Reappraisal Reappraised" (1960) 3 *Historical Journal* 17. Compare, more broadly, AV Dicey, *Law and Public Opinion in England During the Nineteenth Century* (2nd edn., London, Macmillan, 1962), p.211 *et seq*; Sir Ivor Jennings, "In Praise of Dicey" (1935) 13 *Public Administration* 128.

[3] As demonstrated by the fact that the level at which it is appropriate to set income tax—as the major source of funding for government expenditure—is nowadays a matter of public controversy, whereas in the mid-nineteenth century the controversial question was whether income tax should be introduced to fund *any* state expenditure: see Roy Jenkins, *Gladstone* (London, Macmillan, 1995), pp. 148–57. For a general account of the development of the rôle of the state, see PP Craig, *Administrative Law* (4th edn., London, Sweet & Maxwell, 1999), chs. 2 and 3.

[4] *Law and Administration* (2nd edn., London, Sweet & Maxwell, 1997), p.1.

[5] Carol Harlow and Richard Rawlings identify three prevailing types of perception, which they label "red light", "green light" and amber theory—*supra* n.4, chs. 2 to 4; see also Martin Loughlin's distinction, in *Public Law and Political Theory* (Oxford, Clarendon Press, 1992), between conservative normativisim, functionalism and liberal normativisim.

[6] See C Harlow and R Rawlings, *supra* n.4, chs. 2 to 4, esp. pp. 75–8.

focus on the allocation and control of state power, it is plain that the emergence and development of a distinctive system of public law in the United Kingdom has largely been in response to a widening perception, in the twentieth century, that the rôle of the state was expanding, and that existing political institutions were inadequate to control the state as it grew.[7]

Unlike many Continental legal systems, English law does not contain a concept of the state *per se*.[8] In consequence, the range of powers which are defined as being of a "public" character and subject to control by public law are not identified using any concept of the state.[9] Instead, a more *ad hoc* series of tests—relating to the source and to the nature of any given power—is nowadays used in order to determine whether that power should be categorised, for the purposes of amenability to judicial review, as being of a "public law" or "private law" nature.[10] While such tests may be criticised for generating an uncertain boundary-line between public and private law, they nonetheless play an equivalent rôle to the tests used in Continental legal systems to demarcate the state, tests which can themselves produce uncertain boundaries.[11] It thus remains meaningful to talk of English public law as being concerned to identify and to police the exercise of power by the state—provided one appreciates that the term "state" is being used in a descriptive rather than a legal-conceptual sense.[12]

There are numerous examples of the connection between any given theorist's or judge's view of the rôle of the state and their view of the appropriate

[7] For examples taken from a variety of constitutional and political perspectives, see *JUSTICE/All Souls Review of Administrative Law, Interim Report* (1981); WA Robson, "Administrative Justice and Injustice: A Commentary on the Franks Report" [1958] PL 12; R Crossman, *Socialism and the New Despotism* (Fabian Tract No. 298, 1956); HWR Wade, "Law, Opinion and Administration" (1962) 78 LQR 188 at 189 ("The vast powers of modern government had no place in Dicey's scheme of things, and he felt little concern with the great problem, as we now see it: how far is power to be controlled by law?"); Sir William Wade and CF Forsyth, *Administrative Law* (7th edn., Oxford, Clarendon Press, 1994), pp.1–7.

[8] Instead, the somewhat malleable concept of the Crown is used: compare *Town Investments* v. *Department of the Environment* [1978] AC 359, esp. at 380–1 (Lord Diplock); *M* v. *Home Office* [1994] 1 AC 377. See further JWF Allison, *A Continental Distinction in the Common Law: A Historical and Comparative Perspective on English Public Law* (Oxford, Clarendon Press, 1996), pp. 104–7.

[9] Allison argues for this and other reasons that it is inappropriate for English law to draw a substantive distinction between public and private law: *supra* n.8, at 34–41, 107–9. In response, see Paul Craig, "Public Law and Control over Private Power" in Michael Taggart (ed.), *The Province of Administrative Law* (Oxford, Hart, 1997) pp. 207–8.

[10] See, e.g., *R* v. *Panel on Take-overs and Mergers, ex p. Datafin* [1987] QB 815; *R* v. *Disciplinary Committee of the Jockey Club, ex p. Aga Khan* [1993] 1 WLR 909; *R* v. *Insurance Ombudsman Bureau, ex p. Aegon Life Assurance* [1994] CLC 88.

[11] See Paul Craig, *supra* n.9, at 207–8.

[12] For analysis of attempts to provide a working definition of the state, see Patrick Dunleavy and Brendan O'Leary, *Theories of the State: The Politics of Liberal Democracy* (London, Macmillan, 1987), esp. ch.1.

rôle for public law. Professor AV Dicey famously argued in the 1880s that the English notion of the rule of law stood, *inter alia*, for:

> "equality before the law, or the equal subjection of all classes to the ordinary law of the land administered by the ordinary law courts; the 'rule of law' in this sense excludes the idea of any exemption of officials or others from the duty of obedience to the law which governs other citizens or from the jurisdiction of the ordinary tribunals; there can with us be nothing really corresponding to the 'administrative law' (*droit administratif*) or the 'administrative tribunals' (*tribunaux administratifs*) of France. The notion that lies at the bottom of the 'administrative law' known to foreign countries is, that affairs or disputes in which the government or its servants are concerned are beyond the sphere of the civil courts and must be dealt with by special and more or less official bodies. This idea is utterly unknown to the law of England".[13]

Dicey was in fact mistaken in his view of the nature of French law and of the absence of any type of administrative law in England.[14] For present purposes, however, the important feature of his analysis lies in its implicit link between the perception that the state played a limited rôle in day-to-day life and the perception that it was undesirable to seek to control the state other than through the ordinary law applicable to everyone.[15] For, as Jeffrey Jowell has suggested, Dicey was an "unreconstructed Whig [who] had, throughout his life, believed in a *laissez-faire* economic system and had resisted the increasing regulatory role of the State".[16]

By the end of the twentieth century, by contrast, it became commonplace to justify the emergence of a distinctive body of public law, encapsulated in the development of the application for judicial review, by reference to the notions that the functions of the executive branch of the state—considered as a whole—have grown substantially, while Parliament's ability to control the executive has shrunk.[17] Lord Mustill, for example, suggested in his dissenting judgment in the *Fire Brigades Union* case that while the executive should ideally be controlled by Parliament:

> "In recent years . . . the employment in practice of these specifically Parliamentary remedies has on occasion been perceived as falling short, and sometimes well short, of what was needed to bring the performance of the executive into line with the law, and with the minimum standards of fairness implicit in every Parliamentary delegation of a decision-making function. To avoid a vacuum in which the citizen

[13] AV Dicey, *An Introduction to the Study of the Law of the Constitution* (10th edn., London, Macmillan, 1959), pp. 202–3; see also pp. 193–5.

[14] See WA Robson, *Justice and Administrative Law* (3rd edn., London, Stevens, 1951).

[15] See further the references discussed *supra* at n.5, together with PP Craig, "Dicey: Unitary, Self-Correcting Democracy and Public Law" (1990) 106 *LQR* 105.

[16] Jeffrey Jowell, "The Rule of Law Today", in Jeffrey Jowell and Dawn Oliver (eds), *The Changing Constitution* (3rd edn., Oxford, Clarendon Press, 1994), p.60.

[17] See the materials detailed in *supra* n.5.

> would be left without protection against a misuse of executive powers the courts have had no option but to occupy the dead ground in a manner, and in areas of public life, which could not have been foreseen 30 years ago. For myself, I am quite satisfied that this unprecedented judicial role has been greatly to the public benefit".[18]

More succinctly, Lord Templeman has suggested that "judicial review is a remedy invented by the judges to restrain the excess or abuse of power".[19]

The reasons for Parliament's loss of ability to control are several, but principal among them would appear to be the growth of organised and disciplined political party machines, particularly in the House of Commons—now by far the stronger of the two chambers—in the wake of the move towards universal suffrage, finally achieved in 1928.[20] With only very occasional exceptions, MPs depend upon the party machine to be elected and re-elected, and the party machines impose strong whipping systems on MPs in relation to House of Commons votes. In consequence, the ability of the legislature to exercise meaningful control over the executive has greatly diminished. Simultaneously, however, the functions of the state have expanded, particularly with the growth of the welfare state and the nationalisation of several key industries, until the election in 1979 of a Conservative Government committed to reducing the state's rôle.[21]

The expansion of the state has had important consequences for the way in which the relationship between citizen and state—and between institutions of the state—is structured by law. Many aspects are now regulated by more, and more complex, legislation, both primary and secondary. Indeed, the inexorable rise in the amount of legislation has continued regardless of the political complexion of the government of the day—for example, the Conservative Governments in power between 1979 and 1997 were as strongly committed as their Labour predecessors to using legislation to achieve their policy goals. The volume of legislation has attracted widespread criticism.[22] The pressures remain in place, following the election in 1997 of a Labour Government with new policies and fierce competition among ministers for access to parliamentary time.[23]

18 *R* v. *Secretary of State for the Home Department, ex p. Fire Brigades Union* [1995] 2 AC 513 at 567–8.

19 *R* v. *Secretary of State for the Home Department, ex p. Brind* [1991] 1 AC 696 at 751. Lord Templeman is here referring to the substantive principles of judicial review as opposed to the application for judicial review procedure, which was put in place by RSC Ord. 53 and by the Supreme Court Act 1981, s.31.

20 See further, e.g., HWR Wade, *Constitutional Fundamentals* (London, Stevens, 1980), pp. 40–2.

21 For analysis, see Alan Sked and Chris Cook, *Post-War Britain: A Political History* (4th edn., London, Penguin, 1993), chs 13–15.

22 *Report of the Hansard Society Commission on the Legislative Process* (London, 1992), pp. 10–13, citing both the CBI and the TUC.

23 Exacerbated by the large amount of time taken up in the 1997–98 session by constitutional reforms.

Developments in the public sector have affected the state as both a regulator and service provider. For example, the second half of the twentieth century saw significant new controls in the areas of immigration, planning and the protection of the environment from pollution. Housing, education and social security have all seen the enactment of new rights for individuals.[24] Particularly spectacular has been the growth of education law from a relatively modest, fragmented level in the nineteenth and early twentieth centuries, through the landmark Education Act 1944 to the regular enactment of new legislation in the 1980s and 1990s, reflecting the decision of successive governments that most aspects of educational provision should be the subject of standards set in accordance with central government policy and not left to the professional judgements of teachers or the discretion of local education authorities.[25] Included within this are new rights for parents, for example in relation to decisions as to the admission of pupils to or expulsion from school and pupils with special educational needs. These, in turn, have seen the establishment of new tribunals[26] and have provided a fertile area for litigation. Social security law has undergone a series of transformations reflecting changes of policy as to where money should be targeted, the appropriate balance between rules and discretions, and the most suitable model(s) for the resolution of disputes.[27]

A parallel development has been the way in which certain relationships between institutions of the state have become the subject of detailed regulation by legislation. An example is provided by the relationship between local government and the Conservative central Government in the 1980s and 1990s. In this period, the government sought by a series of legislative mechanisms, some remarkably complicated, to control both capital and revenue spending by local authorities. Issues that were previously settled according to conventional understandings were now resolved through legislation and litigation.[28] An analogous experience is to be anticipated following devolution, with the Scotland Act 1998 and the Government of Wales Act 1998 setting up demarcation lines around the powers of the Scottish Executive and Parliament and the National Assembly for Wales which are certain to lead to litigation as the

[24] e.g. rights of the homeless: Housing (Homeless Persons) Act 1977, now found in modified form in Part VII of the Housing Act 1996; rights to support of persons in need of care: National Assistance Act 1948; Part III of the National Health Service and Community Care Act 1980.

[25] Consolidated in the Education Act 1996 and the School Inspections Act 1996. See the summary by N Harris in *Cross on Local Government Law* (9th edn., 1996), para. 20-01.

[26] Education Appeals Committees; Special Educational Needs Tribunals.

[27] See, generally, M Harris and M Partington (eds), *Administrative Justice in the 21st Century* (Oxford and Portland, Oregon, Hart, 1999).

[28] The story is illuminatingly told by M Loughlin in *Legality and Locality: the Role of Law in Central-Local Government Relations* (Oxford, Clarendon, 1996). The courts eventually signalled an unwillingness to intervene except in the clearest cases of abuse of power: *R* v. *Secretary of State for the Environment, ex p. Nottinghamshire County Council* [1986] AC 280; *R* v. *Secretary of State for the Environment, ex p. Hammersmith and Fulham London Borough Council* [1998] 1 AC 521.

devolved institutions seek to mark their independence from Whitehall and Westminster.[29] Furthermore, a distinctive new regime of rights and remedies relating to public procurement has been created under the auspices of European Community law, the full potential of which has yet to be realised.[30]

In later sections of the chapter, it will be argued that the factors identified in this section can explain many significant twentieth century developments in public law, together with likely future developments. It should also be noted that the growth of judicial review may well have had an internal momentum of its own. This will be considered in the next section.

The growth of public law litigation

One of the notable developments of the latter half of the twentieth century has been the explosion of public law litigation, mainly, but not exclusively, through the application for judicial review. The business of courts and tribunals has significantly increased over the course of the twentieth century.[31] To this should be added statistics covering references to the proliferating band of ombudsmen, both public and private sector, and the development of formal complaints mechanisms across business and the public sector.[32] A wide variety of factors can be identified as contributing to this explosion. Some can be seen as arising from general changes in society; others from changes particularly in the area of public law. At the more general level, it is widely perceived that individuals are less inclined to defer to authority and more likely to use the law as a vehicle for challenging unwelcome decisions or actions. In the context of public law, judicial review has emerged in a coherent form from the 1950s onwards. The two key elements were: first, the systemisation and development of the substantive principles of law; and, secondly, the creation of a streamlined application for judicial review procedure with a first step that did not

[29] At the time of writing the position in Northern Ireland remains in the balance.

[30] Public Works Contracts Regulations 1991, SI 1991/2680); Utilities Supply and Works Contracts Regulations 1992, SI 1992/3279); Public Services Contracts Regulations 1993, SI 1993/3228); Public Supply Contracts Regulations 1995, SI 1995/201).

[31] See SH Bailey and MJ Gunn, *Smith and Bailey on the Modern English Legal System* (3rd edn., London, Sweet & Maxwell, 1996), p.49. Figures for tribunals can be found in the Annual Reports of the Council on Tribunals. A context for these figures is provided by research that shows that about half of members of the public who experience non-trivial justiciable problems fail to achieve any kind of resolution of their problem, and that in about eight out of ten problems no legal proceedings are commenced, no ombudsman is contacted and no ADR process used: H Genn, *Paths to Justice* (Oxford and Portland, Oregon, Hart, 1999), pp. 176, 177.

[32] See the discussion of the "complaints explosion" of the 1980s by T Williams and T Goriely in M Harris and M Partington (eds), *supra* n.27, ch. 6.

necessarily involve an appearance in court. The principles of judicial review were only the subject of in-depth analysis in the latter part of the twentieth century. Leading the way was the first edition of de Smith's *Judicial Review of Administrative Action* in 1959. Previously, there was significant learning attached to the different remedies available in the public law context[33] and attention had been paid to particular issues, such as the doctrine of jurisdictional error.[34] However, it was only when connections began to be made within the bewildering mass of case law accumulated over the centuries that a proper understanding began to develop. This process of development has involved both the spreading of awareness of the existence of this body of principles and the deepening of understanding as the principles have been refined through academic and judicial debate.

The process can be observed within the judiciary, beginning with the pioneering efforts of Lords Greene[35], Denning,[36] Reid[37] and Diplock,[38] and now with the cadre of judges appointed to the Crown Office list, many of whom have made significant contributions to both the development of the principles through case law and the literature of administrative law.[39] The spreading of understanding can also be seen in the development of the specialist administrative law Bar,[40] the greater prominence of administrative law within the curriculum of many law schools,[41] the inculcation of at least a basic awareness of judicial review among administrators[42] and the steady stream of judicial

[33] See, e.g., FH Short and FH Mellor, *The Practice on the Crown Side of the King's Bench Division* (2nd edn., 1908).

[34] e.g. DM Gordon, (1929) 45 *LQR* 458, (1944) 60 *LQR* 250, (1960) *UBCLR* 135, (1960) 76 *LQR* 306, (1966) 82 *LQR* 263, 515.

[35] *Associated Provisional Picture Houses Ltd* v. *Wednesbury Corporation* [1948] 1 KB 223.

[36] There are numerous examples, including *R* v. *Northumberland Compensation Appeal Tribunal, ex p. Shaw* [1952] 1 KB 338 (also Lord Goddard in the Divisional Court: [1951] 1 KB 711); *R* v. *Gaming Board* [1970] 2 QB 417.

[37] e.g. *Ridge* v. *Baldwin* [1964] AC 40; *Anisminic Ltd* v. *Foreign Compensation Commission* [1969] 2 AC 147.

[38] e.g. *Council of Civil Service Unions* v. *Minister for the Civil Service* [1985] AC 374.

[39] See, e.g., Lord Woolf MR: "Public Law—Private Law: Why the Divide?' [1986] *PL* 220, *Protection of the Public—A New Challenge* (London, Stevens, 1990), "Droit Public—English Style" [1995] *PL* 57; Sir John Laws: "Is the High Court the Guardian of Fundamental Constitutional Rights?" [1993] *PL* 59, "Law and Democracy" [1995] *PL* 72, "The Constitution: Morals and Rights" [1996] *PL* 622, "Public Law and Employment Law: Abuse of Power" [1997] *PL* 455, "The Limitations of Human Rights" [1998] *PL* 254; Sir Stephen Sedley: "Public Law and Contractual Employment" (1994) 23 *ILJ* 201, "Human Rights: A Twenty-first Century Agenda" [1995] *PL* 386.

[40] The Administrative Law Bar Association was founded in 1986.

[41] Administrative Law is part of one of the core elements of qualifying law degrees; judicial review seems often to have an increasingly prominent part in courses on Constitutional Law or Public Law.

[42] Illustrated by the publication by the Treasury Solicitor's Department of *The Judge over your Shoulder* in 1987; M Sunkin and AP Le Sueur, "Can Government Control Judicial Review?" (1991) *CLP* 161. Awareness does not, however, necessarily lead to conformity: S Halliday, "The Influence of Judicial Review on Bureaucratic Decision-Making" [2000] *PL* 110.

review cases that have received widespread publicity in the media. There must now be very few institutions in the public sector that have not been called upon to respond to a judicial review application.[43]

The deepening of understanding is also important in giving those participating in the preparation and determination of cases a solid basis for their work. For example, if judicial review had ever consistently functioned (or had been widely perceived as functioning), purely as a vehicle for right wing judges to resist the spreading of "eccentric principles of socialistic philanthropy"—to quote the unfortunate, if revealing, words of Lord Atkinson in *Roberts* v. *Hopwood*[44]—then legislative intervention to restrict the judirisdiction would have been inevitable and justified. Instead, the courts have developed a body of principles that are generally flexible enough to cope with the wide variety of situations that come before them, and which usually enable judges to provide a reasoned justification for their decisions (with some exceptions—we are not saying that all judges always get it right). Judges from the Crown Office List have in many cases clearly become familiar with the processes of the public sector institutions with which they deal, and the practical constraints within which they work, allowing them to make and support differentiated judgments as to the quality of those processes by the very fact of being able to observe and compare the good and the bad.

Another important dimension is that it is now established that judicial review principles apply to a broader range of situations than was the case fifty years ago. Both the prerogative orders and the principles of natural justice now extend to administrative acts as well as judicial.[45] It is now understood that many decisions cannot neatly be pigeon-holed into one category or the other; that, analytically, decisions really range on a spectrum from the purely "administrative" to the purely "judicial"; and that the place of a decision on this spectrum may at most influence the *content* of the requirements of natural justice. The restriction of the scope of the prerogative orders to judicial and quasi-judicial actions disappeared without any fuss after *Ridge* v. *Baldwin*.[46] It is now established that judicial review principles apply to the exercise of powers under the royal prerogative (subject to continuing debate as to the proper

[43] Including the University of Nottingham (*R* v. *University of Nottingham, ex p. Ktorides* [1998] *COD* 26 and Cambridge (*R* v. *University of Cambridge, ex p. Beg* [1999] Ed CR 674) but not yet, it seems, the University of Oxford.

[44] [1925] AC 578 at 594.

[45] See *Ridge* v. *Baldwin, supra* n.37 (prerogative orders; *audi alteram partem*); *Re HK (an Infant)* [1967] 2 QB 617 (*audi alteram partem*); *R* v. *Secretary of State for the Environment, ex p. Kirkstall Valley Campaigns Ltd* [1996] 3 All ER 304 (*nemo judex in sua causa*).

[46] See, e.g., *R* v. *Hillingdon London Borough Council, ex p. Royco Homes Ltd* [1974] QB 720 where certiorari was granted straightforwardly in a planning case.

definition of such powers),[47] and to institutions exercising governmental functions even if not established by statute or the prerogative.[48]

Turning to the content of the principles, all errors of law will normally now be regarded as causing a body to act *ultra vires*.[49] There is a trend—possibly initiated by academic writing[50]—to provide a more structured explanation for intervention on the ground that a decision is *Wednesbury* unreasonable[51] or irrational.[52] Courts will now highlight the point that a decision interferes with human rights without sufficient justification,[53] or is inhumane,[54] or uncertain,[55] or interferes unfairly with a legitimate expectation arising from an earlier unequivocal representation.[56] Furthermore, the statutory grounds of appeal found especially—but not only—in the areas of planning, compulsory purchase and highways, have been given a broad rather than a narrow interpretation.[57] Not all changes to the grounds of review have made life easier for the applicant, however. For example, it has been held that decisions expressly approved by Parliament may be subjected to less intense scrutiny.[58] The test for bias now asks whether there is a real danger or likelihood of bias, not merely a reasonable suspicion (although the difference between the two tests is small).[59]

[47] See *R* v. *Criminal Injuries Compensation Board, ex p. Lain* [1967] 2 QB 864; *Council of Civil Service Unions* v. *Minister for the Civil Service, supra* n.38; Sir William Wade and CF Forsyth, *supra* n.7, pp. 247–9, 382–6.

[48] See *R* v. *Panel on Take-overs and Mergers, ex p Datafin plc, supra* n.10.

[49] See *Anisminic Ltd.* v. *Foreign Compensation Commission, supra* n.37; *R* v. *Lord President of the Privy Council, ex p. Page* [1993] AC 682.

[50] J Jowell and A Lester, "Beyond *Wednesbury*: Substantive Principles of Administrative Law" [1987] *PL* 368.

[51] i.e. "so unreasonable that no reasonable authority could ever have come to it": per Lord Greene MR in *Associated Provincial Picture Houses Ltd.* v. *Wednesbury Corporation, supra* n.35 at 230.

[52] Lord Diplock in *Council of Civil Service Unions* v. *Minister for the Civil Service, supra* n.38 at 410.

[53] *R* v. *Ministry of Defence ex p. Smith* [1996] QB 517 at 554–6.

[54] cf. *R* v. *London Borough of Brent, ex p. D* (unreported, 19 December 1997), where Moses J held that while Parliament could not normally have intended an illegal immigrant to claim assistance under the National Assistance Act 1948, the public policy that a person may not take advantage of his or her own wrongdoing was overridden by "the law of humanity": the applicant's right to life and at least a minimum standard of health.

[55] *R* v. *Barnet London Borough Council, ex p. Johnson* (1990) 89 LGR 58; cf. challenges to bylaws on this ground: *Percy* v. *Hall* [1997] QB 924.

[56] e.g. *R* v. *Inland Revenue Commissioners, ex p. Preston* [1985] AC 835; *R* v. *North and East Devon Health Authority, ex p. Coughlan* [2000] 2 WLR 622.

[57] *Ashbridge Ltd.* v. *Minister of Housing and Local Government* [1965] 1 WLR 1320 per Lord Denning MR at 1326, cited subsequently in numerous cases.

[58] *R* v. *Secretary of State for the Environment, ex p. Nottinghamshire County Council, supra* n.28; *R* v. *Secretary of State for the Environment, ex p. Hammersmith and Fulham London Borough Council, supra* n.28, per Lord Bridge at 594–7.

[59] *R* v. *Gough* [1993] AC 646. Note, however, the extension of the rule surrounding the disqualification of judges from hearing a matter in their own cause: *R* v. *Bow Street Metropolitan Stipendiary Magistrate, ex p. Pinochet* [1999] 1 All ER 577.

The courts will now only intervene on the ground of failure to comply with a procedural requirement after considering the consequences for the applicant of that non-compliance.[60] The overall trend has clearly been expansionist and it is noteworthy that it is cases that attempt to restrict the bite of judicial review that have come under greatest pressure in subsequent case law.[61] For some, it is a matter of constitutional discomfort that in developing judicial review, the judges are in practice also determining the limits of their own jurisdiction—a power that would be energetically denied to other public bodies in the absence of express (as opposed to implied) parliamentary approval.[62] For those who share this concern, the Human Rights Act 1998 will provide clear parliamentary support for the further development of judicial review in cases falling within its scope.[63]

Turning to the procedural side, there is little doubt that the introduction of the application for judicial review procedure by statutory instrument in 1977 (taking effect on 11 January 1978)[64] transformed the position of the applicant. Instead of the complete procedural separation of applications for the prerogative orders and actions seeking a declaration or injunction, with separate bodies of law governing their scope and availability, a unified procedure was now available that was issue- rather than remedy-driven. The unified procedure's requirement that the applicant must first obtain leave (now permission) before the matter was allowed to proceed could be seen as an added burden, given that applicants for declarations and injunctions had not previously had to do this (the leave stage was modelled on the old arrangements for the prerogative orders). The leave stage has been criticised on the basis that the process whereby applications are first made *ex parte* and in writing to a judge is unreliable.[65] However, it has been defended as enabling proceedings to be launched on a reasonably firm basis and weak cases to be abandoned without the

[60] *R* v. *Immigration Appeal Tribunal, ex p. Jeyeanthan* [1999] 3 All ER 231.

[61] See, e.g., the doubts expressed about the *Gough* test in *Pinochet, supra* n.59; an analogous example might be the outflanking of *Western Fish Products Ltd* v. *Penwith District Council* [1981] 2 All ER 204 by the development of the substantive "legitimate expectation" principle.

[62] This has helped fuel debate about the constitutional basis of judicial review: see the essays in CF Forsyth (ed.), *Judicial Review and the Constitution* (Oxford, Hart, 2000).

[63] It is undoubtedly true that the judges themselves sometimes feel the need to address this discomfort. See *infra.*

[64] The Rules of the Supreme Court (Amendment No. 3) 1977, SI 1977/1955, introducing a new RS C Order 53: Application for Judicial Revie w Express authority covering the key elements was subsequently provided in the Supreme Court Act 1981, s. 3 1 Order 53 has been set out in amended form in Schedule 1 to the Civil Procedure Rules 1998, SI 1998/3132, as amended. The original changes were largely based on the Law Commission's *Report on Remedies in Administrative Law* (Law Com. 73, Cmnd. 6407, March 1976).

[65] AP Le Sueur and M Sunkin, "Applications for Judicial Review: the Requirement of Leave" [1992] *PL* 102. There is also a risk that good cases may be ruled out at the leave stage: in 1987–89, for example, over 10 per cent of successful final applications only obtained leave at a renewed oral hearing: L Bridges *et al., Judicial Review in Perspective* (2nd edn., London, Cavendish 1996).

expense of a court hearing.[66] The leave stage may also facilitate a settlement, such as by an offer by the authority to reconsider the matter. The new judicial review procedure also affected time limits. The old time limit for the prerogative orders was six months, but the applicant must now apply for permission promptly and in any event within three months from the date when the grounds for the application first arose.[67] The court may extend time if there is good reason, but a remedy may still be refused if to grant it would be likely to cause substantial hardship to, or substantially prejudice the rights of, any person or would be detrimental to good administration.[68] The courts are thus able to deal with the issue of delay pragmatically in the light of the circumstances of the case.[69]

Particularly important is the fact that the requirements of standing (that the applicant have a "sufficient interest in the matter to which the application relates")[70] have for the most part been interpreted liberally and without regard to older precedents suggesting a restrictive approach limiting standing to those whose common law rights are at stake.[71] The position as to the availability of interim relief has also been regularised.[72] The courts have also, after much arguably unhelpful litigation, decided not to regard the application for judicial review as the exclusive remedy where the circumstances of the case raise both public and private law issues,[73] and have accepted that public law issues can be raised collaterally, for example as a defence to a prosecution.[74] It might therefore be felt that courts are now seeking to operate a procedural regime that generally enables attention to be focused on the merits of the substantive arguments rather than on technicalities.

The number of applications for leave (permission) to apply for judicial review has risen from 533 in 1981 to 4,539 in 1998,[75] notwithstanding the cre-

[66] See, e.g., Lord Woolf MR, "Public Law—Private Law: Why the Divide?", *supra* n.39; Law Com No 226, *Administrative Law: Judicial Review and Statutory Appeals*, Part V.

[67] RSC Ord. 53, r. 4.

[68] Supreme Court Act 1981, s. 31(6).

[69] See *R* v. *Dairy Produce Quota Tribunal, ex p. Caswell* [1990] 2 AC 738; *R* v. *Criminal Injuries Compensation Board, ex p. A* [1999] 2 WLR 974.

[70] RSC Ord. 53, r. 3(7).

[71] *R* v. *Inland Revenue Commissioners, ex p. National Federation of Self-Employed and Small Businesses Ltd* [1982] AC 617; *R* v. *Secretary of State for Foreign Affairs ex p. World Development Movement Ltd* [1996] 1 WLR 386.

[72] See RSC Ord. 53, r. 3(10).

[73] The law took a wrong turn with *O'Reilly* v. *Mackman* [1983] 2 AC 237 but matters have been improved by *Roy* v. *Kensington and Chelsea and Westminster Family Practitioner Committee* [1992] 1 AC 624 and *Trustees of the Dennis Roy Pension Fund* v. *Sheffield City Council* [1998] 1 WLR 840.

[74] *Boddington* v. *British Transport Police* [1998] 2 WLR 369.

[75] *Judicial Statistics 1981*, Table A.6(a); *Judicial Statistics 1998*, Table 1.13. In the early part of the century, the average annual number of prerogative writs sought was between 100 and 200: see *Civil Judicial Statistics 1931* (Cmd. 4187), pp. 4–5. What is now judicial review counted for only a part of this business.

ation of rights of appeal to replace judicial review in areas such as homelessness.[76] In 1998 there were 1,346 applications for judicial review disposed of compared with 3,530 actions disposed of in the Queen's Bench Division.[77] The proportion of judicial review disposals in the business of the Queen's Bench Division is increasing.[78] The developments outlined in this section of the chapter must help to provide an explanation for this phenomenon. For it might well be said that judicial review has developed an internal momentum of its own: the more accessible the jurisdiction has (in general) become—through the development of substantive principles and rules of procedure—the more attractive an option judicial review may seem to the would-be litigant.[79] Looking to the future, most if not all of the foreseeable pressures will tend to lead to further increases in the business of public law litigation. We will return to this issue later in the chapter.

Contrasting Judicial Attitudes to the Rôle of Judicial Review

The factors considered in the previous sections of the chapter help explain the rise of judicial review in general. It is also important to note, however, that the degree to which a court will feel it appropriate to develop judicial review in any *individual* case will depend upon that court's views as to the proper boundaries of judicial review, of the rôle of the jurisdiction in relation to Parliament and government, and of the degree to which it is appropriate for courts to be deferential to elected institutions. A court's basis for its views on issues of this type must ultimately, as a matter of logic, rest upon its perceptions concerning the proper functioning of the constitution, which will be influenced by its perception of the shape and functions of the state—although such links are only sometimes revealed in the cases. There are numerous examples of the influence of factors of this type in the case law: a few will be illustrated here.

The first concerns the prevailing judicial view of the need for protections for public authorities in relation to the application for judicial review procedure. In seeking to justify the introduction of the exclusivity rule in *O'Reilly* v. *Mackman*, for example, Lord Diplock suggested that:

[76] Housing Act 1996, s.204.

[77] *Judicial Statistics 1998*, Tables 1.13, 3.5.

[78] In 1992, the comparable figures were 870 and 7,193: *Judicial Statistics 1992*, Tables 1.13, 3.5.

[79] We note, however, the far-from-complete statistical data concerning the impact of judicial review: G Richardson and M Sunkin, "Judicial Review: Questions of Impact" [1996] *PL* 79.

"The public interest in good administration requires that public authorities and third parties should not be kept in suspense as to the legal validity of a decision the authority has reached in purported exercise of decision-making powers for any longer period than is absolutely necessary in fairness to the person affected by the decision".[80]

There was, in consequence, a "need, in the interests of good administration and of third parties who may be indirectly affected by the decision, for speedy certainty as to whether it has the effect of a decision that is valid in public law".[81] The linkage between the rationale for having procedural protections and the perceived functions of the state is made clear in Lord Woolf's extra-judicial suggestion that good administration demands speedy certainty in relation to the validity of a public body's decisions since public bodies, unlike private organisations, administer on behalf of and in ways which affect the whole community.[82] Prevailing judicial perceptions of the rôle of the state thus had a key influence on the judiciary's decision to introduce and to enforce a rule—exclusivity—which had a dramatic influence on judicial review in the 1980s.

Another example can be seen in the case law concerning public interest standing. The *Gouriet* case has been categorised as denying any real role in judicial review to litigants who wish to bring challenges in the public (rather than their personal) interest.[83] With one notable exception in the form of the *Rose Theatre* case,[84] however, more recent case law has allowed pressure groups which are sufficiently expert in the subject-matter of the decision they are challenging, and/or sufficiently representative of a broad swathe of opinion which could not otherwise secure effective representation in court, to seek judicial review of relevant public law decisions.[85] Indeed, the *Dixon* case has even gone so far as to say that only a busybody will be denied standing at the leave stage.[86] This change of stance plainly indicates a revised perception of the role of judicial review. By insisting that an applicant must possess a private right or interest, a court is suggesting that judicial review is not the appropriate forum for the ventilation of questions concerning the public interest. By implication, the

[80] See *supra* n.73, at 280–1.

[81] *Ibid.*, at 284.

[82] "Public Law—Private Law: Why the Divide?", *supra* n.39, *Protection of the Public—A New Challenge*, *supra* n.39.

[83] *Gouriet* v. *Union of Post Office Workers* [1978] AC 435; see further PP Craig, *supra* n.3, at 685–90.

[84] *R* v. *Secretary of State for the Environment, ex p. Rose Theatre Trust Co.* [1990] 1 QB 504; the practical effect of Schiemann J's reasoning would have been effectively to confine judicial review to the holders of a private right or interest.

[85] *R* v. *Inspectorate of Pollution, ex p. Greenpeace (No.2)* [1994] 4 All ER 329; *R* v. *Secretary of State for Foreign Affairs, ex p. World Development Movement*, *supra* n.71.

[86] *R* v. *North East Somerset County Council, ex p. Dixon* [1998] Env LR 111.

only appropriate course of action for those with public interest concerns is to lobby Parliament or government. By allowing public interest challenges into judicial review, by contrast, the courts are accepting that judicial review can play a stronger role in the political process—for pressure groups which fail successfully to lobby to prevent a decision being taken can still seek to challenge the legality of that decision after the event.

Further examples of the role of factors of this type might include the *Wednesbury* case law concerning the varying degree of leeway the courts will afford the decision-maker depending upon whether the impugned decision involves questions of human rights or sensitive policy,[87] and the majority and minority views in the *Fire Brigades Union* case concerning how far it was appropriate for a court to remedy a minister's apparent defiance of Parliament's wishes, rather than leaving the matter to Parliament.[88] Many other examples can be found. They are linked by a common element: for they demonstrate that a court's willingness to find that judicial review will lie in a given case—or to develop the parameters of the jurisdiction—depends on that court's view of its proper place in the constitutional structure of the United Kingdom.

Future prospects

There are a number of factors which are likely to contribute to a further expansion of judicial review. Some of these are pressures inherent within the jurisprudence. Others are the result of the significant legislative developments comprised in the Labour Government's programme of constitutional reforms.

The recent—and likely future—development of the public law/private law distinction provides a useful illustration of the interaction between constitutional change and the parameters of judicial review. This stems from certain quite profound alterations to the shape and ambit of the state in the last twenty years. As Mark Freedland has observed:

> "British governments from 1979 onwards have sought to restructure much of the process and most of the institutions of public administration with the aim of achieving greater efficiency by introducing the discipline of market forces or the closest available analogy to them".[89]

[87] Typified by *R* v. *Defence Ministry, ex p. Smith, supra* n.53. For a sensitive policy case, see *R* v. *Secretary of State for the Environment, ex p. Nottinghamshire County Council, supra* n.28.

[88] *R* v. *Secretary of State for the Home Department, ex p. Fire Brigades Union, supra* n.18. For analysis, see E Barendt, "Constitutional Law and the Criminal Injuries Compensation Scheme" [1995] *PL* 357.

[89] Mark Freedland, "Government by Contract and Public Law" [1994] *PL* 86 at 86–7.

The 1980s witnessed the privatisation of many previously state-owned industries, together with the establishment of autonomous regulatory bodies in areas of economic life which might previously have been regulated directly by the government. The early 1990s saw the emergence of "contracting-out" and the transfer of many "operational" aspects of central government work to Next Steps Agencies.[90] The cumulative effect has been to reduce the size of the state, which may well, as Murray Hunt has argued, have been "reconceived on the model of market ordering",[91] something which has plainly survived the change of government in 1997.

It is unclear how well public law has coped with this reconception. A promising start was made in *R* v. *Panel on Take-overs and Mergers, ex p. Datafin*, where the Court of Appeal found that the Take-over Panel—a self-regulatory body without a visible statutory source of authority, but which carried out the vital task of policing City trading—was in principle amenable to judicial review.[92] Prior to *Datafin*, the courts had generally required a body to derive its authority from statute or from the prerogative for it to be open to judicial review. *Datafin* expanded the range of criteria to which courts could look. Sir John Donaldson MR stated that "possibly the only essential elements" were "a public element, which can take many different forms, and the exclusion from the jurisdiction of bodies whose sole source of power is a consensual submission to its jurisdiction".[93] Lloyd LJ envisaged an assortment of tests: while "the source of the power will often, perhaps usually, be decisive", if the body was "exercising public law functions, or if the exercise of its functions have public law consequences, then that may . . . be sufficient to bring that body within the reach of judicial review".[94] The public law functions of the Panel were thus sufficient to bring it within the scope of judicial review, despite its lack of a clear statutory source of authority. Furthermore, being concerned to control "the realities of executive power",[95] the Court of Appeal dismissed the idea that the applicants had voluntarily submitted to the Panel's jurisdiction by trading in the City knowing of its regulatory powers: the City was not a mere club that one could leave or enter at will.

[90] For general discussion, see Ian Harden, *The Contracting State* (Buckingham, OUP, 1992); Dawn Oliver and Gavin Drewry, *Public Service Reforms: Issues of Accountability and Public Law* (London, Pinter, 1996); Chris Willett (ed.), *Public Sector Reform and the Citizen's Charter* (London, Blackstone, 1996); Michael Taggart (ed.), *The Province of Administrative Law, supra* n.9; Carol Harlow and Richard Rawlings, *Law and Administration, supra* n.4, ch.5.

[91] Murray Hunt, "Constitutionalism and the Contractualisation of Government in the United Kingdom" in M Taggart (ed.), *supra* n.9, at 21.

[92] See *supra* n.10.

[93] *Ibid.*, at 838.

[94] *Ibid.*, at 847.

[95] *Ibid.*, at 838 (Sir John Donaldson MR).

In *R* v. *Disciplinary Committee of the Jockey Club, ex p. Aga Khan*,[96] however, the Court of Appeal sought to limit the scope of judicial review in a way that is hard to reconcile with *Datafin*. The Court held that the Jockey Club was not subject to judicial review, notwithstanding the fact that it effectively exercised monopoly control over horse racing. The reasoning of the members of the Court of Appeal was arguably inconsistent. For Hoffmann LJ, the crucial issue was that the Jockey Club was not exercising governmental functions, in that there was no actual or potential governmental interest in regulating horse racing.[97] Sir Thomas Bingham MR and Farquharson LJ adopted divergent approaches to this issue, but for both judges the key factor was that the Aga Khan had agreed to be bound by the Club's rules when racing his horses—in other words, he fell within the "consensual submission" exception set out in *Datafin*, and his remedies were confined to the law of contract.[98] This is hard to reconcile with *Datafin* since the Aga Khan did not appear to have any greater choice in his dealings with the Jockey Club than the *Datafin* applicants had in their dealings with the Take-over Panel—yet the "consensual submission" exception was successfully invoked by the Club but not by the Panel.

Aga Khan has encouraged courts to rule that judicial review is unavailable where the respondent either derived its power from contract, or had a contractual relationship with the applicant, *regardless* of whether the respondent also performed public law functions.[99] This has meant that the amenability to judicial review of bodies performing identical regulatory functions has varied depending upon whether each body's source of power was statutory or contractual.[100] In addition, given the use of contracts in the processes of "contracting-out" and privatisation, it has become uncertain which (if any) of the bodies set up using these processes will be open to judicial review—prompting concerns about the growth of an accountability deficit since private law remedies may not always be open to members of the public against such bodies either. Mark Freedland has suggested that public law has failed to produce a sufficiently sophisticated response to the growth of "government by contract", and that—by privatising some of its functions—a public body might

[96] *Ibid.*; see further N Bamforth, "The Scope of Judicial Review: Still Uncertain" [1993] *PL* 239.

[97] *Datafin, supra* n. 10 at 930–3.

[98] *Ibid.*, at 924 (Bingham MR), 928, 930 (Farquharson LJ).

[99] *R* v. *Lord Chancellor, ex p. Hibbit and Saunders* [1993] *COD* 326; *R* v. *Insurance Ombudsman Bureau, ex p. Aegon Life Assurance, supra* n.10.

[100] For example, the Ombudsman cases: *R* v. *Advertising Standards Authority, ex p. the Insurance Service* (1990) 2 Admin LR 77; *R* v. *Code of Practice Committee of the British Pharmaceutical Industry, ex p. Professional Counselling Aids* (1991) 3 Admin LR 697. Another controversial decision turning on the presence of a contract is *R* v. *East Berkshire Health Authority, ex p. Walsh* [1988] QB 152; see also the cases discussed in SH Bailey, BL Jones and AR Mowbray, *Cases and Materials in Administrative Law* (3rd edn., 1997), pp. 629–34.

possibly place them beyond the reach of public law.[101] Murray Hunt is less pessimistic about public law's ability to respond, but acknowledges that the *Aga Khan* approach to "consensual submission" may make it difficult for courts to do so consistently.[102]

In this respect, privatisation and "contracting out" provide a good example of the capacity of constitutional change to generate debate about the appropriate parameters of judicial review. Interestingly, a further constitutional change—the enactment of the Human Rights Act 1998—might provide a partial solution to the difficulties. This is via the concept of "spill-over", more commonly associated with European Community law.[103] Section 6 of the Human Rights Act 1998 imposes a duty on public authorities to abide by Convention rights. During the Act's passage, the Home Secretary asserted that the Government intended a public authority to be defined "[by] reference to the concept of a public function".[104] If, in consequence, the scope of Human Rights Act judicial review for breach of section 6 comes to turn on the nature of the respondent's functions, it is at least arguable that courts will feel encouraged—for the sake of consistency—to focus on the same question in non-Human Rights Act cases, thereby reducing the importance of the source (whether statutory *or* contractual) of the respondent's authority in determining its amenability to review. Judicial responses to Community law suggest that the likelihood of such a "spill-over" is uncertain: the need to promote consistency between Community and non-Community cases has encouraged the House of Lords to find that injunctions should be available against the Crown in domestic as well as Community cases,[105] but has not encouraged the open acknowledgement—at least prior to the Human Rights Act—of proportionality as a free-standing ground of judicial review.[106]

The grounds of judicial review are also likely to develop, due both to the logical extension of existing substantive principles of judicial review and to the enactment of the Human Rights Act 1998. Under the first heading, the Court of Appeal's decision in *R* v. *North and East Devon Health Authority, ex p. Coughlan* seems once again to confirm—after a period of doubt—that substantive legitimate expectations, based on fairness as distinct from *Wednesbury* unreasonableness, have a place in English law.[107] Other likely developments

[101] See *supra* n.89, at 98–104.

[102] See *supra* n.91, at 33–8.

[103] See Gordon Anthony, "Community Law and the Development of UK Administrative Law: Delimiting the 'Spill-over' Effect" (1998) 4 *EPL* 253.

[104] HC Deb. vol. 314 col. 409.

[105] *M* v. *Home Office*, *supra* n.8.

[106] *R* v. *Secretary of State for the Home Department, ex p. Brind*, *supra* n.19.

[107] See *supra* n.56. The court endorsed the position taken by Sedley J in *R* v. *Ministry of Agriculture, Fisheries and Food, ex p. Hamble Fisheries (Offshore) Ltd.* [1996] 2 All ER 714, notwithstanding its disavowal by the Court of Appeal in *R* v. *Secretary of State for the Home*

under this heading include the extension of the scope of judicial review for mistakes of fact;[108] the development of the duty to give reasons as an aspect of procedural fairness alongside developments in openness in government (which are likely to be real although never sufficient to satisfy all critics);[109] and the confirmation of a liberal approach to the rules of standing, although it should be noted that standing in Human Rights Act judicial review will be confined to "victims" of rights-violations and will be narrower than in most pre-existing cases.[110]

Implementation of the Human Rights Act 1998 is likely to prove a transforming event, although perhaps not as far-reaching as some would maintain. So far as it is possible to do so, primary and subordinate legislation must be read and given effect to in a way which is compatible with Convention rights.[111] However, this does not affect the validity, continuing operation or enforcement of any incompatible primary legislation, or any incompatible subordinate legislation if primary legislation prevents removal of the incompatibility.[112] Here, a "declaration of incompatibility" may be made.[113] Furthermore, section 6 provides that it is unlawful for a public authority (including a court or tribunal) to act in a way which is incompatible with a Convention right, except where it could not act any differently as the result of primary legislation or it was acting so as to give effect to or enforce primary legislation which cannot be read to be compatible. It is to be expected that this will have an effect at all levels across the public sector. Additional judges are to be appointed; training has been organised for both judiciary and civil servants; legislation and procedures are being reviewed for compatibility with Convention rights.[114] However, it was not intended that the Act should apply

Department, ex p. Hargreaves [1997] 1 WLR 906. See also *R* v. *Secretary of State for Education and Employment, ex p. Begbie* [2000] 1 WLR 1115.

[108] See T Jones, "Mistakes of Fact in Administrative Law" [1990] *PL* 467; M Demetriou and S Housemann, [1997] *JR* 27; M Kent QC, [1999] *JR* 239.

[109] See *R* v. *Higher Education Funding Council, ex p. Institute of Dental Surgery* [1994] 1 WLR 242; *R* v. *Secretary of State for the Home Department, ex p. Doody* [1994] 1 AC 531; Citizen's Charter *Principles of Public Service* (Cm. 1599, 1991) At the time of writing, the Freedom of Information Bill was passing through Parliament.

[110] Note the widespread criticism accorded to the restrictive approach adopted by Schiemann J in *R* v. *Secretary of State for the Environment, ex p. Rose Theatre Trust Co, supra* n.84, distinguished in *R* v. *HM Inspectorate of Pollution, ex p. Greenpeace (No. 2), supra* n. 84 and *R* v. *North East Somerset County Council, ex p. Dixon, supra* n. 86.

[111] 1998 Act, s. 3(1). "Convention Rights" are specified in s. 1(1) and include ECHR Articles 2 to 12 and 14, Articles 1 to 3 of the First Protocol and Articles 1 and 2 of the Sixth Protocol.

[112] 1998 Act, s. 3(2).

[113] *Ibid.*, s. 4.

[114] *Human Rights News*, issued by the Human Rights Task Force; Home Office *Human Rights Act 1998 Guidance for Departments* (see the webpages of the Home Office Human Rights Unit: *www.homeoffice.gov.uk/hract*).

directly as between private citizens (save under Section 3), and it seems unlikely that the Act can be strained by interpretation so as to have that effect.[115]

In terms of the grounds of judicial review, it seems overwhelmingly likely that the Human Rights Act will herald the open recognition of proportionality, which has previously been available where decisions are subject to directly effective Community law, but not otherwise.[116] This change will be prompted by *Smith* v. *United Kingdom*,[117] where the European Court of Human Rights ruled that the domestic protection of Convention rights under *Wednesbury* review—even under Sir Thomas Bingham MR's formulation whereby the more substantial a public authority's interference with fundamental rights, the more a court would require by way of justification to be convinced that the interference was reasonable[118]—did not guarantee an effective remedy from the standpoint of Article 13 of the Convention. For the *Wednesbury* standard involved too high a threshold of review to allow domestic courts properly to question whether the interference with the applicants' Convention rights involved a pressing social need or was proportionate, that is, was necessary and no more than necessary for achieving the Convention-approved aim of (on the facts) protecting national security. The message of the case seems clear: proportionality is a stronger standard of review than *Wednesbury* unreasonableness, and is the appropriate standard for domestic courts to apply in judicial review cases involving Convention rights.

General judicial observations about the likely effects of the Human Rights Act have been offered in two recent domestic cases. In *R* v. *Secretary of State for the Home Department, ex p. Simms*, Lord Hoffmann suggested that the Act was to be understood in terms of a new, human rights-driven "principle of legality", which meant that Parliament could not override fundamental rights in legislation by "general or ambiguous words" since there was too great a risk that "the full implications" of the "unqualified meaning" of such words may pass unnoticed in the democratic process.[119] Unless human rights were overridden by express language or necessary implication, the courts would always assume that the general language of statutes, and of subordinate legislation,

[115] See N Bamforth, "The Application of the Human Rights Act 1998 to Public Authorities and Private Bodies" [1998] *CLJ* 159; G Phillipson, "The Human Rights Act, 'Horizontal Effect' and the Common Law: a Bang or a Whimper" (1999) 62 *MLR* 824; Sir Richard Buxton, "The Human Rights Act and Private Law" (2000) 116 *LQR* 48. Broader views have been advanced by other writers, including Sir William Wade, "Human Rights and the Judiciary" [1998] *EHRLR* 520; M Hunt, "The Horizontal Effect of the Human Rights Act" [1998] *PL* 523.

[116] *R* v. *Secretary of State for the Home Department, ex p. Brind, supra* n. 19; *R* v. *Secretary of State for Health, ex .p Eastside Cheese Company* (1999) 1 LGLR 335.

[117] (2000) 29 EHRR 493. The Convention proportionality test is laid down in detail in *Handyside* v. *United Kingdom* (1976) 1 EHRR 737; *Sunday Times* v. *United Kingdom* (1979) 2 EHRR 245; *Dudgeon* v. *United Kingdom* (1981) 4 EHRR 149; and *Smith* v. *United Kingdom.*

[118] In *R* v. *Ministry of Defence, ex p. Smith, supra* n.53.

[119] [1999] 3 All ER 400 at 412.

was intended to be read subject to the basic rights of the individual. In addition, while the Act would allow the fundamental human rights protected by the common law to be supplemented by those protected by the Convention, since much of the Convention already reflected the common law, its "adoption . . . as part of domestic law is unlikely to involve radical change in our notions of fundamental human rights".[120] If Lord Hoffmann's view is shared by the judiciary more broadly, then the main impact of the Act on judicial review will be that it creates a new human rights-based legality principle of review which can apply whenever Convention rights are in issue. How this will fit in with any proportionality test has yet to be seen.

In *R* v. *DPP, ex p. Kebeline*, Lord Hope suggested that the Convention "should be seen as an expression of fundamental principles rather than as a set of mere rules. The questions which the courts will have to decide in the application of these principles will involve questions of balance between competing interests and issues of proportionality".[121] This being so, judicial deference to Parliament or the executive would not be banished under the Human Rights Act. Where difficult policy choices have to be made between the rights of the individual and the needs of society, it will be appropriate for the judiciary to defer to the executive or legislature. Where questions of social or economic policy are involved, a "discretionary area of judgment" will be available to the executive, within which the courts will tend to be deferential. By contrast, courts are more likely to intervene where the rights at stake are of high constitutional importance or are of a kind which they are especially well placed to assess. How far this signals a difference from pre-Human Rights Act judicial review, in which judicial deference in sensitive policy cases was common, is open to question. On a wide reading, Lord Hope's "discretionary area of judgment" might be felt to parallel Sir Thomas Bingham's approach to *Wednesbury* review in *ex p. Smith*[122]—but reflection suggests that this cannot be so given the European Court of Human Rights' rejection of the Bingham approach in *Smith* v. *United Kingdom*, suggesting that Lord Hope's approach may in fact involve less deference.

Whatever the effects of the Human Rights Act on the grounds of review, the Act is likely to alter the structure of judicial review cases falling within its scope. The courts' focus in judicial review has traditionally been on the nature of the wrong—that is, the *ultra vires* action—allegedly committed by the public authority.[123] Courts thus ask whether the public authority has acted outside

[120] *Ibid.*, at 413.

[121] [1999] 4 All ER 801 at 844.

[122] See *supra* n.53.

[123] In *R* v. *North East Somerset County Council, ex p. Dixon*, Sedley J thus asserted that "Public law is not at base about rights, even though abuses of power may and often do invade private rights; it is about wrongs—that is to say misuses of public power", *supra* n.87, at 331.

the scope of its statutory powers, or unreasonably, or unfairly. The drafting of most Convention rights means that the starting point in Human Rights Act judicial review will, by contrast, be on the nature of the right allegedly infringed and on whether that infringement can be justified.[124] Laurence Lustgarten and Ian Leigh have thus suggested that courts will have to ask what aim the rights-restriction sought to achieve; how severe the need for the restriction was; and whether the impact on the restricted right was significant, and if so whether some less significant option might have been available.[125] They argue that the second issue will need to be assessed in the light of detailed factual information concerning the nature and extent of the problem government was seeking to address, and question whether the existing judicial review procedure—which does not allow for extensive factual inquiry—will prove adequate for this task.[126] Whether or not this is proves to be correct, the Act will plainly herald a far more assertive use of the *terminology* of rights in judicial review cases.

In *Simms*, Lord Hoffmann suggested that the Human Rights Act would require courts, while acknowledging parliamentary sovereignty, to apply "principles of constitutionality little different from those which exist in countries where the power of the legislature is expressly limited by a constitutional document".[127] In the long run, this may turn out to be one of the key consequences of the post-1997 programme of constitutional reform. For both the Human Rights Act and the devolution legislation give courts the power to engage in essentially "constitutional" decision-making, whether this is to judicially review government action using broad Convention principles, or to pronounce on the legality of measures passed by the devolved assemblies.[128] In the twenty-first century, we might therefore expect to see much more explicit articulation of clearly constitutional standards in judicial review than has been the case for most of the twentieth century.

[124] M Taggart, "Tugging on Superman's Cape: Lessons from Experience with the New Zealand Bill of Rights Act 1990" [1998] *PL* 266 at 277–9; Lord Irvine, "The Development of Human Rights in Britain" [1998] *PL* 221. Such an approach seems evident in Lord Steyn's judgment in the *Simms* case: *supra* n.119, at 407 *et seq.*

[125] "Making Rights Real: the Courts, Remedies, and the Human Rights Act" [1999] *CLJ* 509 at 523.

[126] *Ibid.*, at 523, 525–6.

[127] *Ibid.*, at 412.

[128] In the context of devolution, see P Craig and M Walters, "The Courts, Devolution and Judicial Review" [1999] *PL* 274.

Conclusion

It has been argued that constitutional change has a key influence over the development of judicial review, a process which has also had an internal momentum of its own. Looking to the future, it seems likely that the judicial review caseload will continue to rise, due to a combination of continuing internal momentum and the constitutional developments noted above. Of course, litigation has to be financed. While the costs of litigation may not be an overriding concern for some applicants, many are supported by legal aid. Here it is noteworthy that the recent guidance on the granting of civil legal aid may increase rather than reduce the number of legally-aided applicants.[129] Cases which will produce real benefits for the public at large, or which raise significant human rights issues, or are of overwhelming importance to the client, will have a particularly high priority for funding. It is unlikely that the appointment of a few additional judges will be sufficient to deal with the resultant business. This might generate additional delay in the resolution of cases, a hardening of the criteria for the grant of permission to seek judicial review, a greater disinclination to accept a case where there are alternative remedies, and an increase in pressure on advocates to limit the number of points taken. On the other hand, the introduction of case management by the judges may facilitate the settlement of cases, echoing the anticipated effects of the Woolf reforms in civil procedure.[130]

In any event, attempts to inhibit access to the courts may fall foul of the identification of such access as a fundamental right protected by the common law and by the European Convention via the Human Rights Act. There has even been speculation that in the event of an attempt to remove the judicial review powers of the courts, certain judges might defy a clearly worded Act of Parliament.[131] It seems that the role of judges in the twenty-first century may have effectively (but not formally) been entrenched. This being so, it is to be hoped that the parliamentary approval conferred by the Human Rights Act 1998 on the development of judicial review in the human rights context will come to be matched by clearer and more principled decision-making across all areas of public law. More generally, the current articulation of constitutional

[129] See *Access to Justice Act 1999: The Funding Code*, Part 7; *The Funding Code: A New Approach to Funding Civil Cases: Report to the Lord Chancellor following consultation*, available from www.legal-aid.gov.uk/web2/devel/papers.htm.

[130] See D Gladwell, "Modern Litigation Culture: The First Six Months of the Civil Justice Reforms in England and Wales" (2000) 19 *CJQ* 9. A review of the Crown Office List, chaired by Sir Jeffery Bowman, reported to the Lord Chancellor on 21 March 2000. See further [2000] JR 67–78.

[131] Lord Woolf MR, "Droit Public—English Style", *supra* n.39, at 69.

rights carries with it the challenge of developing adequate remedies, both in theory and in practice—possibly reversing Dicey's third axiom concerning the rule of law.[132]

[132] AV Dicey, *supra* n.13, pp. 195–202.

11

Environmental Law

TIM JEWELL AND COLIN REID

Law has a long history of addressing environmental problems. The result, however, has been law *about* the environment rather than *environmental law*. Whilst essentially semantic, this distinction does bring some important consequences. A legal approach which is simply the application of well-established techniques of administrative, criminal, or tort/delict law to environmental issues, in much the same way that such techniques can apply to any other area of activity, has limitations. Whilst rumours of the maturing of environmental law abound—founded, for example, on nascent principles and ideas which can be seen as a basis for "an" environmental law[1]—the longer term question is whether this alone will ensure the development of a coherent or effective response to environmental threats. For if we are going to take environmental issues seriously, not only must specific rules dealing directly with key environmental issues be forged, but law as a whole must assimilate environmental concerns and assist, or at least not obstruct, more environmentally beneficial activity.[2]

A chapter such as this can only raise questions, however, and very big questions do arise. Fundamentally, the issue may simplistically be one about some "ultimate goal", well beyond the particular, often immediate, concerns of lawyers (whether academic or in practice). For example, what would an "environmentally sound" society actually require? A key problem is that different arguments which share a concern to change society by having greater regard for the environment may have very different conceptions of the ideal solution. Various sorts of anthropocentric and biocentric ideas will at times conflict,[3] whilst experience of liberal democracy and its reliance on deregulated private

[1] M Purdue, "Integrated Pollution Control in the Environmental Protection Act 1990: A Coming of Age of Environmental Law?" (1991) 54 *MLR* 534.

[2] G Winter, "Perspectives on Environmental Law—Entering the Fourth Phase" (1989) 1 *Journal of Environmental Law* (JEL) 38.

[3] A convenient, if critical, account of different justifications is given in A Gillespie, *International Environmental Law, Policy and Ethics* (Oxford, Clarendon Press, 1997).

enterprise suggests that it may be profoundly ill-equipped to develop any real sense of "ecological rationality", or to "ecologically modernise" despite shared environmental concern.[4] As with the evolution of ideas of Western democracy itself, one consequence is a readily agreed legal reaction against some of the worst (environmental) excesses, with a subsequent fragmentation of agreement about what to do next, or how to do it.

What is evident since that initial legal reaction, however, is a growing consensus as to some aspects of environmental policy. The most prominent of these internationally and, more recently, nationally is "sustainable development". Having its origins even before the 1987 Report of the World Commission on Environment and Development,[5] and the focus of international activity since,[6] this amorphous concept is now an established part of the Community legal order, plays a prominent part in UK policy, and features in UK legislation too.[7] There remain considerable problems with both its definition[8] and implementation, as a glance at its consideration in the most recent UK policy illustrates.[9] It is the very generality of sustainable development as an organising concept which secures its wide appeal, yet which presents the primary obstacle to its effective implementation. This is particularly so if its social and inter-generational aspects are taken seriously.

The political resonance of sustainable development is complemented by the emergence of other principles, which are perhaps subordinate to it, but which may have more immediate appeal to the lawyer or policy-maker. Most prominent here are the preventive, precautionary and polluter pays principles.[10] There are signs that practical measures, putatively based on such aspirations, are being put in place. Yet here too the limitations of current policy approaches and of legal mechanisms present massive obstacles to the necessary revolution in how we think about, and address, environmental problems.[11]

[4] V Plumwood, "Inequality, Ecojustice, and Ecological Rationality", reproduced in J Dryzek and D Schlosberg, *Debating the Earth* (Oxford, Oxford University Press, 1998); A Gouldson and J Murphy, *Regulatory Realities: The Implementation and Impact of Industrial Environmental Regulation* (London, Earthscan, 1998).

[5] World Commission on Environment and Development, *Our Common Future* (Oxford, Oxford University Press, 1998).

[6] e.g., at the 1992 UN Conference on Environment and Development, Rio de Janeiro.

[7] EC Treaty, Art. 6; *A Better Quality of Life: A Strategy for Sustainable Development for the UK* (Cm. 4345, 1999); Environment Act 1995 (EA 1995), s. 4; Natural Heritage (Scotland) Act 1991, s. 1; Government of Wales Act 1998, s. 121.

[8] "It is a pity that the issue which everyone on the planet will have to tackle at some point has acquired this impenetrable title. It is even more problematic that no definition exists which can be understood by everyone and built into their lives": *Down to Earth—A Scottish Perspective on Sustainable Development* (Edinburgh, Scottish Office, 1999), p. 4.

[9] *A Better Quality of Life*, *supra* n. 7.

[10] E.g., EC Treaty, Art. 174(2).

[11] We return to some of these ideas below, but a valuable introduction to the precautionary principle in particular is provided by R Harding and E Fisher (eds), *Perspectives on the Precautionary Principle* (Sydney, Federation Press, 1999).

Our purpose in this chapter is therefore to explore some of these obstacles, how they are being approached, and the prospects for the next few years. We look first at aspects of the context in which environmental law must now develop, and the challenges that presents for its further evolution. This, as befits the subject, requires a broad outline view, embracing physical, scientific, and political considerations. Secondly, we consider some of the general implications of that changing context for the further evolution of environmental law. Invariably, this too must be selective. It will, however, provide a framework for the third section, which is a specific consideration of waste reduction, management and disposal, one of the most enduring problems in, but most vital components of, UK environmental law. Through that consideration we aim to consider some ways in which sustainable development may—or may not—be pursued through environmental law.

The Challenge for Environmental Law

Physical

We are increasingly aware of the range of human impacts on the environment, locally and globally. Consequently, many obvious impacts have been, or are being, addressed. Whilst the sufficiency of controls over environmental harm remains highly contentious, it is indisputable that they have had at least some beneficial effects. It is becoming all too apparent, however, that that is not enough.[12] The devastating effects of chemical production in the nineteenth century, contributing to the mean age of death in parts of the Midlands being just eighteen or nineteen, are now a thing of the past.[13] The systemic problems of waste are being addressed, although not yet to similar effect (see below p. 221). In relation to water pollution also, major discharges are subject to well-established controls, which have contained much gross pollution, yet water quality is now affected by a cumulation of other factors, including diffuse pollution, abstraction, run-off and altered drainage, which demands a more flexible and diverse legal response. We must also tackle the additional consequences of environmental controls themselves, for example, in disposing of

[12] For an insightful analysis of the strengths and weaknesses of traditional approaches to pollution control see: D Robinson, "Regulatory Evolution in Pollution Control", in T Jewell and J Steele (eds), *Law in Environmental Decision-Making: National, European, and International Perspectives* (Oxford, Clarendon Press, 1998).

[13] A Markham, *A Brief History of Pollution* (London, Earthscan, 1994), ch. 6, although this is now attributed as much to commercial fuel-use decisions as to effective regulation: B Clapp, *An Environmental History of Britain since the Industrial Revolution* (London, Longman, 1994).

sewage sludge, or addressing increased flooding risks from drainage and land use changes.[14]

Greater still are the difficulties facing the conservation of nature. Only in very few cases is the main threat to wildlife posed by direct persecution or killing. Instead, wildlife is under the greatest pressure from loss or deterioration of habitat, changes in agricultural practices, water abstraction, diffuse pollution (including from overseas), foreign species adding competition or affecting the gene pool, and potentially from genetically-modified crops (both the risks of contamination, and the consequences of changing agricultural practices). Tackling such issues forces us to address the big questions referred to above. How *should* we balance the needs of wildlife with the livelihoods of communities? What is it that we are trying to conserve, when the "balance of nature" has been altered by human action for centuries? How can we separate natural and man-made fluctuations? Further interventions may cause as many environmental problems as they resolve and the impacts of human activity seem to out-pace the ability of present political and legal structures to respond to them.

Changes in the physical environment itself also pose new challenges to existing law. For example, established property and tort law are incapable of providing a just response to a policy of managed retreat from the coastline, inevitable if the rises in sea-levels predicted by some materialise. Equally, providing by statute for other ameliorative measures, such as replenishing beaches with marine-won aggregates, will themselves bring uncertain environmental consequences and present what are, frankly, bizarre legal problems.[15] As these few examples suggest, the environment itself presents a moving target for policy or legal instruments. The physical sustainability of development is a key criterion against which the success of contemporary environmental policy and law is measured. Whilst agreement on the centrality of sustainability is heartening, its practicalities remain far from clear.

Scientific

A related issue, but one bringing additional complication, is the role of science in creating an understanding of environmental problems, and in contributing to their solution. The starting point here is a simple one: as we discover more about the physical world and human impacts on it, we discover more that is

[14] *Improving Scotland's Water Environment* (SEPA, 1999); H Cameron, "The Problems of Sewage Disposal" (2000) 77 *Scottish Planning and Environmental Law* L(SPEL) 8.

[15] S McFarland, *et al.*, "Recent Beach Nourishment Schemes in the UK: Some Preliminary Observations", (1994) 25 *Ocean and Coastal Management* 143; T Jewell, "Marine Mineral Extraction", in Freshfields' Environment Group (eds), *Tolley's Environmental Law* (London, Butterworths Tolley, 1999).

potentially harmful. Consequently, what was once accepted as good practice is now prohibited as posing unacceptable "risks". Equally, our own technological and scientific advances also create new environmental problems: the visible dangers of smog have been replaced by the less visible but no less serious dangers of nitric oxide and greenhouse gases. This is often presented as merely a technological challenge. Seen as such, there is no threat to the perceived orthodoxy of science in environmental policy-making—that environmental policy should be based on "sound science".[16] But the reality is more complex.

Science is not about certainties, but hypotheses and experimentation—as one of the most recent reports of the Royal Commission on Environmental Pollution forcefully reminds us.[17] Yet there is a disjunction between this often under-emphasised characteristic of the scientific process, and the expectation that science can provide solutions to environmental problems. That expectation is under siege, and not only in an environmental context. A prominent feature of much recent debate is growing scepticism of the capacity of science. For example, the crisis in the United Kingdom over bovine spongiform-encephalopathy (BSE) is a commanding illustration of how the confidence of those developing new, putatively risk-free, forms of cattle feed proved to be catastrophically unfounded. Other contexts provide further examples: nuclear power, anti-malarial pesticides, DDT.

BSE is a crucial lesson for two further reasons. First, it suggests how particular scientific uncertainties can have important legal implications. It proved difficult enough to identify the link between cause and effect for policy purposes, far less to meet the standards which are a precursor to a legal solution. Even now, and despite vast effort, it has not been possible to prove conclusively what the exact mechanism of causing and transmitting BSE and its derivatives actually is. This sort of scientific uncertainty is at the heart of, and explains pressures to give effect to, the precautionary principle.[18] Indeed, implementation of the principle at a domestic level may require a maturing of the legal process beyond familiar standards and burdens of proof.

The second reason for the potency of the BSE example is that it reveals a broader recognition of the limitations of scientific thinking. It shows very publicly that science will not be able to provide answers to crucial questions of when something is "safe" or when it presents an "acceptable" risk. These are essentially matters for social and political, rather than physical, science.[19] Whether or not a particular environmental "risk" is "acceptable" becomes crucially dependent on who is asked to decide, and within which legal

[16] *This Common Inheritance* (Cm. 1200, 1990), paras 1.16–17 (headed "Fact not Fantasy").

[17] *Setting Environmental Standards*, 21st Report of the Royal Commission on Environmental Pollution (Cm. 4053, 1998).

[18] Harding and Fisher, *supra* n. 11, at 10.

[19] Editorial, "BSE: Madness in the Method" (1996) 26 *The Ecologist* 45.

framework.[20] It is a question deeply-rooted in competing values and rights claims, and thus entails matters of institutional design, and the distribution of decision-making functions. This is not an original observation. However, the confluence of the various developments outlined here does suggest an urgent need for integrated thinking about methods of resolving environmental problems. This must confront some core assumptions about when and how law might intervene to control environmental harm. As the Royal Commission put it:

> "The fundamental purposes of [such] new approaches is not to produce a "right" answer, but to illuminate the value questions raised by environmental issues in order to identify the policies around which consensus is more likely to form and to enable decisions to be better informed and more robust".[21]

Precision may not be obtainable, but a refinement of legal and policy tools has become an urgent necessity.

Political

Some key points of the political context have important implications for the shape of UK and EC environmental law, and to waste law in particular. The first, obvious, point is that environmental law has to develop in an international and global context. At its simplest, a recognition of the global consequences of our impact on, for example, climate and sea-levels has been added to a long-established recognition of direct transboundary harm. A start has been made internationally in addressing global risks,[22] but not only is there still a long way to go before these produce real effects, but it has been argued strongly that such measures are doomed to failure by virtue of their reliance on a state-centric system in an era of globalisation.[23]

The arguable impotence of states effectively to control the environmental impacts of transnational corporations moves the focus to the relationship between trade and the environment.[24] This was one of the big issues consid-

[20] e.g., controversy surrounds developments in planning where perceptions of risk have been recognised as material considerations, contrasted with the provable risks which are the more usual fare of pollution regulators: *Newport County Borough Council* v. *Secretary of State for Wales* [1998] Env LR 174; N Stanley, "Public Concern: The Decision-Maker's Dilemma" [1998] *JPL* 919; J Gilles, "Public Concern as a Material Planning Consideration" (1999) 76 *SPEL* 130.

[21] See *supra* n. 17, at para. 7.43.

[22] P Birnie and A Boyle, *International Law and the Environment* (2nd edn., Oxford, Clarendon Press, 2000).

[23] T Evans, "International Environmental Law and the Challenge of Globalization", in Jewell and Steele, *supra* n. 12.

[24] The rapidly growing literature includes: A Ziegler, *Trade and Environment Law in the EC* (Oxford, Oxford University Press, 1996); *World Trade and the Environment*, House of Commons Select Committee on the Environment, 4th Report (1995–96 HC 149); D Geradin, *Trade and*

ered by the Ministerial Conference of the World Trade Organisation (WTO) in Seattle in December 1999, where the extent to which environmental concerns can feature in the regulation of trade was extremely contentious, for both delegates and demonstrators. This is a complicated matter where one can find odd bed-fellows, since trade mechanisms can be used either to bolster environmental protection, by denying access to markets unless certain minimum standards are met, or to undermine such protection, by outlawing environmental standards as an obstacle to free trade.[25]

Trade and the environment is obviously a very significant issue within the European Community also, where the possibility of differing environmental standards distorting competition or restricting free movement of goods has been one of the key driving forces behind much environmental legislation. The issue can arise in unexpected situations: legislative measures to limit the movement of waste and to protect a sub-species of bee have each led to litigation in the European Court of Justice on the basis that the laws infringe the free movement of goods.[26] Yet, at the same time, EC environmental activity has been criticised as being just as concerned with state protectionism under the guise of environmental protection as it has been with genuine attempts to address the tensions between environmental protection and commercial interests in economic growth.[27] It remains the case that there is not the same degree of political agreement within the EU as to the necessity of environmental laws at European level as there is in respect of the single market project itself, however characterised.

Within the United Kingdom, rapidly changing perceptions of the nature and role of the state have led to significant changes which affect the development and implementation of environmental policy and law. Constitutional changes, taken with new approaches to regulation and to the delivery of services, mean that environmental policy has to operate against a background very different from that in the 1970s, when modern environmental law started to emerge. These changes either provide an unheard-of opportunity for environmental reform, which the trends in environmental policy already referred to would demand, or (more realistically) an unsteady foundation upon which to construct environmentally-informed systems of decision-making. Three particular examples are amongst the most prominent: devolution, privatisation, and a new emphasis on human rights.

Environment (Cambridge, Cambridge University Press, 1997); A Fijalkowski and J Cameron (eds), *Trade and Environment—Bridging the Gap* (London, Cameron May, 1998).

[25] See T Schoenbaum, "Free International Trade and Protection of the Environment: Irreconcilable Conflict" (1992) 86 *AJIL* 700.

[26] Case C-2/90 *Commission* v. *Belgium* [1992] ECR I-4431 and Case C-67/97 *Criminal proceedings against Ditlev Bluhme* [1999] CMLR 612, respectively.

[27] J Scott, *EC Environmental Law* (London, Longman, 1998).

Devolution poses new challenges for the law within the United Kingdom.[28] In essence the issues here are similar to those grappled with for years within the EC:[29] a need to co-ordinate and allocate legislative and policy tasks to the most appropriate governmental level, maintaining an appropriate balance between consistency and integration where necessary, whilst avoiding excessive central control. This task, though, is a new one for our administrators, and the challenge of co-ordinating policy and legislative action is complicated by the fact that the divide between Westminster and the devolved administrations is drawn in different places for Scotland, Wales and Northern Ireland.[30] The Scottish authorities have had the most power devolved to them, and "the environment" is frequently identified as an area within their remit.[31] Yet not only are some important environmental issues reserved to Westminster—including most energy issues and rail, marine and air transport—but the tools available to the Scottish administration are also limited, since taxes and excise duties are reserved matters, as are issues which fall within the sphere of consumer protection and product standards, including "eco-labelling".[32] The formulation and implementation of environmental policies which meet the United Kingdom's international and European obligations whilst accommodating the different priorities, constraints and administrative structures across the United Kingdom will require all of the authorities to come to terms with a new way of working.[33]

A related issue is a more general trend to reconsider the ways in which "communities" participate in environmental decision-making. On one level this debate is based on the steps to broaden rights of access to environmental information,[34] but it extends to a reconsideration of the role of local government, and of the communities it represents.[35] At European level too, regulatory tech-

[28] See generally C Reid, "Devolution and the Environment", in A Ross (ed.), *Environment (Hume Papers on Public Policy)* (Edinburgh, Edinburgh University Press, 2000).

[29] And in other states with strong federal or devolved governmental structures, e.g. Belgium, Germany, and Spain which matches the United Kingdom in its "asymmetrical" arrangements.

[30] Scotland Act 1998, Government of Wales Act 1998, Northern Ireland Act 1998; significant environmental responsibilities contained in the Greater London Authority Act 1999 add a further layer to this picture. See generally: UK Round Table on Sustainable Development, *Sustainable Development—Devolved and Regional Dimensions* (1999).

[31] e.g., *Scotland's Parliament* (Cm. 3658, 1997), p. 6.

[32] Scotland Act 1998, Sch. 5, Heads A.1, C.7, C.8, D and E.

[33] Illustrated in the very title of *The Air Quality Strategy for England, Scotland, Wales and Northern Ireland: Working Together for Clean Air* (Cm. 4548, 2000).

[34] Directive 90/313/EEC on access to information on the environment; Environmental Information Regulations 1992, SI 1992/3240.

[35] Some idea of recent discussions can be gleaned from the DETR Consultation Paper, *Modernising Local Government: Local Democracy and Community Leadership* (1998) (reproduced in (1998) 10 *Environmental Law and Management* 177), and from the development of "community planning" in Scotland (see J McFadden, "Report of the Community Planning Working Group" (1998) 70 *SPEL* 119; B Illsley and M Lloyd, "Pathfinders for Community Planning" (1999) 74 *SPEL* 82).

niques which provide for greater (implementing) discretion in Member States are increasingly in evidence, [36] and reflect criticisms of the opaqueness of the European decision-making process which are at least part of the background to UK reforms.

The nature of environmental regulation has also been transformed by changes in the role which the state sees for itself, most notably demonstrated through privatisation. The energy, transport and the water industries are key areas where enterprises have been removed from state control to a more distant relationship (although not uniformly across the United Kingdom). This process has produced some major environmental gains, most notably the separation in many areas of operator and regulator ("poacher and gamekeeper"),[37] but also losses, since privatised bodies must focus on their narrow goals, especially producing a profit, with limited regard for environmental or social considerations. A crucial element in environmental law thus becomes the regulatory mechanism for privatised utilities, and whether their economic regulation can promote changes in their environmental performance. This creates a great opportunity to ensure that environmental and social issues can be clearly addressed, but also a risk that they will be consigned permanently to the side-lines. Indeed, the UK Round Table on Sustainable Development has been very critical of the balance struck between environmental duties and commercial interest in the regulatory schemes which provide for the "arm's length" regulation of the water, gas and electricity industries, and of the regulators' views in these cases that sustainable development is a "political matter", which is implicitly beyond their concern.[38] No steps have yet been taken to rectify the systemic imbalances against environmental protection identified by the UK Round Table. An additional point is that the commercial cycle of privatised industry, particularly where large infrastructure facilities must be paid for, may inevitably constrain future action. In the *National Waste Strategy: Scotland*,[39] SEPA notes that existing contractual arrangements for waste disposal may contain minimum disposal quantities which can act as a disincentive to the development of waste reduction and recovery systems.[40]

[36] Both in the choice of regulatory instrument and whether to intervene at all: R Khalastchi and H Ward, "New Instruments for Sustainability: An Assessment of Environmental Agreements under Community Law" (1998) 10 *JEL* 257.

[37] C Reid, "The Changing Pattern of Environmental Regulation: British Forestry and the Environmental Agenda" (1997) 9 *JEL* 23, 33–6.

[38] In its Report, *Economic Regulation* (1998), para. 53.

[39] SEPA (1999), at 26.

[40] Similarly if an area decides on the building of a large waste incinerator, it will need a guaranteed supply of waste over many years to justify the capital costs, whilst the financial backers of other environmental infrastructure projects, e.g. sewage treatment facilities built under the Private Finance Initiative or as Public Private Partnerships, may want some guarantee as to the useful life of the plant, and a commitment that it will not be rendered futile by a change in standards or required processes.

The explicit legal recognition of human rights in UK law creates a final new dimension. Given the recent emergence of environmental issues as central concerns, it is not surprising that environmental rights are not expressly included in the catalogue of rights under the European Convention on Human Rights which are now to be protected in the United Kingdom.[41] Nevertheless, environmental law will be affected. Rights under the Convention can be claimed to secure protection against the harm to life or property caused by environmental damage, but only in fairly extreme cases. On the other hand, there are also possibilities of using the rights to thwart the impact of protective measures, especially by claiming that regulatory measures are an undue interference with property rights. From either side there may be criticisms that decision-making procedures do not secure a fair and public hearing before an independent and impartial tribunal.[42]

The Current Shape of Environmental Law

Taken together these factors, amongst others, are transforming the context within which environmental regulation must operate, but not evenly or consistently. Trends towards globalisation and towards devolution pull in opposite directions, while the protection of individual human rights may render some collective environmental controls less effective. Similar tensions exist in many areas. The debate in Scotland over land reform has revealed on the one hand a desire to free landowners from the last vestiges of the feudal restraint, but at the same time a concern to recognise that they have certain obligations to the public interest and future generations not to manage their land in a way damaging to the community or the environment.[43] The outcome, though, is that environmental law has changed dramatically in recent decades.

[41] Human Rights Act 1998; the potential scale of the impact has been amply demonstrated in Scotland where the prohibition on the devolved authorities' acting in breach of the Convention rights has generated considerable litigation, albeit centred on matters of criminal procedure.

[42] See, e.g., the arguments raised in *Powell and Rayner* v. *United Kingdom* (1990) 12 EHRR 355 (whether aircraft noise amounted to an infringement of the right to respect for private life and home (Art. 8)); *Buckley* v. *United Kingdom* (1997) 23 EHRR 101 (whether refusal of a gypsy's application for planning permission to site a caravan amounted to a breach of respect for her home (Art. 8) and to discrimination (Art. 14)); *Lopez Ostra* v. *Spain* (1995) 20 EHRR 277 (severe pollution can be a breach of the right to respect for private and family life and home (Art. 8)); *Guerra* v. *Italy* (1998) 26 EHHR 357 (failure to prepare and publicise emergency plans for hazardous plant amounted to breach of respect for the private and family lives of those living nearby (Art. 8)); *Matos e Silva Lda.* v. *Portugal* (1997) 24 EHRR 573 (whether designation of a nature reserve was a breach of the landowner's peaceful enjoyment of his possessions (First Protocol, Art. 1)), *Bryan* v. *United Kingdom* (1996) 21 EHRR 342 (whether the appeal procedure in the town and country planning legislation provides an "independent and impartial tribunal" (Art. 6)).

[43] Land Reform Policy Group, *Identifying the Solutions* (Scottish Office, 1998); the eventual

Looking back, several major trends can be identified, which may represent the foundations for its further development. These include:[44]

- importance: environmental law is no longer a matter for a few particularly harmful or dirty industries but touches all of our lives in various ways, if only through the passing on of costs involved in meeting higher environmental standards for industrial production and waste disposal;
- international dimension: much of the law now stems from international or European initiatives and meeting internationally agreed targets will lie at the heart of policy over the next few years;
- principles: although there are major difficulties over their interpretation and application, certain key principles form a basis for structuring more specific rules—polluter pays, preventive principle, precautionary principle, sustainable development;
- fixed standards: in part, at least, as a result of EC measures, environmental law has moved away from its very heavy reliance on flexible standards, requiring firms to employ "the best practicable means"[45] to avoid pollution, to the adoption of fixed, numerical standards for emissions and water and air quality, although the underlying requirement to use the "best available techniques" remains;[46]
- process and product standards: the law is no longer concerned simply with "end-of-pipe" controls, but endeavours to limit harmful environmental impacts by regulating the processes which industry adopts and the products which it makes;
- integration: the different impacts of our activities on the environment are increasingly being dealt with not in isolation but in an integrated way, as shown both by the creation of authorities which have wide remits (the Environment Agency and the Scottish Environmental Protection Agency)[47] and the development of regulatory regimes which consider a range of environmental issues;
- diversification of methods: the law is no longer limited to a "command-and-control" approach but utilises a wide range of legal mechanisms to achieve its goals (management agreements, taxes, labelling);
- promotion of shared responsibility: the diverse techniques noted above help to bring home to individuals and companies that the environment is

legislative proposals reflect only a small part of the complex debate: *Land Reform—Proposals for Legislation* (SE/1999/1).

[44] C Reid, "Environmental Law: Sifting through the Rubbish" 1998 *Juridical Review* 236; J Steele and T Jewell, "Law in Environmental Decision-Making", in Jewell and Steele, *supra* n. 12.

[45] e.g., Alkali etc. Works Regulation Act 1906, s. 2.

[46] e.g., Directive 96/61/EC, Art. 10, on integrated pollution prevention and control.

[47] T Jewell and J Steele, "UK Regulatory Reform and the Pursuit of 'Sustainable Development': The Environment Act 1995" (1996) 8 *JEL* 283.

affected by their own decisions and that the creation of environmental protection bodies does not mean that nobody else need consider the matter;

- openness: public access to environmental information and opportunities for a degree of participation in many procedures means that environmental regulation is no longer an activity carried out behind closed doors but is open to public gaze;
- greener government: there is a belated recognition of the importance of government itself demonstrating that it is living up to the higher environmental standards imposed on others.

These developments have gone some way to enabling environmental law to address the most readily identified environmental dangers. Crucially, though, the present position remains a long way from that called for if claims of seeking sustainable development are to be achieved. Transitional issues require as much consideration as ultimate goals. The power of fairly straightforward legal measures to change behaviour is clear; for example, it was the change in duty which stimulated the market for lead-free petrol to such an extent that removing the differential would probably now make very little difference to sales. Other transitional problems are harder to solve. Increasing energy costs seems an obvious way to discourage inefficient use of energy, but the ability of poorer sections of society to respond is constrained—despite the long-term pay-back, they may not have the capital to replace old and inefficient heating systems, or they may live in rented social housing where they have no direct control over the heating systems and insulation. Integrated thinking about the environment and the distributive consequences of proposals is therefore an important challenge for ideas of sustainability.

More diffuse problems are even more intractable to simple legal solutions. The best way of reducing air pollution from traffic is to reduce car journeys.[48] A variety of legal techniques can be used to promote this goal—prohibitions on driving in congested areas, economic penalties on parking, fuel or road use, or economic subsidies for public transport. Yet the most effective way to reduce journeys is simply for people to live near enough for them to walk or cycle to their places of work, leisure, education and basic shopping. To achieve this requires urban living to become the preference not just of the unattached young but of families and the old. This in turn requires huge efforts not just in planning for appropriate housing and other facilities, but also policies on crime, education, home-ownership and employment which will promote new ways of thinking. There are many obstacles to developing legal responses to accommodate the polycentricity of environmental problems, informed by their social and economic implications.

[48] See generally *A New Deal for Transport: Better for Everyone* (Cm. 3950, 1999).

It is therefore necessary for environmental law to be seen as one of a wider range of mechanisms for formulating and giving effect to environmental policy. It has to play its part in a greening of government and industry, both through creating direct obligations and through separate initiatives which together create a climate which rewards sustainable conduct and penalises the unsustainable. Government at various levels is committing itself to policies[49] and targets[50] and the mechanisms are being put in place to ensure that a commitment to environmental protection is actually carried through into practice. There is still a long way to go, but international[51] and domestic reporting mechanisms, such as the Environmental Audit Committee of the House of Commons,[52] are starting to hold government to account, applying pressure to ensure that other mechanisms actually deliver what they might promise in reflecting environmental concerns throughout policy.

Managing the Creation and Disposal of Waste

In this section we explore quite how these obstacles are being addressed, in the particular context of the creation, management and disposal of waste. The starting point is inauspicious. Although some of the earliest statutory controls over "accumulations" of noxious matter date from 1848,[53] as recently as 1989 the House of Commons Environment Committee reported that:

> "never in any of our enquiries into environmental problems have we experienced such a consistent and universal criticism of existing legislation and of central and local government as we have during the course of this enquiry . . . [Department of the Environment] inaction has been a catalogue of neglect. . . there has been a vacuum of central guidance, legislative change and leadership on waste management issues".[54]

Perhaps partly as a result of this rebuke, but more likely driven by EC measures,[55] legal controls over waste have been transformed. They now provide a

[49] *A Better Quality of Life, supra* n.7; a more precise obligation is the requirement under s. 121 of the Government of Wales Act 1998 for the National Assembly for Wales to prepare a scheme for promoting sustainable development.

[50] Such as the sustainable development indicators in *A Better Quality of Life, supra* n. 7, ch. 3.

[51] e.g., Protocol on Substances that Deplete the Ozone Layer (Montreal) 1997 (as amended), Art. 7.

[52] A Ross, "Greening Government: the role of the House of Commons Environmental Audit Committee" (2000) 12 *JEL* (forthcoming); see also the reports of the UK Round Table on Sustainable Development.

[53] Public Health Act 1848; Nuisances Removal and Diseases Prevention Act 1848.

[54] *Toxic Waste*, 2nd Report (1988–89 HC 22), para. 190.

[55] Not least 20 Directives on waste between 1975 and 1996.

vivid and under-appreciated illustration of a quiet revolution in environmental law. That revolution reveals much of the transformation of environmental law as a whole in recent years, and points towards how environmental law may respond to the context in which it now finds itself.

This revolution may owe something to the distinctive features of the waste problem. Waste is universal, and is produced on a massive scale.[56] In the absence of some self-restraint, as economic wealth increases so will the volume and range of wastes. Equally, a far larger class of people has responsibility for waste creation than—perhaps—in many other spheres: there are innumerable producers, transporters and disposers of waste. Traditional "command-and-control" responses simply cannot have the same effectiveness here as in respect of point-source discharges to water or the atmosphere. The trade-environment interface also has a particular resonance in waste policy: there can, for example, be a trade in industrial, household and commercial wastes, of a sort impossible to envisage for other matters of environmental concern. These factors help to explain the recent prominence of waste and its disposal as an issue of European concern.

Policy

The impacts of wider developments on waste policy are easy to discern. Policy has been unified very recently with the development of a national waste strategy, under legislation in 1995.[57] The policy replaces obligations on local authorities to prepare local waste disposal plans—localised, land use orientated plans with few explicitly environmental aspirations. The new strategy is centred on four basic ideas: proximity and self-sufficiency; the precautionary principle; the polluter pays principle; and the waste hierarchy (with reduction being the preferred solution, before reuse, recovery and finally disposal). This is a marked development from earlier versions, and is an explicit attempt to place waste policy more securely within the sorts of sustainability ideas considered above.[58] Heavy criticism of those early efforts was based on their fail-

[56] Incomplete estimates suggest that 70–100 million tonnes of commercial and industrial waste, and 27 million tonnes of municipal waste are created in England and Wales every year (*A Way with Waste* (DETR, 1999) Part 2, ch. 2); in Scotland it is estimated that 11.9 million tonnes of waste are disposed to landfill sites annually (*National Waste Strategy: Scotland* (SEPA, 1999), p. 10).

[57] EA 1995, s. 92 inserting ss. 44A (England and Wales) and 44B (Scotland) into the Environmental Protection Act 1990 (EPA 1990).

[58] "This Strategy . . . takes into account the underlying principle of sustainable development. Much greater resource efficiency is required throughout all industrial, commercial and household practices in order to consume fewer natural resources and generate less waste. Where waste cannot be minimised in volume, its potential hazards must be reduced, it must be disposed of in more appropriate ways and value must be recovered from it": *National Waste Strategy: Scotland*, *supra* n. 56, at 6.

ure to appreciate the scale of change necessary to meet recycling and recovery targets, along with the minimalist attempts they made to shift the costs of waste management and disposal onto waste producers, whoever they may be.[59] What is not clear, of course, is whether the new policy will enable these criticisms to be overcome.

It is the attempt to involve all those involved in the life-cycle of waste—or "waste chain"—which is therefore the dominant feature of the strategy: the first conscious attempt to develop a collective responsibility for waste. Waste producers (industrial, commercial and household), the waste management industry, local authorities (through the planning system as well as in their role as waste collectors), central government and the environment agencies (as regulators), and the voluntary and not-for-profit sector (through voluntary environmental improvement initiatives) all have a part to play in achieving the reductions in waste production and the changes in waste treatment which are necessary to move towards a more sustainable position.[60] The need to co-ordinate local and regional measures, in pursuit of both national and European targets and local needs is a good illustration of the institutional integration necessary for the implementation of environmental policy.

Other strands of waste policy bring other implications. The most prominent of these currently is landfill policy, given the imminent implementation of the Landfill Directive.[61] Although having its main focus on one disposal option, and one which is highly developed in the United Kingdom, this directive has wide implications. In particular, it will require progressive reductions in the proportion of biodegradable waste going to landfill, and thus has implications for choice of disposal options. Indeed, even on the targets suggested by the UK Government (which fall below those in the Directive) an additional eight to twenty-six million tonnes of incinerator capacity may be required by 2015: the equivalent of up to one hundred and thirty new incinerators. This requires a forced reconsideration of strategic priorities, with knock-on effects for land-use planning and atmospheric pollution. Coping with the transference of pollution becomes a keener concern.

In the long term, though, it is not waste regulation that is required but reduction:

[59] The original strategy was *Making Waste Work: A Strategy for Sustainable Waste Management in England and Wales* (Cm. 3040, 1995). More recently see: *Less Waste. More Value*, DETR Consultation Paper on the Waste Strategy for England and Wales (June 1998) (B Pontin, (1998) 10 *ELM* 180) *A Way with Waste*, Draft Waste Strategy for England and Wales (DETR, June 1999) and now *Waste Strategy 2000: England and Wales* (Cm. 4693, May 2000). After two consultative drafts in 1997 and May 1999, the *National Waste Strategy: Scotland* was published in December 1999.

[60] *National Waste Strategy: Scotland*, *supra* n. 56, at 21–5.

[61] Directive 1999/31/EC; *Sustainable Landfill*, House of Lords Select Committee on the European Communities, 17th Report (1997–98 HL 83), para. 59.

"Waste reduction is not just an option: it is an imperative. We need to create, through education and example, a new social spirit in which Government, industry and citizens positively want to see waste reduced at all stages".[62]

In combination, these policy trends suggest a prominent shift towards a more proactive waste policy, and one which depends for its success on more than merely legal intervention. In many respects, the degree of specificity and the centralised nature of the standards set will make assessment of national compliance easier to judge than has been the case in the past. However, in 1998 the House of Commons Environment Select Committee reiterated earlier criticisms of the implementation of waste policy.[63] Implementation therefore remains deeply problematic. Institutional co-ordination also remains patchy. However, it is through the nature and variety of implementing mechanisms that waste management may now exemplify the diversity required of environmental law if polycentric environmental problems are to be taken seriously.

Pursuing Sustainable Waste Management

As the focus shifts from waste disposal to the entire cycle of waste production and management, the interactions with other areas of policy increase. This in turn raises questions as to the limits of environmental policy. The preliminary question of definition is therefore a fundamental one. There should be no gaps to allow harmful activities to escape control, but excessive regulation can stand in the way of environmentally beneficial activities. Yet defining "waste" is far from straightforward. What is waste to one person is a valuable raw material to another, and too wide a definition may provide a disincentive to the very sorts of waste recovery developments which policy wishes to encourage. At one level this is just a technical issue. The solution for waste has been to adopt the wide definition used in EC law, based on the notion of material that the holder wishes to discard, but to modify this through many qualifications and exemptions.[64] There remain difficulties and the long debate over aspects of the scrap

[62] *Sustainable Landfill*, *supra* n. 61, at para. 149.

[63] "It is important to stress from the beginning of our Report our profound disappointment, on the basis of the evidence we have received, that waste management in this country is still characterised by inertia, careless administration and ad hoc, rather than science-based, decisions. Lip-service alone, in far too many instances, has been paid to the principles of reducing waste and diverting it from disposal. Central Government has lacked the commitment, and local government the resources, to put a sustainable waste management strategy into practice": *Sustainable Waste Management*, 6th Report (1997–98 HC 484), para. 17.

[64] EPA 1990, s. 75(2) (as amended by EA 1995, Sch. 22); Waste Management Licensing Regulations 1994, SI 1994/1056. This is an approach which will be familiar from planning, e.g., with wide exceptions applying to use classes and permitted development, often to encourage forms of economic activity despite their known environmental impacts, or to avoid regulation where such impacts are limited.

metal industry serves as an example. In that case, a balance has been sought between the desirability of encouraging the recovery of materials from waste, and the undesirability of doing so in the environmentally careless ways which are all too common.[65]

The peculiar nature of waste has raised a different issue, however. Unlike direct emissions to air or discharges to water, waste products can be transferred and traded. The question has thus arisen of whether waste can benefit from EC rules relating to the free movement of goods, so that any restrictions on its movement require justification within the criteria set out in the EC Treaty. The conclusion of the European Court of Justice was that this is indeed the case.[66] Those devising initiatives to deal with waste, particularly to give effect to the proximity principle, must therefore ensure that the requirements of the laws designed to protect free movement are satisfied. But neither this conclusion, the difficulties of definition or even the issue of the Treaty basis of Community environmental action have found straightforward solutions.[67] Recent Treaty amendments may focus greater attention on this issue, particularly the newly-emphasised obligation to integrate environmental protection measures into all aspects of EC activity,[68] but even in well-established policy areas it is not clear how the balance between trade and the environment will be struck.

Beyond definitional concerns, delivering waste policy also calls for the use of a wide range of legal mechanisms. The starting point for the development of legal regulation is familiar: the foundational waste disposal licensing system established by the Control of Pollution Act 1974 bore many of the hallmarks of other environmental regimes. However, it was that system, operated by local authorities, which drew the criticism set out above. Nevertheless, a licensing scheme remains at the heart of the current regime, under the Environmental Protection Act 1990. There are perhaps three major points to notice, however. First, the scope of the scheme is extended so that it covers not only waste disposal, but also waste management. This can be viewed simply as an evolutionary step, slightly extending the boundaries of existing controls, but it does in fact represent a major change of approach. The law no longer concerns itself simply with final environmental impacts, but seeks to regulate waste management from creation to disposal. This is an important point: a "cradle-to-grave" system which seeks to reduce a problem before it arises is clearly preferable to simplistic "end-of-pipe controls". It does, however, increase the complexity of the issues to be addressed.

[65] e.g. (1995) 248 *ENDS Report* 32.

[66] Case C-2/90 *Commission* v. *Belgium* [1992] ECR I-4431.

[67] Generally see H Somsen, "Dynamics, Process, and Instruments of Environmental Decision-making in the European Union", in Jewell and Steele, *supra* n. 12.

[68] EC Treaty, Art. 6.

Secondly, the licensing scheme itself reflects many of the features which have emerged as environmental regulation has become more sophisticated. There are provisions for a degree of openness in the administration of the system, the regulator is given the legal powers of entry and inspection to enable effective enforcement, there are provisions to create personal criminal liability so that offenders cannot hide behind the corporate veil, and licences may be reviewed and revised as our scientific knowledge of dangers, or our perceptions of these, change. Ultimately, enforcement still lies through the criminal law, but there are complementary statutory civil liabilities imposing simpler and stricter tests than the common law, and which arise from harm caused by disregarding key obligations in criminal law.[69]

These features of the scheme fit well with precautionary and preventive ideals, but it is also clear that a licensing system which must focus on certain defined activities cannot by itself deal with all aspects of waste production and treatment. Accordingly, the third point is that the licensing scheme is only part of the overall attempt to control the production, handling and disposal of waste. Licences can be used to control some of the most obvious and significant dangers created by waste, and are apt where they are linked to a particular location, but are not suitable for dealing with more diffuse problems. These must be tackled by means of other legal techniques.

A crucial element in dealing with the wider issues, therefore, is that of integrating waste measures with other controls, particularly other environmental controls. The land-use planning system has always been a crucial part of the regulation of the waste industry. Indeed, it can be argued that it was the extent and effectiveness of planning controls in limiting some of the worst features of waste sites that enabled the introduction of specific controls to be delayed for so long. There remains a formal link between the planning and waste regimes,[70] and this has been modified to give greater emphasis to waste policy in planning decisions, but further integration is required if environmental priorities are to direct decision-making rather than be merely appended to it.[71] Even now, however, a developing understanding of environmental risks can allow the introduction of a wider range of views as to the "acceptability" of development than have traditionally affected pollution licensing regimes.[72] This is almost certainly an unintended benefit of the integration we have described, but it may nonetheless allow some of the tensions between purely scientific assessment of risk and the assessment by the communities affected by waste-related development to be better accommodated.

[69] EPA 1990, ss. 37 (variation of licences), 64 (public registers), 73(6) (civil liability), 157 (personal liability); EA 1995, s. 108 (powers of entry).

[70] e.g., waste management licences can be granted only for sites with planning permission: EPA 1990 s. 36(2); see PPG 10, *Planning and Waste Management* (1999).

[71] See e.g., *R* v. *Bolton Metropolitan Council, ex parte Kirkman* [1998] *JPL* 787.

[72] See *supra* n. 20 and associated text.

At a strategic level, new waste sites will have to be provided to cope with future wastes and the planning system has a key role in ensuring such provision—simply exporting waste is not an acceptable solution for any region—as well as in ensuring that the sites do not harm the local environment. To the extent that incineration and energy recovery are to play a greater role, the links between waste management and air pollution controls must be strengthened, whilst the forthcoming Integrated Pollution Prevention and Control system ("IPPC") not only applies to waste management sites but requires the issue of waste to be considered in relation to all facilities to which it applies.[73]

A further aspect of integration is "cross-compliance", the idea that observance of laws and standards in one area will be taken into account in regulatory decision-making in another. In the waste regime only a "fit and proper person" can be granted a waste management licence and this takes account not only of technical competence but also of any conviction of the applicant or a related person for offences against a wide range of environmental provisions.[74] When introduced, this requirement may have been partly an attempt to impose some control on an industry notoriously badly-run in part, but it is also a far-sighted attempt to break away from the compartmentalised approach to environmental regulation. Cross-compliance therefore provides an important tool for breaking down the barriers between the different elements of environmental policy. Its likely omission from IPPC respect is therefore regrettable.[75]

A similar attempt to break from traditional thinking is shown in the introduction of the statutory "duty of care". This requires waste producers, carriers and recipients to take reasonable care to ensure that waste is treated in compliance with the law, does not escape and is properly labelled when passed on to another person.[76] The aim is to ensure that producers take responsibility for what happens to the waste after it leaves their hands, whilst those further down the waste chain must ensure that they are properly informed so that the waste can be handled appropriately. As opposed to a command-and-control structure enforced by the regulatory body, there should therefore be a self-enforcing structure emphasising the inter-dependence of those throughout the waste chain. The scheme may not be working as well in practice as had been hoped,[77] but the conceptual innovation is an important one.

[73] Directive 96/61/EC, to be implemented by regulations under the Pollution Prevention and Control Act 1999.

[74] EPA 1990, ss. 36(3), 74.

[75] *Third Consultation Paper on the Implementation of the IPPC Directive* (DETR, January 1999); (1999) 11 *ELM* 87.

[76] EPA 1990, s. 34. Failure to discharge the duty is an offence.

[77] M Poustie, "A Load of Rubbish? The Duty of Care for Waste Revisited" (1997) 60 *SPEL* 28.

Further innovation can be seen in the prominence of economic instruments in managing waste, the most obvious of which is the landfill tax.[78] The imposition of a tax on the weight of material disposed of to landfill is a simple example of the use of a tax to encourage people to adjust their conduct, reducing the quantity of waste going to landfill either by reducing the amount of waste produced or diverting it to methods higher up the waste hierarchy. It would be worthy of note simply as one of only a few examples of such environmental taxes, but demands further attention because of its complementary system of tax credits. That system permits landfill operators to pay some of the money which is due in tax to registered environmental bodies, provided that the operator also makes a contribution from its own funds.[79] This entails two features of increasing importance. First, there is an element of indirect hypothecation (the dedication of taxes raised from a particular activity to a related purpose), an issue which is now featuring in debate in several other areas of environmental policy, most notably transport.[80] Secondly, the operators are not centrally required to devote the sums in a particular way, but within certain fairly broad limits are left with a choice over whether and how to do so. Putting such ideas into practice is itself not straightforward, of course. Setting the level of the tax to provide a sufficiently strong incentive to reduce landfill without encouraging fly-tipping is one issue—which, unusually, sees a Commons Select Committee proposing far higher increases in the tax than proposed by government[81]—as is ensuring that the tax does not act as a disincentive to environmentally beneficial activity.[82] Again, however, the departure from a direct command-and-control approach is obvious.

Recycling initiatives also feature economic measures, such as local recycling credits in England and Wales,[83] but other techniques are also being used. Even if the law sets clear obligations, the long-term future of recycling depends just as much on the development of markets at an international level. In the past, fluctuations in the price and demand for materials such as waste-paper have led to carefully segregated waste simply being buried in landfills. Initiatives such as Remade Scotland are trying to stimulate markets,[84] and although legal

[78] Finance Act 1996, Part III.

[79] *Ibid.*, ss. 51–56; Landfill Tax Regulations 1996, SI 1996/1527, Part VII.

[80] e.g., *Breaking the Logjam: The Government's Consultation Paper on Fighting Traffic Congestion and Pollution through Road User and Workplace Parking Charges* (DETR, 1998).

[81] *The Operation of the Landfill Tax*, House of Commons Select Committee on the Environment, 13th Report (1998–99 HC 150), para. 15.

[82] e.g., the Landfill Tax (Contaminated Land) Order 1996, SI 1996/1529, provides an exception to tax liability where soil or other material derived from the clean-up of contaminated land is itself landfilled.

[83] EPA 1990, s. 52; Environmental Protection (Waste Recycling Payments) Regulations 1992, SI 1992/462.

[84] *National Waste Strategy: Scotland*, *supra* n. 56, at 16; Remade Scotland is a joint venture between the Scottish Executive, SEPA, the Convention of Local Authorities in Scotland, two

measures on the composition of packaging and other products[85] and enabling authorities to become involved in projects[86] can try to overcome obstacles to effective recycling, other factors will dominate overall progress.

Measures aimed at promoting waste recovery also illustrate two further elements of implementing environmental policy: the use of targets and the willingness to let industry have a degree of control over how environmental goals are to be achieved. Targets are now widely used at a variety of levels to quantify the environmental improvements to be achieved, whilst leaving room for discretion as to how these can best be accomplished, yet their full legal significance has still to be addressed. The goal may be clear, but setting the target may be the easiest step in the process. The target-based approach entails a recognition that there are several ways of reaching the goal, which in turns means that responsibility for its achievement must be divided between the different methods and parties concerned. Given the complexity of the physical situation, the number of parties who may be involved (especially in areas such as waste where everyone is a producer of waste to some extent) and potential fragmentation of control structures (especially in view of devolution and privatisation), identifying and enforcing responsibility for meeting the targets is not straightforward. Contractual arrangements have been central to such sharing of responsibility in the past[87] but we are only just beginning to explore the further legal mechanisms necessary to ensure the effective allocation and implementation of targets.[88] The appropriate legal response when one party fails to meet its share has also still to be examined. A failure by any one party may necessitate greater demands on others, especially if an international or EC target is to be met, but how and to what extent are these others to be compensated, especially if the defaulting party cannot really be blamed for the failure?

The flexibility in determining how a target is to be met is one element of investigating alternatives to direct regulation. Such indirect forms of regulation reduce the burden of direct enforcement for all concerned, and avoid the rigidity of formal legal prescription, which can stifle innovation. Under the voluntary accreditation system operating in the context of packaging waste, for example, accredited reprocessors issue notices to those businesses supplying them with waste, which are subsequently accepted by the Agency as proof of

packaging waste bodies (see *infra*) and Shanks Waste Solutions who provide financial support through landfill tax credits.

[85] Directive 94/62/EC, Art. 9 and Annex II; Producer Responsibility Obligation (Packaging Waste) Regulations 1997, SI 1997/648; Proposal for a Directive on End-of-Life Vehicles (COM (1997) 358 final).

[86] EPA 1990, s. 55.

[87] Contracts remain the main vehicle through which waste producers, collectors and disposers regulate their relationships, and form the basis of the packaging schemes through which individual producers can satisfy their legal obligations.

[88] Allocation of targets to the devolved administration is expressly provided for in the Scotland Act 1998, s. 106.

the suppliers' compliance with their own obligations.[89] This enables sub-legal enforcement to take place, unhindered by criminal or civil burdens of proof in a formal sense, or context. This is more suggestive of self- or co-regulatory ideas than direct legal intervention of the more familiar kind, and is effectively an economic sanction on both reprocessors and their suppliers. This approach can be taken further with the potential for voluntary measures to contain the main substance of the desired environmental behaviour, whether within the framework of an agreement with government taking the place of formal legal controls,[90] or as an element in the ultimate shape of legal controls themselves.[91] The overall effectiveness of such agreements remains difficult to assess, and there are difficulties relating to openness and public involvement, enforceability and the potential for free-riders, but at its best this voluntary approach can provide real benefits.[92]

Concluding remarks

In some respects, it is the very generality of waste policy that is the cause of its problems. Whilst progress has been made, and waste controls have more positive features than in 1974, they are still hindered by the general and aspirational character of environmental policy. Yet what does become very clear from this brief overview is how broadly it is necessary to consider the waste problem at large. On one view, the law on waste has come a long way from simply controlling when and where waste could be dumped in a hole in the ground; it has begun to tackle the major cultural shift necessary to fulfil the aspirations of sustainable development. In this sense, it is beginning to reflect many of the broader trends in environmental law with which we began. Much is derived from EC measures. These, in turn, reflect wider international concerns, and they are increasingly based on prevention rather than cure. Some polluters (or potential polluters) will have to pay both for the regulatory mechanism and for any harm done, and economic instruments and other new techniques are used to secure objectives in ways which attempt to emphasise shared, not individual, responsibility. Many of these will have to be taken further, especially in relation to household waste: persuading households to take

89 SI 1997/648, *supra* n. 85; T Jewell, "Voluntary Accreditation of Reprocessors of Packaging Waste" (1998) 10 *ELM* 268.

90 ELNI (ed.), *Environmental Agreements: The Role and Effects of Environmental Agreements in Environmental Policies* (London, Cameron May, 1998).

91 e.g. the current discussions on energy efficiency and climate change levy tax rebates; see (1999) 291 *ENDS Report* 3, (2000) *ENDS Report* 3.

92 C Reid, *Nature Conservation Law* (Edinburgh, W. Green, 1994), pp. 34–6; K Last, "Habitat Protection: Has the Wildlife and Countryside Act 1981 Made a Difference?" (1999) 11 *JEL* 15.

more responsibility for their own waste is a huge challenge, but devices such as charging schemes might provide a way ahead. Equally, some significant elements are not yet reflected in the legal framework, especially, perhaps, a means of obtaining the basic information on overall waste production and disposal methods upon which a definitive strategy can be soundly based.[93]

For other issues, at least the seeds of the way ahead are present. There have already been some steps towards integrating waste measures with other controls, but more has to be done to make sure that different policies and rules do not pull in opposite directions. This is a concern of the whole of environmental law. Do waste issues carry enough weight in the land-use planning system?[94] Does the law on waste dovetail with contaminated land controls, which themselves require co-ordination between local authorities and environment agencies? It is also an issue which affects the relationship between environmental policy and the rest of the law. Do the rules of property law which allow for property to be abandoned fit with the concept that waste producers should retain a degree of continuing responsibility for their waste, as shown in the duty of care and the fact that waste management licences can only be surrendered in particular circumstances? Do company law and the law of insolvency[95] assist or obstruct this continuing responsibility? Do the rules of tort and delict provide satisfactory solutions in the wake of the new liabilities for waste and related matters?[96] Similarly, the adjectival aspects of the law must also be considered. Do court procedures and the rules on issues such as standing enable the obligations that have been created to be effectively enforced? Given the range of strands to the policies, is there the degree of public participation in decision-making processes necessary to achieve the emerging collective ambition? Are the structures in place to ensure that governmental authorities at all levels can co-operate effectively in devising and delivering sustainable policies?

The most prominent lesson, perhaps, is that there is strength, not weakness, in diversity. Environmental problems are so complex that they cannot be tackled by a simple approach. Any one issue interacts with so many other matters—environmental, economic, commercial and social—that law and policy across a wide front must combine to work towards a more sustainable future. Getting the individual pieces right is hard enough, even before the attempt is made to put them together in a coherent way, but that is the challenge if a more sustainable future is to be achieved. Waste law began by dealing with the issue

[93] A statutory obligation to provide information is recommended by SEPA: *National Waste Strategy: Scotland*, *supra* n. 56, at 45.

[94] A formal link between development plans and the Waste Strategy is also recommended: *National Waste Strategy: Scotland*, *supra* n. 56, at 45.

[95] See *Re Celtic Extraction Ltd.* [1999] 4 All ER 684.

[96] EC White Paper on Environmental Liability (COM (2000) 66 final).

of ultimate disposal and has evolved through a "cradle-to-grave" approach, towards looking at matters from "conception[97] to decomposition". The rest of environmental law must take the same path, and the rest of the law must assist, or at least not obstruct this progress. If law is to pursue environmental purposes—or even just to implement environmental policy—then all of law, and all lawyers, must rise to the environmental challenge.

[97] Or even contraception.

12

Labour Law

KEITH EWING AND GILLIAN MORRIS

Introduction

Labour law is derived from a multiplicity of sources, spanning common law and legislation; private and public law; and latterly EU law. Extra-legal sources, most notably collective agreements, also have an important (and unusual) role to play in determining legal rights and obligations. This diversity of sources in itself means that the shape of labour law is subject to a variety of influences, both direct and indirect; to take but one example, the central importance of the economic torts to industrial action law means that the outcome of commercial litigation can, tangentially, significantly alter workers' rights. However, such diversity also exposes labour law to a particularly wide range of ideological forces, which are often inconsistent in their nature. Historically the courts were the mainspring of the values underpinning labour law, and the common law continues to play a crucial role today, not least through judicial activism in implying terms into individual contracts.[1]

In the post-war period in particular, however, labour law has been viewed as integral to the social and economic policies of all major political parties, and no government since the early 1960s has failed to leave its mark on the subject, which its successor, although not erasing that mark entirely, has in turn fundamentally reformed.[2] Labour law has thus served as a direct reflection of the political complexion of the government in power. In addition to these domestic influences, EU developments have exposed labour law to a range of doctrines and industrial relations practices rooted in continental Europe, not all of which mesh easily with UK traditions and structures of worker

[1] See generally S Deakin and G Morris, *Labour Law* (2nd edn., 1998), ch. 4. On developments in the important area of trust and confidence, see D Brodie, "Beyond Exchange: The New Contract of Employment" (1998) 27 *Industrial Law Journal* 79.

[2] For a magisterial analysis of this area during the post-war period until 1990, see P Davies and M Freedland, *Labour Legislation and Public Policy* (1993).

representation. Contemporary labour law is thus complex and, in many respects, incoherent.

Our task in this chapter is to predict the future shape of labour law. Any such prediction requires first an understanding of the influences which have brought labour law to where it is today; only then can we consider how far these influences will continue to prevail, and the impact which forthcoming developments may have upon them. We first examine the labour law inherited by the Conservative Government when it entered office in 1979. We then assess the legacy of the period 1979–97, which, despite the change of government, remains of lasting significance. There follows an analysis of the current Government's programme of reform, and, equally importantly, those areas which it has chosen essentially to preserve. We then consider the changes which are on the horizon in the area of European social policy, and discuss the likely implications of the forthcoming human rights agenda for labour law. The conclusion draws together the threads of our discussion to highlight what we envisage will be the primary influences upon the development of labour law in the foreseeable future.

The Development of British Labour Law

The twentieth century was one of great instability in the development of British labour law. It is sometimes argued that for much of the period the dominant characteristic was the principle of legal abstentionism or collective *laissez faire*, by which it is meant that the overriding strategy was to keep the law out of industrial relations. But this now seems wide of the mark, and reflects a narrow reading of the position and a narrow conception of the law, or at least State power grounded in law.[3] The twentieth century was in fact one of legally grounded (administrative and statutory) intervention in the employment relationship, to overcome the traditional principles of the common law based on freedom of contract, and freedom from interference with the performance of a contract.[4] Indeed there were several quite different forms of intervention designed to protect the worker from the power vested in the employer by the common law; to regulate the employment relationship and working conditions; and to protect workers' organisations from common law liability.

[3] See more fully, K Ewing, "The State and Industrial Relations: 'Collective Laissez-Faire' Revisited" (1998) 5 *Hist Stud Ind Rel* 1.

[4] For a classic account of the common law position, see *Quinn* v. *Leathem* [1901] AC 495, especially per Lord Lindley.

From the First World War to the Second World War

It is tempting to follow the traditional explanation of British labour law and to focus on the immunities introduced for trade unions and their officials by the Trade Disputes Act 1906—Labour's "Magna Carta". But as already suggested there is more to it than this. So far as direct regulation of working conditions is concerned, the twentieth century began with an inheritance which included the regulation by statute of the method of payment of wages, and the regulation by statute of measures designed to protect the health and safety of factory workers and others.[5] But the early twentieth century also saw experiments with minimum wages and the regulation of working time. These took different forms, but because it was not legislation of general application it does not follow that State regulation of working conditions was neither real nor significant. The strategy initially was to target particular industries (as in the case of the coal miners) or particularly vulnerable groups of workers (as in the case of the working time restrictions on female factory workers) directly by legislation.[6]

So far as collective bargaining is concerned, it is true that there was not in this country until very recently any direct statutory support for collective bargaining.[7] But it does not follow from this that the State was indifferent to the process. A system of joint regulation promoted by the Ministry of Labour (established with statutory authority) emerged in the aftermath of the First World War, based on the report of the Whitley Committee on Post-War Reconstruction in 1917.[8] Between 1917 and 1921—and again after 1934—the Ministry of Labour actively encouraged the creation of industry wide, multi-employer collective bargaining arrangements.[9] By 1946, partly as a result of State support by means of the discretionary statutory powers of the Ministry of Labour, no fewer than 85 per cent of the British working population were covered by collective agreements or by trade board awards, a truly remarkable figure which speaks volumes about the nature and extent of State

[5] See generally Deakin and Morris, *Labour Law*, *supra* n. 1, ch. 1.

[6] A good account of the campaign for minimum wage regulation in the mines is to be found in R Page Arnot, *The Miners: A History of the Miners' Federation of Great Britain, 1889–1910* (1949).

[7] Employment Protection Act 1975, ss. 11–16. See also Industrial Relations Act 1971, ss. 44–60.

[8] Cd 8606 (1917). See R Charles, *The Development of Industrial Relations in Britain 1911–39* (1973), and R Lowe, *Adjusting to Democracy: The Role of the Ministry of Labour in British Politics 1916–39* (1986).

[9] See Ewing, *supra* n. 3, at 22–6. The government as employer also played a part by introducing bargaining arrangements for the civil service. See S Fredman and G Morris, *The State as Employer: Labour Law in the Public Services* (1989), pp 10–11.

intervention.[10] It was a system based on autonomous and independent trade unions free from State interference.[11]

From the Second World War to Social Contract

But although we can point to a number of emerging and dominant characteristics of labour law and industrial relations in the first half of the twentieth century, it would be a mistake to conclude that this was a strategy built on an enduring political consensus:[12] indeed from 1922 to 1934 under the influence of a different political leadership, there was a marked withdrawal of State support for collective bargaining, although many of the institutional structures remained largely in place.[13] 1927 also saw the introduction of the first legislation in peacetime since the extension of the franchise in 1867 restricting the freedom of trade unions, legislation extracted as part of the reparations demanded after the General Strike.[14] This legislation was repealed in 1946, when State support for collective bargaining and other forms of joint regulation of working conditions had been revived, to find formal expression in the bargaining duties in the nationalisation statutes.[15] State support on a different scale was to be found in what would now be referred to as Social Dialogue between government and what what we would now refer to as the "Social Partners" on incomes policy.[16] This is a practice which was to continue during much of the post war period, reaching its apotheosis during the "Social Contract" period from 1974 to 1976.[17]

The Social Contract era was in fact the culmination of a form of State regulation of employment conditions which had developed throughout the twentieth century. It was a period which saw the expansion of legislation designed to regulate the employment relationship directly: it was universal in coverage (in the sense of not being confined to specific sectors), and covered an expand-

[10] Ministry of Labour and National Service, Report 1939–1946 (Cmd 7225, 1947), p. 275.

[11] Freedom was secured by three major statutes: Trade Union Act 1871, the Trade Disputes Act 1906, and the Trade Union Act 1913. See generally, C Grunfeld, *Modern Trade Union Law* (1966).

[12] It was in fact a matter of great political controversy, as reflected by the United Kingdom's failure to ratify ILO Convention 1 on Hours of Work despite British involvement in its drafting. See K Ewing, *Britain and the ILO* (2nd edn., 1994), ch. 4.

[13] Though there were also attempts at regulation during the two brief spells of Labour Government, in 1924 and then again from 1929–31. See Ewing, "The State and Industrial Relations", *supra* n. 3, at 14–16.

[14] Trade Disputes and Trade Unions Act 1927, introducing restrictions on industrial action for political purposes, picketing, trade union political activities, and the closed shop in local government.

[15] On which see, O Kahn Freund, *Labour and the Law* (2nd edn., 1977), p. 69.

[16] For a good account, see S Beer, *Modern British Politics* (1965), ch. 7.

[17] See Davies and Freedland, *Labour Legislation and Public Policy*, *supra* n. 2, ch. 8.

ing range of issues arising in the course of the employment relationship: but not yet a national minimum wage, or regulation of working time.[18] It was a period which saw the continuation of State support for collective bargaining:[19] but it was support which was to collapse, partly as a result of a coincidence of drafting failures and the untimely (but perhaps not so coincidental) emergence of judicial review as a pikestaff on which to impale ACAS, the unfortunate agency with statutory responsibility to administer the procedure.[20] It was finally a period which saw the continuation of parliamentary support for independent and autonomous trade unions, in particular by strengthening the immunities from tortious liability for organising industrial action. But this too was to lead to an unseemly conflict with the courts about the scope and extent of these immunities.[21]

The Conservative Legacy

The 1979–97 Conservative Governments saw labour law reform as an essential element in its programme of economic deregulation and liberalisation, which was designed to promote free market competition and, correlatively, to reduce the size of the public sector.[22] Trade unions were characterised as legally over-privileged bodies, which by their very nature distorted the operation of the labour market and, through the mechanism of the closed shop, threatened the freedoms both of employers and workers. Collective bargaining was also seen as an undesirable constraint upon a market which required the individualisation of the employment relationship in order to function properly. The "unique" character of trade unions was said to justify an unprecedented degree of statutory intervention in their internal affairs, ostensibly to secure union democracy and prevent the abuse of union power, but with the effect in

[18] On the Social Contract period, see Lord Wedderburn of Charlton, "The New Structure of Labour Law in Britain" (1978) 13 *Israel Law Rev* 438.

[19] Following the Donovan Report in 1968 and the changing nature of collective bargaining, it was a strategy grounded in direct legal intervention aimed at promoting collective bargaining at the enterprise level in particular.

[20] For analysis, see B Simpson, "Judicial Control of ACAS" (1979) 8 *ILJ* 69.

[21] See especially *Duport Steels* v. *Sirs* [1980] ICR 161.

[22] There is a wealth of literature on this area. Good starting points are Davies and Freedland, *supra* n. 2; Lord Wedderburn of Charlton, "Freedom of Association and Philosophies of Labour Law" (1989) 18 *Industrial Law Journal* 1; K Ewing, "Economics and Labour Law in Britain: Thatcher's Radical Experiment" (1990) 28 *Alberta Law Review* 632; W Brown, S Deakin and P Ryan, "The Effects of British Industrial Relations Legislation 1979–1997' (1997) 161 *National Institute Economic Review*, 69. On public sector reforms, see S Fredman and G Morris, *The State as Employer: Labour Law in the Public Services*, *supra*.

practice of prejudicing their ability to function as effective organisations.[23] Parliament rather than the courts took the lead in reducing the scope for lawful industrial action by narrowing the statutory immunities against liability in tort for organisers of industrial action, and imposing increasingly complex balloting and notification requirements for immunity to be retained.[24]

These policies therefore marked not only a reversal of those of its immediate Labour predecessor, but also of the approach to industrial relations which had prevailed for much of the century. They were joined by a whittling down of statutory employment protection rights, and in some cases their complete removal, in favour of a return to the common law concept of the individual contract of employment. This strategy, again, was not confined to rights which had been introduced or enhanced by the Government's predecessor, such as unfair dismissal protection (the qualifying period for which was raised in stages from six months to two years and whose upper limit on compensation was allowed to stagnate).[25] Rather, it extended to decades-old provisions, such as the nineteenth century Truck Acts, whose constraints on fines and deductions from wages were seen as an anachronistic impediment to freedom of contract, and the wages councils, whose minimum rates for low paid and badly organised groups, dating back to 1909 and 1918, were regarded as distorting market competition.[26]

EC law served as a brake in some areas upon labour market liberalisation. The principle of equal pay for equal work, enshrined in Article 141 (now 119) of the EC Treaty, could not be dispensed with, however antipathetic to the Government's agenda. Nor could the obligations preserving employees' contractual rights in the event that the undertaking for which they worked was transferred, although this proved a major source of difficulty to the extensive programme of competitive tendering in public services. However, the Government refused to countenance further social policy inroads from the Community, other than in the field of health and safety, to the extent, finally, of forcing its European partners to adopt an Agreement on Social Policy (the "Social Chapter" to the Maastricht Treaty) from which the United Kingdom was exempt. It was, perhaps, fortunate that it did not have to live long with the consequences of its "own goal" challenge to the Treaty base of the Working

[23] See further S Fredman, "The New Rights: Labour Law and Ideology in the Thatcher Years" (1992) 12 *Oxford Journal of Legal Studies* 24; P Elias and K Ewing, *Trade Union Democracy: Members' Rights and the Law* (1987).

[24] See S Auerbach, *Legislating for Conflict* (1990); K Ewing, *The Right to Strike* (1991).

[25] See B Hepple, "The Fall and Rise of Unfair Dismissal" in W McCarthy (ed.), *Legal Intervention in Industrial Relations: Gains and Losses* (1992).

[26] See S Deakin and F Wilkinson, "The Law and Economics of the Minimum Wage" (1992) 19 *Journal of Law and Society* 279; R Dickens *et al.*, "Wages Councils: Was there a Case for Abolition?' (1993) 31 *British Journal of Industrial Relations* 516.

Time Directive, adopted as a health and safety measure by qualified majority voting under the former Article 118a, in which the European Court of Justice, in interpreting health and safety as "a state of complete physical, mental, and social well-being that does not consist only in the absence of illness or infirmity",[27] opened the door to the adoption of a wider range of social protection measures under this procedure.

The Labour Government's Programme of "Fairness at Work"

The advent of a Labour Government in 1997 has undoubtedly heralded a less hostile approach towards employment protection and trade unionism. One symbolically important first step was to end the United Kingdom's opt-out from the "Social Chapter", and in doing so agree to implement the directives on parental leave, part-time work, and European Works Councils which had been negotiated under it.[28] Another was the early introduction of legislation implementing, for the first time, a national minimum wage, although the level at which it was initially set (£3.60), and the modifications for younger workers, were disappointing to many.[29] However, it has not brought a return to the past. The mantra of labour market "flexibility", enshrined in the government's election manifesto, remains crucial, although tempered by the values of "fairness", "partnership" and "family-friendly" policies proclaimed in the White Paper, *Fairness at Work*.[30]

How have these values been translated into practice? Unfair dismissal protection has been enhanced by a reduction in the qualifying period to one year,[31] and an increase in the upper limit of the compensatory award from £12,000 to £50,000.[32] Employers can no longer require workers on fixed term contracts to exclude their rights to claim unfair dismissal.[33] Highly significantly, the personal scope of labour law has expanded in some cases to include

[27] Case C-84/94 *UK* v. *Council of the European Union* [1996] ECR I-5755; see B Fitzpatrick, "Straining the Definition of Health and Safety?' (1997) 26 *Industrial Law Journal* 115.

[28] See C Barnard, "The United Kingdom, the 'Social Chapter' and the Amsterdam Treaty" (1997) 26 *Industrial Law Journal* 275.

[29] National Minimum Wage Act 1998; National Minimum Wage Regulations 1999, SI 1999/584. See B Simpson, "A Milestone in the Legal Regulation of Pay: The National Minimum Wage Act 1998' (1999) 28 *Industrial Law Journal* 1 and "Implementing the National Minimum Wage—the 1999 Regulations" (1999) 28 *Industrial Law Journal* 171.

[30] Cm 3968 (1998).

[31] Unfair Dismissal and Statement of Reasons for Dismissal (Variation of Qualifying Period) Order 1999, SI 1999/1436.

[32] Employment Relations Act 1999, s. 34(4).

[33] *Ibid.*, s. 18.

a wider category of dependent labour than the traditional "employee"; the National Minimum Wage Act 1998 and Working Time Regulations[34] extend to the broader category of "workers", and agency and homeworkers are specifically brought within their reach. The Secretary of State has been also been empowered to extend existing rights (such as unfair dismissal) to workers currently outside them, although at the time of writing this power has yet to be exercised.[35]

All workers have been granted the right to be accompanied by a "single companion", who may be either a fellow worker or a trade union official, when required or invited by their employer to attend a disciplinary or grievance hearing at which they "reasonably" request to be accompanied.[36] However, a number of reforms are qualified in nature. The "family-friendly" leave rights are unpaid, raising fears that only the better off will be able to afford them. A power in the National Minimum Wage Act to require employers to indicate workers' hourly rates was not exercised because of representations that it would be too costly, making it extremely difficult for workers with complex pay structures to determine their position. The Working Time Regulations have been modified to remove employers' duties to maintain detailed records of those who opted to work more than the maximum permitted hours, and the range of those outside their protection has been broadened.[37] To this extent, rights have been firmly located in the context of commercial considerations.

The key concept of "partnership", whilst rhetorically attractive, has proved difficult to define. It is clear that it is not to be equated with the promotion of trade unionism and collective bargaining, which are regarded as only one plank in labour market policy. There is some evidence that the complexities of the long-awaited statutory procedure for mandatory recognition of trade unions enshrined in the Employment Relations Act 1999 are encouraging some employers to enter voluntary recognition agreements, so "bargaining in the shadow of the law".[38] The procedure embraces lessons learned from the operation of the 1975 procedure in specifying the criteria for designating a bargaining unit and the method of assessive support for recognition, and in imposing a duty on employers to co-operate with the balloting process.[39]

[34] SI 1998/1833.

[35] Employment Relations Act 1999, s. 23.

[36] Employment Relations Act 1999, ss. 10–13.

[37] The Working Time Regulations 1999, SI 1999/3372.

[38] See G Gall and S McKay, "Developments in Union Recognition and Derecognition in Britain 1994–1998" (1999) 37 *British Journal of Industrial Relations* 601.

[39] Trade Union and Labour Relations (Consolidation) Act 1992, Sch. A1, inserted by the Employment Relations Act 1999. See S Wood and J Godard, "The Statutory Union Recognition Procedure in the Employment Relations Bill: A Comparative Analysis" (1999) 37 *British Journal of Industrial Relations* 203; Lord McCarthy, *Fairness at Work and Trade Union Recognition: Past Comparison and Future Problems* (1999). For a detailed analysis of the recognition procedure, see G Morris and T Archer, *Collective Labour Law* (2000).

However the procedure itself is subject to important limitations. First, the scope of mandatory recognition is relatively narrow, being confined to "pay, hours and holidays". Secondly, if the employer itself fails to comply with the collective bargaining "method" imposed by the Central Arbitration Committee (CAC), which is charged with operating the procedure, the sanction is restricted to specific performance of that method, in comparison to its Social Contract predecessor which provided for the imposition of improved working conditions by the CAC.

Thirdly, the procedure itself is capable of being thwarted if an employer voluntarily recognises any other union, regardless of its level of support among the workforce and (usually) even if it lacks a certificate of independence. Even where there is a recognised union, the capacity of individual employers and workers to negotiate terms and conditions of employment which deviate from those collectively agreed has been explicitly affirmed, although there is an enabling power to introduce a very limited measure of protection for those who do not wish to move to personal contracts.[40] The statutory recognition procedure is paralleled by a mechanism for compulsory derecognition of unions which have been recognised via the statutory procedure, and the CAC is required to assist the parties to agree, *inter alia*, to end the bargaining arrangements in the same way as it assists a recognition application. There is thus no policy preference for the maintenance of collective bargaining arrangements. Indeed, the prohibition against requiring contractors to recognise trade unions (but not against denying recognition), introduced by the Conservative Government, remains intact.[41]

It is also instructive to assess how much of the Conservative legacy has remained untouched. The law governing the organisation of industrial action has remained in its essentials, although some minor but important changes have been made to the pre-action balloting and notification requirements.[42] The fact that the law remains more restrictive than in comparable systems is not regarded as a matter for apology. Some changes have been made to the position of individuals who take industrial action; their (long-standing) exclusion from unfair dismissal protection if dismissed for participating in industrial action has been redressed (though not fully),[43] but the status of industrial action as a breach of contract, rather than as a suspension, remains untouched.

[40] Employment Relations Act 1999, s. 17. At the time of writing, regulations to implement this power have not been issued.

[41] Trade Union and Labour Relations (Consolidation) Act 1992, ss. 186–7.

[42] Employment Relations Act 1999, s. 4 and Sch. 3. On the changes in the area of collective labour law in general, see K Ewing "Freedom of Association and the Employment Relations Act 1999" (1999) 28 *Industrial Law Journal* 283; Lord Wedderburn of Charlton, "Collective Bargaining or Legal Enactment: The 1999 Act and Union Recognition" (2000) 29 *Industrial Law Journal* 1. For a comprehensive analysis of the current law, see G Morris and T Archer, *Collective Labour Law supra.*

[43] Employment Relations Act 1999, s. 16 and Sch. 5.

The reform of the law relating to the internal affairs of trade unions introduced by the Conservative Government also remains in place in its essentials, although the symbolically significant (but under-used) office of the Commissioner for the Rights of Trade Union Members has been abolished and much greater powers accorded to the Certification Officer.[44] This means that the United Kingdom continues to violate ILO standards in a number of important areas.[45] Protection against discrimination by employers against trade union members has been enhanced but it is far from comprehensive in its coverage.[46] Insofar as the present legislation represents the industrial relations settlement for this Parliament there is no imminent indication that these provisions will be changed, and there is every sign that they will continue to represent the framework within which industrial relations are conducted for the foreseeable future.

Human Rights and Labour Law

At an international level, human rights have always been central to labour law. To date, however, domestic courts and employment tribunals have, in general, paid scant regard to international labour standards, and, indeed, they have rarely been prayed in aid by advocates. The Human Rights Act 1998 will change that, although it is important to emphasise that there is a limited range of employment issues to which it can apply. These include freedom of expression, freedom of religion, surveillance of employees, and other aspects of respect for private life, such as sexual orientation.[47] All the avenues afforded by the Act to argue that actions are incompatible with Convention rights will be significant to labour law. The obligation to read and give effect to legislation in a way which is compatible with Convention rights will be crucial to the statutory concept of constructive dismissal; it can undoubtedly be argued that action which breaches a Convention right, such as the right to respect for private life or freedom of expression, constitutes a breach of the (expanding) duty of trust and confidence owed by the employer to the employee.

[44] *Ibid.*, s. 29 and Sch. 6.

[45] See T Novitz, "International Promises and Domestic Pragmetism: To What Extent will the Employment Relations Act 1999 implement International Labour standards Relating to Freedom of Association" (2000) 63 *MLR* 379.

[46] Employment Relations Act 1999, ss. 2, 3, Sch. 2.

[47] See generally B Hepple, "The Impact on Labour Law" in B Markesinis (ed.), *The Impact of the Human Rights Bill on English Law* (1997); Sir Gavin Lightman and J Bowers, "Incorporation of the ECHR and its Impact on Employment Law" [1998] *European Human Rights Law Review* 560; K Ewing, "The Human Rights Act and Labour Law" 27 *Industrial Law Journal* 275.

In this respect authorities which support the view that the employee can claim to have been constructively dismissed, and thereby mount an unfair dismissal claim, without resigning from the employment on the basis that the existing employment contract has been breached will be significant.[48] Convention rights are also likely to be important in determining whether a dismissal is fair; if a dismissal breaches such a right, the duty on tribunals to act compatibly with the Convention should lead them to conclude that it is unfair as not being a substantial reason or not otherwise reasonable in the circumstances. That duty will also be relevant when the courts are considering existing common law rights; the scope of the employer's managerial prerogative and the corresponding duty on employees to obey lawful and reasonable orders will need to be interpreted in the light of the Convention. Finally, those employed by "pure" public authorities will have the right to bring proceedings directly against their employer for violating a Convention right; whether those employed by bodies with mixed public and private functions will have this right will depend upon whether employment is regarded as a "private" act. It is widely assumed that employment will be so regarded, although as one of us has argued elsewhere, there are strong grounds against such an interpretation.[49]

In some areas, particularly collective labour law, the European Convention on Human Rights has afforded little or no support to labour standards: to take but two examples, the (individualistically-orientated) European Court of Human Rights has refused to regard the right to strike as integral to freedom of association, in contrast to the supervisory organs of the tripartite specialist International Labour Organisation; and the superficial approach of the (now defunct) Commission to the ban on union membership at Government Communications Headquarters undermined the impact of ILO condemnation.[50] Moreover, the Court, to date, has refused, on spurious grounds, to apply Convention rights to access to employment, and decisions by the Commission that contractual obligations which clashed with the exercise of Convention rights did not, because they had been "voluntarily" undertaken, constitute an interference with the right are ripe for review.[51] It will be open to domestic courts to take a wider view of the application of Convention rights than Strasbourg, and it is to be hoped that in the area of employment they take

[48] *Hogg* v. *Dover College* [1990] ICR 39; *Alcan Extrusions* v. *Yates* [1996] IRLR 327.

[49] G Morris, "The Human Rights Act and the Public/Private Divide in Employment Law" (1998) 27 *Industrial Law Journal* 293.

[50] For a general critique of the ECHR and collective labour standards see Ewing, *supra* n. 47; on the treatment of GCHQ by international bodies, see G Morris, "Freedom of Association and the Interests of the State" in K Ewing, C Gearty and B Hepple (eds), *Human Rights and Labour Law: Essays for Paul O'Higgins* (1994).

[51] See G Morris, "The European Convention on Human Rights and Employment: To Which Acts Does it Apply?" [1999] *European Human Rights Law Review* 496.

that opportunity. The Human Rights Act 1998, in inviting inquiry into the interpretation of concepts such as freedom of association and the justifications for limiting Convention rights, will open the door to argument based on the wider range of labour standards, in particular those emanating from the ILO. In assessing the relevance for labour law of the human rights agenda much will depend on the willingness of courts and tribunals to embrace the less restrictive and more developed jurisprudence of these other international bodies.

The Influence of Europe

From a slow start EU law has had a profound impact on the shape of British labour law.[52] It has also represented an important source of restraint on the development of domestic legislation, particularly during the Thatcher/Major-years. At a time when labour market deregulation was in vogue in Britain, as we pointed out *supra*, EC law proved to be an irritant: it protected some existing forms of intervention inherited by the Conservatives from the previous Labour Government, and required fresh regulation on a range of other matters. Developments at Community level were also to see an endorsement for trade unions and collective bargaining, again contrary to the drift of domestic labour market policy. Particularly after Maastricht in 1992, social dialogue become a more prominent feature of the social policy-making process, and the role of collective agreements as a means of implementing social policy Directives was reinforced. Neither process is without difficulty,[53] though the Maastricht reforms have now been fully incorporated unto the EC Treaty.[54] There is not yet any legally binding community instrument which directly guarantees the right to freedom of association or collective bargaining.

European Labour Law

What has been the enduring influence of European labour law on the British scene? In the first place, and particularly in recent years, it has seen a broadening of the base of the discipline to make it more inclusive: hence the protection for part-time workers, a development anticipated to some extent by judicial developments.[55] Secondly, EC law has been responsible for extending the

[52] See generally B Bercusson, *European Labour Law* (1996).

[53] For a consideration of some of the issues, see B Bercusson, "Democratic Legitimacy and European Labour Law" (1999) 28 *ILJ* 153.

[54] EC Treaty, Title XI.

[55] For example, *R* v. *Secretary of State for Employment, ex parte EOC* [1994] IRLR 176.

scope of social protection: for the first time in Britain we now have comprehensive (though not fully comprehensive) provision for the 48-hour week, and the protection of workers in the event of a business transfer: it seems unlikely that either would have been introduced otherwise than in implementation of community obligations.[56] And thirdly, EC law has led to a deepening of policy initiatives taken in this country, particularly in the area of equal pay and sex discrimination which may well have been introduced notwithstanding obligations arising under EC law. But it is by no means clear whether this would have extended as far as equal pay for work of equal value, or parental leave—limited though both of these initiatives undoubtedly are.

There is now also a considerable body of Community law imposing a duty on employers to consult about a range of issues: collective redundancies, transfer of undertakings, and health and safety at work.[57] (There are also the European works councils.)[58] This form of arrangement perhaps reflects the practices in a number of European labour law systems where collective bargaining takes place at the level of the industry or sector, and works councils or similar bodies exist to represent the voice of the workers in the enterprise. Trade unions may be represented and may indeed dominate these bodies, but it is nevertheless a form of representation quite unfamiliar to our system which increasingly is based on enterprise-based collective bargaining. Although recognised trade unions may perform this consultative role mandated by EC law, the problem arises because trade unions are recognised in only a minority of workplaces, with collective bargaining density having fallen sharply since 1980 to perhaps no more than about 40 per cent of the labour force, though this may begin to increase with the assistance of the new trade union recognition legislation.[59] But in the absence of a recognised union, the representation gap can be filled only by non union forms of representation.

European Social Policy: Future Prospects

In the short term there is a feeling of unfinished business, in the sense that there are still draft directives which remain to be implemented. The most important here is the Draft Information and Consultation Directive which proposes to extend the current obligations to inform and consult workers representatives to include any significant changes to working conditions. Designed to apply to national level companies employing more than fifty

[56] Directives 92/85/EC and 77/187/EEC respectively.

[57] Bercusson, *European Labour Law*, *supra* n. 52, ch. 33.

[58] Directive 94/45/EC. For analysis, B Bercusson, *European Works Councils—Extending the Trade Union Role* (Institute of Employment Rights, 1997). Now, the Transnational Information and Consultation of Employees Regulations 1999, SI 1999/3323.

[59] See *supra*.

people, this would be significant for two reasons. The first is that it would reinforce the possibility of an emerging twin-track approach to worker representation in the British system: one based on independent trade unions; and the other on works councils or similar bodies. The initiative could help bring together the current rag-bag of measures, and at the same time could provide trade unions with another opportunity to secure a representative role in the workplace. The second reason why the initiative is significant relates to the remedies proposed in the event of the failure to comply with the duty to inform and consult. Following the rather contemptuous approach of Renault Vilvoorde to existing consultation procedures, it is proposed that in the event of a serious breach,[60] any change to working conditions or any dismissal should be void and of no legal effect.

In the longer term, it is by no means certain how the development of European social policy will affect British labour law. We are moving very quickly into unchartered waters, in which no-one will be able to predict with any certainty the consequences of either enlargement of the EU on the one hand,[61] or the impact of the single currency on the other. The Commission has signalled the need for a new agenda expressing concern that European growth and employment rates have fallen behind the USA.[62] The focus of the new agenda it seems is "to build a competitive and inclusive knowledge-based economy which promotes strong and sustained growth, full employment and social cohesion".[63] There is no sense that this will lead to a significant expansion of new rights for workers: with more than 15 million people looking for work, the first objective is full employment; so we may expect a rash of job creation initiatives, with the focus on the employment chapter to the EU Treaty introduced at Amsterdam in 1997.[64] There is also a commitment to "economic reform" in "labour, product and capital markets aimed at stimulating innovation and entrepreneurship", sometimes a synonym for de-regulation or more benignly "labour market flexibility" (though not usually so benign for employees).

[60] *Comité de Groupe European Renault* v. *Société Renault*, Nanterre Court of First Instance, 4 April 1997 (English translation of judgment).

[61] On which see *IGC: Reform for Enlargement* (Cm 4595, 2000).

[62] Commission Communication to the Parliament, the Council, the Economic and Social Committee and the Committee of the Regions, Strategic Objectives 2000–2005.

[63] *Ibid.*

[64] EC Treaty, Title VIII.

Labour Law's Future: Building on "Fairness at Work"

Before contemplating the future of labour law in Britain, it would be wise to reflect on the present. Perhaps more than any other discipline (with the possible exception of social security law), labour law has undergone a series of profound changes over the last two decades: a sharp ideological revision was fastened onto the regime inherited from the 1970s; and onto this synthesis a new framework reflecting a new ideology (though perhaps not as profound as the one which it replaces) has been grafted. The future is likely to be dominated at one level by the teething problems associated with the implementation of the present. So far as the trade union recognition provisions in particular are concerned, the experience of other countries and our experience in the 1970s suggests that a great deal of legal time and intellectual effort will be spent navigating the new procedures.[65] This is a journey which is likely to be made even more interesting by the unpredictable effect of the Human Rights Act 1998, which may leave a mark of some kind on labour law as on other disciplines. Whether that mark will be benign or malignant, and whether it will be real and permanent, remains to be seen.

Economic Influences

But future developments are unlikely to be dominated only by the implementation of recently enacted measures. Labour law in recent decades has been nothing if not dynamic, and there is a strong sense that it will continue to adapt as an instrument for the delivery of social and economic policies. This could be both a concern for those wishing to see further development of the traditional functions of protecting workers from the power of employers under the contract of employment, and of promoting strong trade unions in the workplace and in society generally. The emphasis in the future will be in promoting fairness and efficiency, and in promoting competitiveness in the global economy, a strategy which the British Government is anxious to export to Europe. Indeed before the election in 1997, the Prime Minister re-assured voters that even after Labour's reforms, Britain would remain the most lightly regulated labour market in Europe. It remains the case that enterprise flexibility continues to be a reality even after the Labour reforms of 1997–2000: the recognition legislation does not apply to small businesses;[66] workers continue

[65] For experience in the USA and Canada, see Institute of Employment Rights, *Need to be Heard at Work?* (1998).

[66] Trade Union and Labour Relations (Consolidation) Act 1992, Sch. A1 (as inserted by the Employment Relations Act 1999).

to be unprotected from unfair dismissal for up to a year of employment;[67] and there is no formula for the up-rating of what is a low national minimum wage.

We may thus see a change of focus of traditional labour law, with more and more emphasis on State initiatives designed to promote employment, and to enhance the quality of the labour force through education and training in a fast changing economy. An example of the former at the time of writing is the New Deal; the cash incentives to be provided to unemployed workers, designed to encourage labour mobility, encouraging people to move to where the jobs are, is another—a modern equivalent of the Redundancy Payments Act 1965? Not unrelated to this is the merging of the Benefits Agency and the Employment Service. So far as education and training are concerned, a number of work-based initiatives have already been taken: these include the life-long learning initiative in which trade unions also participate;[68] and perhaps more modestly the contents of the Teaching and Higher Education Act 1998; this provides that some sixteen and seventeen-year-olds have a right to reasonable time off work in order to study for recognised qualifications. Trade unions recognised under the new statutory recognition procedure may also have the right to be consulted by the employer about training.

Political Influences

In view of the recent history of British labour law, it is difficult to believe that *Fairness at Work*[69] represents an enduring settlement or that a broad consensus can be built around its terms. It is true that the new Conservative leadership has accepted the principle of the national minimum wage: but there is a great deal of scope for argument about what the level should be (which ought at least to meet the European decency threshold).[70] As ever, much will depend on the outcome of general elections: while the Labour Party has struck an accommodation with the Thatcher/Major changes of the 1980s and 1990s, it is too early to say whether the present Conservative leadership will strike a similar accommodation with the Labour reforms of the 1990s. Although the differences between the parties is closer than it has been in the past, political developments will still matter, in the sense that Labour governments are more likely to respond to pressure for further improvements in employment protection legislation: more willing to act as a broker of the conflicting claims of busi-

[67] Employment Rights Act 1996, s. 108 (as amended).

[68] On which see A Giddens, *The Third Way and its Critics* (2000), p. 150.

[69] Cm 3968 (1998).

[70] The Council of Europe decency threshold for the purposes of Article 4(1) of the Social Charter is now 60 per cent of the national average wage (having been 68 per cent). See Council of Europe, *European Social Charter: Committee of Independent Experts, Conclusions IV-2, vol 1* (1998), p. 51.

ness and organised labour. In that sense there will inevitably be issues to be addressed. One such issue is employer surveillance of workers,[71] now ripe for regulation in the near future—just as whistleblowing was ripe for regulation in the Public Interest Disclosure Act 1998.[72]

A more difficult issue where it might be expected that the colour of the government in power might be expected to make a difference is in relation to international obligations, with which Britain is not yet in full compliance. This is a result largely of the legislative and other changes introduced by the Conservative Administrations in the 1980s and 1990s: these obligations include several arising under ILO Conventions 87 and 98 and the Council of Europe's Social Charter of 1961—all ratified by the United Kingdom.[73] It is true that important steps have recently been taken in the direction of compliance: the ban on trade unions at GCHQ was lifted; unfair dismissal protection was introduced for strikers (for at least eight weeks);[74] and trade unions are no longer required to inform the employer of the identity of employees to be balloted in an industrial action ballot.[75] But there are continuing questions about (i) the incomplete response in the Employment Relations Act 1999 to the decision in *Associated Newspapers* v. *Wilson* (and the so-called "Ullswater" amendment) permitting discrimination against trade unionists;[76] (ii) the complete ban on secondary and solidarity action;[77] and (iii) the current narrow definition of a trade dispute.[78]

Conclusion

Despite the great labour law changes which have taken place throughout the twentieth century, there are also great continuities and recognisable themes. Even the strategies of the last twenty years or so are not without parallel: the Thatcher/Major period has echoes in the period from 1922 to 1934, though the form of restraint was different; mainly passive neglect rather than active restriction. It also has echoes for a much shorter period in the Labour

[71] See M Ford, *Surveillance and Privacy at Work* (Institute of Employment Rights, 1998).

[72] D Lewis, "Public Interest Disclosure Act 1998' (1998) 27 *ILJ* 325.

[73] On the ILO, see S Mills, "The International Labour Organisation, the United Kingdom and Freedom of Association: An Annual Cycle of Condemnation" [1997] *EHRLR* 35; on the Social Charter, see K D Ewing, "Britain and the Social Charter" (2000) *EHRLR* (forthcoming).

[74] Employment Relations Act 1999, Sch. 5, inserting a new s. 238A to the Trade Union and Labour Relations (Consolidation) Act 1992.

[75] Employment Relations Act 1999, Sch. 3; cf. *Blackpool and The Fylde College* v. *NATFHE* [1994] ICR 648.

[76] [1995] 2 AC 454; and Trade Union Reform and Employment Rights Act 1993, s. 13.

[77] Trade Union and Labour Relations (Consolidation) Act 1992, s. 224.

[78] *Ibid.*, s. 244. See *UCL Hospital Trust* v. *UNISON* [1999] IRLR 31.

Government's ill-fated *In Place of Strife*;[79] and in the Industrial Relations Act 1971, seen at the time as a failure, but in reality a harbinger of things to come.[80] By the same token, the current strategy of the new Labour Government is also consistent with strategies adopted in the past, though the rationale is perhaps now very different: no longer a desire to maintain industrial peace (1917–21), or promote Keynesian style demand management (1934 onwards), or a commitment to the principles of industrial democracy (1975). The goal now it seems is partnership, though paradoxically reliance on the new statutory recognition procedures may not be the least fractious way of creating a consensual relationship. Nevertheless, State intervention is designed to facilitate collective bargaining,[81] in the expectation that bargaining structures will develop in the shadow of the law, as they did from 1917, the law at that time being the Trade Boards Act 1918.

Only the reckless would predict the content of labour law in the future. But it is perhaps possible to indicate the directions of future development and the factors which will shape its progress. Like every other discipline, labour law will carry the burdens of its past—in this case, the values of the common law (which are not wholly incapable of change) and the nature and form of legislative protection; policy-makers may also continue to learn from the mistakes of the past, as in the recognition provisions of the Employment Relations Act 1999. But labour law will also be influenced by brutal economic considerations: by the need to ensure a flexible and skilled labour force in a competitive global economy. This seems likely to place a premium on promoting equality of opportunity in terms of labour market access and in improving the quality of human capital and the skills base of the labour force. It also seems likely to place a premium on low barriers to those who wish to exploit entrepreneurial opportunities; a premium on training and inclusion; and the elimination of discrimination and the enhancing of opportunity.[82] But it would be a mistake to overlook the traditional functions of the discipline.[83] Political pressure will inevitably continue for better legal protection for workers and their trade unions from the inhospitable common law which provides the legal basis for so much of the social power exercised by employers.

[79] Cmnd 3888 (1969).

[80] See B Weekes, M Mellish, L Dickens and J Lloyd, *Industrial Relations and the Limits of the Law* (1975).

[81] Though perhaps not now to promote collective bargaining: the statutory duty of ACAS (removed by the Trade Union Reform and Employment Relations Act 1993, s. 43) to promote collective bargaining has not been restored.

[82] See generally, A Giddens, *The Third Way*, *supra* n. 68.

[83] As proposed by Institute of Employment Rights, *Employment Rights: Building on Fairness at Work* (2000).

13

Company Law

JOHN BIRDS AND JOHN PARKINSON

Company law at the beginning of the twenty-first century is at an important stage in its development. The independent body set up by the Government to conduct a fundamental review of core company law,[1] with a view to legislation in the next Parliament, is scheduled to issue its final report in 2001, and can be expected to recommend many significant changes both of form and substance. The aim is to simplify the law by stripping away unnecessary accretions and to provide a framework that is conducive to efficient wealth creation, while at the same time ensuring that a proper balance is struck between the interests of all the parties involved in the enterprise. Company law scholarship is changing too. While rightly continuing to concern itself with traditional doctrinal analysis, the subject has extended its horizons. The study of company law is now enriched by insights from a variety of other disciplines, and lawyers in turn are contributing to the growth of a genuinely inter-disciplinary field, especially in relation to corporate governance. Theory is of particular importance in company law because a number of questions that are fundamental to it, for example, whether companies are property, or a set of contractual relationships, or social institutions, are not objectively answerable but depend on different philosophical positions about the nature of corporate organisation and its relationship with society. These positions and associated characterisations of the company support different views about the need for regulation, its legitimacy, and the form it should take. This chapter will give first a very brief and selective account of theoretical issues of current interest in company law and then go on to look at a number of important topics in the law and the likely impact of the Company Law Review.

[1] See Department of Trade and Industry, *Modern Company Law for a Competitive Economy* (London, 1998). John Parkinson is a member of the Steering Group overseeing the Review. He writes here in a personal capacity.

Control in public companies

A long-standing issue in company law is the "separation of ownership and control".[2] The concern is that in companies with widely dispersed shares the absence of effective shareholder supervision means that directors are free to act in their own interests at the expense of the shareholders (and putatively, of society as a whole) and that incompetent managements are able successfully to resist removal. Work by economists on the theory of the firm has refocused this debate and drawn attention to the range of mechanisms, additional to directors' duties and shareholder "voice", available to secure managerial accountability and reduce the costs associated with uncontrolled discretion. These include monitoring by non-executive or "outside" directors, performance-related pay schemes, and the role of markets in providing managers with appropriate incentives and deterrents. Concerns nevertheless remain about the effectiveness of individual components of the disciplinary framework and, indeed, of the framework overall. Hostile take-overs, for example, do not appear to be particularly targeted at under-performing companies.[3] One form of accountability which might be strengthened to compensate for weaknesses elsewhere is board monitoring, to which we return below.

Despite the preoccupation with the separation of ownership and control in the English-speaking world, comparative research has shown that widely dispersed shareholdings in public companies are the exception rather than the rule internationally. More commonly, companies face an "insider" system of governance dependent on the holding of large share blocks by banks, other companies, and families, rather than an "outsider" system in which shareholders are typically "uncommitted", but managers are exposed to pressure from an active market in corporate control. The contrasts are not confined to methods of securing managerial accountability and their effectiveness. There are also indications that the outsider system facilitates the rapid redeployment of capital from contracting to developing sectors, but that the insider system is more supportive of wealth-creating, co-operative relationships between a company and its employees and suppliers.[4] As to the reasons for the differences between systems, one literature has suggested that shareholder dispersal, at

[2] The classic work is A A Berle and G C Means, *The Modern Corporation and Private Property* (1932, rev. edn., New York, 1967).

[3] See e.g. J Franks and C Mayer, "Hostile Takeovers and the Correction of Managerial Failure", (1996) 40 *J Fin Econ* 163.

[4] See CPB Netherlands Bureau for Economic Policy Analysis, *Challenging Neighbours: Rethinking German and Dutch Economic Institutions* (1997).

least in the USA,[5] is not necessarily the product of economic, evolutionary forces, so much as the result of political intervention designed to forestall the concentration of financial power.[6] A different view, opening up a potentially fruitful area for comparative legal research, has sought to explain the prevalence of block-holding in insider systems by reference to inadequate legal protection for minority shareholders, thereby inhibiting the development of deep equity markets.[7] Recognition of differences between systems has in turn provoked investigation into the extent to which there is, or will be, convergence in response to the pressures of globalisation, or should be deliberate adaptation (in either direction) through legislative change.

In whose interests should companies be run?

An even more fundamental issue, tackled from a variety of theoretical perspectives, is whose interests company law should seek to protect. This question has a long pedigree, ranging through the Berle-Dodd debate of the 1930s in the USA,[8] governmental interest in this country in the 1970s in the wider responsibilities of companies[9] and in employee participation,[10] and in its most recent guise, a number of different stakeholder theories of the company.[11] These include versions with an ethical motivation, for example, which argue that participants in the company should not be treated merely as a means of maximising shareholder wealth, but as ends worthy of respect in their own

[5] This analysis is unconvincing as regards the United Kingdom: see G P Stapledon, *Institutional Shareholders and Corporate Governance* (Oxford, 1996), at 230–3; see also B S Black and J C Coffee, "Hail Britannia?: Institutional Investor Behavior Under Limited Regulation", (1994) 92 *Mich Law Rev* 1997.

[6] See M Roe, *Strong Managers, Weak Owners: the Political Roots of American Corporate Finance* (Princeton, 1994).

[7] See R La Porta, F Lopez-de-Silanes, A Shleifer and R Vishny, "Legal Determinants of External Finance", (1997) 52 *J Finance* 1131.

[8] See A A Berle, "Corporate Powers as Powers in Trust", (1931) 44 *Harv L Rev* 1049; E M Dodd, "For Whom are Corporate Managers Trustees?', (1932) 45 *Harv L Rev* 1145; Berle, "For Whom Corporate Managers *Are* Trustees: A Note", (1932) 45 *Harv L Rev* 1365; Dodd, "Is the Effective Enforcement of the Fiduciary Duties of Corporate Managers Practicable?", (1935) *U Chi L Rev* 194; Joseph L Weiner, "The Berle-Dodd Dialogue on the Concept of the Corporation", (1964) 64 *Colum L Rev* 1458; P Ireland, "Back to the Future? Adolph Berle, The Law Commission and Directors' Duties", (1999) 20 *Co Law* 203.

[9] See, for example, Department of Trade and Industry, *Company Law Reform* (Cmnd 5391, London, 1973).

[10] See Department of Trade, *Report of the Committee of Inquiry on Industrial Democracy* (the Bullock Report) (Cmnd 6706, London, 1977).

[11] For a survey, see M B E Clarkson, *The Corporation and its Stakeholders: Classic and Contemporary Readings* (Toronto, 1998).

right.[12] The importance of the contribution made by stakeholders, particularly employees, to the success of the company, the extent to which stakeholder welfare is bound up with the fortunes of the business, and arguments based on reliance by stakeholders and implicit promises by management about continuity of relationships, are also put forward as providing a moral case for protecting stakeholder interests through company law mechanisms.[13]

Over the last few years an economic version of stakeholder theory has also been developed. A key element in it is the economic importance of investments by participants in the company that are "firm-specific" or "sunk".[14] Examples include the acquisition by an employee of knowledge or skills that are of value only in the context of the particular firm, or the construction by a supplier of machinery dedicated to the needs of a specific customer. The duration and open-ended character of the returns to these investments mean that they are difficult to protect contractually, thereby giving those who make them a "stake" in the company that is at risk in much the same way that shareholders' investments are at risk.[15] This perspective accordingly invites a reconceptualisation of the company, as an enterprise made up of all the groups, not just the shareholders, which have made investments in it. It points to the need to provide improved protection for stakeholders if they are to have appropriate incentives to invest at a socially efficient level.

Law and economics

The stakeholder model shows that the application of economic thinking does not necessarily lead, as is sometimes suggested, to conservative policy

[12] See e.g. W Evan and R Freeman, "A Stakeholder Theory of the Modern Corporation: Kantian Capitalism", in T Beauchamp and N Bowie (eds), *Ethical Theory and Business Ethics* (3rd edn., Englewood Cliffs, 1988), p. 67. For essays on communitarian theories of the company, see L E Mitchell (ed.), *Progressive Company Law* (Oxford, 1995).

[13] See, for example, J W Singer, "The Reliance Interest in Property", (1988) 40 *Stan L Rev* 611; K Stone, "Labour Markets, Employment Contracts, and Corporate Change", in J McCahery, S Picciotto, and C Scott (eds), *Corporate Control and Accountability: Changing Structures and the Dynamics of Regulation* (Oxford, 1993), p. 61.

[14] See, for example, M M Blair, *Ownership and Control: Rethinking Corporate Governance for the Twenty-First Century* (Washington, 1995), especially ch. 7; L Zingales, "Corporate Governance", in P Newman (ed.), *The New Palgrave Dictionary of Economics and Law* (London, 1998), vol. 1, p. 495; G Kelly and J Parkinson, "The Conceptual Foundations of the Company: A Pluralist Approach", (1998) 2 *CfiLR* 174.

[15] For the traditional analysis justifying shareholder exclusivity, see, for example, F H Easterbrook and D R Fischel, *The Economic Structure of Corporate Law* (Cambridge, Mass, 1991), especially chs 1 and 3; J R Macey and G P Miller, "Corporate Stakeholders: A Contractual Perspective", (1993) 43 *U of Toronto L J* 299; O Williamson, *The Economic Institutions of Capitalism: Firms, Markets, Relational Contracting* (New York, 1985), ch. 12.

prescriptions. Rather, as here, it might indicate a need for legal intervention, aimed at increasing aggregate wealth, which also has socially progressive effects. An example would be to improve the flow of information to employees to facilitate better bargaining, which might in turn lead to greater job security. Of course, there are other changes in company law that might be considered desirable that will conflict with the requirements of the economic goal of efficiency. Here, the role of economic analysis is to provide guidance (often necessarily tentative and based on contestable hypotheses) about the economic effects of different policy choices. How conflicts between values themselves should be resolved is a moral or political question and not an issue that can be settled by economic reasoning.[16]

Such forbearance is not always apparent in law and economics writing on the company, however. The question of the desirability of policy interventions designed to improve the position of groups other than shareholders is often foreclosed by suggestions that such changes will inevitably exact a high price in efficiency terms and be liable to harm those whose interests they are meant to serve.[17] These conclusions tend not to be based on empirical evidence, but to flow from a particular conception of the company as a "nexus of contracts", together with *a priori* reasoning about the operation of market forces. In a similar way it is often argued that regulation aimed at increasing efficiency is unnecessary or will be damaging, since the relevant measures would have been adopted already were they likely to yield benefits.

The contract model is useful as an analytical device: a way of thinking about the efficient allocation of risk, returns, and control rights in a company. It is much less helpful, however, when taken too literally, as though it involved a descriptively accurate account of the processes by which corporate governance structures (legal and regulatory rules and rules determined by private ordering)[18] come into existence. No doubt competitive forces are at work in shaping governance arrangements, but institutional path-dependency, entrenched self-interest, and weak competitive pressure in the relevant markets mean that we should be highly sceptical about the evolutionary theory on which claims about optimality rest. Survival indicates that some threshold of efficiency has been crossed, but not that existing arrangements are necessarily the most efficient ones that are practicably realisable nor that other arrangements with different distributive consequences might not also have good survival properties. Insistence that a company *is* a nexus of contracts narrows the scope for

[16] See S Deakin and A Hughes, "Economic Efficiency and the Proceduralisation of Company Law", (1999) 3 *CfiLR* 169, at 171, and citing R Posner, *The Economics of Justice* (Cambridge, Mass, 1982), as espousing a contrary view.

[17] See, for example, Macey and Miller, "Corporate Stakeholders", *supra* n. 15.

[18] Legal rules from this perspective are transaction-cost saving devices that shadow the bargain the parties would have reached if they had addressed the issue: see Easterbrook and Fischel, *The Economic Structure of Corporate Law*, *supra* n. 15, at 14–15.

legitimate debate about the role of regulation in these areas, by raising strong, but ill founded presumptions about the efficiency of the *status quo*.

The "scope" of company law

Turning now to the Company Law Review and the law itself, one of the early issues considered by the Review is the fundamental question, touched on above, of whose interests company law should seek to protect.[19] One reason why this issue of the "scope" of company law is important is a concern that many British companies are failing to develop and sustain long-term, co-operative relationships with their employees, customers, and suppliers, despite their importance to competitive success.[20] The Review is considering whether the current law, in which shareholder interests are overriding, is compatible with the development of these relationships in appropriate cases, or whether a "pluralist" approach should be adopted, in which directors are required to balance the interests of relevant stakeholders with a view to maximising their wealth as a group. The case for the latter position draws on arguments about contractual incompleteness that were briefly mentioned earlier. Another question as regards "scope" is whether it is sufficient to rely on "external regulation", that is, controls such as environmental, health and safety, and consumer law, to curb the adverse effects of corporate behaviour, or whether the objectives of companies should themselves be modified, so that limiting these effects becomes more comprehensively a part of the company's goal structure. Both these issues raise questions about whether there should be changes in directors' duties, requiring them to take account of a wider range of interests than just those of the shareholders, and whether there should also be structural changes, for example, modifying the shareholders' exclusive right to appoint the board.

What the conclusions will be on these issues is not yet clear,[21] but one likely response is a significant increase in disclosure. The information that companies are required to disclose in their accounts has to date largely been backward-looking and the emphasis has been on accounting for tangible assets. Such information gives only a very partial indication of the company's future

[19] See Company Law Review Steering Group, *Modern Law for a Competitive Economy: the Strategic Framework* (London, 1999), ch. 5.1.

[20] See RSA Inquiry, *Tomorrow's Company: The Role of Business in a Changing World* (London, 1995); Commission on Public Policy and British Business, *Promoting Prosperity: A Business Agenda for Britain* (London, 1997), chs 1 and 4.

[21] It is expected that the Steering Group's provisional conclusions will be published in a further consultation document in March 2000.

earning capacity, and lack of information about "soft" assets, such as human capital and the structure of the company's internal and external relationships, may mean that they are undervalued by the capital market. Failure of share prices fully to reflect investment in these assets may deter managements from making them and contribute to adverse short-term pressures. Disclosure of information about such matters as employment policies and training and the company's relationships more generally should help correct these pressures and encourage directors, shareholders, and other interested parties to enter into a dialogue about strategy and the company's competitive position.

Disclosure can also be used to regulate company behaviour, to supplement more direct regulatory techniques. Most companies recognise the importance to the success of the business of protecting their reputation in relation to environmental, social, and ethical issues. Companies with low standards are liable to come under various forms of pressure, including boycotts, from consumers, employees, NGOs, and capital markets, among others, with consequent damage to profitability. For this form of control to work well, however, corporate performance in the relevant areas must be reasonably transparent. A number of companies already report voluntarily on environmental, and also a range of social and ethical issues,[22] but there is much to be said for making such reporting mandatory for all companies of sufficient economic significance. Bringing reporting within a statutory framework should also facilitate the development of reporting standards that will promote consistency and comparability of the material disclosed.

Non-statutory regulation: the structure of the board

Companies are subject to a complex pattern of regulatory jurisdictions. In addition to common law and statute, various types of non-statutory rules apply in key areas. In particular, companies must prepare accounts in accordance with standards laid down by the Accounting Standards Board, the Financial Services Authority Listing Rules impose a range of obligations on quoted companies, and the take-over process is governed by the City Code on Takeovers and Mergers.[23]

[22] See PIRC, *Environmental and Social Reporting: A Survey of Current Practice at FTSE 350 Companies* (London, 1998). It has been suggested that voluntary reports tend to be selective, concentrating on "good news" and are of limited value in enabling the performance of companies to be compared: see P Kirkman and C Hope, *Environmental Disclosure in UK Company Annual Reports* (Cambridge, 1992).

[23] Although the latter may have to be put on some sort of statutory basis if the proposed 13th EC Directive is agreed.

There are undoubted advantages in non-statutory regulation in terms of the speed with which rules can be changed and the flexible way in which they can be applied. There are, on the other hand, questions about the legitimacy of "private" rule-making and the effectiveness of the sanctions available in the absence of statutory under-pinning. As the Review points out,[24] the current regulatory framework is the result of *ad hoc* decisions rather than any grand design. The Review has accordingly embarked on a principled examination of the appropriate division between statutory and non-statutory controls and how to allocate regulatory functions in such a way as to avoid overlaps and make the best use of the available competencies.

An important example of non-statutory regulation concerns the structure and composition of the board of directors. The Companies Act 1985 does not define the functions of directors, leaving their role and the division of responsibilities between the board and the shareholders to the company's constitution. The office of chairman of the board is not recognised in the Act, nor does it distinguish between executive and non-executive directors. There are, however, provisions that apply to listed companies in relation to some of these matters. These are now contained in the Combined Code,[25] which consolidates the work of the Cadbury[26] and Hampel Committees[27] on corporate governance, and the Greenbury Group on directors' remuneration.[28] The Code, among other things, provides that the board should comprise at least one-third non-executive directors, a majority of whom should be independent of management, and recommends that the positions of chief executive and chairman of the board should be split to prevent an excessive concentration of power. There is no obligation as such to comply with the provisions, but rather an obligation (imposed by the Listing Rules) to disclose whether or not there has been compliance, and if not, the reasons. The company's governance arrangements thereby become reasonably transparent, and the assumption is that directors of non-conforming companies will come under pressure from shareholders unless they can provide a convincing explanation of why the circumstances of the company are such that compliance would be inappropriate. This approach to enforcement has obvious advantages in terms of flexibility and the avoidance of over-regulation. It also seems to have been fairly effective in securing compliance, the evidence suggesting that a large majority of companies are following the main guidelines.[29]

[24] *The Strategic Framework*, *supra* n. 19, at para. 5.5.4.

[25] *The Combined Code: Principles of Good Governance and Code of Best Practice* (London, 1998).

[26] *Report of the Committee on the Financial Aspects of Corporate Governance* (London, 1992).

[27] Committee on Corporate Governance, *Final Report* (London, 1998).

[28] *Directors' Remuneration: Report of a Study Group chaired by Sir Richard Greenbury* (London, 1995).

[29] See PIRC, *Compliance with the Combined Code: A Study Prepared for the Company Law Review* (London, 1999).

There is, however, a case for considering whether some of the Code's provisions should be put into statute and made mandatory, since a "voluntary" approach is often least likely to be effective in those companies in which reform is most needed. Another important issue concerns the content of the Code. The recommendations of the Cadbury Committee on non-executive directors were the culmination of two decades of activity by the Bank of England and other City and industry bodies designed to encourage companies to improve internal monitoring of management.[30] The presence of a strong independent element on the board is not just a matter of "hygiene" and avoiding financial scandals, but is of prime importance in ensuring that companies are competently and energetically managed. The Review is likely to consider whether the requirements of the Combined Code as yet go far enough in securing internal accountability. One concern is that as executive directors play a part in the selection of non-executives, appointees are unlikely to be truly independent and candidates expected to adopt a rigorous attitude to their monitoring responsibilities are unlikely to be chosen. Another is that since they are often in a minority on the board, non-executives have no ability to discipline or remove members of the management team, though it is open to them to seek the assistance of shareholders in so doing. There is some evidence to suggest that while non-executives are fully aware of their strategic role (contributing to the development of strategy from a relatively dispassionate viewpoint), they are less sure of their monitoring responsibilities.[31] There are also indications that non-executives in this country (as distinct from the USA) do not play an active role in removing poorly performing managements.[32]

The role of the common law

Historically, many of the principles of company law were developed by the judges drawing on, in particular, doctrines of equity and partnership law. The governing statutes laid down the basic formalities and parts of the constitutional framework, and conferred personality on the registered company, but said nothing or very little about key areas of company law. These included the effect of the grant of personality and when that personality might be ignored, the capacity of the company or the authority of those acting on its behalf, what were the duties of the key participants, namely the directors and members or

[30] See J Charkham, "The Bank and Corporate Governance: Past, Present and Future", (1993) *Bank of England Quarterly Bulletin* 388.

[31] See KPMG, *The Role and Responsibilities of Non-Executive Directors* (London, 1999).

[32] See J Franks, C Mayer, and L Renneboog, "Who Disciplines Management in Poorly Performing Companies?" (mimeo).

shareholders, how those duties were to be enforced and when breach might be forgiven, what was the exact role of the directors especially as regards their relationship with the company in general meeting, and what it was proper or improper to do with the capital raised by the issue of shares. The importance of the common law principles that dealt with these areas of the subject has diminished with the growth in companies legislation particularly, although not exclusively, since Britain's entry into the European Community and the consequential impact of the European harmonisation programme. So, there are now detailed statutory rules on, among other things, the capacity of a company and the authority of its board of directors, on some aspects of directors' duties and on share capital, and the role of the judges in these respects is confined to interpreting the statutory rules.[33]

However, common law principles are still critical across a range of areas of company law, even sometimes being used to supplement the statutory rules. A classic example is the common law principle of maintenance of capital, which has been relied upon in recent case law notwithstanding the existence of detailed statutory rules governing its application.[34] Perhaps most important are the basic fiduciary principles affecting directors, and the body of law which determines when a majority of a company's members may be under some sort of duty to the minority.[35] What, it may be asked, is likely to be the role of such common law principles in the foreseeable future? It may be easier to seek to answer that question by asking instead what is likely to be the role of the legislation.

Modernisation and simplification of the companies legislation is likely to be a principal consequence of the Review of Company Law, as we have already indicated. In addition to this, it is thought that there are two issues to be considered. The first relates to those common law areas of company law that may be perceived to be defective and where only statutory reform can cure the defects. Despite successive reforms, it is highly arguable that the last vestiges of the doctrine of ultra vires need to be removed from company law, and it seems certain that the Review will so recommend.[36] Legislation could also encapsu-

[33] Many, though not all, of these statutory rules derive from EC Directives. It seems likely that the EC harmonisation process will not be as influential in the next few years as it has been over the past thirty years. There are undoubted problems in reforming and modernising British company law in the light of hitherto strict EC-imposed regimes; see especially Company Law Reform Steering Group, *Modern Company Law for a Competitive Economy: Company Formation and Capital Maintenance* (London, 1999).

[34] *Aveling Barford Ltd* v. *Perion Ltd* [1989] BCLC 626, *Barclays Bank plc* v. *British & Commonwealth Holdings plc* [1996] BCLC 1. It is probably fair to say that the basic *principle* of maintenance of capital is not actually set out in statutory form.

[35] Although in practice this latter issue is likely to arise now by way of a petition brought under s. 459 of the Companies Act 1985 alleging unfair prejudice, rather than under the common law.

[36] Company Law Reform Steering Group, *supra* n. 33, para. 2.35. The only matter for regret will be the removal from consideration of some of the most entertaining cases in company law history, for example *Re Introductions Ltd* [1970] Ch 199.

late appropriate principles of maintenance of capital completely,[37] although the Review seems hitherto more concerned with tidying up and, where possible, simplifying the current statutory rules.[38] As recently recommended by the Law Commission,[39] the law governing the derivative action will surely before long be put into statutory form, together with the basic common law principles underlying one limb of the rule in *Foss* v. *Harbottle*. It is not yet clear whether the Review will consider the "internal affairs" limb of the rule, which precludes a minority shareholders' action in respect of alleged internal irregularities.[40] Certainly the likely reform of section 14 of the Companies Act 1985, to clarify the effect of a company's constitution,[41] which is currently principally a matter determined by a rather confused body of case law, ought to be accompanied by such an examination, as many would say that the case law on the procedural aspects is equally confusing.

The second issue concerns more fundamental codification. It would clearly be possible for the Review of Company Law to recommend that company law be codified with all the basic principles enshrined in statute. The arguments in favour of and against codification generally have been rehearsed on many previous occasions. Arguments in favour include that codification promotes certainty and accessibility, so that those affected by a body of law are better able to know what it says. Arguments against include the dangers of stultification of the law. The Law Commission's recent comprehensive examination of the issue in the context of company directors' duties, accepting the argument about stultification, concluded against complete codification but in favour of a partial "code" of directors' duties, principally because of the need for directors to have a basic knowledge of what the law requires of them.[42]

It seems highly likely that the Review will follow this line of thinking both as regards the bulk of company directors' duties and any other area where codification might be feasible. There are, however, areas of common law where it is difficult to envisage even partial codification. Probably the most obvious is the body of law determining when the courts will lift the corporate veil. The range of circumstances where this may occur is so vast, perhaps encompassing any body of the law in which a company may be involved. It is also impossible to envisage exactly what could be set out in statutory terms by way of general principle, except what would be a rather bland provision that, while a company is generally a separate legal person, it may not be so when used as a façade

[37] What is appropriate is a matter for debate: see E Ferran, "Creditors' Interests and 'Core' Company Law", (1999) 20 *Co Law* 314.

[38] See Company Law Reform Steering Group, *supra* n. 33.

[39] *Shareholder Remedies* (Law Com No. 246, Cm 3769, London, 1997).

[40] This was outside the Law Commission's terms of reference.

[41] Company Law Reform Steering Group, *supra* n. 36, at paras 2.6–2.8.

[42] *Company Directors: Regulating Conflicts of Interest and Formulating a Statement of Duties* (Law Com No. 261, Scot Law Com No. 173, London, 1999), Part 4.

or for fraudulent purposes. That is not to say that statute ought not to tackle some areas where injustices, mostly to people dealing with a corporate vehicle, may sometimes occur, for example in connection with groups of companies, as discussed *infra*. It is expected that the Review will address these issues.

For a variety of reasons, therefore, it is thought that some common law principles will have a role to play in the company law of the future. What is equally clear, however, is that the common law will occupy a smaller volume of company law than is the case at present, and that many sections of existing texts that summarise the effect of case law will be of mainly historical relevance.

Types of company

In relation to the types of company that are available, our law contrasts sharply with the laws of our European partners (and indeed of some other common law jurisdictions). Despite calls for change over many years, and despite the increased number of dispensations for private companies, we still have a largely unitary system of company law based on the original Victorian model. It is fairly easily demonstrated that many of the requirements of the legislation are inappropriate for smaller companies, and it is arguable that many company law doctrines have become confused because of their failure to distinguish between the very different circumstances of the huge multi-national listed public company at one end of the scale and the small incorporated business at the other. Much of our discussion at the beginning of this chapter is irrelevant so far as smaller companies are concerned.

The question of the appropriate law for economically different types of company is one that is occupying the Review. So far at least, it seems to be proceeding on the basis that the right to form a limited company at minimal expense, and gain the privileges of incorporation and limited liability, should be maintained. Much of the public discussion has assumed that the private limited company would continue to be "deregulated". Indeed it seems possible that the current measures providing exemptions from formalities and disclosure obligations[43] will become automatic for companies up to a certain size and may well be extended; additional obligations will be imposed if and when a company is or becomes bigger.[44] Thus, none of the Consultation Papers has

[43] Especially regarding accounts and audit and the provisions for elective and written resolutions.

[44] So, the classifications of companies as "small" or "medium-sized" should become redundant. There seems little doubt that the basic distinction between private and public companies will remain. A Working Group of the Company Law Review is looking at the special needs of small and closely-held companies.

hitherto addressed the question of the abuses of limited liability, presumably on the basis that this issue is satisfactorily addressed by the provisions in the Company Directors Disqualification Act 1985 and the Insolvency Act 1986.[45] Further, any notion that there might be completely separate legislation for private and public companies seems unlikely to dominate the reform agenda.[46]

It is thought, therefore, that the basic categorisation of companies under the Companies Act 1985 (probably continuing to include unlimited and guarantee companies) will remain largely as it is now, with some modernisation and simplification of the requirements on formation[47] and, as indicated, "progressive regulation". What will be more different will be the range of alternatives available to many types of business. There is the immediate prospect of the limited liability partnership being available under the Limited Liability Partnerships Bill that is before Parliament at the time of writing. This will provide a corporate vehicle for two or more participants, with limited liability and considerably fewer formalities than apply to the limited company. It is not, as early proposals were, restricted to "professional" partnerships, although it will be taxed as a partnership rather than under the tax regime for companies. This new form of business association may in the fairly near future prove to be as popular as the private limited company for some small businesses.

One or two other alternatives may well have emerged from Europe by then. The idea of a European company has been around for many years, but more recently the perhaps over-ambitious idea of a corporate form that was wholly European has been modified in favour of a proposed body that would be governed partly by European law and partly by the law of the Member State in which it registers.[48] Even though the demand for such a body from business may not be that high, political will seems likely to drive the proposal into law, so that the European company should exist as a genuine alternative for larger companies within a few years. A more recent interesting proposal is for a European private company. This has not come from the European Commission, rather from a group working under the auspices of the Paris Chamber of Commerce that appears to have consulted widely with European professional and business associations.[49] Only time will tell whether or not it is officially adopted within the European Union, but it does offer the prospect of an alternative form that is truly governed by European law.

The students and practitioners of company law in the foreseeable future may therefore be faced with a much wider choice of business association than

[45] Although some would argue that existing measures are not necessarily sufficient—see also the further moves towards a "rescue culture" in the Insolvency Bill currently before Parliament.

[46] See *The Strategic Framework, supra* n. 19, ch. 5.2.

[47] See Company Law Reform Steering Group, *supra* n. 33.

[48] See the text produced in April 1996.

[49] Chambre de Commerce et d"Industrie de Paris, Conseil National du Patronat Français *La Société Privée Européenne: une société de partenaires* (Paris, 1998).

is the case at present.[50] Academics will have to consider whether the dominance of the registered company form within "company law" courses can be justified, and the scope for inter-disciplinary research comparing and evaluating the different forms will surely increase.

Groups of companies

The fact that very many businesses are organised in groups of companies is well documented, yet company law pays relatively little attention to this, except as regards the preparation of the annual accounts and for a limited number of other statutory purposes. From time to time the question arises in the context of whether the separate legal personality of companies within a group should be ignored, but the answer is, at best, "hardly ever".[51] Yet for many years there has been widespread concern (including judicial concern)[52] that liability for the actions of one member of a group cannot normally be imposed on other members.[53] The Review has not at the time of writing considered this issue, but it is thought that it will be doing so, as it is a central issue of corporate practice that surely must be addressed, even if ultimately no or little change were to be made to the existing law.[54]

One model for change was provided by the draft Ninth EC Directive, which would have allowed groups to choose between a regime imposing group liability or one in which the financial and managerial independence of the group members was preserved. Although this particular proposal failed to attract support,[55] it is likely that the issue will arise at the European level again, and, as has been cogently argued,[56] it would be sensible for Britain to develop ideas that might have an influence on any European proposals. Alternative approaches can be found in other common law countries,[57] and the jurispru-

[50] It should be noted that the Law Commission is also currently reviewing the law of partnership.

[51] *Adams* v. *Cape Industries plc* [1990] Ch 433.

[52] *Re Southard & Co Ltd* [1979] 1 WLR 1198.

[53] See generally *Insolvency Law and Practice* (Cmnd 8558, London, 1982), ch. 51. Of course the possibility exists of a holding company being liable under the Insolvency Act for fraudulent or wrongful trading.

[54] Another issue is whether or not to retain the general statutory definition of holding and subsidiary company for purposes other than group accounting or whether to adopt the rather broader definition used for the latter.

[55] And is probably too rigid. It does not seem to work well in Germany, which provided the model for the draft Directive.

[56] E Ferran, *Company Law and Corporate Finance* (Oxford, 1999), pp. 42–3.

[57] Judicially-created in the USA and under statute in countries such as Australia and New Zealand.

dence of the European Court of Justice reveals a much more flexible approach than that of the British courts.[58] On the other hand, it is not easy to decide on the proper approach to groups, and many would probably regard any change to the existing position as undue interference with their long-standing freedom to organise their business affairs. However, it is thought that there ought to be some basis for imposing group liability for the benefit of "small" creditors and the victims of torts committed by a part of a group,[59] and we would foresee some change in the law to accommodate this within the foreseeable future.

Information technology and company law

It is trite now to observe that information technology will have a rapidly increasing effect on business activity, and companies and other forms of business association are already grappling with issues arising out of the growth of e-commerce. What is of more interest to company lawyers as such is the scope that information technology increasingly provides for alternative mechanisms for companies to conduct their affairs.[60] It is arguable that the law would now regard the use of IT as permissible for directors' meetings and shareholders' meetings where the number involved made it practicable and there was real contemporaneous communication between all participants, although it is perhaps not clear whether audio communication by itself, that is without some form of video link, would suffice. As importantly, communication with shareholders and other interest groups by way of fulfilling the disclosure requirements of company law could be facilitated by the use of e-mail and the Internet, including electronic bulletin boards, and voting on company resolutions could thereby be made more meaningful.

The Department of Trade and Industry and the Company Law Review have, separately, already addressed many of these issues. The DTI is certain to take powers, under the Electronic Communications Act 2000, to enable companies, with the agreement of their shareholders, to transmit information electronically to them or to place information on a website or other electronic forum. This will cover the annual accounts and directors' report, notices of meetings and proxy forms. Shareholders may also be permitted to lodge proxies

[58] See, for example, *SAR Schotte GmbH* v. *Parfums Rothschild SARL* [1992] BCLC 235.

[59] There is hardly great concern for the position of major creditors such as banks and other financial institutions who are well able to protect themselves.

[60] The Registrar of Companies allows the submission of some information by electronic means, a process which has speeded up recently, and it has for some years now been possible to dispense with paper records: see the Companies Act 1985, ss. 707, 707A.

electronically. A wider range of issues is considered in one of the Consultation Documents published in October 1999.[61] The starting point of this is the broader one that the annual general meeting is ineffective in fulfilling its role in the governance of public companies. The possibility of public companies being able to dispense with the AGM is canvassed, although it is recognised that detailed requirements would be required to find another satisfactory method for communication with, and decision-making by, shareholders. Alternatively, provisions could be introduced to facilitate the holding of meetings using information technology, including audio-visual techniques and the Internet. As a minimum, permitting electronic voting is a likely result of the Review and perhaps the norm, at least for institutional shareholders, within the next few years. While it is difficult to envisage exactly what form company law should take in the near future to accommodate information technology, in the light of the rapidity of change in that technology, within a generation, at the very least it is thought that, in addition to the changes already mentioned, the legislation will contain provision enabling the law governing meetings and disclosure to be kept under constant review, with provision for changes in the light of developments in technology.[62]

Conclusion

It is too early to be able to give a definitive indication of the shape of British company law within the medium term. The Company Law Review will not report finally until the Spring of 2001, and the Government's response, which may well come after the next general election, may not adopt all its recommendations. There will then be the task of piloting reforming legislation through Parliament. However, we are confident that we have provided at least some useful pointers to the ways in which the subject is likely to move in the early years of the twenty-first century. There is a real likelihood of implementation of the most substantial changes to the subject since the registered company form first became available in early Victorian times.

[61] Company Law Review Steering Group, *Modern Company Law for a Competitive Economy: Company General Meetings and Shareholder Communication* (London, 1999).

[62] See *ibid.*, at para. 64.

14

Socio-Legal Studies

SALLY WHEELER AND PHIL THOMAS

Socio-legal studies as a descriptor of academic activity has now firmly established itself within the scholarly community.[1] A bold statement perhaps but markers of its success abound. Two commentators William Twining and Nikki Lacey, to whose views we turn in more detail later in this chapter, pass judgement thus: "[s]ocio-legal studies is coming of age and achieving critical mass and has enormous potential" and

> "[t]he importance of socio-legal research is now so widely acknowledged . . . that it is inconceivable that anyone could emerge from a reputable law faculty as ignorant of socio-legal scholarship as I was when I graduated in 1979".[2]

Socio-legal studies has its own professional association which holds an annual conference and other academic events, produces a newsletter and makes research grants to the academic community. The membership of this association, the SLSA, has risen steadily since its inception in Edinburgh in 1990. There are a number of very successful academic journals such as the *Journal of Law and Society* and *Social and Legal Studies*[3] based in the UK that offer publishing opportunities for work that can be described as socio-legal. There are also similar journals in Australia and Canada.[4] As an academic phenomenon—the reason for this choice of descriptive noun becomes clear in the

[1] P Scott, *The Meanings of Mass Higher Education* (Open University Press, Milton Keynes, 1995) p.149.

[2] W Twining, *Blackstone's Tower: The English Law School* (Sweet & Maxwell, London, 1994) p.145 and N Lacey (1994) No 12 *Newsletter of the Socio-Legal Studies Association* 12. In respect of Lacey the authors believe that this was a "recut" of the contribution that she made to the seminar organised by the ESRC in April 1993 as part of their review of Socio-legal studies. Her comments elsewhere are considerably less generous: "socio-legal research . . . has all too often been premised on both a poorly theorised account of social institutions and an insufficient attention to the democratic legitimacy of proposed changes"see N Lacey, "Normative Reconstruction in Socio-Legal Theory" (1996) 5 *Social and Legal Studies* 131 at 143.

[3] These journals are published by Blackwells and Sage respectively .

[4] For example in Australia *Law in Context* and in Canada *Canadian Journal of Law and Society.*

discussion below—socio-legal studies has been recognised by the Research Assessment exercise, unit 36 for the purposes of the 1996 and the 2001 exercise and by funders of research such as the ESRC and the Home Office.

Our concern in this chapter is not to rehearse the history of the development of socio-legal studies or to examine the relationships that it has with other disciplines or sub-disciplines within the academy. These areas are more than amply covered in a range of materials. For example there are at least two collections of essays that contain material on its development from the early years stage,[5] at least one journal special issue and one collection of essays[6] which offer material on the relationships between law and other disciplines which can be said to encapsulate socio-legal studies, and numerous monographs,[7] readers,[8] and textbooks[9] which take a socio-legal stance in discreet areas of legal study. Instead this chapter tries to be more strategic than it is historical or descriptive. It looks at particular issues for socio-legal studies and how they have changed over time, for example the question of disciplinary definition. It examines the factors that have allowed socio-legal studies to take hold within Law Schools in particular and flourish in the way that it has. This necessarily requires us to look at Legal Studies in comparison with other disciplines that have experienced similar change, for example those in the Arts and Humanities such as English. It also pulls us towards the question of the funding of research and whether the type of funding that has been available to socio-legal studies has shaped it in one way rather than another. Of relevance here is the issue of policy and the role that policy plays and should play within socio-legal studies. In looking at issues such as these we hope to be able to map the strategic events within the genesis of socio-legal studies and offer some ideas for questions and difficulties that will present themselves in the future.

[5] P Thomas (ed), *Socio-Legal Studies*, (Dartmouth, Aldershot, 1997) and K Hawkins (ed), *The Human Face of Law: Essays in Honour of Donald Harris* (OUP, Oxford, 1997).

[6] D Galligan (ed), *Socio-Legal Studies in Context: The Oxford Centre Past and Present* (1995) 22 *JLS* and P Thomas (ed), *Law's Frontiers* (Dartmouth, Aldershot, 1996).

[7] The most prestigious series of monographs is that produced by Oxford University Press and badged under the title "Oxford Socio-Legal Series". Production of this series began in 1983 and authorship of monographs is not restricted to researchers based at the Centre for Socio-legal Studies Oxford. Prior to 1983 Macmillan publishers produced this series. In more recent years other publishers have moved into the monograph market for example Dartmouth, Cambridge University Press and Cavendish. However in some cases this interest has been short lived. Dartmouth cancelled their Socio-Legal series in February 1999 after engaging for only 3 years or so with the market.

[8] In 1993 at the SLSA annual conference hosted by Keele University a number of members of the SLSA executive committee set up jointly with Oxford University Press an Oxford Readers in Socio-Legal Studies series. The idea behind the series was to produce a series of books in which were reprinted key articles, essays or book chapters that would provide, together with the editor's introductory essay, an overview of the socio-legal field in chosen areas. Among these areas were "punishment", "criminal justice", "business enterprise" and "family law". OUP ceased to publish this series in 1998 for financial reasons.

[9] S Wheeler and J Shaw, *Contract Law: Cases, Materials and Commentary* (OUP, Oxford, 1994).

Twining in his review of the English Law School makes the point that the landscape of academic thinking about and around legal studies has radically changed in the last twenty years or so from predominantly doctrinal scholarship and offers us an account of the range of scholarly activities that now take place.[10] This is certainly true and interestingly Posner makes the same point about legal studies in America.[11] For Posner this has occurred for three reasons. First the breakdown of immediate post war consensual politics in the 1970's, second the rise of interest in scientific methods of inquiry, and third the technical perfection of doctrinal analysis such that scholars who wish to be innovators have to establish their innovation outside the existing paradigm. The first point is hardly replicated in the UK. We have to question whether there was post war consensual politics and whether in fact there was government without opposition for much of the 1970's and 1980's. The second and third reasons do not really merit serious discussion.

We have to return to Twining for greater illumination. His point is a most welcome one; that law is not and never has been an autonomous discipline. It can not stand lone without reference to the problematics of experienced life, as if it were a given value neutral testimony.[12] Engagement with French philosophy has moved jurisprudence away from English liberalism and German rationalism. The deconstructionalists from Derrida onwards have encouraged the development of modes of analysis that regard truth and objectivity as illusion of Western dominated thought. Nothing comes as value free. These are ideas that we return to in our discussion of Critical Legal Studies but there is no doubt that they have permeated beyond specifically Critical thinking about Law. The freedom created by the advent of postmodernism results in a space for intellectuals to put law where it belongs in the social world alongside the influences and ideas of "psychology, statistics, sociology, moral philosophy, economics [and] history".[13] Law is not alone in being infiltrated in this way, other disciplines such as English, History and Sociology[14] find themselves in the same position. Thus in the case of law it is hardly surprising that what emerges is interdisciplinary scholarship in the form of socio-legal studies.

[10] W Twining, *Blackstone's Tower: The English Law School* (Sweet & Maxwell, London, 1994) p.144.

[11] R Posner, "The Decline of Law as an Autonomous Discipline: 1962–1987" (1987) 100 *Harv Law Rev* 761.

[12] R Tur and W Twining (eds), *Essays on Kelsen* (OUP, Oxford, 1986). This discussion is in the introduction which although is attributed as a joint piece of work the authors make explicitly clear that Tur was primarily responsible for the first part and Twining the second. See pages 21, 27, 29, and 31.

[13] *Ibid*, p. 21.

[14] J Ellis, *Literature Lost: Social Agendas and the Corruption of the Humanities* (Yale University Press New Haven, 1997), E Fox-Genovese, "Literary Criticism and the Politics of *The New Historicism*" in H A Vesser (ed.) *The New Historicism* (Routledge, London, 1989) and A Megill "Grand Narrative and the Discipline of History" in F Ankersmit and H Kellner (eds.) *A New Philosophy of History* (Reaktion Books, London, 1995) 151.

If we reject a description of the evolution of socio-legal studies from its inclusion within the funding opportunities provided by the then Social Science Research Council or from the beginning of the SLSA onwards as possible starting points for examining socio-legal studies on the grounds that then we would be offering an institutional history divorced from intellectual development then a starting point for discussion is less obvious. Socio-legal studies is the only chapter in this collection, apart from legal education for obvious reasons, that is not a substantive area of law within that defined by the law school curriculum. As such it is very unlikely to be found there. This offers a starting place of sorts because if there is one thing that all scholars involved in the legal community and its satellite communities agree upon from a definitional standpoint it is that socio-legal studies is not a substantive subject within the canon of legal education. From that point on differences emerge. Despite the impression given not least by the layout of this collection socio-legal analyses of all areas of substantive law are possible. Indeed it would be entirely possible, if not desirable, to offer a socio-legal account of each of the discrete areas of legal study included within this edited collection. To write in general but also exclusive terms about something which one passionately believes is entirely inclusive is very difficult. From this point on differences on definitional issues emerge.

In 1983 Donald Harris, then the Director of the Centre for Socio-Legal in Oxford espoused that socio-legal studies was "the study of law and legal institutions from the perspectives of the social sciences". This was undoubtedly an accurate description of the work that the Oxford Centre was then undertaking—large-scale projects a feature of which was the collaboration between academics of different disciplines. The description provided by Harris lends itself to a bygone era of multi-disciplinary work made possible by the "block funding" of institutions such as the Oxford Centre by the Social Science Research Council. Reasonably secure long term funding allowed a group of social scientists broadly defined to work together.[15] The most well known example of this collaboration is the Misfortune Study or as it became known in published form the Compensation Study.[16] This study involved academics from law, social administration, sociology, economics, social psychology and history. It offered a view of the compensation system for accident and illness victims from all of these perspectives.[17] The material revealed by the Study was further

[15] For accounts of this period see A Ogus, "Reflections on the Developments in Britain of Interdisciplinary Approaches to Law: Utility and Disutility" (1999) 50 *NILQ* 421and K Hawkins, "Prologue: Donald Harris and the Early Years of the Oxford Centre" in K Hawkins (ed), *The Human Face of Law: Essays in Honour of Donald Harris* (OUP, Oxford, 1997).

[16] D Harris et al , *Compensation and Support for Illness and Injury* (OUP, Oxford, 1984).

[17] In addition to the main volume referred to in the note above two other volumes were published to give a historical and methodological background to the study: P Bartrip and S Burman, *The Wounded Soldiers of Industry: Industrial Compensation Policy 1833–97* (Clarendon Press,

examined not only in more specialist journals and edited collections but also in works that have come to be regarded as modern classics. We think here particularly of Hazel Genn's *Hard Bargaining*,[18] which should feature on every tort reading list in the common law world.

The current position is that socio-legal scholars are more likely to find themselves working as lone scholars backed by institutional funding within a discrete academic unit or as a part of an externally funded team spread across several academic institutions. Socio-legal studies undertaken in this way are far more likely to produce output that is interdisciplinary in nature. The "socio" in socio-legal studies means to us an interface with a context within which law exists, be that a sociological, historical, economic, geographical or other context. For these scholars to be able to place themselves within the academy a more specific descriptor for socio-legal studies is required. The issue has become that of whether socio-legal studies is an approach to the study of law and legal phenomena or a discipline in its own right. The question for these scholars appears to be what the label socio-legal studies says about their work. Thomas for example formulates the range of alternatives thus "a new discipline, a sub-discipline and if so of what, an approach, a methodology, a political position or paradigm".[19] Within these alternatives Thomas lays out the consequence of disciplinary status for socio-legal studies as a negative. This label he feels is something which will stand for tradition and familiarity rather than innovation and novelty. Thomas ultimately ties his own colours to the mast of "paradigm".[20] For him it inserts into the world of academic lawyers a review of values and standards that will allow academic legal studies[21] to develop and change. Other socio-legal scholars provide a different answer. Within the same essay collection as Thomas, Wheeler sees the definitional question as one answered by the term "movement".[22] This was a term chosen to signify the forward progression of socio-legal studies from marginality within most law schools to the predominant form of scholarship undertaken there.

Oxford, 1983) and M Maclean and H Genn, *Methodological Issues in Social Surveys* (Macmillan, London, 1979).

[18] (OUP, Oxford, 1988).

[19] P Thomas, "Socio-Legal Studies: The Case of Disappearing Fleas and Bustards" in P Thomas (ed), *Socio-Legal Studies* (Dartmouth, Aldershot, 1997) p.3.

[20] P Thomas (ed), *Socio-Legal Studies* (Dartmouth, Aldershot, 1997) p.19. This develops from his idea in "Socio-Legal Studies in the UK" in F Bruinsma (ed), *Precaire Waarden, Liber Amicorum Voor Por. Mr A A G Peters* (Gouda Quint, Netherlands, 1994).

[21] We should make it clear that socio-legal studies can make a similar contribution across the whole range of humanities and social sciences. The membership of the SLSA and its executive committee reflect this. The reference to "academic lawyers" and "academic legal studies" should be understood in the spirit in which it was made; in a collection of essays which attempted to set out, largely for the benefit of doctrinal legal scholars, the achievements and future agendas of socio-legal studies in relation to discrete areas of law.

[22] S Wheeler, "Company Law" in P Thomas (ed), *Socio-Legal Studies* (Dartmouth, Aldershot, 1997) pp.285, 302 n.39.

The need for a definition comes from the desire to both defend and proselytize socio-legal studies. The defence is to attacks mounted by the sociology of law movement, now represented it seems almost exclusively by Roger Cotterrell, and more latterly by the Critical Legal Studies movement. The proselytizing of socio-legal studies has been undertaken to encourage funders external to the academy of the value of socio-legal research while within the academy the object of conversion has been in the main doctrinal legal scholars. By contributing to discussions around definition there is a danger that socio-legal scholars condemn their work through their own anxious protestation. Indeed there are those within socio-legal studies who espouse just this view—that participation in the search for definition engages with largely derogatory views about the intellectual nature of socio-legal studies without sufficiently emphasising its strengths.[23] However in our view engagement around definition has changed somewhat in recent years. What occurs now is the conveyance of the intellectual excitement of socio-legal studies and the unique nature of its methodology that is different from that of say doctrinal legal studies or analytical jurisprudence.[24] It remains important for those whose institutional location is in a traditional law school to be able to explain, but not necessarily any more to defend, what their research agenda consists of.[25]

Socio-Legal Studies and the Sociology of Law

The traditional reference point to the engagement of sociology of law and socio-legal studies is an article by Campbell and Wiles in 1976. This set out the view of sociologists of law that socio-legal studies was "anti-theoretical, concerned with social engineering through existing social order and not with explaining that order or transcending it by critique".[26] Their understanding of socio-legal studies appears to be that it has no theoretical base either of its own or borrowed from anywhere else, that it is entirely orientated towards the acquisition of empirical data (which it does presumably without encountering

[23] B Hutter and S Lloyd Bostock, "Law's Relationship with Social Science: The Interdependence of Theory, Empirical Work and Social Relevance" in K Hawkins *The Human Face of Law* (OUP, Oxford, 1997) p.19 at pp.19–25.

[24] The "masterclass" on socio-legal research was the most popular of session of its type at the 1999 SPTL conference in Leeds.

[25] Until recently both Hutter and Lloyd Bostock conducted their research within the portals of the Oxford Centre, a very different research environment to that found in traditional law schools.

[26] C Campbell and P Wiles "The Study of Law in Society in Britain" (1976) 10 *L&S Rev* 547 at 548–9.

any of the debates around methodology pervasive in "true" social science) and that it produces at best material for a legal reform audience.[27] This polemic is transformed into a critique by Roger Cotterrell. His position is that socio-legal study as a methodology is too reactive to a policy audience as it does not take law or legal categories as problematic but prefers instead at what legal agencies do. His contrast is to "social studies of law" which apparently do this.[28] We would suggest that Cotterrell has a narrow conception of what constitutes socio-legal studies. His paradigm is of small-scale studies, which examine whether a particular set of legal rules reflects the practice that is undertaken in the area of their operation.[29]

We have two objections to the construction of socio-legal that is offered by the sociologists of law. The first is that there is no recognition that the very least that the law in context type of study—that is persistently taken to be representative of socio-legal studies—does is to create some building blocks for socio-legal theory. While the starting point is undoubtedly extant legal categories, procedures and actors, their end-point is to suggest a focus on practices that have not previously been the focus of attention, for example the importance of non-legal sanctions, the role of negotiation in the legal field, the role played by legal actors in shaping law and the processes of law and the effect of litigation choices on the creation of legal precedent. It is worth at this point referring back to the Compensation Study. This was a large-scale piece of work that has been described as "atheoretical". [30] What is rarely pointed out is that the work which was undertaken as a result of its findings has been instrumental in keeping the accident compensation system on the policy agenda long after the recommendations of the Royal Commission chaired by Lord Pearson have been forgotten.[31] In addition to keeping issues on the policy agenda the Study was also the beginning of inquiries into "complaining behavior"—

[27] Hutter and Lloyd-Bostock, supra n.23, sum up the Campbell and Wiles contribution as one that is "warning of the intellectual poverty and ultimate sterility of socio-legal studies".

[28] R Cotterrell, *Law's Community* (OUP, Oxford, 1995) see especially chapter 14 at p.311.

[29] R Cotterrell, *The Sociology of Law* (Butterworths, London, 1992) where his citations are to S Macaulay, "Non-Contractual Relations in Business: A Preliminary Study" (1963) 28 *Am Soc Rev* 55 and H Beale and T Dugdale, "Contracts Between Businessmen: Planning and the Use of Contractual Remedies" (1975) 2 *Brit J of Law & Soc* 45. As Hutter and Lloyd Bostock point out Cotterrell is not the only academic to pursue a generalised picture of socio-legal studies from the very specific. Their example is the author of the 6th edition of Lloyds Jurisprudence (Stevens, London, 1995). Socio-legal studies is critiqued as "atheoretical" and "pragmatic" on the basis that several jury studies of the 1970's and 1980's did not ask questions that the author thought appropriate.

[30] A Ogus, supra n.10 at 423. Ogus makes the point that theoretical engagement within socio-legal studies did not occur until post 1984. We would not agree with this, see the text accompanying notes 33 and 34.

[31] For a reprise of recent developments and future ideals within the sphere of damages for personal injury see A Burrows, *Understanding the Law of Obligation* (Hart Publishing, Oxford, 1998) pp.182–91.

asking why some people used law and why others might not—from a psychological/legal perspective rather than an economic/legal perspective.[32]

Our second objection is that within the broad church inherent to socio-legal studies there are many examples of work that could not of themselves ever be described as "atheoretical" or "policy orientated". As examples of this we would offer Doreen McBarnet's *Conviction*[33] and Yves Dezaley and Bryant Garth's *Dealing with Virtue.*[34] *Conviction* has become a classic within socio-legal studies. It took as its starting point the legal concepts which underpin the criminal justice system but unlike other contemporary studies of the criminal process its conclusions were not couched in the language of deviant behaviour by those applying the rules but instead that it was the very nature of the values of the process that worked against defendants. Dezaley and Garth's work involved applying Pierre Bourdieu's concepts of "field" and "habitus" to the formulation of international arbitration rules. The use of ideas such as "cultural capital" broke new ground within socio-legal studies. As Garth pointed out the application of Bourdieu's theory allowed the authors to ask different questions of their fieldwork participants.[35] The result is an account of how legal actors trained in a particular national system, and thus imbued with the ruling concepts of that system, contribute to the construction of a "global legal field". This occurs through their competing with each other, both personally and in respect of regulatory regime, for the legal services market. A final parting observation would be that while Sociology of Law is at most marginal to curriculums in both Sociology and Law and has little foothold in the academic research community, socio-legal studies has gone from strength to strength.[36]

Socio-legal Studies and the Funding Environment

The relationship between socio-legal studies, funding for such, and the proximity to policy was brought home to the socio-legal community in 1994. This was brought about by the coincidence of a number of events which are briefly summarised below. We have already referred to the "block funding" that the Oxford Centre received. The Economic and Social Research Council, the suc-

[32] S Lloyd-Bostock and L Mulcahy, "The Social Psychology of Making and Responding to Complaints. An Account Model of Complaint Processes" (1994) 16 *Law and Policy* 123.

[33] (Macmillan, London, 1981).

[34] (University of Chicago Press, Chicago, 1996).

[35] Both of us (Wheeler and Thomas) were fortunate enough to be present at Garth's discussion of this work with David Campbell at an Author Meets Critic session at the 1997 SLSA Conference in Cardiff.

[36] M Travers, "Putting the Sociology Back into the Sociology of Law" (1993) 20 *JLS* 438 at 442–4.

cessor to the Social Science Research Council brought this funding to an end in 1992. While this was not a positive for socio-legal studies in terms of the loss of a physical location and an exclusive intellectual home, it did raise the possibility that the money released would be available to fund socio-legal studies nationally. In 1993, with this possibility in mind perhaps, the ESRC announced its intention to review socio-legal studies. Also in 1993, in response to a Government White Paper on Science, Engineering and Technology urging that a greater emphasis be placed on economic competitiveness, the ESRC set up a series of Users Forums in relation the range of subjects/disciplines that it was responsible for funding. The Socio-legal Studies Users Forum had representatives from Government Departments, legal services such as the Law Society and the private sector such as the Consumers' Association. Professor Martin Partington, then Chair of the SLSA was appointed by the ESRC to consult with both the academic community and with the Users Forum so that a bid for a socio-legal studies programme could be drafted and submitted to the ESRC Programmes Board. Partington has written up his experiences in putting together the programme bid in essay form and this forms a useful insight into the current debates and tensions within the socio-legal community.[37]

The context within which Partington was working was the mission of the ESRC "to support high-quality research . . . that will contribute to economic competitiveness, the quality of life and the effectiveness of public services and policy".[38] Partington's approach to formulating the bid was, very properly, to consult as widely as possible with the socio-legal studies community and with the newly formed Research Users Forum, of which he was secretary. What is immediately obvious from his account is that socio-legal scholars certainly did not view themselves as agents of the policy process and were reluctant to become so. Many academic respondents to Partington's consultation exercise were excited about the prospect of funding being released specifically for a programme aimed at the core intellectual concerns of socio-legal studies and about the quality of access networks that could be built through the Users Forum. However there were also reservations expressed about the desirability for researchers in becoming enmeshed in a Government driven research agenda. This fear came from the idea of the close involvement of the Users Forum, which might then extend to its members dictating areas and priorities for research in a political environment, which identified users as "commerce, government and the professions".

The programme bid was unsuccessful. No documented reasons for this failure exist but a rumour current at the time was that it felt that the bid lacked

[37] M Partington, "Socio-Legal Research in Britain: Shaping the Funding Environment" in P Thomas (ed), *Socio-Legal Studies* (Dartmouth, Aldershot, 1997).

[38] Taken from the website of the ESRC under the heading "Our Role".

sufficient engagement with economics in a disciplinary sense and regulation in a policy sense.[39] This, if true, further discredits the charge that socio-legal studies is too close to the policy making process. No doubt we all remember the emphasis that was placed at that time on the need for policy to be articulated in the economic discourse of the New Right.[40] Socio-legal studies was not seen to be delivering in this area. One might have expected Law and Economics and regulatory economic perspectives to have come to the fore during the 1980's in particular if socio-legal studies was indeed simply an expression of perceived policy reform needs but this was not the case.[41]

The need for the socio-legal scholars to interface with Research Users as a condition of obtaining ESRC funding has continued. The ESRC's Thematic Priorities, first announced in 1995 and revised in 1997, were developed in consultation with the User community, and, while it is possible to obtain funding outside these Priorities by means of a grant application, the majority of the ESRC research budget is devoted to funding under the Thematic Priorities. In order to secure ESRC funding a proposal generally has to receive very positive reviews in respect of making a significant contribution to methodological development, theoretical development and have policy relevance. No mean feat we would say.[42] Other funders of socio-legal work from both the Government sector, for example the Department of Health and the Home Office, and the private sector such as the Nuffield Foundation and the Rowntree Trust use methods such as tender and contract relationships to secure value for money and specific deliverables. The steady decline in Higher Educational institutional funding from Government which is unlikely to change in the short to medium term pushes and will continue to push socio-legal studies scholars' towards participating in these processes as the only way to secure money to buy time for research. The agendas of these funders are such that their preferences are likely to be for research that has an immediate policy relevance.

There are numerous challenges for socio-legal studies in this type of environment. One is whether it will be possible to produce quality work that will develop socio-legal theory still further. There is no evidence from recent SLSA conferences and editions of the *Journal of Law and Society* to suggest that this challenge is not being taken up but it remains a concern for the future. Another is the issue of the adequacy of the methodology that is being employed within socio-legal studies. Of course this issue is not one that exists only in the con-

[39] Discussions at the Research Users Forum to which Wheeler was a party in May 1996, as an ex officio member (SLSA Chair).

[40] A Abbott, *Department and Discipline* (Chigago University Press, Chicago, 1999) 194.

[41] A Ogus "Law and Economics in the UK: Past, Present and Future" (1995) 22 *JLS* 26.

[42] P Hillyard and J Sim "The Political Economy of Socio-legal Research" in P Thomas (ed) *Socio-Legal Studies* (Dartmouth, Aldershot, 1997) 45 at 63.

text of funded research but it is one that has been brought to the fore by the concerns of many potential research funders. They have voiced their consternation at the level of engagement or indeed lack of it with methodology that is sometimes revealed in socio-legal funding applications. The difficulty for those within socio-legal studies is the need to embrace the methodological cultures of not only the starting discipline but also the partner discipline.[43] This problem is exacerbated by the huge bottom-up growth in socio-legal studies in recent years. The result is that many incoming post-graduates, who usually have a single discipline background, receive supervision on their chosen topic within socio-legal studies from a supervisor or team of supervisors, who while excelling in their own disciplines, have no inter-disciplinary perspective. There is then every chance that this lack of inter-disciplinary methodology will permeate further down the research chain as these students become supervisors themselves. Recent ESRC decisions on the future shape of research postgraduate funding: that students should have a first year of research training funded followed by three funded years to complete a Ph.D. will assist in combating this problem. However many post-graduates are self-funded or receive institutional scholarships. There needs to be input from the socio-legal community to try and overcome the training shortfall by engaging with both students and supervisors.[44]

Socio-Legal Studies and Critical Legal Studies

Notable by its absence from this collection is Critical Legal Studies. Critical Legal Studies engages traditional doctrinal legal scholarship on its own terms and thus should have much greater potential for debate with it than socio-legal studies. Its exclusion says much about the failure of the critical legal studies project to impose itself as a serious alternative paradigm of dealing with law to the "liberal legalism" and analytical jurisprudence of doctrinal scholarship. Predictions that Critical Legal Studies could rival the Legal Realism of the 1930's in terms of the disruption caused to traditional legal scholarship have

[43] Hillyard and Sim, supra n.42, are of the view that the problem is that law is distinct from other social sciences and that socio-legal studies has become trapped within law schools. Legal academics in their view have little training in social science research or methodology and so there is every chance that socio-legal research will adopt the discourse of lawyers. We could not possibly agree with a view as parochial as this.

[44] The problem of single discipline students and post-graduate studies in socio-legal studies was recognised as long ago as 1987 by the Oxford Centre, see the Centre for Socio-Legal Studies *Annual Report* 1986-87 at p33.

proved unfounded,[45] but so, however has the charge that Critical Legal Studies has died.[46]

Critical Legal Studies stands on the periphery of the legal academy as part of an intentional statement about it underlying *credo*, its representation of the other.[47] That representation occurs through the trashing of established legal principle as unnecessarily privileged and the offering of counter-principle.[48] This has often been taken as an intentionally polemical deconstruction leading to an ultimately nihilistic position. However this masks what both Teubner and Goodrich have described as a "love of law"[49] and fails to recognise that in much of this work there is a reconstructive discourse[50] which urges that the events and deliberations cast as value neutral by the liberal legal voice be set within the larger political sphere. In opposition to value neutral liberal theory Critical Legal Studies offers values drawn from a variety of ethical starting points—feminist theory, critical race theory, Levinas' ethics of alterity to name but a few. There is no unity of ethical position within the paradigms mentioned here nor is there in Critical Legal Studies generally.

Lacey in her plenary address to the SLSA conference held in Leeds in 1995 suggested that socio-legal studies could not hope to progress along the reformist agenda and by implication as an academic discipline unless it embraced much more fully a theorised understanding of relevant social institutions. Once again, as in our discussion of the Sociology of Law movement, we would take issue with her conception of socio-legal studies as one that focuses narrowly on the overtly empirical but presumably extreme examples make effective comparisons. We would interpret her to mean that in a society presented with new opportunities through technology, globalisation and an

[45] A Hunt, *Explorations in Law and Society* (Routledge, London, 1993) p.139.

[46] P Kahn, *The Cultural Study of Law* (Chicago University Press, Chicago, 1999) 29.

[47] Goodrich puts forward another rationale for the failure of Critical Legal Studies to revolutionize Law Schools and that is the lack of personal commitment shown by figures within the movement. He makes this charge in respect of both American and British critical legal scholars, see P Goodrich "Sleeping with the Enemy: An Essay on the Politics of Critical Legal Studies in America" in J Leonard (ed), *Legal Studies as Critical Studies* (SUNY, Albany, 1995) p.299 at pp.304–7 and P Goodrich, "The Critic's Love of the Law: Intimate Observations on an Insular Jurisdiction" (1999) 10 *Law and Critique* 341 at 357 respectively. This is not a position, which would necessarily occur to those outside the inner sanctum of Critical Legal Studies, and as a critique it is bitterly ad personam in places.

[48] For a fuller explanation of this see N MacCormick, "Reconstruction after Deconstruction: Closing in on Critique" in A Norrie (ed), *Closure or Critique* (Edinburgh University Press, Edinburgh, 1993) p.142. For an example see C Dalton, "An Essay in the Deconstruction of Contract Doctrine" (1985) 94 *Yale LJ* 997.

[49] G Teubner, "The king's many bodies: The Self-deconstruction of law's hierarchy" (1997) 31 *Law and Society Rev* 763 at 773 and Goodrich (1999) supra n.47 at 344.

[50] See Lacey, supra n.2 at 139. She comments thus "Notwithstanding the iconoclastic and polemical self-presentation of "trashing", there was always a concern with how things could have been, and might have been different. It wasn't just an irresponsible, existential enjoyment in shaking up the world."

expanding interest in rights what socio-legal studies must not forget is that part of its future challenge is:

> "addressing the ethics of power as measured through the constitution and regulation of new social aggregates and forms of subjection, the equalities and inequalities, tolerance or exclusion, that they imply."[51]

We would see this as articulating an appropriate mission for the next century and beyond and thus an appropriate place to end.

[51] P Goodrich, "Social Science and the Displacement of Law" (1998) 32 *Law and Society Review* 481at 489.

15

Commercial Law: Confining the Remedial Boundaries

SARAH WORTHINGTON AND ROY GOODE*

Most appraisals of the current state of the law conclude that changes, however welcome, have been too slow and too limited. The message is usually that much remains to be done, and that it would best be done as soon as possible. Suggestions for further essential intervention are then advanced. This essay takes a different stance. The general thesis advanced here is that the function of commercial law is being stymied by too much intervention. Less would be better. In particular, it is suggested that the function of commercial law would be altered, for the worse, by the current impetus to alter the remedial consequences of a breach of contract between commercial parties.[1]

The object of concern is the gathering momentum in favour of the introduction of "restitutionary damages", or "disgorgement of profits", for breach of contract.[2] The Law Commission,[3] the judiciary[4] and academics[5] have all

* The second-named author would like to make it clear that any credit for this paper belongs almost entirely to Sarah Worthington, by whom it was written, and that his own contribution was limited to the injection of a few ideas and critical comments, endorsement of the resulting product and, as a corollary, an equal responsibility for any shortcomings.

[1] Although the focus of this essay is on commercial parties, the analysis has general application.

[2] The Law Commission prefers the term "restitutionary damages": Law Commission Report (No 247), *Aggravated, Exemplary and Restitutionary Damages* (1997) ('LCR'). Here "disgorgement" or "disgorgement of profits" is preferred. It is a more accurate descriptive term. Moreover, it is less likely to engender confusion with the remedy of "restitution" for unjust enrichment, which bears no relationship to "disgorgement" or "restitutionary damages", either in its cause of action or its assessment of quantum.

[3] LCR recommendations 7–9 and Draft Bill, clause 12, suggesting that the common law ought to be allowed to develop unimpeded, but that, in addition, restitutionary damages ought to be available where the defendant's wrong (other than a breach of contract) was committed with "deliberate and outrageous disregard of the plaintiff's rights". Restitutionary damages for breach of contract should be left to common law development: para 3.44.

[4] *A-G* v. *Blake* [1998] Ch 439 (CA), 458–9, suggesting (obiter and without argument or elaboration) that disgorgement for breach of contract might be appropriate where the breach

indicated their support. A disgorgement remedy compels a defendant to pay over any profits made, or expenses saved, as a result of a breach of contract.[6] The quantum of the remedy therefore depends upon the defendant's profits, not upon the claimant's reliance or expectation losses. A simple example illustrates these remedial alternatives. Suppose S agrees to sell goods to B for £10,000. Suppose, too, that S later obtains a better offer from C—perhaps because C has an urgent supply deadline to meet—and decides to breach the contract with B and instead sell the goods to C for £13,000. Suppose, finally, that on the day the goods were due to be delivered to B their market price is £11,000. B can mitigate any reliance or expectation losses[7] arising from S's non-performance by seeking alternative supplies in the market. On the assumed facts, this is likely to make B's reliance loss minimal. Her expectation losses—the sum of money required to put her in the same position as she would have been in if the contract had been properly performed[8]—are more substantial. They include the extra £1,000 needed to obtain alternative supplies plus any additional costs incurred in obtaining these substitutes. But the disgorgement remedy, if it were available, would entitle B to insist that S pay over the £3,000 profit that S has gained from the breach of contract.[9]

The overriding sentiment behind the disgorgement remedy is an intuitive moral view that no one should be entitled to profit from a wrong. Despite the generality of this sentiment, few if any adherents of the remedy suggest that it should apply to every profitable breach of contract.[10] The thesis of this essay is that it should apply to none.[11] The contrary view would have adverse conse-

consisted in doing exactly what the contract expressly prohibited or in delivering shortfall performance. An appeal to the House of Lords has been heard.

[5] See, eg, G Jones, *Goff & Jones: The Law of Restitution*, 4th edn, (London: Sweet & Maxwell, 1993) ("Goff & Jones"), pp 714–34; P Birks, *An Introduction to the Law of Restitution*, rev'd edn, (Oxford: Clarendon Press, 1989) ("Birks"), p 326–7; Sir William Goodhart QC, "Restitutionary Damages for Breach of Contract" [1995] RLR 3; P Jaffey, "Restitutionary Damages and Disgorgement" [1995] RLR 30, 40 and "Disgorgement and Confiscation" [1996] RLR 92, 93, 96; H McGregor, "Restitutionary Damages" in P Birks (ed), *Wrongs and Remedies in the Twenty-First Century* (Oxford: Clarendon Press, 1996) ch 9, p 209.

[6] This was the remedy ordered by the Israeli Supreme Court in *Adras Building Material Ltd* v. *Harlow and Jones GmbH* (1988) 42 (1) PD 221, translated in [1995] RLR 235, on facts similar to those outlined in the example in the text.

[7] Such losses being the normal measure of contractual damages: *Surrey County Council* v. *Bredero Homes Ltd* [1993] 1 WLR 1361, 1364 *per* Dillon LJ; *Johnson* v. *Agnew* [1980] AC 367, 400 *per* Lord Wilberforce.

[8] *Robinson* v. *Harman* (1848) 1 Ex 850, 855; 154 ER 363 *per* Parke B.

[9] Whether the remedy is proprietary or personal is not addressed in this essay. It is assumed throughout that the remedy is personal, notwithstanding certain precedents suggesting the contrary (see, eg, *AG for Hong Kong* v. *Reid* [1994] 1 AC 324).

[10] See notes 2–4, above. Goff & Jones, p 721, come close to this, suggesting that the remedy ought to be available whenever the profit could not have been generated "but for" the breach.

[11] This does not mean that situations advanced by disgorgement adherents as warranting the remedy should go unremedied, only that the remedy should not—and need not—be analysed or quantified as disgorgement: see especially the discussion of amenity damages (Section 4) and

quences for commercial law. It would fundamentally alter the nature of commercial agreements, coercing performance by presenting parties with the alternative of mandatory redistribution of wealth and risk by the courts. Moreover, since the proposed jurisdiction is unclear, its introduction would increase the level of uncertainty in commercial agreements. Even without this uncertainty, the additional remedial jurisdiction would increase the costs of insurance against potential liability.[12]

Two introductory points are necessary. First, the chosen focus on restitutionary damages might seem unacceptably narrow for an essay designed to address issues of general significance in commercial law. This is not so. Rights and remedies are intimately linked: alter one, and the other is immediately changed.[13] Any change to the legal remedies available upon breach of a commercial contract will necessarily alter the content of the obligations agreed to by the parties. The immediate effect between the contracting parties and the potential ripple effect on third parties are sure to be significant. Secondly, the chosen focus might also seem unduly foolhardy given that the issue is currently under consideration by the House of Lords. This is especially so since the odds seem to favour a decision contrary to the thesis advanced here.[14] Be that as it may. The issue is important. This essay may be the first in this volume (but surely not the only one) to have the counter-argument put by the highest authority.

recovery of overpayments (Section 8) below. Nor does it mean that true disgorgement (analysed and quantified as such) is never a remedial option: a breach of fiduciary obligation, eg, warrants such a remedy. But this essay does suggest that disgorgement should not be adopted as a remedy for breach of contract.

[12] In *Surrey County Council* v. *Bredero Homes Ltd* [1993] 1 WLR 1361, 1370, Steyn LJ considered both these grounds compelling.

[13] Austin, *Lectures on Jurisprudence* 3rd edn, (1869) Lecture XLV, 787ff.

[14] Much has been written in this area. See especially D Friedmann, "Restitution of Benefits Obtained Through the Appropriation of Property or the Commission of a Wrong" (1980) 80 *Col LR* 504; R Sharpe and S M Waddams, "Damages for Lost Opportunity to Bargain" (1982) 2 OJLS 290; G Jones, "The Recovery of Benefits Gained from a Breach of Contract" (1983) 99 LQR 443; I M Jackman, "Restitution for Wrongs" [1989] CLJ 302; D Friedmann, "The Efficient Breach Fallacy" (1989) 18 *J Leg Studies* 1; J Beatson, *The Use and Abuse of Unjust Enrichment* (Oxford: Clarendon Press, 1991) ch 8; R O'Dair, "Restitutionary Damages for Breach of Contract and the Theory of Efficient Breach: Some Reflections" (1993) 46 CLP 113; E McKendrick, "Restitution and the Misuse of Chattels—The Need for a Principled Approach" in N Palmer and E McKendrick (eds), *Interests in Goods* 2nd ed, (London: Lloyds of London Press, 1998) ch 35; L D Smith, "Disgorgement of the Profits of Breach of Contract: Property, Contract and 'Efficient Breach'" (1994) 24 *Can Bus LJ* 121.

1. The current position

The current position, at least for the moment, is still that disgorgement is not available as a remedy for breach of contract.[15] The cases which adherents cite in support of the disgorgement remedy for breach of contract can all be analysed as either expectation damages for breach of contract, compensatory damages for a proprietary tort[16] (or restitution of an unjust enrichment derived from unauthorised use of property), or disgorgement for breach of an equitable obligation. Moreover, this is how they are generally analysed by the court.[17]

Some scholars have argued that, notwithstanding this, these cases provide support for the existence of the disgorgement remedy. Regardless of the overt reasoning adopted by the judges, it is asserted that the damages awarded must be restitutionary—they cannot be compensatory—where the claimant would never under any circumstances have waived the breach in return for a compensating payment.[18] So where notional licence fees are awarded for breach of restrictive covenants,[19] or notional rents for use of mooring bays,[20] the assertion is that these remedies must be restitutionary, measured in a fashion which strips the defendant of gains (or expenses saved), because they cannot possibly be compensating the claimant for something the claimant would never have agreed to for a fee.[21] This seems to miss the point of compensatory remedies entirely. It is almost universally the case that a claimant would prefer performance over a money remedy; and in many of these cases the claimant would not consent to the breach if permission were requested in advance. But the purpose of a damages remedy is to repair the unwanted harm, it is not to give claimants what they would have wished for in an ideal world. The quadriplegic injured in a car accident would undoubtedly refuse to consent in advance to a

15 *Tito* v. *Waddell (No 2)* [1977] Ch 106, 332 *per* Megarry V-C; *Johnson* v. *Agnew* [1980] AC 367, 400 *per* Lord Wilberforce. Also see *Teacher* v. *Calder* (1899) 1 F(HL) 39, [1899] AC 451, 467 *per* Lord Davey; *The Siboen and the Sibotre* [1976] 1 Lloyd's Rep 293, 337 *per* Kerr J; *Surrey County Council* v. *Bredero Homes Ltd* [1993] 1 WLR 1361, 1364 *per* Dillon LJ.

16 *Wrotham Park Estate Co Ltd* v. *Parkside Homes Ltd* [1974] 1 WLR 798; *Surrey County Council* v. *Bredero Homes Ltd* [1993] 1 WLR 1361; *Jaggard* v. *Sawyer* [1995] 1 WLR 269. Also see R Sharpe and S M Waddams, "Damages for Lost Opportunity to Bargain" (1982) 2 OJLS 290; S Stoljar, "Restitutionary Relief for Breach of Contract" (1989) 2 JCL 1.

17 See S Worthington, "Reconsidering Disgorgement for Wrongs" (1999) 62 MLR 218 and the references cited there.

18 See, eg, Sir W Goodhart, "Restitutionary Damages for Breach of Contract: The Remedy that Dare Not Speak Its Name" [1995] RLR 3; J Beatson, *The Use and Abuse of Unjust Enrichment* p 233; P Birks, "Civil Wrongs: A New World" in *Butterworths Lectures 1990–91*, pp 75–6; Virgo, G, *The Principles of the Law of Restitution* (Oxford: Clarendon Press, 1999), p 458.

19 *Wrotham Park Estate Co Ltd* v. *Parkside Homes Ltd* [1974] 1 WLR 798.

20 *Penarth Dock Engineering Co Ltd* v. *Pound* [1963] 1 Lloyd's Rep 359.

21 See *Clydebank Engineering Co* v. *Don Jose Ramos Isquierdo y Castaneda* [1905] AC 6.

breach of the tortfeasor's duty of care in return for an agreed sum, but the remedy is no less compensatory for that. So too with expectation and reliance losses awarded to contractual claimants. The real difficulty with these cases is that there is no ready market enabling an uncontroversial valuation of the benefit denied to the contracting party by the breach. But difficulties in assessing damages do not (and should not) suggest resort to a disgorgement remedy. It seems to be a fundamental misconception to suggest that, because the claimant would not have consented to a breach, these cases provide support for a wide-ranging use of the disgorgement remedy.[22]

The only unequivocal judicial support for the disgorgement remedy for breach of contract comes from *obiter dicta* of the Court of Appeal in *AG* v. *Blake*.[23] This is the case which is now under consideration by the House of Lords. Blake was a former MI5 agent who defected and later escaped to Moscow. In breach of his contract and the Official Secrets Act 1989, he wrote an autobiography which was published in the UK. Since Blake was outside the jurisdiction, he was not amenable to the procedure by which the profits of his crime might have been confiscated upon his conviction for his offence. In these circumstances, the Attorney-General was granted an injunction restraining Blake from receiving any benefit from the publication. This was described by the court as a public law remedy designed to uphold the integrity of the criminal law. This aspect of the case is not relevant to the present discussion. What is of immediate concern is the court's suggestion that the private law of contract might have entitled the Attorney-General to claim disgorgement of the profits made by Blake. In an extended discussion of "restitutionary damages" for breach of contract, the court indicated that such damages should be available in at least two situations: first, where the defendant had saved expense by skimping on the agreed performance under the contract; and, secondly, where the defendant had made a profit from doing the very thing which he or she had agreed not to do.[24] In both of these instances, the Court regarded compensatory damages as an inadequate remedy if regard were paid to the objects which the claimant sought to achieve by the contract. Moreover, in both these

[22] Some claims that these cases illustrate restitutionary damages are even more broadly based. For example, in *AG* v. *Blake* [1998] Ch 439 (CA), at 457, it is said that "In reality the doctrine [that damages for breach of contract are exclusively compensatory] is already subject to exceptions, for the gain (or saving of expense) made by the defendant is sometimes used as the measure of the plaintiff's loss." But this ignores the fact that what is avowedly being measured *is* the plaintiff's loss, *not* the defendant's gain (or saving). For example, the value of an asset *to the plaintiff* might be assessed on the basis of the sale price received for it by the defendant (ie the defendant's gain), but if the defendant chooses to give the asset away, so that the defendant derives no gain, this convenient measure of the plaintiff's loss will of course be abandoned. In truth, the defendant's sale simply provides ready evidence of the market price of the asset.

[23] [1998] Ch 439. Approving the analysis, see G Virgo, "Clarifying Restitution for Wrongs (note on *Attorney-General* v. *Blake*)" [1998] RLR 118.

[24] *Ibid.* 458.

cases the profits in question would be occasioned directly by the breach; the breach would not merely provide the defendant with the opportunity to make the profits. These two general features were seen as critical in defining the various classes of contractual breach which might merit restitutionary damages.[25]

These comments were clearly obiter. They were not essential to the court's decision. Moreover, they were delivered without the benefit of argument from counsel because the Attorney General had declined to press the contractual claim. Perhaps, too, they were contrary to authority.[26] However, now that this case is before the House of Lords, all of these concerns are eliminated. The issue is material, and the House has heard considered argument. Moreover, on an issue such as this, it surely cannot be decisive that the authorities are against the disgorgement remedy for breach of contract. This is too easy an argument for maintaining the status quo. If the argument is to be won by either side at this level, it must be because the views advanced represent the preferable legal position. The House of Lords is not averse to changing laws it perceives to be flawed, however it might describe what it is doing.[27] Indeed, this approach has to command support: there is no merit in retaining a law which is no longer appropriate (or which perhaps never was appropriate) simply because it has the backing of history. That said, it must also be true that a rule which has stood the test of time should not be dismissed lightly.

All of this means that the issues have to be addressed from first principles. There are several arguments which are commonly advanced in favour of the disgorgement remedy for breach of contract, some of general application and some aimed at identifying a more limited class of cases where the remedy is seen as appropriate. These arguments need to be assessed carefully before the case against the disgorgement remedy can be made confidently.

2. Wrongdoers should not be able to profit from their wrongs

The first assertion of those who advocate disgorgement for breach of contract (or for any other wrong) is that it is unacceptable for the law to allow wrongdoers to profit from their wrongs. Crime should not pay—nor should civil wrongs. The moral force of this sentiment is so powerful that it hardly seems

[25] *Ibid.* 458–9.

[26] G H Treitel, *The Law of Contract*, 10th edn, (London: Sweet & Maxwell, 1999), at p 869.

[27] See, eg, *Kleinwort Benson Ltd* v. *Lincoln City Council* [1998] 3 WLR 1095, [1998] 4 All ER 513 (HL). Also see the Privy Council decision in *AG for Hong Kong* v. *Reid* [1994] 1 AC 324 (PC).

possible to mount a contrary argument.[28] Who could possibly argue that crime *should* pay? But the argument goes deeper than that. It appears to have two strands. The first is that no one should benefit by taking what is rightfully another's. The existing law deals tolerably well with this. Physical assets cannot be stolen with impunity, nor can they be used without their owners' consent; contracting parties cannot simply refuse to perform their side of the bargain. In all these circumstances the law ensures that what is rightfully another's is given to that other, either in specie or in its monetary equivalent. The laws of torts, contract and unjust enrichment—with their remedies of compensatory damages, expectation damages and restitution—all ensure that this is the case. In these situations the disgorgement remedy is not needed to ensure that parties obtain what is rightfully theirs.

The other strand of the argument is more difficult. It suggests that a party should not be able to make a collateral profit by committing a wrong against another. For example, a person should not be able to keep the £1,000 fee he was paid to assault another, or the £50,000 profits generated by selling secrets,[29] or the £3,000 profits generated by breaching a contract of sale and selling to a more willing buyer.[30] In these instances the profit generated by the wrongdoer is not related to the value of what is rightfully the victim's. The wrongdoer may be quite prepared to "reinstate" the victim—and will be legally obliged to do so. The tortfeasor will have to pay compensatory damages for trespass to the person; the contract-breakers will have to pay expectation damages for breach of contract. But should they, in addition, have to pay over the profits gleaned from their breaches?[31]

The law *could* proceed on this basis. It does not at the moment. Either stance requires justification. If disgorgement is demanded simply because it is seen as unfair and inequitable for a wrongdoer to profit, then there is little justification for reallocating those resources to the victim of the wrongdoing, over and above any sums necessary to give the victim what is rightfully his or hers. Better for the general good of all that the gains be dedicated to the common

[28] Although, taken to its logical conclusion, this sentiment would require the law to specifically enforce all obligations where the defendant is likely to make a collateral profit from breach: see Section 3 below.

[29] As in *AG* v. *Blake* [1998] Ch 439 (CA).

[30] As in the illustration given at the start of this essay.

[31] Whether the claimant is entitled to these profits *in addition* to damages is a nice question. Arguably if the profits would not have been generated but for the breach, then the damages claim is an "expense" incurred in generating the profits and should be deducted. This would mean, eg, that in the example given at the start of this essay, the contract-breaker would be liable to pay over the profits of £3,000, or the expectation damages of £1,000 and the *net* profits of £2,000, but not both the £1,000 expectation damages *and* the total profits of £3,000. See, eg, *Tang Min Sit* v. *Capacious Investment Ltd* [1996] AC 514; *Baltic Shipping Co* v. *Dillon* (1993) 176 CLR 344; *Cullinane* v. *British "Rema" Manufacturing Co Ltd* [1954] 1 QB 292; *George Mitchell (Chesterhall) Ltd* v. *Finney Lock Seeds Ltd* [1983] AC 803.

pool—that they be paid over to the state. Certainly the limited aim of profit stripping does not compel the conclusion that the victim of the wrong should benefit from the disgorgement remedy. But the matter does not end there. Even if the desire is only to eliminate the possibility of making gains from wrongs, the obligation to pay those gains over (whether to the state or to the victim) will immediately alter the characteristics of the wrong. It cannot be otherwise, however much we might want it to be so. This means that even if the aim is simply to prevent wrongdoers from profiting from their wrongs, the disgorgement remedy forces consideration of the nature of the underlying obligation and the extent to which its modification is desirable.

If the profits of wrongdoing are stripped from the wrongdoer, then the inevitable consequence is that potential wrongdoers are pressurized to perform their obligations to the letter.[32] On its face, this seems to be no bad thing. In fact, it is often advanced as an independent reason for favouring the disgorgement remedy. However, there are persuasive countervailing arguments, and it is these (which are outlined in the next section) which frustrate adoption of the superficially easy course of profit-stripping for the simple purpose of denying wrongdoers a profit from their wrongs.

3. Parties should abide by their promises

A separate but related reason advanced in favour of the disgorgement remedy is that it has a powerful deterrent effect. It induces parties to abide by their promises. This is seen as advantageous, not only for the individual counterparty but also for the general integrity of contract law (or any other branch of the law to which the remedy might be applied).[33] Again, the assertion is rarely rationalised. Its validity is generally assumed to be intuitively obvious.

Clearly a disgorgement remedy has, and is intended to have, a deterrent effect. The empirical evidence can be found within the criminal law, where disgorgement in favour of the state can now be ordered,[34] and within fiduciary law, where disgorgement in favour of the fiduciary's principal is the standard remedy for breach of the fiduciary's duty of loyalty. In both categories, a profit-generating wrong loses its impetus if the profit is confiscated. Economic analysis explains these results on the basis that self-interested actors will not be

[32] The reason why this is so is explained in the next section.

[33] D Friedmann, "Restitution of Benefits Obtained Through the Appropriation of Property or the Commission of a Wrong" (1980) 80 *Col LR* 504; D Friedmann, "The Efficient Breach Fallacy" (1989) 18 *J Leg Studies* 1.

[34] See Criminal Justice Act 1988 s 71, as amended by the Proceeds of Crime Act 1995 s 1; also see the more draconian Drug Trafficking Act 1994 s 2(3).

motivated to act if the benefits of the activity are appropriated in their entirety to the principal.

It seems counter-intuitive to suggest that this remedial incentive to perform a contract specifically, according to its agreed terms, is undesirable. Nevertheless, this is arguably so. The reason is rooted in a fundamental and often unarticulated conception of the purpose and function of the law. The specific function of commercial law is to enable commercial parties—and markets—to survive and prosper. But the means adopted by any society—or market—to achieve these ends will differ. They will reflect the particular political and moral values which are seen as worthy of advancement. The evolution of a society's legal rules depends entirely on the priorities accorded to these different values. The common law tradition (along with many other legal traditions) reflects a conviction that individual liberty reigns supreme. The impositions of the law are therefore geared to preserve individual liberty to the greatest extent possible. If individual liberty is accorded such pre-eminence, then individual autonomy will be condoned by the law except where it positively inhibits or conflicts with society's advancement. On the other hand, if individual liberty is not accorded a pre-eminent position, but instead society's advancement and prosperity is seen as the worthier value, then the legal rules will have to reflect this by compelling individuals to act for the greater good. The common law does not compel individuals to act altruistically for the benefit of the society. Instead, it allows individual autonomy a free rein, although only up to the point where the autonomy of another is infringed. In general, therefore, the law protects citizens from harmful interference by others;[35] it does not demand that its citizens be sustained and nurtured by others.

All of this is reflected in the common law's pre-occupation with remedies which are designed to repair harms rather than remedies designed to compel performance. For example, the law does not compel citizens to be careful by imposing "double damages" rules, even though we might all prefer others to be careful. Instead, it merely compels the wrongdoer to compensate the victim for the harm caused. The same is true of all tort obligations, even though they are all obligations which are regarded as sufficiently important to be imposed by the law rather than bargained for. The law imposes these obligations because it sees advantages for society in having all citizens protected against certain harms, and yet it does not go so far as to impose remedies which compel adherence to the chosen standards; it simply requires the wrongdoer to make compensation.

If this is true of obligations imposed by the law, then it ought to be even more true of obligations "purchased" between individuals. This is in fact the case. By and large the remedy for a breach of contract simply requires the

[35] J S Mill, *Utilitarianism, Liberty, Representative Government* (London: Everyman ed; 1910), p 73.

defendant to put the claimant into the position, so far as money can do so, that the claimant would have been in had the contract been carried out.[36] The claimant has purchased the right to be put into a particular position in the future. The harm suffered by the defendant's breach is that the anticipated goal is not achieved. The defendant is not obliged to perform, merely to make good expectations.[37] The law guards very jealously the jurisdiction to compel actual performance of an agreed obligation. Contracts are specifically enforceable only when damages would not adequately compensate the claimant *and* where compulsory performance would not work an injustice on the defendant. Moreover, this protective element in respect of the defendant is judged at the time the order to perform is due to be carried out, not at the time the parties made the contract and might have considered their respective positions in relation to specific performance.

This restrictive approach to enforcing performance is even more evident in the courts' approach to situations where the parties themselves have inserted terms designed to compel performance in specie rather than permit a breach which would otherwise only be compensated for (and no more) in money. A penalty clause is one which provides for a "payment of money stipulated as *in terrorem* of the offending party"[38] to force performance of the contract. Such a clause is unenforceable to the extent that it provides for recovery in excess of the claimant's loss.[39] Although it may be relatively easy for parties to contract around these rules, the sentiment behind them is significant: the law is set against attempts to compel the specific performance of promises.[40]

There are two obvious exceptions to this general compensatory approach. The first is the entire branch of the law classified as criminal law. There punishment and deterrence are the order of the day. But these remedies are avail-

[36] The claimant's "expectation" or "performance" interest is protected: see D Friedmann, "The Performance Interest in Contract Damages" (1995) 111 LQR 628. Where it is not possible to award damages on this basis, the claimant may be allowed to recover the losses incurred by the claimant in reliance on the contract. This protects the claimant's "reliance interest": see *Anglia Television Ltd* v. *Reed* [1972] 1 QB 60; L Fuller and W Perdue, "The Reliance Interest in Contract Damages" (1936) 46 Yale LJ 52.

[37] *Co-operative Insurance Society Ltd* v. *Argyll Stores (Holdings) Ltd* [1998] AC 1.

[38] *Dunlop Pneumatic Tyre Co Ltd* v. *New Garage & Motor Co Ltd* [1915] AC 79, 86; *Jobson* v. *Johnson* [1989] 1 WLR 1026. Also see *Workers Trust and Merchant Bank Ltd* v. *Dojap Investments Ltd* [1993] AC 573 (re deposits).

[39] *Jobson* v. *Johnson* [1989] 1 WLR 1026.

[40] Moreover, this remains the approach of the courts even if the parties confine the "penalty" to disgorgement of profits made in breach of contract. This is sometimes mooted as not "penal" because it does not strip the defendant of any more than the ill-gotten gains—it does not put the defendant in a worse position than if the contract had not been breached, which is usually the effect of penalty clauses, and even of expectation and reliance damages. Notwithstanding this, courts will assess each situation on its merits to determine whether the remedy is in substance a penalty. The same approach is evident in the equitable jurisdiction to provide relief from forfeiture. Also see H Collins, "Fairness in Agreed Remedies" in C Willett (ed), *Aspects of Fairness in Contract* (London: Blackstone, 1996) p 97.

able only in respect of wrongs which the society has especially and carefully classified as unacceptable behaviour. The criminal law represents a statement of the types of conduct which make it impossible for a society to survive and prosper. Such transgressions merit a deterrent remedy, whether by fine or by imprisonment. Moreover, such a remedy is warranted notwithstanding loss to the victim or profit to the transgressor.[41] The profit and loss elements do not define when the activity is wrong; nor do they delimit the punishment which is ordered—although they may add another factor in its assessment.[42] The nature of the wrong also reinforces the practice that these profits, when disgorged, are disgorged in favour of the State, not the victim of the crime. The victim is merely compensated for loss. The categorisation of the activity as criminal is done for the protection of society in general, not specifically for the protection of individual victims.

The second class where deterrence is the order of the day is with equitable obligations—fiduciary obligations and obligations of confidence. As with criminal law, these obligations too are imposed by operation of law, even though the context is often overtly contractual and the fiduciary or confidant is paid to act in that capacity. These obligations are strictly limited in their ambit, however. They are imposed only where there is no other effective means of regulating the relationship between the parties,[43] and they reflect the rare circumstances where the law obliges one party to act altruistically for the benefit of another, not self-interestedly. The remedies are designed to deter breaches[44] and, especially where the obligation of confidence is concerned, the duty often has statutory supplements.[45]

[41] This was the situation in *AG* v. *Blake* [1998] Ch 439 (CA). Blake's conduct warranted punishment notwithstanding that the information revealed was no longer confidential or that the Crown did not suffer any loss as a result of the revelations. Indeed, it warranted punishment whether or not Blake had benefited from the crime. The additional disgorgement remedy simply reinforced and made complete the demands for full punishment in the circumstances. All of this is reiterated in the designation of the activity as criminal in the Official Secrets Act 1989. What made that case appear unpalatable was not the general inadequacy of the law in dealing with the situation, but the fact that this specific "criminal" was beyond the jurisdiction of the court so that the available responses could not be implemented. Jurisdictional problems ought not to be solved by wholesale changes to the fundamental underpinnings of the law.

[42] The same is true of murder, for example. Murder is assessed to be a crime regardless of any profit-making, or even profit-motivation, associated with it. This is not to say that proper punishment does not profit-strip. The same is true of disclosure of national secrets (even if no longer secret).

[43] S Worthington, "Fiduciaries: When is Self-Denial Obligatory?' [1999] CLJ 500.

[44] To provide an effective deterrent, the remedy must strip the profits from the defendant. However, there seems to be no necessary reason for paying the profits over to the claimant (provided the claimant has not suffered a collateral loss). This is especially so where the defendant is insolvent, and the disgorgement remedy works to the advantage of the disgorgement claimant but to the disadvantage of the defendant's other creditors: see V. Finch and S Worthington, "The Pari Passu Principle and Ranking Restitutionary Rights" in F Rose (ed), *Insolvency and Restitution* (London: LLP: 2000) (forthcoming).

[45] Individual interests in commercially sensitive information are protected by intellectual

Outside the criminal law and the law of equitable obligations, the only exception to this "preservation from harm" principle—and the correlative promotion of individual liberty and autonomy—seems to arise where the courts award punitive (or exemplary) damages[46] for certain torts, and perhaps also aggravated damages for certain breaches of contract.[47] This is rarely done, and appears to have clear parallels with the courts' jurisdiction in respect of contempt of court and abuse of process. In essence, the courts are expressing disapproval of defendants who show contempt for the legal system itself.[48] With this as the stated aim, the focus is on the particular qualities of the defendant's conduct, not on whether the conduct generates losses for the claimant or profits for the defendant.

From all of this certain generalisations are possible. The introduction of a disgorgement remedy for breach of contract would undoubtedly work to compel the specific performance of contractual obligations. Such a remedy would fundamentally recast the expectations of risk and wealth allocation between the parties. If the defendant committed a breach of contract, the claimant could recover compensatory damages (if the contract provided a winning bargain for the claimant), or disgorgement of the defendant's profits (if the defendant had discovered a still more profitable bargain), or the defendant's saved expenditure (if, for some reason, performance by the defendant were more expensive than compensatory substitute performance, or if the latter were not available as a remedy). With the option of disgorgement as a remedy, the risk imposed on a defendant who enters into a contract is not simply to meet the claimant's expectations of contractual performance. It is to do this, or, at the claimant's whim (albeit only on the defendant's breach), to meet some alternative measure. The resulting pressure on the defendant to perform to the letter is clear. This would alter dramatically the conventional notion of contract and the pre-eminence currently accorded to individual liberty and autonomy. Moreover, permitting recourse to a disgorgement remedy would also call into question the rationale underpinning the rule against penalties which assumes that the parties can only provide for genuine pre-estimates of loss.

property legislation (where the remedies are sometimes compensatory and sometimes require disgorgement). Community interest in national security is protected by the Official Secrets Act 1989.

[46] *Rookes* v. *Barnard* [1964] AC 1129, 1221 and 1226 *per* Lord Devlin: the remedy is designed primarily to punish the defendant for cynical wrongdoing and to deter the defendant from engaging in unacceptable conduct in the future. LCR, paras 5.70–72, suggests that punitive damages are inappropriate for breaches of contract.

[47] Aggravated damages are avowedly compensatory, so the focus should be on the claimant's loss and not on the defendant's conduct. However, such damages are often awarded in situations which strongly parallel those meriting exemplary damages awards, so an analogy between the two is commonly drawn.

[48] See the additional comments made later.

It follows that the disgorgement remedy should not be introduced unless this is the impact intended. Moreover, if the intention *is* to compel specific performance, then the analogy with the criminal law would suggest that disgorgement is not sufficient as the sole motivator: defendants should be compelled whether or not they have profitable alternatives open to them. Alternatively, if the intention is to compel specific performance so as to preserve the integrity and status of the institution of the law of contract[49] and prevent parties from flouting its goals, then the analogy with exemplary damages would suggest that the disgorgement is a crude tool since it takes no account of the deliberate and contemptuous nature of the defendant's conduct. In ignoring this factor, it will punish and exempt different defendants inappropriately.

All of this suggests that there is no general case for the award of the disgorgement remedy for breach of contract. Perhaps, however, there are specific cases where the disgorgement remedy might be appropriate. Most adherent propose only a limited sphere of operation. These suggestions for more restricted classes are the subject of the next few sections.

4. Disgorgement where damages are otherwise inadequate

It is sometimes suggested that the disgorgement remedy is appropriate when expectation or reliance damages for breach of contract are inadequate.[50] In these limited circumstances, the disgorgement remedy is seen as able to supplement existing remedial responses without altering the fundamental nature of the law of contract and its emphasis on individual autonomy. In this vein, it is argued that the law of contract would be seriously defective if it did not include this additional option. Without it a claimant would be deprived of an effective remedy because the law had failed to attach sufficient value to the claimant's legitimate interest in having the contract duly performed.[51]

The inference is clear. It is that the traditional contractual measure of compensatory damages produces a figure which inadequately represents the value

[49] Jackman, I M, "Restitution for Wonrgs" [1989] CLJ 302, especially p 320, suggests that the institution of contract law is adequately protected by compensatory damages, although he recognises the moral drive to punish deliberate offenders.

[50] See, eg, *AG* v. *Blake* [1998] Ch 439, 457. Also see D Friedmann, "The Performance Interest in Contract Damages" (1995) 111 LQR 628; B Coote, "Contract Damages, *Ruxley* and the Performance Interest" (1997) 56 CLJ 537; G Jones, "The Recovery of Benefits Gained from a Breach of Contract" (1983) 99 LQR 443, 452.

[51] *AG* v. *Blake* [1998] Ch 439 (CA), 457.

the claimant legitimately places on the expected performance. To suggest that disgorgement of the defendant's collateral profits provides the only possible way out of this difficulty seems patently unsound. If damages are truly inadequate, then it seems preferable to devote attention to proposing an alternative model for their assessment.

As it is, the common law has several strategies for dealing with situations where damages are difficult to assess. The most familiar are orders for specific performance[52] and injunctions.[53] As noted earlier, this jurisdiction is carefully regulated.[54] The circumstances of the case are assessed at the time the order is made, not at the time the parties enter into their contract.[55] Moreover, the claimant's interest in performance is not the sole determinant. The impact of the order on the defendant is also material. The court's task is to determine whether the claimant's potential harm warrants infringement of the defendant's autonomy by insisting on performance (or some other order) rather than confining the claimant to a damages claim. Indeed, such is the value placed on personal autonomy that it is rare that a defendant will be compelled to provide some *personal* service (and provide it in person)[56] as opposed to the more common requirement that the defendant transfer an asset or provide some other benefit (including services which do not need to be performed by the defendant personally). These orders provide a claimant with substantial advantages. However, the advantages do not include access to a disgorgement remedy. The remedy is consistently compensatory.[57] The cases on injunctions

[52] Some commentators have suggested that the disgorgement remedy ought to be available where the defendant has breached a specifically enforceable contract: J Beatson, *The Use and Abuse of Unjust Enrichment* (Oxford: Clarendon Press, 1991) p 17; R Nolan, "Remedies for Breach of Contract: Specific Enforcement and Restitution" in F Rose (ed), *Failure of Contracts: Contractual, Restitutionary and Proprietary Consequences* (Oxford: Hart Publishing, 1997) p 35; R O'Dair, "Restitutionary Damages for Breach of Contract and the Theory of Efficient Breach: Some Reflections" (1993) 46 CLP 113. Also see *Williams* v. *Roffey Bros & Nicholls (Contractors) Ltd* [1991] 1 QB 1, but contrast *Surrey County Council* v. *Bredero Homes Ltd* [1993] 1 WLR 1361, 1371 *per* Steyn LJ.

[53] *Hoffmann-La Roche (F) & Co AG* v. *Secretary of State for Trade and Industry* [1975] AC 295 (HL), 360–1 *per* Lord Diplock; *American Cyanamid Co* v. *Ethicon Ltd* [1975] AC 396, 406–10 *per* Lord Diplock. Also see *Lumley* v. *Wagner* (1852) 1 De GM & G 604; *Sky Petroleum Ltd* v. *VIP Petroleum Ltd* [1974] 1 WLR 576.

[54] See *Co-operative Insurance Society Ltd* v. *Argyll Stores Ltd* [1998] AC 1 (specific performance); *Jaggard* v. *Sawyer* [1995] 1 WLR 269 (injunctions and damages in lieu).

[55] And the order can be refused, even where it is a contract for the sale of land where such orders are the norm: *Patel* v. *Ali* [1984] Ch 283.

[56] Unless the state of the personal relationship between the parties is considered immaterial to the satisfactory performance of the contract.

[57] Using the term broadly, to include all remedies quantified by reference to the *claimant's* position (whether the assessment is of expectation or reliance damages, or restitution for subtractive unjust enrichment), rather than the *defendant's* profits.

(and damages in lieu) have been mentioned already,[58] but the same is equally true of specifically enforceable contracts.[59]

These equitable orders are not the only option where compensatory calculations are difficult. The common law is becoming increasingly sophisticated in its appreciation of the various issues which are material in assessing compensatory damages. For example, the law now recognises that a claimant may have a legitimate interest in the proper performance of a contract intended to provide benefits to non-contracting third parties rather than to the claimant. Compensatory damages (perhaps amounting to cost of cure) can be claimed for the breach of such contracts.[60] Similarly, the law recognises that a claimant may have legitimate non-pecuniary reasons for entering into contracts. Compensatory damages (whether cost of cure or amenity damages) can also be claimed for the breach of such contracts.[61] Of course, the usual rules of remoteness and foreseeability[62] apply in assessing such claims, so that defendants can realistically judge their likely liabilities and will not be required to pay compensation in respect of unexpected and unpredictable temperamental reactions from the claimant.[63] But this direct approach to the difficulties in assessing compensation, whatever its shortcomings, is surely better than resorting to disgorgement damages which bear no necessary (or likely)

[58] See Section 1 and S Worthington, "Reconsidering Disgorgement for Wrongs" (1999) 62 MLR 218 and the references cited there.

[59] *Lake* v. *Bayliss* [1974] 1 WLR 1073. Also see *Lamine* v. *Dorrell* (1705) 2 Ld Ray 1216 (conversion); *Biggerstaff* v. *Rowatt's Wharf Ltd* [1896] 2 Ch 93, 103 (sale of goods). In the context of contracts of sale, the claimant's permitted access to the proceeds of any unauthorised sale by the defendant to third parties is often taken to be a disgorgement remedy, but see, eg, R Nolan, "Remedies for Breach of Contract: Specific Enforcement and Restitution" in F Rose (ed), *Failure of Contracts: Contractual, Restitutionary and Proprietary Consequences* (Oxford: Hart Publishing, 1997) p 35, 57 and P Watts, "Remedies for Breach of Contract: Specific Enforcement and Restitution—A Comment", *ibid*, p 61at p 62.

[60] See the approach adopted by Lord Griffiths in *Linden Gardens Trust Ltd* v. *Lenesta Sludge Disposals Ltd* [1994] 1 AC 85. Whether such damages ought to be held for the benefit of the non-contracting third party suffering the practical detriment is a nice question. Contrast the more forced approach adopted in *Beswick* v. *Beswick* [1968] AC 58. Also see Contacts (Rights of Third Parties) Act 1999.

[61] *Ruxley Electronics and Construction Ltd* v. *Forsyth* [1996] AC 344 (HL), 360–1 *per* Lord Mustill, 374 *per* Lord Lloyd. The idea of "consumer surplus" and its importance in the law was first propounded and explained by Harris, Ogus and Phillips, "Contract Remedies and the Consumer Surplus" (1979) 95 LQR 581. Also see E McKendrick, "Breach of Contract and the Meaning of Loss" (1999) 52 CLP 37.

[62] *Hadley* v. *Baxendale* (1854) 9 Ex 341.

[63] *Dillon* v. *Baltic Shipping Co*(1993) 176 CLR 344, 367, 369 *per* Brennan J. This appears consistent with the Court of Appeal decisions in *Hayes* v. *James & Charles Dodd* [1990] 2 All ER 815 and *Watts* v. *Morrow* [1991] 1 WLR 1421, which suggest that damages for disappointment, distress, vexation, injured feelings, loss of enjoyment etc are only recoverable where (i) they arise from physical discomfort or inconvenience, or (ii) the contract itself was to provide enjoyment, pleasure, peace of mind or relief from stress. *Ruxley Electronics and Construction Ltd* v. *Forsyth* [1996] AC 344 (HL) indicates that a "reasonable" defendant will be expected to appreciate the amenity value inherent in many modern contracts.

relationship to the claimant's losses. Such an approach may well lead to an increase in the orders for cost of cure and amenity damages as the courts pay more regard to the subjective concerns which motivate both commercial and consumer contracts (especially the latter).

It has been suggested that the artificiality in valuing the loss of amenity only serves to indicate that compensatory damages are inadequate and that restitutionary damages are preferable.[64] However, the case most often cited in this context—*Ruxley Electronics and Construction Ltd* v. *Forsyth*[65]—demonstrates the deficiencies inherent in adopting the disgorgement approach rather than confronting any difficulties directly. In that case there was no profit made or expense saved by the contractor in building a pool shallower than requested, notwithstanding the well-recognised amenity component in the arrangement between the parties. Disgorgement would not have given the claimant an adequate remedy. The real difficulty simply had to be faced. The court refused to award specific performance or cost of cure, and so the resulting loss of amenity had to be valued. So, too, with the commonly cited hypothetical example of the photographer commissioned to take photographs at a wedding. If the photographer does not turn up, especially if his absence is motivated by a more lucrative job offer, then there is a common perception that monetary damages are inadequate and that disgorgement should be ordered as a punitive and deterrent remedy. But this reflex is surely not the most appropriate response. By focusing on the photographer's profits, some claimants will be denied any adequate remedy and others will receive a remedy totally unrelated to their losses. Whether or not the photographer's breach is profit-generating, it is better for the court to grapple with the difficult task of placing a money value on amenity and aggravated damages.[66] If the breach is also profit-generating, then this may add to the claimant's aggravation, but it is unlikely to affect the other (more substantial) components of a properly assessed compensatory damages claim.

The response that all of this is too hard—and that disgorgement provides a readily accessible measure—will not do. There is no sense in complaining that compensation is inadequate and then adopting a strategy which is unrelated to solving that problem. The real difficulty with these cases is that the claimant desperately wants specific performance, but the court cannot (for practical reasons[67]) or will not (for reasons of waste[68]) order such performance (or sub-

[64] Eg, G Virgo, "Clarifying Restitution for Wrongs (note on *Attorney-General* v. *Blake*)" [1998] RLR 118, 124.

[65] *Ruxley Electronics and Construction Ltd* v. *Forsyth* [1996] AC 344 (HL).

[66] Clearly the claimant's loss cannot be adequately measured by the impact of the breach on her predicted financial status.

[67] As with the photographer who does not turn up. So, too, in *AG* v. *Blake* [1998] Ch 439 (CA), although had Blake been amenable to the jurisdiction of the court, surely he could have been subjected to an injunction to prevent publication of his story. Again, the problem in this case is not the inadequacy of the existing law, but its territorial limitations.

[68] As in *Ruxley Electronics and Construction Ltd* v. *Forsyth* [1996] AC 344 (HL).

stitute performance or cost of cure damages).[69] Once a court has made its assessment that it cannot or will not protect the claimant from harm by giving the claimant precisely what was bargained for, it then has to determine to what lesser extent it will remedy the harm. The difficulty in doing this is equally present whether or not profits have been made by the defaulting defendant. Any strategy for solving the difficulty needs to recognise this, and to avoid becoming trammelled by an understandable desire to punish the profitable wrongdoer.

5. Disgorgement from a cynical contract-breaker

Cynical contract-breakers attract a high degree of personal opprobrium. Because of this, they are often perceived to be likely candidates against whom a disgorgement remedy ought to be directed.[70] Nevertheless, the considered view of many commentators is to the contrary.[71] One justification for the stance is pragmatic: it is too difficult to determine who is cynical and who is not when it comes to breaching contracts.[72] A more principled response recognises that there is no necessary link between the cynical nature of the breach and either the level of profits generated by the defendant or the inadequacy of the compensatory damages recoverable by the claimant[73] (and disgorgement should be ordered only where compensatory damages are inadequate[74]). This

[69] The fact that damages are inadequate is often intrinsically related to the sense that the damage cannot be repaired: the revealed secrets cannot be retracted, (less certainly) the built houses cannot be demolished, the retained goods cannot be used as the claimant preferred, alternative sources of supply cannot be accessed. Sometimes this is a justifiable recognition that the losses are not easily quantifiable—but it rarely if ever follows that the unquantifiable losses are in any way related to the profits made by the contract-breaker. Blake's revelation of the "secrets" would have been equally problematic whether it was for profit or not. As indicated earlier, the profit stripping must be associated with a justifiable desire to compel the defendant to perform; the damages assessment must perform as best as can be done the task of making the claimant whole again.

[70] See, eg, P Birks, "Restitutionary Damages for Breach of Contract: *Snepp* and the Fusion of Law and Equity" [1987] LMCLQ 421.

[71] *AG* v. *Blake* [1998] Ch 439 (CA), 457; LCR Part III and para 6.2.

[72] *Surrey County Council* v. *Bredero Homes Ltd* [1993] 1 WLR 1361, 1370 *per* Steyn LJ; *AG* v. *Blake* [1998] Ch 439, 457. In Sir W Goodhart, "Restitutionary Damages for Breach of Contract: The Remedy that Dare Not Speak Its Name" [1995] RLR 3, 11, it is suggested that disgorgement ought to be available unless the defendant can show that the breach occurred for reasons outside the defendant's control.

[73] Eg, G Virgo, "Clarifying Restitution for Wrongs (note on *Attorney-General* v. *Blake*)" [1998] RLR 118, 123. In *AG* v. *Blake* [1998] Ch 439 (CA), at 457, the matter was simply stated to be irrelevant. In *AG* v. *Guardian Newspapers (No 2)* [1990] 1 AC (HL), at 261, Lord Keith suggested that a natural desire to deprive a deliberate wrongdoer of profit is not a valid ground for departing from the normal measure of damages for breach of contract.

[74] *AG* v. *Blake* [1998] Ch 439 (CA), 457.

is true, but it masks the more fundamental problem,[75] which is that there is no necessary link between the level of profits generated by the breach (whether cynical or not) and the inadequacy of the compensatory damages recoverable by the claimant. It is therefore difficult to see how the two were ever linked in the first place, without then going on to look for circumstances which are material to both (or to either).

This absence of inter-dependency does not eliminate the desire to punish cynical wrongdoers. However, it is better in these circumstances to direct the punishment to the behaviour itself, and to admit openly that it is not the harm to the victim, or the benefit to the wrongdoer, but the style of breach which is under attack. There are several routes to this end. Sometimes such wrongs are criminal, marking society's formal assessment that this type of behaviour is unacceptable. Many frauds fall into this category. But even where the wrong is not serious enough to be categorised as criminal, it is recognised that deliberate wrongs somehow offend against the institutions constructed by society for the protection of all. This is especially so where the obligations are imposed by the general law (as with torts). In the face of such "contempts" of the general law, the court exercises a limited discretion to award punitive (or exemplary) damages.[76] The purpose of such an order is to express the court's disapproval and punish the defendant accordingly; it is not to compensate the claimant, nor to strip the defendant of ill-gotten gains. The punishment is intended to be proportionate to the behaviour judged unacceptable; it is not limited by its collateral profit-generating features. It would be a poor system of punishment if it were so limited. However, these non-criminal routes do not catch many cynical contract-breakers. Even in the face of clear evidence of a cynical breach of contract, courts appear to regard the wrongdoer with far more equanimity than they reserve for other deliberate wrongdoers. The distinction seems to reflect a perception that the flouting of "bought" obligations inflicts less institutional harm than the flouting of externally "imposed" obligations. That said, even though the general rule is that punitive damages are not available for a deliberate breach of contract,[77] something similar can sometimes be obtained, in the guise of compensation for injured feelings or "aggravated damages", where the defendant's conduct is considered particularly outrageous.[78]

If this largely unchallenged position of the cynical contract-breaker is regarded as morally unacceptable, so much so that there is an overriding sense that the law should intervene, then elsewhere it has been suggested that an

[75] See Section 4 above.

[76] See *Rookes* v. *Barnard* [1964] AC 1129.

[77] *Perera* v. *Vandiyar* [1953] 1 WLR 672.

[78] *Addis* v. *Gramaphone Co Ltd* [1915] 1 KB 1. The LCR suggested that the analysis of the Court of Appeal in *A B* v. *South West Water Services Ltd* [1993] QB 507 was unduly restrictive in assessing the availability of exemplary and aggravated damages: see LCR Part IV, especially paras 4.2–4.4, 4.24–4.28.

approach based on analogies with the equitable obligations of good faith and loyalty might provide an avenue for a principled development of the law.[79] On this basis, but (again by analogy) only in the limited circumstances where the contractual relationship would otherwise be unworkable, bad faith profit-generating activities might be punished by requiring disgorgement. At first sight this may seem an attractive route for the eradication of the problem of cynical contract-breakers. However, it does not reflect equity's current approach. Even where equity insists that powers and duties be performed in good faith (bona fide and for proper purposes), it does not visit breaches with a disgorgement remedy. The equitable remedy is confined to injunctive relief if the circumstances permit, or avoidance of the impugned transaction if third party rights would not be affected, or equitable compensation for the losses thereby caused. Equity's intervention is exclusively compensatory.

In short, it is difficult to justify converting distaste or outrage in the face of cynical profit-making breaches into a generalisable rule requiring disgorgement. The response is better seen as genuinely punitive, directed at the style of the behaviour and not the magnitude of the benefits secured. This is the approach currently adopted with civil and criminal wrongs, and reflects a preferable alignment of wrong and remedy.

6. Situations where the profits are generated directly by the breach

In *AG* v. *Blake*,[80] the Court of Appeal suggested that disgorgement was an appropriate remedy in the exceptional circumstances where compensatory damages were inadequate *and* the defendant had profited directly from the breach. The second condition is limiting. Disgorgement is impossible unless there are profits, and the need for the profits to arise *directly* from the breach provides a remoteness test.

Every quantification of damages needs to be subjected to remoteness tests, otherwise defendants would be exposed to unacceptable risks. However, the test advocated by the Court of Appeal for the disgorgement remedy is so restrictive that it appears to neutralise the jurisdiction at its inception. Satisfaction of a "but for" test is not enough. A breach which enables the defendant to take up a more profitable alternative contract is not regarded as sufficient to warrant the disgorgement remedy, even when the alternative

[79] S Worthington, "Reconsidering Disgorgement for Wrongs" (1999) 62 MLR 218.
[80] [1998] Ch 439, 458.

opportunity could not have been taken up but for the breach of contract.[81] If this is true for unauthorised resales or service contracts, then consistency suggests that there should be no disgorgement of the profits generated by building extra houses in breach of a restrictive covenant,[82] or selling secrets in breach of contract.[83] In these latter cases the profits are produced by the further steps of designing, building and selling attractive houses to willing third parties, or writing, publishing and marketing a book to the eager public. The breach itself is not the sole source of the profits; other factors contribute.

If the remoteness test denies a disgorgement remedy whenever there are mixed contributions to the profits generated by the defendant, then it seems that recovery must inevitably be confined to "expenses saved" as a direct result of non-performance or defective performance. This element of "profit" is probably recoverable in any event, and in a less limiting form, using compensatory principles.[84] On this basis, the remoteness test advocated for the disgorgement remedy would deny the jurisdiction any practical value. Moreover, it would leave unremedied the very cases where moral sensibilities are most seriously affronted.

Notwithstanding this, the Court of Appeal suggested that there were two particular situations which met the double requirement that the profits be derived directly from the breach and that compensatory damages be inadequate. These were cases where the defendant's breach consisted in doing precisely what the defendant had contracted not to do, and cases where the defendant provided skimped contractual performance. These classes are considered separately in the next sections.

7. Situations where the defendant has done precisely what he or she agreed not to do

As already noted, the Court of Appeal in *AG* v. *Blake*[85] suggested that the disgorgement remedy was appropriate where the defendant's breach of contract consisted of doing precisely what the contract compelled the defendant not to do. The rationale for such a category is not at all clear. At a theoretical level, it seems indefensible to suppose that doing something which the defendant promised not to do is any worse that not doing something which the defendant

[81] *Ibid.* Also see *Teacher* v. *Calder* [1899] AC 451.
[82] *Wrotham Park Estate Co Ltd* v. *Parkside Homes Ltd* [1974] 1 WLR 798 (CA).
[83] *AG* v. *Blake* [1998] Ch 439 (CA).
[84] See Section 8 below, and the general comments in Section 4 above.
[85] [1998] Ch 439, 458.

promised would be done.[86] The categorisation does not necessarily reflect any difference in the significance of the promise to society in general, or the likely injury to the plaintiff, or the culpability or mala fides of the defendant. Moreover, the sense that the distinction is illusory is compounded if reliance is to be placed on the express words of the contract. Blake's conduct surely merits the same response regardless of whether his contract expressly obliged him "not to disclose" or, alternatively, "to keep secret" the information he gained in the course of his work as a government agent. And if reliance is to be placed on *implied* obligations not to act in certain ways, then is seems the rule must become one of universal application. A contract whereby A agrees to supply goods to B contains no negative stipulation, but the courts will surely infer a "not" obligation, be it an obligation not to supply nothing, or not to supply shoddy goods, or not to supply C instead of B. We know the courts will do this, because in some cases they have even gone so far as to support such inferred obligations by injunction[87] and (more rarely) by giving the owner a proprietary interest in the promised asset.[88] Certainly they protect such implied "not" obligations by compensatory awards.

Does it make any difference that the "not" obligation is an obligation specifically not to make a collateral profit?[89] This is the form of implied obligation imposed on fiduciaries and confidants. It can also be imposed expressly between contracting parties.[90] Then disgorgement is commonplace. However, the earlier discussion shows how particular the courts are in implying such obligations or in permitting the parties to specify them. There is a realisation that these obligations and their associated remedies come with a penal deterrent, and the circumstances where this is permitted are strictly supervised. If the disgorgement remedy were restricted to this limited class of "not" obligations, it would not be disgorgement for breach of contract but disgorgement for breach of equitable duties (or perhaps compensation or restitution for misuse of property).

In summary, it seems this category should be dismissed as inappropriate and ineffective in defining a class of breaches for which the disgorgement remedy might be appropriate.

[86] But contrast [1998] Ch 439, 458, citing P Birks, "Restitutionary Damages for Breach of Contract: *Snepp* and the Fusion of Law and Equity" [1987] LMCLQ 421, 434: "If you promise not to pursue a particular profit-making activity and then do pursue it, nothing is more apt than that you should make restitution of your profits." But, unlike a fiduciary promising loyalty, Blake did not promise not to pursue profit-making activities; he simply promised not to disclose without authority, whether for profit or not (see [1998] Ch 439, 452).

[87] *Howard E Perry & Co* v. *British Railways Board* [1980] 1 WLR 1375, 1383; *Sky Petroleum Ltd* v. *VIP Petroleum Ltd* [1974] 1 WLR 576.

[88] This is commonly done in contracts for the sale of land, and contract for the sale of rare chattels, but also see *Barclays Bank Ltd* v. *Quistclose Investments Ltd* [1970] AC 567.

[89] The Court of Appeal in *AG* v. *Blake* [1998] Ch 439 (CA) appeared to start from this specific "not" obligation and then generalise to all "not" obligations: see footnote 86 above.

[90] *Reid-Newfoundland Co* v. *Anglo-American Telegraph Co* [1912] AC 555.

8. Situations where the defendant has skimped on performance

The Court of Appeal in *AG* v. *Blake*[91] also suggested, as a second category, that the disgorgement remedy was appropriate where the defendant's breach of contract involved skimped performance. In these circumstances the court suggested that a defendant ought to be required to disgorge the "expenses saved" as a result of the breach. This, too, is a strange category to nominate as warranting a disgorgement remedy. There seems no reason to suppose that injury from skimped performance is somehow necessarily worse for either society in general or the individual claimant in particular, nor that such performance necessarily compels a more censorious treatment of the defaulting defendant. Moreover, in practice there is often little to distinguish "skimped" performance from "defective" performance. If this distinction is blurred, then the category of breaches where it is suggested disgorgement might be warranted seems almost all-embracing.

In most cases of skimped performance, what is needed to preserve the claimant from harm is "cost of cure" damages. Such damages will enable the claimant to have the work done properly, according to the agreed terms, thereby putting the claimant in the position he or she would have been in had there been no breach of contract. This is the measure of damages which courts will often award.[92] However, courts will not make wasteful or pointless orders. This has two consequences.

First, even if the claimant has suffered a loss from the skimped performance, if the cost of cure is out of all proportion to the benefit which the claimant would obtain from proper performance, then the courts will not award damages at this level.[93] Instead, they will award damages assessed at the difference between the value to the claimant of the work which was actually done and the value to the claimant of the work which ought to have been done.[94] This second, alternative, measure of damages has been criticised on the basis that it leaves the claimant inadequately compensated. This is because the sum awarded—which depends upon an assessment of the value to the claimant of

[91] [1998] Ch 439, 458.

[92] *Mertens* v. *Home Freeholds* [1921] 2 KB 526; *Hoenig* v. *Isaacs* [1952] 1 TLR 1360.

[93] eg *Jacob & Youngs* v. *Kent* 129 NE 889 (1921).

[94] Note that this measure of damages is assessed from the *claimant's* perspective (ie the value difference to the claimant), not the defendant's perspective (ie the expenses saved by the defendant). See *East Ham Corporation* v. *Bernard Sunley and Sons Ltd* [1966] AC 406; *White Arrow Express Ltd* v. *Lamey's Distribution Ltd* [1995] NLJ 1504. Sometimes this measure will exactly match the cost of cure measure (eg *Dean* v. *Ainley* [1987] 1 WLR 1729; Sale of Goods Act 1979 s 51(3)), but sometimes it can be dramatically different (eg, *Ruxley Electronics & Construction Co Ltd* v. *Forsyth* [1996] AC 344; *Peevyhouse* v. *Garland Coal Co* 382 P 2d 109 (1962)).

the work actually done and the work which ought to have been done—does not make due allowance for "consumer surplus".[95] This is the extra value, over and above the market valuation, that the claimant placed on having the work done as requested, not as delivered. The criticisms of the law's shortcomings in this area are real. Many contracts are entered into for non-pecuniary advantages. However, these criticisms have been partly assuaged by the decision in *Ruxley Electronics & Construction Co Ltd* v. *Forsyth.*[96] That case allowed an owner to claim damages for "loss of amenity" when a pool-builder constructed a pool which was several inches shallower than the one bargained for. As noted earlier, in cases such as these where the real complaint is that the assessment of damages does not properly remedy the harm, it seems far better to address the problem directly rather than to advocate a disgorgement remedy—which bears no necessary relationship to the claimant's loss.[97]

Secondly, because the court will not make pointless or wasteful orders, it follows that if the claimant has suffered no real loss from the breach (even when amenity damages are factored in), then the court will not award any remedy. Damages are not designed to provide a gratuitous benefit to the aggrieved party.[98] This is so, even if the result is to allow the defendant to reap a windfall in saved expenses. *Tito* v. *Waddell (No 2)*[99] is illustrative. In that case, certain islanders claimed for breach of contract but recovered only nominal damages against a phosphate mining company that had agreed, as part of the terms upon which the island would be mined, that the landscape would be reinstated upon completion of the project. When that time came, the mining company refused to perform, thus saving itself considerable expense. The islanders were deemed to have no real interest in cure, since they had moved to another island many miles away and were unlikely to return to their original homes. In cases such as these, two approaches, not one, prompt demands for a disgorgement remedy.

The first is the familiar desire to prevent the wrongdoer—the contract-breaker—from profiting from the breach. The earlier arguments need not be

[95] Again see Harris, Ogus and Phillips, "Contract Remedies and the Consumer Surplus" (1979) 95 LQR 581 and E McKendrick, "Breach of Contract and the Meaning of Loss" (1999) 52 CLP 37. Despite its name, a "consumer surplus" is not necessarily limited to consumer (rather than commercial) contracts. Both types of contracts can be entered into in order to acquire non-financial benefits, although the name does recognise that this will be more common with consumer contracts. For example, a gallery commissioning re-decoration work may attach a "consumer surplus" value to the manner in which the work is done, yet this is not a "consumer" contract.

[96] [1996] AC 344.

[97] In the *Ruxley* case, for example, it seems the defendant saved nothing in building a shallower pool: he had quoted the same price for both depths.

[98] *Ruxley Electronics & Construction Co Ltd* v. *Forsyth* [1996] AC 344, 357. Also see *Staniforth* v. *Lyall* (1830) 7 Bing 169; *Taylor* v. *Bank of Athens* (1922) 27 Com Cas 142.

[99] [1977] Ch 106. Also see Landlord and Tenant Act 1927 s 18(1) (and cp *Joyner* v. *Weeks* [1891] 2 QB 31).

rehearsed.[100] They suggest that moral indignation is not a sufficient reason to ground the demand for a disgorgement remedy. The second approach is more persuasive. It suggests that a claimant in this position has paid more than was warranted for the defendant's contractual performance, because the claimant's payment was assessed on the (subsequently unfounded) assumption that the defendant had additional obligations to perform. The claimant should therefore be able to recover this wasted expenditure, so the argument goes, on the basis of a partial failure of consideration. The disgorgement remedy is merely a convenient assessment of the extent of the claimant's over-payment.[101] If the contract is a divisible contract, then this approach will work. If the contract is not, then two rules might prevent resort to a claim in unjust enrichment. First, the breach must entitle the claimant to terminate the contract: restitution is not available if the contract is still on foot. Secondly, the current law (admittedly under pressure for reform) suggests that restitution is not possible unless there has been a total failure of consideration.[102] In most cases this second requirement will not be met, even in the unlikely event that the first is. Nevertheless, if this approach works, it attracts none of the criticisms reserved for the disgorgement remedy. It is not a disgorgement remedy; it is a straightforward claim for restitution of an unjust enrichment, being the over-payment for contractual benefits not received.

However, the real issue is what should be done about alleged over-payments in the more common case where the unjust enrichment approach is unavailable (perhaps because the breach does not entitle the claimant to terminate the contract) and yet the court refuses to order substantial compensatory damages (because it judges the claimant's position—even if amenity values are factored in—to be not materially different as a result of the skimped performance). The fact that the claimant's position is not materially different as a result of the skimped performance does not gainsay the claimant's assertion that more has been paid to reach that position than was warranted under the terms of the agreement. The claimant then wants compensation for the alleged over-payment. This is so whether the defendant has saved expenses or not. Moreover, the claimant wants the shortfall assessed on the basis of the claimant's loss through over-payment, not the defendant's gain through saved expenditure; the two may not be equivalent.[103] Finally, the claimant does not want the claim

[100] See Section 2 above.

[101] Clearly it is not an accurate assessment, since the defendant's "saved expenses" do not include the profit element which would undoubtedly have been charged to the claimant as part of the over-payment for the unfulfilled service. However, if the claimant chooses to claim less in damages than the full entitlement, the defendant is hardly likely to complain.

[102] The Law Commission Consultation Paper, "Pecuniary Restitution on Breach of Contract", (Law Com No 65, 1975) recommended that the rule be abolished, but the Report (Law Com No 121, 1983) dropped the recommendation.

[103] A "luxury" service is often charged out at a much higher rate than the real cost to the provider. Consider the difference in price between first class and economy airline seats. A person

to abate because the defendant is entitled to rely on some restitutionary defence; the claimant wants full recovery—full compensation—notwithstanding such factors. These features demonstrate the error in suggesting that adoption of the disgorgement remedy is a convenient means of reaching the desired compensatory ends. This is not what is suggested here.

Here it is suggested that contract law—perhaps with some minor adjustments—is already equipped to deal with the situation. The Romans would have styled the claim as an *actio quanti minoris*. The Sale of Goods Act 1979 s 53(1)(a) provides its statutory equivalent. The general law, too, delivers a similar response. Even cases such as *White Arrow Express Ltd* v. *Lamey's Distribution Ltd*,[104] where the claimants unsuccessfully attempted to recover over-payments in respect of an "enhanced" delivery service which they had not received, do not deny this. The claimants in that case were stymied in their efforts, not because the law was unable to meet the situation, but because of the way they had framed their claim.[105] This may need attention. If claimants are forced to frame their claims with such care so as to avoid being caught out, then reform may be necessary. But the need for reform reflects procedural, not substantive, shortcomings in the law. Compensatory damages are—as they should be—adequate to cope with cases where the claimant has overpaid for a contractual benefit which has not been received.

The familiar American case of *City of New Orleans* v. *Fireman's Charitable Association*[106] is illustrative. The defendant entered into a contract with the claimant to provide a fire-fighting service. The defendant in fact provided less than the agreed cover, deploying fewer men and horses and shorter lengths of hose. The defendant's savings from this skimped performance were substantial. However, the court held that the claimant's damages were nil, since the reduced service had not prevented the defendant from putting out any fires. This case is often cited by restitution lawyers as a clear illustration of the need for a disgorgement remedy. However, the the earlier discussion of *White Arrow Express Ltd* v. *Lamey's Distribution Ltd*[107] suggests that an appropriately framed *compensatory* claim would entitle the claimants to recovery of their overpayments: the contract was for the provision of a "luxury" fire-fighting service where only a "basic" service was provided. If this is true, then the conventional assessment of compensatory damages would not produce a result which is "inadequate".[108] There is therefore no call for a supplementary

who has paid for the former and received the latter wants to recover the overpayment, not the airline's "expenses saved".

104 [1995] CLC 1251 (CA); The Times, 21 July 1995.

105 H Beale, "Damages for Poor Service" (1996) 112 LQR 205, and the references cited there.

106 9 So 486 (1891).

107 [1995] CLC 1251 (CA). See the text associated with footnote 105 above.

108 In fact, compensatory damages will often be more advatageous to the claimant than disgorgement: see footnotes 101 and 103 above.

disgorgement remedy—in fact, on the arguments advanced earlier, its introduction could radically alter the commercial sense of the agreement between the parties.

This conclusion ignores one important feature of many of these cases. At the heart of demands for a disgorgement remedy is often a deep-seated suspicion that these defendants are cynical contract-breakers, and that they therefore deserve to feel the full force of the law's opprobrium. This factor has already been considered.[109] If this is the real complaint, then the better response, it seems, is to identify and deal with these cases by focusing directly on the conduct complained of, not on the incidental profits generated.

In summary, the category of skimped performance also seems to be an unnecessary and inappropriate target for the proposed introduction of a disgorgement remedy.

9. Peripheral problems with the disgorgement remedy

So far the analysis has centred on criticisms of the potential bases which might underpin awards of a disgorgement remedy for breach of contract. If such a jurisdiction is to be introduced, then defining its limits is a primary concern. However, even if this central problem were solved, there would be still further difficulties.

In *Surrey County Council* v. *Bredero Homes Ltd*,[110] Steyn LJ suggested that a disgorgement remedy imposed to deprive cynical contract breakers of the fruits of their breaches would add uncertainty to the resolution of commercial and consumer disputes, deliver a windfall to claimants, deter economically valuable activity, and increase insurance costs. These consequences are commonly conceded, although advocates of the disgorgement remedy do not regard them as compelling.[111]

But these are not the only concerns. There is the twin problem of confining and quantifying the disgorgement remedy itself. The Court of Appeal in *AG* v. *Blake*[112] was concerned to ensure that the remedy did not catch gains which

[109] See Section 5 above.

[110] *Surrey County Council* v. *Bredero Homes Ltd* [1993] 1 WLR 1361 (CA), 1370.

[111] Eg, Sir W Goodhart, "Restitutionary Damages for Breach of Contract: The Remedy that Dare Note Speak Its Name" [1995] RLR 3, 10, suggests that these commercial reasons ought only to protect defendants where the claimant could have obtained substitute performance.

[112] *AG* v. *Blake* [1998] Ch 439 (CA), 458.

were too remote.[113] The gains had to be "occasioned directly by the breach, which does not merely provide the defendant with the opportunity to make them".[114] Some of the difficulties associated with this formulation have already been addressed.[115] In addition, the defendant's "gains", even if not too remote, may exist as real profits or as deemed savings of expense. In either case, if only those profits solely referable to the breach are to be disgorged, then some account must be given for the defendant's contributions of time, skill and effort. This too can be difficult.[116]

There is also the question of onus of proof. If disgorgement is simply regarded as a remedial alternative to compensatory damages, then claims for the remedy will need to be established only on the balance of probabilities. However, some commentators have recognised that disgorgement imposes a penalty on the defendant.[117] It is the equivalent of a confiscation order. The injustice to the defendant of a mistaken order for disgorgement greatly exceeds the injustice to the claimant of a mistaken acquittal. In these circumstances procedural and evidential rules are often weighted in the defendant's favour. This is the common practice of the criminal law. Both the Law Commission[118] and the judiciary[119] have recognised the implications if the civil law is to impose such penalties.[120]

Finally, if the aim is to protect the claimant's performance interest, then the disgorgement remedy only achieves this indirectly, by removing one incentive to breach. If the performance interest is so prized, then some other means ought to be found to ensure that *all* claimants are protected, not simply those engaged with defendants motivated to pursue profit-making breaches.

All of this is undoubtedly difficult on the facts presented to the court in *AG* v. *Blake*.[121] *Blake* is a hard case—so hard that there is a clear temptation to

[113] Also see R. Nolan, "Remedies for Breach of Contract: Specific Enforcement and Restitution", in F D Rose (ed.), *Failure of Contracts—Contractual, Restitutionary and Proprietary Consequences* (Oxford: Hart Publishing, 1997) ch 3.

[114] *AG* v. *Blake* [1998] Ch 439 (CA), 458. Also see the discussion in *Halifax Building Society* v. *Thomas* [1996] Ch 217 (CA).

[115] See Section 6 above. Also see R O'Dair, "Restitutionary Damages for Breach of Contract and the Theory of Efficient Breach: Some Reflections: (1993) 46 CLP 113; M Chen-Wishart, "Restitutionary Damages for Breach of Contract" (1998) 114 LQR 363.

[116] Eg, contrast *Boardman* v. *Phipps* [1967] 2 AC 46 (HL) and *Guiness Plc* v. *Saunders* [1990] 2 AC 633 (HL).

[117] P Jaffey, "The Law Commission Report on Aggravated, Exemplary and Restitutionary Damages" (1998) 61 MLR 860, 861–3, 868–9; P Jaffey, "Restitutionary Damages and Disgorgement" [1995] RLR 30, 39 and the references cited there.

[118] LCR paras 4.99–4.101, although arguably "weighting the normal civil standard of proof in the defendant's favour" does not adequately safeguard the defendant.

[119] *Rookes* v. *Barnard* [1964] AC 1129. LCR paras 5.2–5.3, 5.29, 5.38.

[120] However, it has to be said that these concerns are not reiterated in the treatment of fiduciaries and confidants who are required to disgorge.

[121] [1998] Ch 439.

grant a disgorgement remedy because the particular circumstances seem insoluble on the basis of existing law. Three features make *Blake* such a hard case. First, there is the moral outrage that an ex-MI5 agent, entrusted with issues of national security, could deliberately reveal matters agreed to be secret and yet remain beyond the reach of the English courts. Secondly, the legitimacy of this moral outrage is confirmed by the knowledge that, had Blake been amenable to the jurisdiction of the court, the criminal law could have provided a satisfactory remedy. Finally, there is exasperation in the realisation that the state institutions—the law itself—is being flouted and thereby brought into disrepute.[122] All of this underpinned the successful intervention by the Attorney-General on public law grounds.[123] Whether it is enough to justify a disgorgement remedy for breach of contract is another matter. The rules of precedent would convert such intervention into a general rule with application outside these particularly difficult circumstances.[124] The discussion so far suggests that this would be an unnecessary and unwarranted advance.

10. Reasons against the introduction of a general disgorgement remedy for breach of contract

If the arguments advanced so far are accepted, then no compelling reason has yet been proposed in favour of adoption of the disgorgement remedy for breach of contract. On these grounds alone, the case against the disgorgement remedy might conceivably be considered won. But to leave the discussion at this stage would be to adopt an essentially negative approach. The final question must be, are there any compelling reasons for confining damages for breach of contract to the expectation and reliance measure, and excluding the possibility of disgorgement?

The answer must be yes. The general aim of commercial law is to support parties in their engagements in market transactions. This aim is best achieved,

[122] And even on the facts of *Blake*, the intervention permitted by the introduction of a disgorgement remedy for breach of contract is only effective because the royalties due to Blake had not yet been paid to him *and* were owed to him by a publisher amenable to the jurisdiction of the UK courts.

[123] It has been suggested that the injunction ordered by the Court of Appeal on public law grounds could not achieve the desired ends. For example, the publisher could simply pay similar sums to Blake on some other account (eg for another published piece, no matter how short). However, this is a common problem: a disgorgement remedy for breach of the contract between Blake and the Crown could equally easily be avoided by precisely the same mechanisms.

[124] Indeed, the Court of Appeal seemed keen to state the principle in general terms, thus making it less likely than usual that the decision would, in the future, be confined to its particular facts.

it seems, if the courts confine awards of compulsory performance and limit the measure of damages awarded.[125] This approach is better for the parties and better for society as a whole. If the penalties for a breach of contract are too severe, then commercial parties will be deterred from entering into binding agreements. They will not be prepared to take the risk that unforeseen consequences may cause them to breach their contract and thereby incur either substantial personal liability[126] or significant loss of personal autonomy. In terms of social cost, too, fewer resources are wasted if contractual remedies shun compulsory performance and instead impose duties which minimise harm but which are conditional upon the parties themselves mitigating their losses.

These are general considerations. They favour conventional minimal legal intervention. Most of the time this intervention will require the contract-breaker to bear the burden of the breach, regardless of whether the breach was intentional, or negligent, or caused by some unforeseen catastrophe. But the argument in favour of minimal intervention does not change even if the breach is intentional and either profit-generating or expense-saving. Such breaches are usually motivated by the realisation that a better deal can be done elsewhere, or that the original contract is uneconomic. To decide whether a breach is advantageous to the contract-breaker in these circumstances requires the contract-breaker to factor into the equation the costs of compensating the counter-party. The modern law, if it is to give fair consideration to the plight of the claimant, must require this measure of compensation to incorporate sums in recognition of any consumer surplus or injury to feelings (aggravated damages) where either of these is warranted. However, even with this added requirement to compensate the claimant in full, there will be situations where a breach is economically advantageous to the contract-breaker. Adoption of a wealth-maximising criterion in determining the rules of commercial law would condone efficient breaches of contract. If the circumstances are such that the defendant will be better off, and the claimant will be no worse off, then society too will be better off , in economic terms, as a result of the breach.[127] Adherence to the theory of efficient breach is therefore inconsistent with adoption of the disgorgement remedy. If defendants were required to disgorge the profits of a breach, then they could never be better off as a result of a

[125] H Collins, *The Law of Contract* (1997, Butterworths: London) ch 17.

[126] Goetz and Scott, "Enforcing Promises: An Examination of the Basis of Contract" (1980) Yale LJ 1261.

[127] This is the standard of Pareto efficiency. See R A Posner, *Economic Analysis of Law* 4th edn, (Boston, Mass: Little Brown & Co, 1992) pp 117–126. For criticisms of the theory of efficient breach, see D Friedmann, "The Efficient Breach Fallacy" (1989) 18 JLS 1; L Smith, "Disgorgement of the Profits of Breach of Contract: Property, Contract and 'Efficient Breach'" (1992) Can Bus LJ 121; R O'Dair, "Restitutionary Damages for Breach of Contract and the Theory of Efficient Breach: Some Reflections" (1993) 46 CLP 113.

deliberate breach; there would then be no incentive for them to search for more efficient market opportunities.

But not everyone is persuaded by these efficiency arguments. There is a powerful rival analysis which sees the law as required to perform a more social function, paying greater regard to individual power relationships and personal circumstances in working out the most appropriate—rather than the most economically efficient—remedy in the circumstances. But this lobby too is better served by minimalist legal intervention designed to preserve individual liberty while securing protection from harm. This protection is best delivered by general compensatory awards supported by a narrowly circumscribed discretion to order (or refuse to order) specific performance or protective injunctions or aggravated damages if the particular circumstances warrant such intervention. The advantage of a discretion operating at this level is that it can be applied in a context-sensitive and individually tailored manner. The remedy is specifically targeted to the wrong.

11. Conclusions

The ideas underpinning this essay can be set out very simply. They all derive from a conviction that commercial practice is best supported by a law which promotes individual autonomy and protects market participants from harm. The introduction of a disgorgement remedy for breach of contract would fatally upset this balance. It would be a blunt remedial instrument, poorly suited to achieving its stated aims and likely to have wide-ranging adverse consequences. The better approach is to maintain (or, if necessary, adopt) specific, focused, context-sensitive strategies to meet the perceived difficulties.

If disgorgement were introduced as a general remedy for breach of contract, it would certainly satisfy a common and often strongly felt moral need to strip wrongdoers of their ill-gotten gains. But it would do this at the cost of promoting the specific performance of contractual obligations. This is the generally intended effect of disgorgement remedies. Neither society, nor contracting parties, nor the integrity of the institution of contract law require this as a generalised response to contractual arrangements. The consequential impositions on individual autonomy are not matched by any equivalent advances in protection from harm. In any event, it is better to adjudicate upon orders for specific performance at the time that performance is to be ordered, and in the light of its likely impact on both parties to the deal.

Nor is disgorgement warranted where compensatory damages are inadequate. If compensatory damages truly are inadequate, then the better response is to address the problem directly. The claimant's loss when a contract is breached is not necessarily linked in any meaningful way to the defendant's gain. Using one to remedy the other is therefore a strategy likely to be doomed to failure. These difficulties are not eliminated by selecting specific categories of breach as likely to leave claimants under-compensated. The basic difficulty persists: the claimant's loss is not related to the defendant's gain.

Nor is the disgorgement remedy warranted where the desire is simply to deter unacceptable conduct. If a particular type of breach is unacceptable and warrants a deterrent remedy, then it is unacceptable whether or not the defendant makes a collateral profit. The problem, again, is that the unacceptable behaviour is not necessarily related to the generation of profit. The remedy should reflect this. It should focus directly on the behaviour, not on the peripheral issue of profits. This means that a punitive order targeted at the wrong is likely to be a more appropriate and effective deterrent than disgorgement. This approach is equally apt in the case of cynical contract breakers. If such behaviour is deemed unacceptable by society, then a punitive response is warranted, and this remains true whether or not the breach was profit generating.

In short, the disgorgement remedy should not be embraced. It is not likely to deliver adequate compensation to claimants or effective deterrents against defaulting defendants. This is because there is a fundamental disjunction between the problems being addressed and the solutions being advocated. The harms suffered by a claimant, or the classes of contractual breach deemed unacceptable, are simply not linked to the size of the defendant's profits or the ability to generate them. Compulsory disgorgement is therefore unlikely to solve these particular conundrums and is sure to distort the general commercial landscape. By contrast, a remedy for breach of contract which enables recovery of the claimant's loss is well-suited to advancing the aims of commercial markets. Those aims centre on the promotion of individual autonomy and the protection of market participants from harm. What the commercial law of the future does need to do, however, is to ensure that those losses are assessed on a properly responsive commercial basis. In particular, commercial contract law needs to recognise that losses take many forms, and that those suffering amenity damages or losses associated with overpayments for benefits not received must be adequately recompensed.

Postscript

The opinions of the House of Lords in *AG v Blake* were delivered on 27 July 2000. As predicted in this chapter, the House (by a majority of 4:1) held that there was no reason in principle why a breach of contract could not be remedied by an account of profits (a term they preferred to restitutionary damages and, presumably, to disgorgement). Such a remedy was warranted only in exceptional circumstances, and the case before them was sufficiently exceptional.

Space and timing do not permit a detailed assessment of the judgments or their ramifications. As might be expected, Lord Hobhouse's dissenting opinion seems, to these authors, to have more to recommend it than the majority view. Lord Nicholls gave the leading judgment for the majority.[128] He said:

> "It will be only in exceptional cases, where those remedies [of damages, specific performance, injunction or fiduciary accountability] are inadequate, that any question of accounting for profits will arise. No fixed rules can be prescribed. The court will have regard to all the circumstances, including the subject matter of the contract, the purpose of the contractual provision which has been breached, the circumstances in which the breach occurred, the consequences of the breach and the circumstances in which relief is being sought. A useful general guide, although not exhaustive, is whether the plaintiff had a legitimate interest in preventing the defendant's profit-making activity and, hence, in depriving him of his profit."

He held, further, that the Court of Appeal's categorisation (skimped performance and negative obligations) did not assist in making the necessary decision. Nor, he agreed, did the cynical nature of the breach, or the fact that the breach enabled the defendant to enter into an alternative profit-generating contract, of themselves, suggest that an account of profits was warranted. On the facts here, however, he viewed the Crown as having a legitimate interest in preventing Blake from profiting from the disclosure of official information, whether classified or not, while he was a member of the secret service or after: Blake should not have a financial incentive to break his contractual undertaking. This view was confirmed by the perceived analogies between Blake's contractual undertaking and a fiduciary's or a confidant's equitable obligations.[129] An account of profits was seen as appropriate in all three cases.

Lord Hobhouse disagreed. He saw this as awarding the Crown a remedy for a cause of action which it did not have. He divided legal remedies into those which enforced performance of an obligation and those which gave a substitute for performance. In the former category were orders to specifically perform, to make restitution or to account. In the latter category were orders to pay compensation, whether for torts or for breaches of contract. Since Blake was neither a fiduciary nor a confidant, nor a holder of Crown property, there were no unspent obligations which the Crown could enforce against him. It could only sue for breach of contract. The remedy for this was confined to compensation, quantified to provide substitute performance. The precedents went no further than this, he thought; they did not support awards measured according to the gain made by the defendant. Accordingly, he thought that the Crown could not be given an account of profits without doing violence to principle, no matter how strong the policy suggesting that criminals such as Blake should be deprived of the fruits of their criminal conduct.

The majority, it seems, perceived both a gap in the law and the need to fill it with the remedy of an account of profits. These authors remain of the view, with Lord Hobhouse, that the arguments in favour of either assertion are not compelling. The concerns raised in this chapter are left unaddressed in the analysis advanced by the majority.

In conclusion, perhaps the most remarkable feature of this extraordinary saga is that the House of Lords has had the opportunity to adjudicate upon matters which the parties themselves had not elected, at any stage, to put into play.

[128] Lord Goff and Lord Browne-Wilkinson simply agreed, with Lord Browne-Wilkinson amending the form of the order in a manner which, with respect, seems more consistent with the majority assertion that the remedy was not proprietary. Lord Steyn also agreed, but added his own confirming comments.

[129] Although Blake was not a fiduciary and the information was not confidential.

16

Consumer Law into the Next Millennium: A Serious Service Fault?

JOHN LOWRY AND DAVID OUGHTON

Introduction

Consumers of goods enjoy the protection of a guarantee of the quality of the products they receive,[1] but the same cannot be said for the consumer of services given that the service provider is only liable on proof of fault.[2]

Sadly, from a consumer perspective the service industry has its fair share of "cowboy" operators who are prepared to cut corners and take advantage of the inexperience of some of their customers. Recent case law and concerns expressed by the Office of Fair Trading illustrate the point. For example, the builder employed to construct a swimming pool to the depth of seven feet six inches in *Ruxley Electronics & Construction Ltd* v. *Forsyth*[3] in fact, constructed a pool to the depth of six feet, thereby saving himself additional costs, but was not required to remedy the defect so as to give the consumer the end result requested. Similarly, the car servicing industry has been informed that it is to be the subject of an Office of Fair Trading enquiry on the ground that, "the nature of the service leaves many consumers at risk of being exploited by traders doing the work. This is a sector in urgent need of investigation."[4] This has been followed by a more recent statement of concern about the car

[1] Sale of Goods Act 1979, s. 14(2). Moreover where goods are required for some specific purpose made known to the seller, the Sale of Goods Act 1979, s. 14(3) requires the goods to be fit for that particular purpose, provided it is reasonable for the consumer to rely on the skill and judgement of the seller in selecting goods appropriate for the identified purpose. Similar terms are also implied into other contracts for the supply of goods under the Supply of Goods and Services Act 1982, ss. 4(2) and (4) and under the Supply of Goods (Implied Terms) Act 1973, ss. 10(2) and (3).

[2] Supply of Goods and Services Act 1982, s. 13.

[3] [1994] 3 All ER 801.

[4] See *Fair Trading News* (Office of Fair Trading, July 1999) "Lifting the bonnet on car servicing", available on http://www.oft.gov.uk

servicing sector which indicates that in the last decade the number of consumer complaints regarding car servicing and repairs has more than doubled.[5] The statement continues by identifying a number of areas of concern including the failure of garages to give information on what work is to be done; the fact that faults are often introduced during routine servicing and that work, generally, can be very shoddy. In the same sector, the Office of Fair Trading has identified a recent instance in which a car mechanic was sentenced to fifteen and a half months imprisonment for contempt of court when, after previous fines and a suspended sentence, he continued to provide poor quality work, in breach of an order made under the Fair Trading Act 1973, Part III.[6]

It is not just the car servicing sector which has attracted consumer complaints. Recent newspaper headlines have highlighted matters such as the mis-selling of pensions and mortgages by financial institutions. Widespread concern over holiday disasters has led to the introduction of a form of strict liability for tour operators in the form of the Package Travel, Package Holidays and Package Tours Regulations 1992.[7] Furthermore, the glass and glazing industry has produced grounds for consumer dissatisfaction over the years for late completion of work and shoddy workmanship.

The primary difficulty is to ascertain how best the consumer interest is to be protected. Some might argue that a stronger mechanism of administrative control of the service sector might pay dividends. For example, it is virtually impossible to set up business in Germany as a builder without first having secured approval from a relevant trade guild. As a result only recognised and appropriately qualified traders may deal with consumers.

Current thinking in the Department of Trade and Industry seems to suggest that the preferred governmental approach is to look for an expansion in the number of trade association codes of practice under the guidance of the Office of Fair Trading, within the powers conferred on that body under the Fair Trading Act 1973.[8] Unfortunately, voluntary codes of practice have a number of drawbacks which make their use, as an instrument of consumer protection, less than desirable. In particular, there is no guarantee that all traders in a given sector of trade will be members of a relevant trade association. Furthermore, the history of the use of self-regulation as a mode of consumer protection illustrates that some trade associations do not enforce their code of practice as vig-

[5] Office of Fair Trading, *A Driving Force for Change* (January 2000). Available on http://www.oft.gov.uk/html/trading/ftr23–01.htm. The car servicing market is valued at £9 billion *per annum* and most recent surveys show that this market attracted 27,000 complaints.

[6] See *Fair Trading News* (Ofiice of Fair Trading, October 1999), "Mechanic jailed for shoddy work", available on http://www.oft.gov.uk

[7] SI 1992/3288, introduced to implement the EC Directive 90/314/EC on Package Travel, Package Holidays and Package Tours.

[8] See *Modern Markets, Confident Consumers* (DTI, 1999), ch. 4. Available on http://www.dti.gov.uk/consumer/whitepaper

orously as might be expected by consumers. In addition, there are known difficulties associated with the fact that codes of practice are not rules of law and therefore, there may be a diminished ability on the part of the trade association to apply appropriate sanctions in the face of a breach of the code by a member trader. Also there is not always an adequate redress mechanism provided for by trade association codes of practice, with the result that a consumer may be informed that a member trader has breached a code of practice, but is not required to give full compensation in respect of the loss suffered by the consumer. It is our contention that it would be desirable to develop a more specific civil law remedy for consumers along the lines of the guarantee of quality and fitness for purpose given to the consumer of goods under the Sale of Goods Act 1979, section 14(2) and (3).

The Varieties of Service Contracts

The provision of pure services encompasses a wide variety of day-to-day activities.[9] Typical examples range from professional advisors such as doctors, lawyers, accountants, surveyors, and architects. The consumer may also require pure services from providers of leisure (including tour operators), vehicle servicing, carriers, film processors and cleaning services.[10] Of growing significance are financial services such as insurance, including investment vehicles such as ISAs, and consumer credit. However, unlike other pure services, those of a financial nature generally involve a long-term commitment on the part of the consumer. It will be demonstrated that many so-called pure service contracts ultimately involve the delivery of a finished product and it is upon this element of the transaction that the protective anxiety of consumer law should focus.

The Current Regime of Protection: the Unmet Needs of the Service Consumer

The Supply of Goods and Services Act 1982, section 13, implies a term into contracts for the supply of services that the provider will exercise reasonable care and skill, thereby codifying the common law position before 1982,

[9] See Supply of Goods and Services Act 1982, s. 12(1). This definition excludes contracts for services such as contracts of employment or apprenticeship: (s. 12(2)). Other exclusions include the services of advocates, company and building society directors and arbitrators (see SI 1982/1771; SI 1983/902 and SI 1985/1).

[10] Other obvious examples include furniture removals and window cleaning. See further, *Service Please* (London, National Consumer Council, 1981), p. 4 *et seq.*

importing a general negligence standard which is considerably less onerous a duty than that to which suppliers of goods are subject.[11] Accordingly, it remains the case that the consumer of services is in a considerably worse position than the consumer of a defective product.

Whether the consumer sues in contract under section 13 of the 1982 Act, or in tort under *Donoghue* v. *Stevenson*,[12] he or she is confronted with the numerous policy considerations which limit the imposition of fault-based liability.[13] More particularly the crucial issue, upon which hangs the measure of protection the law is prepared to allow the consumer, is the court's classification of the damage suffered. If the consumer's loss is categorised as property damage, then provided the settled principles of negligence which govern liability for misfeasance are satisfied, liability for losses which are not considered too remote a consequence will follow. But, if the consumer's loss is viewed as purely economic, the full weight of policy considerations will be brought to bear by the court as a means of limiting or circumventing the service provider's liability. It is to this scenario we now turn.

The Conundrum Posed by Pirelli and Murphy

Take the following situation: P engages O, a firm of consulting engineers, to design a chimney for his house. The chimney is built according to O's specifications which also stipulated the requisite construction materials. However, the specified cement proved to be unsuitable and cracks appeared at the top of the chimney rendering the structure unsafe. The chimney is dangerous and has to be partly demolished and rebuilt.

If the approach of the House of Lords in *Pirelli General Cable Works Ltd* v. *Oscar Faber & Partners*,[14] were to be followed, P would be able to establish liability by recourse to settled principles governing property damage. The consultant engineers would be treated as the producer of a qualitatively defective product for, on facts analogous to the above hypothetical, Lord Fraser of Tullybelton expressed the opinion that the plaintiff had received a damaged article when, but for the defendant's negligence, he would have had a sound one.[15]

[11] See further, Woodroffe, *Goods and Services—The New Law* (London, Sweet & Maxwell, 1982) and Oughton and Lowry, *Textbook on Consumer Law* (London, Blackstone Press, 1997), ch. 8. It has been cogently argued that the standard required of the supplier of consumer services is too low: see Stephenson and Clark, National Consumer Council Paper (1985). Cf. the views of the Law Commission in Report No. 156 (Cmnd 9773, 1986), para. 2.24.

[12] [1932] AC 562.

[13] See, further, Brazier and Murphy, *Street on Torts* (London, Butterworths, 1999), p. 210 *et seq.*

[14] [1983] 2 AC 1.

[15] *Ibid.*, at 16.

At its base level, the simplicity of Lord Fraser's solution is attractive. Provided the tri-partite test laid down by Lord Bridge in *Caparo Industries plc* v. *Dickman*[16] is satisfied, a legal duty of care will be owed by the service provider. For property damage, as with physical injury, the focus of the court is generally bound up with principle rather than issues of policy.[17] This is not to say that the determination of the appropriate parameters and intensity of a defendant's duty of care is necessarily a straightforward exercise. Indeed, complexities do arise because of the nebulous nature of the duty concept and because the delineation of a defendant's particular duty of care is necessarily a fact intensive process.[18] This is manifestly apparent in negligence actions for losses arising out of non-feasance where the conceptual basis of liability continues to remain blurred.[19] But the *Pirelli* approach in categorising the loss suffered as a result of the defective design service as representing property damage avoids the pitfalls of the policy considerations which underlie liability for pure economic loss. If *Pirelli* had been allowed to stand on its face value, the consumer's position in establishing negligence liability would at least be relatively straightforward.[20] However, this was not to be.

The approach taken in *Pirelli* now has to be read in the light of the landmark decision of the House of Lords in *Murphy* v. *Brentwood DC*.[21] Although stopping short of actually overruling *Pirelli*, the reasoning adopted by the House of Lords in *Murphy* proceeds on the basis that *Pirelli* should be viewed as falling within *Hedley Byrne* principles relating to negligent advice.[22] The one important difference in the majority of consumer transactions is that it is generally very likely that there will be a contractual relationship between the service provider and the consumer. As a result, it should not be difficult to establish the necessary degree of proximity required by the law and that harm to the consumer is foreseeable. However, it is still clear that the requirement that it

[16] [1990] 2 AC 605 at 617–18. In Lord Bridge's view the test for determining the existence of a legal duty of care requires affirmative answers to the following: Was the damage to the plaintiff reasonably foreseeable? Was the relationship between the plaintiff and the defendant sufficiently proximate? Is it just and reasonable to impose a duty of care?

[17] Foreseeability without more is not sufficient to create a legal duty of care, all three limbs of Lord Bridge's test, *supra*, must be satisfied; see *Marc Rich & Co AG* v. *British Rock Marine Co Ltd* [1996] AC 211.

[18] In *Marc Rich & Co.* v. *Bishop Rock Marine Co, ibid.*, Lord Steyn adopted the view of the majority of the Court of Appeal, [1994] 3 All ER 686 at 692–3, that the three requirements for a duty of care are not to be treated as wholly separate and distinct requirements but rather as convenient and helpful approaches to the pragmatic question whether a duty should be imposed in any given case. In the end whether the law does impose a duty in any particular circumstances depends upon those circumstances.

[19] See *Smith* v. *Littlewoods Organisation Ltd.*[1987] AC 241 and Murphy, [1996] *CLJ* 43.

[20] This is not to suggest, however, that fault-based liability is the preferred option over strict liability (as to which, see *infra*). The point is that if liability were to remain negligence-based, the loss should be viewed as property damage.

[21] [1990] 2 All ER 908.

[22] [1990] 2 All ER 908 at 919 per Lord Keith.

should be just and reasonable to impose liability on the defendant applies to cases of physical and property damage as well as to economic loss.[23] However, it is suggested that if the duty to provide a service of an acceptable standard of quality and fitness were to be enshrined in statute, the possible difficulties of establishing a duty situation would be reduced. The problem caused by the distinction between acts and words is that words of advice such as those given by architects and engineers lead to the performance of the act of building and may be inseparable.[24] Moreover, the interpretation given of *Pirelli* in *Murphy* ignores an express *dictum* of Lord Fraser to the effect that the engineers in *Pirelli* were not liable for negligent advice.[25] Yet it has since been authoritatively decided that *Hedley Byrne* liability will extend to economic loss caused by a negligent performance of a service. In *Henderson* v. *Merrett Syndicates Ltd*,[26] Lord Goff said that this wider principle "rests upon a relationship between the parties, which may be general or specific to the particular transaction, and which may or may not be contractual in nature".[27]

While the extension of *Hedley Byrne* liability to cover negligent performance of services is to be welcomed, at least in so far as it extends the level of consumer protection, nevertheless it is suggested that the better approach would be to draw a rebuttable inference to the effect that service providers, where appropriate, are to be viewed as suppliers of finished products so that consumers can avoid the pitfalls of establishing fault and rely, instead, upon strict liability.

Contracts for the supply of goods and contracts for the supply of services

It can be seen from the foregoing discussion that the range of services available to consumers is very wide and that affecting that range of services are a number of policy issues which might suggest that they be treated differently from contracts for the supply of goods. However, one particular type of service provision is so close in nature to a contract for the supply of goods as to be almost indistinguishable. Where a consumer contracts for the supply and installation of a bathroom suite by a plumber or where a consumer contracts

[23] See *Marc Rich & Co.* v. *Bishop Rock Marine Co* [1996] AC 211.

[24] See Stapleton, (1991) 107 *LQR* 249.

[25] [1983] 2 AC 1 at **. See also Oughton, Lowry and Merkin, *Limitation of Actions* (London, LLP, 1998), p. 260 *et seq* on the limitation issues raised by this case.

[26] [1995] 2 AC 145.

[27] *Ibid.*, at 180. But cf. *Stovin* v. *Wise* [1996] AC 923 on the continued relevance of the "general reliance" theory.

with a carpenter for the construction of a set of display shelves, there is both a supply of goods and a supply of services. What is clear under the present state of the law is that if the goods supplied by the plumber or the carpenter are inherently defective, there is a guarantee of the quality of those goods under the Supply of Goods and Services Act 1982, section 4(2). But if the defect in the end product is said to emanate from the provision of the service rather than from an inherent defect in the goods supplied, liability rests on the ability of the consumer to prove that the service provider was at fault under the Supply of Goods and Services Act 1982, section 13.

Distinguishing between a contract for the supply of goods and one for the supply of services is very difficult. For example, if a man is admitted to hospital and is injected with a spinal anaesthetic and suffers paralysis because of undiscoverable defects in the anaesthetic, the liability of the anaesthetist is fault-based.[28] But where cows are injected with a defective serum by a veterinary surgeon and die as a result of those defects, the veterinary surgeon may be liable without proof of fault on the basis that he has given a guarantee of the quality of the serum.[29] Admittedly, the example of the anaesthetist is one in which liability rested on the tort of negligence, but the position would be the same had he provided his services pursuant to a contract. Here the highest level of expected contractual performance, in the absence of an express or implied promise to guarantee a successful result, is that the anaesthetist will exercise reasonable care and skill, since in medical science all things, or nearly all things, are uncertain.[30]

The tests used to distinguish a supply of goods from a supply of services do not make it easy to separate the two varieties of contract.[31] Moreover, it is relatively easy to think of examples of sale of goods contracts which involve an element of labour, and service contracts which involve a supply of goods. For example, in the former category are contracts to sell a piece of machinery subject to a stipulation that it must first be removed from its location.[32] The case law seems to treat a contract to paint a portrait as a contract for the skill of the artist.[33] In some instances there is both skill involved in the manufacture of

[28] *Roe* v. *Minister of Health* [1954] 2 QB 66.

[29] *Dodd* v. *Wilson* [1946] 2 All ER 691.

[30] See *Thake* v. *Maurice* [1986] 1 All ER 497 at 511 per Nourse LJ. See also *Perlmutter* v. *Beth David Hospital* 122 NE 2d 792 (1955).

[31] Some of the difficulties created by the older case law may derive, at least in part, from the now defunct requirement that contracts for the sale of goods valued at more than £10 had to be evidenced in writing under the provisions of the Statute of Frauds 1677. A good example can be found in *Lee* v. *Griffin* (1861) 1 B & S 272 where there was an oral contract for the manufacture and sale of two sets of false teeth, but the buyer died before payment had been made. Since the contract was regarded as one of sale, the executor of the deceased was able to have the contract declared unenforceable.

[32] *Underwood* v. *Burgh Castle Cement Co Ltd* [1922] 1 KB 343.

[33] *Robinson* v. *Graves* [1935] 1 KB 579. Cf. *Isaacs* v. *Hardy* (1884) Cab & El 287.

goods and further collateral skill involved in their installation, in which case, the transaction is most likely to be regarded as one for work and materials.[34]

In seeking to classify a contract as one for the supply of goods or one for the supply of a service, three general features need to be taken into consideration. One is to ask what is the substance of the contract so as to ascertain if the contract is, in essence, one for the skill of the provider or whether it is one for the supply of an end product. Alternatively, a distinction might be drawn on the basis of the comparative value of the supply of goods element set against the value of the service element.[35] Thirdly, if the contract involves the conveyance of property in goods it will be governed by the Sale of Goods Act 1979 provided that conveyance of property is not entirely incidental to the transaction. Generally, following the decision in *Robinson* v. *Graves,* the first of the preceding tests is applied, namely, that it is necessary to identify the substance of the contract. However, it is difficult to see why a contract to paint a portrait should be treated any differently from the contract to produce a set of false teeth in *Lee* v. *Griffin.* In each case there is a supply of goods combined with the exercise of a considerable degree of skill on the part of the artist or the dental technician. Moreover, in *Robinson* v. *Graves* there were also comments which seemed to suggest that the value of the skill used in painting the portrait was in excess of the value of the end product, but as has been noted above, this test was rejected in *Lee* v. *Griffin.* Perhaps the strongest justification for the very pragmatic decision in *Robinson* v. *Graves* is that if the court had regarded the contract as one for the sale of goods, the "purchaser" would have been able to break his contract with impunity on the ground that there was no written evidence of the existence of the contract, valued at more than £10, which was a requirement at the time. What this suggests is that it is virtually impossible to draw a sensible distinction between a contract for the sale of goods and a contract for work and materials where the two types of contract meet at the edges. Many other examples can be given. For example, when a party of diners attend a restaurant for a meal, they might be seen to purchase goods, especially in circumstances in which the meal served involves little expert preparation,[36] but it would not be too difficult to imagine circumstances in which a group of diners attended a restaurant because of the international reputation of the head chef, in which case it might be argued that the substance of the contract was the skill of that chef rather than the simple supply of an end product.

[34] *Anglo-Egyptian Navigation Co* v. *Rennie* (1875) LR 10 CP 271 (contract for work and materials where there was skill in manufacturing a boiler and skill in installing it). But cf. *Phillip Head & Sons Ltd* v. *Showfronts Ltd* [1970] 1 Lloyd's Rep 140 (sale despite the presence of skill in stitching together more than one piece of carpet and skill in fitting the carpet).

[35] A test decisively rejected in *Lee* v. *Griffin* (1861) 1 B & S 272 at 278 per Blackburn J.

[36] *Lockett* v. *A & M Charles Ltd* [1938] 4 All ER 170.

Arguments against the imposition of strict liability on the part of service providers

The traditional view is that the nature of a supply of services is such that it should be treated differently from a contract for the supply of goods. This is apparently the case because the sheer number of different types of contract covered by the phrase "supply of a service" is so great, ranging from the delivery of goods to an offshore oil rig to the repair of a domestic washing machine.[37] Because of this very wide range of affected contracts, it has been considered inappropriate in the past to add to the terms already implied at common law and under the Supply of Goods and Services Act 1982. In response to this, it is argued that by careful definition, it would be possible to reduce the range of contracts covered by any proposed reform. In the first place it is argued that any reform should apply only in relation to consumer transactions, which, for the purposes of other legislation, has been effectively done by an appropriate statutory definition.[38] Moreover, it is not suggested that all contracts involving the supply of a service to a consumer should be subject to a guarantee of fitness for purpose. For example, it might be undesirable to impose on a professional adviser such a duty, since the matter on which advice is given could be clouded in uncertainty to the extent that a guarantee of success could not be given. It would be unfortunate if a solicitor were to be taken to guarantee the success of future litigation in every case. Similarly, since the seeds of mortality are sown in everyone, it would be improper to impose on a surgeon an obligation to guarantee the success of a future surgical procedure. It would also be unrealistic to expect a financial adviser to guarantee the long-term performance of an investment vehicle such as an ISA product or an endowment policy. In contrast, where the supply of a service involves the provision of a tangible end product, it is suggested that a guarantee of the quality of not just the goods supplied, but also the work which goes into installing those goods ought to be given. In this way, the consumer is guaranteed the quality of not just the double glazing units supplied by the contractor but also the quality of the work which goes into fitting those units.

It has also been argued that in the case of a supply of goods, it is ultimately possible to trace the goods back to their originator, the manufacturer, who can be held responsible for any defects in them. In contrast, the supplier of a service is the originator of his "product" with the result that there is no one higher up the chain of distribution to whom responsibility may be deflected.

[37] See Law Commission, *Implied Terms in Contracts for the Supply of Services* (Law Comm. No. 156, Cmnd. 9773, 1986), para. 1.09.

[38] See Unfair Contract Terms Act 1977, s. 12; Consumer Protection Act 1987, s. 20(6).

However, the position of a service supplier is considerably stronger than that of a producer of goods, since the EC Product Liability Directive[39] and the Consumer Protection Act 1987 have subjected the manufacturer of consumer goods to a form of strict liability, under which it is not necessary for the consumer to prove fault on the part of the producer of a defective product. If the producer of goods is subject to a regime of strict liability, there appears to be little reason for taking a different view of service providers who also supply goods.

It is suggested here that the consumer of services has the same expectations of quality and fitness of the end-product as does the consumer of goods and that the consumer of services ought to be given adequate protection. This was certainly the understanding of the European Commission when they attempted to introduce a general set of rules governing the supply of services to consumers in 1990.[40] In their view, while many services are characterised by their "one-off" nature (which is sometimes intangible) and the fact that the service "disappears" at the time of damage to the consumer,[41] there is nevertheless an expectation on the part of consumers, who have little technical knowledge, that services provided will be reasonably safe.[42]

A further argument in favour of the privileged position of service providers is that, in many cases, the service provided is long-term in nature, whereas sales of goods tend to be one-off transactions that are complete relatively quickly. This may be true of the advisory services provided by professionals, but the same cannot be said of "supply and install" contracts such as car-servicing contracts and contracts to fit double glazing units. It is this last group of consumer contracts which repeated reports of the Office of Fair Trading and other bodies interested in consumer protection have identified as the ones which give rise to substantial consumer dissatisfaction.

Perhaps the greatest difficulty associated with a guarantee of quality and fitness in the context of a consumer services contract is that it is not always appreciated how difficult performance of the contract may prove to be. It may be the case that serious difficulties in performance of the contract may arise after the supplier's services have been contracted for. For example, a consumer might employ a builder to construct an ornamental pond in his back garden, only to discover that the nature of the land is such that substantial excavation work has to be carried out to remove rubble left behind by the house builder, before work on the pond can commence. In such a case, the increased cost of the work might make it uneconomic to continue with the contract at the price

[39] Directive 85/374/EEC.

[40] Draft Directive on the supply of consumer services (COM (90) 482 final, SYN 308, 91C, 12/11), OJ 1991 C12/8.

[41] *Ibid.*, recital 11.

[42] *Ibid.*, Art. 1(3) and recital 11.

originally agreed. In response to this, it is argued that the service provider, being a specialist, is more likely to be aware of the problems which might be encountered and ought to be able to make express provision for such events in the contract. Moreover, all that is suggested here is that the service provider should give a warranty of quality and fitness, as opposed to the condition applicable to contracts for the sale of goods, breach of which will give rise to a right of rejection. It might also be appropriate to allow the use of exemption clauses, subject to a requirement of reasonableness, so as to limit the possible extent of liability on the part of the service provider.

Strict liability already exists in certain areas of service provision

Although the general view of liability for defective services is that the service supplier is only liable on proof of fault, a closer examination of the true position reveals that in a number of cases a different regime prevails. If the service supplier is a bailee, as is the case with a number of suppliers of consumer services such as garages and laundries who take in consumer goods for repair, the bailee is only liable if he is at fault, but in such cases, the burden of proof is reversed.[43]

A similar approach to consumer services, in general, was adopted by the European Commission when they proposed the draft Directive on the supply of consumer services.[44] Although, the basic principle underlying the proposal was that a supplier of services should only be liable for defects causing damage to the health and physical integrity of consumers or their tangible property where caused by the fault of the provider, the burden of proving lack of fault was placed on the supplier. Clearly the intention was to bring consumer services law as close as possible into line with the introduction of a strict liability regime for producers of goods. However, the attempt at reform was introduced into a climate of political hostility during the adoption of the "subsidiarity" principle. There appeared to be little political will to take the matter further[45] despite the fact that a common principle applicable across the entire consumer

[43] *Houghland* v. *RR Lowe (Luxury Coaches) Ltd* [1962] 1 QB 694. It seems the same approach may not apply to the owner of a car park, since there may not be a voluntary transfer of possession sufficient to give rise to a bailment: *Ashby* v. *Tolhurst* [1937] 2 KB 242; *Fred Chappell Ltd* v. *National Car Parks Ltd*, *The Times*, 22 May 1987. Cf. *Ultzen* v. *Nichols* [1894] 1 QB 92.

[44] See *supra* n. 40.

[45] In the light of this hostility, the proposed Directive was withdrawn and a later Commission Communication (COM (94) 260) indicated that the intention was to concentrate on specific service sectors where particular needs could be established.

service sector might have liberated trade by reducing uncertainties regarding insurance costs borne by suppliers in competing Member States.[46]

In relation to what may be called "design and build" contracts of service, the courts have been prepared to impose a standard higher than that of reasonable care. On this basis, the supplier of the service may be deemed to have undertaken to produce a particular outcome.[47] In *Greaves & Co (Contractors) Ltd* v. *Baynham Meikle & Partners*,[48] the designers of a warehouse floor were taken to have impliedly warranted that the floor would be reasonably fit for the use of forklift trucks. The circumstances showed that the customer had made it clear that such trucks would be used. Furthermore, there had been a warning by the British Standards Institution that traffic vibration could cause cracks in the type of floor recommended by the defendants. Lord Denning MR reasoned that the common intention of the parties was:

> "that the engineer should design a warehouse which would be fit for the purpose for which it was required. That common intention gives rise to a term implied *in fact* . . . In the light of that evidence it seems to me that there was implied in fact a term that, if the work was completed in accordance with the design, it would be reasonably fit for the use of loaded stacker trucks. The engineers failed to make such a design and are, therefore, liable".[49]

While Browne and Geoffrey Lane LJJ concurred, both were at pains to emphasise that the decision laid down no general principle in relation to the obligations and liabilities of professional men. Nevertheless, although the decision concerned a business transaction, it is suggested that the approach adopted by Lord Denning would be of considerable benefit in reinforcing the position of consumers if it were to be applied to consumer services generally.

The decision in *Greaves & Co. (Contractors) Ltd* v. *Baynham Meikle & Partners* would seem to suggest that design services fall into a separate category in which the courts are more prepared to imply higher standards on the part of service suppliers in a manner which may be more easily equated with the position of the supplier of goods. But, in the field of building design services, it is important to relate the designer's obligations to those of the main contractor under his contract with the building owner.[50] Thus although a building designer may be taken to guarantee that his design will be fit for its

[46] Weatherill, *EC Consumer Law & Policy* ((Harlow) Addison, Wesley, Longman, 1997), p. 101.

[47] Where the contractual supplier of a service guarantees a result, this is likely to be an express term of the contract. However, the problem with express contractual terms is that the consumer must know exactly what he or she wants and negotiate with the supplier to that end. Since consumers are not experts, they may be unsure what they require and in consequence their contracts reflect this imprecision. Accordingly, the contractual expectations of consumers might be better achieved if the law were to imply certain basic standards.

[48] [1975] 3 All ER 99. See also G. K. *Serigraphics* v. *Dispro Ltd* (unreported, CAT 916, 1980).

[49] Greaves, *supra* n. 48, at 103–4.

[50] See *Independent Broadcasting Authority* v. *EMI Electronics Ltd* (1980) 14 BLR 1.

intended purpose, this liability may be negated by an express or implied term in the main contract to the effect that the main contractor has guaranteed the quality of the end product.[51]

In one particular area of consumer service provision, namely, the package holiday sector, steps have already been taken to improve the position of the consumer through the introduction of a stricter form of liability. Until the introduction of the Package Travel, Package Holidays and Package Tours Regulations 1992[52] the liability of a tour operator was clearly fault-based. For example, in *Wall* v. *Silver Wing Surface Arrangements*[53] the Walls booked a holiday in Tenerife in rooms on the third floor of a hotel which the defendants had inspected prior to including it in their brochure. Unknown to the defendants, the owners of the hotel had padlocked the gate at the end of a fire escape, with the result that it could not be used. A fire having broken out, the plaintiffs decided to make alternative escape plans by tying together a number of sheets to create a "rope". Sadly the knots did not hold and Mrs Wall was very seriously injured when she fell to the ground. In the absence of negligence on the part of the tour operators, no liability attached. Moreover, Hodgson J found it inconceivable that, had the officious bystander suggested to the parties the inclusion of a term to the effect that the consumers would be reasonably safe in using the hotel, the tour operators would have agreed to this. Specific emphasis was placed on the fact that a tour operator has no control over the running of the hotels or other travel services provided by third parties. All of this does not mean that the holiday-maker is unprotected at common law, since much will turn on the particular undertakings of the parties. If the tour operator has entered into an express agreement to provide all the services contracted for, then it will not matter if the failure to take care is comprised in the act of a third party employed by the tour operator, since the tour operator has undertaken personal responsibility towards the customer.[54]

The problem of identifying what terms can be implied into a package holiday contract is less of a stumbling block following the adoption of the EC Package Travel Directive as part of English law. Under the Package Travel, Package Holidays and Package Tours Regulations 1992, the tour operator is now liable for the "improper performance of the contract",[55] whoever in the contractual matrix is responsible for the failure to fulfil the consumer's expectations. The only escape for the tour operator arises where it can be proved (by the tour operator) that the improper performance is not due to the fault of the tour operator himself or a service provider engaged by the tour operator. Thus

[51] *Ibid.*, at 47–8 per Lord Scarman. See also *Samuels* v. *Davis* [1943] KB 526.
[52] SI 1992/3288.
[53] Unreported, 1981.
[54] *Wong Mee Wan* v. *Kwan Kin Travel Services* [1996] 1 WLR 38.
[55] SI 1992/3288, reg. 15(1).

if a holiday-maker were to step out of a hotel into the path of an on-coming vehicle driven by a local taxi driver, the tour operator would not be liable unless the taxi driver had been employed by the tour operator to take the holiday-maker on a trip. Similarly, the holiday-maker cannot be heard to complain if the improper performance is due to the fault of the consumer.[56]

At first sight, what the Regulations do is to impose strict liability on the tour operator, but closer scrutiny of the wording of the Regulations and the Package Travel Directive show that the tour operator is responsible for the proper performance of the *obligations* under the contract.[57] As a result, it is necessary to ascertain what those obligations are. If a court determines that the contract merely obliges the tour operator to exercise reasonable care, then the effect of regulation 15(1) will not be to impose strict liability, but merely to satisfy a fault-based standard. For example, suppose a tour operator were to state that a particular hotel has a swimming pool and this did prove to be the case. The tour operator will probably be taken to have complied with his contractual obligations even if the chlorination system failed to operate properly so that swimming in the pool became unsafe, unless it could be said that an unsafe swimming pool is not a swimming pool at all. In contrast, the tour operator would be liable if the promised pool had been turned into a sunken garden by the hotel owner during the low season.[58]

Conclusion

Despite the latitude which English law accords to service providers, other jurisdictions favour a much stricter approach. For example in Australia, subject to certain limited exceptions,[59] section 74(2) of the Trade Practices Act 1974 implies on the part of the supplier of a service, a warranty that the service will be reasonably fit for the purpose made known to him, whether "expressly or by implication", by the consumer, and that the service is of such quality that it might reasonably be expected to achieve the desired result. Incorporating such a provision into English law would not represent such a root and branch reform which, at first sight, it might appear to be. There already exists a body of case law which proceeds, at least in part, along these lines.

The Australian provision is also significant to the extent that it does not imply a condition of quality and fitness allowing rejection, but merely a warranty, giving rise to a remedy in damages. Furthermore, difficult cases involv-

[56] *Ibid.*, reg. 15(2). See also *Hartley* v. *Intasun* [1987] CLY 1149 (late arrival at airport).

[57] SI 1992/3288, reg. 15(1).

[58] See Grant and Mason, *Holiday Law* (London, Sweet & Maxwell, 1997), p. 120.

[59] These consist of, predominantly, professional advisory services and financial services.

ing unanticipated risks could be dealt with by the courts along lines already established under the Sale of Goods Act 1979, section 14. For example, if the consumer were to state his requirements in very general terms and unanticipated risks were to arise in the performance of the contract, it ought to be possible for the courts to limit the range of purposes regarded as "normal" for the purposes of the guarantee of reasonable or satisfactory quality.[60] Likewise, if there is any element of fault on the part of the consumer in using the "product" of the contract in an unanticipated manner, it would be possible to limit the supplier's liability to what could be reasonably expected in the circumstances.[61]

While it is accepted that there are different considerations applicable to many contracts for the supply of services, it is suggested that in the case of "supply and install" contracts the parallels with sale of goods contracts are so close that it would be possible to give a guarantee of both the supply of goods element and the service element. This might have the effect of increasing the costs of small-scale service providers, since most would want to look into the cost of obtaining appropriate insurance cover. But, ultimately, those costs would be passed on to the entire consumer community rather than being concentrated on the individuals who presently suffer as a result of a defective service element in the contracts they enter into.

[60] In *Aswan Engineering Establishment Co* v. *Lupdine Ltd* [1987] 1 All ER 135, buckets not stated to be required for export to a very hot Middle Eastern state were considered to be of merchantable quality if they were fit for export purposes generally and since the buyer had not stated his specific requirements other than in very general terms, the requirement of fitness for purpose was considered to impose no higher duty on the seller than a duty to supply goods which were of merchantable quality.

[61] *Heil* v. *Hedges* [1951] 1 TLR 512.

17

Criminal Law

RICHARD CARD AND ANDREW ASHWORTH

The social and technological contexts of the criminal law at the start of the third millennium differ markedly from those at the start of the twentieth century. The Internet, the equivalent in importance of the introduction of printing, has transformed global communications and commerce.[1] It provides new challenges for the criminal law. So does the Human Rights Act 1998, whose implementation will bring into sharp focus the need for the criminal law to be adequately defined and to be compatible with the European Convention on Human Rights 1950.

In November 1999, the Performance and Innovation Unit established by the Prime Minister predicted fundamental changes in the early part of the new millennium.[2] It identified five "drivers of change", three of which—globalisation, changing attitudes and values, and scientific innovation—will certainly impact on the criminal law.[3]

The rate of change is now so fast that it is difficult to gaze far into the future. In assessing the outlook, we have borne in mind not only the above considerations but also the fact that for the foreseeable future government policy (whichever of the two major parties is in power) will include low taxation and a continuing drive for cost-effectiveness. But governments are not the only players here, and we will refer also to the role of the courts and of academic lawyers.

[1] For an overview of telecommunications and crime which identifies, *inter alia*, current and emerging forms of criminality involving telecommunication systems, and the problems of dealing with them, see Grabosky and Smith, *Crime in the Digital Age* (New Brunswick, New Jersey, Transaction Publishers/Annandale, New South Wales, The Foundation Press, 1998).

[2] The Unit is part of the Cabinet Office. What is in the text was reported in *The Observer* on 21 November 1999. It is obtainable on www.cabinetoffice.gov.uk/innovation/1999/strategic-mainpage.htm

[3] The other two "drivers" identified were demographics and the environment.

Reform and modernisation of the substantive law: a stocktake of law reform proposals

In the last third of the twentieth century whole chunks of the substantive criminal law were substantially reformed and modernised, so as to make them fit for their purpose, often as a result of the recommendations of the Law Commission and the Criminal Law Revision Committee (CLRC). The following list indicates notable examples. The law of offences against property was essentially recast by the Theft Acts 1968 and 1978 (both based on CLRC reports),[4] the Criminal Damage Act 1971 and the Forgery and Counterfeiting Act 1981 (both based on Law Commission reports).[5] The common law offences of conspiracy and attempt were replaced (save for conspiracy to defraud and, possibly, conspiracy to corrupt public morals or to outrage public decency) by the statutory offences of conspiracy and attempts by Part I of the Criminal Law Act 1977 and the Criminal Attempts Act 1981 (both based on Law Commission reports).[6] The major offences against public order, hitherto common law offences of some imprecision, were abolished and replaced on the Law Commission's recommendation[7] by the statutory offences of riot, violent disorder and affray in Part I of the Public Order Act 1986. That Act also introduced a number of new offences and re-designed some existing provisions, although it is far from a comprehensive code of public order law.

These examples give the lie to any allegation that the Law Commission has had little effect in terms of actual criminal law reform. Further evidence is provided by the overall statistics for Law Commission reports in the area of substantive criminal law for the period 1966–95 inclusive. In that period there were twenty-four Law Commission reports recommending legislative reform (particularly in terms of simplification and modernisation) in this area. Seventeen of them led to legislation enacting their recommendations (wholly or almost wholly). The fate of three subsequent reports (on money transfers obtained by deception, involuntary manslaughter and corruption) is described *infra.* This overall success rate can be compared with that for reports in the other two areas on which the Law Commission has particularly concentrated since its inception. Twenty out of twenty-eight reports on land law,

[4] *Eighth Report: Theft and Related Offences* (Cmnd 2977, 1966); *Thirteenth Report: Section 16 of the Theft Act 1968* (Cmnd 6733, 1977).

[5] *Criminal Law: Report on Offences of Damage to Property* (Law Com No. 29, 1970); *Criminal Law: Report on Forgery and Counterfeit Currency* (Law Com No. 55, 1973).

[6] *Criminal Law: Report on Conspiracy and Criminal Law Reform* (Law Com No. 76, 1976); *Criminal Law: Attempt, and Impossibility in Relation to Attempt, Conspiracy and Incitement* (Law Com No. 102, 1980).

[7] *Criminal Law: Offences Relating to Public Order* (Law Com No. 123, 1983).

which recommended legislative reform, were implemented in the period 1966–95, and twenty-four out of twenty-eight such reports in the area of family law.

Of the CLRC's ten reports running from its *Eighth Report: Theft and Related Offences*[8] in 1966 to its last, *Eighteenth Report: Conspiracy to Defraud*[9] in 1986, eight made recommendations for legislative change to the substantive criminal law. Three of them have not been implemented, and two of the remainder have only been implemented in part.

The success of the Law Commission, in particular, must not, however, conceal the fact that there are swathes of the criminal law which remain unreformed, unmodernised and unsimplified despite Law Commission and CLRC reports: offences against the administration of justice (report published in 1979);[10] offences against religion and public worship (1985);[11] criminal libel (1985)[12] are possibly minor examples since, apart from perversion of the course of justice, charges for any of these offences are extremely rare. Towering over these unreformed areas is the whole area of offences against the person, fatal and non-fatal. Despite recommendations for the reform of this area of the law by the CLRC (in 1980)[13] and, in respect of non-fatal offences, by the Law Commission (in 1993)[14] whose recommendations have been accepted in principle by both the then and subsequent governments, legislation has not yet been forthcoming. A subsequent report, published by the Law Commission in 1996, dealt with involuntary manslaughter.[15]

The reform of offences against the person law ought to be a high priority in the new millenium. The law on non-fatal offences does not deal adequately with modern situations, and through its unclear and outdated language is liable to continue to create scope for legal argument with cases having to go on appeal for clarification. Given its overall statutory structure, there is little that the appellate courts can do but "patch up" the law in this area. The Law Commission has been supported in its criticism of the law in this area by calls for reform by the appellate courts.[16]

[8] Cmnd 2977 (1966).

[9] Cmnd 9873 (1986).

[10] *Offences of Interference with the Course of Justice* (Law Com No. 96).

[11] *Offences against Religion and Public Worship* (Law Com No. 143).

[12] *Criminal Libel* (Law Com No. 149).

[13] *Fourteenth Report: Offences Against the Person* (Cmnd 7844).

[14] *Legislating the Criminal Code: Offences against the Person and General Defences* (Law Com No. 218). In July 1997 the Government announced that it proposed to introduce legislation to reform the law of non-fatal offences (HC Deb, vol. 299, col. 578–579). It then waited until February 1998 to issue a consultation paper on the Law Commission's proposals (a novel procedure) as a first step in the process (*Violence: Reforming the Offences against the Person Act 1861* (Home Office, 1998)).

[15] *Legislating the Criminal Code: Involuntary Manslaughter* (Law Com No. 237).

[16] *Lynsey* [1995] 3 All ER 654 at 654–5, per Henry LJ; *Mandair* [1994] 2 All ER 715 at 725, per Lord Mustill.

It is not just in the area of substantive offences that reform is required. Governments have shown little interest in the general principles of the criminal law. The Law Commission report on the *Mental Element in Crime*[17] (published in 1978) met with no legislative response, nor did its report published in the previous year on *Defences of General Application.*[18] Both, however, provided a basis for provisions contained in the draft Criminal Law Bill, referred to *infra.*

Sexual offences law also requires attention if it is to accord with changing social values and attitudes in the early years of the new millenium and to avoid discrimination against the homosexual community incompatible with the Convention rights under the Human Rights Acts 1998. Piecemeal reform of sexual offences law has occurred since the 1960s, notably by the changes made in respect of male homosexual buggery and gross indecency (age of consent etc.) by the Sexual Offences Act 1967 and by the re-casting of the offence of rape by the Criminal Justice and Public Order Act 1994. On the other hand, wide-ranging proposals made by the Criminal Law Revision Committee in 1984 in its *Fifteenth Report: Sexual Offences*[19] have not—with isolated exceptions—been given legislative effect, nor were the recommendations in its *Seventeenth Report: Prostitution: Off-Street Activities.*[20] Equalising the age of consent for homosexual and heterosexual relations, and the introduction of an offence of sexual intercourse or activity with an under eighteen-year-old where an abuse of trust is involved, in 2000 are steps in the right direction but the law will still intrude unnecessarily into sexual relations where neither party is open to abuse or exploitation and it will still be discriminatory against male homosexual activity (by the requirement that sexual activity between "consenting adults" must be in private—which it is not if a third person is present). It is to be hoped that the comprehensive review announced in June 1998 of the current legislation relating to sexual offences produces a report reflecting contemporary attitudes to sexual behaviour, sexual orientation and sexual exploitation, which is compatible with modern interpretations of the European Convention on Human Rights and is given legislative effect.

Looming over everything is the failure of successive governments to implement the Law Commission's recommendations for the codification of the substantive criminal law. Until this is done, that law will remain incoherent and inconsistent, inaccessible and uncertain, and far from reasonably comprehensible. In addition, the failure to codify is a major obstacle to the systematic development of the criminal law.

[17] Law Com No. 89.
[18] Law Com No. 83.
[19] Cmnd 9213 (1984).
[20] Cmnd 9688 (1985).

Consistent with the terms of the Law Commission Act 1965, it has been the aim of the Law Commission, since its Second Programme of Law Reform in 1968[21] that there should be a Criminal Code, initially covering the general principles of criminal liability and certain specific offences, and subsequently criminal procedure, evidence and sentencing. Building on the draft Criminal Code Bill, prepared for it by a group of distinguished academic lawyers,[22] the Law Commission put forward in 1989 a comprehensive draft Criminal Code Bill,[23] covering offences against the person, offences against property, sexual offences and public order offences, as well as the general principles of liability. Much of this draft Code simply restated in simpler and consistent terminology the existing law. Parts of it, however, resolved matters of incoherence or uncertainty under the present law, while other parts incorporated various proposals for reform made in modern times. It became clear that a Bill as large as the Criminal Code Bill would present logistical difficulties for Parliament, and that this might increase government's reluctance to give parliamentary time to it, since it offered it no political or strategic advantage. Consequently, the Law Commission decided to put forward a number of shorter Bills on discrete areas of law as a way of progressing codification. When enacted these Bills would eventually be consolidated into a Criminal Code Act. However none of its three draft Bills to implement this strategy, on *Offences against the Person and General Defences*, on *Involuntary Manslaughter* and on *Corruption*, has yet been enacted.[24]

The delay in codifying the substantive criminal law has been the subject of adverse comment by judges. In *Baker*,[25] Brooke LJ, a former Chairman of the Law Commission, giving the judgment of the Court of Appeal, said:

> "[T]his case provides yet another illustration of the pressing need . . . for Parliament to codify these defences to common offences like assault and criminal damage in order to make them clear and accessible to both the criminal law practitioners . . . and to the public at large . . . [A]s judges we are very well placed to see how, to use the vivid phrase of Henry LJ in *Lynsey*[26] 'bad laws cost money and clog up courts with better things to do'. Convicted offenders are still having to wait an

[21] Law Com No. 14, Item XVIII.

[22] *Codification of the Criminal Law: A Report to the Law Commission* (Law Com No. 143, 1985).

[23] *Law Commission: A Criminal Code for England and Wales* (Law Com No. 177, 1989).

[24] See Law Com No. 218 (1993), Law Com No. 237 (1996) and Law Com No. 248 (1998) respectively.

[25] [1997] *Crim LR* 497, CA. The words quoted do not appear in the brief report; they do appear in the transcript available on LEXIS. His Lordship discussed the non-implementation issue extra-judicially in "The Law Commission and Criminal Law Reform" [1995] *Crim LR* 911. The former Lord Chief Justice has also called extra-judicially for a Criminal Code: "A Criminal Code: Must We Want for Ever?" [1998] *Crim LR* 694.

[26] [1995] 3 All ER 654 at 655. Henry J expressed similar statements to those of Brooke LJ ([1995] 3 All ER 654 at 659).

> unacceptably long time, often in custody, before their appeals are heard . . . In our judgment this case would not have troubled this court at all if the relevant principles had been set out clearly in codified form . . . We hope very much that the executive and the legislature will soon be able to afford a higher priority to important technical measures designed to codify the criminal law and to make it more accessible to those who have to use it than has apparently been possible in recent years".

In addition, as the former Chairman of the Law Commission has argued the "bringing home" of the ECHR by the Human Rights Act 1998 reinforces the need for the certainty which a Code could bring, if the principle of legality is to be observed.[27] However, it should be borne in mind that much of the content of the existing code is controversial—notably, the law on sexual offences and the law of homicide—as are some of the areas of criminal law it excludes (e.g. serious offences committed with motor vehicles and serious environmental and safety offences). It is therefore important not to allow the pursuit of formal and procedural virtues such as clarity, consistency and reasonable precision, necessary as these are, to obscure the deeper substantive issues about the limits of the criminal sanction and the grading of offences.

Social and technological change

The criminal law at the start of the third millennium needs to adjust to reflect changing social attitudes and values. One has to doubt whether society needs the protection in 2000 of the clutter of ancient offences, such as the following examples. The continuing need for the offence under section 3 of the Vagrancy Act 1824 of "simple" begging in public or for the offences under section 4 of the Vagrancy Act 1824 of "sleeping rough" (i.e. wandering abroad and lodging in a barn, unoccupied building, open air, tent etc., and not giving a good account of oneself) and of begging with the exposure of wounds or deformities, is doubtful.[28] The same may be said of offences under section 28 of the Town Police Clauses Act 1847 (and its counterpart the Metropolitan Police Act 1839), which contains a mind-boggling list of outmoded offences, such as slaughtering cattle in a street, rolling or carrying any cask, tub or hoop or wheel on the pavement, other than in the course of loading or unloading a cart or for crossing the pavement, flying a kite in the street, shaking a rug or mat in the street (except a door-mat before 8 a.m.), ordering or permitting a window cleaner to stand on a window-sill to clean the windows of premises of which

[27] Hon. Mrs Justice Arden "Criminal Law at the Crossroads: The Impact of Human Rights from the Law Commission's Perspective and the Need for a Code" [1999] *Crim LR* 439.

[28] In 1976 a Home Office Working Party on Vagrancy and Street Offences recommended the reform of these offences.

one is the occupier, depositing ash or nightsoil in the street, and keeping a pigstye in the street.

To the extent that conduct of such types requires the intervention of the criminal law, it can be dealt with where necessary by other more focused legislation, such as the Refuse Disposal (Amenity) Act 1978, the Highways Act 1980, the Environmental Protection Act 1990 and road traffic legislation.

The law must also continue to adjust to the impact of technological advances, as it did in the 1990s. The Computer Misuse Act 1990, essentially enacting the recommendations of the Law Commission,[29] was necessary to deal effectively with computer hackers, hackers who intend thereby to facilitate the commission of a serious crime and those who without authority modify computer material. The House of Lords' decision in *Preddy*[30] about the inapplicability of the offence of obtaining property belonging to another by deception, contrary to section 15 of the Theft Act 1968, to obtaining advances credited to a bank account, because the credit obtained was not property belonging to another, led to a speedy reference to the Law Commission, an equally speedy report,[31] and a swift enactment of the report's recommendations (an offence of obtaining a money transfer by deception) by the Theft (Amendment) Act 1996. Money talks!

The law needs to be adjusted to deal adequately with other technological advances. The summary offence of possession of an indecent photograph of a child, contrary to section 160 of the Criminal Justice Act 1988 as amended, needs several further amendments if the law is to achieve its goal and if the innocent are to be protected. Another example would be the much-heralded advent of cyber-narcotics, about which the criminal law is silent. A further area of technological advance which has left the law behind is fraud in the context of cashless trading and trading over the Internet. Where an alleged deception involves unauthorised use of a cheque or credit card, the various offences of obtaining *by* deception under the Theft Acts 1968 and 1978 can only be proved by a perversion of the requirement of a causal relationship between the deception and what has been obtained.[32] The Law Commission's provisionally proposed separate offence of intentionally or recklessly causing a legal liability to pay money to be imposed on another (e.g. a bank), knowing that the other does not consent to this and that one has no right to do so,[33] is one way of dealing with the problem. Another problem with these deception offences, made even more important by the development of e-commerce over the Internet, is

[29] *Computer Misuse* (Law Com No. 186, 1989).

[30] [1996] AC 815, HL.

[31] *Legislating the Criminal Code: Offences of Dishonesty (Money Transfers)* (Law Com No. 243).

[32] *Charles* [1977] AC 177, [1976] 3 All ER 112, HL; *Lambie* [1982] AC 449, HL.

[33] *Legislating the Criminal Code: Fraud and Deception* (Law Com Consultation Paper No. 155, 1999).

that, because there cannot be a deception unless someone is induced to believe that something is true which is false,[34] there are inherent limits on their application where the fraud is practised in a computer or other machine; one cannot deceive a machine.[35] This does not matter too much if one obtains another's property by in-putting false information into a machine, because theft may be committed. On the other hand, if something else is obtained by such means, like an insurance policy, overdraft rights or increased overdraft borrowing, a job, services or the evasion of liability to pay money, no substantive offence is currently committed. The problem would be resolved (wholly or partly, depending on the definition given to "a service") if the Law Commission's provisional conclusion that it should be criminal to obtain a service without the permission of the person providing it, albeit without the deception of a human mind, either by extending the offence of theft or by creating a separate theft-like offence[36] is enacted, but obviously the other types of such fraud would remain outside the law. These problems, which originate in the fact that the CLRC's *Eighth Report: Theft and Related Offences*[37] adopted, modernised and applied to new offences the notion of false pretences in the Larceny Act 1916, are perhaps not surprising in the light of the fact that the use of cheque or credit cards in this country was in its infancy in 1966 and that "trading" over the Internet or with a machine was an unimagined phenomenon when the report was published.[38] One can appreciate how fast the context has changed when a great modernising statute just over thirty years old itself requires modernisation.

The Internet

The virtual instantaneity of the channels of communication provided by the Internet, their ability to transcend national boundaries,[39] their accessibility and breadth of reach, and the difficulties of authenticating the identity or location of someone posting a message on it, and hence the available anonymity of such a person, make the Internet an attractive medium for various activities which may offend the existing criminal law. The Internet is used for the per-

[34] *Re London and Globe Finance Corpn Ltd* [1903] 1 Ch 728 at 732; cited with approval in *DPP* v. *Ray* [1974] AC 370 at 379 and 384, per Lords Reid and Morris.

[35] Law Commission Consultation Paper No. 155, *supra* n. 33, para. 8.36 *et seq.*

[36] *Ibid.*, para. 8.58.

[37] Cmnd 2977 (1966).

[38] Grabosky and Smith, *Crime in the Digital Age, supra* n. 1, at 154.

[39] Several of the papers in the [1998] *Criminal Law Review, Special Edition, Crime, Criminal Justice and the Internet,* deal with the consequences of this in respect of the traditional regulatory powers of states.

petration of various kinds of fraud and money laundering (e.g. via the use of smart cards),[40] for drug-trafficking and for the dissemination of obscene material,[41] child pornography,[41] racist material[42] and material liable to prejudice a fair trial. A threat to kill has been made over the Internet.[43] Stalking over the Internet is increasingly common.[44] The increasing sophistication of Internet-users (e.g., the use of encryption techniques, password protected files and methods of hiding files on a computer disk) mean that detection of those responsible for such activities is hard. Even if they are detected, their use can escape regulation by a simple relocation of site.

The Internet is simply an international network of millions of computers, via "Internet service providers" (commercial organisations or public institutions) who provide access via their computers to other networks of computers, without any centralised storage location. There is no single, centralised entity, governmental or non-governmental, in any state, let alone globally across the one hundred and fifty-plus states "on the Internet", which regulates the Internet. Indeed, the nature of the Internet means that it is not technically feasible for a single entity to control all the information posted on it. This is one reason why the Internet is very difficult to regulate. Although the services offered by a service provider vary, the provider normally also offers e-mail, free webspace and access to newsgroups (i.e. discussion groups which communicate via the Internet), all of which require data to be stored on the service provider's computers for access by "customers".

English criminal law at the start of the third millenium can only hope to deal effectively with originators of Internet material who are detected if those persons are already within its jurisdiction (or elsewhere in the United Kingdom).

How, then, is the Internet to be regulated? One option is to impose responsibility on Internet service providers, either via secondary liability for offences committed by users (after all providers have the right of control over them) or via a specific offence built around a duty to block access to material deemed unlawful or offensive. Not only does the latter technique raise worrying issues

[40] See Grabosky and Smith, *Crime in the Digital Age*, *supra* n. 1, chs 7–9.

[41] *Fellows* [1997] 2 All ER 548, CA. Also see news features in *The Independent*, 28 August 1996; *The Guardian*, 18 September 1996; *The Times*, 21 November 1995; *The Daily Telegraph*, 25 March 1996, 22 May 1996 and 13 November 1996.

[42] See US Anti-Defamation League Report, *High-Tech Hate: Extremist Use of the Internet* ([October] 1997). See the Home Secretary's condemnation of racist abuse on the Internet (14 September 1998), at http://www.coi.gov.uk/coi/depts/GHO/GHO98Q3.html

[43] *Daily Telegraph*, 15 December 1999.

[44] For examples, see Ellison and Akdeniz, "Cyberstalking: The Regulation of Harassment on the Internet" [1998] *Criminal Law Review, Special Edition, Crime, Criminal Justice and the Internet* 29 at 31–2. For more recent examples, see *The Guardian*, 16 October1999; 29 November 1999.

about censorship,[45] but either approach raises issues about the reality of a service provider's ability to vet material on the Internet, estimated at two hundred thousand additions a day in 1999,[46] although it is somewhat easier to block access to identified newsgroups (such as those of a paedophile nature).

One has to conclude that the criminal law of individual states is incapable alone of dealing effectively with the new medium. It seems that the answer must lie in the use of other methods as well. It has been suggested that the solution could lie with "a new multi-layered governance approach". This would involve public and private bodies at a national and supranational level and "new self[47]-regulatory solutions".[48] An approach along these lines has, indeed, been endorsed by the *Action Plan on Promoting Safer Use of the Internet*, adopted by the European Parliament and the EU Council in 1999, which speaks in terms of the promotion of industry self-regulation and content-monitoring (for example, dealing with content such as child pornography or content which incites hatred), and of encouraging industry to provide filtering tools and rating systems.

The *Action Plan* is far from perfect. Industry self-regulation and content monitoring may be of limited value for the reasons given above. Filtering software can be crude in its effect, blocking out unintended material and unduly restricting the right to communicate and receive information. As the House of Commons Select Committee on Culture Report, *The Multi-Media Revolution*,[49] stated, although international initiatives will have an important impact on national Internet regulation, "the question is whether attempts at regulation can be anything more than optimistically indicative rather than genuinely effective". Nevertheless, the plan contains the seeds of a more effective regime than mere reliance on the criminal law. Like the references to diversion and decriminalisation infra, it would lead to diminished reliance on the criminal law, although the reasons for the change are different. A reversal of the trend of recent years of seeking to deal with every social problem "after the event" by making it an offence, which has not been notably successful, would be welcome.

45 See Akdeniz, "Child Pornography on the Internet" (1998) 148 *NLJ* 451.

46 *The Guardian*, 18 November 1999.

47 "In this way of thinking 'self' both means as an individual solution (e.g. individual protection from cybercrime), or as a more collective solution (e.g. codes of conduct for ISPs or the introduction of hotlines and user organisations)": *ibid.*

48 Ellison and Akdeniz "Cyberstalking: The Regulation of Harassment on the Internet", *supra* n. 44. Also see House of Lords Select Committee on Science and Technology, *Info Society, Agenda for Action in the UK* (1995–96 HL 77) para. 5.50.

49 Vol I (1997–98 HC 520–I).

Globalisation

International travel, communications (especially the Internet), business networks and so on pose increasing strain on the application of criminal law. There are major jurisdictional and enforcement problems where victims and perpetrators are in different states, whether the conduct involved is fraud, Internet child pornography, an Internet threat to kill, or whatever. The jurisdiction rules in English criminal law have been extended in recent years, in statutes such as the Sex Offenders Act 1997 and Part I of the Criminal Justice Act 1993 (implemented in 1999). But other difficulties, such as extradition and the obtaining of evidence from witnesses abroad, must then be surmounted.

Traditionally, mutual assistance in obtaining and collecting evidence and the service of process by one state at the request of another is obtained through bilateral and multilateral treaties. The situation can be complex because different states are party to different treaties drawn in different terms. In Europe the basis of mutual assistance is the Council of Europe Convention on Mutual Assistance in Criminal Matters 1959, ratified by the United Kingdom in 1991 following the enactment of the Criminal Justice (International Co-Operation) Act 1990. The Act's provisions are not limited to states party to the Convention, although whether a request for assistance by a non-party state will be complied with depends on what other treaty provisions there are with that state. Under the Act, a request, whether inwards or outwards, for service of overseas process or for obtaining of overseas evidence is processed through the Home Secretary (in practice, through a unit in the Home Office which channels it and co-ordinates its execution). This can cause considerable delay, partly because of the volume of requests and partly because of the complex and bureaucratic nature of the process.[50] Difficulties can also arise because of the absence of a framework enabling our enforcement agencies to ask foreign agency to intercept communications, and because assistance is usually supplied (and is required by the 1959 Convention to be supplied) in the manner provided for the law of the requested state (which may affect the admissibility in this country of the evidence obtained).[51] The implementation in the United Kingdom of the EU Convention on Mutual Legal Assistance in Criminal Matters 2000, some aspects of which require legislation, will improve the situation as between the parties to the Convention. An important feature of the new Convention is that assistance is to be given in the manner indicated by the requesting state, unless that is contrary to the law of the requested state. Other important features are that the Convention provides for the direct transmission

[50] House of Lords Select Committee on the European Communities Ninth Report paras 36 and 37.

[51] *Ibid.*, para. 35.

of requests for mutual assistance between judicial authorities without the involvement of central authorities, that it provides a basis for co-operation in the use of modern technological methods, for example, the hearing of evidence by live television links, that it permits joint investigation teams to be established on an *ad hoc* basis involving investigators from the requesting state and from the state in whose territory the investigation is conducted, and that it provides for the interception of communications in one state at the request of another.

In addition, the adoption of a proposal, made by the United Kingdom, for the concept of mutual recognition of court decisions would lead to a regime where each EU Member State recognised as valid the judicial decisions of a criminal court, before as well as after conviction, with the minimum of formality. The proposal involves the abolition of dual criminality restrictions, expedited extradition procedures based on the judicial backing of arrest warrants (similar to the system already in operation between the United Kingdom and Ireland), and the mutual recognition of judicial orders or warrants for the tracing, seizure and production of evidence. Neither this proposal nor the EU Convention involves the harmonisation of domestic substantive law.[52] A major problem which is also unresolved is getting witnesses to come from abroad to give evidence in this country; witnesses abroad cannot be compelled to go to give evidence before an English court. As a result, injustices to the accused or to the prosecution will inevitably continue to occur. Admittedly, if a witness is prepared to testify but not to travel to do so, documentary evidence from the witness is admissible under section 23 of the Criminal Justice Act 1988,[53] but this is a second best because the witness cannot be cross-examined. The narrow range of cases[54] where live TV link evidence may be given abroad must be extended if the opportunity presented by the EU Convention is to be seized.

The difficulties sometimes arising from reliance on international co-operation may be surmounted if some kind of international or supranational legal system, for certain purposes at least, could be agreed. Two major steps in that direction are the Hague (Rwanda and former Yugoslavia) War Crimes Tribunals, and the embryonic establishment of a Permanent International Criminal Court, whose statute is now awaiting the required ratification by sixty states. However, experience with the *Corpus Juris* proposals suggests that the Permanent International Criminal Court may represent the high watermark of international co-operation for the moment, and that ideas for other forms of international criminal legal systems are premature. The *Corpus Juris* is a report[55] prepared for consultation as part of the European Legal Area

[52] *Ibid.*, paras 134 and 135.

[53] i.e. witness outside United Kingdom and not reasonably practicable to secure his attendance.

[54] Criminal Justice Act 1988, s 32; Criminal Justice Act 1988 (Commencement No 12 Order) 1990.

[55] The Report is reproduced as Appendix 3 of the Report referred to *supra* n. 50.

Project. It addresses the problems resulting from the fact that, because the EU creates a commercial territory without frontiers, while retaining the independent criminal jurisdiction of each Member State, there are particular difficulties in national authorities investigating and prosecuting major frauds and other crimes on the Community's budget. The *Corpus Juris* proposes in respect of these a common regime of substantive criminal law (including offences) and rules of evidence and procedure, which would be applicable in the courts of EU Member States with a supranational body with power to direct prosecutions. Its adoption would require Member States to modify their substantive and adjectival law but only in respect of the limited category of offences covered by it. In this limited sphere, there would be a "two-track system". The offences, procedures and evidential rules of the *Corpus Juris* would sit alongside the English law. Central to the *Corpus Juris* system would be a new official, the European Public Prosecutor (EPP), and his staff, with responsibility for investigating offences, deciding whether to prosecute, and bringing and discontinuing prosecutions. The EPP would only be politically accountable to the EU Council for the exercise of his functions, although it might be that he would be subject to the same limited degree of supervision by the English courts as the DPP. The *Corpus Juris* also creates a new type of judicial officer, the "judge of freedoms", whose functions would be exercised by national judges in each state, and who would ensure that the rights of an accused were protected by exercising control over the investigatory powers of the EPP, over preliminary procedures for gathering evidence (in search and telephone-tapping) and pre-trial steps in the procedure (such as remands in custody).

As the opposition to the *Corpus Juris* on the part of the UK Government and others[56] indicates, substantial difficulties must be overcome if any form of international criminal legal system is to be introduced. The opposition to the *Corpus Juris* has been based partly on its implications for national sovereignty in relation to a range of criminal offences.[57] Eurosceptics see it with alarm as a template for a European criminal justice system. Political objections of this type may be overcome in time. Current perceptions of state sovereignty may preclude acceptance of international criminal legal systems in specific areas for a few years but increasing globalisation is inevitably going to accelerate a reduction in the importance of national sovereignty and may make such a solution irresistible before long, perhaps initially on a regional basis where the greater commonality of interest and understanding would assist in acceptance of the idea. In the interim, improved arrangements for mutual assistance along the lines described *supra* must be the answer.

Opposition to the *Corpus Juris* also highlights the problems to be overcome

[56] Including the House of Lord's Select Committee on the European Communities in its *Ninth Report* (1998–99)

[57] *Ibid.*, at n. 50, para. 46.

under a twin-track approach blending different domestic systems. Although the *Corpus Juris* seeks to meld the inquisitorial and written traditions of continental Europe with the adversarial and oral ones of English law, the result is overall closer to the continental system. The *Corpus Juris* does not fit happily with the largely accusatorial procedure employed by English law, nor does the absence of a jury at the trial stage.[58] Moreover, the role of the EPP is inconsistent with the "Philips principle", i.e. that the role of investigator and prosecutor should be kept distinct. Introducing a two-track system in England with these fundamental differences, as the *Corpus Juris* proposes, is fraught with problems. It seems that there must be a good deal of harmonisation of national rules before a twin-track system can be acceptable. In this respect, it should be noted that, as of the end of the second millennium, the UK Government prefers "convergence" or "approximation" of criminal laws rather than their "harmonisation".[59] The constitutional problems of harmonisation which some states may have in some areas may be an even bigger hurdle to harmonisation than political issues.

Diversion and decriminalisation

In times when the ambit of transnational and international criminal law is likely to increase, might the increased pressure to reduce the costs of the criminal justice system, which continues to offer a reason for "streamlining" criminal procedure (e.g. paper committals, plea before venue, and the proposed reduction of the right to elect jury trial), have an impact on the criminal law itself?

The large number of crimes with low penalties (and often strict liability) in English law offers the opportunity for substantial decriminalisation. The adoption of this idea, akin to a proposal by Justice in 1980,[60] would continue developments of the last twenty years. Convictions for non-imprisonable offences, other than a number of non-regulatory offences, no longer form part of a person's criminal record,[61] and the fixed penalty system has been extended, notably in relation to endorsable and non-endorsable road traffic offences by the Transport Act 1982. The fixed penalty system in effect decriminalises the offences concerned where the procedure is used, as it normally is, because the case will not go to a criminal court unless, during the suspended

[58] *Corpus Juris*, Art. 26.

[59] Report, *supra* n. 50, para. 134.

[60] Justice, the British Section of the International Commission of Jurists, *Breaking the Rules*.

[61] National Police Records (Recordable Offences) Regulations 1985, SI 1985/1941, as amended.

enforcement period, the offender requests a court hearing. A more extreme model takes matters completely out of the criminal sphere by introducing civil penalties, not necessarily fixed ones, levied by the appropriate authority, without any right of "appeal" to the criminal courts. The Inland Revenue has for some considerable time had power to exact civil penalties in respect of income tax evasion, misdeclaration to the Inland Revenue and other conduct resulting in the non-payment of income tax. The Customs and Excise has long-standing powers of seizure and forfeiture. More recently, the Finance Act 1985 decriminalised many offences relating to VAT. It replaced the criminal law and the jurisdiction of the criminal courts by introducing administrative penalties. Fixed penalties are raised by an assessment made by the tax authority on a "balance of probabilities" basis, in response to which the person to whom it is directed can either pay up or appeal against it to an independent tribunal. On appeal, the onus of proof is on him and not the tax authority. Similar civil penalties have been substituted for criminal offences in the area of customs duty and are widely used against bootleggers.[62] Lastly, the Act 2000 Financial Services and Markets provides a form of civil penalty for market abuse.

While diversion and decriminalisation of minor offences may be viewed with some favour, it is to be hoped that there will not be a more general adoption of some modern examples of the criminal law being used to enforce civil orders in non-regulatory areas: for instance, the civil law provisions for an interim possession order,[63] breach of which is a summary offence under the Criminal Justice and Public Order Act 1994, and the civil law provisions for an anti-social behaviour order or for a sex offender order, under the Crime and Disorder Act 1998, breach of which is an either-way offence punishable with up to five years' imprisonment. The attraction of this for Parliament seems to be that the initial order can be made free from the evidential constraints of the criminal law and on the basis of a lower standard of proof, although not (it would seem) simply on the balance of probabilities,[64] but that the criminal

[62] McFarlane "Regulating European Drug Problems" (1999) 149 *NLJ* 1075 at 1076.

[63] County Court Rules, SI 1981/1687, Ord. 24, Part II.

[64] It is wrong to regard the law of evidence as providing distinct and separate standards of proof. The standard of proof on a claimant or applicant in a civil case varies according to the seriousness of what has to be proved. Although there is *dicta* suggesting that a civil court never adopts the criminal standard of proof even where allegations of a criminal nature are being made (*Bater* v. *Bater* [1951] P 35 at 37, per Denning J), case law suggests that allegations of a criminal or similar nature have to be proved to the criminal standard of beyond reasonable doubt. In *Khawaja* v. *Secretary of State for the Home Department* [1983] 1 All ER 765 at 783, Lord Scarman said that in the context of habeas corpus the difference between the criminal and civil standards was "largely a matter of words". In civil cases where the allegation is one of murder or child abuse the standard of proof has been held to be beyond reasonable doubt (see *Halford* v. *Brooks*, *The Times*, 3 October 1991). Lower down the scale of things, it has been held in binding-over proceedings (strictly civil proceedings) that the criminal standard applies. Thus, it would seem that the standard of proof in the present type of cases is certainly higher than mere balance of probabilities.

sanction and specific arrest powers attached to the breach of order offence can be a more effective means than a civil remedy of dealing with a breach of the order. At this point, all that has to be proved beyond reasonable doubt is breach of the order (normally without reasonable excuse if an excuse is raised) not the factual basis of the order proved in the more relaxed civil law way.

Both decriminalisation and the tendency to create civil-criminal hybrids raise human rights issues that are too frequently ignored. The very reason for governments choosing a civil-criminal hybrid is sometimes to avoid the extra protections conferred by Article 6(2) and 6(3) of the European Convention upon those "charged with a criminal offence": the European Court has been vigilant about such techniques, and has on several occasions held that a procedure classified as civil in domestic law should be treated as criminal.[65] The same applies to decriminalisation: whatever alternative procedure is adopted, probably some form of administrative procedure, it will be necessary to ensure that an accused person has the right of access to a court so as to challenge the allegation upon which the imposition of a penalty is based. Even apparently modest fines can have a significant financial impact on some people.

Impact of the Human Rights Act 1998

Unless steps are taken in advance, the early years of the new millennium will see a flurry of judicial declarations of incompatibility and much judicial reconstruction of criminal law to avoid incompatibility with the Convention rights under the Act.

In terms of general principles, the jurisprudence of the European Court of Human Rights indicates that the law on the following needs to be addressed so as to ensure compatibility with a Convention right: the defence of insanity[66] (Article 5);[67] use of force in public or private defence, at least where the consequences are fatal[68] (Article 2);[69] entrapment[70] (Article 6(1));[71] strict liability and reverse onus provisions[72] (Article 6(2));[73] and the right of parental chas-

[65] e.g. *Benham* v. *United Kingdom* (1996) 22 EHRR 293; *Schmautzer* v. *Austria* (1996) 21 EHRR 511; *Garyfallou AEBE* v. *Greece* (1999) 28 EHRR 344.

[66] See *Winterwerp* v. *Netherlands* (1979) 2 EHRR 387, ECHR.

[67] Right to liberty and security of the person.

[68] See *McCann* v. *United Kingdom* (1996) 21 EHRR 97, ECHR; *Andronicou and Constantinou* v. *Cyprus* (1998) 25 EHRR 491, ECHR.

[69] Right to life.

[70] See *Teixeira de Castro* v. *Portugal* (1999) 28 EHRR 101, ECHR.

[71] Right to fair hearing.

[72] See *DPP, ex p Kebeline* [1999] 4 All ER 801, HL.

[73] Presumption of innocence.

tisement[74] (in relation to which legislation to limit this to a right to smack was announced in January 2000)[75] (Article 3)[76].

Likewise a number of offences need to be addressed: male homosexual sexual offences, in terms of the rule that consensual conduct is criminal unless "in private" between "consenting adults"[77] (Article 8);[78] offences relating to a failure by gypsies or travellers to leave land when directed (Articles 8 and 11);[79] offences relating to raves and to aggravated trespass; offences relating to processions and assemblies; offences relating to obscene publications; offences of incitement to racial hatred; contempt of court; criminal libel; and incitement to disaffection (Articles 10 and 11).[80] In addition, any offence where the meaning of an element is a question of fact for the jury or magistrates under English law is liable not to be justifiable under any article which permits necessary interference if "prescribed by law" on the ground that the offence lacks sufficient certainty to satisfy that term.[81] Although not strictly within the realms of substantive criminal law, or indeed the criminal law at all,[82] the law relating to breach of the peace, and the law on binding over (recommended for abolition without replacement by the Law Commission in 1994),[83] need to be addressed (Article 5, in particular).[84]

Since Parliament is unlikely to plug the various gaps itself, at least in the near future, much power will be left in the hands of the judiciary in interpreting the Human Rights Act and the European Convention. On many issues there will be a choice of two tendencies, a minimalist (reading human rights down) and a maximalist (giving effect to human rights except so far as restrictions really are necessary and permissible in Convention terms).[85] If judges decide to issue declarations of incompatibility, the government will have the decision whether or not to amend the "offending" law by the fast-track procedure provided in the Human Rights Act. If judges use their interpretive powers under section 3 of the Act to reconstruct statutes in ways not congenial to government, the

[74] See *A* v. *United Kingdom* (1999) 27 EHRR 611, ECHR

[75] *The Guardian*, 18 January 2000.

[76] Right not to be subjected to inhuman or degrading treatment.

[77] *Dudgeon* v. *United Kingdom* (1981) 4 EHRR 149, ECHR.

[78] Right to respect for private life.

[79] Right to freedom of assembly and association.

[80] Right to freedom of expression.

[81] See *Legislating the Criminal Code: Fraud and Deception* (Law Com Consultation Paper No. 155, 1999), paras 5.33–5.53.

[82] Glanville Williams, "Arrest for Breach of the Peace" [1954] *Crim LR* 578 at 583, citing *Davies* v. *Griffiths* [1937] 2 All ER 671 (breach of the peace); *Veater* v. *G* [1981] 2 All ER 304 at 307, per Lord Lane CJ (binding over).

[83] *Binding Over* (Law Com No. 222, 1994).

[84] See *Steel* v. *UK* (1999) 28 EHRR 603, ECHR; *McLeod* v. *United Kingdom* [1998] 2 FLR 1048, ECHR; *Hashman and Harrup* v. *UK* [2000] *Crim LR* 185, ECHR.

[85] Compare R Buxton "The Human Rights Act and the Substantive Criminal Law" [2000] *Crim LR* 331 with A Ashworth "The Human Rights Act and the Substantive Criminal Law: A Non-Minimalist View" [2000] *Crim LR* 564.

latter's only course will be to put forward amending (or reaffirming) legislation through normal parliamentary channels, a course it will not welcome when there is already said to be a log-jam of bills and proposals for legislation.

Judges and the criminal law

Although the judges will undoubtedly have a central role in determining the impact of the European Convention in English criminal proceedings, little has been said thus far about their function in developing the common law and in interpreting criminal legislation. Much of the law of homicide, and the general part of the criminal law, remains in the common law. The judges have created a new category of general defence, in duress of circumstances,[86] but have also stated that it is not for them to create a new category of defence, in involuntary intoxication.[87] The House of Lords has attempted to define intention four times in twenty-five years, but has still stopped short of offering a comprehensive definition.[88] The House of Lords has produced at least one decision that has been widely ignored,[89] and its major decision in *Caldwell* has withered away through its failure to convince lawyers and academics and, despite Lord Roskill's attempt to revive it in 1985, it has largely disappeared from view in legal practice. So-called objectivism has also been evident in other decisions,[90] but subjectivism has won the day on several occasions,[91] in form if not in substance.[92]

Many of these divergent decisions reflect deep differences of opinion on normative questions about the criminal law: although many judges still tend to write their judgments as if principles can be deduced from previous decisions, there has been an increasing tendency to cite academic writings and expressly to adopt suggestions made by some writers. This may reflect a changing approach among counsel, in what they place before the court, or a greater willingness of contemporary appellate judges to travel beyond *Archbold*. The divergence of judicial decisions also serves to demonstrate some of the limitations on the codification project. For, as argued earlier, the principal virtues of codification lie in the formal values of certainty, clarity, accessibility and even judicial accountability. But the substance of any code must be based on choices

[86] *Conway* (1989) 88 Cr App R 159; *Martin* (1989) 88 Cr App R 343.

[87] *Kingston* [1995] 2 AC 355, HL.

[88] *Hyam* v. *DPP* [1975] AC 55; *Moloney* [1985] AC 905; *Hancock and Shankland* [1986] AC 455; *Woollin* [1999] AC 92.

[89] *Anderson* [1986] AC 27.

[90] e.g. *Graham* (1982) 74 Cr App R 235; *Brown* [1994] 1 AC 212; *Adomako* [1995] 1 AC 171.

[91] e.g. *Gladstone Williams* (1984) 78 Cr App R 276; *Shivpuri* [1987] AC 1; *Gomez* [1993] AC 422; *B* v. *DPP* [2000] 2 WLR 452.

[92] *DPP* v. *Morgan* [1976] AC 182.

of the kinds confronted by the judges and discussed by academics; too often it is assumed that some of these choices (e.g. in favour of a "subjective" doctrine of mistake) are uncontroversial, and that "consistency" dictates that all instances (e.g. of mistake) call for the same legal response, when on normative grounds it might be argued otherwise.

Academics as educators and commentators

Forty, or even thirty, years ago criminal law textbooks were thin on the ground. Now there is a choice among several, together with a smaller group of text-and-materials books. The number of journals in which writers on criminal law can publish has not increased so significantly, and indeed even within those journals most of the articles are on evidence or procedure. Relatively few scholarly articles on the substantive criminal law are published, and most of those focus on topics in the general part. Yet it could be said that criminal law scholarship is far more diverse than it was some years ago. In the 1960s it was possible to identify the typical academic criminal lawyer as a liberal subjectivist (male, white . . .) codifier. Even if there was some kind of consensus then, there is none now.

There is a group of liberal subjectivist writers who still have a high reputation and who receive frequent approving references from the judiciary. Some in this group have ceased to offer arguments for the subjectivist point of view, regarding the debate as *passé* and treating any intrusion of objectivism as an atavistic aberration. But is the objective-subjective division as clear, either in legal or in moral terms, as is often assumed? Perhaps this was one point on which Lord Diplock in *Caldwell* was right. Certainly there is a group of philosophical neo-liberals, among whom Antony Duff is prominent, who argue that traditional forms of legal subjectivism are unconvincing even on their own premises (e.g. advertent recklessness), as well as creating moral distinctions that are insubstantial. Other writers on the philosophy of the criminal law question the moral credentials of some parts of the apparatus of subjectivism, such as fair labelling, the principle of correspondence, and the rejection of "constructive" liability.[93] The communitarian tendency in some of this writing appears in a stronger form in critical legal scholarship on criminal law, notably in the work of Nicola Lacey, Celia Wells, Peter Alldridge and Alan Norrie.[94] Much critical writing has a low normative content, however, and is directed

[93] e.g. J Gardner, "Rationality and the Rule of Law in Offences against the Person", [1994] *Camb LJ* 502; J Horder, "A Critique of the Correspondence Principle", [1995] *Crim LR* 759.

[94] e.g. A Norrie, *Crime, Reason and History* (1993); N Lacey and C Wells, *Reconstructing Criminal Law* (2nd edn., 1998); P. Alldridge *Relocating Criminal Law* (1999).

more at exposing incoherence and contradictions in the language used by the judiciary and by other academics, particularly of the liberal subjectivist group.

Allowing for the crudeness of the subjective-objective terminology and of this broad typology of writers on criminal law, we may conclude by proposing the need to press forward with at least two academic enterprises. The first is teaching the criminal law in a way that is critical, that is, at a minimum, not simply propounding and explaining the existing rules. Whether the critique be internal or normative, or even both, it is surely essential to the academic exercise. Often it will require some pruning of topics to be covered in the course, and hard decisions may be forced increasingly upon us as modularisation and the claims of new subjects gain the ascendancy. A second enterprise is writing about the criminal law in ways that not only reflect those concerns of teachers but also, on at least some occasions, confront the normative questions that have to be addressed by law-makers. As academics our research and our reflections should enable us to criticise some approaches and to propose viable approaches (let us not say, solutions) to legislative and judicial problems. Some will do this as guardians of human rights, others will reject the alleged individualism of the human rights culture, or the particular Convention we have imported into domestic law, or the power the Human Rights Act gives to the judiciary. Some will emphasise the political nature of many decisions on criminalisation and decriminalisation, others will continue to regard the criminal law as a branch of applied moral philosophy. This is not to argue that as academics we have the responsibility to formulate proposals for legal change, but rather to assert that, diverse as we are in our perspectives, we possess the knowledge base from which to make a significant contribution.

18

Character Evidence and Criminal Procedure

JOHN JACKSON AND MARTIN WASIK*

Introduction

There is a deep paradox at the centre of the use of character evidence in the criminal process. On the one hand, criminal records are increasingly used at many stages of decision-making before and after trial. It is generally taken for granted, for example, that this information is relevant for police officers investigating crime[1] and making decisions on arrest,[2] for magistrates who hear bail applications, and for prosecutors who decide whether to prosecute and what to charge. After conviction the offender's record plays an important part in the pre-sentence reports of probation officers, in sentencing decisions,[3] and in decisions affecting a prisoner's custodial regime and early release under licence. Criminal records have an increasing role in drawing suspects into the criminal process, as police officers obtain instant access to them through computer technology.[4] Beyond the criminal process criminal record information is increasingly being used by employers and other organisations,[5] and recent legislation has made provision for a statutory system of access to records for

* Professor Wasik's contribution to this essay is based upon research carried out at Manchester University during 1998 when he was a British Council/Leverhulme Trust Senior Research Fellow. Thanks are due to both organisations for their generous support.

1 According to *Gowan* [1982] Crim LR 821, an "experienced professional criminal" may expect a vigorous interrogation from the police, whilst similar questioning of a man of good character might be regarded as oppressive or unfair (cf. *Hudson* (1980) 72 Cr App R 163).

2 An officer's knowledge of the suspect's record may well influence his or her perception of whether there are "reasonable grounds" to arrest.

3 M Wasik and A von Hirsch, "Section 29 Revised: Previous Convictions in Sentencing" [1994] *Criminal Law Review* 409.

4 See A Hoey, "Techno-Cops: Information Technology and Law Enforcement" (1998) 6 *International Journal of Law and Information Technology* 69.

5 B Hebenton and T Thomas, *Criminal Records* (1993).

the purposes of vetting candidates for employment, and applicants for licences.[6]

There has been remarkably little critical analysis of the use of criminal record information, whether within or outside the criminal process. Article 8 of the European Convention on Human Rights 1950 provides for a right to respect for the privacy of the individual, but there may be derogation from this principle as provided by law and necessary in a democratic society. The Article permits the principle to be subordinated to the interests of the prevention of crime, or for the protection of the rights and freedoms of others. Hence the need for the police, and for the employers of carers and others in positions of trust, to have access to criminal record information. Little thought has been given, however, to how important this information *really* is, certainly for *all* employers. There are important countervailing values in allowing convicted persons to "live down" their previous convictions. The Rehabilitation of Offenders Act 1974, which recognises these legitimate concerns, has been very significantly undermined over the past twenty years. Similarly, although there is a literature on the relevance of past criminal convictions to sentencing, there has been little thought given within the criminal process as to how useful it *really* is for the police and prosecutors to rely on criminal convictions. There is the well-known risk that police will tend to rely on "rounding up the usual suspects". Having identified someone whose profile appears to fit the offence under investigation, evidence which does not assist in implicating that suspect may be subconsciously overlooked, or deliberately withheld.

Against this general trend towards increasing reliance on criminal convictions, however, there endures the basic principle of law that an accused's criminal convictions, and more generally his or her "bad character", should not be admitted or used during the course of a contested criminal trial. There are, of course, some exceptions to the principle. The prosecution may, in certain circumstances, lead evidence of bad character where the evidence has a sufficient degree of relevance to the issues in the case—commonly referred to as "similar fact" evidence, even though the grounds of relevance do not *necessarily* depend on the closeness of the similarity between the past character evidence and the facts of the offence charged.[7] In addition, if the accused conducts his or her defence in a certain way, such as by raising evidence of his or her own good character, or by making imputations on a prosecution witness or on the deceased victim of the crime, the prosecution may reveal details of the accused's record.[8] Notwithstanding these well recognised exceptions, however, the principle has remained largely intact, despite a growing trend within the

[6] S Uglow, "Criminal Records Under the Police Act 1997" [1998] *Criminal Law Review* 235.

[7] See I Dennis, *The Law of Evidence* (1999), p. 578.

[8] Criminal Evidence Act 1898, s. 1(f).

law of evidence towards the admission of all relevant evidence before the trier of fact, subject where appropriate to warning from the judge.

Pannick has argued that the exclusionary rule rests upon "patronising assumptions" about the irrationality of those who are called for jury service, and that it proceeds on the wrongheaded basis that hiding information from juries will somehow help them to decide criminal cases.[9] There is some judicial support for greater openness, with Lord Griffiths pointing out that the exclusionary rule is something of a throw back to the days when "jurors were often uneducated or illiterate and the penal laws were of harsh severity, when children could be transported, and men were hanged for stealing a shilling and could not be heard in their own defence".[10] The Law Commission, however, at the end of a detailed review informed by empirical evidence,[11] found themselves unable to recommend any substantial change from the *status quo*.[12] Given the emphasis placed at trial on the exclusion of character evidence, in a process where the defendant's past has nonetheless been made known to all the professional participants, the question must be asked whether too much time has been invested in trying to protect the small number of defendants who end up contesting cases in front of juries, at the expense of the much larger number of defendants who plead guilty before trial. The rules at trial do have an effect on earlier decisions, in so far as those involved will know that evidence of the defendant's bad character cannot be used at trial. Nevertheless, the traditional focus on the exclusion of bad character evidence from the jury is a classic example of what Twining has called "court-centredness" in the Anglo-American rules of evidence and evidence scholarship. Much is made of the dangers of juries being ill-equipped to deal with the prejudicial effect of character evidence.[13] But is this a convincing reason for dwelling so exclusively on trial rules? Can we really be so confident that the array of professional participants who make decisions throughout the rest of the criminal process are not similarly prejudiced by record information in similar ways?

In this chapter we aim to stem the tide of jury and trial-centredness by focusing on the use, effect and dangers of character evidence *throughout* the criminal process. When we come to consider the trial phase we will see that, in fact, character evidence is adduced at trial much more frequently than is commonly thought, and that the strategy of exclusion is very difficult to operate in non-jury trials. We will then examine the central question of the relevance of

[9] D Pannick, "Juries Can Cope with a Defendant's Form", *The Times*, 8 October 1996.

[10] *H* [1995] 2 AC 596, at 613.

[11] Law Commission, *Previous Misconduct of a Defendant* (Consultation Paper No. 141, 1996).

[12] J McEwan, "The Law Commission Dodges the Nettles on Previous Misconduct" [1997] *Criminal Law Review* 93.

[13] W Twining, "Identification and Misidentification in Legal Processes: Redefining the Process" in S Lloyd-Bostock and B Clifford (eds.), *Evaluating Witness Evidence* (1983), pp. 255, 261–2.

character evidence, and consider whether the strategy of exclusion at trial should be replaced by more careful monitoring of the use of character evidence throughout the criminal process, with clearer guidelines laid down for all participants.

Criminal records in criminal justice decision-making

Recent work on the dynamics of criminal justice decision-making has shown that the final disposition of a criminal case is crucially affected by "up-stream" negotiations prior to the trial, and by the way the case is "constructed" by the police and prosecution authorities.[14] It is important to realise that when a defendant is convicted at trial the criminal record he or she then acquires is itself a product of these practices. For example, modern policy on cautioning is to avoid "repeat" cautioning unless there are highly exceptional circumstances. This means that the presence of a previous caution will effectively determine whether a defendant's case is referred to the prosecutor. In the prosecutor's file it then becomes important again, with a good record making prosecution less likely. In the decision to prosecute, there is discretion over whether to proceed with one charge, or several. If it is alleged that offending has taken place on several occasions over a period of time, the prosecutor may proceed on the basis of sample counts, rather than prosecute all the alleged instances. Thus, in the event of conviction, the choice over charge will have a crucial effect on the record. Case outcome is also affected by charge and plea negotiation. The prosecutor may be prepared to accept a plea of guilty to a lesser charge than that originally preferred, in order to save court time and public money and, perhaps, to protect vulnerable witnesses. Cretney and Davies, for example, have shown how section 18 woundings are routinely negotiated to section 20 assaults in return for a guilty plea in domestic violence cases.[15]

A further important element here is the broad definition of many common criminal offences. Because offences such as robbery, burglary, theft, deception and handling are compendiously drafted, the legal labels appearing in a person's record will correspond inexactly to the underlying criminal behaviour. Some of the offences, such as theft and deception, overlap very substantially.[16]

[14] M McConville, A Sanders and R Leng, *The Case for the Prosecution* (1991).

[15] Section 18 and s. 20 of the Offences Against the Person Act 1861. See A Cretney and G Davis, "Prosecuting Domestic Assault" [1996] *Criminal Law Review* 162. See also A Mulcahy, "The Justification of Justice: Legal Practitioners' Accounts of Negotiated Case Settlements in Magistrates' Courts" (1994) 34 *British Journal of Criminology* 411.

[16] *Gomez* [1993] AC 442.

Others cover a wide range of seriousness. As was pointed out by the Lord Chief Justice recently, the seriousness of house burglary "can vary almost infinitely from case to case".[17] The Court of Appeal often makes remarks of this kind when asserting that it is next to impossible to lay down sentencing guidelines for particular offences, since so much turns on the particular facts. Yet these problems are just as acute when the police, the prosecution authorities, or the sentencing court, are considering the significance of an offence of burglary on the defendant's record. They will generally know nothing about the defendant's past offences beyond the stark entry in the record, and offence labels are relatively uninformative. Where, for example, several defendants have been involved in an offence, playing very different roles, their resulting criminal records are likely to be indistinguishable. The cumulative effect of these, and other, complex and interrelated up-stream decisions can be to produce a picture of the defendant's law-breaking which, as reflected in the legal category of the offence for which he is convicted, bears only an approximate resemblance to what actually took place.

Despite these limitations, a defendant's criminal record is still generally taken to be an objective and impartial record of their past dealings with the criminal justice system. This is perhaps what Walker means when he observes that although other factual matters before the court may be difficult to assess, "previous convictions are indisputable".[18] In fact, however, information in criminal records is subject to a range of problems of inaccuracy, differences of interpretation, and bias. Following official exposure in the early 1990s that criminal record systems were in a "terrifying state of inaccuracy",[19] the Government introduced a computerised criminal record system, known as Pheonix, from 1995. The quality of criminal record information has, despite its obvious importance, attracted surprisingly little interest from academic researchers, but occasional reports since 1995 indicate that problems of inaccuracy persist. In 1998 Phillips and Brown found that only five of the ten police stations in their survey had reliable data on previous convictions,[20] and in 1999 Corre and Wolchover confirmed earlier evidence that when determining bail in magistrates' courts, decision-makers are often hampered by criminal records which are out of date or inaccurate.[21] Weis has observed that for individuals having frequent contact with the criminal justice system, the likelihood of errors on the record become significantly greater: "a long, complicated

[17] *Brewster* [1998] 1 Cr App R (S) 181.

[18] N Walker, *Why Punish?* (1991), p. 98.

[19] Law Society's evidence to the House of Commons Home Affairs Committee, Third Report, *Criminal Records* (1990).

[20] *Entry Into the Criminal Justice System* (Home Office Research Study No. 1985, 1999), p. 22.

[21] N Corre and D Wolchover, *Bail in Criminal Proceedings* (1999), p. 309. For earlier studies to the same effect see P Cavadino and B Gibson, *Bail* (1993), p. 106.

offence history is probably less valid, and less reliable, than a recent, simple one".[22]

Apart from the question of *accuracy* of records, it should be stressed that the acquiring of a criminal record is not a straightforward matter of recording objectively verifiable facts—it is a complex interactive process. It is also one which is subject to *bias*. Persons from certain social backgrounds, and from certain ethnic groups, and perhaps males rather than females, are more likely to be investigated by the police and thereby to acquire a criminal record. Once having a record, its stigmatising effect is likely to attract further police attention. Criminal record, then, is not just relevant to criminal justice agencies through the immediate case file, but also through the history of past encounters which the defendant carries about with him or her. The enduring legacy of labelling theory in criminology has been its stress on the importance of the official criminal justice *response* to law-breaking, rather than the pathology of the individual offender, or the inherent nature of the wrongful act. It now seems rather obvious that when a criminal "label" has been attached to an individual defendant, later criminal justice decisions will be affected to a significant extent by the existence of that label.[23] Perhaps most significant of all, however, is the extent to which the acquiring of a record may be influenced by discriminatory enforcement practices. There is abundant and long-standing research evidence that black suspects are more routinely investigated by the police, more frequently processed through the formal criminal justice system, and hence will acquire criminal records more readily and easily than whites.[24] The most comprehensive modern study found that a higher proportion of black defendants than white defendants had entered the criminal justice system as a result of police action, such as stop and search, and that 6 per cent of blacks had already been known to the police when arrested, as compared with 3 per cent of whites.[25] Unfortunately, these factors are generally overlooked when evidence of character and record is relied upon at various stages of the criminal justice process. For example, *sentencing* practices which give greater weight to the defendant's criminal record are indirectly discriminatory. So-called "three-strikes" sentencing laws have been shown to operate disproportionately against blacks in the USA because they are driven by criminal record—thus "black offenders are 21 per cent more likely and Hispanic offenders are 28 per cent more likely than similar white offenders to receive a mandatory sentence".[26]

[22] J G Weis, "Issues in the Measurement of Criminal Careers" in A Blumstein (ed.), *Criminal Careers and Career Criminals* (1986), vol. II, pp. 1, 33.

[23] R D Schwartz and J H Skolnick, "Two Studies of Legal Stigma" in H S Becker (ed.), *The Other Side* (1964), p. 103.

[24] Much of the relevant research is usefully summarised in Frank Belloni and Jacqueline Hodgson, *Criminal Injustice* (2000).

[25] R Hood, *Race and Sentencing* (1992).

[26] D Schichor and G Sechrest (eds.), *Three Strikes and You're Out* (1996), p. 274.

The use of character evidence at the trial

The Principles of Criminal Evidence

To attempt to explain why character evidence is used so extensively throughout criminal justice decision-making but is generally banned from use at trial, it is necessary to have regard to the purposes of the criminal trial and the principles of criminal evidence that have been developed over the years.

Many decisions in the criminal process are influenced as much by *forward looking* concerns, about the degree of risk posed by a suspect or offender as with looking backward into the precise circumstances of the offence charged. Character evidence is relevant to questions of risk, since it provides a picture of the accused's criminal history, albeit one which contains the inaccuracies and distortions we discussed earlier. Assessments of offender risk, however, generally operate in criminal justice at a crude level of analysis, and are imbued with mistaken or misleading "common sense" assumptions. It is true that someone who has been convicted and imprisoned for a criminal offence is much more likely to commit a further similar offence than a person chosen at random from the population as a whole.[27] On the other hand, people tend greatly to overestimate the likelihood that a *particular* convicted person will reoffend in a similar way.[28] We know that more than one-third of men born in 1953 had been convicted of a standard list (non-motoring) offence before the age of forty.[29] The majority of those convicted, however, do not reoffend at all. Of those that do, research shows that most reoffend in a *different* way on the next occasion. Philpott and Lancucki[30] found, for example, that of 435 persons convicted of violent offences in 1971, 51 per cent had not been reconvicted eight years later. Of those who had, their first reconviction was for an offence of violence in 16 per cent of cases, but in the remaining 33 per cent of cases it was for a different kind of offence, most frequently theft or handling. The Law Commission has recently touched on another aspect of criminal record, in relation to the criteria for bail, and the extent to which existing English law is compliant with the European Convention on Human Rights 1950.[31] While it is accepted that the defendant's criminal record is relevant to the risk that he or she may abscond or commit further offences while on bail, the Commission sketches the European

[27] D Farrington *et al.*, *Understanding and Controlling Crime* (1986).

[28] J Roberts and N White, "Public Estimates of Recidivism Rates: Consequences of a Criminal Stereotype" (1986) 28 *Canadian Journal of Criminology* 229.

[29] *Criminal Statistics England and Wales 1998* (2000), ch. 9.

[30] GJO Philpotts and LB Lancucki, *Previous Convictions, Sentence and Reconviction* (Home Office Research Study No. 53, 1979).

[31] Law Commission, *Bail and the Human Rights Act 1998* (Consultation Paper No. 157, 1999).

Court jurisprudence which eschews the use of overly broad risk assumptions based on the criminal record. The Court has insisted that bail should be refused only where inferences drawn from the record have been properly and reasonably derived.[32]

The trial process, in contrast, is essentially a *backward looking* truth-finding inquiry into the guilt of the accused. One of the key tenets of what Twining has called the "rationalist tradition of evidence scholarship" is a belief that human beings are competent to discover the truth,[33] albeit that evidence about the past is typically a matter of probabilities. The characteristic mode of reasoning is inductive, by which one starts with certain basic data and moves by way of inductive generalisation towards a probable conclusion. An attempt is sometimes made to explain the ban on bad character evidence at trial on grounds of irrelevance to the issue of guilt.[34] But if we accept that a person's past crimes are relevant to questions of risk about their future conduct, then we must accept that such evidence is also relevant in determining a question of historical fact about a particular occurrence, especially when used in conjunction with other evidence. Evidence about a person's propensity can be linked with other incident-specific evidence in a way that suggests strongly that the person committed a given crime, even if the same propensity evidence, by itself, would not justify that inference.[35]

If the character ban in criminal trials is to be justified, then it is necessary to rely on principles other than truth-finding. In his influential book on the principles of criminal evidence Zuckerman has argued that, apart from the need to discover the truth, other important principles are at stake in the criminal trial.[36] One of these is the protection of the innocent, or the "presumption of innocence". Although the rationalist tradition of evidence scholarship is founded on the belief that human beings are competent to find the truth, it does not deny that errors may be made in the evaluation of evidence. While character evidence can sometimes be relevant to guilt, there is a risk that juries will give too much weight to the character evidence. This concern is borne out, to some extent, by jury research. We know that mock jurors are more likely to convict a defendant if they are told that he or she has a recent previous conviction for a similar offence.[37] The principle of protecting innocent defendants may, then, require that character evidence, which tends to increase the risk of mistaken conviction, may have to be excluded, or at least carefully regulated.

[32] See e.g. *Toth* v. *Austria* (1991) 14 EHRR 551.

[33] W Twining, "The Rationalist Tradition of Evidence Scholarship" in *Rethinking Evidence* (1990), p. 32.

[34] See *DPP* v. *Boardman* [1975] AC 421, at 451, per Lord Hailsham.

[35] R C Park, "Character at the Crossroads" (1998) 49 *Hastings Law Journal* 717, at 723.

[36] A A S Zuckerman, *The Principles of Criminal Evidence* (1989).

[37] See W R Cornish and A P Sealy, "Juries and the Rules of Evidence" [1973] *Criminal Law Review* 208; Law Commission, *supra* n. 11, Appendix D.

Apart from the danger of giving too much weight to character evidence, scholars have identified another form of prejudice which may arise. This is the risk that allowing in such material may make juries convict otherwise than on the evidence.[38] Zuckerman has argued that the reception of character evidence threatens a further principle of evidence, which is that in a criminal trial the accused stands to be tried, acquitted or convicted only in respect of the offence with which he or she is charged.[39] Recent mock jury research suggests that a jury is more likely to convict a defendant when evidence of a particularly unpleasant past conviction, such as a sexual offence against a child, is revealed to them.[40] Here, conviction on the basis of prejudice, and in the face of the evidence, seems a real possibility.

The Exclusionary Approach

Fears about the consequences of admitting character evidence at trial have resulted in efforts to devise a test of exclusion which would counter these fears whilst still allowing the admission of strongly probative character evidence. Rules have been developed to assist judges in striking the right balance in this respect. The courts have identified forbidden chains of reasoning, and various categories of relevance, in the search for a workable approach. Lord Hershell's classic formulation of the similar fact rule in *Makin* v. *AG for New South Wales*[41] made a distinction between (i) character evidence adduced for the purpose of leading to the conclusion that a person is likely from his criminal conduct or character to have committed the offence, and (ii) character evidence adduced to prove a fact in issue. This distinction has proved unworkable[42] and, after considerable judicial soul-searching, the courts have concluded that no clearer rule can be devised than that the prosecution may not adduce evidence for the purpose of proving an accused's bad character unless the probative force of the evidence is sufficiently great to make it just to admit it, notwithstanding its prejudicial effect in showing the defendant's guilt of another crime.[43]

[38] See e.g. R Lempert, "Modelling Relevance" (1975) *Michigan Law Review* 1027. The Law Commission also distinguished this kind of "moral prejudice" from the kind of "reasoning prejudice" discussed earlier, see *supra* n. 11, para 7.2.

[39] See *supra*, n. 36, at 222–3.

[40] Law Commission, *supra* n. 11.

[41] [1894] AC 57.

[42] Certain cases are only explicable on the basis that the similar fact evidence was admitted to show propensity, see e.g. *Straffen* [1952] 2 QB 911. Indeed it has been argued that reasoning from similar fact evidence to guilt necessarily involves reasoning from propensity, see A E Acorn, "Similar Fact Evidence: and the Principle of Inductive Reasoning Making Sense" (1991) 11 *Oxford Journal of Legal Studies* 63. For recent discussion of the role of propensity in similar fact evidence, see M Redmayne, "A Likely Story!" (1999) 19 *Oxford Journal of Legal Studies* 659.

[43] *DPP* v. *P* [1991] 2 AC 447, at 462, per Lord Mackay.

Although the exclusionary approach to evidence of bad character is still endorsed in most common law jurisdictions, questions are increasingly being asked about whether it can be justified. As we have seen, keeping juries in the dark sits ill alongside the exposure of criminal record information to other decision-makers both before and after trial. Of course, these participants are not using criminal records to adjudicate on guilt, but they are used to help determine many other decisions affecting individuals, such as arrest, bail, prosecution and charge. One response here is to claim that the principles of the presumption of innocence, and of confining the verdict to the charge, have such significance at the trial stage that special steps must be taken to exclude character evidence there. While we can justify the use of character evidence by the police *before* trial on the ground that they would be in dereliction of their duty if they did not have regard to past crimes in the investigation of crime, at trial an anti-inductivist stand is justified on the moral basis of the presumption of innocence.[44] But this does not explain why the presumption of innocence should be given such special weighting at trial, nor why such an extreme anti-inductivist stance is necessary. Civil jurisdictions which also attach significance to principles such as the presumption of innocence do not generally exclude character evidence at trial.[45]

Even if we could justify the exclusionary approach, it is not always recognised how often evidence of an accused's character is in practice admitted at trial. Focus on the extent to which character evidence is relevant to guilt obscures the practical fact that criminal records are often admitted on the narrower issue of the defendant's credibility *as a witness.* The character evidence of *witnesses* is commonly revealed during the criminal trial, often during cross-examination. In his study of Wood Green Crown Court in London Rock found that, almost as a matter of course, counsel would so "blackguard" the other side's witnesses that they were no longer believable.[46] In his words, under cross-examination, victims and prosecution witnesses would be asked about matters touching on their "title to credit"—their way of life, their associations, their past convictions, their disinterestedness, and their integrity.[47] Rock ascribed this to the adversarial nature of the trial, which was dedicated to pitting the testimony, credibility, and reputation of witnesses against each another. The result was that there was little that counsel were not allowed to say.

There has recently been heightened concern about the lack of consideration and courtesy extended to victims and witnesses in the adversarial trial, and

[44] Z Bankowski, "The Jury and Reality" in M Findlay and P Duff (eds.), *The Jury Under Attack* (1988), pp. 8, 17.

[45] M Damaska, "Propensity Evidence in Continental Legal Systems" (1994) 70 *Chicago-Kent Law Review* 55.

[46] P Rock, *The Social World of an English Crown Court* (1993), p. 34.

[47] *Ibid.*

judges have been exhorted to restrict the amount of character evidence admitted to discredit their testimony. These exhortations have not always been heeded and judges have been criticised for admitting evidence of the complainant's sexual history too readily, despite legislative attempts to curb its use.[48] Recent attempts to restrict the use of character evidence against particular kinds of witnesses stand in sharp contrast to the long established "shield" afforded to defendants since 1898. What is not always recognised is how easily defendants can lose this shield. This can happen in a variety ways. Despite the ban on the prosecution adducing the defendant's bad character there has never been any bar on defendants adducing evidence of their own *good* character, and if this happens the prosecution may then cross-examine on their bad character. The "tit for tat" rule whereby imputations cast on an opponent's witness permit the opponent to cast imputations against one's own witness can also have the effect of exposing an accused's conviction. Although the character evidence is admitted in these circumstances solely for the purposes of going to the credibility of an accused's evidence,[49] many commentators have pointed out the difficulty of distinguishing between an issue of credibility and an issue of guilt,[50] as for example where the issue in dispute is a sexual one concerning what happened between two persons in private.[51] Defendants who give evidence against a co-defendant also risk putting their character in issue.

All in all, the Crown Court study conducted for the Royal Commission on Criminal Justice in 1993 found that by virtue of the operation of these rules about 20 per cent of defendants with a criminal record had their record revealed to the jury.[52] Since that time the courts have relaxed the evidential constraints on character evidence still further. In *DDP* v. *P*[53] the House of Lords adopted a less stringent approach towards the admissibility of similar fact evidence, and decisions since *P* have shown that its effect has been to create a more liberal admissibility regime.[54] The decision of the House of Lords in *H*[55] has further loosened the constraints on the admissibility of similar fact evidence by shifting consideration of one key aspect of the probative force of the evidence—namely the question of possible collusion on the part of

48 See e.g. J Temkin, "Sexual History Evidence—The Ravishment of Section 2" [1993] *Criminal Law Review* 3 for a critique of the judicial response to s 2 of the Sexual Offences (Amendment) Act 1976. For the latest legislative attempt to restrict sexual history evidence, see ss. 41–3 of the Youth Justice and Criminal Evidence Act 1999.

49 *McCleod* [1994] 1 WLR 1500, at 1512–13, per Stuart-Smith LJ.

50 See e.g. Zuckerman, *supra* n. 36, at 94–7.

51 *Funderburk* [1990] 1 WLR 587.

52 M Zander and P Henderson, *Crown Court Study* (RCCJ Research Study No. 19, 1993), para 4.6.6.

53 [1991] 2 AC 447.

54 See e.g. *Channing* [1994] Crim LR 924; *Ryder* [1994] 2 All ER 859; *Wharton* [1998] Crim LR 668.

55 [1995] 2 AC 596.

multiple complainants—from the judge to the jury. Where the defendant faces a series of offences where the evidence on each is not cross-admissible, a recent House of Lords decision has held that there is no duty on the judge to order separate trials even where there is a strong risk of prejudice, such as in sexual cases.[56] Turning to decisions on the cross-examination of the accused on bad character, the courts have long recognised that the trial judge has a discretion whether to permit such cross-examination, notwithstanding that a defendant has lost his or her so-called shield.[57] Recent decisions have emphasised, however, that judges do not have to exercise their discretion to exclude previous convictions merely because they are for similar offences, with the risk that juries will use them to infer guilt rather than as relevant to credibility.[58]

Apart from the occasions when character evidence is openly admitted as evidence, there are other occasions when this evidence leaks out to the jury inadvertently. Munday[59] has catalogued a range of situations when this occurs, such as where the defendant admits under questioning that he or she has been in prison before, or witnesses reveal that the defendant has a previous record. It is always open in such situations for the judge to stop the trial, but a more common option is for the judge to direct the jury to disregard the evidence, a feat almost impossible to accomplish, equivalent as one commentator has put it,[60] to "unbiting the apple of knowledge". These difficulties are compounded in non-jury trials, where the judge or magistrates act at the same time as the tribunal of law and the tribunal of fact. They can all the more easily be exposed to inadmissible evidence *before* the trial, through access to documents, and *during* the trial, through having to make rulings on whether a defendant has lost his or her shield. Of course, steps can be taken to remove, as far as possible, any inadmissible evidence from the tribunal. In magistrates' courts magistrates are prevented from acquiring knowledge of the defendant's previous convictions but, as one of the authors has shown, this can cause difficulties when the tribunal of law is supposed to warn the defence that it is taking a course of action which will result in loss of the defendant's shield.[61] One way of dealing with this problem in the magistrates' courts would be to give an enhanced role to justices' clerks, requiring them to alert the defence, but this would remain a problem in cases where stipendiaries sit alone without legally qualified clerks or in non-jury trials

[56] *Christou* [1996] 2 WLR 620.

[57] See e.g. *Selvey* v. *DPP* [1970] AC 304.

[58] See e.g. *Burke* (1985) 82 Cr App R 156; *Powell* [1986] 1 All ER 193; *McCleod* [1994] 1 WLR 1500; *Wainwright* [1998] Crim LR 665.

[59] R Munday, "Irregular Disclosure of Evidence of Bad Character" [1990] *Criminal Law Review* 92.

[60] M Damaska, "Reflections on the Character of Evidence in Continental and Anglo-American Systems" (unpublished paper, 1988).

[61] M Wasik, "Magistrates: Knowledge of Previous Convictions" [1996] *Criminal Law Review* 851.

presided over by a judge sitting alone.[62] In any event, the leave of the magistrate or judge is required before the prosecution can seek to cross-examine under section 1(f) of the 1898 Act, with the consequence that magistrates and judges are exposed to the character evidence before ruling on its strict admissibility.

Apart from the problems of exposure to inadmissible evidence caused by the role of the tribunal in non-jury cases, there is also the difficulty that non-jury tribunals have usually built up an experience over time that enables them either to know, or to make a well informed guess, about a defendant's criminal record. It has been suggested that there is a widespread problem of persons appearing regularly before a local bench where it is difficult to find magistrates who are not already familiar with their record.[63] On top of this, magistrates may well be able to make informed inferences about an accused's record from the way the trial is being conducted. In a survey conducted by one of the authors of the procedural and evidential difficulties that emerge when trial judges try serious criminal cases on their own (in Diplock cases in Northern Ireland), a senior judge reported that it was not difficult to work out whether a defendant had a criminal record.[64] If a defendant has a clean record it is a matter that is usually trumpeted early on in a case. Another judge compared the situation to the Sherlock Holmes story of "the dog that didn't bark in the night"—if no mention is made of the defendant's clear record, it can be assumed that he has not got one.[65]

Of course, it is often claimed that a tribunal with professional experience built up over time is less likely to be affected by prejudicial material than is a lay jury unversed in the rules of evidence and procedure. Strong views have been expressed on the question whether professional judges, or magistrates, are as affected by prejudicial character evidence as lay persons. On the one hand, the legal experience of judges and magistrates should place them in a better position to guard against forbidden chains of reasoning, and their professional role should militate against extra-legal prejudices stemming from an accused's bad character.[66] On the other hand, case-hardening may make

[62] This mode of trial is more common in the United Kingdom than is commonly thought. For the prevalence of criminal trials presided over by sheriffs without a jury in Scotland see G Maher, "Reforming the Criminal Process: A Scottish Perspective" in M McConville and L Bridges (eds.), *Criminal Justice in Crisis* (1994). For the prevalence of so-called "Diplock" trials without jury in Northern Ireland, see J Jackson and S Doran, *Judge without Jury: Diplock Trials in the Adversary System* (1995).

[63] P Darbyshire, "Previous Misconduct and Magistrates' Courts—Some Tales from the Real World" [1997] *Criminal Law Review* 105

[64] J Jackson and S Doran, *supra* n. 62, at 244.

[65] Caution may be needed in making this assumption about magistrates' courts, where research suggests that good character evidence is not always raised: J Vennard, *Contested Trials in Magistrates' Courts* (Home Office Research Unit No. 71, 1982).

[66] R C Park, "Character Evidence Issues in the OJ Simpson Case—Or, Rationales of the Character Evidence Ban, with Illustrations from the Simpson Case" (1996) 67 *University of Colorado Law Review* 747, at 771.

professionals more cynical, and more inclined to use knowledge of an accused's previous convictions as a confirmation of guilt. In the Diplock survey, judges themselves were divided about the impact of previous convictions. One judge admitted that one could never be sure about the extent to which one was influenced subconsciously by such evidence, but others thought the record of the defendant did not make a whit of difference to their reasoning.[67] There is little research evidence on whether professional judges or magistrates react differently to character evidence than juries, although in Kalven and Zeisel's classic study of the American jury[68] there was some evidence to suggest that judges *were* influenced by prior record for a similar crime. The Lord Chancellor's Department has recently commissioned research on the effects on magistrates of learning that a defendant has a previous conviction.[69]

The Relevance of Character Evidence

We can conclude that the exclusionary approach is less effective in preventing disclosure of a defendant's past than is sometimes thought. Research indicates that disclosure of bad character, particularly where it relates to previous convictions similar to those charged, does have an impact on juries and although the evidence in relation to judges and magistrates is less conclusive, it may well have an impact on them as well. This raises the central question of the *relevance* of character evidence, both to issues of guilt and credibility, and the question whether lay and professional persons are capable of handling such evidence in a manner which reflects its true weight.

In an influential article, Davies[70] has summarised the respective psychological literature on these issues. She has charted three phases in the literature. In the 1950s and 1960s psychological literature supported the common sense belief that a defendant's previous character was relevant to the probability of his or her doing or not doing an act charged, on the ground that human behaviour is governed by stable personality *traits* that produce generally consistent behaviour in widely divergent situations. By the mid-1960s, however, this reliance on trait theory was being called into question by an alternative theory known as social behaviour theory (or specificity theory or situationism), according to which behaviour depends on environmental factors so that response patterns, even in highly similar situations, often fail to be related. Methodological flaws in both these theories have more recently prompted a third, more cautious,

[67] See *supra* n. 62, at 244.

[68] H Kalven and H Zeisel, *The American Jury* (1966), pp. 127–30.

[69] S Lloyd-Bostock, "Decline of the 'Little Parliament': Juries and Jury Reform in England and Wales" (1999) 62 *Law and Contemporary Problems* 7, at 32.

[70] S M Davies, "Evidence of Character to Prove Conduct: A Reassessment of Relevancy" (1991) 27 *Criminal Law Bulletin* 504.

response whereby it is now accepted that behaviour is simultaneously a function of disposition, situation, and their complex mutual interaction.

Davies concluded that evidence of previous misconduct *may* be useful to trial fact-finders, if one takes account of factors such as the similarity between surrounding circumstances, the number of prior instances, proximity in time, and whether the conduct is inherently likely to be repeated. At the same time, she argued that generalised descriptions of a person's character traits are much less useful in predicting single instances of behaviour. Evidence of a prior conviction will *rarely* be a good indicator of whether a person will intentionally give false testimony. If the prior conviction used to impeach is for an offence not involving dishonesty, one must generalise on the basis of a general readiness to commit criminal acts in order to suggest that the witness cannot be believed, and psychologists of all persuasions would agree that such a generalisation cannot be inferred from one or two criminal acts. Even where the previous offence did involve dishonesty, that conviction may be irrelevant to the question whether the witness is lying on oath, because of the very different situational factors operating. Turning to the literature on the prejudicial effect of character evidence, there is a large body of work[71] which shows that the phenomenon known as "fundamental attribution error" causes human decision-makers to attribute too much importance to dispositions and to overlook important situational differences. Some recent studies are more favourable to lay reasoning,[72] but only where the assessors of character are well acquainted with the person whose character is in question, and they are given information about specific acts in their situational settings, rather than in the form of a global traits.

There have been innumerable warnings about the dangers of generalising from psychological laboratory conditions to the real life processes of the courtroom.[73] In real life there are the problems discussed *supra*, concerning inaccuracy and bias in character evidence presented to the court, and the fact that previous convictions may not be a true reflection of an accused's criminal history. Park has urged caution about the significance of these studies for law reform. In relation to the attribution error studies, for example, he explains that the question is not how good or bad lay reasoning is in general, but whether triers of fact are more accurate in determining whether the defendant committed the crime if they are given evidence about his or her commission of other crimes at other times.[74] In relation to this, he contends that the research implications are two-sided—not just that *jurors* might attach too much importance to disposition evidence, but that *judges*, in using their discretion to

71 *Ibid.*, at 527.
72 *Ibid.*, at 531–2.
73 See e.g. M King, *Psychology In and Out of Court* (1986).
74 *Ibid.*, at 739–41.

exclude evidence on the ground that it will prejudice the jury, may make attribution errors in deciding what might prejudice a jury. For the jury, the policy implications of the research are again unclear, as it suggests that human beings will continue to make dispositional attributions, and to overestimate their power, whether or not they are given specific information about an accused's past character. Park has also warned about the dangers of generalising from psychological studies of *non*-criminal behaviour to conclusions about the probative value of criminal behaviour.[75] Studies show, for example, how difficult it is to predict from one instance of ordinary behaviour that another such instance will occur, but it could be that a single instance of extreme behaviour (such as commission of murder) does demonstrate a higher propensity to commit another instance of extreme behaviour of the same type.[76]

Allowing for the difficulty in deriving policy guides from the psychological evidence, there are still enough pointers to suggest that the "exclusionary rule and exceptions" approach to character evidence is misguided. This is indeed the conclusion that the courts and policy-makers have reached in relation to similar fact evidence. As Davies has argued, the ingredients of "probative value" and "potential for prejudice" of character evidence are complex and variable.[77] Any *rule* to the effect that similar past crimes are not probative in a propensity sense to guilt makes little sense, and the courts have accepted that a categorical approach, specifying exceptions to such a rule, should be abandoned in favour of a careful balancing exercise weighing the probative value of the evidence against its prejudicial effect on a case by case basis. It may be that the kind of "structured discretion" approach favoured by the Law Commission is therefore the best way forward. It must be recognised, however, that this leaves the door open to the kind of biases and stereotyping that we have seen attaches to other phases of the criminal process. Mention has already been made of the distorting effects of "rounding up the usual suspects" in police investigations, and similar considerations apply at the trial level. While accepting that evidence of prior crimes may be relevant in a propensity sense to show guilt, it should be remembered that criminal defendants are much more likely to have committed prior bad acts than a randomly selected person from the general population.[78]

The psychological evidence suggests that judges should be much stricter in admitting character evidence for the purpose of assessing credibility.[79] There is no need for a new rule of evidence to achieve this, since character evidence

[75] R C Park, *supra* n. 35, at 733–5.

[76] *Ibid.*, at 737–8.

[77] See *supra* n. 70, at 534.

[78] R J Allen *et al*, *Evidence: Text, Cases and Problems* (2nd ed., 1997), p. 303.

[79] See R Munday, "The Paradox of Cross-Examination to Credit—Simply Too Close for Comfort" (1994) 53 *Cambridge Law Journal* 303; P Roberts, "All the Usual Suspects: A Critical Appraisal of the Law Commission's Consultation Paper No 141" [1997] *Criminal Law* Review 75.

introduced for such a purpose generally lacks probative value. It should be for the party seeking to cross-examine on the basis of character to show its particular relevance to credit. The Law Commission canvassed such an idea in its Consultation Paper,[80] but drew back from it on the ground that any proposal to restrict character evidence in general exceeded its terms of reference. The Commission's suggestion that this proposal would impose a higher standard of legal relevance for character evidence than for other evidence is, in our view, questionable in the light of the low probative value that character has in relation to credibility. Indeed, the proposal that bad character imputations should be made only where they would substantially undermine the witness's credibility is not far removed from existing and long-standing common law boundaries in cross-examination. According to Sankey LJ in *Hobbs* v. *Tinling*,[81] such questions are only proper if they are of such a nature that the truth of the imputation conveyed would *seriously affect* the opinion of the court on the credibility of the witness. The real problem, then, would seem to be that trial judges have been unwilling to circumscribe cross-examination to this extent. More stringent limits on cross-examination as to credit would have the desirable effect of protecting witnesses from indignity. It would also take the sting out of the iniquities in the "tit for tat" rule. Defendants would generally be restricted to casting imputations which went directly to the facts in issue. In such a case, under the Law Commission's proposal, there would be no loss of the shield.[82]

There remains the question whether defendants should be allowed, as at present, to adduce evidence of *good* character. Just as *bad* character evidence is much less helpful in assessing the credibility of witnesses than is commonly thought, so *good* character evidence is equally unhelpful. Apart from the psychological research that stresses situational factors as well as character traits, there are dangers in the trial context of reading too much into the defendant's clean record, just as there is in reading too much into his or her previous misconduct. The wisdom of allowing defendants to assert their own good character is doubtful, as is the general requirement on judges to give a propensity direction to juries.[83] The accused who has determinedly "kept his hands clean" in preparation for a major "job", and the artful dodger who has offended at will while evading the clutches of the law, are both no doubt pleased that judges should inform juries that their clean record may have a bearing on their propensity to commit the first offence with which they are charged.[84] All that

[80] See *supra* n. 11, paras 12.91–12.100.
[81] [1929] 2 KB 1.
[82] See *supra* n. 11, para. 12.79
[83] See *Vye, Wise and Stephenson* [1993] 3 All ER 241. The position is different in Australia, see most recently *Melbourne* v. *The Queen* [1999] HCA 32.
[84] Zuckerman, Jackson and Doran, (1993) *All ER Rev* 208–9.

good character generally means is that the defendant has a clean record,[85] and this tells us precious little about his or her propensity to commit the offence charged.

Conclusion

Character evidence is used throughout the criminal process, and is more commonly admitted at the trial, against defendants as well as other witnesses, than is commonly thought. Yet throughout this chapter we have drawn attention to the dangers of attributing too much weight to character evidence. This suggests that there should be much more careful *monitoring* of the use of such evidence throughout the criminal process.

Mention was made, above, of the bias that can be caused by the use of criminal records against defendants. Article 14 of the European Convention guarantees a right to enjoyment of the rights and freedoms of the Convention without discrimination on any ground such as sex, race, colour, language, religion, political or other opinion, national or social origin. Given the importance that record plays in accounting for the differential treatment of suspects and defendants with and without a record throughout the criminal process, there is a need to monitor carefully how defendants come to acquire a criminal record in the first place. Section 95 of the Criminal Justice Act 1991 requires the Secretary of State to publish such information as he considers expedient in order to enable those involved in the criminal justice system to avoid improper discrimination on grounds of race, sex or any other improper grounds. A number of publications have been produced under this power,[86] but much more work needs to be done not only in monitoring policing decisions but in monitoring the decisions of prosecutors and sentencers as well. As part of these equity monitoring procedures it would be useful to track the extent to which persons with certain kinds of backgrounds are disproportionately processed through the system, and to compare the outcomes of their cases.

[85] Although it was accepted by the House of Lords in *Aziz* [1995] 3 WLR 53 that a trial judge has a discretion to decline to give any character directions where it is considered an insult to common sense to give them as where a defendant without previous convictions is shown beyond doubt to have been guilty of serious criminal conduct.

[86] See e.g. Home Office, *Race and the Criminal Justice System* (1992), (1994), (1995), (1997), *Gender and the Criminal Justice System* (1992), *Does the Criminal Justice System Treat Men and Women Differently?* (Research Findings No. 10, 1994), *The Sentencing of Women* (1997), *Statistics on Race and the Criminal Justice System* (1998). There have also been publications in Scotland and Northern Ireland under s. 306 of the Criminal Procedure (Scotland) Act 1995 and art. 56 of the Criminal Justice (NI) Order 1996.

As well as monitoring the *outcome* of cases, it can be argued that more also needs to be done to build in safeguards for defendants in the *process* of cases. One way in which the European Court of Human Rights has satisfied itself that decision-makers have conformed with requirements of the European Convention, such as the need to ensure that pre-trial detention does not exceed a reasonable time, is by scrutinising the reasons given for decisions.[87] It may be that judges should also be required to record reasons when making decisions to admit character evidence. The Law Commission has helpfully suggested certain factors which ought to be taken into account in deciding whether to admit similar fact evidence.[88] To ensure that these have been taken into account properly, judges and magistrates should arguably have to record their reasons for the admission of that evidence.

When it comes to the use of character evidence by the tribunal of fact, we have seen that the traditional approach, of trying to prevent the revealing of the defendant's bad character, does not protect the defendant from prejudice when the evidence is disclosed. One way of monitoring the use of such evidence would be to follow the continental requirement that the tribunal of fact should give a reasoned opinion demonstrating that its factual findings have a firm basis in evidence.[89] The European Court of Human Rights has stressed the importance of giving reasons in the criminal trial. In the context of drawing inferences from silence, and in ensuring that convictions should not depend solely or mainly on adverse inferences from silence, the Court has emphasised the importance of a reasoned judgment.[90] Although the Court has never endorsed the need for exclusionary character rules, it could be argued that a tribunal of fact which relied disproportionately on character evidence to convict would result in the defendant not receiving a fair trial. When a jury is exposed to character evidence, the inscrutability of the verdict makes it impossible to know just what reliance has been placed on that evidence. One way of compensating for this is to require careful directions to be given to the jury. The Court of Appeal has recognised that legislation permitting juries to draw adverse inferences from the defendant's silence could breach Article 6 of the Convention unless juries are given very carefully framed directions on that matter.[91] Of course, one can be sceptical of the precise effect that directions will have on juries, just as one can be sceptical of the effect which the requirement to give reasons might have on a professional judge. There is, however, evidence that mock juries do listen to judicial directions on evidence and try their best to heed them.[92]

87 See e.g. *Letellier* v. *France* (1991) 14 EHRR 83.
88 See *supra* n. 11, paras 10.79–10.80.
89 Damaska, *supra* n. 45, at 66.
90 *Murray* v. *United Kingdom* (1996) 22 EHRR 29.
91 *Burchall* [1999] Crim LR 311.
92 See e.g. Cornish and Sealy, *supra* n. 37.

The effectiveness of directions will, however, depend very much on how they are framed, and one may be sceptical about judicial directions which require juries to disregard character evidence which they have already heard, or to use that evidence as relevant to credibility but not guilt.[93] It has been submitted that the general irrelevance of character evidence as going to the credibility of witnesses should result in judges being much more vigilant about admitting evidence for that purpose. This would restrict the amount of character evidence admitted during the trial but, for reasons already discussed, character evidence is still inherently likely to spill out during the course of the trial. More attention needs to be given to giving juries relevance directions, spelling out to them the general *irrelevance* of character, and explaining why such evidence is generally so regarded. A further question is whether such a direction should be given even when character evidence has *not* been admitted. Jury research has concentrated on the effect upon mock juries of revelations about the defendant's record. Very little is known, however, about the ways in which perceptions of character (whether of the defendant, or of witnesses) feature as an issue in jury deliberations more generally. More research needs to be done on this, and on the impact on juries of character directions, whether or not the defendant's record has been made known to them. More generally, it has been suggested that more needs to be done to maximise the respective contribution that juries and judges make to the task of reconstructing reality in the courtroom.[94] The judge has traditionally given directions to the jury on how to approach the facts but there is little interaction between judge and jury during the trial and little opportunity for judges to be assured that their directions are understood by juries. The inscrutability of the final verdict will probably continue to be a feature of the jury trial in the common law world for some time but this need not mean that steps could not be taken to encourage more open dialogue between judges and juries.[95] This also points to the need for judges and juries to act in partnership, in order to produce as accurate a verdict as possible.

Finally, if judges are to be given a more active responsibility in guiding juries on character issues, steps must be taken to ensure that judges themselves are made aware of the distorting effects of character evidence and of the stereotyping dangers that such evidence can produce. Cultural awareness training needs to become a more significant feature of training schemes for all practi-

[93] See e.g. R L Wissler and M I Saks, "On the Efficacy of Limiting Instructions: When Jurors Use Prior Convictions Evidence to Decide on Guilt" (1985) 9 *Law and Human Behavior* 37.

[94] J Jackson and S Doran, "Judge and Jury: Towards a New Division of Labour in Criminal Trials (1997) 60 *Modern Law Review* 759.

[95] One example is the procedure adopted by Judge Dann in Phoenix Arizona who distributes sets of instructions to jurors before the trial and encourages them to write down questions for him during the trial: see S Adler, *The Jury: Trial and Error in the American Courtroom* (1994), pp. 228–40.

tioners in the criminal justice system. Aside from monitoring the outcomes and processes of individual decisions, this suggests that there is also a need to monitor the practises of all those who are involved in criminal justice decision-making. Professionals have rightly been jealous of their independence and suspicious of State interference. But as they are entrusted to take ever greater responsibility for decisions, mechanisms of accountability need to be strengthened to satisfy the public that they are properly entrusted with such responsibility. The identification of "institutionalised racism" within the Metropolitan Police by the Macpherson Report[96] is a warning to all professions which work within the criminal justice system that their structures need to be constantly reviewed to avoid unfair discrimination.

[96] See *The Stephen Lawrence Inquiry,* Report of an Inquiry by Sir William Macpherson of Cluny (Cm 4262, 1999).

19

Does Medical Law Have a Future?

MARGARET BRAZIER AND NICOLA GLOVER

Introduction

If a volume of essays on law's futures had been prepared in the middle of the twentieth century, medical law would have been absent from the literary feast. Perusal of the Law Reports before 1980 will reveal no more than a handful of reported cases which address either the civil liability of doctors or how the law should respond to controversial problems of medical ethics. Everything has changed today. At the start of this new century, medical law flourishes. It is established as a thriving area of scholarship. Claims for compensation for medical negligence rise inexorably.[1] Hardly a day passes without the popular media highlighting a medical law controversy, be it retention of children's organs or yet another tragedy when a mentally disturbed ex-patient kills or mutilates his unfortunate victim. Medical law is a matter of national importance, even regarded by some as a national scandal. Frank Dobson, when Secretary of State for Health, declared:[2] "The only place for a lawyer in the NHS is on the operating table". Mr Dobson will be disappointed. Medical law will not go away because government wills it. Most importantly medical law is much, much more than simply medical negligence claims against doctors and hospitals. Fundamental issues of the boundaries of human rights are the central concern of what we still style medical law. Key questions of the responsibilities which individuals, families and society owe to the more vulnerable members of our community need answers. Nonetheless, in this chapter, we reflect on whether our subject, which has little obvious history, does have a future?

[1] In 1996–97 litigation cost the NHS close to £300m: *Hansard*, 24 March 1998, 165–6. The House of Commons Public Accounts Committee has estimated that the NHS has £2.8bn to meet in outstanding liability claims: (2000) 320 *British Medical Journal* 270.

[2] *The Guardian*, 30 April 1998.

We could have addressed an endless list of topical developments: how the law will respond to cloning, cryonic preservation, head transplants or virtual surgery would each generate a chapter of its own. Scholarship among lawyers and ethicists in this field is too often driven by the pace of scientific developments. Making an informed choice of which controversial and demanding area of medicine to respond to defeated us. What we seek to do is to argue that, while the law's relationship with medicine and science will continue to dominate public and scholarly debate in 2050, medical law as we have known it for the last twenty years is unlikely to exist. We plead guilty to a degree of hyperbole and a large measure of crystal ball-gazing.

Kennedy's and Grubb's classic work describes medical law as "essentially concerned with the relationship between doctors (and to a lesser extent hospitals and other institutions) and patients".[3] Montgomery in 1997 rejects the restriction of the subject to the "clinical medical context". Entitling his text, *Health Care Law*, Montgomery addresses the United Kingdom's international obligations to tackle health problems and government's responsibility to ensure access to health care for its citizens.[4] The differences between these two approaches is more than just nomenclature. Medical law which focuses on a relationship between doctors and patients remains in essence a creature of private law. Albeit NHS patients have no contractual relationship with their doctors, echoes of contract still haunt their encounters. Health care law is located more firmly in public law. Doctors are shifted to the margins of debate. The needs, and even rights, of individual patients must be viewed within a wider context of protecting health and promoting public goods.

A shift from medical law to health care law seems inevitable. The Law Reports portray a bygone age. Cases on informed consent, standards of care, or treating patients with mental incapacity still appear to reflect a system of care where care is delivered within a one to one relationship between doctor and patient. The fact that NHS care is almost always team care is overlooked. Developments in the NHS will gradually change that picture. The replacement of doctors by other professionals in many contexts of care will force the law to rethink its conceptualisation of disputes about provision and standards of publicly-funded health care. We suggest, however, that what we now call medical law will undergo much greater upheaval than simply a change of name. Society's understanding of illness is in flux. Neat divisions of physical and mental illness broke down some time ago. The current preoccupation with autonomy and individual rights ignores the fact that disease and disorder fail to recognise such rights. Medical law, as it approaches middle age, must confront challenges deriving both from how we regard [ill] health and how we seek to respond to its demands.

[3] *Medical Law: Text and Materials* (2nd edn., Butterworths, 1993), p. 3.
[4] J Montgomery, *Health Care Law* (Oxford University Press, 1997), p. 1.

What is Illness?

Reports that a Scottish surgeon carried out surgery on two patients to amputate their legs below the knee generated a media frenzy early in 2000. Neither patient suffered from any physical condition requiring amputation. The surgeon defended his conduct robustly. He argued that both patients suffered from apotemnophilia, a psychological condition which resulted in a fixation that they were meant to be an amputee.[5] Without surgery, such a person might resort to desperate measures, such as hacking off their own leg. The surgeon's employing NHS Trust immediately prohibited further such operations, even though both operations were carried out privately at no cost to the NHS. Yet the law permits transexual surgery involving much greater mutilation of the body. What is different about amputation to allow the individual to live in the body which he believes that he belongs in? Amputation becomes a treatment for body dysmorphia.

The amputee's tale becomes a debate about illness. If a convincing case is made that the person is *sick* and amputation offers *cure*, bizarre behaviour becomes lawful. If the person is classified as simply having a perverse desire to have his leg chopped off, and seeks the services of a butcher not a doctor, a criminal offence is committed.[6] Medicalising choices to grant such choices respectability is a recurring theme of law's relationship with medicine. Very often debate about the ethics of some novel fertility treatment is trumped by claims that infertility is a disease, therefore any process offering cure must be legitimated. The technology to establish pregnancy in a person without a uterus is already in place. Imagine a male to female transexual seeking such assisted conception, can she be denied the benefit of treatment which will "cure" her fatal "defect"? At a more mundane level consider the controversy over Viagra. What is usually disputed is who falls into a category of people having a medical *need* for the drug. Just wanting Viagra because it improves sexual performance is not enough. Illness makes choices legitimate and transforms wants into rights.

Perhaps our use of examples demonstrate too narrow an understanding of health. The World Health Organisation has defined health[7] as "a state of complete physical, mental and social well-being and not merely the absence of disease or infirmity". Such a definition embraces a host of human desires. Thus amputation could be regarded as essential to the individual's well-being for who, but he, can define his own well-being. Failing sexual potency is

[5] See (2000) 320 *British Medical Journal* 331.
[6] See generally *Consent in the Criminal Law*, (Law Commission Consultation Paper No. 139).
[7] *Constitution of the World Health Organisation* (Geneva, WHO, 1948).

self-evidently detrimental to many of its sufferers. They may not be ill but they are not well. A right to be well begins to look infinitely elastic and predominantly subjective.

Human wants expressed as health needs create a paradox. Medicalisation legitimates choices which might otherwise fall foul of the law. At the same time it infantilises the choice-maker.[8] Her choice is subjected to medical discretion. Persuade a doctor that a need is a health need and you may be permitted to engage in otherwise prohibited conduct. Currently the price paid for realising that choice, be it for Viagra, or fertility treatment, or just effective sleeping pills, is submitting yourself to judgements not just about your immediate request but often your whole lifestyle. Doctors will judge whether your need is real and whether you deserve what you ask for.

A case can be made that the medical role is to protect the patient, to ensure that she comprehends the risks inherent in what she seeks and provide a guarantee of competence on the part of her "helpers", the doctors. Such a role would however be essentially advisory. However unusual the patient's request, once adequate advice was proffered, the doctor should respond and provide what is asked for. Doctors would cease to be gatekeepers of certain kinds of treatment. Gatekeeping of any kind is being overtaken by technology. British legislation on fertility treatment requires that British clinics take account of the welfare of any child likely to be born as a result of treatment. British regulators restrict access to Viagra by classifying it as a prescription-only medicine. Yet those who want to buy sperm or Viagra can do so easily via the Internet. The wealthy and knowledgeable have several means by which to evade British regulations limiting access to medicines or technology.[9]

The ease with which some individuals can bypass "medical" barriers to realising their desires casts doubt on the future viability of any gatekeeping role for doctors or the law. The debate on what constitutes illness could alter radically. If society concedes that a settled desire for bizarre surgery, or a wish to enhance sexual potency, or just a good night's sleep, justifies the satisfaction of that want, why maintain a pretence of illness? Why restrict the freedom of a third party to assist in the realisation of that want? Consumer protection laws could (in theory) offer sufficient guarantee of the quality of goods supplied and standards of service provision. Professional regulation could develop to maintain adequate levels of competence in service providers. Discarding concepts of illness and according legitimacy to the desire itself will not compel unwilling doctors to participate in conduct contrary to their personal or professional

[8] Elegantly discussed by McLean, see Sheila McLean, *Old Law, New Medicine* (Pandora Press, 1999), pp. 5–24.

[9] Procreative tourism is already well under way, see, for example, L Nielsen, "Procreative Tourism, Genetic Testing and Law" in N Lowe and G Douglas (eds), *Families Across Frontiers* (Kluwer, 1996), p. 831.

ethics. No surgeon will be forced to perform amputations which she considers to be unjustifiable self-mutilation. Laws will cease to be a means of preventing other doctors, or new breeds of professionals, meeting the customers, demands. No doubt a market will develop to meet demand.

Such a future, where medical law is subsumed in consumer law, may be seen as a logical development of regarding medical law as a sub-set of human rights. Currently illness is the peg on which a number of human rights claims are advanced. Yet if there is an untrammelled right to assistance in founding a family the rationale of why the person seeking to found a family needs help might be dismissed as irrelevant. If respect for privacy restricts the State's rights to interfere in consensual activity between willing participants, on what basis can X be barred from helping Y dispense with an unwanted limb? The jurisprudence of the European Court of Human Rights does not promote such "liberality" at present.[10] Civil law traditions of the dignity and non-commensurability of the human body appear to stand in the way of such a development. However, unless the law can settle upon some coherent and defensible definition of illness, the elasticity of concepts of illness may snap. With illness no longer as a precondition of entitlement to access to technology and drugs, a world evolves in which, for the few, medicine in all its forms is just another good to be bought freely in the marketplace.

Individuals, communities and health

In this *Brave New World*, those few may be happy. Lawyers need not fear it. Technology will fail. Customers and medical services retailers will fall out. Contract law will flourish again in this world. It will be a small world. Removing legal barriers to the use of medical technology to satisfy desires, does not mean that the NHS (if it survives) will fund such wants as every patient demands. Publicly-funded medicine will still have to grapple with what constitutes illness. Radical changes in systems for allocation of resources must come and litigation to challenge rationing decisions will rise dramatically. Other fundamental questions about the role of law will also surface if we move towards such a divided world of access to medicines and technology.

Expanding definitions of illness coupled with the present tendency to prioritise self-determination as *the* basic human right in medical law, assume that health is essentially a personal concern. Classic definitions of personal liberty and modern human rights law all qualify liberty by accepting that restrictions on personal liberty to prevent harm to others are justifiable. Article 8 of the

[10] See *Brown* v. *United Kingdom* (1997) 24 EHRR 39, ECHR.

European Convention of Human Rights 1950 imposes significant qualifications on a right to respect for private and family life. The State may limit the exercise of such rights in the interests of (*inter alia*) "the economic well-being of the country, for the prevention of disorder or crime, for the protection of *health* or *morals*, or the protection of the rights and freedoms of others". Article 8 provokes several questions in the context of access to medicines and technology. Restrictions on what we are allowed to do with our bodies, or permit others to do, have traditionally been debated in the context of morals. Sado-masochistic acts are prohibited as immoral. Self-mutilation unsanctioned by the legitimacy of illness may fall short of moral standards. The likelihood of a sufficient consensus on morals still justifying prohibitions on consensual activity in 2050 seems slim. More important may be the question of how far protection of health justifies restrictions on the gratification of desires dependent on such access. The contented amputee will perceive no harm to him from the satisfaction of his want. Nor is any third party obviously harmed by him.

Laws restricting access to medicine on grounds of protection of health will be subjected to scrutiny. Whether prohibitions on access to certain kinds of services can be justified in terms of protecting the patient (or customer) herself may be doubted. The law permits voluntary participation in many risky activities. We are not barred from engaging in, for example, bungee-jumping albeit we risk life and limb. The law protects our welfare by policing standards of provision of equipment and services and offering generous redress if the failure of services provided results in injury. Providing the law can guarantee "medical" choices are informed choices, consumers of medicines and medical technology might contend that what they need is effective consumer protection, not paternalist direction.

Must protection of health as a justification for infringement of free access to medicine involve evidence that granting X what he seeks may damage Y? Even in our *Brave New World*, prohibiting conduct directly harmful to other individuals or public health may be justified. There is abundant evidence that easy access to antibiotics has increased the levels of antibiotic resistance in the community endangering medicine's capacity to combat infectious disease. Our cavalier or misguided use of antibiotics could leave you at the mercy of untreatable disease. Certain kinds of drugs carry a significant potential for misuse either by their immediate user or a third party into whose hands they fall. Overuse of tranquillisers or sleeping drugs may result in increased incidence of accidents. Used recreationally, as with the sleeping drug Temazepam, such medicines may increase crime rates. The criminally-minded, given unrestricted access to lethal medicines, may more readily dispose of unwanted relatives. Restricting access to poisons and drugs with a significant potential to result in harm should not be a difficulty.

Such restrictions would form but a small part of the picture, and concern the more minor issues in the future of medicine. Analogous arguments about physical harm to others are harder to find among the more high profile dilemmas of modern medicine. In relation to fertility treatment British law does presently impose restrictions on access grounded in protecting the interests of others. Section 13(5) of the Human Fertilisation and Embryology Act 1990 requires clinics offering treatment to take account of the welfare of the child to be born and of any existing children who may be affected by the birth. Section 13(5) is almost universally condemned as discriminatory against people who cannot, or choose not to, procreate naturally. Even where proposed treatments risk the birth of a child with physiological abnormalities some have argued that the risk assessment is a matter for the putative parent(s). The consumer's choice should not be constrained.

Restrictions dependent on evidence that allowing X to have the treatment of his choice will result in readily recognisable harm to Y will be minimal. Much more pertinent will be questions of whether proponents of consumer choice will accept the logical consequences of such a system and how far (if at all) the need to provide health care for the community as a whole justifies restricting the liberty of a part of that community.

In 2000, while illness is utilised to legitimise certain human wants, illness is also sometimes invoked as an excuse for abdicating personal responsibility for health. There is a reluctance to recognise that individuals may be responsible both for their own ill-health and for their conduct when "ill". Some degree of moral, even legal responsibility in relation to transmitting infectious disease is gradually gaining credence.[11] Suggestions that lifestyle-related illness should be categorised as self-inflicted with consequences in terms of priority for publicly-funded health care are generally rejected.[12] Those who elect to participate in a medical services market will be able to do so only if they possess the funds to do so. For many, health insurance will be the source of such funds. Lifestyle is likely to dictate premiums. Smokers and heavy drinkers will be penalised. The riskier the service a person seeks the higher the cost will be. A culture of choice allows the consumer to dictate what he will pay, as much as what he will buy. If a transsexual is prepared to embark on the risks of an extra-uterine pregnancy and can meet the cost, who else's business is her choice?

Those choices becomes the business of others once migration between different worlds of health care is contemplated. The transsexual pregnancy is established. The sexually eager youth buys Viagra. Disaster strikes. The transsexual's child is born premature and very sick. Her life too is at risk. The youth suffers a brain haemorrhage. Their insurance cover is exhausted. The NHS is

[11] See M Brazier and J Harris "Public Health and Private Lives" (1996) *Med L Rev* 171.

[12] See the debate among clinicians exploring coronary bypass surgery for smokers (1993) 306 *British Medical Journal* 1047.

left to deal with the consequences. The cost to the public purse is increased because the private market procedures, which NHS clinicians might have declined to perform, have catapulted the consumers into incontrovertible *illness*. There is ample evidence today that the NHS picks up the burden of privately-funded care, given that many private clinics lack intensive care facilities. Privately-funded fertility treatment has increased the burden on specialist neonatal units within the NHS.

Migration between private and public health care is commonplace today. The growing popularity of complementary medicine, largely available only in the private sector, enhances this trend. Consumers already pick and choose. Soon hard choices will be unavoidable. Should such migration be restricted? Can the NHS withhold treatment from, or give a low priority to, a person whose choice to access unrestricted private care contributed to the illness for which he now seeks treatment? Such a result is almost unthinkable. Turning away the dying victim of medical disaster from intensive care, however foolish his initial choice may have been, may violate a State's responsibility to protect life. But could the detrimental effect on publicly-funded health care be used to justify restrictions on a burgeoning private market?

In the world we speculate on, which allows unrestricted access to medical technology for those who can pay, the NHS will not just continue to carry the cost of paying for others' mistakes and disasters, its own costs will escalate. The truly unhealthy will for the most part be excluded from the consumer market. The NHS will bear the cost of treating the poor, with their much greater risk of ill-health, and the cost of treating those with chronic or incurable illness. The expectations of its patients will be raised by what they perceive as available on the other side of the divide.[13] Failure by the NHS will become even more likely to generate litigation, itself imposing intolerable strains on NHS budgets. The existence of decent public health care could be threatened by the extension of liberty for those able to exercise it. Such arguments are already being heard. In *Heil* v. *Rankin*[14], counsel arguing for a 100 per cent rise in levels of damages for pain and suffering acknowledged that such an outcome would adversely affect the NHS by increasing the cost of litigation. Nonetheless he contended that such a consideration was legally irrelevant. The entitlement of medical accident victims to appropriate levels of compensation should not be diminished by the impact on the service of escalating litigation costs. Individual rights should not cede precedence to community needs. Others disagree: Lord Woolf M.R. expressly acknowledged the potential injury to the N.H.S. arising from escalating levels of damages. The philosopher, John Harris, has argued that claimants in medical

[13] And note that once it is conceded that X is ill, a blanket exclusion on treatment for his or her condition may become unlawful; see *R* v. *North West Lancashire Health Authority, ex p A*, [2000] 1 WLR 977.

[14] [2000] 2 WLR 1173, CA.

negligence suits against the NHS should have their claims rationed in competition with patients seeking treatment from the same limited budget.[15] The basic nature of resort to law to obtain redress for NHS errors will inevitably have to be re-analysed. The present model, with its unspoken assumption that what is in issue is just a variant of the normal form of personal injury claim where patient X seeks redress from Doctor Y for Y's personal negligence, cannot survive.

In those cases where in form at least what is in dispute is the duty owed by a doctor to a patient the law's conceptualisation of the relationship between the two may need to alter. The tort of negligence has never accommodated that relationship entirely comfortably. Negligence might well fit claims for a failure to perform a medical procedure adequately but fails to recognise the crucial nature of communication in patient/doctor encounters. The unending debate on "informed consent" swings between paternalism and a myth of patient self-sufficiency which rarely meets the reality of illness. Teff's "therapeutic alliance" is passed by as the pendulum swings.[16] The courts, in past years, tended to reinforce the paternalistic nature of the doctor/patient relationship. Lord Diplock in *Sidaway* v. *Board of Governors of the Bethlem Royal Hospital and the Maudsley Hospital*[17] perceived the doctor's duty as to do what he judged best for his patient. "Doctor knows best" is a remedy many legal scholars have devoted the past fifteen years to attacking. The opposite end of the spectrum, untrammelled patient choice, may fail to represent reality, or to meet all patients' desires. The English courts have moved away somewhat from Diplock in *Sidaway*.[18] Nonetheless the judiciary continue to try to accommodate doctor/patient relationships within a tort model inadequate to recognise the delicate balance between a person's need and right to a sense of control over his or her fate and the dependency which illness brings with it.[19] The rights of the ill are not necessarily identical to the rights of the well. The complicated nature of trust between patient and professionals calls for a recognition of that relationship as a *fiduciary* relationship.[20]

The Canadian Supreme Court has followed that route, expressly endorsing fiduciary principles at the heart of health care law. In *McInerny* v. *MacDonald*,[21]

[15] J Harris, "The Injustice of Compensation for Victims of Medical Accidents" (1997) 314 *British Medical Journal* 1821.

[16] H Teff, "Consent to Medical Procedures: Paternalism, Self-Determination or Therapeutic Alliance" (1985) 101 *LQR* 432.

[17] [1985] AC 871 at 895, unless of course the patient himself might have the "training and experience" to make it "natural" for him to make his own decisions!

[18] Most notably in *Pearce* v. *United British Healthcare Trust* [1999] PIQR P53.

[19] See A Campbell, "Dependency Revisited: the Limits of Autonomy in Medical Ethics" in M Brazier and M Lobjoit (eds), *Protecting the Vulnerable: Autonomy and Consent in Health Care* (Routledge, 1991), p. 101.

[20] See P Tucker, "Good Faith: In Search of a Unifying Principle for the Doctor-Patient Relationship", (1998) 5 *Journal of Law and Medicine* 372 and P Bartlett, "Doctors as Fiduciaries: Equitable Regulation of the Doctor-Patient Relationship", (1997) 5 *Med L Rev* 193.

[21] (1992) 93 DLR (4th) 415.

it was observed that a patient "shares intimate information" in a consultation with his doctor because the doctor-patient relationship is trust-based in nature.[22] It was recognised that trust is vital in order to encourage reciprocity between the doctor and patient.[23] However, so far, the development of a fiduciary-based relationship in Britain has been frustrated.[24] Conventional principles of negligence continue to be stretched to meet demands beyond their capacity.

A further difficulty besets the courts response to "medical" litigation. The existence of health professionals other than doctors is barely acknowledged. Patient complaints and lawsuits often result from failures in communication, and the role of non-medical professionals in communication is vital. A patient undergoing surgery is likely to have, at best, an hour or so of direct contact with the surgeon. Far more of his or her care will be provided by junior doctors, nurses, auxiliary staff, and even volunteers. The NHS, in contrast to private medicine, provides a service, a service delivered by a multi-disciplinary team. Now that hospital doctors are covered by NHS Indemnity, the practical advantages of suing an individual doctor are less. The focus of litigation must become the NHS provider's discharge of a duty to provide a competent service regardless of through whom that service is delivered.[25] The question of whether limits on resources should affect what constitutes a reasonable level of service will not go away.[26]

The courts will need to adapt to a radically altered publicly-funded health service. The introduction of NHS Direct[27] allowing telephone and Internet access to health advice, the development of health check booths in shopping centres, presage the availability of a much more "anonymous" form of health care. The relationship between health care provider and patient will be totally different to that between a patient and a general practitioner, or a patient undergoing hospital treatment today. Indeed in a sense there will be no *relationship*. The element of trust crucial to many forms of health care is absent. Health professionals, from several different backgrounds and disciplines, from conventional and complementary medicine, will dispense advice without prior knowledge of the patient. Loyalty, of professional to patient, or vice versa, will not be a factor in the encounter. Measures such as NHS Direct are designed to ease the burdens on the NHS and increase patient choice. They could be seen as mirroring the consumer-oriented services which, we suggest,

[22] See also *Kenny* v. *Lockwood* (1932) OR 141 (CA) and *Henderson* v. *Johnston* (1956) OR 789.

[23] In *Breen* v. *Williams* (1996) 186 CLR 71, the Australian Supreme Court of New South Wales, Australia, rejected the earlier approach taken by the Canadian Supreme Court in *McIneny*.

[24] *R* v. *Mid-Glamorgan F.H.S.A., ex parte Martin* [1995] 1 WLR 110, CA.

[25] See *M* v. *Calderdale Health Authority* [1998] Lloyds Med Rep 157.

[26] See *Brooks* v. *Home Office* (1999) 48 BMLR 109.

[27] www.nhs.direct.nhs.uk.

will emerge in the private sector. Will they do so? Or will shopping for medicine offer a recreation for the "worried well" and fail to meet the needs of the sick? When the NHS consumer is dissatisfied, either because he cannot "buy" entire well-being, or because she is truly sick and the absence of records and prior acquaintance with her health provider mean her illness goes undiagnosed, the chances are that the "patient's" grievances will add a further cost to the NHS litigation burden.

Caring for the vulnerable

Resort to claims of human rights enables those able to articulate such claims to enhance their access to the medical technology of their choice. The clamour of those who seek satisfaction of their subjective judgements of their health needs may drown out the voices of the vulnerable. As a beleaguered public health system attempts to accommodate the rights of its more able patients, how the law defines and enforces the rights of, and responsibilities to, especially vulnerable members of the population will prove equally challenging. The current debates surrounding the care of patients suffering from mental disorder or impairment do no credit to the law or policy in this arena. The growing numbers of very elderly people in our society, a proportion of whom suffer from some degree of dementia, and most of whom lack the money and health to assert their own rights, will exacerbate the difficulties of mental health law.

The past two decades have witnessed upheaval in policy in relation to the care and control of the mentally ill. Mental health legislation, up to and including the Mental Health Act 1959, centred largely, though not exclusively, around institutional care provision. Patients whose mental disorder prevented them caring for themselves or created a risk that they might harm others were removed from the community. Their rights were minimal and often disregarded. Behaviour which contravened society's norms could too easily be classified as illness. The Mental Health Act 1983 retained an emphasis on institutional care but the role of the community as a potential care environment began to emerge more strongly. Caring for mentally disordered and impaired patients in the community came to be recognised as a better approach. Detention in hospital was to be a last resort and implemented only for short periods of acute illness. The 1983 Act recognised that patients' rights to liberty and autonomy should be restricted only when their welfare or the safety of others demanded such restrictions. Vulnerable patients should not simply be removed from sight and left at the mercy of doctors or families.

Throughout the 1980s community care was popularly embraced by the psychiatric care profession. However, community care had no sound statutory foundation. Nor was the purported care adequately funded.

The 1983 Act recognised the need to acknowledge patients' rights but neither statute nor common law offered meaning to such rights. Lacunae in the law flowered like weeds in a garden. The absence of clear principles governing how patients lacking mental capacity could lawfully be treated for physical illness forced the House of Lords to allow doctors to give proxy consents for their patients.[28] The shift away from use of formal powers of compulsory detention allowed doctors to invoke vague concepts of best interests to detain a patient without the patient enjoying any of the safeguards of his rights built into the 1983 Act.[29] The behaviour within the community of patients who were discharged from hospital, but still ill, gave rise to a spate of legally dubious attempts by doctors to require patients in the community to submit to continuing treatment.[30] The law failed patients and doctors. Two different pressure groups expressed concerns. The first asserted that patient rights were cavalierly ignored. The second believed that patients posed grave dangers to others. The two joined forces in calls for legislation to clarify the legal basis of changing psychiatric practice. The Mental Health (Patients in the Community) Act 1995 was the result of these demands. It introduced the supervised discharge order, placed community care on an official footing, and provided the psychiatric patient with the opportunity for more freedom whilst also ensuring the protection of third parties. The 1995 Act was heralded as the solution to secure a firmer equilibrium between patient rights to liberty, patient welfare and the protection of the wider community.

Criticism of community care policy did not abate. Enthusiasm for community care diminished in light of a continuing series of incidents, in which formerly detained patients harmed themselves and others. Each incident led to an inquiry[31] which highlighted the failures of the care policy. Depressingly, each report outlined broadly similar failures in the policy. The media focused on lack of legislative powers to control patients in the community, or failure to exercise powers to re-detain patients. Investigations of the tragedies of community care highlighted the absence of effective means of ensuring that the patient in the community had

[28] *Re F* [1990] 2 AC 1, HL.

[29] *R* v. *Bournewood Mental Health and Community NHS Trust* [1998] 3 All ER 289, HL.

[30] See, for example, *R* v. *Hallstrom ex p W* [1986] 2 All ER 306. See generally P Fennell, *Treatment Without Consent: Law, Psychiatry and the Treatment of Mentally Disordered People since 1845* (London, Routledge, 1996).

[31] E.g. The Woodley Team Report, *Report of the Independent Review Panel to East London and The City Health Authority and Newham Council* (London, East London and The City Health Authority and Newham Council, 1995); Steering Committee, *Report of the Confidentiality into Homicides and Suicides by Mentally Ill People* (London, Royal College of Psychiatrists, 1996); J Ritchie, *et al.*, *Report of the Inquiry into the Care and Treatment of Christopher Clunis* (London, HMSO 1994).

secure accommodation and continuing contact with mental health services. Reports demonstrated an absence of health care as much as control.

Mental health services and mental health law needed to be modernised. In 1998, the Government appointed an expert committee which was commissioned to review the Mental Health Act and to consider recommendations for reform. The committee's recommendations were adopted and included within the government's consultation paper *Reform of the Mental Health Act 1983—Proposals for Consultation.*[32] The proposals are intended to develop a more comprehensive mental health service. It is accepted that with the changes in care patterns, long spells of in-patient treatment in a hospital setting are no longer necessary or desirable. The 1983 Act does not offer sufficient flexibility for care and treatment in an age where technological advance and expanding professional skill and knowledge can harness the community as an effective care environment. The consultation paper also recognises the need to achieve greater transparency and clarity in the legislation's application. The express inclusion of principles which underlie the provisions within the new mental health legislation would enable such clarity to be achieved. For example, use of the least restrictive environment of care should be encouraged; where informal care is an option, informal care should always be considered before recourse to compulsory powers; and, patients should, as far as possible, be involved in developing and reviewing their care plans. Furthermore, while the patient's views should be considered, the safety of the patient and the public should be a key consideration when determining the question of whether compulsory powers should be imposed. Where compulsory powers are thought necessary decisions will be made with reference to express principles.

One of the principal objectives of the proposed reforms is to extend powers to control patients living in the community. Compulsory powers will be available to ensure treatment and supervision of patients outside hospital. The history of the review of mental health law explains this emphasis on *control.* But it would be wrong to suggest that rights, so prominent in other "medical" law controversies, are ignored. New laws will highlight the need for procedural justice. The two-stage process of admission for assessment and treatment is to be replaced by a simpler process of a single application to admission to compulsory care and treatment. After twenty-eight days an automatic review of each compulsory care "order" will take place. It has been expressly recognised that, where possible, the least restrictive care environment should be used. The tribunal will, therefore, have to decide not only whether the patient should be subject to a compulsory care and treatment order under the 1983 Act, but also whether this should take place in hospital or in the community. For the first time compulsory orders may well apply in the community as well as in

[31] Department of Health, *Reform of the Mental Health Act 1983—Proposals for Consultation* (Cm. 4480, London, HMSO, November 1999).

hospital. Irrespective of where the care and treatment is provided, the patient's right to due process is taken seriously.

A number of problems look set to continue to bedevil mental health law. Just as what is meant by "illness" remains unclear in the context of claims to medicine and medical technology by people wanting those services, so too the definition of *mental* illness remains elusive. The experience of recent years has amply demonstrated that boundaries between physical and mental illness make little sense. An obstructed bowel can result in mental confusion, yet is the patient mentally ill? A mentally-ill pregnant woman may refuse the surgery necessary to save her life and her baby's, but is a Caesarean section treatment for her mental illness?[33] For the doctor, the relationship of physical and mental illness is a fascinating question of scientific and clinical judgement. For the philosopher, the issue revolves around fundamental questions of human personality. For the lawyer, and the law, its importance lies in our endorsement of laws which authorise removing rights of self-determination from the mentally ill, while rarely invoking coercive measures against the physically ill. Mental illness allows doctors to impose treatment patients do not want. Justification of why and when patients diagnosed as suffering from one sort of illness lose their right to make their own decisions however (apparently) bizarre or irrational[34] such decisions may be is insufficiently explored.[35] Extending coercive powers, not only under overt reforms of mental health care but also within proposed reforms to permit the indefinite detention (outside the Mental Health Acts) of dangerous persons with severe personality disorder,[36] risks a return to mental health law prior to 1959 where anti-social behaviour as defined by the standards of the day is equated to mental illness.

A second difficulty for mental health law is paradoxically whether doctors and lawyers will *use* new mental health laws when they should. In arguing that there are risks that definitions of mental illness may be manipulated to permit unjust deprivation of liberty, we do not suggest that there are not significant groups of people who should properly be treated within a framework of compulsory care. Their illness has deprived them of the capacity to look after their own interests and/or have adequate regard to the interests of others. However at present a number of psychiatrists, and on occasion the courts,[37] view resort to the Mental Health Act 1983 with ambivalence. They judge that for a person to be subjected to formal detention under the Act brings with it an ineradicable social stigma. Detention in hospital, or any imposition of compulsory

[33] Yes, according to *Tameside and Glossop Acute Services Trust* v. *CH (a patient)* [1996] 1 FLR 762.

[34] See *St George's Healthcare NHS Trust* v. *S* [1998] 3 All ER 673, CA.

[35] Though see DPT Price, "Civil Commitment of the Mentally Ill" (1994) 2 *Med L Rev* 321.

[36] See, now, The Dangerous People with Severe Personality Disorder Bill and see Home Office/Department of Health, *Managing Dangerous People With Severe Personality Disorder—Proposals for Policy Development* (London, HMSO, 1999).

[37] See, for example, *Re W* [1992] 4 All ER 627, CA.

treatment, necessarily has disadvantages—whether it is the fact that such measures are taken under the label of the Mental Health Act which is problematic must be doubted. When a person cannot articulate his objection to what is done to him, or is under eighteen, informal powers are utilised to just the same end as the Mental Health Act without the concomitant rights that Act grants. Patients who are informally detained lack access to mental health review tribunals and currently to the after-care prescribed for formerly detained patients by section 117 of the Mental Health Act. They are deprived of their liberty just as effectively as if they were formally detained.

The use of informal care means to treat those who cannot object, but to use the Mental Health Act for those who remain articulate, is to stigmatise the latter. It is yet another false boundary in our understanding of illness. There are the mentally ill who are "dangerous", but articulate, and are often seen as "mad and bad". Mental health legislation exists to control them. Then there are the mentally ill whose condition prevents them caring for themselves and are dangerous only to themselves. They are "sick and sad". Society must look after them, but distinguish them from the "mad and bad"; nor, given their inability to speak for themselves, will society bother too much about their rights?

Our fears may be exaggerated. However, further evidence that the law is in some confusion in dealing with different categories of the mentally ill is offered by the troubled history of reform of the law relating to decision-making on behalf of mentally incapacitated persons. A programme of law reform quite separate from review of mental health legislation has been under way for several years. The Law Commission consulted widely, and in 1995 produced a report proposing a new Mental Incapacity Bill.[38] The Bill would have provided a new legislative framework for authorising decision-making on behalf of people unable to manage their own affairs, be they financial, health, welfare or other personal matters. Political controversy over relatively insignificant parts of the Report relating to clinical research and withdrawal of treatment from patients in a persistent vegetative state resulted in the then Government shelving the Report. The Labour Government conducted a further consultation and now proposes to introduce many (but by no means all) of the Law Commission's proposals.[39] The importance of clarifying the law governing health care decisions on behalf of people unable to make their own decisions must not be underestimated. The number of people who will fall into this category is likely to rise sharply in the next fifty years. A growing population of very elderly people who are at risk of succumbing in the latter years of life to dementia will contribute to that rise. The capacity of medicine to keep alive people who at some point in life (on occasion at birth) suffer devastating

[38] *Mental Incapacity* (Law Commission Report No. 231, London, HMSO, 1995).

[39] *Making Decisions: The Government's Proposals for Making Decisions on Behalf of Mentally Incapacitated Adults* (Cm 4465, October 1999).

brain damage will add to the numbers. The Mental Incapacity Bill now backed by government will operate a presumption of capacity. Incapacity must be proven. A person will lack capacity if at the time of making a decision, he or she is unable by reason of mental disability to make a decision on the matter in question, or is unable to communicate a decision. A person will be regarded as incapable of making a decision if, at the time of making the decision, the person is "unable to understand or retain the information relevant to the decision, or unable to make a decision based on that information".[40] Mental disability is defined as "any disability or disorder of the mind or brain, whether permanent or temporary, which results in an impairment or disturbance of mental functioning".[41] Mental disability operates as a threshold to the exercise of decision-making powers by others. It is a threshold built in to protect against paternalistic intervention which might judge that imprudence equals incapacity. But the scope of mental disability is broad. Physical illness affecting the mind would seem to fall squarely within it. In departing from the language of mental disorder found in the Mental Health Act, the Law Commission noted the equation of "mental disorder" with narrower concepts of psychiatric illness. In this context, the proposed reforms both recognise the fragility of boundaries between physical and mental illness, and, paradoxically, they reinforce distinctions between psychiatric and other illnesses.

Once incapacity is established, decisions made on the patient's behalf will continue to be made on a "best interests" test. Nonetheless that test is revolutionised. No longer will "best interests" be defined by responsible professional practice and be in effect no more than a requirement not to be negligent. Statutory criteria will be prescribed. These criteria seek to balance the welfare needs of patients with respect for whatever residuary ability they retain to express their own preferences. Their ascertainable past and present wishes must be considered, the views of families and carers must be canvassed and participation in decision-making by the patient encouraged as far as possible. Recognising that many people, once fully mentally competent, would seek to have some say in what happens to them if struck down by age, injury or disease, proposals for continuing powers of attorney would permit individuals to execute a power of attorney to entrust decisions relating to health care to a proxy chosen by them, just as they can now entrust decisions on financial and property matters to the agent of their choice under the Enduring Powers of Attorney Act 1985. Proposals on mental incapacity aim to create a coherent framework to ensure that decisions are made by the appropriate person with appropriate safeguards. Supervised by a radically reformed Court of Protection, new laws aim to recognise that rights must be respected but that ill-

[40] *Ibid.*, para. 1.6.
[41] *Ibid.*, para. 1.6.

ness may render rights of self-determination of much less real substance than a right to be cared for with respect.

Alas, a spectre haunts the picture and threatens to undermine the success of laws which offer promise of just treatment of vulnerable patients whose needs depends on others. Among the proposals from the Law Commission not acted on by government are the recommendations for public law protection of vulnerable adults analogous to measures already in place in relation to children. Proposals (*inter alia*) to empower social services to intervene to supervise and protect vulnerable adults and to create an offence of ill-treating or wilfully neglecting a person without capacity will not be implemented. Yet there is growing evidence of abuse of vulnerable adults, especially elder abuse.[42] A certain naivety is apparent in government decision-making. Proposals that in prescribing how a person without capacity be cared for, the law should pay some overt regard to the interests of carers are rejected. Decisions must in theory rest exclusively on the interests of the person involved, be they decisions taken by doctors or families. Evidence that in many instances for patients in the community, the interests of cared for and carer cannot be divorced is ignored. Evidence that on occasion "carers" do not care is also ignored. The community's collective responsibility fades into insignificance.

Mental health law will change dramatically in the early years of the new century. The emphasis on laws focusing so much on individual rights and powers may frustrate the good intentions of law reformers. The continuation of two sorts of mental health law, a reformed Mental Health Act 1983 and proposed Mental Incapacity Act will re-inforce stereotypes of those said to be mentally ill. Above all, confining serious discussion of rights to the balance of rights to autonomy and liberty and the need to care and control, overlooks the most important right of all, the right to decent levels of basic care, shelter, food, and everyday services. Many patients are well enough to live independently in the community despite suffering from mental disorder or mental incapacity. Their state of mind is fragile and neglect of the body and its basic needs will tip them further towards disorder or incapacity, triggering the need to involve the law. Past experience has shown that failure to provide a strong support structure for vulnerable people has had devastating consequences.

In conclusion

Law's relationship with medicine and health will continue to provide fertile ground for scholars in 2050. The shape of the subject will be markedly differ-

[42] See Doh, *Joint Investments Plan Guidance, Older People Including Those Who Have Mental Health Problems* at www.doh.gov.uk/pub/docs/doh/jipop.pdf

ent with an emphasis on doctors fading away. Whether health law is a discrete sub-discipline may be disputed. A subject born of family law, tort and jurisprudence may be submerged in consumer law and public law, with the criminal justice system becoming ever more prominent. The fate and name of our subject is however a trivial concern. The question which will vex our grandchildren is this. Will the law develop a capacity to define and enforce an entitlement to *basic* health care sufficient to ensure that those who are ill can obtain treatment? Such an entitlement will fall short of endorsing every claim to medical services which a particular individual might desire. It can only be, as Article 25 of the Universal Declaration of Human Rights provides, a right to a standard of care *adequate* to sustain health. The legislature and the courts will need to grasp the nettle of defining what degree of illness generates a responsibility incumbent on the State to provide treatment. The courts will have to grapple with the uncomfortable notion that on occasion other rights must cede priority to a right to treatment when ill. Unrestricted access to what medicine has to offer and unrestricted access to compensation for NHS accidents may have to be curtailed. Health is not a purely personal matter. The community must recognise that a responsibility to treat the sick requires some sacrifice of individual wants.

20

Family Law's Futures

REBECCA BAILEY-HARRIS AND
JUDITH MASSON

Introduction

Family law poses a particular challenge for prophetesses scanning the horizon of the next three decades. The development of law in this field is determined by a complex interplay of factors: social structure, social policy and political expediency. One may be reasonably confident that social trends apparent at the end of the last millennium will continue, in that the rates at which individuals embrace forms of family relationship outside marriage , and exit from successive formal marriages, will not diminish substantially.[1] However, recent past history has demonstrated all too clearly that the law reform agenda is determined as much by political expediency as by social realities and community demand.[2] Despite these real difficulties, we will be bold and make twin assumptions. The first is that society in the coming decades will become increasingly pluralist, multi-cultural and secular, and the second is that this will be recognised and supported by successive governments and reflected in legislative developments. On this basis we may witness a significant change in the "landscape" of family law.

It seems probable that both family formation and modes of family dispute resolution over the coming decades will increasingly be determined by

[1] See Lewis, *Marriage, Cohabitation and the Law: Individualism and Obligation* (LCD Research Paper Series, 1/1999); Lewis, *Individualism and Commitment in Family and Cohabitation* (LCD Research Paper Series, 8/1999), p. 1–2: "In one generation the numbers marrying have halved, the numbers divorcing have trebled and the proportion of children born outside marriage has quadrupled"; Lewis, "Marriage, Cohabitation and the Nature of Commitment" (1999) 11 *Child & Family Law Quarterly* 355. Note however that figures in *Population Trends* (1999) indicate a fall in divorce rates over the past three years: [2000] *Family Law* 4.

[2] Classic examples are the withdrawal of the Family Homes and Domestic Violence Bill 1995, the abandonment of the Adoption Bill 1996, and the non-implementation of Part II of the Family Law Act 1996.

individual choice reinforced by a promotion of individual responsibility, the latter linked to a continuing settlement culture. However, policy dilemmas relating to the appropriate role and interests of the State in matters of family regulation are unlikely to disappear. In the future as in the past, family law is likely to reflect an ongoing tension between the competing interests of party autonomy and State paternalism, an issue we return to at various stages of this chapter. Even in an increasingly pluralist landscape certain absolutes will remain. One virtual certainty is the continuing of protection of the rights of the child where conflicts exist with parental claims in a multi-valued society, although there may be shifts in the approach to and content of that protection.

What will be the principal legal (as opposed to sociological and political) influences on the substance of family law in this country over the coming decades? The first is internal: full implementation[3] of the Human Rights Act 1998, with the interpretation of the substantive Convention rights by our own courts. As the last century turned into the present commentators argued that the Act's potential influence in this field (as in others) cannot be overestimated.[4] New judges are to be appointed to cope with the anticipated increased demands on judicial time, and it is estimated by the Lord Chancellor's Department that human rights issues may be raised in 50 per cent of cases. The substantive Articles of the Convention for the Protection of Human Rights and Fundamental Freedoms most likely to have particular impact on domestic family law[5] are Article 2 (right to life), Article 6 (right of access to a court and right to a fair hearing), Article 8 (protection of private and family life), Article 12 (right to marry and found a family) and Article 14 (prohibition of discrimination in access to the substantive Convention rights). A period of uncertainty is inevitable before a body of domestic jurisprudence on the interpretation of Convention rights is built up, and our courts[6] may chose to depart[7] from more conservative Strasbourg jurisprudence on the interpretation of relevant articles.[8] Looking to other legal systems, it is interesting to speculate on the respective influences

[3] 2 October 2000, in England and Wales. The Act is already in operation in Scotland.

[4] Swindells *et al.*, *Family Law and the Human Rights Act 1998* (Family Law, 1999); H Conway, "The Human Rights Act 1998 and Family Law: Parts I and II" [1999] *Family Law* 811 and [2000] *Family Law* 30.

[5] Even prior to the implementation of the Act, it has become increasingly common practice to invoke Convention Articles in family law cases: e.g. *Re C (HIV Test)* [1999] 2 FLR 1004; *Re J (Abduction: Wrongful Removal)* [2000] 1 FLR 78; *Re X (Parental Responsibility Agreement: Children in Care)* [2000] 1 FLR 272; *Re N (Leave to Withdraw Care Proceedings)* [2000] 1 FLR 134. Note however the recent judicial exhortations to restraint: *Daniels* v. *Walker* (2000) The Times, May 17; Re L; *Re V; Re M; Re H* (2000) The Times, June 21 per Thorpe LJ.

[6] Sedley, "Human Rights: A Twenty-First Century Agenda" [1995] *Public Law* 386.

[7] As they will be entitled to do so by determining their relevance or otherwise: Human Rights Act 1998, s. 21).

[8] See e.g. on Art. 8: *Cossey* v. *United Kingdom* [1991] 2 FLR 492; *Kerkhoven* v. *Netherlands* (Application No. 15666/89, 19 May 1992); *XY and Z* v. *United Kingdom* 24 EHRR 143; *McMichael* v. *United Kingdom* 20 EHRR 205.

which mainland European civilian legal concepts and those from other Commonwealth jurisdictions will have on the family law of this country.

Our overall prediction is that over the next three decades family law will become dominated by a "*menu carte*" of different categories of relationships, their nature, content and consequences increasingly determined by individual choice rather than by traditional "family values" ideology. This prediction is fortified by research published at the end of the last century which found that marriage was increasingly viewed by the younger generation as a matter of choice.[9] The same research found that despite gloomy predictions in the last century of the negative effects on personal relationships of a growing commitment to an ideology of individualism, in fact commitment remains important, but it now means subtly different things to young persons choosing between marriage and cohabitation. It is not clear that one form is superior to another, nor that parental commitment to children differs according to family form.

Constituting the legal family

We make the prediction that over the coming decades individuals will find themselves increasingly free to choose from a *menu carte* of legally recognised relationships, the content of that *carte* reflecting both mainland European and Commonwealth influences. What is not easy to predict is the extent to which the various relationships will resemble or differ from each other in their legal consequences, nor whether the whole extent of the *carte* will be freely available to every individual. For instance, will marriage be available to same-sex partners as well as to heterosexuals? Will registered partnership be an option only for same-sex partners, or open to all?

It is unthinkable that traditional marriage, so firmly embedded in our culture, will disappear from the future landscape of family law. Notwithstanding a likely growth in the recognition of the demands of multi-culturalism, dwindling numbers of practising church-goers and increasingly vociferous calls for equality rights for homosexuals, it is most unlikely that the traditional monogamous and heterosexual character of marriage[10] will be eroded any more in this century than in the last two. Some argue there is no pressing need to change the traditional precepts of marriage if a range of alternative legally recognised relationships is available to individuals; others, by contrast, argue that in a pluralist society each family form should be freely accessible to each individual.[11]

[9] Lewis, *supra* n. 1.

[10] *Hyde* v. *Hyde* (1866) LR 1 P & D 130.

[11] An argument perhaps reinforced by Articles 8 and 14 of the European Convention on Human Rights.

Whatever the ideological attractions of that latter argument, we consider the creation of same-sex marriage to be politically unrealistic in the foreseeable future.[12] The coming decades may nevertheless witness some more limited reforms to the institution of marriage. Parliament, influenced not least by the Human Rights Act 1998,[13] should without delay address the issue of transsexuals' capacity to marry by recognising the reality of gender reassignment surgery and reverse the injustice perpetrated by *Corbett* v. *Corbett (orse Ashley)*.[14] An increasing promotion of individual choice in personal matters may result in further liberalisation of ceremonial requirements under the Marriage Act 1948, going beyond the relatively modest reforms as to venue effected by the Marriage Act 1994 which proved popular with celebrities and the press alike at the end of the last century. We may reach the point in this country where (climate permitting) couples have the facility to tie the knot at home, on the beach or in a park, as they have long enjoyed in, for example, Australia.[15] Moreover divorcees wishing to remarry are likely to be made more welcome by the Church of England.[16]

By the end of the last century, the recognition of unmarried cohabitation (defined to exclude same-sex couples) was scattered across a range of statutes in areas including inheritance family provision, transfer of and succession to protected tenancies, occupation orders and fatal accidents claims.[17] Yet there was no consistency of policy; by contrast to rights in other areas, successive governments were reluctant to address the claims of cohabitants to asset distribution on relationship breakdown, despite concerted calls for reform from a range of professionals.[18] Nor did the legislature approach cohabitation as a real civil status, as opposed to a factual situation with legal consequences, despite "the choice that now exists between marriage and cohabitation whenever a new intimate relationship is initiated".[19] Strong pressure for further reform will come not only from social realities but also from the Human Rights Act 1998.

What is less predictable is the precise model of legal recognition of a new status, and whether European or Commonwealth—particularly Australian-models will prove the more influential. The first choice to be made is that

[12] R Bailey-Harris, "Lesbian and Gay Family Values and the Law" [1999] *Family Law* 560 at 564.

[13] In this context, of particular relevance are Articles 8, 12 and 14 of the ECHR.

[14] [197I] P 83.

[15] Marriage Act 1961 (Cth).

[16] *Marriage After Divorce* (January 2000).

[17] For an overview, see Barlow, *Cohabitants and the Law* (Butterworths, 1997).

[18] See e.g. Bailey-Harris, "Law and the Unmarried Couple: Oppression or Liberation?" (1996) 8 *CFLQ* 137; Thorpe LJ and Bailey-Harris in *Dividing the Assets on Family Breakdown* (Family Law, 1998), pp. 8–9 and ch. 5 respectively; Harper, "Cohabitation Law: The Way Forward" [1999] *Family Law* 435; Family Law Committee of the Law Society, *Proposals For Reform of the Law* (September 1999); SFLA, *Cohabitation Report* (April 1999) summarised in Gouriet "Cohabitation Update" [2000] *Fam Law* 210.

[19] Lewis, *supra* n. 1, p. 89.

between the "opt-in" model of registered partnership and the conferring of legal consequences on a defined relationship by operation of law, with the possibility of some "opt-out" contractual facility. The former appeals to party autonomy and individual choice, but is criticised by paternalists for its inability to protect a vulnerable partner where the other is unwilling to register, for its inadequacy when parties are unaware of rights, and for low rates of take-up in European countries.[20] The latter model, conversely, is strongly paternalistic but may be criticised for imposing "Marriage Mark II" on those who reject that institution.[21] Registered partnership (commonly but not necessarily confined to same-sex relationships)[22] is essentially a mainland European approach; the alternative model of attaching legal consequences to a defined unmarried relationship has been widely adopted by the Australian States and Territories following prototype legislation in New South Wales in 1984.[23] The second model is currently favoured by two of the leading legal practitioners' organisations in this country.[24]

The second issue is the definition of relationship. Will new legislation be aimed essentially at couples, adopting the "cohabitation model", and if so, will the definition be same-sex inclusive? With two exceptions this is the Australian approach[25] which (with two recent exceptions referred to *infra*) has been confined to heterosexual "cohabitation".[26] English legislation has to date been reluctant to recognise same-sex partnership as "cohabitation", preferring instead inclusion under a wider (and therefore more neutral) definition such as "family member"[27] or "associated person".[28] Such coyness may disappear in future. The Property (Relationships) Act Amendment Act 1999 in New South Wales and the Property Law Amendment Act 1999 in Queensland, provide models in extending the definition of "de facto spouse" to include cohabitants of the same sex.[29] Moreover, that amending legislation in New South Wales demonstrates that the two definitional approaches need not be mutually exclusive, since it simultane-

[20] Bailey-Harris, *supra* n. 18; Tatchell, *Gay Times*, November 1996; Eekelaar, "Registered Same-Sex Partnerships and Marriage: A Statistical Comparison" [1998] *Family Law* 561.

[21] An argument also levelled against registered partnership: "The Spirit of the New French Registered Partnership Law: Promoting Autonomy and Pluralism or Weakening Marriage?" (2000) 12 *CFLQ* 1.

[22] Available only to same-sex partners in e.g. Denmark, Norway, Sweden, Iceland, Greenland, Spain, Germany, Luxembourg. In the Netherlands and France it is available to all.

[23] De Facto Relationships Act 1984 (NSW), renamed the Property Relationships) Act in 1999; Property Law (Amendment) Act 1987 (Vic), De Facto Relationships Act 1991 (NT), De Facto Relationships Act 1996 (SA), De Facto Relationships Act 1999 (Tas). See Finlay, Bailey-Harris and Otlowski, *Family Law in Australia* (5th edn., Butterworths, 1997), pp. 196–9, 326–38, 345–8.

[24] Law Society and Solicitors Family Law Association, see *supra* n. 18.

[25] Not exclusively: see the Domestic Relationships Act 1994 (ACT) and the Property (Relationships) Legislation Amendment Act 1999 (NSW).

[26] See the statutes listed *supra* n. 23.

[27] Rent Act 1977, Sch. 1, para. 3(1), as interpreted in *Fitzpatrick* v. *Sterling Housing Association Ltd* [1999] 2 FLR 1027.

[28] Family Law Act 1996, s. 63.

[29] See Millbank, (1999) 13 *Australian Journal of Family Law* 93, at 93–4.

ously confers rights on "a close personal relationship (other than a marriage or de facto relationship) where there is domestic support and personal care".[30] In this country both the Solicitors Family Law Association and the Law Society [31] favour a definition inclusive of same-sex partners.

The third issue is the extent to which the various relationships offered on the *menu carte* differ from or resemble each other in legal consequence. How extensive in substance is the field of choice? This question admits of no easy answer. An obvious objection to similarity is the undesirability of forcing on parties the very hallmarks of an institution which they have attempted to reject.[32] But conversely, similarity in legal consequence may make the choice of family form less mercenary. What do individuals themselves expect—sameness or difference in the choice they make? Lewis's recent research concluded that "most people in the sample felt that it was proper to treat marriage and cohabiting parents the same".[33] Whether this is true of financial consequences is perhaps more debatable.

Terminating Legal Relationships

Judicial divorce in this country has undergone a marked transformation, both conceptually and procedurally, in its relatively short history of a century and a half. The Matrimonial Causes Act 1857 was innovative in procedure rather than substance; it created a new secular court but retained the fault-based (and discriminatory) grounds which had formerly founded divorce by private Act of Parliament after the requisite prior order from the ecclesiastical court.[34] In 1969 the Divorce Reform Act 1969 took the radical step of making irretrievable breakdown of marriage[35] the sole ground for divorce, and the subsequent introduction and extension[36] of the so-called "special procedure"[37] for undefended petitions has reduced the judicial role to a mere formality in the vast majority of cases. The end of the last century saw fresh proposals for divorce reform which for the first time were government-driven[38] and were strongly

[30] Property (Relationships) Act 1984 (NSW) as amended, s. 5(b).

[31] See *supra* n. 18.

[32] See criticisms of PACS in Steiner "The Spirit of the New French Registered Partnership Law: Promoting Autonomy and Pluralism or Weakening Marriage?" (2000) 12 *CFLQ* 1.

[33] See *supra* n. 1, p. 89.

[34] McGregor, *The History of Divorce in England* (Heinemann, 1957), p. 17; Stone, *Road to Divorce: England 1530–1987*, p. 388.

[35] See the important preceding reports *Putting Assunder* (1966) and *The Field of Choice* (Cmnd 3123, 1966).

[36] Introduced in 1973 and extended to all uncontested cases in 1977.

[37] Well described by Waite LJ in *Pounds* v. *Pounds* [1994] 1 FLR 775 at 777.

[38] Green Paper, *Looking to the Future* (Cm 2424, 1993); White Paper, *Looking to the Future* (Cm 2799, 1995).

critical of continuing fault-based foundations which exacerbate hostilities. But the curious history which followed the passing of the Family Law Act 1996 makes the future of divorce law in this country extremely difficult to predict. In June 1999 the Lord Chancellor unexpectedly announced that Part II of the Act (divorce based on a process over time) would not after all be implemented as planned in 2001. No satisfactory explanation has been given for the Government's sudden change of heart, nor at the time of writing is any indication of policy forthcoming. Thus we are left with the absurdity of a heavily criticised divorce process still in operation, and increasing calls for the eradication of fault considerations,[39] but no government response, due no doubt to pre-election nerves about tackling any issue with "family values" implications. The crystal ball is particularly murky here.

We nevertheless predict with some confidence that at some point in the not-too-distant future true "no fault" divorce will be introduced in this country, although it is difficult to be precise about details. How will irretrievable breakdown of marriage be established—mutual or unilateral demand, irreconcilable differences, separation,[40] or a process over time? Will the coming decades see an abandonment of the long-established notion that legal procedures are capable of "saving" at least some marriages? This found expression in eighteenth century judicial pronouncements[41] and persisted through the Green and White Papers, *Looking to the Future*[42] into Part II of the Family Law Act 1996; the aim of the period for reflection and consideration was to promote reconciliation in at least some cases. Yet critics have long questioned the assumption that divorce law and procedure affect behaviour.[43] Moreover, if we move to a *menu carte* of legally recognised relationships, there may well be reciprocal influence in the ways in which each can be terminated. Divorce may come to resemble simple de-registration of a registered partnership, and the latter could be subject to certain formalities. A related question is whether divorce will become purely administrative, seemingly a logical progression from the "special procedure", but it is interesting to note the problems recently

[39] See e.g. Rae [1999] *Family Law* 745; Report on Interdisciplinary Conference [1999] *Family Law* 746; Smart [1999] *Family Law* 801; Walsh [2000] *Family Law* 3.

[40] As for instance in the Australian Family Law Act 1975 (Cth), ss. 48–9.

[41] "When people understand that they must live together, except for a very few reasons known to the law, they learn to soften by mutual accommodation that yoke which they know they cannot shake off" per Sir William Scott in *Evans* v. *Evans* (1790) 1 Hag Con 34–7; 161 ER 477.

[42] See *supra* n. 38.

[43] See e.g. Davis and Murch, *Grounds for Divorce* (Clarendon Press, Oxford, 1988); Davis, "Divorce Reform: Peering Anxiously into the Future" [1995] *Family Law* 564; Bailey-Harris, "Rhetoric and Reality in Divorce Reform" [1995] *Family Law* 618; Richards, "Divorce Numbers and Divorce Legislation" [1996] *Family Law* 151; Eekelaar, "Family Law; Keeping Us 'On Message'" (1999) 11 *CFLQ* 387.

experienced by the French Minister of Justice in convincing her county of the merits of a wholly administrative divorce process.[44]

Achieving economic justice on relationship breakdown

Hitherto a wide judicial discretion has characterised reallocation of assets between divorcing couples[45] and, by contrast, formalism between their unmarried counterparts.[46] Here too it is extremely difficult to predict the Government's plans. One possibility for the coming decades is a greater emphasis (either through amendment of section 25 of the Matrimonial Causes Act 1973 or, in default thereof, by judicial interpretation of the existing provision) on substantive rather than formal equality on divorce. Comparatively neglected in England in the past, there are very recent signs of a growing interest in this issue. In 1998 the Lord Chancellor referred to the Ancillary Relief Advisory Group only the formal equality model embodied in the Family Law (Scotland) Act 1985 [47] and also found in deferred community models elsewhere.[48] Some Canadian and Australian cases[49] as well as feminist writings [50] have focused instead on substantive equality of outcome, namely the objective of equalising between the parties the economic consequences of marriage and its breakdown. There are now some indications that this approach is beginning to emerge in the Family Division here. Recent cases have emphasised that the "clean break" objective in section 25A is not a principle or presumption and may be inappropriate where one party is financially vulnerable as a result of role-division in the relationship. In *SRJ* v. *DWJ (Financial Provision)*[51] where

[44] Bailey-Harris, "Family Law Reform in France" (1999) *Int Fam Law* 108.

[45] *Report of the Lord Chancellor's Advisory Group on Ancillary Relief* (July 1998); *Piglowska* v. *Piglowski* [1999] 2 FLR 763.

[46] Through continued application of the general law of property, trusts and proprietory estoppel as the vehicle for dispute resolution.

[47] Creating the presumption of equal division of matrimonial property on divorce.

[48] On the German model, see Lucke, "Dividing the Assets on Family Breakdown: The German Civil Code", in Bailey-Harris (ed.), *Dividing the Assets on Family Breakdown* (Family Law, 1998), ch. 3.

[49] *Moge* v. *Moge; Women's Legal Education and Action Fund (Intervener)* (1993) 99 DLR (4th) 456; *Waters* v. *Jurek* (1995) 20 Fam Law 196; *In the Marriage of Mitchell* (1995) 19 Fam LR 44.

[50] See e.g. O'Donovan, "Principles of Maintenance: An Alternative View" 1978) 8 *Family Law* 180; O'Donovan, "Should All Maintenance of Spouses be Abolished?" (1984) 45 *Modern Law Review* 424; Didduck and Orton, "Equality and Support for Spouses" (1994) 57 *Modern Law Review* 681; Bailey-Harris, "The Role of Maintenance and Property Orders in Redressing Inequality" (1998) 12 *Australian Journal of Family Law* 3; K Dunn, "Splitting the Difference" (1998) 12 *Australian Journal of Family Law* 214.

[51] [1999] 2 FLR 176. See also Wilson, J "Ancillary Relief Reform: Response of the Judges of the Family Division" [1999] *Family Law* 159.

the husband's resources might increase in the future, a nominal periodic payments was held to be justified in order to keep alive the possibility of compensating the wife for lost opportunity costs attributable to the marriage. There is also evidence of growing academic interest in the "equality issue" in ancillary relief.[52] Will it also permeate the financial consequences of breakdown of other relationships on the *menu carte*, or will marriage alone be regarded as representing a special commitment which alone confers the right to equalisation?

The nature of the parental child support obligation has given rise to considerable debate over the past decade,[53] albeit obscured by the highly technical nature of primary and secondary legislation.[54] At the time of writing, the government plans to make significant changes to the method of assessment from late 2001.[55] Will the crystal ball disclose in the child support legislation a different construct of the family,[56] whereby the obligations of step-parenthood and other forms of social parenthood are more overtly acknowledged?[57] The Government's reform proposals go some way in this direction, in that the terminology of "non-resident" is to replace the stigmatising "absent" parent, and under the much simplified formula liabilities towards step-children will assume far greater significance. But it remains to be seen whether more radical reconstruction will occur.

The role of contract in determining financial obligations

Future governments are likely to continue a policy of promoting settlement and agreement in the resolution of family disputes, rationalised on grounds of individual empowerment as well as reduction of stress and costs. In the

52 Eekelaar, "Should s 25 Be Reformed?" [1998] *Family Law* 469; Cretney "Trusting the Judges: Money After Divorce" in *Current Legal Problems 1999* (OUP, 2000), vol. 52, at 304–8.

53 Parker, "Child Support: Rights and Consequences" (1992) 6 *Int J of Law and the Family* 148; Eekelaar and Maclean, *Maintenance After Divorce* (Clarendon Press, Oxford, 1986), p. 107 *et seq.*; Eekelaar, *Regulating Divorce* (Clarendon Press, Oxford, 1990), p. 103 *et seq.*

54 Child Support Act 1991; Child Support Act 1995; Child Support (Maintenance Assessment and Special Cases) Regulations 1992, SI 1992/1815.

55 White Paper, *Children's Rights and Parents' Responsibilities* (Cm 4349, 1999); Barton [1999] *Family Law* 704; Pirrie [1999] *Family Law* 838; Child Support, Pensions and Social Security Bill 1999.

56 Diduck, "The Unmodified Family: The Child Support Act and the Construction of Legal Subjects" (1995) 22 *J of Law & Society* 527, at 530.

57 The Child Support Act 1991 obligations are imposed only on parenthood which is biological, adoptive or recognised under the Human Fertilisation and Embryology Act 1990; support obligation may currently be imposed on a step-parent under the Matrimonial Causes Act 1973, s. 254).

financial field, this points towards increased recognition of pre-nuptial[58] and cohabitation contracts. Such contracts raise complex issues of social policy which merit fuller analysis than has to date appeared in government publications.[59] The extent to which their terms should be conclusive exposes the classic tension between party autonomy and State paternalism. In striking a fair balance, the legislation must embody safeguards to protect the interests of a vulnerable party and of the State at two stages:[60] when the contract is made and when the relationship breaks down. It would be reasonable to require, as a minimum precondition to validity, certification that each party has received independent legal advice. The extent to which contractual terms can subsequently be departed from is far more difficult. A simple judicial power to depart on the broad ground of unfairness would be an undue erosion of contractual freedom, whereas substantial injustice produced by unforeseen change of circumstances might be an acceptable compromise. An underlying practical question is the degree of popularity which such contracts would enjoy beyond the world of the international super-rich.

Parents' rights and parenting

The Human Rights Act 1998 will undoubtedlly affect child law although its impact may be more muted than some of the extravagant claims suggest.[61] Public law and local authority practice in child care will come under closer scrutiny—decisions to place children away from home and limit family contact conflict with the parents' "right to family life" in Article 8 of the European Convention on Human Rights but Strasbourg jurisprudence accepts that this can be necessary to protect children.[62] Close attention was paid to the Convention when the Children Act 1989 was drafted[63] and the courts have tended to take a conservative approach in children's cases and supported local authorities' protectionist approaches.[64] Private law is not immune; the courts

[58] Currently not specifically enforceable and taken into account only as one factor under s. 25(2) of the Matrimonial Causes Act 1973: *F* v. *F (Ancillary Relief: Substantial Assets)* [1995] 2 FLR 45; *N* v. *N (Foreign Divorce: Financial Relief)* [1997] 1 FLR 900; *N* v. *N (Jurisdiction: Pre-Nuptial Agreement)* [1999] 2 FLR 745.

[59] Green Paper, *Supporting Families* (1998), para. 4.22 *et seq.*; *Summary of Responses to the Consultation Document* (1999); see the criticisms by Barton [1999] *Family Law* 137 and Hodson [1999] *Family Law* 199, at 265.

[60] *Supporting Families, supra* n. 59, failed to differentiate the two stages: see para. 4.23.

[61] J Herring, "The Human Rights Act and the Welfare Principle in Family Law—Conflicting or Complementary?' [1999] *CFLQ* 221.

[62] *Olsson* v. *Sweden* (1989) 11 EHHR 259; *Johansen* v. *Norway* (1996) 23 EHHR 33.

[63] J Fortin, *Children's Rights and the Developing Law* (Butterworths, 1998), p. 53.

[64] *Re KD (a minor)(ward: termination of access)* [1988] 1 All ER 577.

are public authorities and therefore under an obligation to interpret the law in conformity with the Convention.[65] Findings of fact which family courts have shied away from will be crucial in any case where the right to family life will be curtailed. Courts will no longer be able to escape the consequences of their own decisions by failing to enforce them.[66]

The old certainties about what makes a proper family are gone, concerns lie not with who carers are but what they do, and the extent of their commitment to the child:

> "The Government's interest in family policy is primarily an interest in ensuring that the next generation gets the best possible start in life. Children need stability and security".[67]

It recognises its role in providing support for all, particularly at times of crisis and intervening when children's welfare is threatened. Family law will continue to be primarily concerned with disputes about children, and in handling these it will communicate with litigants, lawyers and the wider community principles and platitudes about family life.

Parenthood, not marriage, has become the defining relationship for much of family law; changing social structures and developments in reproductive technology mean that its difficulties and conflicts are faced within an ever-widening range of adult relationships between parents, step- parents, partners and relatives. The broad power of the court to award parental responsibility by reference to the elastic concept of welfare will continue to allow it to accommodate novel disputes between biological and social parents as well as those who claim a relationship with a child, but provides no simple certainty about what the answer should be or the process by which it should be determined.[68] The family justice system faces the challenge of dealing with more disputes not just because relationships are more fragile but because the social system has rejected prescriptive definitions of suitable carers and encouraged individuals to pursue their claims.[69] Disputes appear more complex partly because parents feel able to raise issues such as domestic violence and sexuality which used to be hidden from the courts. If the family justice system is not to be crushed under an impossible caseload, it will have to be more effective in promoting agreement, diverting conflicts from the courts and reducing opportunities for harassment by litigation.[70]

65 R Buxton, "The Human Rights Act and Private Law" (2000) 116 *LQR* 48.

66 *Hokkanen* v. *Finland* [1996] 1 FLR 289; *Ignaccolo-Zenide* v. *Rumania* (Application 31679/96).

67 Ministerial Group on the Family, *Supporting Families* (1998), p. 52.

68 J Dewar, "The Normal Chaos of Family Law" [1998] *MLR* 467, at 480.

69 For example Maidment concluded in 1979 that a key reason fathers failed to obtain custody was that they did not apply for it: S Maidment, *Child Custody and Divorce* (Croom Helm, 1984), p. 61.

70 B Hale, "The View from Court 45" [1999] 11 *CFLQ* 377, at 385.

The majority of unmarried fathers will have parental responsibility[71] but there will continue to be many other carers who have no recognised relationship with children they are looking after. Despite the "privatisation"[72] of relationships by the Children Act 1989, the courts have retained control over legal relationships between carers and children; parents have not been able to confer parental responsibility on non-parents except through guardianship to take effect on death.[73] The use of court proceedings to acquire status has not proved attractive.[74] A proposal that parents should be able to give parental responsibility to a step-parent by formal agreement was made in the Adoption Law Review and included in the draft Adoption Bill.[75] Such a provision could form the basis for clarifying the status of any social parents like the *menu carte* for adult relationships but it would cut across restrictions on caring by non-relatives[76] and undermine controls on unsuitable carers.[77] The desire to protect children and concerns about family abuse will constrain further moves towards privatisation; the State knows that it cannot control what partners parents take but will remain extremely cautious about endorsing them so as to avoid responsibility.

Domestic violence is widespread; knowledge about its prevalence and about its impact on children and carers means that it can no longer be ignored in post-separation arrangements for children's welfare.[78] Zero-tolerance and proactive policing will, unfortunately, not eliminate it; the family justice system will need to use its powers to control violence and protect children. The policy of promoting parental contact, now reinforced by the Human Rights

[71] Following the acceptance of the proposal that joint registration of birth should confer parental responsibility on unmarried fathers: see Lord Chancellor's Department, *The Procedures for the Determination of Paternity and the Law on Parental Responsibility for Unmarried Fathers* (1998).

[72] A Bainham, "The Privatisation of the Public Interest in Children" [1990] *MLR* 206.

[73] Children Act 1989, ss. 5, 6.

[74] J Masson *et al.*, *Mine, Yours or Ours?* (HMSO, 1983), p. 85; E Bullard *et al.*, *Custodianship: Caring for Other People's Children* (HMSO, 1991).

[75] *Adoption: the Future* (Cm 2288, 1993), para. 5.21; DH and WO, *Adoption a Service for Children: Consultation Paper and Draft Bill*, cl. 85. The requirement for the agreement of both parents would effectively have limited these agreements to step-parents marrying a previously unmarried parent or one whose spouse had died. However, since providing parental responsibility to someone else does not diminish that of existing holders this seems excessively cautious.

[76] Such as private fostering: see Children Act 1989, Part IX and *Re H (a minor) (s.37 direction)* [1993] 2 FLR 541; it would also make it more difficult to control commercial surrogacy and non-agency adoption arrangements.

[77] Unless registration of the agreement were subject to the sorts of police checks and restrictions which apply to adoption and foster placements: Children (Protection from Offenders) (Miscellaneous Amendments) Regulations 1997, SI 1997/2308; Protection of Children Act 1999.

[78] A Mullender, and J Morley, "Domestic Violence and Children: What do we Know from Research?" in A Mullender, and J Morley (eds), *Children Living with Domestic Violence* (Whiting and Birch, 1994); A Mullender, "Children Living with Domestic Violence" (1996) *Adoption and Fostering* 20.

Act, precludes simple solutions. However, better support for families with serious problems[79] cannot mean continuing to expect mothers to protect children and comply with court orders made in favour of violent fathers. The existence of contact centres which provide a safe location but do not ensure children's well-being or supervision have been part of the problem rather than the solution by facilitating contact which would not otherwise have been ordered. Providing good practice guidance for case-workers in the court welfare service will not support and protect women and children;[80] more robust steps will be required to show that policy is "joined up" throughout the family justice system. New Zealand legislation provides a model[81]—the court is precluded from making orders for custody or unsupervised contact in favour of a person who has used violence against the other party or the child unless it "is satisfied that the child will be safe".[82] Requiring judges to consider violence issues will create a basis for appeal for women, counter the pressure not to infringe the father's rights and provide a safeguard for courts which might otherwise be trapped into enforcing odious orders.

Children's rights

Listening to children is a recurrent theme in research[83] and abuse inquiries which is echoed in government reports and guidance.[84] Within public law this is largely an implementation issue reflecting cultural resistance at all levels to valuing children's perceptions, and beliefs that adults, particularly professionals, know and will do the best for children. The extent to which new structures, a Children's Rights Commissioner and local children's rights officers[85] will succeed in changing the culture remains uncertain.

[79] Ministerial Group on the Family, *Supporting Families* (1998), p. 56.

[80] Contrary to the beliefs of the Advisory Board on Family Law, Children Act Sub-Committee: see *Consultation Paper on Contact Between Children and Violent Parents: the Question of Parental Contact Where There is Domestic Violence* (1999), pp. 45, 53.

[81] Guardianship Act 1968, ss. 16B, 16C and Domestic Violence Act 1995.

[82] Guardianship Act 1968, s.16B(4).

[83] C Smart, and B Neale, *Family Fragments* (Polity Press, 1999); J Masson, and M Winn Oakley, *Out of Hearing* (Wiley, 1999); M Winn Oakley, and J Masson, *Official Friends and Friendly Officials* (NSPCC, 2000).

[84] R Waterhouse, *Lost in Care: The Report of the Inquiry into Children's Homes in North Wales* (H.C 201, TSO, 2000). W Utting, *People Like Us* (TSO, 1997); *The Government's Response to the Children's Safeguards Review* (Cm 4105, 1998); DH, HO, DFEE and NAS, *Working Together to Safeguard Children* (2000), para. 7.11.

[85] The exact role of the Children's Rights Commissioner remains uncertain. The position was first announced as a way of ensuring that the new regime for residential care maintained expertise in children's residential care: *Modernising Social Services* (Cm 4169, 1998), para. 4.41. However, no specific provision was included in the draft Care Standards Bill 2000; the role was reannounced in the response to the Waterhouse Report in February 2000.

Changing parental behaviour poses more difficulties. The avowed role of government will remain supporting and advising parents, not "lecturing or hectoring" them.[86] There is ambivalence about how far messages in legislation can and should be used to influence parenting. To use legislation rhetorically, without expectations of enforcement, devalues law, and challenging behaviour, rather than restating widely accepted views risks wholescale disobedience.[87] Constructing divorce as a crisis for children justified State intervention, including the use of divorce law for messages about post-divorce parenting.[88] But new messages about children and parental separation cannot just be directed at married parents. The definition of parental responsibility, already a vehicle for messages to parents in Scotland[89] provides a way of indicating the importance of listening to and consulting children.

Children's views about their care both within families and by public authorities also challenge adults' understandings about their welfare. Children who are separated from their families stress the importance of sibling relationships, even with brothers and sisters with whom they have never lived.[90] Family law has given little attention to relationships between separated children and allowed them to be controlled by their carers.[91] This is also a rights issue, raising questions about the extent of the right to family life, parents' rights to control their children's family relationships and what the State must do to assist children living with their parents but separated from siblings with whom they want contact.

The very restrictive approach to children's applications in private law proceedings which consigns them to the High Court is unsustainable[92] but it is unlikely that there will be a general shift to give children party status and representation in all disputes concerning them. Cost, the resistence to intervention in the family and the acceptance that arrangements on separation should generally be left to parents will continue to provide high barriers to general provision for children's representation. The creation of CAFCASS[93] (the Child

[86] Ministerial Group on the Family, *Supporting Families* (1998), foreword and para. 9.

[87] Hence the rejection of laws banning corporal punishment (loving smacks) by parents: *Protecting Children, Supporting Parents* (1999).

[88] "Recent legislation . . . is best understood as setting out general aspirations about how to divorce well": J Dewar, "The Normal Chaos of Family Law" [1998] *MLR* 467, at 483. See also J Eekelaar, "Family Law: Keeping 'On Message'" [1999] 11 *CFLQ* 387.

[89] Children (Scotland) Act 1995, ss. 1, 2.

[90] A Mullender, and A Kearn, *I'm Here Waiting* (BAAF, 1997); J Masson, C Harrison, and A Pavlovic, *Lost and Found* (Ashgate, 1999); C Thomas *et al.*, *Adopted Children Speaking* (BAAF, 1999).

[91] *Re S (contact: application by sibling)* [1998] 2 FLR 897; *Re F (contact: child in care)* [1995] 1 FLR 510. Children's direct contact is easily controlled but e-communication will give children power to make and continue relationships themselves.

[92] *Practice Direction* [1993] 1 FLR 668. It discriminates against child applicants in breach of ECHR, Art. 14.

[93] Lord Chancellor's Department, *Support Services in Family Proceedings* (1998); a bill to establish the new service was announced in the Queen's Speech in November 1999.

and Family Court Advisory and Support Service) will provide a potential source of representation where judges think this is necessary and also a source of advice for children.[94] But these new roles will have to vie with existing obligations to provide reports and represent children in public law cases in a service which will be subject to new pressures to act speedily and consistently with limited resources.[95] One likely consequence is the reduction of resources for representation and reporting in public law cases.[96]

Improving child care

What of the future of child care? A comparison of the concerns about the state of care for children in 1946 and 1998 gives no basis for optimism about the ability of those who have directed or operated it to deliver quality services for children and young people away from home.[97] Inquiries have repeatedly identified major failings in the system, poorly qualified staff and managers, low morale, lack of resources but knowledge of the problems has not enabled those with responsibility to find solutions.[98] Within the context of half a century of failures, the suggestion that the next decades will bring the care that "any good natural parent"[99] would provide and that "there should be no difference in aspirations for looked after children than all children"[100] seems overly ambitious. Improving the management of care services by target-setting, inspection and enforcement is identified by the Department of Health as the key to improving the care of looked after children. Through its *Quality Protects*[101] programme, the Government has set new objectives for children's services; local authorities must achieve specific targets, in relation to, for example, the placement and educational attainment of children in the public care so that at least three in four care-leavers obtain at least one GCSE (or its equivalent) and that no more than one in six children have more than three placements in any

[94] N Fricker, "The New Children and Family Courts Advisory Service" [2000] *Fam Law* 102.

[95] To comply with ECHR, Art. 6, see R White, [2000] *New LJ* 192.

[96] The new management structure will be expected to end the wide variations in time spent on (and cost of) cases (see e.g. SSI, *The Panel Managers Annual Workshop 1999* (Department of Health)) and to fit in with the Best Value system (see *infra*).

[97] J Masson, "From Curtis to Waterhouse: State Care and Child Protection in the UK from 1945 to 2000" in J Eekelaar *et al.* (eds), *Cross-Currents: Family Law in England and the United States since 1945* (OUP, forthcoming).

[98] Social Services Inspectorate, *Social Services Facing the Future: Annual Report of the Chief Inspector of Social Services 1997/8* (1998).

[99] *The Government's Response to the Children's Safeguards Review* (Cm 4105, 1998), para. 2.3.

[100] *Children Act Report 1995–1999* (Cm 4579, 2000), para. 5.3.

[101] DH, *Quality Protects* (Circular LAC (98)28, 1998); *Children Act Report 1995–1999* (Cm 4579, 2000), paras 1.17–1.25.

one year. Inspection of care services will cease to be a local authority function and become the responsibility of the new National Care Standards Commission.[102] For the first time local authority fostering and adoption services will be subject to the same standards as the independent sector under regulations issued by the Secretary of State. Where the Commission reports that local authority is failing to meet the required standards, the Secretary of State will be able to take over the management of the service. However, there is no evidence that directly run social services will be able to deliver what local authorities have failed to do.

Recruitment to social work is in crisis, many posts are unfilled and applications for training in steep decline.[103] The foster care system too is in crisis.[104] From the current viewpoint it seems unlikely that social services departments will be able to maintain the current level of care provision, let alone develop the quality services demanded. The care system will have to shrink. This will require not only a change in culture, refocusing away from child protection investigations, but also the development of services which can truly support families and divert children from substitute care. The legal framework already exists for services for children in need and inter-agency co-operation so that health and education can take a greater role in supporting families.[105] But the barriers to implementation have to be surmounted.[106]

The ideology of rescue has dominated children's services. Despite the very obvious evidence of its inadequacy, the care system has been assumed by parents, social workers and the courts to be able to look after children better than their parents. Presenting the accommodation of children as a service to families has allowed it to be used for long periods, without proper planning, coercively and without the adequate assessment of alternatives.[107] Children's interests have been overlooked on the assumption that an agreement between the parents and the State provided adequate protection[108] and that it was better to avoid court proceedings where possible. Social work policies and practices have largely been based on beliefs about what is good for children rather

[102] Care Standards Bill 2000.

[103] R Waterhouse, *Lost in Care* (2000), para. 54.05 and Conclusions 35, 36 and 62; D Brindle, *The Guardian, 27* January 2000.

[104] Select Committee on Health (1998: para. 50, rec 22).

[105] Children Act 1989, III and Sch. 2, especially para. 1A.

[106] The introduction of the new duties in the Children Act 1989 did not increase the proportion of social services expenditure on family support: *Children Act Report 1995–1999* (Cm 4576, 2000), para. 9.12

[107] J Hunt, et al., *The Last Resort* (TSO, 1999); J Packman, and C Hall, *From Care to Accommodation* (TSO, 1998). Local policies appear to have had a stronger influence on admissions to the system than underlying need (Cm 4579, 2000), para. 9.41.

[108] It is not clear that such a view can be sustained after the Human Rights Act . In *Nielsen* v. *Denmark* (1989) 11 EHRR 175, the ECHR rejected a claim by a 12-year-old boy that his Art. 5 rights had been breached by placement in a psychiatric ward at the request of his mother.

than evidence of what works. In the future, the need to justify decisions in terms of children's rights and expenditure in terms of "Best Value"[109] will require "evidence-based" practice. There is already a substantial research literature about care services although there are many gaps, for example about the impact of contact on children who will not return to their birth families during childhood[110] and the risk factors associated with adoption breakdown: knowledge about both of these will be crucial in determining the form of permanent substitute care.

The Future of Adoption

In the 1990s both Conservative and Labour Governments promoted adoption as the way of ensuring proper care for children who could not return to their parents and chided local authorities for giving insufficient priority to it.[111] Although it is generally accepted that most children who are looked after are not "potential candidates for adoption"[112] local authorities will have to make adoption an integral part of their child care service and speed up the time taken between the decision to plan an adoption and the making of the order.[113] Developing adoption requires substantial resources to recruit, prepare and support adoptive parents. Ongoing social work support will be necessary.[114] The crisis in fostering is due, in part, to the failure of social services departments to take seriously their role in supporting damaged children in placement; the fact that children have been adopted will not automatically resolve their difficulties or enable carers to cope alone. It is also far from clear that there are large numbers of would-be adoptive parents for older children, particularly when developments in reproductive technology and inter-country adoption will enable more childless people to obtain babies to care for.

[109] Department of Environment, Transport and the Regions, *Modern Local Government: In Touch with the People* (Cm. 4014, 1999), ch. 7; Circular 10/99, *Local Government Act 1999: Part 1 Best Value.*

[110] D Quinton *et al.*, "Contact Between Children Placed Away from Home and their Birth Families: Research Issues and Evidence" (1997) *Clin Ch Psychol and Psychiat* 2, at 393–413.

[111] SSI CI (96)4; DH Circular LAC 98(20); Ministerial Group on the Family, *Supporting Families: Summary of Responses to Consultation Paper* (1999), para. 6.12; (Cm 4570, 2000), para. 2.48.

[112] R Parker, *Adoption Now: Messages From Research* (1999), p. 96 Cf. P Morgan, *Adoption and the Care of Children* (Institute of Economic Affairs, 1998).

[113] SSI, *For Children's Sake: an SSI Inspection of Local Authority Adoption Services* (1996); R Parker, *Adoption Now: Messages From Research* (1999).

[114] N Lowe, *et al.*, *Supporting Adoption: Reframing the Approach* (BAAF, 1999); R Parker, *Adoption Now: Messages From Research* (Wiley, 1999).

The desire to promote adoption will raise questions about the nature of adoption and when the rights of, and legal relationship between, birth parents and children can be overidden. For the majority of children, adoption no longer entails "a fresh start" with complete severance of earlier relationships and the creation of a new identity. Adoption agencies' policies and practices in post-adoption contact developed rapidly in the 1990s;[115] many adopted children want contact with their natural families.[116] What then should the legal framework for permanent family care be? Will it be possible to recognise commitment and provide security for a child in the new family whilst simultaneously acknowledging that the child has other parents who will continue to play some part in his or her life? Residence orders which are revocable, of limited effect and last only until a child is sixteen are inadequate. But the traditional notion of adoption fails to reflect the continuing importance birth families have to children (and *vice versa*). Past experience suggests that carers who commit themselves to children want the recognition of parenthood that adoption brings[117] and that children want their family arrangements to be normalised so that they have parents who care for them. *Inter vivos* guardianship or irrevocable residence orders lasting throughout childhood,[118] supported by appropriate documentation, could provide the basis for new substitute parenting but the term "adoption" will be difficult to displace.

Adoption against the wishes of a parent will not automatically breach the European Convention but it must be "necessary" for the protection of the rights of the child and the adoptive parent. Freeing for adoption is problematic since it ends the legal parent and child relationship, leaving the child without any family, and precludes the parents' formal involvement in the adoption process. The widely used basis for dispensing with agreement, unreasonably withholding,[119] will not provide an adequate basis for arguing that adoption is *necessary*, particularly if it is accepted that parental responsibility through a residence order would properly reflect the carer/child relationship. Although an adoption applicant who has been the child's *de facto* carer for many years may have the right to have that relationship recognised,[120] a residence order may be considered appropriate if contact with parents is to continue. A test for non-consensual adoption based on the significant superiority of adoption to

[115] SSI, *Moving Goalposts* (1995).

[116] C Thomas, *et al.*, *Adopted Children Speaking* (BAAF, 1999); R Parker, *Adoption Now: Messages From Research* (Wiley, 1999).

[117] Neither custodianship nor joint custody which were introduced by the Children Act 1975 proved to be attractive options.

[118] Such provisions were proposed in *Review of Adoption Law* (1992), para. 6.6 and *Adoption: The Future* (Cm 2288, 1993).

[119] Adoption Act 1976, s. 16(2)(b).

[120] *Soderback* v. *Sweden* [1999] 1 FLR 250.

the child's welfare would fit better with the European Convention[121] but would not permit all adoption orders made in the past. Consequently, there will have to be greater emphasis on negotiating approval of adoption arrangements with birth families and securing family care without old style adoption.

The recognition of legal relationships will challenge the requirement for joint adopters to be married but change is unlikely to follow swiftly. The European Convention on the Adoption of Children[122] currently permits joint adoption only by married couples. More importantly, the greater involvement of birth families in the selection of adoptive families is likely to reinforce conventional notions of what makes a good family. Although the right to adopt after a period of care may be recognised there can be no right to create family life by adoption. Choice of placement will continue to be dominated by the child's needs and, consequently, adoption placements with lesbian and gay individuals will continue to be made, particularly if alternative placements are not available.[123]

The current practice of the courts to refuse orders in relation to post-adoption contact so that the adoptive parents are "in the driving seat"[124] is also problematic. It discriminates against the family relationships children have with birth parents and fails to protect the family life children and birth parents were having prior to the adoption, in circumstances where it has accepted that the relationship should continue. To fit with the Human Rights Act and children's and parents' expectations about the continuation of relationships, future adoption will need to look more like post-divorce parenting. Written parenting plans will set out the expectations of birth and adoptive families or each other and of the adoption agency. Agencies will arrange support and provide mediation services to help both sets of parents make adjustments in ways which promote the child's development.

Redress for those harmed in the care system

Throughout the 1990s there was a growing awareness that something had gone terribly wrong in the provision of care for children living away from home. This was not only a problem in the United Kingdom; widescale abuse and neglect in care homes and State residential schools was the subject of inquiries

[121] *Review of Adoption Law* (1992), para. 12.6; *Adoption: The Future* (Cm 2288, 1993), paras 5.4, 5.5.

[122] Cmnd 3673, 1967.

[123] R Parker, *Adoption Now, supra* n. 116, at 39; M Owen *Novices, Old Hands and Professionals: Adoption by Single People* (BAAF, 1999).

[124] Per Butler-Sloss LJ in *Re T (adoption: contact)* [1995] 2 FLR 251, at 253.

in Canada and Australia.[125] In the words of Sir William Utting, former Chief Inspector for the Social Services Inspectorate, "There are no grounds for complacency . . . even the best organisations are not immune from infiltration by determined abusers".[126] The police became substantially engaged in investigations of "historic" abuse; men were charged and convicted on the basis of these investigations and the evidence of adults some of whose complaints as children had been dismissed as "wicked lies".[127] Inquiries, similar to those held in relation to the deaths of individual children in care in the 1970s and 1980s, were held to examine the circumstances in residential homes in Staffordshire, Leicestershire and most notably North Wales.[128] The inquiries explored the processes of the abusers and the reasons why they had remained uninvestigated for such long periods. The Government commissioned a further report to consider what needed to be done to ensure the safety and well-being of all children living away from home, appointed a Taskforce to improve standards in residential care and set targets for local authorities through the *Quality Protects* programme.[129]

The establishment of abuse of trust by officers in charge and negligence by care authorities raises questions about the redress available to individual victims. Although compensation had already been paid to the victims of "Pindown", the question of providing redress for historic abuse has set considerable challenges for the legal system. Issues of liability, limitation and proof are raised within a context where local councillors may be profoundly ashamed of what has occurred, insurance companies want to fight claims, and allegations that complainants are dishonestly seeking compensation are repeated. Only where there has been a major public inquiry is the basis for a claim clear, but this is an exceptionally expensive way of establishing a victim's rights.

Local authorities had largely avoided liability for negligence relating to the child care system. Following the decision of the House of Lords in *X* v. *Bedfordshire*[130] that the local authority should have immunity from liability in

[125] Law Commission of Canada, *Discussion Paper on Institutional Abuse* (1998); Human Rights and Equal Opportunities Commission Report, *Bringing Them Home: Report of the National Inquiry into the Separation of Aboriginal and Torres Strait Islander Children from their Families* (1997); J Cashmore *et al.*, *Systems Abuse: Problems and Solutions* (New South Wales Child Protection Council, 1994).

[126] W Utting, *People Like Us* (1997), pp. 1, 5.

[127] All but two of the police forces are working on or have completed enquiries into historic cases of abuse in children's homes: C Wolmar, *The Guardian*, 16 February 2000.

[128] A Levy, and B Kahan, *The Pindown Experience and the Protection of Children* (Staffordshire County Council, 1991); A Kirkwood, *The Leicestershire Inquiry 1992* (Leicestershire County Council, 1993); R Waterhouse, *Lost in Care* (TSO, 2000).

[129] *The Government's Response to the Children's Safeguards Review* (Cm 4105, 1998).

[130] [1995] 2 AC 633; applications were made to the European Court of Human Rights: *Z. and others* v. *United Kingdom* (Application No. 29392/95). The Commission has expressed the opinion that there was violation of Arts 3 and 6.

relation to its child protection functions, a series of applications relating to negligent care causing harm through abuse by foster-carers or lack of education were struck out.[131] However, following the decision of the European Court of Human Rights in *Osman* v. *United Kingdom*[132] it appeared that a blanket approach to immunity was unsustainable. In *Barrett* v. *Enfield*[133] the House of Lords held that a local authority could owe a duty of care in relation to operational aspects of its decisions about children in its care. *Osman* also provides a possible answer for the limitation point.[134]

Redress limited to pecuniary compensation cannot truly compensate victims for what has occurred. Victims may also want retribution (the conviction of the perpetrator); protection for others at risk through the care system; recognition of their suffering (through findings that their account is credible) and acknowledgment of the agency's responsibility through an apology.[135] In Canada, the widespread abuse of children in care homes and, particularly, residential schools which were compulsory for Native American children led to the use of ADR to meet these wider needs and to award compensation without the high costs in time, resources and emotions which civil proceedings would have entailed.[136] The size of the problem and the practicalities of investigating individual cases also make this a particularly appropriate way of handling claims, although evidence from Canada suggests that it may lead to lower awards. However, there appears to be no move to develop novel ways to handle these claims in England and Wales; victims individually and in groups will need to pursue their cases through the courts and the Criminal Injuries Compensation Authority.

Conclusion

Prophesy demands speculation not only on the future of substantive law but also on methods of dispute resolution. Family structures are changing, but the problems which currently lead families to turn to lawyers—namely disputes over children and finances—will remain. It is less clear what part the law and the family justice system as currently configured will continue to play in their

[131] *H* v. *Norfolk County Council* [1997] 1 FLR 384; *Holtom* v. *Barnet London Borough Council*, *The Times*, 30 September 1993.

[132] [1999] 1 FLR 193, ECHR.

[133] [1999] 2 FLR 426, HL; applied in *S* v. *Gloucester County Council: Tower Hamlets London Borough Council and Havering London Borough Council* [2000] 1 FLR 825.

[134] The acceptance that local authorities had immunity means that time can only begin to run following the decision in *Osman*.

[135] The Association of Directors of Social Services did issue an apology in January 2000.

[136] R Bessner, *Institutional Abuse in Canada* (Law Commission of Canada, 1998), Pt IIC.

resolution. Reduction in legal aid will lead to a reduced role for lawyers, although their services will no doubt remain popular with the self-funding client, which itself may skew the future nature of specialised legal practice. At the same time a new profession of family mediation is developing, and the relationship between each profession's involvement in family dispute resolutions awaits refinement. The emphasis on negotiated solutions, already entrenched in all areas of private family law,[137] is likely to gain ground in public law proceedings relating to children. The settlement culture and the rise of mediation will have its costs as well as benefits. The rule vacuum that the current discretion-based system creates provides space for negotiation, but rules may provide a securer base for developing fair solutions where the protection of lawyers is not available.

[137] See e.g. Bailey-Harris, Barron and Pearce, "Settlement Culture and the Use of the 'No order' Principle under the Children Act 1989" (1999) 11 *CFLQ* 53; *White* v. *White* [1998] 2 FLR 310; *Re L; Re V; Re M; Re H* (2000) The Times, June 21, per Thorpe LJ.

21

Unjust Enrichment

KIT BARKER[1] AND LIONEL SMITH[2]

Introduction

The future is always a dangerous playground. It has a unique capacity for throwing up unforeseen topography and changes in social attitude, which regularly trip its predictors up and prove them embarrassingly wrong. Unjust enrichment law holds special risks in this respect, because its development to date has been short and controversial. Although its ancestry is long-standing[3] and it has relatives overseas, the subject as it exists in England and Wales is still officially less than ten years old.[4] It is far from mature and much of the anxiety and frenzied activity of its youth has yet to subside. Moreover, as with so many adolescents elbowing their way into the world, it has created about it a storm of controversy, which renders a clear vision of its direction and future ambitions difficult. There is even still disagreement about the name the subject should bear.[5]

We nonetheless look to the future, clouded as it is. In doing so, we have decided to focus on two issues—the role of remedies in unjust enrichment law and the interaction between unjust enrichment and trusts—rather than attempting a comprehensive prediction of everything that may transpire in the next thirty years. This is a pragmatic limitation exercise, given the space available. In adopting it, we ignore significant questions. For example, we set aside the topical, structural question whether rights of recovery will continue to

[1] Writing here on Remedies.

[2] Writing here on Trusts.

[3] Baker, "The History of Quasi-Contract in English Law" in W Cornish, R Nolan, J O'Sullivan, G Virgo (eds), *Restitution: Past Present and Future* (Oxford, Hart, 1988), ch. 3; Jones, "The Role of Equity in the English Law of Restitution" in E Schrage (ed.), *Unjust Enrichment: the Comparative Legal History of the Law of Restitution* (Berlin, 1995), p. 149.

[4] *Lipkin Gorman (a firm)* v. *Karpnale Ltd* [1991] 2 AC 548.

[5] See Birks, "Misnomer" in W Cornish *et al.* (eds), *Restitution: Past Present and Future, supra* n. 3, ch. 1.

develop incrementally by reference to particular proven categories ("unjust factors"), or will get absorbed by something akin to a common law version of the civilian *condictio indebiti*.[6] We also avoid speculation about the future of the new defence of change of position. The latter will continue to impact crucially upon the way the law balances rights of recovery against individual and societal interests in the security of transactions and receipts in the new millennium. Our only excuse for neglecting these matters is that we might otherwise—by seeking to say something about everything—end up saying nothing of significance about anything. At the same time, it will become clear that much of what *is* said in the following pages does little to settle existing controversy.

Remedies

The analytical framework erected for unjust enrichment law currently has two phases: a cause of action phase and a (recently much invigorated) defence phase. As the subject matures, a third will be added: remedies.[7] In a sense we started here. English law traditionally focused on forms, not causes of action. Nonetheless, modern thinking about remedies has been limited, because this is really the icing on the cake: the end, rather than the beginning, of a journey of increasing intellectual sophistication in our thinking about the nature and content of rights. What follows is a broad sketch of the way in which this remedial "map" may come to look.

Some of its features are instantly controversial. For example, the reader will see that it identifies confiscation and prevention, as well as restitution, as remedies for unjust enrichment. This itself presupposes a vision of unjust enrichment law as spanning the public/private law divide and it assumes a particular, controversial role for the unjust enrichment concept as a broad organisational tool, or "umbrella", beneath which a series of sometimes quite different actions for unjust gain can defensibly be collected.[8] The map also assumes the feasi-

[6] For recent allusion to this issue, see *Kleinwort Benson* v. *Lincoln City Council* [1999] 2 AC 349, at 408–9, noted by Meier and Zimmermann in (1999) 115 *LQR* 556. There are powerful arguments against the introduction of the civilian approach: Birks, "No Consideration: Restitution after Void Contracts" [1993] 23 *UWALR* 195, at 217–20.

[7] See *contra*, Birks, "Rights, Wrongs and Remedies", (2000) 20 OJLS 1. Professor Birks advocates precisely the reverse. Rather than incorporating a remedial agenda into unjust enrichment law, he advocates the eradication of the language of remedy from private law altogether. Some of the aims underpinning this strategy are laudable, but it seems, with respect, disproportionate to them; entailing as it does the erasure of much of the learning of Blackstone and Austin upon which English legal thought is usually based.

[8] A Burrows, *The Law of Restitution* (London, Butterworths, 1993) ("Burrows"), p. 1; *Muschinski* v. *Dodds* (1985) 160 CLR 583, at 617, per Deane J. Note, however, that neither would

bility of a strategy of integration between common law and equitable restitutionary remedies, which may be difficult to put into immediate practice without legislative intervention. Optimistically, it anticipates the day when we no longer talk separately of equitable and common law damages, *quantum meruit*, *quantum valebat*, accounts of profits, "money had and received" and "money paid", but rather of the principles according to which monetary restitutionary awards are measured and quantified. As these are identified and understood, and as the whole range of remedial solutions implicitly described by the current range of claims is realised, further adjustments may be possible to the first two stages of our analytical apparatus. It may be possible, for example, to reduce the role of certain restitutionary "defences" such as "counter-restitution impossible"[9] and/or the "passing on" of loss,[10] replacing them with a system of deductions from, or set-offs against, monetary awards.[11] We may also be able to rid ourselves of some residual limitations upon restitutionary causes of action, such as the requirement that failures of consideration must be "total" before they can afford rights of recovery.[12] For there is some evidence that this restriction has in the past been partly attributable to courts' unwillingness to engage in difficult quantification issues.[13] A better grasp of quantification principles may therefore release rights to expand further to their logical limits, replicating the liberating effect that more careful thinking about defences has already had upon their scope.

The gains from this vision are flexibility, logic and the better tuning of unjust enrichment law to the objectives it is designed to meet: more precise justice. A broader range of more differentiated and sensitive responses becomes available, unobstructed by forms of action and historical barriers between equity and law. It is a vision which rejects the hobnailed philosophy of all or nothing. The flexibility implied by the map does not mean, however,

place confiscation within the unjust enrichment rubric. See also, *contra*, Hedley, "Unjust Enrichment" [1995] 54 *CLJ* 578.

[9] *Clarke* v. *Dickson* (1858) EB & E 148.

[10] This defence was rejected in English law in *Kleinwort Benson Ltd* v. *Birmingham City Council* [1997] QB 360, but it is not clear whether this was because passing on can only ever be relevant in claims for loss, or because the gains the claimant had made in the case were too remote to be taken into account. The defence was left open in public law cases involving taxation.

[11] Equity has side-stepped the former defence in this way: *Spence* v. *Crawford* [1939] 3 All ER 271. The concerns underlying the passing on defence (that the claimant may be left with a windfall) could equally be met by deducting from the claimant's monetary award a sum representing the gains he had received as a direct consequence of his transaction with the defendant.

[12] *Hunt* v. *Silk* (1804) 5 East 449; *Whincup* v. *Hughes* (1871) LR 6 CP 78. In practice, courts have subtly evaded this requirement: see, e.g. *Rover International Ltd* v. *Cannon Film Sales Ltd (No. 3)* [1989] 1 WLR 912.

[13] P Birks, *An Introduction to the Law of Restitution* (Oxford, Clarendon Press, 1985, rev'd 1989) ("Birks"), pp. 242–3. There are, however, other concerns: McKendrick, "Total Failure of Consideration and Counter-Restitution: Two Issues or One?" in P Birks (ed.), *Laundering and Tracing* (Oxford, Clarendon Press, 1995), p. 219.

that courts will have an unfettered discretion to choose between remedial options. Some remedies (monetary restitution, for example) are likely to be available automatically, though the way in which they are quantified will vary. Others (proprietary and specific relief) will be available only in limited circumstances. The process is not an arbitrary pick-and-mix. Nonetheless, we are likely to drop the assumption that there is, in every case, an automatic association between particular causes of action and particular remedial responses and the task of our courts will then be to define and consistently apply the factors which bear upon the availability of the various options. This they will probably do in much the same way as they currently do in contract and tort, when deciding on the balance of monetary and injunctive relief, or the relative availability of damages based on market loss or "cost of cure".

Bearing in mind the controversy of this type of approach, the following remedial map is proffered together with some observations and predictions based around it. The reader will note that the map gives examples of the various different types of unjust enrichment remedy. Some of these are themselves controversial, either because there is a dispute as to whether they in fact serve to combat unjust enrichment at all (as in the case of the resulting trust, for example); or (as in the case of subrogation) because they are probably better analysed as techniques (ways of obtaining remedies) rather than as remedies themselves. Space precludes a full defence of these features, which are elegantly defended elsewhere.[14]

Prevention

Prevention is normally left off the map. This is because we have in the past focused on a law of "restitution," not "unjust enrichment". That is inappropriate in a modern rights-based system[15] and blinkers us. If we remove our goggles, however, we soon see that both public and private unjust enrichment law can operate in preventive fashion. Courts can thus preempt criminal profit by forfeiting inheritance interests,[16] confiscating property,[17] imposing resulting[18] or constructive[19] trusts; or, as recently illustrated in *Attorney General* v.

[14] References to much of the literature can be found in Barker, "Rescuing Remedialism in Unjust Enrichment Law: Why Remedies are Right" [1998] *CLJ* 301 at 304–5.

[15] Birks, *supra* n. 5, p. 1.

[16] *Goff and Jones on the Law of Restitution* (5th edn., London, Sweet & Maxwell, 1998), pp. 802–10; Virgo, "The Law of Restitution and the Proceeds of Crime" [1998] 6 *RLR* 34, at 46–61; Jones, "Stripping a Criminal of the Profits of Crime" (2000) 1 *Theoretical Inquiries in Law* 59 at 65.

[17] Criminal Justice Act 1988, Part VI (as amended by the Proceeds of Crime Act 1995); Prevention of Terrorism (Temporary Provisions) Act 1989; Drug Trafficking Act 1994.

[18] *Cleaver* v. *Mutual Reserve Fund Life Association* [1892] 1 QB 147.

[19] See American cases cited by Jones, *supra* n. 16, at 65–9. The possibility of English courts using the constructive trust to combat fraud is raised by Lord Browne-Wilkinson in *Westdeutsche Landesbank Girozentrale* v. *Islington LBC* [1996] AC 669, at 716.

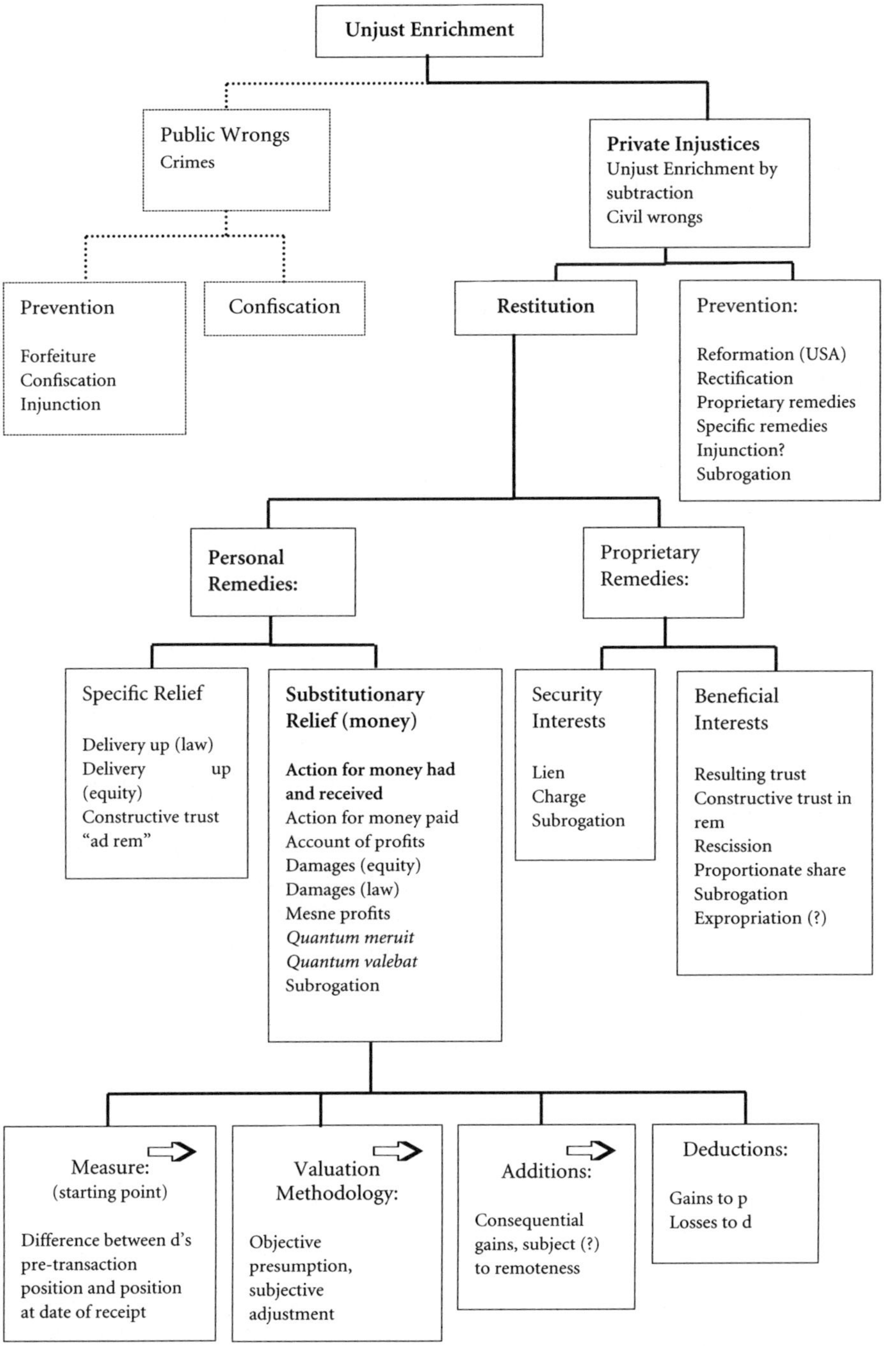

Figure 1: Unjust Enrichment: A Remedial Map (current remedial emphasis indicated in bold

Blake,[20] by issuing injunctions. The remedies in such instances either prevent any gain being made in the first place, or—as with the trust device—prevent further gain being derived from it.

Prevention features in private unjust enrichment law too, though more rarely. The *Restatement* thus mentions private transactions in which courts anticipate unjust gain by reforming (rewriting) the terms of documents.[21] Some cases involving subrogation can only be explained in this way.[22] Moreover, in *Attorney General of Hong Kong* v. *Reid*,[23] the Privy Council recently granted a constructive trust over the property investments of a dishonest fiduciary, on the basis that they were derived from his bribe. This had the effect not only of stripping him of his pre-trial profit, but of preventing him obtaining any post-trial gain, either through personal enjoyment of the property itself, or its future investment or use.

Prevention will always be exceptional for practical, liberal and economic reasons. Where the facts surrounding enrichment disclose a civil wrong, it may well be possible for a claimant to obtain an injunction to restrain the wrong itself, in contract or tort. Prevention of gain from the wrong is then otiose. We also, of course, tend to find out about unjust enrichment only when it has already happened. Even if neither of these practical considerations were to prevail, however, most free market societies will be reluctant to lay down prior restraints on profit because this is restrictive of personal liberty and antithetical to the general consensus that gain, unlike loss, is a social good: something to be encouraged.

There are two bases for exceptional interference. One is to do *ex ante* what the law would otherwise do *ex post*. Where, for example, the receipt of gain would ordinarily lead to confiscation by the State (in public law) or to restitution (in private law), prevention may be justified, even if it is rarely feasible. This is simply averting today what we would otherwise have to put right tomorrow. The other basis—predominant in the criminal cases, but also carrying across into private law cases such as *Reid*—is deterrence. The public interest in such instances may be so strong as to trump the respect we ordinarily afford to a person's liberty to profit.

[20] [1998] Ch 439. This is a broad but exceptional power, in support of the policy of the Criminal Justice Act 1988. A narrower jurisdiction to issue interlocutory relief was described in *Chief Constable of Kent* v. *V* [1983] QB 34.

[21] *US Restatement of Restitution* (2nd tent. Draft, 1983), comment h to s. 8. Our own "contractual" remedy of rectification arguably achieves similar things.

[22] e.g. *Banque Financiere de la Cité* v. *Parc (Battersea) Ltd* [1998] 2 WLR 475, noted by Mitchell [1998] 6 *RLR* 144 and some cases on indemnity insurers' subrogation rights, cited in Burrows, *supra* n. 8, at 78–82.

[23] [1994] 1 AC 324.

Confiscation

Confiscation contrasts with restitution. It involves the seizure of gains by the State, rather than their transfer to a private party at whose expense they have been obtained. Actions are State-controlled and respond to public wrongs (crimes), rather than private injustices, such as mistakes or torts. They are quantified differently[24] because their aims are different. For whereas the primary function of restitution is to do corrective justice[25] (to erase the effects of private injustice by restoring parties to their pre-transactional positions), the main purpose of confiscation is to deter public wrongdoing.

There are four reasons for putting confiscation on the map. First, it targets gains acquired through wrongdoing, albeit wrongdoing of a more serious and public nature than that encountered in private law. Secondly, the rise of organised crime (in particular drug-trafficking) has recently prompted government to place increased priority upon it. This priority is at a premium when public money is short. Indeed, confiscation could, if used more broadly, become an imaginative source of public funding—a way of putting gains made at the public expense to constructive public use. The confiscated profits of environmental crime could be used in a targeted way for clean-up. The profits of "victimless" financial crimes such as insider-dealing could be fed into closer industry-regulation, according to public demand, and so on. Thirdly, some of the deterrent aims underpinning confiscation clearly carry across into private law, as *Reid* poignantly illustrates. Public and private values are defiantly resistant to confinement within our rigid legal categories. Fourthly, many crimes, such as fraud and public nuisance, also constitute private wrongs, so that there are bound to be cases where confiscation and restitution potentially overlap. There are signs of competition between the two[26] and we cannot deal with the overlaps if we ignore one half of the picture.

Two important questions about the relationship between confiscatory and restitutionary remedies are foreseeable, which will require resolution in the

[24] Three differences are immediately apparent: (1) whereas restitutionary remedies are sometimes limited by reference to a plaintiff's loss, loss is irrelevant to the State's entitlement to confiscate the profits of crime; (2) a very generous approach is taken to the quantification of confiscatory awards under current drug-trafficking legislation, which requires proof of only a very loose correlation between crime and profit. The approach to this correlation in cases of civil wrongdoing is much stricter; (3) courts in civil cases can adjust restitutionary awards to take account of a wrongdoer's own skill and initiative in generating profit (*Boardman* v. *Phipps* [1967] 2 AC 46). Not so in cases involving crime.

[25] E Weinrib, *The Idea of Private Law* (London, Harvard, 1995), pp. 140–2; "Restitutionary Damages as Corrective Justice" [2000] 1 *Theoretical Inquiries in Law* 1; Barker, "Unjust Enrichment: Containing the Beast" (1995) *OJLS* 458, at 468–74; Virgo, *The Principles of the Law of Restitution* (Oxford, OUP, 1999), pp. 4–6. See *contra*, H Dagan, *Unjust Enrichment* (Cambridge, CUP, 1997), pp. 31–2.

[26] *Halifax Building Society* v. *Thomas* [1996] Ch 217.

short to medium term. First, is restitution ever available for "pure" crime (that which is not also a civil wrong) ? Secondly, where the same conduct is wrongful both criminally and under our civil system, which remedy—confiscation or restitution—is appropriate ? The answer to the first question is likely to be "no", *if* (but only if) confiscation is adequate to strip the criminal of his profit and the victim of the crime is unidentifiable, has sustained no personal harm, or has been fully compensated.[27] This is the basic stance detectable in *Halifax Building Society* v. *Thomas*.[28] But there will be exceptions, where the State fails to confiscate, or is incapable of confiscating.[29] Likewise, if a private victim can show that he has been *harmed* by crime, he has in truth suffered a *private* injustice too and should be entitled, as he is in the law of public nuisance,[30] to bring a private action (in this case for restitution, rather than for compensation) based nominally on the "public" wrong. In truth, the crime in such cases discloses both a public and a private grievance. The result is that restitution should probably be available to fill the gaps left by the criminal law for deterrent purposes, as commentators have suggested,[31] but also, perhaps, that it should be available where crimes have had specific, detrimental effects on private interests.

The second question is easier. If the facts present both a crime and a restitution-yielding civil injustice, both confiscation and restitution are logically available. The issue becomes one of policy and is probably best resolved in the following way. Where the effect of the restitution action(s) is to strip away all of an offender's gain, the confiscation claim should normally be dropped, since its objectives (deterrence) will have been indirectly met.[32] But where criminal gains are in-exhausted by restitution actions, the State should be entitled to claim the surplus. The priority of restitution over confiscation can be justified on the basis that the purpose of the public action is ultimately nothing other than the protection of our collective private interests. Where one such private interest has been provably affected, it should therefore claim first place in the queue.

[27] It is for this reason that no *direct* link is drawn on the map in figure 1 between public injustices and restitution.

[28] [1996] Ch 217. The court was reluctant to extend restitution into areas in which Parliament has legislated for confiscation. Cf. also Law Comm. Rep No. 247, para. 3.27.

[29] Virgo, *supra* n. 16, at 38–9; Jones, *supra* n. 16, at 70.

[30] In nuisance, this right is limited to those who can show "special" damage, in order to avoid potential floods of claims.

[31] See Virgo, Jones, *supra* n. 16.

[32] Under the CJA 1988, s. 71(1C), a court's duty to make a confiscation order softens into a power, where the victim "has instituted, or intends to institute" a civil claim.

Restitution

Restitution is the heartland of unjust enrichment.[33] The majority of cases involve monetary relief, but attention will in future come to focus upon a broader range of more differentiated remedies; and upon the formulation of criteria governing their availability, quantification and overlap. The map indicates a number of groupings. Remedies are either personal or proprietary.[34] Personal remedies are in practice monetary, though they might also be specific—that is, providing a right to the return of a thing *in specie*, without affording the claimant all the normal incidents of a proprietary interest, such as the right to claim priority in insolvency.

Proprietary remedies are divisible into those which confer beneficial interests in property (together with the full range of beneficial incidents which attach to such interests, including the right to claim priority and accretions in value) and those which confer security interests, such as the equitable lien (which do not). In principle, it should be possible to combine different remedies, where this is necessary to achieve full restitution.[35] It should also be possible to combine such remedies with compensatory awards, provided that a court does not unwittingly compensate twice for the same loss.[36] Though English law has formally set its face against this and requires plaintiffs to elect between restitution and compensation,[37] this seems unnecessary; it could in some circumstances lead to injustice; and there are, in fact, some cases[38] in which courts seem covertly to have tolerated combined awards through subtle manipulation. A system which increasingly respects the concurrency of actions should also respect the concurrency of compatible remedies and it should do so overtly.

How will existing remedial patterns change, with regard to restitution? Monetary remedies will almost certainly continue to dominate, though the development of quantification principles will increase their sophistication and reduce the importance accorded to old jurisdictional barriers. The continued

[33] No distinction is made in Figure 1 between "restitution" and "disgorgement", though the latter term may arguably be useful in identifying cases in which the monetary value of defendant's gain is paid to a plaintiff even though the plaintiff has suffered no material loss: Smith, "The Province of the Law of Restitution" (1992) 71 *CBR* 672, at 696.

[34] The word "proprietary" here signals that a plaintiff is entitled to a secondary right *in rem* over a defendant's gain, not that her cause of action is founded on any continuing legal or equitable right in property.

[35] *Restatement of Restitution* (2nd tent. Draft, 1983), s. 8 and Illustration 1.

[36] *Ibid.*, ss. 15–18; Burrows, "Reforming Non-Compensatory Damages" in W Swadling and G Jones (eds), *The Search For Principle* (Oxford, OUP, 1999), p. 295 at 304–6.

[37] Patents Act 1977, s. 61(2); *United Australia Ltd* v. *Barclays Bank* [1941] AC 1; *Tang* v. *Capacious Investments Ltd* [1996] 1 AC 514, PC. See also *Baltic Shipping Co* v. *Dillon (The Mikhail Lermontov)* (1993) 176 CLR 344;

[38] Cf. *e.g.*, *Rogers* v. *Parish* [1987] QB 933.

priority of these is predictable not simply because English law has, in contrast to continental systems, [39] always preferred substitutionary to specific relief, but also because the law has come to recognise more and more negative and intangible forms of gain, which cannot, by definition, give rise to specific or proprietary relief. Much of our economic wealth now exists as abstract rights which never assume anything akin to a proprietary form; and which have meaning only in terms of their monetary value. Credit, not property, is the vogue in our new, fast-moving world-economy.

Two predictions are possible in respect of the way that claims for monetary relief will be handled. First, awards will come to account in a more detailed way for a defendant's preferences. There are signs of this in *Ashman*,[40] but the limits are not known. In that case, the defendant trespasser was a wrongdoer, but the value of her gain was still subjectivised when it came to assessing mesne profits. How far will this go? Traditionally, there has been some resistance to subjectivity in quantification (as opposed to liability) matters,[41] but the tide has turned. The difference between objective (market-based) and subjective approaches to gain may be less extreme than supposed, because most people (by definition) value things at the market rate. Nonetheless, where they can prove they genuinely valued them at a lower rate; and that they were not a conscious wrongdoer, or a wrongdoer by choice[42] (or possibly, that they were no more at fault than the plaintiff),[43] there is a case for allowing their own values in. This would bring the law into line with the approach to valuation methodology taken in loss-based claims, where innocent claimants, though they are normally assumed to value what they have lost at the market rate, can successfully argue additional subjective detriment. As in the valuation of loss, so in the valuation of gain. The methodological assumptions and the libertarian values which underpin them, must be the same.

Secondly, it is probable that Professor Birks' influential "two-measure"[44] approach to the quantification of restitutionary awards will, in the long run, be displaced and supplemented by an analysis which is both simpler and more complex. The simplicity will derive from the recognition that in measuring gain, there is only one basic "measure", not two. Birks currently depicts two—

[39] Englard, "Restitution of Benefits Conferred without Obligation," in *International Encyclopedia of Comparative Law,* vol. X, ch. 5, paras 57, 206.

[40] *Ministry of Defence* v. *Ashman* [1993] 2 EGLR 102.

[41] See, e.g. Goff and Jones (4th edn., London, Sweet and Maxwell, 1993), p. 29. The position changes in the 5th edn., see pp. 29–30.

[42] This may explain the result in *Ashman, supra* n. 40. Mrs Ashman did wrong, but had little practical choice other than to do so, by virtue of her circumstances.

[43] This is the position under the *Restatement of Restitution* (1937), s. 155.

[44] *Birks, supra* n. 13, at 75–77, 358; P Birks, *Restitution, The Future* (Sydney, Federation Press, 1992), ch. 5; (ed.) *Laundering and Tracing (*Oxford, Clarendon Press, 1995), p. 320. Some cases have begun to refer to this taxonomy: see e.g. *Agip* v. *Jackson* [1990] Ch 264; *Bruyninckx* v. *Bruyninckx* (1995) 4 BCLR (3d) 341.

the value a defendant initially[45] received and the value surviving in his hands at the time of trial, but there are difficulties. Certainly, there are two measures of *loss* in private law—expectation and reliance. The former is the difference between a claimant's post-transaction position and his anticipated (expected) position; the latter between his post-transaction position and his pre-transaction position. But this twin-pronged analysis is possible only because there are two logically different baselines of a claimant's entitlement (two alternative positions he can claim to be legally entitled to occupy), against which the loss can be assessed. In claims for restitution, by contrast, there is only one legal baseline against which a defendant's *gain* can be measured (only one position he is legally entitled to occupy): his pre-transaction position. This fact reveals that Birks' distinction is not one that private lawyers would ordinarily construe as a distinction of "measurement" at all: it is one about two different ways in which a defendant's post-transaction position can be assessed.

There are two, more substantive difficulties. First, it is hard to see why a court assessing a defendant's post-transaction position should ever take *as a starting point* the amount he happens to have left at the time of trial, rather than the amount he has received up until that point. If the law's premise is that a person should not *make* unjust gains at another's expense, it is gains *made*, not gains *kept* that count. Whilst it may be that a defendant *ends up* for some legitimate reason being accountable only for what he has left, the basic assumption must surely be that he is *prima facie* liable for that which he originally got. This makes the existence of a second "measure" of monetary restitution decidedly suspect.[46] Secondly, the two-shot solution to quantification problems apparent in Birks' approach is unlikely to prove flexible enough without a good deal of distortion. The *Restatement* mentions cases where a wrongdoing defendant has been held liable for additional gains made from a gain initially received, but which have disappeared again by the time of

[45] There is some ambiguity here. At one point (*Laundering, ibid.* at 320) he implies that the "value received" measure is defined so as to ignore anything that happens "subsequently". At another, (*Birks, supra* n. 13, at 75, n. 2), he clearly says that the measure includes not just the amount initially received, but subsequent gains too, provided they are not too remote. The latter approach does not provide a stable, basic measure and the view taken here (see further the text, *infra*) is that it is best to adopt the former position. Value upon initial receipt is therefore the basic measure, to be adjusted to account for "consequential" gains, as necessary.

[46] *Burrows, supra* n. 8, at 373. The cases Birks cites in favour of it are best explained in other ways; either (i) the claim is for a proprietary remedy, so as to be necessarily limited to the value of the property claimed, or (ii) the plaintiff in practice failed to request the full amount received in its statement of claim (*Banque Belge pour L'Etranger* v. *Hambrouck* [1921] 1 KB 321), or (iii) the court tacitly reduced the size of the plaintiff's award from value received for reasons of policy or justice, e.g., in order to share the losses occasioned by a defendant's insolvency across a broad group of creditors: *Sinclair* v. *Brougham* [1914] AC 398 (where the award was effectively personal, but reduced in size); *Re Wrexham, Mold & Connah's Quay Railway Co* [1899] 1 Ch 440.

trial.[47] Liability here fails to coincide exactly with either the first or second measure.[48] Similar difficulties obtain where courts add interest to the amount initially received; or where deductions are made from awards to take account of a defendant's own in-put to a gain. The complexity of these adjustments will, it seems, ultimately defy any two-shot approach to quantification.

It therefore seems probable that in assessing monetary awards, the law will in the long term end up using a single basic "measure" of restitution (the difference between a defendant's pre-gain position and his position on its initial receipt), but that it will then develop more complex principles according to which awards may then be (a) increased to account for consequential gains or (b) decreased on moral or policy grounds. The starting point will be simpler and more stable, the principles of adjustment more complex.

Despite the supremacy of monetary relief, there is some scope for greater use of personal, specific remedies in unjust enrichment law, both at law and in equity.[49] Our increased exposure to continental thinking and recent calls for the provision of an intermediate remedial option, half-way between remedies operating *in rem and in personam*,[50] make this more likely. Specific relief could, if existing analogies are anything to go by,[51] prove useful in cases in which a plaintiff has a particular, subjective interest in an asset, which a defendant has unjustly received from him, so that return of the asset accords the most perfect form of corrective justice. The availability of such an option might, in theory,[52] be made independent of the question of whether or not property in the asset had been retained by a plaintiff. Some of the advantages of proprietary remedies for unjust enrichment would thereby be replicated, without including the controversial right to claim priority in a defendant's insolvency.

Proprietary restitutionary remedies are most controversial and it is significant that the pattern of their availability is changing. Indeed, we are now

[47] *Restatement of Restitution* (1937), illustrations 3,4 to s. 151. The position is less clear in the United Kingdom *Birks, supra* n. 13, at 351, cites *Heathcote* v. *Hulme* (1819) 1 Jac & W 122 as authority against such liability, but see *Eden* v. *Ridsdales Railway Lamp Co & Lighting Co* (1889) 23 QBD 368.

[48] The way in which Birks would apparently deal with such a case would be to include subsequent gains within the "first measure" of restitution: see *supra* n. 45. But this, as indicated, creates an unstable, fluctuating yardstick of measurement.

[49] The ancient equitable jurisdiction to order delivery up of chattels was apparently not superceded when the same remedy became available at common law: see R Meagher, W Gummow and J Lehane, *Equity: Doctrines and Remedies* (3rd edn., Sydney, Butterworths, 1992), p. 630.

[50] See, e.g, Goode, "Property and Unjust Enrichment" in A Burrows (ed.), *Essays on the Law of Restitution* (Oxford, Clarendon Press, 1991), p. 217, at 222; "Proprietary Restitutionary Claims" in W Cornish *et al.* (eds), *Restitution Past Present and Future, supra* n. 3, at 63.

[51] Torts (Interference with Goods) Act 1977, ss. 3–7 and RSC Ord. 45, r. 4.

[52] In practice, rights *in specie* tend to prevail in circumstances in which legal or equitable title persists. In the former instance, the remedy is sought in tort; in the latter, a trust pertains, granting the claimant the right not simply to specific relief, but also to a beneficial interest.

catching the first glimpses of a potentially very different landscape. In the past, such remedies were deployed conservatively, in the sense that they were used to replicate (conserve) pre-existing property interests, rather than to create new, "first-time" interests, where none existed before.[53] This reflected the corrective (restorative) rationale of private law. It is clear, however, that some cases are now awarding proprietary remedies without reference to the conservative philosophy. Public law cases of criminal confiscation always provided examples of this, but until *Lord Napier and Ettrick* v. *Hunter*[54] and *Reid*,[55] the civil law eschewed it. *Reid*, it is fair to say, has caused a shock wave, precisely because it contemplates using private law to expropriate property rights compulsorily, without recourse to legislative sanction. The result is that it has been interpreted either as a sign of a dangerous, new judicial power to engage in property redistribution; or authors have sought (unsuccessfully, it is suggested) to reconcile it with the traditional, conservative thesis.

There is, however, a third possibility: that *Reid* is a symptom of a more general, functional approach to unjust enrichment remedies. Mr Reid was guilty, remember, not just of a breach of fiduciary duty, but also of a pernicious crime and one committed against the Crown at that. The functional analogy between the trust and confiscation is close and it seems possible that the former was, on this occasion, used in furtherance of the deterrent policies normally (but not exclusively) associated with public wrongdoing. We have already seen civil courts intervening against gain in support of the policies of the criminal law,[56] by issuing injunctions. Reid may simply be an example of the exceptional use of a different equitable remedy to a similar, public end: to achieve maximum deterrence through maximum gain—stripping and prevention.

The potential of the trust to shift the landscape of unjust enrichment law from obligation to property is so fundamental that we devote a significant part of the next section to it. But *Reid* is important not simply because of the remedy used, but because of the type of remedial functionalism it supposes to be acceptable. That functionalism assumes that in some (though not necessarily all, or even the majority of) cases, there is no single, "automatic" remedy for unjust gain, but that courts have some degree of *choice* in picking the response which is "adequate" or "appropriate", given its effects and the law's purposes. On occasion, it seems to say, courts may look forward to the individual and social effects of remedies, not simply back, to the past pattern of rights.

This type of functionalism has a bad press in private law. It is associated with "palm tree justice" and unconstitutional, purposive, judicial action. If we are

53 See Birks' "Proprietary base" theory, which is premised on this vision: *Birks*, *supra* n. 13, at 378–9; "Establishing a Proprietary Base" [1995] 3 *RLR* 83, at 84.

54 [1993] AC 713.

55 [1994] 1 AC 324.

56 See *supra* n. 20.

truthful, however, judges have always looked to the effects of remedies when deciding whether to allow them and have, whatever they say, taken account of policy as well as right, though the fact has regularly been buried deep beneath a panoply of legal concepts.[57] In Canada and the USA, the influence of policy is more obvious and it is notable, of course, that it is in those jurisdictions that both a separate remedial agenda and a more radical use of the proprietary remedy have emerged. It now seems possible that we may follow them in part, even if we do not embrace proprietary remedies themselves quite with the same transatlantic gusto. The benefits of a more flexible remedial strategy of this type may have been underestimated and the dangers significantly overstated.[58] The benefits are a clearer depiction of the factors bearing upon decisions about remedial form; more integrated remedial solutions as between common law and equity; greater differentiation between different remedial possibilities and the avoidance of damaging elisions of, or confusions between, ideas relating to cause of action (when is restitution available) and response (how and in what amount is it to be made?).[59] By contrast, judges should be able to meet the main dangers of remedialism—lack of discipline in the ranks—by structuring decision-making by reference to more clearly identified moral and policy factors.

The Trust

Some fundamental questions about trusts and unjust enrichment need to be resolved in the near future. One question is whether a person is strictly liable in unjust enrichment for receiving trust property. Another is when trusts arise as a response to unjust enrichment. On both of these questions, the law is contested and subject to significantly different understandings in different quarters.

Receipt of Trust Property

The claim known as "knowing receipt of trust property" is traditionally thought to require that the defendant had, or should have had, some level of

[57] For this point, effectively made in the context of proprietary remedies, see, D Wright, *The Remedial Constructive Trust* (Sydney, Butterworths, 1998); Rotherham, "Restitution and Property Rites: Reason and Ritual in the Law of Proprietary Remedies" (2000) 1 *Theoretical Inquiries in Law* 205; Barker, "The Remedial Constructive Trust" (1999) 13 *TLI* 204, at 207.

[58] Barker, *supra* n. 14; Wright, *supra* n. 57.

[59] One manifestation of this type of elision which occurred in Canada, but which has subsequently been set right, was the description of the constructive trust as a "third head of obligation" based on unjust enrichment: cf. *Murdoch* v. *Murdoch* [1975] 1 SCR 423, at 455; *Rathwell* v. *Rathwell* [1978] 2 SCR 436, at 454.

awareness that the property received was subject to a trust. A typical statement is that of Hoffmann LJ, as he then was, in *El Ajou* v. *Dollar Land Holdings plc*:[60]

> "the plaintiff must show, first, a disposal of his assets in breach of fiduciary duty; secondly, the beneficial receipt by the defendant of assets which are traceable as representing the assets of the plaintiff; and thirdly, knowledge on the part of the defendant that the assets he received are traceable to a breach of fiduciary duty".

A most formidable argument has been made that a defendant who receives trust property should be strictly liable to the beneficiary in unjust enrichment, subject to defences.[61] This argument has persuaded at least one judge, although not yet in a judicial capacity.[62] The basis of the argument has shifted over the years. Initially, it was that the claim known as "knowing receipt" was actually a claim in unjust enrichment, and so it was a mistake to think that it should require fault.[63] More recently, it has been acknowledged that "knowing receipt" is best seen as a form of equitable wrongdoing, but the argument asks why it should not be possible to leave this claim to one side, and sue the defendant in unjust enrichment, a possibility which (the argument must suppose) has lain unnoticed for many years.[64]

The courts, however, remain unmoved. The Court of Appeal has continued to hold that fault is required for the claim in knowing receipt. In *Brown* v. *Bennett*,[65] the formulation set out above from *El Ajou* was said to be "a paradigm example of its proper expression". More recently, the Court has indicated that "notice" will suffice for liability.[66] The House of Lords has indicated that the plaintiff must establish some level of awareness of the trust on the part of the defendant, without specifying exactly what level is required.[67]

It seems that this requirement of fault can be justified in principle. It must be remembered that claims for receipt of trust property are, in one crucial respect, unlike most cases of unjust enrichment. Most claims in unjust

60 [1994] 2 All ER 685, at 700; remitted [1995] 2 All ER 213.

61 Birks, "Misdirected Funds: Restitution from the Recipient" [1989] *LMCLQ* 296.

62 Lord Nicholls of Birkenhead, "Knowing Receipt: The Need for a New Landmark" in W Cornish *et al.* (eds), *Restitution: Past, Present and Future*, *supra* n. 3, at 231.

63 Birks, "Misdirected Funds: Restitution from the Recipient" [1989] *LMCLQ* 296; Birks, "Persistent Problems in Misdirected Money: A Quintet" [1993] *LMCLQ* 218, at 228–9.

64 Birks, "Equity in the Modern Law" (1996) 26 *UWALR* 1, at 72; Birks, "Property and Unjust Enrichment: Categorical Truths" [1997] *NZLR* 623, at 651–4. This is the version to which Lord Nicholls subscribes.

65 [1999] 1 BCLC 649.

66 *Twinsectra Ltd* v. *Yardley* [1999] Lloyd's Rep Bank 438, at para. 114. The meaning of "notice" in this context is discussed by Gardner, "Knowing Assistance and Knowing Receipt: Taking Stock" (1996) 112 *LQR* 56, at 60–4. See also *Houghton* v. *Fayen* [2000] 1B CLC 511, CA; *BCCI (Overseas) Ltd* v. *Akindale*, unreported, 14 June 2000, CA, each phrasing the fault requirement differently.

67 *Westdeutsche Landesbank Girozentrale* v. *Islington London BC* [1996] AC 669, at 707D. In *Citadel General Assurance Co* v. *Lloyds Bank Canada* [1997] 3 SCR 805, 152 DLR (4th) 411, the Supreme Court of Canada adopted a carelessness standard.

enrichment do not depend on any showing that the plaintiff held a proprietary interest in the subject matter of the enrichment at the time of the defendant's receipt. They depend, instead, on a showing of enrichment, an inquiry which is divorced from proprietary rights in specific assets. Claims to recover mistaken payments, or the value of services, illustrate this clearly. But a claim in knowing receipt is defeated if the defendant acquired the property in circumstances which eliminated the plaintiff's preexisting equitable interest. In other words, the claim in knowing receipt depends upon equitable proprietary rights. Because such rights are systematically invisible, defendants have never been strictly liable for interfering with them.

Two possible futures therefore lie ahead. One future is strict liability, subject to defences, bringing this claim into line with the common law.[68] But the profound change which this would bring about should not be underestimated. No-one can tell when an asset is subject to a trust, and so this approach represents a huge shift, against historical tradition, towards *prima facie* liability. The defences will have much more work to do, particularly on behalf of those whose business it is to deal with money. Banks, stockbrokers, lawyers, and others will routinely be required to go to trial to establish their defences, no matter how honest and careful are their procedures. The other future resists "the temptation of elegance"[69] and accepts that being a trust beneficiary is inherently more risky than being the holder of a legal title.[70]

Trusts Arising by Operation of Law

The vexed question of when trusts arise to reverse unjust enrichments is currently dominated by the speech of Lord Browne-Wilkinson in *Westdeutsche*.[71] The suggestion there that trusts can only arise when the trustee's "conscience is affected"[72] is capable of a number of interpretations. What is crucial in that formula is the meaning of the word "trust". If it means "situation in which beneficial ownership is divorced from nominal ownership" then the speech would have far-reaching effects indeed.[73] But it does not appear that this was meant at all. The word "trust" in Lord Browne-Wilkinson's formula means something more. It means a relationship whose characteristics go beyond the

68 *Lipkin Gorman (a firm)* v. *Karpnale Ltd* [1991] 2 AC 548.

69 R Goff, "The Search for Principle," reprinted in W Swadling and G Jones (eds), *The Search for Principle* (Oxford, OUP, 1999), at 318.

70 The matter is fully discussed in Smith, "Property, Unjust Enrichment and the Structure of Trusts" (2000) 116 *LQR* 412, where the requirement of fault is defended.

71 See *supra* n. 67.

72 *Ibid.*, at 705.

73 As demonstrated in Swadling, "Property and Conscience" (1998) 12 *Trust Law International* 228.

proprietary, and include the full range of personal obligations which an express trustee owes to his beneficiary.[74] This is evident within the speech, in particular where Lord Browne-Wilkinson rejected the "separation of title" argument, in which it was suggested that there is a trust where one party holds a legal title and another holds the equitable beneficial ownership of the same asset.[75] His terminological choice is also evident in his statement that if there was a trust, the recipient would be personally liable, regardless of fault, for any subsequent payment away of trust money.[76] Because Lord Browne-Wilkinson held that "[i]n the absence of fraud courts of equity have never awarded compound interest except against a trustee or other person owing fiduciary duties",[77] it followed that the bank could not succeed in its claim for compound interest unless it could prove a trust in the sense that Lord Browne-Wilkinson used that word. Whether his usage will become widely accepted is one of the questions whose answer must await future developments.

But the crucial point is that nothing Lord Browne-Wilkinson said entails that equitable proprietary rights (as distinct from personal obligations) cannot arise until the conscience of the legal title-holder is affected; such a position would be incompatible with a great deal of law. It is true that he doubted the reasoning in *Chase Manhattan Bank NA* v. *Israel-British Bank (London) Ltd*,[78] suggesting that the result in the case—that a mistaken payee holds the payment on trust for the payor—could only be defended on the basis that the conscience of the defendant payee was affected when it learned of the mistake.[79] But he must be taken to have chosen his words consistently; this effect on the payee's conscience was necessary for a trust in Lord Browne-Wilkinson's sense, but not for mere equitable proprietary rights.

But the part of the speech which invites serious prognostication is this:

> "Although the resulting trust is an unsuitable basis for developing proprietary restitutionary remedies, the remedial constructive trust, if introduced into English law,

[74] This point was made by Birks, "Trusts Raised to Reverse Unjust Enrichment: The *Westdeutsche* Case" [1996] *RLR* 3, at 11–12; see also Smith, "Constructive Fiduciaries?" in P Birks (ed.), *Privacy and Loyalty* (Oxford, OUP, 1997), pp. 265–6.

[75] *Westdeutsche*, *supra* n. 67, at 706–7. Contrast Lord Lindley in *Hardoon* v. *Belilios* [1901] AC 118, PC, Hong Kong, at 123: "All that is necessary to establish the relation of trustee and cestui que trust is to prove that the legal title was in [one party] and the equitable title in [the other]"; also Wilson J in *Guerin* v. *Canada* [1984] 2 SCR 335, 13 DLR (4th) 321, at 361: "A trust arises, as I understand it, whenever a person is compelled in equity to hold property over which he has control for the benefit of others (the beneficiaries) in such a way that the benefit of the property accrues not to the trustee, but to the beneficiaries".

[76] *Westdeutsche*, *supra* n. 67, at 703. Such a strict liability does not necessarily arise if "trust" is understood as Lord Lindley and Wilson J understood it: *ibid.*

[77] *Ibid.*, at 701.

[78] [1981] Ch 105.

[79] *Westdeutsche*, *supra* n. 67, at 715.

may provide a more satisfactory road forward. The court by way of remedy might impose a constructive trust on a defendant who knowingly retains property of which the plaintiff has been unjustly deprived. Since the remedy can be tailored to the circumstances of the particular case, innocent third parties would not be prejudiced and restitutionary defences, such as change of position, are capable of being given effect. However, whether English law should follow the United States and Canada by adopting the remedial constructive trust will have to be decided in some future case when the point is directly in issue".[80]

The death of the remedial constructive trust was recently announced, but as in the case of Mark Twain, the report may have been exaggerated.[81] Whether or not with an eye on Lord Browne-Wilkinson's words, trusts arising by operation of law to reverse unjust enrichment are thick on the ground in English courts. In *James* v. *Williams*,[82] the Limitation Act 1980 seemed to bar the plaintiff's claim, to the benefit of the defendant's predecessor in title and so of the defendant. But the result was avoided; the Court of Appeal held that there was a constructive trust all along. In *Heinl* v. *Jyske Bank (Gibraltar) Ltd*[83] the same Court held that where an agent purports to transfer a company's property, but, to the knowledge of the transferee, the agent lacks authority, the property is held on trust for the company. Similarly in *Allied Carpets Group plc* v. *Nethercott*:[84] where a director took an unauthorised dividend he held it on trust for the company. Other trusts are not explicable as examples of subtractive unjust enrichment. In *Yaxley* v. *Gotts*,[85] the Court of Appeal seems to have revivified the doctrine of part performance via the constructive trust. The same court later applied this decision in *Banner Homes Group plc* v. *Luff Developments Ltd*:[86] an oral agreement which is not enforceable as a contract may nonetheless be enforceable via a constructive trust.

Are these trusts remedial or institutional? No-one really knows. They just keep arising. What does the distinction even mean? No-one really knows. The reasoning of the courts generally avoids any confrontation with the wider implications of the proliferation of such trusts; but this is hardly surprising. The lesson of Lord Denning's career has been learned by all. If you want your innovations to last, do not mark them as such. More prosaically, if you want

[80] *Ibid.*, at 717.

[81] Birks, "The End of the Remedial Constructive Trust?" (1998) 12 *Trust Law International* 202; see also Wright, "Professor Birks and the Demise of the Remedial Constructive Trust" [1999] *RLR* 128.

[82] [1999] 3 All ER 309.

[83] [1999] Lloyd's Rep Bank 511.

[84] Unreported, 28 January 2000.

[85] [1999] 3 WLR 1217.

[86] [2000] 2 WLR 772.

your judgments to be upheld on appeal, do not identify them as controversial. Better to cross the Rubicon in disguise.[87]

There are some who are driven near to despair at the prospect of judicial innovation and flexibility, particularly in the context of proprietary rights. It is sometimes suggested that judges may not take account of policy issues in deciding cases.[88] But whatever may be the ideals of moral philosophers, it is almost inconceivable that any judge ever decided a point of law without regard to the consequences, not just for the parties, but for the system. Indeed, testing a proposed rule by its consequences is a kind of built-in mechanism of common law reasoning. No-one believes that the mass of common law rules was created like a system of Euclidian geometry, by backward-looking deduction from a set of unchallengeable axioms. The truth must be that judicial styles lie on a spectrum. Some judges reach sooner than others the limits of their willingness to shape the system.[89] (We may note in passing where on the spectrum lay those judges whom we remember long after they are gone.) If a prediction be permitted which is informed by comparative historical experience, the coming into force of the Human Rights Act 1998 will very quickly alter the calculus of the extent to which judges may legitimately take account of policy. They will be required to do so under the legislation, and this mode of adjudication will tend to spill over into private law.

There is a narrower version of the argument against judicial flexibility, one which objects not so much to innovation as to discretion. This position rests on the unelected authority of the judiciary, and via a kind of social contractarian theory draws the conclusion that judicial discretion is inappropriate.[90] So far as it suggests that equitable doctrines are not genuinely discretionary, but are so in name only, this argument seems inaccurate.[91] So far as it condemns

[87] P Devlin, *The Judge* (Oxford, OUP, 1979), p. 12: "It is facile to think that it is always better to throw off disguises. The need for disguise hampers activity and so restricts the power. Paddling across the Rubicon by individuals in disguise who will be sent back if they proclaim themselves is very different from the bridging of the river by an army in uniform and with bands playing".

[88] Birks, "The End of the Remedial Constructive Trust?" (1998) 12 *Trust Law International* 202.

[89] And of course the same is true of academics. In respect of any judicial innovation, some will say that it goes too far.

[90] Birks, "Equity in the Modern Law" (1996) 26 *UWALR* 1, at 97–9. See now Birks, *supra* n. 7, at 23–4, "this view of the law and of the role of the courts would ultimately threaten the stability of our society."

[91] e.g. Birks, "Review of Wright, *The Remedial Constructive Trust*" (2000) 115 *LQR* 681, p. 684: "The universal discretion formally asserted by the Court of Chancery has long since settled down. We can speak of a right to specific performance as easily and as correctly as of a right to damages at common law". The first statement must be highly controversial; for example, in *Mediterranean Shipping Co SA* v. *Atlantic Container Line AB*, unreported, 3 December 1998, Clarke LJ said, referring to the judgment of Millett LJ in *The Angelic Grace* [1995] 1 Lloyd's Rep 87: "The importance of that last passage is that it recognises that the grant of an injunction, like the grant of any other equitable remedy, is discretionary". Buxton LJ referred to "considerations

discretion as requiring litigants to beg for their rights,[92] it is not wholly fair, since the possibility that some legal responses are controlled by discretion does not, by any stretch of the imagination, entail that the judge may choose to withhold all recourse.[93] Most interestingly, judges themselves seem inclined to the view that, at least in certain kinds of cases, they cannot do their job without discretion. One might postulate a Law of Conservation of Judicial Discretion. If the possibilities for flexible constructive trusts are sharply constrained, as they were for cohabitational disputes by *Lloyds Bank* v. *Rosset*,[94] another doctrine will arise: in this context, proprietary estoppel.[95] It would be futile to try to squeeze all judicial discretion out of our legal system. And it is a mistake to think that a system which permits some discretion somehow fails to meet the ideals of the rule of law.[96]

Perhaps one can only guess at two possible futures. In one, the House of Lords squashes the remedial constructive trust. This would leave two difficult tasks. First, to provide some convincing rationale for the trusts which English law does recognise, which at the same time is circumscribed so as to be consistent with a halt on further development. Attempts along these lines have not been successful to date. The second task would be to stop judges from using other doctrines, such as proprietary estoppel, to achieve exactly the same results which had been denied to them by the law of trusts.

In the other future, English courts will continue to develop this area of the law without any interdict, even if they lack an actual blessing. It might be that

militating against the granting of equitable and therefore discretionary relief". Mummery LJ agreed with both judgments. Birks' second statement about specific performance, even if true, would not establish his first, since specific performance is not all of equity; but in any event it appears that specific performance really is discretionary, although, as is always rightly the case, the discretion is constrained: see e.g. *Mean Machines Ltd* v. *Blackheath Leisure (Carousel) Ltd*, unreported, 13 May 1999, CA; *Co-Operative Insurance Society Ltd* v. *Argyll Stores (Holdings) Ltd.* [1998] AC 1; *Paramadevan* v. *Semelhago* [1996] 2 SCR 415, 136 DLR (4th) 1, paras 20–22.

[92] Birks, *supra* n. 7, 23.

[93] In traditional terms, if equitable responses are subject to discretion, this does not entail that legal ones are as well. See P Devlin, *The Judge* (Oxford, OUP, 1979), p. 201: "Those who live under the rule of law have as their entitlement the right to look first to the law for their protection and to the discretion of a judge only supplementarily in those recesses of justice into which the law is too solid to flow". See also Gardner, "The Remedial Discretion in Proprietary Estoppel" (1999) 115 *LQR* 438, positing a baseline entitlement subject to discretionary variation.

[94] [1991] 1 AC 107.

[95] This is vividly illustrated by *Gillett* v. *Holt* [2000] 2 All ER 289, CA.

[96] See Llewellyn 35, Law of Lawful Discretion: *The Common Law Tradition: Deciding Appeals* (Boston, Little, Brown & Co., 1960; reprinted Buffalo, W.S. Hein, 1996), pp. 217–19. Also, perhaps more poetically: "For it seems to me vital for students—and indeed for the bar and for the appellate bench itself—to awaken not only to the fact that rules alone do not decide any case worth puzzling about but to the companion fact, the comrade-and-brother fact, that the courts do not and cannot simply use the leeways of doctrine as they please. Put shortly, the courts are controlled by the tradition of their office with regard to the manner in which they use the leeways which their office opens up to them": K Llewellyn, *The Bramble Bush* (New York, Oceana, 1951), p. 156. See also Devlin, *supra* n. 94.

a relatively unconstrained doctrine, like that prevailing in North America, would take root and flourish.[97] The next stage of development, still under way in North America itself, would be a settling down and an ordering of the possibilities. Even if trusts become truly discretionary, it is in the nature of our system that particular factors will become crucial in the exercise of that discretion.[98] It may even be that the remedial constructive trust will be seen, in the end, to be something which would better be called something else. Perhaps it is a kind of injunction.[99] But those who insist that if it is badly named it must instantly be renamed are missing the point. Judicial development often starts out with misleading labels. The change from "quasi-contract" to "unjust enrichment" is clearly an improvement; but English law did without "unjust enrichment" for many years. The name changes when the judges are ready, and they are readier when the impetus for change is not merely a good idea but an overpowering need.

More so than anywhere else in the law of unjust enrichment, the matter of trusts arising by operation of law has resisted theorising, not in the sense that theories are absent, but in the sense that none has really won the day. This is a sign of a field of law which is the subject of vigorous judicial development. Such fields are exciting, but at the same time frustrating. Ultimately, academic lawyers may need to accept that for the time being they are cast in the role of observers.

Conclusion

The perilous process of prediction can be reduced to the matter of guessing what will change, and what will not. If our guesses are correct, the law governing liability for receipt of trust property should, at least as a matter of judicial development, resist the wholesale change to strict liability which is advocated from some quarters. It needs, however, a clear restatement as to the required

[97] It is important to stress *relatively* unconstrained. Canadian courts will not countenance a claim for a trust where the plaintiff has no rational connection to the alleged subject matter: *Barnabe* v. *Touhey* (1995) 26 OR (3d) 477, Ont CA.

[98] In Canada, one factor which seems to be emerging is whether the plaintiff had a reasonable expectation of acquiring a proprietary interest: Smith, "Canada: Annual Survey" [1994] *RLR* 102 at 103. That factor is arguably emerging in cases like *Yaxley* v. *Gotts* [1999] 3 WLR 1217 and *Banner Homes Group plc* v. *Luff Developments Ltd* [2000] 2 All ER 117.

[99] Smith, "Constructive Trusts—Unjust Enrichment" (1997) 76 *Can Bar Rev* 539, at 549–50. It seems difficult to find a Canadian case in which a remedial constructive trust had the effect of re-ordering bankruptcy priorities. Indeed in *Bedard* v. *Schell* [1987] 4 WWR 699 (Sask QB) it was held that such a "trust" was not a trust within what was then the Bankruptcy Act, RSC 1970, c B-3, s. 47(a), by which property held in trust by the bankrupt is excluded from property divisible among the creditors.

level of fault. On the other hand, this is a most tentative prediction indeed; powerful voices argue the contrary position, and the matter may be resolved by legislative intervention.

On the other hand, we see change in the wind when it comes to remedies. The legal responses by which unjust enrichments can be reversed are many and varied. What is needed is an ordering and an organisation of these different possibilities, such as the one presented herein. And the most interesting question is how the judges will understand the relationship between liability on the one hand, and remedial possibilities on the other. Will they follow their counterparts elsewhere in the common law world, in recognising a measure of remedial discretion? We have argued that this step is sound in principle, and offers the best hope for the rational development of the law. The other alternative, a renunciation of flexibility, would consign English law to a period of stagnation, in a misguided attempt to reach an unattainable and indeed mythical plateau of legal certainty.

One judge, at least, seems to share our view that flexibility is the way of the future. Lord Millett has said:

> "There are five questions to be asked: (1) Has the defendant been enriched? (2) If so, is his enrichment unjust? (3) Is his enrichment at the expense of the plaintiff? (4) Has the defendant any defence to the claim? (5) What remedies are available to the plaintiff?"[100]

Much of the future of this area of the law lies in that final question.

[100] "Restitution and Constructive Trusts" in *Restitution: Past Present and Future*, *supra* n.3, at 208.

22

Land Law and Trusts

ELIZABETH COOKE AND DAVID HAYTON

Land Law

We are celebrating a millennium; that means it is nearly 2000 years since the famous, and stinging, rebuke to lawyers was delivered:

> "you experts in the law, woe to you, because you load people down with burdens they can hardly carry, and you yourselves will not lift one finger to help them".[1]

The words were not, of course, addressed to us. But they can still make us feel uncomfortable. At the start of a new millennium, how far have we progressed towards a law, and a community of lawyers, whose priority is to relieve hardship and injustice rather than to accentuate them?

Twentieth-Century Land Law

The context in this part of this chapter is land law, with a hint of landlord and tenant, an area where lawyers have made conspicuous efforts to give relief against the rigours of the law which, although codified and reformed by the 1925 legislation, was ill-equipped to meet some of the challenges and demands of the twentieth century—in particular, the demands imposed by wider property ownership and by family breakdown.

The story of those efforts is well known. The solution to some of the century's unexpected developments was to some extent found within the property legislation itself. For example, Benjamin Cherry[2] would not have expected that the overriding interest defined in section 70(1)(g) of the Land Registration Act

[1] Luke, ch. 11, v. 46 (New International Version).

[2] The draftsman of the 1925 legislation; see S Anderson, "The 1925 Property Legislation: Setting Contexts" in S Bright and J Dewar (eds.), *Land Law: Themes and Perspectives* (Oxford, Oxford University Press, 1998) ("Bright and Dewar").

1925 would have eventually protected Mrs Boland;[3] nor could he have foreseen the family-focused jurisprudence that would grow up around section 30 of the Law of Property Act 1925.[4] In many cases, new legislation was needed to adapt the law of property to real life—conspicuously the Matrimonial Homes Act 1967[5] and Part II of the Matrimonial Causes Act 1973. Frequently the courts have had to develop their own solutions, thanks to equity's well-known fecundity. Of these, perhaps the best known and most discussed are the common intention constructive trust,[6] and estoppel;[7] both doctrines continue to be the subject of energetic development.[8]

But neither trusts nor estoppel will provide a solution for the unmarried cohabitant whose need is all the greater because she has never had the resources to make any financial contribution to her family home. Mrs Burns is still not catered for;[9] more generally, there is no jurisdiction for the courts to make financial provision for cohabitants after the breakdown of their relationship.[10] Moreover, there have been instances where the courts have been reluctant to accept, or have actually managed to decline, the helping hand offered by statute. It took a House of Lords decision[11] for the courts to accept that the Domestic Violence and Matrimonial Proceedings Act 1976 really meant what it said and could oust a property owner from his home in favour of a non-owning co-habitant. And while section 25 of the Matrimonial Causes Act 1973 is readily used to effect sweeping redistribution of property in perhaps 99 per cent of cases, the courts have jibbed at applying them to millionaires.[12]

[3] *William & Glyn's Bank Ltd* v. *Boland* [1981] AC 487: a wife's equitable interest in the matrimonial home was protected against the mortgagee. In 1925 she would not have been expected to have such an interest; nor would it necessarily have been seen as a property right that could have been protected by s. 70(1)(g).

[4] *Williams* v. *Williams* [1976] Ch 278. Section 30 has now been replaced by ss. 14 and 15 of the Trusts of Land and Appointment of Trustees Act 1996, whereby the court has jurisdiction to resolve disputes between trustees of land. A property adjustment order for the benefit of children would now more naturally be dealt with under the Children Act 1989, s. 15, Sch. 1.

[5] Replaced by the 1983 Act; see now s. 30 of the Family Law Act 1996.

[6] *Gissing* v. *Gissing* [1971] AC 886.

[7] *Greasley* v. *Cooke* [1980] 1 WLR 1306.

[8] *Midland Bank plc* v. *Cooke* [1995] 4 All ER 562 opened new horizons within constructive trusts; cases such as *Wayling* v. *Jones* (1993) 69 P & CR 170, *Matharu* v. *Matharu* (1994) 68 P & CR 93, and *Sledmore* v. *Dalby* (1996) 72 P & CR 196 illustrate the adaptability of estoppel to new social and moral contexts.

[9] *Burns* v. *Burns* [1984] Ch 317; a cohabitant who had not made any financial contribution to her partner's property was left with no interest in it after 17 years' cohabitation, despite the value of her mothering and home-making role.

[10] Contrast the position elsewhere; e.g. the New South Wales De Facto Relationships Act 1984.

[11] *Davis* v. *Johnson* [1979] AC 264.

[12] For example, *Dart* v. *Dart* [1996] 2 FLR 286, and the remarks of Butler-Sloss LJ at 304–5.

A Problem of Balance

As we make our way into a new century land lawyers are faced with a number of technical challenges. We have still not fully resolved the doctrinal issues thrown up by the 1925 legislation, let alone explored all the mysteries of more recent measures such as the Law of Property (Miscellaneous Provisions) Act 1989[13] and the Trusts of Land and Appointment of Trustees Act 1996. Before long there will, it is hoped, be a new Land Registration Act[14] which will keep us busy for many a year.

Perhaps even more important are what one might call problems of balance, which involve issues which will not go away and can only become more pressing given the climate of change, not only social but also environmental.

A special problem is the difficulty of balancing property rights against "family" interests, by which is meant the needs and (moral) entitlements that are built up within families and exposed on family breakdown. Perhaps the most unhelpful attempt to deal with this is to be found in the Family Law Act 1996, where the level of protection offered against domestic violence depends upon the victim's status as a property-owner or otherwise, and also upon her marital status.[15] Less crude—surely more well-meaning—have been the courts' endeavours to cater for family claimants within the world of constructive trusts, estoppel, and the like; yet the resulting case law is built upon ideas and values often alien to the relationships which give rise to the cases.[16]

Moreover, the courts have had difficulty in balancing the needs of the individual litigant and the wider community, the latter usually unrepresented and invisible. Thus a decision may assist a particular claimant, but leave others to pay a price. The price may be simply the fact of being left with unsatisfactory law, which must always be unacceptably costly. *Peffer* v. *Rigg*[17] must be an example; so too the decision in *Prudential Assurance Co* v. *London Residuary Body*[18]

[13] It is unclear if s.2 is estoppel-proof, for example; consider *Bankers Trust Co* v. *Namdar* (unreported, 14 February 1997, CA); *Godden* v. *Merthyr Tydfil Housing Association* (unreported, 15 February 1997, CA); *Yaxley* v. *Gotts* [1999] 3 WLR 1217.

[14] See *Land Registration for the Twenty-First Century* (Law Com No. 254).

[15] Contrast ss. 33 and 36 (and in particular ss. 33(7) and 36(8)), and consider the enigmatic, perhaps even offensive, s. 41.

[16] A Lawson, "The Things We Do for Love", (1996) 16 *LS* 218; S Gardner, "Re-thinking Family Property", [1993] 109 *LQR* 263.

[17] [1977] 1 WLR 285. The decision (of a judge of the Patents Court) used the doctrine of notice to protect the holder of an unregistered interest, despite the obvious meaning of the Land Registration Act 1925; see C Harpum, *Megarry and Wade's The Law of Real Property* (London, Sweet & Maxwell, 2000), para. 6–105, p. 269. It is unlikely that the decision would be followed.

[18] [1992] AC 386; the decision re-asserted the need for a lease to have a certain term, thereby rendering void a "lease" whose practical effect had become unfair between the parties. The value of the decision is undermined by the fact that by careful drafting the parties could have achieved exactly the same arrangement without offending against the principle of certainty.

where (it has been convincingly argued)[19] a valiant attempt to produce a just result was disguised as an arid doctrinal exercise, leaving the law as to certainty of leasehold terms illogical and arbitrary in its effect. On another level, the price paid may be the fact that certain benefits become more expensive. This certainly happened in the wake of *Boland*,[20] though we are used to that now; it must be a continuing result of the case law flowing from *Barclays Bank plc* v. *O'Brien*.[21] The House of Lords' decision in *Bruton* v. *London and Quadrant Housing Trust*[22] is another example.

Bruton

The case concerned an occupant of property owned by a local authority. The authority had granted a licence to a Housing Association to occupy and use the premises; the Association in turn granted a licence to Gary Bruton to live there. Mr Bruton then claimed the status of a tenant, in order to enforce the landlord's duty to repair under section 11 of the Landlord and Tenant Act 1985.

The Court of Appeal, by a majority, held that he was a licensee. The reasoning,[23] in summary, was:

(1) a party with no estate in the land cannot grant a tenancy, except a tenancy by estoppel;
(2) the Association never purported to grant a tenancy, so there is no inconsistency between the terms of the grant and the licensor's assertion that he has no title and nothing for the parties to be estopped from denying, so there is no tenancy by estoppel;
(3) therefore Mr Bruton is not a tenant.

The House of Lords disagreed with step 1. Their Lordships held that because Mr Bruton had exclusive possession, at a rent, he had a tenancy, following *Street* v. *Mountford*.[24] The Housing Association's want of title made no difference to this; nor did the Association's social purpose constitute a special circumstance that could take the case outside the *Street* v. *Mountford* principle.

[19] S Bright, "Uncertainty in leases: is it a vice?", (1993) 13 *LS* 318.

[20] See *supra* n. 3. The price of the decision is the cost of additional enquiries now made of borrowers by mortgagees.

[21] [1994] 1 AC 180. The benefit of additional protection against undue influence must be balanced against the fact that millions of home-owners must indirectly bear the cost of litigation as the implications of the decision are worked out.

[22] [1999] 3 WLR 150.

[23] See in particular the judgment of Millett LJ, [1998] QB 834 at 842–6.

[24] [1985] AC 809.

On this basis, of course, tenancy by estoppel was a red herring, and must always be one where the issue is "has the claimant a tenancy?".[25]

The House of Lords' decision is both startling and sad. It is startling because it overturns such long-established law. Yes, of course, we have benefited from reminders in recent years that leases are of course contracts;[26] but the suggestion that a lease might be purely contractual, with no need for an estate in land, is completely novel.[27] The decision is, with respect, wrong in trying to sidestep the fundamental principle "*nemo dat quod non habet*".[28]

It is sad because—although the decision gave Mr Bruton what he needed—it must make the task of the defendant and other Housing Associations much more difficult. In the first place, the resources of a charitable organisation are being stretched to make costly repairs. In the second, it has become, it seems, impossible for a Housing Association to grant a licence to occupiers, even where it has only a licence itself and needs (NB needs *for its charitable purposes*) the flexibility involved in granting a licence rather than a tenancy. The long-term result must be poorer provision for the homeless. Their Lordships recognised this, yet felt able only to express regret.[29] Yet their decision was in no sense forced by precedent. If the House of Lords is able to decide that a lease need not be an estate in land, it must also be able to declare that the particular circumstances of this arrangement warranted a finding that this was one of the exceptions to *Street* v. *Mountford*.[30]

Looking Ahead

As this chapter is being written two publications from the Law Commission are awaited. One is the final Report and draft Bill on Land Registration.[31] The other is the long-expected paper on home-sharers.[32] The one deals with land

[25] The urge to digress is irresistible: Lord Hoffmann, [1999] 3 WLR 150 at 157, asserts "it is not the estoppel which creates the tenancy, but the tenancy which creates the estoppel". That is contrary to settled understanding; nor is it supported, as Lord Hoffmann states (at 158), by *Morton* v. *Woods* (1869) LR 4 QB 293. It seems that he has taken the words of Kelly CB out of context. The whole basis of the case was that there was no actual tenancy; tenancy by estoppel was needed to support the "landlord's" right to levy distress.

[26] See for example *Hussein* v. *Mehlman* [1992] 2 EGLR 87.

[27] At the time of writing, the standard works have not been amended in the light of the House of Lords' decision in *Bruton*; so the settled understanding before that decision can be seen in the opening paragraphs of *Hill and Redman* (Issue 29) and of *Woodfall* (September 1995 Issue).

[28] See S Bright, [2000] 116 *LQR* 7.

[29] [1993] 3 WLR 150, per Lord Slynn at 152F, Lord Jauncey at 154B.

[30] In spite of *Family Housing Association* v. *Jones* [1990] 1 WLR 779, by which of course the House of Lords was not bound and where, in any case, the Association's lack of title was not considered.

[31] See *supra* n. 19.

[32] See the Law Commission's 33rd Annual Report (Law Com No. 258), para. 5.7.

law at its most hard-edged; the other with issues of need, relationship, and responsibility. Will the two sit happily together? And will either lead to a better way of balancing the needs of individuals with each other and with those of the community? We must wait and see; but this last century has left the impression that property concepts by themselves are inadequate for the legal regulation of land ownership.[33]

A solution already advocated is to expand our notions of property. The idea is that since property rights are well-protected we can protect more rights by regarding them as property rights; this is a huge and exciting idea, widely discussed elsewhere.[34] Another possibility is to consider which rights are actually more important than property rights, and then to develop the balancing techniques which are so lacking in land law so as to make more room for rights that do not involve ownership.

It would be foolish to suggest that the Human Rights Act 1998 will ride like a knight in armour to the rescue at this point, but it may—given a creative approach by the judiciary—provide inspiration and a starting point.

The Human Rights Act 1998

The incorporation into domestic law of the European Convention on Human Rights 1950, coming into force in October 2000, will have far-reaching implications, and even property lawyers may feel its effects.

Article 1 of the First Protocol states:

> "Every natural and legal person is entitled to the peaceful enjoyment of his possessions. No one shall be deprived of his possessions except in the public interest and subject to the conditions provided for by law and by the general principles of international law.
>
> The preceding provisions shall not, however, in any way impair the right of a state to enforce such laws as it deems necessary to control the use of property in accordance with the general interest or to secure the payment of taxes or other contributions or penalties".

The need for the balancing of rights and interests is inherent in the wording of the article, in particular the references to the public or general interest. In *Sporrong and Lönnroth* v. *Sweden*[35] it was pointed out that:

[33] This is seen even more clearly in the New World where legal conscience has finally caught up, in some measure, with the outrage of colonisation, but finds itself hampered by an inappropriate set of legal concepts. See S Dorset, "Land Law and Dispossession: Indigenous Rights to Land in Australia" in Bright and Dewar, *supra* n. 2.

[34] See for example K Gray, "Equitable Property" [1994] *CLP* 157. Gray quotes, at 210, CB Macpherson, "Human Rights as Property Rights" 24 *Dissent* 72, at 77: "We have made property so central to our society that any thing and any rights that are not property are very apt to take second place".

[35] (1982) 5 EHRR 35 at 52.

> "the Court must determine whether a fair balance was struck between the demands of the general interest of the community and the requirements of the protection of the individual's fundamental rights. The search for this balance is inherent in the whole of the Convention".

Thus in *James* v. *United Kingdom*[36] the Court was able to find that the workings of the Leasehold Reform Act 1967 did not amount to a violation of the rights of the Duke of Westminster under this Protocol; it so found in spite of the fact that property—the reversion on long-leasehold houses—was taken away from him, and in spite of the fact that a number of wealthy tenants actually made a windfall profit by their discounted purchase,[37] because it was able and obliged to look past the individual litigant, past those closely involved with the litigant, and out to the interests of the wider community, where the Leasehold Reform Act was "calculated to enhance social justice".[38] The contrast with the House of Lords' reasoning and priorities in *Bruton* is striking.

The Article protects the right to enjoyment of "possessions", in English, rather than of "property". The French term is "*biens*" and the European Court has adopted a wide-ranging interpretation of the term. "The concept of 'possession' is autonomous and the demonstration of an established economic interest by an applicant may be sufficient to establish a right protected by the Convention."[39] There is much potential for development here; the rights of adverse possessors spring to mind, for example.

Article 8 of the Convention is more the province of family lawyers, but the property lawyer should be alert to its reference to a home:

> "1. Everyone shall have the right to respect for his private and family life, his home and his correspondence.
>
> 2. There shall be no interference by a public authority with the exercise of this right except such as is in accordance with the law and is necessary in a democratic society in the interests of national security, public safety or the economic well-being of the country, for the prevention of disorder or crime, for the protection of health or morals, or for the protection of the rights and freedoms of others".

Again, the issue of balance is writ large here. In the Strasbourg jurisprudence the balancing exercise has been carried out in such diverse contexts as the interference with home life caused by the noise from an airport,[40] the

[36] (1986) 8 EHRR 123.

[37] *Ibid.*, at 153.

[38] *Ibid.*, at 141.

[39] DJ Harris, M O'Boyle and C Warbrick, *Law of the European Convention on Human Rights* (London, Butterworths, 1995), pp. 517–18.

[40] *Powell* v. *United Kingdom* (1987) 9 EHRR 241; the complaint was held by the Commission to be ill-founded.

forfeiture of a lease for non-payment of a service charge by way of rent,[41] and the refusal of planning permission to enable a gypsy to live in caravans on her own land.[42] It must surely have relevance, along with Article 1 of the First Protocol, to applications for possession of land, and particularly in family contexts.

Where could the Human Rights Act 1998 take our courts and the general shape of our land law? The courts are obliged to "take into account" the Strasbourg jurisprudence (section 2), but that wording surely leaves them free to develop their own jurisprudence within the meaning and spirit of the Convention and of that jurisprudence. The challenge must be to find ways out of the dilemmas and impasses of the last century by using the opportunities given by the European Convention, namely:

- to resolve the uncertainty as to the Convention's applicability between private individuals, in favour of the relevance of the Convention and the need for the State to protect individuals against violations by others;[43]
- to explore the meaning of "possessions" and take up the tacit invitation to see this as something broader than merely "property";
- to develop the right to respect for one's home;
- to take seriously the Convention's demand for a balancing of different rights; not only the individual rights to property, possessions and to respect for one's home but also the "public interest" and the need for justice in the community.

None of this will flow automatically from the Human Rights Act 1998. Any instrument that enshrines the right to "possessions" or to property can be regarded as a measure for the protection of the haves rather than the have-nots, a way of entrenching wealth. Hence the fear expressed that "incorporation [of the European Convention] will benefit the wealthy more than the poor and companies more than individuals".[44] Hence the nervousness glimpsed in the deliberations over the reform of land registration.[45] Hence the view that Convention rights could be used to outlaw the whole system of adverse pos-

[41] App. No. 11949/86 v. *United Kingdom* (1988) 10 EHRR 149; again, the complaint was held to be ill-founded because the law relating to forfeiture was "in accordance with the law and necessary in a democratic society for the protection of the rights of others" (at 155).

[42] *Buckley* v. *United Kingdom* (1997) 23 EHRR 101; no violation of Article 8. It was noted, at 129, that "in the instant case the interests of the community are to be balanced against the applicant's right to respect for her "home", a right which is pertinent to her and her children's personal security and well-being".

[43] M Hunt, "The 'Horizontal effect' of the Human Rights Act" [1998] *PL* 423; but see Sir Richard Buxton, "The Human Rights Act and Private Law", [2000] 116 *LQR* 48.

[44] P Sparkes, *A New Land Law* (Oxford, Hart Publishing, 1999), p. 37.

[45] *Land Registration for the Twenty-First Century* (Law Com No. 254), for example at paras 5.20 (p. 75), 5.68 (p. 97). The Scottish Law Commission seems to have been a little more robust; see *Report on the Abolition of the Feudal System* (Scots Law Com No. 168, 1999), p. 92.

session, or to eliminate what survives of our security of tenure legislation.[46] But the Act need not be used thus, given a commitment by the judiciary to use it as an instrument for upholding and balancing rights across the community.

The Act does not provide an instant solution to *Bruton*. Human rights were not in issue in that case; although had it arisen post-incorporation we might have seen Mr Bruton arguing his right to respect for his home, and both parties claiming the right to peaceful enjoyment of possessions. But even on the terms in which the case was actually litigated, might there not have been a different decision had the courts been in the habit—a habit they must now acquire—of looking critically at the law, and at alternative decisions open to them, in the light of the law's impact upon the rights not only of the individuals before them but also of the wider community? Their Lordships in *Bruton* seemed to feel that it would not be legitimate to take the latter interest into account; in a more rights-based jurisprudence that scruple might well disappear.

Any More Rights?

The European Convention on Human Rights is not a magic carpet to take us into an era of flexible and imaginative justice in land law. But it could be a starting point. There is more to do. The Convention enshrines, for example, the right to respect for one's home if one actually has a home; what about a right to a home for those who have none? We are quite a long way away from being able to enact and implement such a right; yet at least one new constitution is prepared to attempt this.[47] Nor are we much nearer the realisation of the idea of community or public rights to the preservation of the countryside and environment.[48] Perhaps the experience of "bringing rights home"[49] will act as a catalyst, not only for the development of new techniques for the balancing of rights, but also for the creation of new rights. Mrs Burns might then be laid to rest by the land law textbooks;[50] and we might be able to say that the new millennium will have been a time of lifting some of the more burdensome consequences of land-ownership.

[46] J Howell, "Land and Human Rights", [1999] *Conv* 287 at 305 and 307. Attempts to use the Convention thus must run up against the legitimate social purpose of both sets of legislation, as well as meeting head on the right both of squatters and of tenants to peaceful enjoyment of possessions and the rights, of some squatters and all tenants, to respect for one's home.

[47] See M Roberston, "Land and Post-Apartheid Reconstruction in South Africa", in Bright and Dewar, *supra* n. 2, at 311, notes that the South African Government's White Paper on housing recognizes housing as "a basic human right" (*Government Gazette*, No. 16178, 23 December 1994).

[48] See Gray, *supra* n. 34.

[49] *Rights Brought Home* (Cm 3782, 1997).

[50] See *supra* n. 9.

Trusts

The Impact of Globalisation

Trusts are created to preserve and to generate wealth, whether they are family trusts, providing an alternative to the operation of the law of succession for four or so generations, or commercial trusts, furthering financial interests in the business world. With the late twentieth century triumph of capitalism over communism and encouragement of citizens to have proprietary stakes in the development of their countries' economies so as to further private and public interests, it follows that there is a very rosy future for trusts as flexible property-owning vehicles.

It seems that the pressures of globalisation will lead to the English trust concept becoming more flexible than is currently understood to be the case. English courts will be forced to refine their notion of what precisely is a trust and of the public policy limits upon a trust when dealing with English assets owned by foreign or local trustees, but governed by an expressly chosen foreign trust law, e.g. that of Suntopia. If the English court then gives effect to rights expressly conferred by Suntopian legislation, why cannot a similar result be achieved under English trust law if the settlor expressly purports to confer such rights?

Under English law, for example, it is regarded as "elementary that a settlor who retains no beneficial interest cannot enforce the trust which he has created"[51] and "a trust for non-charitable purposes" is clearly void because there is no beneficiary,[52] the fundamental "beneficiary principle" requiring there to be a beneficiary to make the trust an enforceable obligation. However, under some foreign trust laws[53] a settlor automatically has a right to enforce his trust, even though not a beneficiary, or has such a right if he appoints himself in his trust instrument to be an enforcer.[54] Indeed, under some foreign trust laws[55] non-charitable purpose trusts are not void but are valid and enforceable if the settlor's trust instrument has appointed someone to be enforcer or, in Bermuda, if the court considers that there is a person with sufficient interest to justify the court allowing such person to enforce the trust.[56]

[51] Lord Millett when a leading QC in "The Quistclose Trust: Who Can Enforce It?"(1985) 101 *LQR* 269 at 287.

[52] *Re Recher's WT* [1972] Ch 526 at 538 per Brightman J.

[53] e.g. Liechtenstein, Taiwan, and proposed Chinese Trust Law.

[54] Cayman Special Trusts (Alternative Regime) Law 1997.

[55] e.g. Cayman Islands, Jersey, Belize, Isle of Man.

[56] Trusts (Special Provisions) Amendment Act 1998, s.12B(1)(d).

What then if, in a trust instrument governed by English law (and under which the settlor is not a beneficiary), the settlor expressly stipulates that he is to have the right to enforce the trust in addition to such rights inherent in the beneficiaries (particularly where such beneficiaries may not yet be alive, ascertained or of full capacity)? What, indeed, if such settlor purports to create a trust to use the income to further the interests of the UK Labour Party (until twenty-one years from the death of the last survivor of all the descendants of Queen Elizabeth II alive at the date of creation of the trust) expressed to be enforceable by the Leader from time to time of such Party—or to use the income (for such perpetuity period) to press for the abolition of vivisection in the United Kingdom and elsewhere, to be enforceable by the Chair from time to time of the unincorporated Anti-Vivisection Society?

If the settlor had taken advantage of the Recognition of Trusts Act 1987 to choose a foreign trust law that upheld the right of the settlor or another expressly appointed enforcer to enforce the above trusts, surely such trusts would have been held to be so enforceable by the English court. One cannot see how the right of such an enforcer would be "manifestly incompatible with public policy"[57] or inconsistent with the irreducible core content of the trust obligation. Indeed, it is the very existence of the enforcer in the non-charitable purpose trust that creates the obligation that is at the core of the trust.

The key to the trust obligation is surely that there must be some person intended by the settlor to have *locus standi* to enforce the trustee's duties. This was recognised by Goff J in *Re Denley's Trust Deed*.[58] After upholding a trust for a purpose that benefited a class of individuals so that they were necessarily intended to have *locus standi* to enforce the trust, he distinguished it from[59] "a purpose trust, the carrying out of which would benefit individuals where that benefit is so indirect or intangible or which is otherwise so framed as not to give those persons any *locus standi* to apply to the court to enforce the trust, in which case the beneficiary principle would apply to invalidate the trust".

This so-called "beneficiary principle" should really be the "enforcer principle": just as a car needs an engine, so a trust needs an enforcer, normally being a beneficiary, but being the Attorney-General or the Charity Commissioners for charitable purpose trusts or an expressly appointed enforcer for non-charitable purpose trusts. It is the existence of the enforcer that gives substance to the obligation of the trustee that is at the core of the trust concept. If the settlor reserves rights as an additional enforcer then this strengthens the trust concept.

[57] Article 18 of the Hague Trusts Convention in Schedule to the Recognition of Trusts Act 1987. See my forthcoming LQR paper "Developing the Obligation Characteristic of the Trust".

[58] [1969] 1 Ch 373; also Grant MR in *Morice* v. *Bishop of Durham* (1804) 9 Ves 399 at 405 stated "there must be somebody in whose favour the court can decree performance".

[59] [1969] 1 Ch 373 at 382–3.

Thus, in a trust governed by English law it should be realised that the settlor can effectively reserve rights as an additional enforcer of his trust and can create a valid non-charitable purpose trust—so long as he provides an enforcer mechanism and restricts the trust to a valid perpetuity period,[60] assuming that the purposes are clear enough to be administratively workable.[61]

In some areas it seems clear what will be the attitude of the English courts when it is an English settlor who transfers English assets to English trustees for the benefit of English beneficiaries but chooses Suntopian law to try to obtain an advantage not permitted by English trust law. What if Suntopian law permits trusts to endure for ever (having abolished the rule against remoteness and the rule against inalienability of income); or permits trusts to endure so long as a material purpose of the settlor subsists (so ousting absolutely entitled beneficiaries' proprietary *Saunders* v. *Vautier*[62] rights to terminate the trust and claim the trust property for themselves); or permits a settlor to settle his own property on himself until bankruptcy or to settle property on another for life such that the life interest cannot be assigned voluntarily or involuntarily (e.g. on bankruptcy); or provides for there to be a valid trust for "beneficiaries" where they have no right to be informed that they be beneficiaries, no right to sue the trustee and no rights in respect of the trust property? In these cases it seems that the English court will not recognise the effect of the foreign law because contrary to English public policy or repugnant to the English trust concept.

On the other hand, where it was a foreign settlor who transferred Suntopian assets to Suntopian trustees for beneficiaries of a trust governed by Suntopian law and, later, the trustees happened to purchase English assets (directly or via an underlying Suntopian company owned by them, the usual method of operation), the English courts will need to examine the issues more closely. If the nature of beneficiaries' rights under Suntopian trust law is a special chose in action[63] against the trustee rather than a proprietary interest in the trust property owned by the trustee, should the English court not accept this? This would mean accepting that the nature of the chose in action, as limited by the settlor, ousts *Saunders* v. *Vautier* rights[64] as well as ousting proprietary tracing processes against third parties (unless the English court considers that the imposition of an equitable lien or a constructive trust is an appropriate procedural remedy for breach of a fiduciary duty) or even against the trustees in

60 *Re Nottage* [1895] 2 Ch 649; *Re Wightwick's WT* [1950] Ch 260; *Leahy* v *Att-Gen for New South Wales* [1959] AC 457.

61 *Re Astor's ST* [1952] Ch 534.

62 (1841) 4 Beav 115, *Stephenson* v. *Barclays Bank* [1975] 1 WLR 88.

63 *Archer-Shee* v. *Garland* [1931] AC 212.

64 See *supra* n. 62.

respect of assets acquired by them for themselves in breach of their fiduciary duty.[65]

However, if English creditors would otherwise be prevented from attacking English assets held on trust for the settlor for life or until bankruptcy it would seem that the English court would make the bankrupt settlor's life interest available for creditors. The position should be similar if the Suntopian trustees purchased English assets for the settlor's son as life tenant to lead an extravagant life in London before becoming bankrupt, where the settlor had purported to create a spendthrift trust[66] under which the life interest could not be assigned voluntarily or involuntarily.

Where perpetuity rules are concerned, if a valid perpetual trust exists under its proper Suntopian law and then, in the course of managing the trust fund, assets happen to be purchased in countries like England, not permitting perpetual trusts, it seems that the English court[67] should accept such trusts rather than impose resulting trusts over English assets. However, if the settlor's perpetual trust is for the benefit of descendants of himself and his siblings but under the governing Cayman Special Trusts (Alternative Regime) Law 1997 such beneficiaries have no rights to sue the trustee or the enforcer and no rights whatsoever in the trust property, it seems that the English court should not hold there to be a trust for those "beneficiaries".[68] Instead, the trust should be regarded as a resulting trust for the settlor, with the trustee having merely a power of appointment to benefit the "beneficiaries", recharacterised as objects of a power, although not even having the right of such an object to apply to the court to have the trustee removed.[69]

European Developments

As just seen, Caribbean developments have stretched the elasticity of the trust concept to breaking point.[70] In mainland Europe a much narrower trust concept is developing, regarding the trust as part of the law of obligations, not part

[65] Under South African trust law beneficiaries only have a proprietary claim against assets rightfully acquired by the trustees in performing their duties: Honore's *South African Law of Trusts* (4th edn., Juta & Co, Cape Town), pp. 23–4.

[66] Popular in the USA: see *Scott on Trusts* (4th edn. by W F Fratcher), para. 152.

[67] Like American courts: see *ibid.*, paras 593 and 600.

[68] See Millett LJ in *Armitage* v. *Nurse* [1998] Ch 241 at 253 referring to "an irreducible core of obligations owed by the trustees to the beneficiaries and enforceable by them which is fundamental to the concept of a trust. If the beneficiaries have no rights enforceable against trustees there are no trusts" and D J Hayton, "The Irreducible Core Content of Trusteeship" in A J Oakley (ed.), *Trends in Contemporary Trust Law* (Oxford, 1996), ch. 3.

[69] *Re Manisty's Settlement* [1974] Ch 17.

[70] See further D J Hayton (ed.), *Modern International Developments in Trust Law* (Kluwer Law International, 1999) ch. 1.

of the law of property. In case law and in legislation there can be found in particular situations of a commercial (as opposed to family) nature the concept of a trustee owning property for the benefit of others which is not his private property but a segregated fund immune from the claims of his private creditors, heirs or spouse. This has led to an international working group producing a book, *Principles of European Trust Law*,[71] setting out eight Principles, a General Commentary thereon, and various National Commentaries. The intention is that this will help civil law jurisdictions to pass legislation that efficiently implements The Hague Convention on the Law Applicable to Trusts and on their Recognition, so far implemented by Italy, The Netherlands, Malta and the United Kingdom in Europe, although Luxembourg and France have signed the Convention.

This Convention, like all Hague Conventions, is concerned with attaining common private international law principles but, inevitably, has an impact on internal laws if local assets held on foreign trusts by a local trustee are not to be available to claims of the trustee's creditors, heirs and spouse. However, if the trustee be a wealthy corporation that will not become insolvent—and does not have heirs or spouses—it can easily function as a trustee in a civil law system, as has happened in Italy. Of course, some day such a corporate trustee will become insolvent, or an individual businessman, who has purported to create client accounts to keep their money separate from his own, will become bankrupt.

Lack of a general segregated fund type of trust concept in Europe means that there is not a level playing field to protect the interests of consumers (e.g. in client accounts being trust accounts) or of commercial lenders (e.g. in having a collective security trustee to look after their secured loans) or of investors (e.g. in collective investment schemes or in buying interests in stocks and shares held by a custodian for speedy, inexpensive dealings in such interests).[72] Special *ad hoc* statutory provision has therefore been made in mainland Europe for safeguarding persons against financial risks, or the risks have to be run or insured against. It seems likely, therefore, that there will need to be a general segregated fund type of trust concept introduced in Europe via an EU Directive, helping to protect consumers, to remove obstacles to European trade and investment and to provide some limited harmonisation of law within Europe.[73]

[71] D J Hayton, S C J J Kortmann and H L E Verhagen (eds) (Kluwer Law International, 1999).

[72] See further The Association of Corporate Trustees, *Report on Commercial Trusts and Trust-like Arrangements in Europe* (October 2000).

[73] D J Hayton, "The Developing European Dimension of Trust Law" (1999) 10 *KCLJ* 48.

English Developments

The Government has already introduced into Parliament the Trustee Bill 2000 in response to pressures[74] for trustees to have wide statutory powers (in default of express provision in the trust instrument) of investment and of delegation to custodians or nominees or to discretionary portfolio managers.[75] It also confers wide powers on trustees to insure the trust property and to charge for their services. All of these powers are much needed and much-welcomed.

However, the new power of investment reflects the wording of the power in section 34 of the Pensions Act 1995 in case any extra wording expressly widening the power might reflect on section 34 when the courts come to interpret it. Thus, in the interests of clarity and flexibility, draftsmen are likely to insert their own express power of investment in trust instruments,[76] e.g. "power to invest or apply the Trust Fund as if they were absolutely beneficially entitled thereto in the purchase or acquisition of any property right or interest of any kind, whether or not income-producing and with or without security, but including derivatives only when used for the purpose of controlling or limiting risk".

Courts, nowadays, of course have woken up to the fact that trustees, like private investors, must take account of modern portfolio theory and have regard to the total return, taking account of income yield and of capital appreciation. There may well be more scope for capital growth (e.g. with the tough taxation of dividend income even for non-taxpayers, leading companies to retain more profits) so that trust instruments need to create flexible trusts whereby capital can be appointed to income beneficiaries where "income" in trust law terms is low.

Reform of perpetuities and accumulations is likely in the next five years to implement the Law Commission's Report with a draft bill on the topic.[77] It is anomalous that England has had a twenty-one year accumulation period[78] instead of a period coterminous with the perpetuity period of royal lives plus

[74] See D J Hayton, "Developing the Law of Trusts for the 21st Century" (1990) 106 *LQR* 87; Law Commission Consultation Paper No. 146 *Powers and Duties of Trustees* (June 1997), and The Treasury, *Consultation Document on Investment Powers of Trustees* (May 1996).

[75] Subject to contrary intent, clause 1 imposes a statutory duty of care in exercising the new statutory powers.

[76] "Or apply" enables the trustees to go beyond a narrow view of "investing" (e.g. purchasing call-options or put-options pursuant to a tax avoidance scheme or purchasing derivatives to protect against exposure to risk). See further the broad Bermudian Trustee Amendment Act 1999, s. 10 power of investment.

[77] *The Rules against Perpetuities and Excessive Accumulations* (Law Com No. 251, April 1998).

[78] The Accumulations Act 1800 being passed due to lengthy accumulations required by Mr Thelluson's will and the fear of MPs that their parents could create will trusts preventing them and their children acquiring income to maintain a satisfactory lifestyle.

twenty-one years or the statutory (eighty year) period as in other trust jurisdictions that retain perpetuity rules. The Bill proposes a 125 year period for the rule against remoteness of vesting and the rule against accumulations of income. Sadly, like the Perpetuities and Accumulations Act 1964, it leaves non-charitable purpose trusts to the rule against inalienability making such trusts void from the outset unless restricted to a lives plus twenty-one years perpetuity period. This seems indefensible.[79]

Indeed, all three rules should be abolished in the twenty-first century.[80] If the underlying assets can always be alienated by the trustees why does it matter that the capital value of the trust fund is to be held by the trustees for ever, only the income being used except to the extent that the trustees may exercise any powers of appointment over capital? The only reason seems to be to prohibit the deceased settlor from ruling the living from the grave for too long by virtue of conditions ensuring, for example, that in order to benefit, the beneficiaries must take the settlor's surname or only marry Catholics and bring their children-beneficiaries up as Catholics and not have permanent residence other than in England. One can tackle this by making such conditions enforceable only for, say, a period of fifty years or outlaw them altogether. Indeed, some conditions may be held to contravene the Human Rights Act 1998 if a broad view is taken of the powers of the court as "a public authority" within Article 8 of the Convention.[81]

In the area of family homes, where the share of a cohabitant or other home-sharer in the home owned by the other is in dispute, the courts have pushed beyond their proper limits the rules relating to resulting trusts, constructive trusts and proprietary estoppels in order to try to reach meritorious results.[82] The Law Commission is about to produce a Consultation Paper to lead in due course to a Report with draft bill appended, so as to achieve meritorious results on clearer principles than is currently the case and so as to enable constructive trust and estoppel interests to develop in more orthodox fashion.

However, it is believed unlikely that the English courts will develop the retrospective remedial constructive trust so as to create a proprietary interest where none existed prior to the court order.[83] Nevertheless, the court of equity

[79] Motivated by human sentiment for "people trusts" (to which the rule against remoteness applies) and against "purpose trusts" (to which the rule against inalienability applies).

[80] As e.g. in Turks and Caicos Islands, Cayman STAR trusts, Manitoba, Wisconsin and Alaska.

[81] See M Hunt, "The Horizontal Effect of the Human Rights Act" [1998] *PL* 423, but contrast the narrow approach of Sir Richard Buxton, "The Human Rights Act and Private Law" (2000) 116 *LQR* 48.

[82] e.g. *Midland Bank* v. *Cooke* [1995] 4 All ER 565, *Wayling* v. *Jones* (1993) 63 P & CR 170.

[83] This would upset statutory priority rules applicable to involvencies (*Re Polly Peck International plc (No. 2)* [1998] 3 All ER 812) while if the defendant is wealthy enough a personal remedy is as good as a proprietary remedy to prevent unjust enrichment of the defendant at the plaintiff's expense.

acting on traditional grounds of conscience has leeway[84] to achieve a meritorious result at the date of its decree by holding that X, who had earlier acquired an interest in specific property from V, is bound by W's interest therein as first decreed prospectively by the court, because in the circumstances X's conscience was affected by W's inchoate rights against V at the time X acquired an interest in the property. Thus, X is bound not by principles of property law but personally by application of a principle of equity that affects his conscience and prevents him from dishonestly exploiting his legal proprietary interest, because he had actual knowledge of W's rights or would have had actual knowledge but for deliberately or recklessly failing to make inquiries of W as to any interest justifying her occupation of the property.

Conscience, involving actual, Nelsonian or "naughty" knowledge, is at the basis of liability in equity as a dishonest accessory to a breach of fiduciary duty, where such accessory had not received for himself property subject to such duty.[85] Where such property had been so received then liability to account in equity ("as a constructive trustee" in the old terminology)[86] ought also to depend on conscience[87] so that such liability should arise if the recipient deals dishonestly with the property instead of returning it to its rightful owner. However, if the recipient, R, honestly dealt with the property in using it to pay off a secured or unsecured debt of his own then equitable subrogation principles ought to prevent him from being unjustly enriched[88] so that the rightful claimant should stand in the shoes of the secured or unsecured creditor paid off with the claimant's money. Where, however, R's debt was not an old debt but a new debt which would not have been incurred but for R's receipt (or justifiably anticipated receipt) of the claimant's property then the defence of change of position[89] should be open to R, as also should be the case if subsequently R made a gift of money to S in consideration of his marriage to R's daughter or spent the money on shares that are now worthless.

Finally, it is hoped that minor but necessary reforms will occur in the next twenty years or so in areas examined by the Trust Law Committee, namely Rights of Creditors against Trustees and Trust Funds,[90] Trustee Exemption

[84] *Ashburn Anstalt* v. *Arnold* [1989] Ch 1 and D J Hayton and O R Marshall, *Commentary and Cases on the Law of Trusts and Equitable Remedies* (10th edn., Sweet & Maxwell), p. 373.

[85] *Royal Brunei Airlines* v. *Tan* [1995] 2 AC 378.

[86] Used by Lord Browne-Wilkinson in *Westdeutsche Landesbank* v. *Islington London Borough Council* [1996] AC 669 at 705 but to be avoided per Millett LJ in *Paragon Finance plc* v. *Thakerar* [1999] 1 All ER 400 at 414.

[87] *Westdeutsche*, *supra* n. 86, at 705, 707, 709 per Lord Browne-Wilkinson, seemingly disregarded in *Houghton* v. *Fayers*, *The Times*, 9 February 2000, where the Court of Appeal held that dishonesty need not be established against the defendant.

[88] *Boscawen* v. *Bajwa* [1995] 4 All ER 769; *Banque Financiere* v. *Parc (Battersea) Ltd* [1999] 1 AC 221.

[89] *Lipkin Gorman* v. *Karpnale* [1991] 2 AC 548.

[90] *Report*, together with consultation papers on Exemption Clauses and Apportionment (Tolley Publishing, April 1999).

Clauses, Trustee Indemnity Clauses[91] and Apportionment between Capital and Income, and in the sphere of resolving internal trust disputes by arbitration or mediation. This sphere is currently being examined by the Trust Law Committee but the existence of incapacitated or unborn or otherwise unascertained beneficiaries creates major problems.[92] The question of a limitation period for claims of persons interested under discretionary trusts and powers also needs to be resolved:[93] the Law Commission[94] is considering this in a general examination of reform of limitation periods, but its proposal of a fixed ten year long-stop period for all claims seems inappropriate for discretionary trusts that can last for over a hundred years under a royal lives perpetuity period.

Conclusions

Through the application of private international law to international trusts governed by a foreign law, English courts will refine and develop the English trust concept, in particular to develop the trust as a more flexible obligation than conventionally considered currently to be the case.

There has been a trend in offshore trusts towards secrecy and confidentiality via "dummy" settlors and "blackhole" trusts,[95] so making life difficult for the Inland Revenue, creditors, heirs and spouses of the settlor or beneficiaries, and also preventing any beneficiary or object of a power of appointment from knowing of the trust until the end of the trust period (so making life easy for the trustees). Mainland jurisdictions are taking steps to ensure more transparency offshore so that they can protect themselves against erosion of their tax base[96] and prevent settlors or trustees acting dishonestly.[97]

[91] Consultation paper published by Macfarlanes, Solicitors and distributed by Society of Trusts and Estates Practitioners (January 2000).

[92] Litigation friends or a representative need to represent such persons but no compromise can be binding without the approval of the court: RSC Ord. 15 r.13(4), Civil Procedure Rule 21.10.

[93] See *Armitage* v. *Nurse* [1998] Ch 241 at 261 indicating how little protection trustees have against a person who is merely the object of a discretionary trust or power as well as against persons with interests in remainder and not in possession. *Jones* v. *Williams* [1999] 3 All ER 309 is out of line with *Armitage*.

[94] Law Com Consultation Paper No. 151 (January 1998).

[95] See D J Hayton (ed.), *Modern International Developments in Trust Law* (Kluwer Law International), 1999, ch. 15.

[96] See OECD, *Report on Harmful Tax Competition* and response of M Gaffney [1998] *Private Client Business* (Issue 6) 311.

[97] See the (Edwards) *Review of Financial Regulation in the Crown Dependencies* (Cm 4109, October 1998) and the Foreign Secretary's White Paper, *Partnership for Progress and Prosperity* (March 1999).

In the twenty-first century, however, as the trust becomes increasingly used to manage efficient succession to a mega-wealthy person's corporate trading and investment interests, it seems very likely that trustees will concentrate on developing a closer relationship with the beneficiaries, educating them about the activities managed by the trustees and involving appropriate beneficiaries in such activities, while also educating them about the proper relationship with the trustees: this should not be a "them" and "us" relationship but a joint relationship based on mutual trust and respect.[98]

Trusts provide a unique "pooling and potting" facility, i.e. putting together assets and then ring-fencing them, whether as a family device, for looking after the young or the elderly or the mentally infirm or a whole dynasty for four generations or so, or as a financial and commercial mechanism[99] for the holding of a collective security or for fund management for investors or pensioners or for holding clients' money. The uses of trusts for the preservation and generation of wealth are as broad as the imagination of man can devise.

In the twenty-first century it is easy to forecast that there will be a much greater use of the trust in financial and commercial affairs. Japan, Taiwan and Russia already have a statutory trust concept while China has nearly finalised its trust legislation. By mid-century it seems likely that no nation of any significant wealth will be without the trust concept. However, it may take a little longer before such concept may be used as an alternative to the law of succession under which on D's death with three children, for example, three-quarters of his estate on death (notionally including gifts made within x years of death) must pass absolutely to those children under forced heirship rules applicable in civil law jurisdictions.

Expansionary development of the trust concept is now in the hands of foreigners, viewing the trust primarily as part of the law of obligations so that beneficiaries do not have proprietary rights, only personal rights against the trustee which afford them a protected priority over the claims of the trustee's creditors, heirs and spouse. However there is scope for the history of the English trust to be repeated on the continent : the *ius in personam* may become regarded as a *ius in personam ad rem* and then develop into an *in rem* proprietary interest (although this may well require legislation when the time is adjudged ripe). This should not be so surprising when one considers European developments from Roman times, as have done the contributors to *Itinera Fiduciae: Trust and Treuhand in Historical Perspective*,[100] leading its editors to

[98] See J Hughes "The Trustee as Mentor" in (1998) *Chase Journal*, vol. II, Issue 2, p. 1.

[99] Further see D J Hayton (ed.), *Modern International Developments in Trust Law* (Kluwer Law International, 1999), chs 8 and 9 and TACT, *Report on Commercial Trusts and Trust-like Arrangements in Europe* (October 2000), Appendix.

[100] R Helmholz and R Zimmermann (eds) (Berlin, Duncker & Humblot, 1998).

conclude:[101] "If, as seems to be happening today, modern European Law incorporates the trust, there is much to suggest that it will be building upon historical foundations".

Indeed, this is reflected in a June 2000 Confidential Report commissioned by the Swiss Government from Professor Theuenoz. He recommends implementation of The Hague Trusts Convention and developing the fiducie into a general concept whereby the fiduciaire holds the assets subject to the fiducie as a separate fiduciary patrimony, so that only his own private patrimony is available for claims of his private creditors, spouse and heirs: draft clauses are appended to the Report. Swiss litigation on this would be a major breakthrough, leading her business and financial competition to respond with litigation of their own.

[101] *Ibid.*, at 44.